THE
RESTAURANTS
OF
NEW YORK

1989 Edition

Seymour Britchky

A FIRESIDE BOOK
PUBLISHED BY SIMON & SCHUSTER INC.
New York
London
Toronto
Sydney
Tokyo

F Fireside
Simon & Schuster Building
Rockefeller Center
1230 Avenue of the Americas
New York, New York 10020

DESIGNED BY EVE METZ

MANUFACTURED IN THE UNITED STATES OF AMERICA

10 9 8 7 6 5 4 3 2 1

ISBN 0-671-65823-9

The following reviews appeared, in somewhat different form, in *Seymour Britchky's Restaurant Letter*: Adrienne, Alo Alo, Ambassador Grill, American Place, Anabelles, Andrée's, Aquavit, Arcadia, Arizona 206, Arquà, Auberge Suisse, Aurora, Au Tunnel, Azzurro, Ballato, Ballroom, Barocco, Le Bernardin, Bice, Le Bilboquet, Bistro Bamboche, Blue Nile, La Bohême, La Boîte en Bois, La Bonne Bouffe, Bouley, Brandywine, Bravo Gianni, Brazilian Pavilion, Brive, Bruno, Bukhara, Cabana Carioca, Café de Bruxelles, Café de la Gare, Café des Artistes, Café du Parc, Café Greco, Café Loup, Café Luxembourg, Café San Martin, Canastel's, Il Cantinori, Canton, Cedars of Lebanon, Cellar in the Sky, Chelsea Central, Chez Jacqueline, Chez Josephine, Chez Louis, Chez Pierre, Chin Chin, Cinco de Mayo, Le Cirque, La Colombe d'Or, Contrapunto, La Côte Basque, Le Cygne, Da Silvano, Da Umberto, Dawat, Eamonn Doran, Ecco, Elio's, Erminia, Eze, El Faro, Felidia, Le Festival, Flamand, Florent, Four Seasons, Frank's, Fu's, Georgine Carmella, Gijo's, Gotham, La Goulue, La Grenouille, Grove Street Café, Gulf Coast, Hasaki, Hatsuhana, L'Hostaria del Bongustaio, Hulot's, Indochine, Jean Lafitte, Jockey Club, John Clancy's, Lafayette, Lattanzi, Lutèce, Le Madeleine, Malaga, Manhattan Ocean Club, Man Ray, Marcello, Marie-Michelle, Maurice, Melrose, Ménage à Trois, La Métairie, Mike's, Miss Ruby's Café, Mocca Royale, Moe's, Montrachet, Il Mulino, Nicola Paone, Il Nido, Nippon, Nishi Noho, Odeon, Omen, Onini, Orsini's, Orso, Palio, Palm and Palm Too, Le Palmier, Paola's, Parioli Romanissimo, Le Périgord, Pesca, Petaluma, La Petite Ferme, Petrossian, Pietro's, Il Ponte Vecchio, Positano, Primavera, Primola, Provence, Prunelle, Quatorze, Rakel, Raoul's, Le Régence, Remi, Restaurant Raphaël, La Ripaille, Ritz Café, Rosa Mexicano, Russian Tea Room, Sabor, Sala Thai, Salta in Bocca, Sam's, Sam's Café, Sandro's, Santa Fe, Scarlatti, Sea Grill, Seryna, Sichuan Pavilion, Sido, Sign of the Dove, Sistina, 65 Irving Place, Smith & Wollensky, Sofi, Sukhothai, Sushizen, Table d'Hôte, Tamu, Tango, Tapis Rouge, Thai Royale, La Tulipe, "21," Union Square Café, Vico, Water Club, Zapata's, Le Zinc.

The following reviews appeared, in somewhat different form, in *New York* magazine: Akaihana, American Harvest, Au Grenier Café, Bangkok Cuisine, Barbetta, Broome Street Bar, La Caravelle, Carolina, Chalet Suisse, Christ Cella, Claire, Coach House, Csarda, Darbár, Gibbon, Jane Street Seafood Café, J. G. Melon, Nanni, Oyster Bar & Restaurant, Pinocchio, Raga, Le Relais, René Pujol, Sal Anthony's, Santerello, Siam Cuisine, Trastevere and Trastevere 84, Vašata, Windows on the World.

CONTENTS

INTRODUCTION

As this last edition of the 1980s goes to press, a picture of what to expect in the 90s moves into focus. It is apparent that Real Estate will continue to dictate the ever tougher rules of the rough and tough restaurant game—and in new ways. While storefront rents soar to levels that, only a year ago, were but fantasies in property owner imaginations, New York—which, contrary to what you thought, took up cohabitation, when it did, solely for purposes of sharing the rent—is now into commercial sharing, too, putting eating places into places that are already other kinds of places, and *will remain* those other kinds of places. It is now clear that "doubling up in hard times" will be a catchphrase right through to the end of the century. Herewith a handful of recent items from the local press that will give you some idea of what to expect in years ahead.

A Fair Exchange

In what is said to be the largest buy-and-lease-back transaction ever consummated, Mr. Donald Trump has purchased the New York Stock Exchange and leased it back to the Exchange for the hours of 10 to 4, five days a week, for a thousand years. It is understood that Mr. Trump's purpose is to convert the floor of the exchange into a "dining arena" each afternoon at 4, when, traditionally, the stroke of a bell signals the close of the day's trading. At the gong hundreds of "Trumpeteers" in three-piece suits and long white aprons will virtually invade the Exchange floor, sweep it, carpet it, and set up row upon row of white-linened executive desks and high-backed, five-spoked, leather-upholstered swivel chairs, into which, it is expected, exhausted brokers, traders, investment bankers, arbitrageurs, waste basket rummagers, criminal lawyers, and other professionals closely connected to the securities industry, will *plotz,* at the end of their frantic day, for cocktails and tranks, while they punch out on desk-top computers dinners they will choose from the menus of New York's 100 best restaurants as selected by a panel of heavy eaters. Orders will be instantaneously faxed to restaurant kitchens, and in most instances the food will be ready to roll by the time a Trumpeteer pulls up in his limo at, for example, Pig Heaven for an order of Chinese dumplings, then at the Second Avenue Delicatessen for a pastrami on rye with cole slaw and Russian dressing, then at the Palm for a slice of its world-famous cheesecake. E.T.A. for a three-course dinner, delivered to the very desk from which it was ordered, will, of course, depend on traffic conditions. Diners will choose wine from Donald Trump's private cellar in Trump Tower, whence bottles will be shot through pneumatic tubes—recently installed in Trump's network of underground rights-of-way—directly to the floor of the Exchange. Starting at around 9 P.M., host Trump will stroll among the tables with a serving cart bearing rare brandies, vintage Cuban cigars, and a computer terminal, at which Trump himself will enter charges for after-dinner drinks, tobacco, and stock tips. At a recent preview, the restaurant, called simply Trump's Market, operated smoothly at full capacity. Insiders familiar with the situation assert that the buy-and-lease-back arrangement rescued the Exchange from imminent bankruptcy. The firm of Baum & Lopata acted as intermediaries representing both parties in the negotiations.

Surprising Announcement by Transit Authority

In disuse as a subway station for more than 40 years, while serving both as a staging area for Transit Police underground operations and as Transit Authority storage space for old turnstiles and chewing gum machines, the IRT local stop at East 18th Street and Park Avenue South ("Fourth Avenue" when last a rider stuck a dime in a slot here) will be rechristened, in cheerful—if illiterate—recognition of the most prominent characteristic of this unique operation, the Noisome Diner. Scheduled to operate 24 hours a day, just like the subway, serving up-to-date interpretations of the food of the forties on both the uptown and downtown platforms, the Diner is seen as a way of bringing together the various population groups who live along the Lexington Avenue line. At present the station is encrusted with years of accumulated filth, and, though a thorough cleaning is planned, Mr. Joe Baum, speaking on behalf of Donald Trump, the principal investor in this imaginative enterprise, has made it plain that *nothing will be changed*. Because reopening the stairways to the street poses security problems, the Diner will be serviced by kitchens to be installed in structures that already exist in Union Square and Madison Square Parks (each park just a one-stop ride for your waiter or waitress). Between courses guests will be diverted by advertising posters still in place for Philip Morris cigarettes and Greer Garson movies (in Technicolor!), while they wait for trains to pull in with their stuffed derma or spaghetti and meatballs. An opening date has not yet been announced, pending certain approval of Mr. Trump's plan for trains to slow down and briefly open their doors as they pass through the station, so that staff and customers can hop on and off. Sam Lopata is the consulting architect.

Midtown Experiment Dismays Educators

An anonymous committee consisting of unidentified presidents and chancellors of certain New York colleges and universities organized a news conference yesterday to protest aspects of an experiment recently initiated in the Main Reading Room of the Public Library, at 42nd Street and Fifth Avenue. The conference was held in a driving rain in Bryant Park, just behind the Library, under the shelter of umbrellas. In an opening statement, an anonymous representative of the committee informed the press that, though committee members realized their protest could provoke retaliation from Donald Trump—holder of mortgages on the lands and buildings of most of New York's educational institutions and principal stockholder in this unique food service enterprise (which, if it proves successful, will be extended to all branch libraries)—the committee felt compelled to disregard the danger and speak out in protest. The spokesman emphasized that the educators do not object, *in principle*, to the sale of food and beverages by vendors plying the aisles of the Main Reading Room, but they do feel that some aspects of the program—modestly named Books 'n' Burgers—among them the crackling sounds of hamburgers, ribs, steaks, free-range chickens, and Maine lobsters on the grills, the tinkle of ice cubes in highballs, and the popping of champagne corks, distract scholars from their studies. The committee, through its spokesman, made clear that for now its principal demand is to be consulted before the printing of the next menu. But it also expressed the wish that sale of the most distracting comestibles be restricted to actual breakfast, lunch, and dinner hours, with in-between times limited to food and drink of a less festive, and in the committee's words, "tea-time" character.

Mr. Trump responded at once in a hastily called conference held in the Reading Room itself. Surrounded by microphones, and in a ringing voice, Trump asserted that Books 'n' Burgers was the quietest, least distracting in-library food vending operation of its kind anywhere, and he challenged members of the committee to come out of hiding and identify themselves and their affiliations.

As Books 'n' Burgers continued to function right through the Trump conference, reporters present were in a position to observe the operation first hand. The basic Books 'n' Burgers unit, though it resembles the carts airlines use to deliver snacks and meals to its passengers, is longer, wider, higher, and altogether a considerably more massive example of food service rolling stock, what with its flaming grill, rotisserie, convection oven, full bar, 300-bottle air-conditioned wine closet, walk-in refrigerator, and espresso machine. In the interest of preserving as much quiet as possible, the wagons roll along on soft rubber tires, but because they are too heavy to be pushed, they are driven by engines specifically designed to produce the absolute minimum of gas emissions and noise. The controls are operated by "Trumpettes," young women in uniforms consisting of library smocks, horn-rimmed reading glasses, and, again in the interest of silence, nothing at all on their carefully pedicured feet. Trained to be as unobtrusive as possible, the Trumpette guides her wagon along her route, pauses at each occupied chair, approaches the reader from behind, and gently interrupts his studies with a soft tap on the shoulder. When the reader turns, the Trumpette, carefully trained to her function, slowly removes her glasses, smiles, and with a toss of her head in the general direction of the mobile unit somewhere behind her, fixes the reader with a look that is at once friendly and inquiring—but, again in the interest of strict library decorum, *without saying a word*. When a male scholar misunderstands the gesture, the Trumpette must urge him back to his chair and explain, in as soft a whisper as possible, that she has in mind Books 'n' Burgers, and not, as one Trumpette was overheard to put it, "flapjacks in the stacks."

A press kit distributed at the Trump conference credits the design firm of Baum & Lopata with menu and wagon graphics, uniforms, and the two-story-high B 'n' B banners that now flank the library entrance.

Le Cirque to Be Restaurant

It has just been announced that Le Cirque, the well-known celebrity hangout on 65th Street—which, until now, has served principally as a "people-watching" and "elbow-rubbing" center for unemployable celebrities, attendant groupies, and regiments of camp followers—is to have restaurant facilities added as an integral part of the ongoing enterprise. In a statement released by Sirio Maccioni, former owner and current floorwalker at the popular East Side boîte, real food prepared by genuine French chefs will be served at scores of tables and chairs that will be placed in among the tables and chairs already *in situ,* which will remain *in situ,* where they will continue to serve their former functions. On the premises today, Mr. Maccioni, a well-known amateur skier, informed reporters that he had traded in his skis for a pair of stilts, which are to be his means of locomotion once the combined operations are in full swing.

The new policy was instituted shortly after Le Cirque was taken over by prominent New York developer Donald Trump. Reached by telephone, Mr. Trump explained that originally he had had no intention of purchasing Le Cirque, but that it had come into his possession quite by accident in the course of his acquisition of the Upper East Side. Once he discovered it was his, Trump continued, he determined immediately that the valuable property's cost effectiveness needed to be beefed up. He added, however, that the idea of installing a restaurant on the premises was not his, but that of his close associates Sam Lopata and Joseph Baum.

Ten Sensible Rules About Going to, Eating in, Paying at and Departing from New York Restaurants

1. RESERVATIONS. Before going to a New York restaurant, telephone to make a reservation. True, reservations are often not accepted, but this is sometimes because the restaurant no longer exists. By telephoning you determine whether the place is still in business, and, if so, whether you can get a table when you want one.

2. NO RESERVATIONS. If a restaurant does not accept reservations, it is probably because it is so busy that it can get away without offering the convenience. Ask if the place is likely to be crowded when you want to go. Sometimes you will get a helpful answer, sometimes an honest one, sometimes both.

3. COMPLAINTS. It's no fun to complain throughout your meal. After all, you go to a restaurant to enjoy yourself, your food, and your companions. But it's a good idea to complain about *something* early on. People who complain are people who seem to know what they want and what they are about, and they get better treatment than the timid or unsure. If you are shy or diffident, or don't know what you want, that's too bad, but it need not be a guarantee that you will not enjoy eating in New York restaurants.

4. SENDING BACK. If you don't like something you ordered, tell the waiter it tastes terrible and send it back. Do the same thing if what should be hot food is cold or if there is anything else clearly wrong with what is brought to you.

5. WINE. If you like wine but don't know much about it, order an inexpensive bottle. Modestly priced wines are the most reliable ones in restaurants. They are what they are. Restaurants are not the place to give yourself a wine education; it is much too expensive and unreliable. Expensive wines in restaurants may be too young or too old, or damaged from poor storage, and if you're unsure of yourself, you may not know why you don't like what you get and whether you really ought to return it. If there is a sommelier (the man with the chain around his neck), his business is to sell you wine (after suitable discussion), pour your first glass, and generally convert the purchase and consumption of a bottle of mild booze into an important event. Few New York restaurants have sommeliers anymore, but those that do generally have pretty good wine stocks. If the sommelier seems like a decent sort and if you want to spring for a fancy bottle, tell him how much you are willing to spend, and he will recommend a bottle at the price, and probably a good one.

6. EMERGENCIES. If you need service at once and are unable to catch your waiter's or captain's eye, the best system is to rise from your chair and approach

11

the nearest responsible member of the staff. The late English conductor Sir Thomas Beecham used to brush dishes to the floor to get attention, but as most dining room floors in New York restaurants are carpeted, this ploy might go unnoticed. Flinging dishes against the walls or ceilings, however, is a surefire way to bring the help.

7. YOUR CHECK. Review it. It's wrong about one time in ten; in your favor about one time in a hundred. Ask for a menu to check the prices if you think you have been overcharged or charged for a more expensive item than the one you ordered. Check the addition. Of course, you may have had a few drinks and a bottle of wine, while the waiter is probably sober, so he may be right, and you may be wrong.

8. TIPPING—HOW. Don't leave your tip under a plate. It simply is not done. If you want to give someone a tip, hand it to him. If you don't spot him, leave the money out in the open where it is easy to see. If you're tipping on a credit-card voucher, write in the tip *and write in the grand total*. If you do not, an emendation may be made favoring the waiter and penalizing you. This is so common that the credit-card companies have a name for it; they call it an "override."

9. TIPPING—HOW MUCH. Par is 15 percent of the before-tax food total, plus some lesser percentage of the liquor and wine. If you are served by both a waiter and a captain, 20 percent is fair, most of it to the waiter, the exact proportion depending on whether the captain did no more than cursorily take your order or if, at the other extreme, he thoroughly explained the menu, prepared sauces and desserts, and helped with the selection of wine.

Reasons for tipping more: You ate the least expensive items on the menu and occupied the table for three hours; the service was terrific; you are feeling expansive.

Reasons for tipping less: The reverse of the above, except that waiters should not be penalized for your depression unless it is their fault.

Sommeliers should be tipped $2 per bottle, but no less than $3 in total if they have been really helpful.

10. DEPARTURE. Leave when you are good and ready. It is your right to eat at your own pace, including lingering over a second cup of coffee. Enjoy possession of a table that others are waiting in line for. Later they will.

A Note on Using This Book

The restaurants in this book have been classified as "inexpensive," "medium priced," "expensive," or "very expensive."

When the book went to press, these categorizations were roughly defined as follows—for a three-course dinner for one, with coffee, not including wine, tax, or tip:

Inexpensive:	Under $25
Medium priced:	$25 to $35
Expensive:	$35 to $45
Very expensive:	Over $45

By the time the book is printed, bound, distributed, and purchased by you, these definitions, in many instances, will no longer be accurate. First, prices in all restaurants seem to go up steadily—that is inflation. Second, if an inexpensive or medium-priced restaurant is doing very well, it may shift from one category to the next—that is the profit motive. A press-time $30 dinner may run to $40 by the time you eat it.

In some few instances specific prices of dishes or drinks or wines are referred to in the text. They are meant to give an impression of the restaurant's pricing policy. The information was correct when written, and the impression is probably still correct, even if the exact price has changed.

The Ratings

★★★★	Excellent
★★★	Very good
★★	Good
★	Good (but not *as* good)
●	Acceptable
○	Unacceptable

Restaurant Listings

BY TYPE OF FOOD

AMERICAN

American Harvest **39**
American Place **40**
Anabelles **43**
Arcadia **48**
Arizona 206 **50**
Broome Street Bar **89**
Carolina **115**
Chelsea Central **124**
Claire **137**
Coach House **138**
Four Seasons **171**
Gotham **181**
Gulf Coast **188**
Huberts **193**

Jane Street Seafood Café **200**
J. G. Melon **203**
John Clancy's **205**
Melrose **225**
Mike's **231**
Miss Ruby's Café **232**
Odeon **247**
Oyster Bar & Restaurant **255**
Ritz Café **304**
Sam's **315**
Sea Grill **323**
"21" **350**
Water Club **358**
Windows on the World **360**

BELGIAN

Café de Bruxelles **95**

Flamand **169**

CHINESE

Canton **110**
Chin Chin **130**

Fu's **175**
Sichuan Pavilion **327**

CZECHOSLOVAKIAN

Vašata **355**

DIVERSE OLD AND NEW WORLD

Brive **86**
Café des Artistes **98**
Coach House **138**
Four Seasons **171**
Gotham **181**

Grove Street Café **187**
Jacqueline's **199**
Ménage à Trois **226**
Odeon **247**
Sam's **315**

18

STEAKHOUSES

SWISS

THAI

VIETNAMESE

BY RATING
★★★★Excellent

★★★Very Good

★★Good

19

★Good (BUT NOT AS GOOD)

●ACCEPTABLE

Fu's **175**   Sam's **315**

BY NEIGHBORHOOD

DOWNTOWN, INCLUDING CHINATOWN AND LITTLE ITALY

American Harvest **39**   Cellar in the Sky **117**
Ballato **61**   Georgine Carmella **177**
Canton **110**   Windows on the World **360**

TRIBECA

Arquà **52**   Moe's **235**
Barocco **67**   Montrachet **237**
Bouley **80**   Odeon **247**
Chanterelle **121**   Tapis Rouge **345**
Ecco **157**   Le Zinc **362**

SOHO

Broome Street Bar **89**   Provence **285**
Cinco de Mayo **133**   Raoul's **293**
Omen **249**   Tamu **342**

GREENWICH VILLAGE, INCLUDING THE EAST VILLAGE

La Bohême **76**   Hasaki **189**
Café de Bruxelles **95**   Indochine **197**
Café de la Gare **97**   Jane Street Seafood Café **200**
Café Loup **102**   John Clancy's **205**
Il Cantinori **108**   Melrose **225**
Chez Jacqueline **125**   Il Mulino **238**
Chez Pierre **129**   Nishi Noho **246**
Coach House **138**   Il Ponte Vecchio **279**
Da Silvano **151**   Quatorze **288**
El Faro **164**   Rakel **291**
Florent **170**   La Ripaille **303**
Gotham **181**   Sabor **310**
Grove Street Café **187**   Sukhothai **338**
Gulf Coast **188**   La Tulipe **348**

EAST SIDE, 14TH STREET TO 33RD STREET

Brandywine **82**   Cedars of Lebanon **116**
Café du Parc **100**   La Colombe d'Or **141**
Canastel's **107**   Le Palmier **261**

22

EAST SIDE, 34TH STREET TO 41ST STREET

EAST SIDE, 42ND STREET TO 50TH STREET

EAST SIDE, 51ST STREET TO 59TH STREET

EAST SIDE, 60TH STREET TO 72ND STREET

EAST SIDE, ABOVE 72ND STREET

Al Bacio 34
Anabelles 43
Andrée's 44
Azzurro 60
Bistro Bamboche 73
Café Greco 101
Café San Martin 105
Csarda 146
Elio's 159
Erminia 161
Flamand 169
Fu's 175
Gibbon 178
Gijo's 179
Hulot's 195
J. G. Melon 203
Lusardi's 210
Malaga 216

Marcello 220
La Métairie 228
Metro 229
Mocca Royale 233
Paola's 262
Parioli, Romanissimo 264
Petaluma 271
Pinocchio 278
Primavera 282
Remi 297
Sala Thai 313
Sam's Café 316
Sistina 331
Table d'Hôte 341
Thai Royale 346
Trastevere and Trastevere 84 347
Vašata 355
Vico 356

WEST SIDE, 14TH STREET TO 41ST STREET

Ballroom 63
Chelsea Central 124
Claire 137
Da Umberto 153
Eze 163
Frank's 174

Man Ray 218
Miss Ruby's Café 232
Onini 250
Periyali 268
Sofi 336

WEST SIDE, 42ND STREET TO 50TH STREET

Au Tunnel 58
Barbetta 65
Cabana Carioca 94
Carolina 115
Chez Josephine 126
Lattanzi 209
Le Madeleine 214

Mike's 231
Orso 254
Raga 290
La Réserve 300
Sea Grill 323
Sushizen 339

WEST SIDE, 51ST STREET TO 59TH STREET

Adrienne 31
Aquavit 46
Bangkok Cuisine 64
Le Bernardin 68
La Caravelle 112
Darbár 149
Jean Lafitte 202

Jockey Club 204
Manhattan Ocean Club 217
Marie-Michelle 222
Maurice 223
Palio 257
Petrossian 274
René Pujol 299

Restaurant Raphaël **301**   Tango **343**
Russian Tea Room **308**   "21" **350**
Sam's **315**

WEST SIDE, 60TH STREET TO 72ND STREET

La Boîte en Bois **77**   Café Luxembourg **104**
Café des Artistes **98**   Santa Fe **319**

WEST SIDE, ABOVE 72ND STREET

Akaihana **33**   Santerello **320**
Au Grenier Café **55**   Siam Cuisine **326**
Blue Nile **74**

OPEN ON SUNDAY

Adrienne **31**   Chez Jacqueline **125**
Akaihana **33**   Chez Louis **127**
Alo Alo **36**   Chez Pierre **129**
Ambassador Grill **37**   Chin Chin **130**
Anabelles **43**   Cinco de Mayo **133**
Arizona 206 **50**   Claire **137**
Au Grenier Café **55**   Coach House **138**
Azzurro **60**   La Colombe d'Or **141**
Bangkok Cuisine **64**   Contrapunto **142**
Bice **70**   Csarda **146**
Le Bilboquet **72**   Darbár **149**
Blue Nile **74**   Da Silvano **151**
La Bohême **76**   Dawat **155**
La Boîte en Bois **77**   Eamonn Doran **156**
Brandywine **82**   Ecco **157**
Broome Street Bar **89**   Elio's **159**
Bruno **90**   El Faro **164**
Bukhara **91**   Flamand **169**
Cabana Carioca **94**   Florent **170**
Café de Bruxelles **95**   Fu's **175**
Café de la Gare **97**   Georgine Carmella **177**
Café des Artistes **98**   Gijo's **179**
Café Greco **101**   Gotham **181**
Café Loup **102**   Gulf Coast **188**
Café Luxembourg **104**   Hasaki **189**
Café San Martin **105**   Indochine **197**
Canastel's **107**   Jane Street Seafood Café **200**
Il Cantinori **108**   Jean Lafitte **202**
Canton **110**   J.G. Melon **203**
Carolina **115**   Jockey Club **204**
Cedars of Lebanon **116**   John Clancy's **205**
Chelsea Central **124**   Lusardi's **210**

25

OPEN LATE (UNTIL MIDNIGHT OR LATER EACH NIGHT THE RESTAURANT IS OPEN FOR BUSINESS)

SUITABLE (BY REASON OF ECONOMY OR MENU OR ACCOMMODATIONS) FOR LARGE FAMILY GROUPS

American Harvest 39
Blue Nile 74
Canton 110
Cedars of Lebanon 116
Christ Cella 131
Csarda 146
Grove Street Café 187
Indochine 197

Malaga 216
Oyster Bar & Restaurant 255
Petaluma 271
Raga 290
Sal Anthony's 311
Sala Thai 313
Sukhothai 338
Thai Royale 346

OUTDOOR DINING AND ENCLOSED GARDENS

Aquavit 46
Barbetta 65
Café Loup 102
Chez Jacqueline 125
Chez Pierre 129
Da Silvano 151
La Goulue 183
Hasaki 189
Lutèce 212

Le Madeleine 214
Odeon 247
Provence 285
Raoul's 293
Le Relais 296
Sal Anthony's 311
Sea Grill 323
Smith & Wollensky 333
Le Zinc 362

BRING YOUR OWN WINE (OR WHATEVER)

Café de la Gare 97
Canton 110
Grove Street Café 187

Table d'Hôte 341
Thai Royale 346

THE
RESTAURANTS
OF
NEW YORK

★★ADRIENNE

700 Fifth Avenue (entrance on 55th Street)
LUNCH, DAILY; DINNER, MONDAY TO SATURDAY.
Reservations: 903-3918.
Credit cards: AE, DC, MC, V.
Very expensive.

You do not experience luxe by looking at it. Luxe, to be luxe, must enfold you. And, sure enough, when you are lost in one of Adrienne's immense armchairs, you find that you may not only sit down, but roll over on your side and curl up in the fetal position. With respect to embrace, however, that is about it, for Adrienne, one flight up the grand staircase, no more enwraps you than can any partitioned-off section of a wide-open landing, which is where you are. Enter this destination, and you do not quite arrive, no environment forms around you. You are at a stopping-off point from which you are out of touch neither with where you have been nor with where you are going, a way station—which is perhaps appropriate to travelers to whom a hotel is just that, but not to New Yorkers out to dinner in search of fantasy and escape. Still, it may be the potted palms that finally undo this place, for they call to mind innumerable hotel lobbies of fact and film. But the dark boudoir pink of the silken walls, the scalloped curtains of mauve satin in the arched windows, the pale yellow linen on the large, well-spaced tables, and the glinting mirrored panels all contribute to the impression that this is not a restaurant at all, only a stage set on which will be performed a broad satire of the newly rich. But look carefully, and you will see that there is about Adrienne an intended look and flavor—of Art Nouveau. The curvilinear wood frames of those armchairs, for example, are in that sinuous style, as are the wall sconces, as are the softly colored Mucha posters that hang, almost invisibly, on a mirrored wall. But those few elements are lost in this place, and you would probably miss the design intent were not Adrienne billed as a purveyor of Mediterranean food, that part of the world being associated with that style of design.

It is perhaps the final undoing of this, how you say, ambience that it is in two unseparated parts. Make a right at the top of the grand stairway, and you are in Adrienne, but make a left, and you are in Le Bistro d'Adrienne, the latter, separated from the former by nothing at all, distinguished from it by a lower-priced menu, the absence of linen from the pink-marble tabletops, hideous side chairs instead of armchairs, a handful of posters distinctly bolder than those Muchas, and, instead of male captains and waiters in tails (they look like orchestra conductors), young women in red-and-white-striped shirts; and though you may well prefer the charms of the Bistro's informal service, it is clearly just the tourist class of the combined establishment, not a restaurant with its own identity, except that it is equipped, as first class is not, with a bar, complete with mixed nuts.

So you are surprised to discover that, in rooms of this nameless posh and lesser posh, designed to offend no one, the food served will be alien to many of the hinterland roomers who drop down from upstairs. Consider, for example, this tuna tartare, three disks of the deep-pink ground raw fish, each of them adorned with a circle of black caviar within which stands—a little yellow eye—half a soft-cooked quail egg, the three-part constructs arranged on a latticework of haricots verts that is strewn with slivers of almond, a good dish for all but the nakedly raw tartare itself, which, though of fresh seafood, lacks the sticky richness and complexity of herbs, seasoning, and other seafood that characterize fish tartares at their best. By "Mediterranean," Adrienne means not only

31

the south of Europe (read France), but the north of Africa, though the salad known as tabouli that you have had in New York's North African and Near Eastern restaurants are rather remote ancestors of this one, in which the greens and grains, gentled by superb oil, are surmounted by a couple of small, firm, moist fillets of the Mediterranean fish called rouget—its flavor, too bad, is fine in one fillet, distinctly off in the other. Order the wild mushroom soup, and your waiter arrives with a soup plate, a great tureen, and a ladle, with the last of which, when he has filled your plate, he is careful to fish out the remaining mushrooms. This is earthy soup, thick and creamy as well, of a nuttiness that derives from the black truffles with which it is prepared. Italy, too, has shores on the Mediterranean, so you find a couple of pasta dishes on the menu, notable among them this shrimp carbonara, the sweet, crunchy, eminently flavorful crustaceans in an herbed sauce, at the center of your plate a mound of broad noodles mingled with more of those wild mushrooms.

What English speakers call John Dory the French call Saint Pierre, a fish that, in the south of France, is a usual component of bouillabaisse. Here the thing is served straight, the browned fillets of the firm white meat dotted with bits of black olive, strewn with strands of fennel, set on a hash of sweet vegetables, and garnished with a dark eggplant dressing, everything on a light but creamy sauce that, by its slight enrichment of them, potentiates all the elements. Order the roasted lobster, and you take a chance worth taking, for the thing has been served overcooked and tough, despite which—as in most of the flawed dishes here—the imaginative idea is just about its redemption. The lobster, in its shell, in a wondrously fragrant pale-green sauce of coriander and olive oil, is strewn with dice of earthy turnip, and garnished with a great mound of crunchy root vegetables arranged over a layer of couscous. Your patience with imperfection is more than tried, however, by this pastilla de pigeon, the dark and tasty meat of the bird, separated from its skin, its bones, and from all its moisture as well, encased in a pot-shaped pastry the sweet spice of which will remind you of your morning Danish. No fault to be found with the rabbit, the browned chunks of pale meat, some on some off the bone, touched with Eastern spices, fragrant of thyme, and mingled with myriad vegetables—baby carrots, turnips, and little onions among them.

In the Bistro: a so-called "herring tartare," slices of firm, tart pickled herring arranged over thin circles of oiled potato, between them a thick cream threaded with herbs; a confit of duck salad in which the good greens, slices of potato, mushrooms, and peas, all in a rich dressing, are surmounted by hot dark strands of spicy preserved duck; a hot brandade, the mash of codfish and potatoes, oily and peppery, baked into a broad soup plate and garnished with the crusts of buttered bread on which you spread the thick stuff; and a navarin of lamb, much good meat in a thick gravy that is just touched with tomato, the hefty stew adorned with strands of root vegetable and tender haricots verts.

You get a decent plate of cheese and fresh fruit in the Bistro, or a sweet-spiced apple charlotte that is a pielike affair of tart and juicy fruit encased in a crackling pastry. In Adrienne itself, the sweets are more polished: a feuilleté of chocolate that is really two rectangles of dark, polished chocolate, with a paler chocolate mousse between them, set in a white, almond-flavored sauce sabayon that is encircled by a lemon sauce; another chocolate dessert, this one described as "à la provençale," and made up of four pointed ellipses of chocolate, under them a chocolate pastry cream on a thin layer of cake that has taken on the green of the pistachio sauce in which these candylike sweets are set; a pear crisp that is a sandwich of two flaky pastries and a filling of moist chunks of pear in a smooth coffee sauce—an unconvincing marriage; and a thing that, though described as "grapefruit supremes," strikes you as, principally, a rich ice cream encased in a cinnamoned, chocolate-decorated white cake, to which the honey-sweetened grapefruit sections, and dabs of shredded dates, are but diverting garnishes.

★★AKAIHANA

2164 Broadway (near 76th Street)
LUNCH, MONDAY TO FRIDAY; DINNER, DAILY.
Reservations: 724-8666.
Credit cards: AE, DC, MC, V.
Inexpensive.

Except for "Health Food" places themselves, only Japanese restaurants are really acceptable to the physical-fitness set. And except for certain Japanese customers (those groups of businessmen who seem to smoke and drink as if bent on calling up Prohibition days), the crowd in Japanese restaurants will sometimes seem as trim, erect, and scrubbed as the corps de ballet just out of the shower. Of course, this is especially noticeable here on the youthful and wanton Upper West Side, where nourishment in eating places is at best a secondary agenda. And you cannot miss it in Akaihana, a bright and shiny box of a place that lures the sound-body types not only with its bean curd, seaweed, and raw fish but also with a setting, of playfully angulate lines and nursery colors, that is notably neat and clean—though it manages to skirt the antiseptic with artful whimsy.

If you want to look like you belong, you will use chopsticks, and you will sit up straight. Leaning forward to shorten the haul is not done. Under the circumstances, you may find sashimi easier to handle than the sometimes fragile sushi bundles. The fluke sashimi is of vivid brightness, the raw fillets intertwined with slivers of lemon; the pungency of mackerel is easy to take when the fish itself is fresh; and the likes of yellowtail and sea bass, though these are not especially flavorful fish, are brought to life by the leaves of fresh ginger with which they are served. Among the sushi items, the octopus is of exceptional silkiness—a shaft of it is served belted to a block of rice with a band of deep-green seaweed. But if you come here when the three principal kinds of tuna are on hand, it is well to concentrate on those, for they set one another off smartly. The regular tuna is dark red and beefy, the toro (fatty tuna) mild and of an almost fluffy texture, the bonito fibrous and a little high. All of them make good sushi.

From among the two dozen dishes listed as appetizers (some of which are also listed as main courses, or can be converted to same by ordering a double portion): kaibashira furai, three plump, rich, deep-fried sea scallops, their flavor clear, their surfaces browned and crisp; hijiki, cool sea-gamy seaweed mixed with strands of root vegetable and flavored, strikingly, with ginger; agedōfu, blocks of soft bean curd, deep-fried until their surfaces are firmed, served in a dark and salty soy sauce that is dotted with button mushrooms; kara-age, chunks of boned chicken that reach you steaming hot, as if just out of the deep fryer, served with mustard and oranges—the citrus makes the dish seem a bit Chinese; shumai, little steamed noodle dumplings stuffed with a spicy pork forcemeat—you eat them with a fiery mustard; and negimayaki, sheets of beef wrapped around shafts of scallion—the meat is rare, and the gently cooked scallions retain some of their bite.

Shio is a method of broiling fish in its skin, with much salt, that causes the fat under the skin to permeate the meat—to excellent effect when things work out right. Akaihana prepares salmon this way (salmon shioyaki) and removes the salty skin before serving it—sure enough, the meat is not itself very salty, but its flavor is notably enriched. And the place frequently offers a deep-fried sea bass, the big slices of it reassembled into the entire beast minus its bones—it comes off as an especially buttery fish, the crusty surface moist with oil and lightly soured with vinegar.

Fresh fruit is usually available for dessert, as well as those peculiar Japanese ice creams.

★ AL BACIO

245 East 84th Street
DINNER. CLOSED SUNDAY.
Reservations: 744-9343.
Credit cards: AE, DC, MC, V.
Expensive.

It is easy to make money. Find out how others are doing it, and do exactly the same thing. People interested in making money, and interested in nothing else, have been at that game for 300,000 years (a recent estimate of the age of the human race). When, however, you contaminate the imitation, put, you should pardon the expression, your "personal stamp" on it, you are guilty of the Artistic Heresy (the sin in which the entrepreneur ranks himself—that is to say, his taste—above that of the market), and you usually sacrifice profit in return for nothing at all—or, often, for disaster. With scores of clubby Italian joints packing them in all over the upper East Side, comes one Roberto Cazzaniga, proprietor here. He could have visited, say, Elio's, Sistina, and Primola, added them up, divided by three, and had a sure thing. But no, he wants to do it *his* way. If he had in mind something on the order of, say, the *Rite of Spring*, or *Ulysses*, or even Maxwell's Plum, his egoism would be glorified by the immensity of his vision. But Cazzaniga does not want to shock anybody. All he wants is to break a few rules and get away with it. Under the circumstances it is easy not to deplore the two-thirds emptiness his place enjoys almost nightly. Who, after all, does not prefer, anytime, a big winner to a petty original?

Your disdain would be tempered by sympathy were it not for the satisfaction and length with which Cazzaniga describes to you his singular concept. His restaurant, he explains, is a Roman garden under a Roman sky. It abjures the clangor and clutter (conviviality) of his competitors, aims for a relaxed comfort (sedateness) that will appeal to the mature (infirm) of all ages. (You take it that the purpose of the background music is to demonstrate how near to inaudibility both Antonio Vivaldi and Billie Holiday can be played.) He even states—in this, and in this alone, he is unique—that his food is merely decent, every bit as good as it has to be, but no better. (He does not, you understand, want to stress you with gustatory sensations that rouse.) With such objectives it is no surprise that the place is better than he intends. The Roman garden, for example is, happily, instead, a comfortable oblong dining room, the banquette down each side upholstered in a blue cloth that simulates those intricately patterned Italian papers—like nineteenth century endpapers—in one of which Al Bacio's small menu is bound. The tables are in two long rows at the banquettes, the facing armchairs in dark-blue slipcovers down to the pale-wood floor. A great vase of flowers stands on the floor at each end of the room, and there is art here and there on the cosmetic-pink walls, most of it so harmless that the one or two truly dreadful pieces stand out. That sky overhead (it must be midnight) is midnight blue, but it is lowered just like a ceiling—by broad stripes of white cloth, on the diagonal, that are stretched across white tracks from which tiny spots cast soft light about the room. And sure enough, the Third Avenue crowd has been avoiding this place as if it were the New Jersey living room they left behind with their first spouse.

And why not? For this polenta with cheese, though the four rectangles of browned cornmeal are covered over with hot melted fontina of strong flavor, is no better than at a dozen other places, and here you cannot see the bar from your table—and even if you could, nary a model is seated at it. So you concentrate on your food, on this grilled eggplant, the thin slices shaped like broad tongue depressers, drenched in oil, and strewn with capers; on this pasta e ceci, the dense soup of noodles and chickpeas that, in this version, lacks the tangy or bitter edge of greens that in certain renditions of this dish offsets its weight, though the sprig of rosemary floated on top adds a good fragrance, and the cheese that is grated on a bit of sharpness. Pretty good pasta dishes: the linguine and shrimp, in their herbed and buttery broth, would be perfect if not for the iodine in some of the crunchy crustaceans; the spaghetti carbonara is the real thing, salty and rich, thick with egg yolks, chunky of its strong and abundant Italian bacon; and, the winner, penne ai carciofi, in which minute slivers of artichoke, deep fried, browned, crisped, are mingled with the hefty pasta in a sauce that is little more than velvety oil and seasoning—add cheese, and the simple dish becomes complex.

Presumably a regional dish from an extremely small region, one in which the citizens have both pea-patch back yards and oceanfront front yards, onto the latter of which squid are washed up, so that on moneyless days the locals can make do with this item—such must be the source of the combination of squid and peas, the pinkish, quite tender, and iridescent meat of the seafood in striking contrast to the emerald green orbs that nestle in its concavities—good food that would taste even better if you had grown up with it. Big browned scallops and thin spears of green asparagus approximately repeat that color scheme in their winy and parsleyed broth. The swordfish is firm and moist, but a bit less than fresh, which is too bad, for the steak is slicked with a rousing tomato sauce that is dotted with capers and strong black olives. But then you go over to the "carne" department, and almost everything goes wrong. The osso buco has taken on almost none of the flavor of the spicy density of vegetables that is the good sauce in which it was cooked— the meat is white and pallid, served long before it is ready. The fritto misto—chunks of calf brain, artichoke, zucchini—suffers for the hard-fibered inedibility of the artichoke leaves, though otherwise this is nicely fried food that is roused by the lemon you squeeze on. You order your filet mignon rare, and even the outside is rare—pale gray, actually —as if the knack of charring, or browning the surface of beef while barely cooking it is beyond this kitchen.

The Parmesan cheese is ok, if not the headiest, most aged in town—you may have yours with a tart, crisp apple. The sweet desserts, displayed on the rolling cart, include a sharp and citric lemon tart on a dark pastry; an uncompromisingly rich chestnut mousse cake encased in chocolate; and a zabaglione torte described also as a tirami sù cake— black cake, a rich tan cream that, by its flavor, seems to put it more in the zabaglione than the tirami sù family.

★ ALO ALO

1030 Third Avenue (at 61st Street)
LUNCH AND DINNER.
Reservations: 838-4343.
Credit cards: AE, DC, MC, V.
Medium priced.

By whim of the interests behind this place, small platforms have been installed high up on the walls, and on them have been placed large figures of misshapen waiters and waitresses standing in grotesque poses, bearing demented expressions. Delighted with the comic effect, the house has hired a live staff that, unable to match the physical appeal of the models overhead, does duplicate their mental state. The random quality of their exertions notwithstanding, the particular crowd that has found this place goes on grazing here. At Alo Alo, only by their raiment can you tell the keepers from the animals.

Actually the two-story-high corner-site installation is as much greenhouse as zoo—not by virtue of any growing things for the livestock to nibble on, rather by way of the massive glass walls almost all around, through which tourists who come to this part of town may pause to watch the specimens feed. Because the barrier between the interior of the restaurant and its surrounding city streets is transparent, the place has something about it of a sidewalk café, what with its clear view of the vehicular and pedestrian traffic through this busy intersection and the dense and casual spread of its unlinened marble-topped tables. Your introduction to the place is the bar, at which you usually spend a waiting period even if you have arrived at the very hour of your reservation. Here you find pairs of salesmen exchanging big talk for the benefit of the young lady nearby who temporarily rebuffed them with the explanation, "I think I'm waiting for somebody." You ask the barmaid to list the available beers, and her pained response makes clear that she has heard the stupid question many times before. She brightens, however, as she returns her attention to an admirer on the other side of the bar, a gentleman suffering from temperature confusion—his collar is turned up, but his shirt is unbuttoned to the belt. Eventually you are led to a table. Like all of them, yours is right beside another, and when your waiter tries to take orders from both tables at once, you refuse to play. You point out that your opponents, having been presented with menus, enjoy an unfair advantage.

But the worst, for which everything that has gone before prepared you, is not yet to come. What you get to eat is not only better than anything else about the place, it is mostly commendable: grilled vegetables, long, thin slices of zucchini, big sheets of egg-plant, crescents of red pepper and yellow pepper, quarters of endive, and a single huge mushroom, all of them blackened a little and dressed—and enriched—with good olive oil; fried eggplant, the thin slices wrapped around a bit of goat cheese and leaves of fresh basil; warm carpaccio, the leaves of raw meat apparently brought up to tepid solely by the heat of the plate on which they are served—they taste like rare roast beef, but they are served with a mound of chopped tomatoes in a tart dressing, a garnish that, very nicely, takes over the dish; veal soup, a hot, clear broth of strong meat-and-vegetable flavor—you find lengths of crisp root vegetable and tender veal at the bottom of the bowl.

You ask for an order of pasta con piselli (pasta with peas), which, the menu states, is "to be eaten with a spoon." Of course it arrives without the spoon. It may also be eaten with a fork. Happily, it consists of firm but tender little pasta shells, big sweet green peas, and slivers of ham, all slicked with butter—you add ground cheese, which fortifies the dish. You order spaghetti alla rugula, which the menu describes as "spaghetti with arugula, Parmesan cheese..." Your waiter asks if you would like yours with Parmesan cheese. This is a primitive kind of dish, little more than buttered and seasoned noodles, the arugula more a color than a flavor—the Parmesan makes the stuff sturdy without altering its satisfying plainness. You get small green gnocchi in a smooth and creamy tomato sauce that is fragrant, a little, of fresh basil. And you get tarocchi, lengths of curled pasta mingled with chunks of tomato, capers, and slices of rather tasteless black olive—an obvious dish, but a vigorous one, the olives notwithstanding. Each day there is a risotto of the day, sometimes a simple and creamy preparation in which the grains of firm rice are combined with Parmesan cheese—a mother's milk kind of dish.

The steamed salmon is fresh but slightly overdone, so that it has lost some of its oil and some of its flavor—the "sauce" of warm, chopped, dressed tomatoes redeems the dish. The handsomely browned chicken has considerable chicken flavor for such a tiny bird, and its mustard sauce is subtle, does not overpower it. The "veal chop with garlic," you figure, is garlic flavored—it is a nice enough little chop, browned and moist, but the garlic is present only as a garnish of whole browned cloves.

You look around and note that almost everyone goes for the monumental chocolate dessert, a layered affair of black cake at the bottom, three inches of rich mousse at the center, curls of pure black chocolate gilded with confectioners' sugar on top. The fruit tarts and the crème caramel are not bad.

Wine is as little as $11, but you may need two bottles, the second for that long dry spell while you wait for your check. The pasta dishes and risotto are available in half orders, but they go for at least 75 percent of the full-order-price—which you learn only when you get your check.

★ AMBASSADOR GRILL

1 United Nations Plaza (at 44th Street)
LUNCH AND DINNER.
Reservations: 355-3400.
Credit cards: AE, DC, MC, V.
Medium priced.

Restaurants in hotels have always been suspect. They fail many ways, but what they lack when they do is a human being behind them, someone with an idea of the restaurant he wants, the rules of the place to follow from the idea. Committees and compromise, inputs from staff men and guidelines from manuals, of such are restaurants in chain hotels, for instance in this corporate place, and you first figure out that you are at the mercy of disembodied regulations when the lady who leads you to your table grabs a couple of menus and a wine list before she does so, and then, instead of leaving the documents with you, walks off with them because, as your waiter subsequently explains, "If you don't ask for them, she can't put them down." (Here in the perfect world, human discretion has been eliminated.) Soon enough it is your waiter's own turn to go through idiotic paces, so when he sets upon your table a perfectly legible printout of the day's special dishes, he then proceeds to recite its contents complete.

You will recall that when the Grill opened in the late seventies, its spiffy interior (the dining room is a design descendant of the velvet-upholstered limousine) was received with approval, its intercontinental menu (the place is hard by the UN) with reservations, its gimmicks (in each multinational basket of breads there stood, like a great sail, a matzo the size of a road map) with slaps upon the thigh. It has since been several things, none of which has caught on with its guests (of an evening you see but a sprinkling of transients from upstairs), with its neighbors (UN delegates prefer a dozen other places nearby, though lower-level functionaries sometimes crowd the bar), or with the city as a whole (few "go out" here). Today, the restaurant serves better food than ever, but the food of Gascony in a setting that is at once cushy and high-tech is only one of the anomalies with which the place is stuck at this point in its erratic search for identity. The dining room is all dark plush and glitter, recessed banquettes around the sides in which you can almost hide, deep armchairs that embrace you, and a level of light that just about undoes the intended intimacy. The light source is the famous ceiling, an installation of clear and mirrored glass that reflects itself upwards in an endless inverted crystalline cascade—very nice, but you do wish it did not illuminate the place like a bathroom. In further argument with the posh appointments is the open grill, all its unbeautiful works exposed, the wall behind it the color of aluminum siding. Get yourself a table along the side, and out of sight of the works, and you will be comfortable, though no matter where you sit, the nursery-pink linen is another off note, as are most of the notes that trickle in from the 88-key doodler in the cocktail lounge.

Actually, the regular menu is in two parts, Gascony on the right, mostly French food of no particular province on the left. From the left: a tartare of two salmons that is not exactly that, rather a coarse-chopped raw-salmon patty, sticky and well-seasoned, surrounded by supple and deep-pink leaves of smoked salmon that contrast with it strikingly despite the near relationship; and warm poached shrimp, three big ones and very crunchy, of sweet, clear flavor in their smooth, fragrantly herbed, and buttery sauternes sauce. From Gascony: a warm salad, a great mound of crisp greens that, moistened with a vinegar dressing that is at once sweet and sour, has buried in it chunks of rich foie gras, nuggets of fresh salmon, and little slivers of garlic; and a skewer of lobster and wild mushrooms in a pool of butter, the morsels of lobster meat very much themselves, even though they have taken on much flavor in the grilling, the woodsiness of the mushrooms a good foil to the seafood.

John Dory (on the left), an estimable European swimmer, is brought here, filleted, and wrapped around an herbed, strongly seasoned, and vegetable-dotted shellfish stuffing to form a kind of seafood sausage—it is grilled, reaches you a little dry, its listed mustard sauce like a lemony hollandaise, the ambitious dish amusing but no more. From Gascony there is this poached hen, the juicy, tender parts, under a thick and deep-green herb sauce, served with a cup of the fatted broth in which the bird was done—you are served also a chunk of judiciously seasoned sausage and an array of whole vegetables, little carrots, a zucchini, a potato in its skin among them. Firm white beans are the bulk of the Gascony cassoulet, the thick sauce in which they are bound redolent of bacon fat, the top of the dish breaded and browned, in it chunks of that bacon, much strong duck, the giblets too, and disks of very sweet-spiced sausage. The sole Gascony finfish listed is salmon yet again, a dull slab of it, with it a candied garlic sauce that seems to be with it but not for it—a pretty arrangement of many vegetables adorns the plate.

The crème brûlée is little more than a rather heavy hot-and-cold custard. You do better with any of the three Gascony desserts: a hot apple pastry, touched with brandy, that is a mingling of the slivered apple with pastry flakes—the vividly fruity sweet is garnished with an intense vanilla ice cream; a poached pear that is of Gascony by virtue of its being done in Gascony wine—the sweet-spiced fruit is purple of its red-wine treatment, is served in a pool of its syrupy poaching liquid, is garnished with a winy pear sherbet; and a prune ice cream, dotted with black patches, that is saturated with Armagnac—alcohol does not freeze readily, so the ice cream, though of high flavor, has the texture of mousse.

★★AMERICAN HARVEST

3 World Trade Center (in the Vista International Hotel)
LUNCH, MONDAY TO FRIDAY; DINNER, MONDAY TO SATURDAY. CLOSED SUNDAY.
Reservations: 938-9100.
Credit cards: AE, DC, MC, V.
Expensive.

"Welcome once again to the American Harvest, at the Vista International Hotel," intones the red-jacketed stripling who, having paralyzed you once before with his air-waves-announcer delivery and brightly smiling but disembodied politesse, takes it that now you are all old friends. He segues into a speech about the foodstuffs American Harvest is "celebrating" this month, and you have not the cruelty to point out to him the inaptness of his language here in this semideserted and therefore slightly depressing dining room. The misfortune of this place is that it is situated in a hotel connected to the World Trade Center. The tourists sleep in the hotel but prefer to eat in the renowned Windows on the World, next door and upstairs. (These circumstances make some of the palaver on the printed menu seem particularly ill-chosen. One paean goes, "Overhead Canadian geese are flying south—a sure sign cooler weather is on the way," and you figure that some of this restaurant's missing patrons read the word and went up to Windows to watch the migration.) Which is too bad, for the Harvest, despite any number of pretensions, is the superior restaurant. Not that the cooking here is anything that will ever get you to pause, stare, and wonder; rather that, under the laid-on-thick, full-color, boosterly nationalism, there is food here that is of a character that is persuasively American. And if such menu nonsense as "Colorado Lamb Chops," "Russell Farm Leeks," and "Kalamazoo Celery Sauce" still makes it difficult for you to take the Harvest seriously, just be prepared to giggle your way through a good dinner.

As much as it extols the country's bounty, the American Harvest solemnizes the American living room. The three big dining areas are lofty, all coordinated sofas and armchairs, carpeting and draperies, with walls of warm wood paneling. The theme is not only America but also Tradition, so there is a quilt on one wall, and elsewhere, in display cases, museum examples of other native handicrafts—furniture, dolls, baskets, and the like. But, for all its national pride, nothing about the place is as endearingly American as its old-world borrowings. That red-coated captain tells you about "spesh-ee-al-ee-tays," explains that the "table-a-doat" is "pre-fix."

Every month the menu changes, presumably to reflect the season, so you will not always find what you read about. In October, Oregon salmon are apparently ripe for the marinating, and if the dill-flavored marinade and the mustard sauce that come with the dish are both a little sugary, the suppleness and fresh sweet-water flavor of the fish cannot be undone. Raw bay scallops are marinated too, in lime juice that is sharp and fragrant with hot spice and fresh coriander—the rich little morsels arrive strewn with slivers of red onion and avocado. The big oyster dish consists of a pair of raw ones and three more pairs—oysters Rockefeller, deviled oysters, and oysters Virginia. They are all fine, served respectively in hot, crusted spinach; seasoned and wrapped in bacon; and lightly breaded and flavored with mustard. Much is made of the Caesar salad, the entire preparation carried out on a stand beside your table, under your very gaze. This is a spectacular version of the familiar dish, composed of impeccable fresh, crisp romaine lettuce and crunchy croutons in a dressing that is sticky with egg yolk, sharpened with anchovy. Naturally, the ham is Smithfield, and to the strong, salty slices of fibrous pink meat you add ripe fruit and melon from a proffered tray of six or seven varieties. Sometimes the

39

house prepares what it calls "seafood in cabbage leaf," hot, sweet logs of tender, coarse-ground fish and shellfish, served under chunks of fresh crabmeat and moistened with a light, buttery sauce that is dotted with chives.

The broiled salmon is so light it is almost fluffy, and its garnish of stewed peaches and its mildly orange-flavored sauce are surprisingly natural with the fish. When the veal is a sautéed veal chop with kidneys, you discover that a bit of the organ meat is like an odd zest to the gentle veal. There are garlic and thyme in the buttery sauce. And when veal is served as a fricassee, the big mound of stew in its creamy sauce is under strands of crisp cucumber—but the meat is not without gristle. The "Trailblazer's Lamb" is a big slab of charcoal-broiled red meat, rather toughened by its overcooking, surmounted by circles of fried onion and moistened by a good dark broth that is largely the blood of the meat—it does not rescue the dish.

John Cage has written of an incident that occurred when Virgil Thomson was driving cross-country with a friend. When they came to Kansas, Thomson fervently urged his companion to race right through the state without pause. The man grew hungry, however, stopped at a diner, and once inside, saw something on the counter and asked the waitress what it was. "Peanut-butter pie," said she. Said Thomson, "You see what I mean?" American Harvest, apparently unfamiliar with the wisdom of Virgil Thomson, has served something called peanut-butter chiffon pie. It calls to mind not only this tale but also the symptoms of lockjaw. Yet the Harvest has also turned out a lovely peach pie on a flaky pastry; firm poached peaches in an intensely sweet-spiced syrup; a hot apple-and-strawberry cobbler served under a crumbly, shortbread pastry; and a so-called apple pound cake that is more like a nut cake threaded with slivers of apple—it is surfaced with a sweet, sticky caramel that will restore the ache to your tired teeth. The brownies are good—light, nutted, powdery on top.

★★AMERICAN PLACE

969 Lexington Avenue (near 70th Street)
DINNER. CLOSED SUNDAY.
Reservations: 517-7660.
Credit cards: AE, DC, MC, V.
Very expensive.

Having been publicly derided for unembarrassedly appending to his menu, like a footnote without a referent, a sententious and self-serving epigraph, L. Forgione, chef and proprietor here, found himself in a hard place. Capitulate to the taunting, drop the quote from the menu, and thus concede its pomposity? Or retain it and remain ridiculous?

Comes not quite to the rescue, compromise. The quote remains, to be sure, but in minuscule type, and in medium-brown ink on dark-tan paper. In black and white, it still goes like this:

> *"The truth is, one must be inspired to cook. For, you know, we always learn from others and end up teaching ourselves."*
> —James Beard, *Friend and Mentor*—

While Forgione is letting you know he is inspired, was an intimate Beard disciple, is self-taught—not to mention reverent—you are reminded that it has always been good

American marketing to wrap the product in veneration of a past that grows in glory as it recedes. Even the name of this place borrows from an old reputation, makes reference to an art gallery of the same name founded by Alfred Stieglitz, in which were shown the early efforts of American painters and photographers, many of whom were later honored for their works (and many of whom were not).

You do wish that the products peddled here were wrapped in something other than self-importance and yesteryear, for this place purveys food that does not need the hype. The surroundings, however, conduce not at all to its appreciation. The room manages to be densely furnished and noisy without being convivial, to be popular and to be not at all a destination. The dull have made it their own, they want it to remain and to remain the same, thank you, and if no one else likes it the way it is, so much the better. You might not have predicted this fate for food once considered advanced. A couple of steps down, and you are in a low-ceilinged store that is one building lot wide, three times as deep. Except for two tables up front that, though not crowded in, seem hardly to be in the restaurant at all, wherever you sit you are privy to those upper East Side conversations in which she finally has him where she wants him and is going to tell him exactly what she goes through all day while he is at the office. He does not respond with a recitation of his own problems because to do so would be to admit he is as henpecked at the office as he is at home. She pauses long enough to note that the restaurant's appointments suggest her eleventh go at her own living room, the time she had the hypnodecorator in—he put her into a trance, covered the walls with raw silk onto which cattle brands had been randomly scribbled, tossed in a handful of framed arts, a mirror, a grape-colored banquette, took his fee and ran before she even had a chance to look around and burst into tears.

Forgione announces his American theme with the top item on his printed menu: "terrine of America's three smoked fish with their respective caviars." It is of course as ridiculous to suggest (as the words do) that only three fish are smoked in America as to suggest that only three kinds of cigarette are smoked in America. Anyway, you figure the dish is here to make a mildly jingoistic rather than culinary point, and sure enough, though the terrine is eminently edible, there is no magic in the juxtaposition of its elements. You are served a square slab, which was cut from a loaf that was formed of four layers of fish mousse alternating with layers of, first, smoked salmon, then whitefish, then sturgeon—the smoked fish are three stripes across a field of herb-speckled white, the whole set in a pool of crème fraîche and ringed with dabs of caviar—orange, pale-pink, and black. The terrine is dominated by the strong flavor of the whitefish, and the caviars are fine, the salmon of plump, bursting globules, the whitefish roe pleasantly sharp, the black roe much more assertive than the best sturgeon caviar. But everything in this dish would be improved if served alone, away from everything else. Opt instead for one of the three-hundred fish America grills, "Montauk" (imported from the Hamptons!) tuna, three rectangles of the fresh red meat, lightly browned in the judicious grilling, rare, and served with a hollandaise that has been roused with lime juice and cilantro. Morsels of fresh lobster and little chunks of woodsy mushrooms are assembled into croquettes, are delicately breaded and gently sautéed, are served, in their winy lobster sauce, with crunchy spears of green asparagus. That, of course, was "New England" lobster, and so when these potato pancakes are identified as "Pennsylvania Dutch," while no background information is given on the salmon served with them, you lift up the fillet to make certain it is not concealing anything. The salmon has had two preparations—it was smoked then grilled, both with restraint, so that, despite two "cookings," it remains itself, and both the fish and the crusty pancakes are enriched with a chived hollandaise. Little pancakes once more, these dotted with bits of scallion, described as griddle cakes, and interleaved with warm disks of a moist, vividly flavored duck sausage, to which the grainy pancakes are a good foil—the dish is strewn with a spicy relish of sweet corn and red pepper. The listed pasta dish is notable for the diversity of its elements and for how well they get along: wide noodles, short lengths of dark, salty ham, grilled shrimp that gained much flavor in their grilling, wild mushrooms, sweet peas, all in a light but creamy sauce that is heady of garlic.

The tail of a lobster is broiled under its spicy stuffing, the stuffing is browned, the lobster is cooked through but remains juicy, and the whole, with its claws, is set in a bourbon sauce that is dotted with slivers of wild mushroom and red pepper—the sparkling food is garnished with a muffin of moist rice that is flecked with bits of vegetable. Salmon again, the substantial fillet "cedar planked," which is to say, baked on a board. The method seals in moisture, and, sure enough, the fresh pink fish, a little rare, is juicy and glistening under its darkened surface, and it is served in an "egg sauce" that resembles scrambled eggs—enriched and very soft, herbed and nubbly, striking with the good seafood. There must be honey in their marinade, for the slabs and parts of quail that, mingled with slices of strong, salty "Ozark country ham," are arranged around the perimeter of your dinner plate are not only crisped and of clear quail flavor, but sweet in an uncloying way—the good bird is garnished with emerald-green snowpeas and with a mound of mashed potatoes that is polished with butter. A good sign: you are not asked how you want your veal chop. And though it reaches you a bit rarer than the pink-but-cooked-through condition that is just right, the chop is well intended, its surface grill-marked and handsomely browned, the green pasta that garnishes it fragrant of herbs, its veal sauce deep and a little winy. Juicy slices of lamb cut from a rare-roasted loin are packed with a pungent stuffing of spinach and goat cheese—the lamb is strong, the blackened edges of each slice are crackling, and the arc in which they are arranged is extended with thin slices of grilled eggplant, the two set in a strong sauce of the lamb's own juice. Carpetbagger steaks—steaks stuffed with oysters—work about one time in ten, otherwise come across as a big mistake. This one tries hard, but the dryness of the overcooked filet mignon is an obstacle not even intrinsic to the dish, and neither the stout red-wine mushroom sauce nor the garlic with which the oysters have been sautéed bridge the disparate elements.

The bread pudding is a grainy-tasting mass in a bourbon sauce—like a whiskeyed crème anglaise—that is dotted with crushed raisins. The hot banana betty is a nice juxtaposition of the sweet-spiced powdered crust, chunks of ripe banana, hot cream. A pitcher of whipped cream accompanies the devil's food cake, but it could as well be a glass of milk, for this is your basic chocolate cake, dark and strong, layered and topped with rich black frosting. Labeled "local," the peach pandowdy is presumably a seasonal availability. When it is on the menu, it is served to you in a round ramekin, the chunks of fresh fruit in a thick, sweet syrup between breadlike pastries, with it another pitcher of the good house whipped cream. The shortcake is made with these berries one time, those another, on occasion both ripe raspberries and, that rarity, sweet and firm little huckleberries.

★★ANABELLES

1294 Third Avenue (near 74th Street)
LUNCH AND DINNER.
Reservations: 772-8100.
Credit cards: AE, MC, V.
Expensive.

Someone had a notion—well, kink of mind—to paint this place, every inch of its extensive walls and ceiling, with broad brush strokes of boudoir mauve. Then someone —maybe someone else, maybe not—had the kink to paint, here and there just under the ceiling, friezes of silhouettes of waiters in long white aprons and white bowties. (The waiters and waitresses here wear black, with long white aprons and white bowties.) Happens, unfortunately, that to any but the most literal eye, the painted black figures, black of hands and face as well, look, in their servantly poses, like stepinfetchit caricatures, or line dancers in a minstrel show. It was probably one of those situations in which, when Anabelles was put together, everyone saw the gaffe, but no one wanted to be the first to acknowledge note of such a thing. Now, if there is any more of that mauve paint . . .

The ceiling is not high, the tables are not far apart, and the surfaces are abetted, in their sound-reflecting function, by rectangular glass mirrors here and there, all of which conditions conspire, particularly in the more densely tabled corners, to a situation in which sound bouncing among the surfaces enjoys a half-life of approximately ten minutes. The floor is carpeted, but you would look funny clinging to it. The help are sweet, and your waitress does not mind allowing as how, what with the noise, a day off from here is like a month in the country.

But, big but, there is nothing laughable about the kitchen. It turns out a fashionable menu—several of the dishes are just about standards of the new-cooking repertoire—in which stylish food is served up in comparatively vigorous renditions: a pink and creamy butternut squash soup, its root flavor mild but vivid, to which crumbled Roquefort and chopped walnuts have been added to striking effect; a carpaccio of fish—the species varies from day to day—that, when it is snapper, is a vaguely pink film of the utterly fresh seafood, tender, ornamented with strands of fresh mint, salted, and garnished, at the center of your plate, with a little mound of seafood salad, of shrimp and lobster, that is unfortunately a distraction from, if not quite a discordance with, that sweet snapper; boudin blanc, the white sausage nutted and meaty and just rich enough, shreds of leek and slices of shiitake mushroom in its creamy sauce; ravioli with cod mousse, the strong flavor of the homey fish somehow not obscured by its startling sauce of capers and herbs—a good, pungent dish.

So much is now known about how yummy is your salmon when rare, that when it is cooked to a point that is perfect by all but the most recent standards, though utterly fresh and full of flavor, it seems not moist enough under its strong, browned horseradish crust. The grilled chicken has real flavor of its own, is moreover adorned with strands of good ham and with cut-up sweet pea pods, is set on rich mashed potatoes. The veal chop is supple and juicy in its sauce, which is sharp of mustard, smoky of tarragon. And the grilled liver, blood pink at the center, reaches you in thick slabs in its lime-and-ginger sauce—the dish may be thought of as liver and onions, for the pudding at the center of your plate is of roasted onions, and as usual that vegetable makes nice music with that meat.

You suspect that the desserts are the responsibility of someone other than the chef, for though the fruited and nutted chocolate bread pudding is intense but not heavy in its chocolate sauce, and the tart tatin is unobjectionable in its pecan-dotted caramel sauce, the poached pear is obvious and insipid under its thick, cinnamon-flavored sauce, and the flat apricot tart is, or does a good imitation of being, a day old.

★★ANDRÉE'S

354 East 74th Street
DINNER. CLOSED SUNDAY.
Reservations: 249-6619.
Credit cards: AE.
Beer and wine.
Medium priced.

You enter to an anteroom, are met at the door by Andrée's cordial husband, are served, often, by one or the other of her amiable young daughters (or by others whose qualifications are apparently other than professional), are visited, at around dessert time, by Andrée herself, all smiles and energy in her kitchen whites. She asks after your well being and then leaves you alone, unless you have questions of your own about her food or restaurant, in which case she lingers, responds with enough evident pleasure almost to persuade you that yours are not the same questions she gets six nights a week. When things are slow you sometimes see Papa standing in a doorway, one arm around an offspring's shoulders—his pride in his children is strengthened by the fact that, though they have been earnestly helping out in the dining room for years now, they have never been tempted to assume a pro's aplomb, still occasionally look a bit surprised when, a dish of food having been set rather tentatively down, its intended proceeds without incident to eat it. In all that, happily, the charm adds more than the absent deftness takes away. Still, it is well that Father uncorks the wine, for though he, too, is not quite to this business born, his poise is enough to preserve some of the ceremony of that event. The restaurant is a bit bigger now than in its early days—in the enlarged back a U-shaped banquette converts the four tables-for-two within it to a seminar of eight. But, what with the lace curtains on the front windows, the sloping floor, the large bare-topped Spanish campaign table of dark wood (it looks like an old family piece among the standard white-linened restaurant tables), and rugs and prints on the walls that appear to have been accumulated over years, rather than chosen all at once by a decorator, the place remains a dining room that is also something of a living room.

Under her umbrella subtitle, "Mediterranean Cuisine," Andrée gathers together dishes of North Africa, southern France, Greece, Italy, Israel, Turkey. Fear not, no stigma of impurity attaches to begetting a meal via a mingling of the cookeries. A distinction is made between "appetizers" and "first courses." The former are less expensive, are mostly vegetarian, include a number of deep-fried items, which reach you hot, handsomely crisped, virtually greaseless, among them kobeba and falafel, the former crusty, grainy wheat shells filled with a meat stuffing that is wildly flavored of Eastern spices, the latter light and well-seasoned bean fritters that are dotted with pine nuts. Other appetizers: taramosalata, the Greek paste of bread and red caviar in a version that is particularly lemony and oceanic, less doughy than most; stuffed grape leaves, hot ones, the rice sweet-spiced and moist within its parchmentlike but tender wrappers; baba ghannoush, the cool paste rich of its oil, sharpened by the somewhat burnt flavor the eggplant takes on in the baking.

Among the more ambitious "first courses" there are always special dishes of the day,

44

which you learn of early on when a member of the staff arrives with a white slate—she holds it under her chin for you to see and simultaneously recites its contents, as if to prove to you, the examiner, that she has mastered her lesson. One such special is given as "shellfish en matelote," a small soup bowl of creamed and lightly tomatoed seafood broth, flecked with herbs, in which you find fresh and tender clams and mussels in their shells, scallops out of theirs and a little overcooked, some of their oily richness boiled away. The regularly listed first courses include shrimp Alexandria, the crisp and clean-tasting crustaceans baked with tomatoes and feta cheese in a tart and briny ouzo- (lico-rice) flavored broth—well-made food, but the Greek affection for combining feta and seafood remains unexportable; panaché de saumon, a small ramekin of rich, smooth salmon mousse spread with a velvety mayonnaise, served with smoked salmon that is moistened with good oil and strewn with capers and strands of onion; ratatouille en croûte, the chunky and well-oiled vegetable stew wrapped in a browned and delicate pastry; merguez au fromage, the sweet-spiced and heavily anise-flavored lamb sausages served with slabs of bland but nicely browned cheese in a thick tomato sauce. Each night there is a pasta of the night, and on occasion the firm noodles are served in a pungently seasoned tomato sauce that is thick with nuggets of eggplant, the entire dish adorned with strands of mozzarella—decent food, if not an inspired creation. Withal, if you eat here but once, your dinner should begin with the house chicken soup, for its like is not readily found in other local eating places. The hot and salty broth is thick and dark with the Egyptian herb called mulokheyyah, which is at once bitter, of vigorous flavor, and headily fragrant—eat this soup rapidly, and your brow grows moist.

What is given as red snapper à l'égyptienne is the whole fish, boned if you prefer, but with the skin on, firm, fresh, and of vivid flavor even in its lemony and saffron-flavored broth—which is thick with chunks of potato and tomato, strands of pepper and onion. The fish couscous—made with snapper, cod, and sea trout—suffers on occasion for the less-than-sweet condition of one variety, though the souplike dish, with potatoes, chick-peas, and strands of almond in its oiled and briny broth, is otherwise fine. There is vegetarian moussaka and there is meat moussaka, the latter a hot mash of chunky, sweet-spiced ground beef in which bits of blackened skin cling to dice of rich eggplant—the dish is topped with a béchamel that is fluffy and handsomely browned. Sometimes you are offered cassoulet, the suitably ponderous mass of firm beans bound in a thick gravy and covered over with slabs of sausage, moist sections of lamb, pork, and duck buried within it. Next to that, the rack of lamb, served to you uncarved, is a delicacy, the charred herbs with which it is surfaced a nice accent to the blood-pink and strong-flavored meat.

The pear poached in white wine is firm and fruity in its syrup. Something called "khochaf" consists of dried fruits poached, it seems, in rose water, with pistachios and pine nuts—a gentle sweet, though consuming the stuff is a bit like drinking perfume with your fruit salad. Good baklava, the honeyed pistachios wrapped in a browned pastry. The chocolate mousse is fresh, dark, and airy under its rich whipped cream. Sometimes there is a hot raspberry tart, the ripe sugared berries of almost liquorlike strength on the flaky pastry—it is served with a little pot of tart crème fraîche.

★★★ AQUAVIT

13 West 54th Street
LUNCH, MONDAY TO FRIDAY; DINNER, MONDAY TO SATURDAY. CLOSED SUNDAY.
Reservations: 307-7311.
Credit cards: AE, MC, V.
Very expensive.

A pair of townhouses seven stories high, one behind the other, surround an atrium through which, halfway up, the buildings are bridged. Between dawn and dusk, daylight floods the glass-domed space, and at certain times of year rays of actual sunlight pierce through to ground level, but at night a moon and a sky full of stars do nothing to relieve the darkness of the hidden vault. This, however, is midtown space, vastly valuable, and now some Swedes, having noted that the base of the atrium would make a singular restaurant setting, have taken possession of it—along with adjacent portions of the two lower stories of the front building—and installed the first serious Scandinavian restaurant to open in New York in decades. It appears that, happily, Swedish restaurant design is not characterized by the desperation for effect with which that pursuit is beset in New York. No element of this place is unconventional, nothing is designed to overwhelm, the restaurant is plainly commodious in a way that is its own stunning effect.

You enter, by descent of a few steps, to the upper floor of this two-tiered place. Here is the informal half of Aquavit, a long stand-up bar, unlinened tables, the comparatively simple Swedish menu supplemented by a short list of the Danish open-faced sandwiches called smorrebrod—they have names (e.g., H.C. Andersen, Tivoli, Havsstrykare), and they have unlikely seeming sets of components (e.g., smoked eel with scrambled egg and chives) that are the evolved culmination of centuries of intrepid Danish sandwich eating. Bypass that café by descending further, and you come to the inner room of Aquavit proper, pale walls, soft light, a banquette under a row of small framed paintings, and a couple of tables right beside the large windows at the back of the room, which look out to the lofty backyard, these sheltered inside accommodations presumably for the convenience of those who are afraid of heights even from the bottom. A few more steps down, and you are in the atrium itself, to your left the sloping west wall of gray ceramic tiles down which a sheet of water endlessly flows; to your right a vertical cliff of polished opal-gray marble; across the way, under four large paintings, another banquette, of gunmetal leather. Within these bounds has been created, by a balance of appointments, an installation that manages to be a cushy interior in the out-of-doors: a random arrangement of creamy-linened tables, little steel lanterns that burn like candles thereon, capacious armchairs of leather and tubular steel around them; dark blue carpeting, of a small geometric pattern, that in this low light seems softly mottled; white birch trees that reach a couple of stories up; and, above the tops of those, and extending almost to the top of the atrium, great two-dimensional kitelike mobiles, of colored cloth mounted on wood slats, that tame but do not quite undo the dark void overhead—a sharp clap of your hands, and the whole place echoes.

Mention Scandinavian food, and the American reflexively thinks of a smorgasbord. No such buffet is presented here, but if your problem is that without one you will not feel you have eaten Swedish, the house lists a smorgasbord plate. It is composed of more elements than can possibly register on a single mind, among them herrings and fish roes, a hard cheese and a livery pâté, cured salmons, salads, more, but though they are fine, you are more likely to come away with a clear idea of what you have eaten if you begin with something unassorted: a thick slice of deep-orange gravlax, firm, supple, and tender, the marinated salmon infused with dill and served with a sparkling dill-and-mustard sauce; a tartare of salmon and oysters, the fresh raw fish and shellfish chopped, seasoned, herbed, and bound together into a light and sticky mass that is at once oceanic and sweet; a salad of dark wild mushrooms that become wondrously earthy in the oil with which they are dressed—fresh greens, walnuts, and hard-cooked quail eggs add, respectively, crispiness, crunchiness, a bit of eggshell; arctic venison pâté, a rectangle of reddish-brown forcemeat, studded with pistachios, in a pastry frame, adorned with lingonberries, and garnished with strands of celery root in a thick dressing—you do wish the pâté were not cool, but still the flavor of the strong meat is clear; a salmon soufflé, about the size of a large egg, on a layer of spinach within a browned puffy-pastry dome—this is not a soufflé as you know it, its weight and texture are those of a quenelle, but the salmon flavor is clear, dramatized by the dilled red sauce in which the construct is set.

You have by now noted that salmon is much of this menu. There are in fact three salmon dishes among the main courses, and of those the juniper-smoked salmon is commended to your attention. The fish is only barely smoked, so that it is not cooked through, yet it takes on a heady smokiness. Then it is cooked, once again lightly, so that when it is served, its center is a deep rosy-pink, it is juicy, and it is of almost dazzlingly complex flavor—the somewhat tart sauce of trout roe is in striking contrast. In Scandinavia, fancy food is often French food in Nordic variations. Thus this Dover sole, the fish halved, skinned, boned, reassembled, done through but not overcooked, and served in a white wine sauce that is lightly browned on the plate—the three fish roes with which it is adorned add gamy zest to the perfectly prepared dish. And thus the turbot, a massive nugget cut from a huge fish, the bones at the center like spikes, the dark skin you peel away almost like leather, the meat firm and of a delicate flavor made nutty by the browned butter your waiter spoons on—a horseradish garnish northernizes the dish. The snow grouse must be a tiny creature, for your serving of its meat is but a few thin leaves—still much is made of the bird, it is in a tart and creamy sauce that is dotted with lingonberries, and it is garnished with a sharp purée of celery root, with a browned and crusted slice of potato tart that is vigorously salted and of strong potato flavor, and with a kind of meatball, presumably of the grouse itself, that is solid, powerfully seasoned, satisfying. Arctic venison again, the thin slices of loin blood-juicy in their spicy, fruity, and much enriched apple and juniper berry sauce. But for red meat that is both closer to home and far from the usual thing, consider the poached tenderloin of beef, the thick disks much like slices cut from a broiled loin, for the rims are browned and the centers rare, but these reach you in a clear and stocky broth in which you find also leeks and little carrots, slightly bitter baby turnips and halves of potato with their skins on, and a marrow bone—you may season the meat with sharp mustard and/or coarse salt.

The rich, dark chocolate cake is notable for the nutty flavor of its almond crust and the intensity of the bright-red raspberry purée in which it is set; the crème caramel for its lightness and for the black raisins in its sauce; the clafoutie for the warm hominess of the cooked Swedish blueberries, the dark and crumbly pastry, the extraordinarily thick and tart crème fraîche served with it; the brambleberry sorbet for the depth of its berry flavor; the so-called smalandsk cheesecake for the nuttiness, grittiness, distinctiveness of the mixed cloudberries, lingonberries, slivered almonds, and for the deep vanilla flavor of the ice cream served with the odd mixture.

You may prefer to drink beer and aquavit with dinner—très, très Scandinavian. There is superb Carlsberg beer on tap and several flavors of aquavit—in Scandinavia caraway is the usual flavor.

★ ARCADIA

21 East 62nd Street
LUNCH, MONDAY TO FRIDAY; DINNER, MONDAY TO SATURDAY. CLOSED SUNDAY.
Reservations: 223-2900.
Credit cards: AE, DC, MC, V.
Very expensive.

Whether by calculation or chance, Anne Rosenzweig, chef here, has built her reputation in part by culinary flattery. She incorporates in her fancy food elements of home cooking that are rarely so honored. The attachment of certain authorities to the humble dishes on which they were reared is thus redeemed. Dress the quail with kasha, make pasta taste like borscht, use crème fraîche like sour cream, construct a dessert of macadamia nuts (the caviar of junk food, a jar was always produced for special occasions), and you are close to uncovering a food critic's most carefully clothed secret: nine times out of ten she would rather have a pastrami on rye. It is not, of course, that those foods are out of place in new contexts, rather that Arcadia does not deserve extra points simply for incorporating, say, smoked whitefish in its seafood salad.

This is a small place. The seating is tight, the booking is tight. You arrive at the hour of your reservation, maybe get seated half an hour later. You are not dealt with in a take-it-or-leave-it manner, you understand, the house fervently does wish that those nursing brandies and coffee refills would vacate, but there you are. That, however, is the lesser of the tightness problems. The greater is the one with which you may well be stuck throughout dinner, for Arcadia, installed in a storefront that would do comfortably as an eight-chair barbershop, strains to seat 50 at dinner. You enter to a small room occupied by a bar and, often, a crowd around it, the two of which it accommodates more or less readily. But someone had the wishful notion, back when this place was laid out, that the room could hold four tables as well, and has since overlooked the visible fact that to eat at any of them is to be stuck between a throng and a hard place. When you reserve a table at Arcadia, you understand, you specify the back room—which is only a little better. Webster defines Arcadia as "a region or scene of simple pleasure and quiet," which surely describes the swath of sylvan mural that segues from spring through winter in its perimetric four-season sweep around the dining room. Having perhaps been mindful that there would be population enough on the banquettes below his painting, the muralist excluded from his quiet region all fauna, sapiens and otherwise.

The peaceful fantasy, however, does not offset the real congestion, for the seating at the straight banquettes along the sides is cheek to cheek to cheek, though if there are two of you, you are better off side by side than face to face, for the smaller tables for two would barely accommodate a game of solitaire. (If you do not smoke, the waiters and waitresses automatically remove the ashtrays, to free up square inches. You may wish to have the obtrusive flowers removed as well.) Still, those tables are not as bad as the two in the narrow center aisle. Seated at one of these, and without Zen training, the incessant pedestrian traffic to your left and right will have you convinced by coffee time that you are caught in a stampede. Happily there is a large table in each of this room's four corners, the only entirely comfortable accommodations in the place. If you are four, arrange in advance for a corner table.

Rosenzweig's inclination to the down home extends to her nomenclature. Consider, for example, this so-called crabmeat cocktail, which does not explain itself until it shows up in a big martini glass, the fresh seafood, all its sweet flavor intact, a mass bound in a saffroned and lemony mayonnaise and set on crisp greens. And it extends to her corn cakes, one of the three ever present dishes on her regularly revised menu. You are served four of these golden disks, they are delicately browned, light, of vivid cornmeal flavor, sweetened a bit by the whole kernels of corn with which they are dotted, and served with a great dollop of crème fraîche—thick and creamy, but you wish it had more tartness and character—that is adorned with minced chives and what are given as "caviars," a gram or two of a black one, two or three of a pale-golden one, the roes dim in the context of this well-made but self-consciously fancified dish. But some of her good ideas are sans cutes, among them this grilled leek, the white stalk—delicately charred and moistened with herbed butter—protruding from a block of flaky puff pastry that is stuffed with a sweet, sharp onion marmalade. But the pasta with salmon, beets, and dill, though eminently edible, is coy theater. That it looks as if it would glow shocking fuchsia in the dark is the least of it. That everyone in the place who gets a copy giggles, then announces that it tastes like borscht, is the point. You do wonder why there is pasta that tastes like borscht when there exists already borscht that tastes like borscht. Culinary humor, maybe. For those who might otherwise miss the joke, there is a dollop of cool thick cream at the center of the dish. (The chunks of good salmon in among the noodles establish that when you add salmon to borscht—or its farinaceous counterpart—you still have borscht.)

The chimney-smoked lobster is another perennial dish, and if you get here just once, it is the main course to have. This is a tiny lobster, done over a fire, an exacting business—too much fire, and the lobster will be dry and stringy. But these crustaceans seem always to arrive moist and supple and juicy in their tarragon butter, and the smokiness they pick up in the making dramatizes but does not obscure the meat's sweet flavor. The dish is served with celery root cakes—they are like potato tarts, buttery within their crusty surfaces, the good root flavor almost subsumed in their vigorous seasoning. What is listed as "Arcadian fish stew" sports two great wings that protrude from the sides of its soup plate, crusts of bread spread with a vibrant garlic sauce, and you may find them the high point of this bouillabaisse variant, for though the soup is saffroned, brandied, touched with citrus, threaded with leeks and tomato, it is of a certain thinness, and though the mussels in their shiny black shells are sweet, the mound of seafood at the center of your plate is overcooked, the scallops have lost their richness, the fish its identity. You are asked how you want your duck steak, and it arrives accurately medium rare in its polished and somewhat fruity port wine sauce—the duck is tender, juicy, of clear flavor, there are slices of earthy wild mushrooms in the sauce, the wild-rice pancakes are crusty, the kale that adds a note of green to the dish is otherwise a dull presence in the lively company. The roast veal shanks are another variant, this one on osso buco, the meat—well cooked, firm, moist, and just falling off the bone, but of little flavor—served with the ricelike pasta grain called orzo, everything in a stocky sauce the acidity of which does not undo the somewhat leaden solidity of this winter food.

Of Rosenzweig's variations on familiar themes, her reinterpretation of cheese and fuit is, it is hoped, the most disastrous: dabs of three cheeses, one of them sweating, two of them drying out, with three crusts of toasted brioche on which slivers of grilled pear have settled into a shriveled and dejected state. The stiff-textured chestnut flan has nothing on plain flan. But the pear and cranberry crisp is light and fruity, accented with bits of crisped sweet pastry, enriched with cinnamon-flavored whipped cream. And, as ever, the chocolate bread pudding—the third perennial—is of a comforting warmth and solid chocolate depth in its lightly brandied sauce.

Talk to the floor staff and they will tell you that since her connection with "21" Rosenzweig works here an average of three nights a week. Some think the food is better when she is on hand. Whatever the reason, few kitchens in New York produce food so superb and also so dreary, the best dishes those that have always been on the menu. The East Side crowd that once filled this place has been in part supplanted by a new set, and though it has been reported that Arcadia requires jackets and ties, guys in pullover sweaters now eat here unmolested.

★★ARIZONA 206

206 East 60th Street
LUNCH, MONDAY TO SATURDAY; DINNER, DAILY.
Reservations: 838-0440.
Credit cards: AE, DC, MC, V.
Expensive.

Odds and ends—including heart-shaped wreaths of red peppers on the walls and a single tomahawk—are all it took to transform a stucco alpine ski lodge (this was briefly Stamperl 206) into a clay hovel of the American Southwest. Cement, adobe, whatever the building material is or is meant to resemble, the stuff was spread with a rubber trowel, for 206 looks like a plastered low-ceilinged cave, complete with fireplace just inside the entrance, built-in rough-hewn wooden benches along the walls, loose cushions on them, and a wide-plank floor that, presumably, is laid over bare earth. The companionably shoulder-to-shoulder seating is at virtually adjacent tables, their wood tops the size of chessboards. Occupied, as it is, by recent seniors, the place throbs a little with the jollity of a sloppy college bar. Look through the front window, and you would guess that most in the crowd are working on burgers, and that the youthful staff, in unisex pink shirts and khaki work pants, hang out here on their nights off, when some of these customers are themselves working the floor. Either way, your waitperson has to get within four inches of your ear to make audible its recitation of the special dishes of the night, for the mating sounds in these hard-surfaced surroundings, taken together with the piped-in Top 10 (which occasionally share their air with Willie Nelson, who settles an old score with Hoagy Carmichael by singing "Stardust"), get first call on your tympana.

But it is not burgers the crowd is on, instead a Californiated version of Mexican and American-southwestern food, with not-so-faint traces of everywhere else on earth. Among the offerings are these bicontinental ravioli, the pasta packages, filled with a hot paste of pungent goat cheese, set in a spicy and brick-red pepper sauce that is strewn with sprigs of fresh coriander, all the elements fine, though this particular new-world sauce with this old-world pasta is an instance of culture shock unresolved; a flour tortilla filled with a creamy and mildly spiced filling that is mostly sweet crabmeat, with it a tart green salsa and well-garlicked cubes of cold tomato; a lamb salad that is several slices of cool, rare meat with crunchy halves of baby artichoke and marinated tomatoes, all in a tangy vinaigrette; and pan-fried sweetbreads, the slivers of organ meat, rich within their crisped surfaces, mingled with sautéed wild mushrooms and bits of bacon and strewn over half a black-skinned, sweet, earthy squash.

Though the tabletops are wee, the dinner plates are the size of ash can covers, so with two plates on one table, the air space over the occupants' laps is inevitably violated. Making it a point not to knee your dinner when you cross your legs, you edge up to the rim of your plate and insert your fork into a transatlantic mound of "seafood risotto with saffron & roast poblano chili," the big grains of wet rice—the dish is soupy—dotted with rich scallops, crisp sweet-tasting shrimp, chunks of lobster, the liquid green and spicy-hot of the chiles ground into it. Hot peppers again, this time rubbed into the surface of a chicken that is breaded, crisped, and served on a layer of kale—the moist meat of the bird is suffused with the flavor of the hot pepper. Because the rib-eye steak is about as thick as it is wide, the fibrous meat is tender and blood-juicy despite the heavy black crust it picked up in the grilling—the good meat is garnished with whole onions. In what is given as "venison black bean chili," morsels of the game meat are mingled with a nubbly mix of beans, corn kernels, whole shallots, all in a fiery black liquid that is enriched by the blood of the venison—the dish is adorned, at the center, with a dollop of sour cream, and you soak up the last of the hot liquid with the toasted corn bread that accompanies it.

Appended to the restaurant is the Café, a so-called grazing establishment in which you select small plates of food from among those that are listed by price category ($6, $8, $10, $12) on blackboards posted here and there. The room is open and airy, especially by comparison to the restaurant proper, and determinedly casual—the seating is on white-painted metal folding chairs with padded seats, the floor is of big red tiles that look like they have been walked on for centuries, and the cooking facilities are right in the room with you, so the help is never out of sight. You wave, and a giddy young man comes by, laughs sympathetically as he takes your order, as if your recitation were really a humorous recounting of minor problems, is beside himself when, presently, he is able to deliver your fried onions, the huge pile of tender, delicately crisped rings, of sweet and clear onion flavor, set beside a pool of hot-spiced chocolate-brown molé sauce. His hebephrenic tittering accompanies also the barbecued oysters, the crisped mollusk meats, in a folded tortilla, roused by their green-pepper sauce; and the fried calamari, in which the circles of somewhat toughened but clear-flavored squid are set in a sauce of tomato and cumin over which another sauce, of black beans and garlic, has been dribbled; and the smoked quail, the grill-marked bird stuffed with peppercorn-dotted wild rice and garnished with a tangy fruit chutney.

Café desserts: a nutted persimmon pudding pie, adorned with whipped cream, that is dull despite its sweet spices; and a layered affair of ice creams and sherbet—the flavors are, respectively, fig, walnut, and cranberry-tangerine—in which the three parts seem to cancel one another out, leaving something that is little more than cold and wet. Restaurant desserts: a sweet-potato empanada that is a hot, sweet-spiced yam mash wrapped in a light pastry and garnished with maple ice cream; an apple pear crisp that is like kids' food, the soup plate of cooked fruit, under a crisped sugary topping, moistened with cool cream; something given as "natillas with anise crème anglaise," which turns out to be a fluffy floating island, the big white meringue strewn with pine nuts and fennel seeds in its licorice-flavored sauce.

Lone Star beer *on tap*—and though light, the creamy stuff has body and sparkle, comes up through clean pipes, is served in clean glasses, holds its head and texture, is good with this food.

★★★ ARQUÀ

281 Church Street (at White Street)
LUNCH, MONDAY TO FRIDAY; DINNER, MONDAY TO SATURDAY. CLOSED SUNDAY.
Reservations: 334-1888.
Credit cards: AE.
Medium priced.

Come here on foot, and your evening is made, for to enter this place after a walk through its gray environs is a change of scene from the coal mines to the seashore. Arquà is your basic urban hideaway (a largely imaginary genre, there never were many examples), a first-class eating place, comfortable and festive, hidden away in an otherwise grim neighborhood. Of course in today's New York, the restaurant is a beachhead rather than an outpost—purveyors of high-tech housewares, secondhand lace, and poster art will inevitably follow.

As if to emphasize the drama of this store in this setting, its interior has been given a paint job of mottled amber that glows warm in the room's abundant light. The furnishings are simple, around twenty white-linened tables in three rows, a plain wood floor, tall windows on the Church Street and White Street sides (the windows on White provide excellent views of the male traffic into and out of the Baby Doll Lounge—"Go-Go Girls" and "Topless Dancers"—across the street), Deco light fixtures on the walls, and great handsome paper lanterns, three of them, hanging from the high ceiling. A barmaid wearing hoop earrings you could toss a basketball through tends the little bar up front, its top of polished brass framed in pale wood, desserts and wines are displayed on a table nearby, next to it a pot of flowers stands on a carved-wood pedestal. Your waiter is in a white shirt, white apron, suspenders, a more-or-less garish four-in-hand—he answers your questions willingly, usually correctly. Early in the evening he waits on folks from the Street who have chosen to eat well before crossing the river—in that crowd, both genders wear suits, carry attaché cases. Things get colorful later on, e.g., this gent in a nose ring, nightmare shirt, and leopard-spotted hair. "*How* did he do that?" whispers an uptown lady, cringing.

Sgombretti are little mackerel, and if you require rousing, begin with these, the fillets of tiny fish, cold and a little sour, piled high with sweet slivers of oiled onion, all in a pool of marinade that has in it thin discs of crunchy, bright-orange carrot. The marinated squid is almost as vivifying, the many rings reach you mingled with chips of crisp celery, the two in a garlicky oil that intensifies the flavor of the tender, vividly fresh seafood. For a bit of satiation along with your stimulation, you will do well with the radicchio alla griglia, for when the red lettuce has been oiled and grilled and charred a little, taleggio is melted over it, the rich stuff seeps in among the hot, crunchy leaves— their slight bitterness is in stunning contrast to the creamy cheese. Solider still is the stuffed artichoke, the heart in four quarters, the quartered stem attached, each part packed with a meaty filling that is overlaid with a glinting strip of good bacon. For utter solidity, as for a hunger unbound, you will opt to begin your dinner with polenta pasticciata, a mound of cornmeal the size of a cake, soft and moist and of a high, grainy cornmeal flavor, upon it chunks of sausage, much fennel in their flavoring, and sautéed onions, the two in a bright red sauce, thin slices of hard Parmesan on top—hot, homey food that you eat your way through in a sweat.

Half-orders of pasta are iffy, sometimes you get them, sometimes not. If you are refused half an order of the gnocchi alle quatro erbe, be glad, settle for a full order, for these white nuggets have both lightness and solidity; though firm, they are soft enough to be reduced between your tongue and palate; and they are adorned with a dollop of tangy tomato sauce and with strands of fresh herbs—the wondrous dish takes on a good edge when you add ground cheese. Pappardelle del dogi are wide, weighty noodles served here with little leaves of radicchio that are in striking textural contrast to the substantial pasta—the good sauce is light, creamy, nubbly with ground sausage. Each day there is a risotto of the day, and you are in luck if you come when the rice is served with cuttlefish and its ink, the glinting black-stained grains, threaded with lengths of the seafood, of an elemental ocean pungency that is deep and sea-gamy. A serving of that rice is a mammoth dune in which a gentleman's fedora could be buried, and though no prizes are given, people do stand around and watch when anyone undertakes to begin his dinner with the aforementioned polenta and continue it with an order of this.

Your grilled swordfish is the size of your dinner plate and half an inch thick, grill-marked outside and juicy inside, sweet and tenderly fibrous, nicely garnished with cool tomatoes adorned with fresh basil. A fish soup appears on the menu, but sometimes a more elaborate one, which your waiter identifies as "Italian bouillabaisse," is offered; this is a collection of sweet little clams in their shells and a couple of crunchy shrimp in theirs, lots of squid and sections of fresh fish, all in a spicy and tomato-redded oil—hefty, vibrant food. The grilled chicken is handsomely browned, moist, takes on some of the flavor of the rosemary with which it is done, is surrounded by chunks of roasted potato that are crusty outside, soft inside. You get those same potatoes with this special-of-the-day veal chop, the bronzed and glistening eye of meat bifurcated longitudinally and packed with taleggio and spinach—unlike most cheese-stuffed veal chops, this one is light, and its tender meat is pink and glistening within its seared surfaces.

The house makes a good version of the rather obvious sweet called tiramisù; unlike most it is not puddinglike, its chocolate, rich cheese, and coffee-flavored ladyfingers all distinct elements in the lively layered affair. The millefoglie is a couple of pale and flaky pastries, a polished custard between them, confectioners' sugar on top. The ricotta cheesecake is cool and moist and light, the flavor of its browned top a zest to it, and it is served with good sauces, one pale and lemony, the other red of fresh raspberries. The firm, grainy-textured pear, purple of the red wine in which it was poached, is heady with the flavor of cloves.

★★★ AUBERGE SUISSE

153 East 53rd Street
LUNCH AND DINNER. CLOSED SUNDAY.
Reservations: 421-1420.
Credit cards: AE, DC, MC, V.
Expensive.

In the slightly honky-tonk visual cacophony that is the Citicorp Center, it is easy not to notice those places that, by their design, and by their situation in this multilevel retail confusion, call little attention to themselves. Moreover, what you do notice of this restaurant as you pass by gives little idea of what it is, for through its glass façade you see little but the short bar. Many who pass the place take it for a mere drinkery. And even when you get inside, you may not be persuaded of its culinary stature, for the cool modern appointments hardly suggest the breadth and color of this establishment's cookery.

The Auberge is of up-to-date materials: a glinting ceiling of metallic acoustic tiles; dark and cushy carpeting; walls of dark, patterned mirror; other walls, and banquettes, of tan and brown suedes and leathers; suede on the chairs, with pale wood and tubular steel. A little candle glints on each of the handsomely set tables, which are clothed in beige linen. The small rooms are, in fact, so slick and glassy that the place could almost pass for one of those trendy new bits of glitz that are popping up all over the formerly industrial edges of this town. You can distinguish this place from one of those, however, not only by its site but by its utterly timeless clientele. The eternally comfortable middle class come here, including many visitors from across the sea. In this restaurant's somewhat modern versions of old world cooking, they find evidence that the Auberge is an enclave, in crass America, of all that is good and decent and Central European.

They also find cold apricot soup, a polished puree, almost like a liqueur in its intense fruitiness, at once substantial and heady. And they find viande de Grison et jambon cru, thin slices of pink ham and dark-red beef arranged like large petals—pink on one side, red on the other—around the circumference of a plate. The ham is smoky, but delicate and tender. The air-dried beef is a little salty, a little gamy, fairly dry, almost fugitive in its lightness. The two meats are garnished with a mound of gherkins and pickled onions. The traditional Swiss dish called raclette is served here in a shallow, round casserole, the bottom of which is coated with the hot and pully melted cheese. It comes directly from the oven, and its pungent fragrance fills the atmosphere around the table. A couple of boiled potatoes are set in the butter-colored, red-peppered cheese. More cheese, this time beignet de fromage, three big dollops of baked Gruyère, fluffy, almost airy, browned, and served with a thick tomato sauce—not an inspired dish but a satisfying one. Some of the best snails in New York are made here. The snails themselves are plump and tender. They are served in one of those flat-top "pans" with six hollows in the surface, in each hollow a juicy morsel, in butter, across the top of the entire production a film of cheese and herbs and spices, like a savory pancake—an exceptional dish.

Switzerland has no coastline, but it does have streams. Accordingly, though fish is not a major element in Swiss cooking, the Swiss do have a way with freshwater varieties. Any sensible trout that knows his time has come would rather be cooked here than anywhere else in town. The fish is poached in wine, and it is served, its bones and skin removed, in a velvety cream sauce that is lightly dotted with chives. The flavor of the fish—sweet, but slightly tart—seems to gleam through the richness of the silken sauce. You can get minced veal here prepared in the manner known as Zurichoise, in which tender slivers of the pale meat, mingled with mushrooms, are served in a pink sauce that is rich, light, brandylike. This dish, like many of the main courses here, is served with a big pancake of rösti potatoes—hot and soft and salty riced potato within the browned and crusty surface. Though most of the food here is what you may justifiably characterize as fancy, some of it is, by design, coarse. The veal sausage, for example, is a great, grilled log of spiced and fatted veal, bursting from its casing, dressed with dark sautéed onions. Perfectly grilled liver is served, rather startlingly, under shafts of hot banana and a big curl of meaty bacon—stunning food. Another length of bacon, this one wrapped around the circumference of a thick filet mignon: The meat is firm and bloody, its flavor intensified by the bacon and its fat. And though the steak is surmounted by foie gras, ham, béarnaise sauce, and a great big mushroom, the complexity does not undo the forthrightness of the beef.

You have probably, by this time, eaten rather richly, so for dessert you may wish to go no further than le colonel, a creamy and icy lemon sherbet soaked in Swiss pear brandy —a rousing sweet. The so-called orange auberge consists of liquored slices of the sweet fruit served with an intense vanilla ice cream and some of this restaurant's rich and pure whipped cream. A couple of mild comedowns are the soufflé glacée (a parfait that is little more than a decent mocha-flavored ice cream) and the carrot cake (which is sometimes a little dry and these days a little dull). That good whipped cream may also be had on fresh berries that have been soaked in kirsch.

★ AU GRENIER CAFÉ

2867 Broadway (near 111th Street)
LUNCH, SUNDAY TO FRIDAY; DINNER, DAILY.
Reservations: 666-3052.
Credit cards: AE, DC, MC, V.
Medium priced.

If you have stood at the foot of the stairs leading to this second-story place, looked up, considered the prospect, and gone elsewhere, come back and look again. That run-down stairwell has been renovated. Pale-blue paint and daintily patterned pale-blue paper now cover the lumpy walls, and the missing banister has been screwed back into place. It is not exactly alluring, but it is no longer frightening. What *is* still frightening is the fellow behind the service bar just inside the restaurant door at the top of the stairs. He is a member of the proprietorial staff, and his aspect is that of the presiding zombie, whose power is such that it need never be used. He sits, still as a monument, his eyes at half-mast, overseeing without looking. Meanwhile, within a few yards of his mooring, his waitress, working enough tables for a team of three plus a host and busboy, is running herself into marathon condition right before his very eyelids. Presently she flies to him to requisition a glass of wine. He rushes to fill her order at the speed of Frankenstein's monster responding to the telephone. The waitress, of course, is a college girl, and this is the Columbia University neighborhood, but the spirit of classless academia has not entered here, for the *patron* knows precisely where his duties end and his underlings' begin—which may be just as instructional to the young lady as her liberal-arts program.

The establishment in which she is getting this tuition-free side of her education is a brick-and-wood shell of a place, odd shaped by way of one diagonal wall that is stocked with wine and topped with a mirror that leans forward, providing an overview of the room to those not directly under it. There are posters on the walls, plants here and there. An old chest of drawers is the coffee station. You eat at unlinened tables of sealed oak. Withal, the place is comfortable, and it gets a crowd that ranges from cohabiting undergraduates wearing, apparently, each other's clothing to tenured ladies and gentlemen in elbow-patched tweed jackets and Shetland sweaters.

The people behind Au Grenier are caterers as well as restaurateurs, so when you have the grilled-mussel appetizer and find that it is of bivalves that have not been properly sorted or cleaned, you conclude that the extensive list of pâtés and salads (deliverable food) is the section of the menu from which to choose your first course. The country pâté is coarse and pungently seasoned, just the right color of pink at the center of the hefty slices, very good with its strong mustard. And if the venison and rabbit pâtés are not exactly redolent of the juniper berries and Armagnac with which, respectively, they are ostensibly prepared, their distinctive meat flavors make them fine alternatives to the standard pâté de campagne. The lentil salad is an utterly satisfying bulk of the peppered little beans mingled with bits of onion and pimento, all in a tart and well-herbed mustard vinaigrette.

Au Grenier is not, however, all picnic food. It actually has its pretensions. Your salmon, for example, is served "en chemise," which is to say wrapped, with spinach and sautéed onions, in a flaky pastry, the entire production set in a smooth white sauce that is flavored with herbs and mushrooms. But most of the food here, whatever it is called, is hefty. The poulet à l'estragon, for example, consists of both halves of a substantial chicken breast, browned but still moist, in a garlicky and tarragon-flavored mushroom sauce. You get fine sweetbreads, the thin slices of rich meat sautéed until crisp, served in a tart, dark sauce that is thick with shallots. An order of roast pork is three giant slices that appear to have been browned after they were cut from the roast—the pale, juicy, weighty meat is livened with a buttery dill sauce. The choucroute is a big mound of strong sauerkraut, studded with juniper berries and overlaid with inches of dark and spicy sausage, lengths of a pink and smoky one, and slabs of that good roast pork—winter food. Naturally, in a place of this kind, there is boeuf bourguignon. This one is a little soupy, but its sauce has a good complexity of flavor—of wine and herbs, vegetables and garlic—and the meat is fine.

Au Grenier obtains good pastries but sometimes serves them a little too cold or a little too old or both. At their best, the apricot and lemon tarts have a fruity sprightliness, the ganache has a deep chocolate intensity, and the napoleon a creamy richness, but you cannot depend on any of them being themselves.

Much is made of wine, with several items on the long list offered by the glass. But get here a little late, and the house will claim to be out of this or that rather than open a bottle to sell you less than all of it.

★★★ AURORA

60 East 49th Street
LUNCH, MONDAY TO FRIDAY; DINNER, MONDAY TO SATURDAY. CLOSED SUNDAY.
Reservations: 692-9292.
Credit cards: AE, DC, MC, V.
Very expensive.

Here is the latest baby of Joe Baum, restaurant impresario formerly of the Four Seasons, Windows on the World, like that. This time Joe is involved in a place that could make it solely as a restaurant, one that, to succeed, need not serve also as an architectural showcase, tourist attraction, circus. For he has with him, imported from France, a chef whose food would draw the public even to a room fitted out only with tables, chairs, and a cashier. But Baum can never go that way. Look at him, and you know why: Baum is the short, slight, anxious chap with the constant cigarette, the one whose studied politesse, idling-engine calm, and smile (at once beatific and feverish) are paid for, you may be sure, in nightmares. He could no more start a restaurant and chance leaving out the showmanship than sit down to a meeting with his lawyer lacking his pack of filter tips. Baum's is theatricality as security blanket, overkill due to fear of failure. The syndrome is of the patient who never believes his success is based on merit, who is convinced that what he has clearly accomplished has really been done by razzle-dazzle, sleight of hand, deception. Accordingly, its good cooking notwithstanding, the restaurant has been (a) designed to a fare-thee-well—the decorator, Milton Glaser, in competition with the merchandise; and (b) laid out more like a saloon than eating place—first-class food is all very well, but money is made on liquor quicker.

In fact, when you enter, it is to the giant bar—the winding counter of polished pink-and-gray granite is shaped like the outline of your hand with the fingers together. In a niche of the elaborately carved wall behind it, there lies a life-size reclining figure, in white plaster, of a sleeping lady draped in cloth, presumably the goddess Aurora on the couch of Tithonus, from which she rises each morning to bring the rosy-fingered dawn to gods and men. The bar is the restaurant's physical center and also its visual center, for there hang from the ceiling over it dozens of baubulous, tiered, hemispheric light fixtures, pink ones, white ones, lavender, all aglow, like clouds tinted by a blushing daybreak. Before the opening of this place, published reports had it that the bar was meant for eating at, but, during the dinner hour at any rate, it is just a bar, supporting the elbows of salesmen and middle managers watering the day's affronts. The scene ensures that, with respect to its more civilized competitors, Aurora will remain the bourgeois interloper in an aristocratic world. In the two parts of the dining room proper, the wings to the east and west of the bar, you walk on Glaser-designed, bubble-patterned carpeting. You eat from bubble-patterned plates (they look like nursery china). You sit in snappy swivel chairs or broad love seats upholstered in tan leather, before tables covered with pale, cream-colored linen. And you are waited on by unfailingly courteous help, the captains in double breasted formals, the waiters in tan-and-ivory uniforms—short jackets and striped pants—that make them look like bellhops. The dining room walls are faced with panels of dark wood hung with great, glowing, presumably dawnlike semicircular sconces, and high up on the molding at the top of the wood paneling, leaning on the plaster walls above (and quite beyond comfortable viewing range), are a dozen or so dawn watercolors by Glaser himself—they look to be in temporary storage, waiting for a place to be hung. Curators from the Whitney, Modern, etc., have not yet been by to choose something for their collections.

All of which you will forget when you turn your attention to the shellfish salad, a seafood array that dazzles for the way each item gets a distinct treatment and yet contributes to the coherence of the complex dish. The elements include: cool shrimp filmed with a dressing that is heady with the fragrance of tarragon; raw littleneck clams, fresh, sweet, and briny, each of them under a dab of tart and tangy red sauce; the claw meat of a lobster, of almost fugitive tenderness and lightness within its herbed dressing; fried oysters, these warm, the plump morsels encased in a gossamer batter coating that, surprise, is hot-spiced; and a garnish of saffron sherbet, a somewhat gimmicky amusement that, anyway, does the dish no harm. Lobster again, this time poached and warm, served in the saffron-flavored broth, thick with strands of lemon rind and emerald-green snow peas, in which the juicy white meat was done—the interplay of lemon and saffron is rousing, striking for its touch of discord. The duck confit salad is a simple affair, chunks and shreds of dark and peppery meat served on spiky chicory leaves that have been moistened with velvety oil. Send for the foie gras sauté, and receive two thin slices of charred, glistening organ meat—though profoundly rich, it is light, almost fluffy, and it is served, strikingly, over circles of black radish and leaves of the sharp green called mâche. On occasion pasta is offered, sometimes a little herbed mound of pale, narrow noodles dotted with plump scallops and chunks of root vegetable, the whole under sea urchin roes—fresh as these may be, they always taste sea-gamy almost to the point of rankness, and the light sauce that moistens the dish, though given as "curry sauce," comes across as a nameless spiciness.

Your captain asks how you want your salmon (rare? medium? well done?). How the chef wants to make it is how you want it, and presently you learn that he makes it blood (figuratively) rare. It arrives lacking not a drop of its undersea moisture, in which state the fresh fish has the quality of ripe, juicy fruit—its tangy but delicate horseradish breading is in stunning contrast to the coral-colored meat, and the dish becomes both rich and complex when you spoon on its buttery dill sauce. The man in the kitchen is not, however, infallible with swimmers. His halibut, for example—four little fillets arranged over a pool of mint sauce and strewn with asparagus spears—is prettily browned but dried in the baking, and the fancy treatment obscures somewhat the character of the fish itself. A touch of overcooking mars also the crêpinette of pheasant, an otherwise dazzling dish in which you get boned sections of the bird folded over fennel greens, giblets in a little sack formed of a crêpe, the flavor of the pheasant distinctive and vivid, the game garnished with glistening mounds of hot shredded cabbage, one white, one red. The orange and the duck have been together a long time, so it is surprising to find them doing new, different things together. Here they are now, this time the fruit a blood orange: The breast of the duck is served in a great arc of rich little slices, and those are strewn with skinned, deep-red citrus sections; the leg at the center of the plate is intact within its crisp skin; and everything is set in a fruity sauce, crimson and tangy. Order venison, and you get three little medallions, at once tender and of a fine, fibrous texture, blood-rich and vaguely livery within their handsomely charred surfaces, the meat set among hot prunes, tablets of crisp apple, and chestnuts in its tart and vaguely sweet-spiced sauce poivrade. The rack of lamb is given as "with gratin of ratatouille," and until it arrives, you figure you know what that means. This "gratin" actually covers the entire plate, and this "ratatouille" is creamy—the vegetables bound in a thick white sauce—over it the four velvety chops of pungent meat.

The apple tart is a great circle, thin overlapping slices of the tangy fruit on a parch-mentlike pastry, at its center an egg of ice cream of intense cinnamon flavor. You see rice pudding on a menu this experimental, and you figure you are in for an experiment. What you are in for is rice pudding, albeit studded with berries—a pleasant enough sweet, but not what you came for. In fact most of the desserts are notable more for perfection (not to be scorned) than originality: the many-layered lemon hazelnut torte, for example, the nuts crunchy, the smooth lemon cream of bright, sweet acidity; the feuilletée of berries, for another, a sandwich of two discs of crisp caramel-sweet pastry, between them a big inch of thick whipped cream studded with berries, the construct served in an eggy, well-liquored crème anglaise.

The menu changes from day to day, so you will not always find what you seek.

★ AU TUNNEL

250 West 47th Street
LUNCH AND DINNER. CLOSED SUNDAY.
Reservations: 582-2166.
Credit cards: AE, MC, V.
Medium priced.

Imagine a fellow moving this decades-old establishment (used to be called *Pierre* au Tunnel) from one site to another, and, in taking advantage of the opportunity, putting together a new installation that would have looked old-fashioned when the old place first opened. People with an unclear recollection of where this place used to be and what it looked like (it was a block to the north and looked vaguely like a tunnel) walk in here and think this is the original place with a new paint job. Presumably you have to admire a respect for the past so devotional that it not only preserves the old days, but recreates them faithfully. The only thing this new incarnation of Au Tunnel lacks is age. It comes off as a brand-new relic. The red carpeting glows, and the stucco walls appear to have been just troweled on. The decorative pottery and the copper pots and pans gleam. Of course there are beams on the ceiling, framed maps and prints on the walls, a deer's head over the fireplace (with a rifle nearby). The half-timbered front room houses the bar, as well as a couple of tables at a red banquette. There is a small mural up here, a whimsical café scene—someone probably had to be unearthed, so convincingly does it replicate this lighthearted, between-the-wars style of illustration, a combination of five-cent-magazine covers and the funnies. The bar is often busy before curtain time, as is the dining room. On weekends the place even gets some after-theater action. Come what may, the waitresses—most of them French—run the place with brusque, somewhat motherly efficiency.

In the course of a day, they probably deliver several dozen orders of this coarse, powerfully seasoned, well-fatted pâté—you eat it with the good, chewy bread, and with strong mustard. If you have that pâté as part of the hors d'oeuvres variés, you get a heavily garlicked, almost purple salami and a cool headcheese as well, the latter bits of meat and organ meat embedded in a firm and fragrantly herbed jelly. You get a big plate of smoked salmon—it is garnished with onions and capers, but is best taken with oil and a little lemon. The cool mussels are sweet tasting, with not a bad one in the lot—a rarity these days—but they are claylike, almost hard under their tangy sauce ravigote. The snails here are above average for the West Side—these are not the little leathery ones, they are big and plump, but their green and garlicky sauce is almost painfully salty.

Have the trout meunière on your first visit here, and it may be your last, for the fish is prepared in nut oil—or a bad imitation thereof—rather than butter, which gives it a dull, lifeless quality. In a place like this you go for the coq au vin, a great abundance of the stew in a strong, dark, and winy sauce that is studded with nicely sautéed mushrooms and whole onions; or you go for the tripe, served here in long, chewy lengths, in a fatted broth that is powerfully seasoned and redolent of root vegetables and herbs; or for the rabbit in its thick white-wine sauce, again with mushrooms and onions, and garnished with a big mound of eggy noodles, or for the tête de veau, great slabs of tongue, rich slices of brain, not to mention a complex cross-sectional slab of meats and cartilaginous meats of various textures and colors, all of which you moisten with a hot, thick vinai-grette that is studded with capers. With many of these dishes, when you have dispatched what you took to be your serving, you discover that, in the iron pot on the edge of your table, more is waiting.

On the marble board, two or three cheeses at room temperature and in good condi-tion: Very good Brie has been had here, though on occasion neither pears nor apples nor any other fruit suitable for cheese and wine is available—the orange you are offered is all wrong. Perfectly nice raspberry tarts and blueberry tarts have been served with whipped cream that is fortified with Grand Marnier. The chocolate cake is given sparkle by the thin shelves of fruit preserves between the layers. The mocha cake, with mocha sauce, is a good standard sweet.

• AZZURRO

1625 Second Avenue (near 84th Street)
DINNER.
Reservations: 517-7068.
Credit cards: AE, DC.
Beer and wine.
Medium priced.

Italian restaurants half-a-building-lot wide are inserting themselves, all over the Upper East Side, into real estate slivers that heretofore mainly accommodated over-the-counter sidewalk-service head shops. The layout of these restaurants is inevitable: a row of tables down each side, an aisle between, a counter at the back, and, beyond that, a kitchen (usually out of sight) the cramped dimensions of which you infer from the brevity of the printed menu. Azzurro, however, differs in a couple of respects from its competitors. The others are dim, candlelit places, all rusticity, and they are hidden away on side streets, while this is a garishly lighted long box of a store right on Second Avenue; and, far from being rustic, it is assertively urban. Its waiters, for example, a collection of swaggering young gents recruited, obviously, on some street corner, are dressed in boldly patterned shirts, bowties the size of mustaches, and baggy pleated pants that hang, from low on their hips, to the very floor (concealing from view the occasional absence, in their shoes, of anything resembling socks). The room they work looks like the sample living room in a renovated tenement going condo. The ceiling here is a vivid shade of post-card-sky blue, complete with recessed lights that, organized in stray clusters, are meant to look like constellations of stars. The long north wall is brick, the one opposite of white plaster, and the place is hung with framed astronomic and geographic engravings, complete with Latin lettering, you should know Azzurro has class. On rainy days a rubber runner is laid on the floor in the aisle between the rows of tables. It is laid there also on dry days.

A couple of blue sheets (they match the ceiling) are the printed menus, historic documents that bear traces of the olive-oiled fingers by which they have been handled apparently since the days of the first printing. They list the likes of this spiedino di mozzarella, a melted-cheese sandwich, actually, the hot mozzarella oozing out from between the well-oiled slices of fried bread, the two triangular sandwich halves dressed with a sharp and salty sauce of pulverized capers and anchovies. Equally rich, but quite another matter, is this cool caponatina, a mellifluous eggplant stew that has an intensity of eggplant flavor you encounter only when the vegetable has absorbed every drop of olive oil it can possibly hold, and when, moreover, it is aggressively seasoned and garlicked.

Do not, however, let your happy selection of appetizers mislead you into thinking that your first judgments of this establishment were ill considered. In fact, it is a rare dinner here that is without at least one gross flaw. Consider for example this capellini con caposanti e gamberi, a dish of thin spaghetti with scallops and shrimp in tomato sauce, in which the shrimp are not merely tainted with iodine, but, apparently, marinated in it. So on your next visit you go for a red sauce without seafood, rigatoni con pomidoro e basilico, and the hefty tubes of noodle arrive in a chunky, oil-rich red sauce that is heady with fresh basil.

The menu lists no specific varieties of finfish, mentions only "fish of the day." Anyway, the fish is grilled (as are all the main courses). And sometimes the grilled item is a slab of grouper that, if it has not been long frozen (to account for its tastelessness and pulpiness), does a terrific impression of having so suffered. But another night you get an eminently decent swordfish steak, its own flavor clear and sweet, the imparted flavor of the grill present but not overwhelming, a garnish of cool roasted red peppers very good with the hot seafood. Then again there is this grilled chicken—which could actually pass for that grouper. And then there is this herbed veal chop, which would be yummy had it been separated from the fire as soon as it was done. But it is all a matter of luck, and another time you find the so-called porterhouse steak (it is really a sirloin) eminently well grilled, the pink, silken meat tender and blood-juicy within its charred surfaces. At Azzurro it is well to know the ropes. One of the ropes to know is that potatoes and a green vegetable come with the main courses. Your waiter will not mention this when he tries to sell you, say, some spinach. Turn him down, you get some anyway. Order some, and you will get spinach and green beans as well—with a charge for the spinach, which otherwise would have been part of your dinner at no cost. It is probably just chance that when the spinach carries no charge it is fine, but that when you pay for it, it is loaded with sand.

Most nights only two desserts are offered: zuccota, a mass of chocolate ice cream beside a mass of strawberry ice cream, the two embraced by a crescent of sponge cake soaked in rum, nuts and candied fruits all about—a rousing excess; and tirami su, among the more restrained versions, a layered affair of cream cheese, chocolate, white cake, liquor, cinnamon on top. These are large servings, and when you ask to split a dessert you get an extra plate and two spoons.

★★BALLATO

55 East Houston Street (near Mott Street)
LUNCH AND DINNER. CLOSED SUNDAY AND MONDAY.
Reservations required for dinner: 226-9683.
No credit cards.
Beer and wine.
Medium priced.

Mrs. Ballato now presides over the late Mr. Ballato's famous hideaway. The old gentleman was something of a professional character; his survivor is anything but. She is slight, blue haired, courteous, sweet. She helps you off with your coat, apologizes for the weather. If she fails to embrace you on your arrival because she does not know you very well, she will at least place a hand on your shoulder when you leave, now that you are old pals. Except that the restaurant is a little more relaxed than it was under the governance of its occasionally bristling founder, the change in proprietary style has changed it very little.

You enter to a small anteroom, wherein a shelf of books and magazines has been installed for the diversion of customers waiting for tables. Your coat is put in a closet, the portal of which is hung with amber beads. There is a glass icebox stocked with wine, cheese, fruit. Farther back the oblong dining room holds two rows of square tables, eleven all told, four chairs at each. The walls are surfaced with broad panels of plain cloth, and they are hung with scores of photos and pictures of John Ballato, framed articles about the restaurant, a Sinatra poster, a good number of Warhol prints, and other assorted contemporary graphics (when SoHo decided to come into existence, it chose a site not far from this place). The rear wall of the dining room hardly exists, for it is wide open to the brightly lit and immaculate kitchen (into which you must enter for the facilities and the pay phone).

The uptown set that used to crowd the curb outside with waiting limousines has deserted Ballato in favor of the slumming that has in recent years been provided for them on their own Third Avenue. But Ballato is still busy. Many of the gentlemen who come regularly look as if they ought to be the mayor of Brooklyn. You would swear that others are off-duty policemen, except that their ladies wear more jewels than a cop's salary can account for. Large families come here (a couple of tables are pushed together), and Greenwich Villagers in search of a better bargain than their own pricey neighborhood offers. It is a comfort-loving rather than a luxury-loving crowd, and they are here for the familiarity of the surroundings, the reliability of the food, the straightforward service.

The baked clams and the mussels reganate are browned and crisped, their breading easy on the dried oregano—they come in pools of parsleyed and buttered broth. Roasted green peppers are stuffed with a pungent meat-and-cheese filling, and they are dressed with a spicy tomato sauce—satisfying food.

Good pasta: lovely green noodles in a sauce that is little more than cream and cheese, the dish ornamented with a sprinkling of sharp red pepper; very good linguine with fresh clams, cloves of browned garlic and much parsley in the briny butter; excellent manicotti, the pillows of pasta stuffed with pully cheese and covered with an honest red sauce that is still bubbling when the casserole reaches your table.

If you can bring yourself to do it, order the octopus. It is served, be warned, in rather undisguised long shafts, but the slightly rubbery meat has a sharp gaminess that is worth learning to like, and the strong red sauce, thick with garlic and onions, will help. On occasion this establishment has served bass that would have pleased much more a couple of days earlier, in a sauce livornese devoid of the olives and capers that title leads you to expect. But the scampi are good—big and crunchy shrimp in a creamy tomato sauce that is thick with rice.

You get a giant portion of brains, and the rich meat arrives sizzling, crusted with seasoned breading. A small spoon protrudes from the dark marrow of the osso buco, the tender meat barely clings to the bone, a thick and gravylike mushroom sauce moistens the meat and its garnish of rice. But better than almost anything in the place is the rolatine of veal, the browned cylindrical packages filled with a spiced stuffing of strong cheese, sausage, herbs, the meat moistened with a sturdy brown sauce.

The menu lists "assorted cheeses," but a decent fontina is all you can usually get. The zabaglione is the usual hot and winy froth, but it comes with a bonus of tissue-wrapped macaroons. When the restaurant is busy your waiter may discourage the zabaglione on the ground that it takes twenty minutes. It takes five. The cheesecake is distinctly Italian —wet, light, and sugary.

★★BALLROOM

253 West 28th Street
LUNCH AND DINNER. CLOSED SUNDAY AND MONDAY.
Reservations: 244-3005.
Credit cards: AE, DC, MC, V.
Expensive.

Tapas, Spanish snacks or hors d'oeuvres, are the main attraction here, cold ones and hot ones, the selection varied from day to day. The cold ones, around fifteen little dishes of this or that, are held before you, all on one tray, by your waiter, while he describes them one at a time. Those you want are put before you there and then. Hot ones—they are fewer in number—you learn about only from his recitation. Many who dinner here regularly limit themselves to these small plates, but the printed menu does list a handful of main courses, cheese and fruit may be selected from the rolling cart, and you choose sweet desserts from those displayed on butcher blocks just inside the entrance. In Spain, eating tapas is an informal business usually undertaken together with the consumption of spirits, especially sherry. Accordingly, the upper level of the restaurant portion of the Ballroom (there is also an attached nightclub) is given over in large measure to a tapas-and-liquor bar (over which hang hams and sides of dried fish, huge ropes of dried red peppers and strings of garlic, sometimes game birds complete with plumage), behind which the usual array of whiskeys and such is augmented by a big selection of sherries. Along the length of the bar, platters of this cold item or that are placed, each flagged with the price of a serving. Locals sometimes stop by for a drink, have a second, sample the tapas, and, what with one thing or another, do not head home until they have done the equivalent of dinner. The dining room is otherwise a somewhat rambling affair illuminated by the soft light of white globes, with palms here and there, pots and pans elsewhere, backlighted stained-glass windows opposite the bar, white tiles on the floors, sheets of white butcher paper on the white-linened tables. The original Ballroom was one of the earliest eating places in SoHo, back when art galleries were most of what was there, and as a gesture of respect to the source of its commerce, that place commissioned a mural in which the then trendy artists and dealers were portrayed sitting around the old Ballroom itself. The work has no appropriateness in this store other than a nostalgic one, but if you want a reminder of those days, here it is, dominating the lower level. A diagram identifying the characters in the scene may be consulted.

Cold tapas: morsels of octopus, tender, not rubbery, of clear pulpo flavor, in a somewhat spicy redded oil that clings to their surfaces; bay scallops in a rather obvious curry sauce that suggests a canned spice mix—a couple of brussels sprouts bulk up the little plate of food; one big squid packed with a fruited and sweet-spiced filling of pork and nuts, served in a tart and chunky tomato sauce; two thick slices of eggplant in a green, fiery Moroccan paste; chorizos in a rare setting, the strong Spanish sausage chopped into little dice and dressed with a spicy vinaigrette that is thick with minced red peppers.

Hot tapas: grilled gambas, the barely cooked-through shrimp of immaculate flavor in their peppery oil, very nice with the strong onions you find on the same plate; a stew of crayfish and morels, very little seafood in those carapaces, of course, but the mushrooms are fine, as are the red peppers with which they are mingled; sautéed shiitake mushrooms in a sweet, well-oiled sauce that is dense with bits of tomato, strands of onion, fresh sweet peas; a couple of quite substantial baby lamb chops moistened with spicy oil, strewn with sprigs of fresh, fragrant rosemary, and garnished with fluffy rice; in season, a single soft-shell crab, judiciously done in olive oil, served with an avocado sauce of which it has no need; fried plantains and yucca, the hefty strips of fruit and root in a napkin-lined basket, bread substitutes more or less, the kinds of pallid starch you must grow up with to love, the bits of garlic with which they are touched not enough to excite them—or, probably, you.

Among the few listed and unlisted main courses, there is a vigorous chicken stew, its dark and lemony sauce laden with fresh, heady cilantro greens, the big chunks of chicken intermingled with onions, potatoes, morels; and an especially rich veal dish, the lean tenderloin roasted within a fattier meat wrapper, the entire construct blackened on the outside, the meat at the core pale and juicy—you are served a thick slice in a sauce that is herbed, winy, dotted with black peppercorns.

The standard, very rich chocolate desserts of the day are available, and they are fresh. The excellent spongecake, firm but not heavy, is moistened with orange liqueur. The pecan pie is notable for the strong coffee flavor of its filler. Your waiter will probably garnish your dessert with the good house whipped cream, maybe with a strawberry or two as well.

In the adjoining club, cold tapas and drinks may be ordered before the show. For a couple of seasons of the year, this is the place (anyway, on this side of the Atlantic) where Blossom Dearie is witty and musical at 6:30 P.M.

★ BANGKOK CUISINE

885 Eighth Avenue (near 53rd Street)
LUNCH, MONDAY TO SATURDAY; DINNER, DAILY.
Reservations: 581-6370.
Credit cards: AE, DC, MC, V.
Inexpensive.

In the dim clutter that is this little place, one fixture stands out especially—an illuminated fish tank, complete with bubbles and swimming fish. Sometimes, during a lull, you will espy a member of the staff staring into the tank, wide-eyed, as if he were getting a preview of paradise itself. Innocence, it appears, is not dead. But to find any in a New York restaurant, you must choose a place that is in the hands of a national group relatively new to the big city. Among the—to us—childlike qualities of the people who run this place are courtesy (the service is invariably sweet), patriotism (portraits of Thai royalty adorn the walls), and piety (small figurines of Buddha and other divines are on display). Even the prices are innocent—that is, low. And the strongest drink you can get is wine. The food itself, however, is far from innocuous. Some of it, in fact, borders on the violent. So as you skip about among the items on the menu, beware of those marked with stars—they look as guileless as anything else you get to eat here, but they are armed.

Some, of course, are more lethal than others. Tod mun pla, for example, carries but a small stiletto. This, the menu informs you, is, of all Thai dishes, the most famous (which may tempt you to repeat certain generalizations about the unfathomability of the East). It consists of deep-fried fish patties that, though they are steamy and fresh, are of almost no identifiable flavor—however, they take on a little life when they are dipped in their tart, sweet, somewhat spicy sauce. What this restaurant calls egg rolls may also elude you. They carry no weapon at all, are like pastry sausages stuffed with clear noodles and bits of meat and vegetables, are disappointing unless you think of them as street food—they would make fine snacks from a vendor. But the satés are good. If you order the beef saté, you are served six short wooden skewers, each of them bearing many thin slices of dark, shiny beef, warm and tender—you dip the meat in a brown, mildly spicy sauce that is thick with chopped peanuts.

There is a printed menu, and there is a blackboard on which are listed a half-dozen additional items. The latter listing is every bit as permanent as the former, and happily so, for it includes the LARGE FLOUNDER TOPPED WITH SHRIMP CURRY. The fish is indeed large, and it is whole, fresh, prettily browned, and covered over with lots of crisp shrimp that are mingled with strands of sweet red pepper and green peppers—little hot ones—in an oil that is at once creamy, fiery, subtly fruited. You get a good chicken dish here, called kai yang—many sections of bird, deep fried and crusty, which you dip into a cool, spicy fruit sauce. The only duck dish is the one listed on the blackboard as ROAST DUCK TOPPED WITH CHEF'S SPECIAL SAUCE $9, but not otherwise described. The item seems inspired—if that is the correct word—by Chinese cookery, consisting as it does of great chunks of the duck, with peppers and pineapple, in a hot brown sauce dotted with green peas. It is well made—the flavor of the duck is vivid despite the competition—but takes getting to know.

If you come here only once—and if you tolerate intense spice—do not pass up the nam sod. This is minced pork served at room temperature (and that condition in itself deters some). But the pale ground meat is studded with whole peanuts and strands of sharp onion, it is moistened with lime juice, and it is made fragrant with a heady admixture of cilantro and bits of fresh ginger—a stunning dish. A couple of good beef dishes: pra neua, a kind of beef salad, the slices of meat mixed with onion and scallions, all in a dark, sour, spicy sauce; and neua pad king, slices of charred beef with onion and mushrooms and strands of scallion greens in a sauce that is flavored with ginger. The noodle dish to have is the one marked with a star—pad Thai. These are fried noodles, a little dry and crackling, slightly sweet, mingled with chopped peanuts, bits of white scallion and green, shrimp and chopped egg, the whole fiery hot.

The desserts are puddinglike and dull.

★★BARBETTA

321 West 46th Street
LUNCH AND DINNER. CLOSED SUNDAY.
Reservations: 246-9171.
Credit cards: AE, DC, MC, V.
Expensive.

Outdoor cafés and dining gardens are showing up around town in record numbers. But for eating out of doors, nothing has so far touched the wooded court that is this establishment's tranquil oasis out back. The peaked white umbrellas, linened tables, and gurgling fountain that fill the clearing are a setting for a classy picnic indeed, with not only moonlight but many of the comforts of indoors to boot, including the occasional cat—they explore in the bushes and walk along the tops of the low garden walls just as if they were sentries on guard.

Its outdoors has always been Barbetta's main lure, but these days the food—which was never less than very decent—is a little better than ever, some of it even first-rate. If you are interested in trying a lot of it, begin with what the menu refers to as the "Grande Antipasto Piemontese" (Piedmont food is this restaurant's specialty). It includes a creamy, emerald-green paste of robiola (rich Italian cream cheese) and fresh basil; a brandied mousse of buttered, well-seasoned liver; slivers of cold eggplant, imbued with oil, rimmed with blackened skin, dotted with tomato sauce and cooled melted cheese; fresh squid in a spanking vinaigrette.

If you liked that basil mixed with cheese, you will like it again in pesto on hot pasta, for the sauce is powerfully fragrant with fresh basil, and the narrow, flat noodles called trenette are cooked to the proper point—tender but firm. Barbetta's primavera sauce, also served on flat noodles, is of a tart tomato brightness that manages to dominate the dish without obscuring the flavors of the fresh green vegetables that are its bulk. Some days lots of rice dishes are offered, but the house pushes risotto Piemontese: The dark, nubbly grain, oiled and moist, is mingled with mushrooms and small slices of liver—an earthy and satisfying dish that is at once primitive and subtle.

The cold whole trout is cooked until its skin is crisped, then marinated until it is tart—an utterly refreshing summer dish. The cold bass is fresh and firm, but its thick mayonnaise is rather heavily salted. Happily, the tuna sauce in this restaurant's vitello tonnato is not recognizably of canned fish—the weighty puree, polished with oil and studded with capers, is spread across broad slices of cold veal that are fibrous but tender, a little crusty at the edges. You may have your veal hot: The paillard is very delicate, barely browned, its blood-pinkness just cooked away, super when you squeeze on a bit of lemon; but the brandied scaloppine with wild porcini mushrooms, though otherwise well prepared, is dominated by an excess of the booze. Good birds: a charred duck, the rich meat strikingly cut by its fruity—not sugary—lemon sauce, and a pot-roasted squab buried in a tomato-and-vegetable sauce that is artfully soured with lemon. Hot slivers of sautéed sweetbread are mingled with wild mushrooms and a dark, winy marsala sauce— the rich meat is very nicely browned.

Sharp Parmesan cheese is usually on hand, as well as strong, biting Gorgonzola. For an Italian restaurant, this place turns out a mean chocolate mousse—thick, dark, bitter-sweet, adorned with whipped cream that is rich yet light. The St-Honoré is mostly a light puff pastry, its syrup glaze caramelized, its custard filling smooth and cool and sweet. Some of the desserts are even Italian, including a zuppa inglese of good sponge cake, a judicious amount of rum, and the house's splendid whipped cream.

When it rains, you eat inside—crystal chandeliers, brocade-upholstered chairs, silken drapes, the works.

★ BAROCCO

301 Church Street (at Walker Street)
LUNCH, TUESDAY TO FRIDAY; DINNER, MONDAY TO SATURDAY. CLOSED SUNDAY.
Reservations: 431-1445.
Credit cards: AE, DC, MC, V.
Medium priced.

A noisy, convivial, thriving place in which the highly conversational customers at the tiny, closely assembled white-linened tables are quite upon one another, to their apparent indifference. The square room is low ceilinged, dimly lit by soft-glowing Deco light fixtures mounted on the walls, and in it you are surrounded by glass—big venetian-blinded windows that look out on the intersection of Walker and Church, a mirrored wall above the black banquette that runs along the room's east side, panels here and there of those glass bricks that look like big ice cubes, all to a slick, slightly glitzy effect. The illumination is not so dim that you fail to discern the exposed pipes and ducts that crisscross the ceiling, the valves and wheels connected thereto. The background music is distinctly audible above the talk. Neckties spotted here, if any, are the whimsical accessories of certain ladies' blouses. This is TriBeCa, Manhattan's frontier, and everyone is up to something, or is young enough still to think so.

The waiters and waitresses pick their way through the furniture and guests, turn to the next blank page of their order pads as they fly, give and receive information and instructions with dispatch, inform that the special sardines of the day (they do not explain why there are unlisted dishes "of the day" when the menu is printed and revised daily) are hardly prepared at all (decapitation aside), being as they are marinated raw and served in the herbed and well-seasoned oil in which they were steeped, skin and bones in place and quite edible, the flavor of the oiled little swimmers at once oceanic and gentle. What is given as "verdure al forno" will seem like caponata to you (the name it goes by another night), but whatever you call it, it comes as a substantial mound of baked and cooled vegetables slicked with olive oil, the chunks of eggplant and tomato, the sliced peppers, the onions and celery and slivers of olive all mingled with sour capers, and quite rousing with the house garlic bread ("fettunta," $2 the hefty slice, crusty outside, soft but chewy inside, the garlic pungent but not overpowering). You are advised that "the chef will not" (as if it is a matter beyond house control) *divide* an order of pasta (much less prepare a half order), so your spaghettini con pomodori freschi, when it arrives in its deep plate, is accompanied by a bare plate onto which the more adroit member of your party transfers approximately 50 percent. This is a perfectly good and simple pasta dish—firm noodles, a tangy and chunky tomato sauce, sprigs of fresh basil—but it is undone by its admixture of hot pepper, an alien presence that has no business (and performs no function) among those straightforward ingredients. You will be more content with the ravioli, their emerald-green hue (unaided, spinach does not create this effect) merely a distraction, for the pasta envelopes are supple, their spinach-and-ricotta filling smooth and rich, their red sauce tangy. But charcoal-gray is today's hot pasta color (squid ink its pigment), against which the rings and lengths of squid with which the long strands of spaghetti are mingled gleam iridescently. The broth of the dish, however, is too thin to be called a sauce, and though the liquid is briny and impressively dusky, it is without the inky sea-gaminess of this stuff at its best.

On a good day Barocco grills a whole fresh snapper, delivers it to you very handsomely packaged in its crisped, metallic-pink skin—the fish is firm, cooked through, juicy, all its snapper flavor intact. On a lesser day, the four giant shrimp that, in their shells, have been peppered, parsleyed, and grilled on a wood skewer are, with respect to three of them, sweet and crunchy, and with respect to one of them, distinctly off. A nicely grilled chicken, its skin crisp, the moist meat done to the bone, has all the flavor of a Cornish hen (none), though the rosemary with which it is prepared helps. Rosemary again—this time it clings to the surface of a judiciously grilled veal chop, suffusing the browned meat with its heady flavor. Your medium-rare lamb chops arrive blood-rare, but they are good anyway, handsomely striped by the grill and redolent of garlic. The steak, though decent, has been fired and nothing else, and in a restaurant of this type, you expect the influence of oil, garlic, an herb, something.

The ricotta cheesecake does this imitation of a cream-cheese cheesecake—it is sugary and heavy on its doughy pastry. The peach tart is many substantial chunks of ripe, fruity fruit on a much better pastry.

★★★★ LE BERNARDIN

155 West 51st Street
LUNCH AND DINNER. CLOSED SUNDAY.
Reservations: 489-1515.
Credit cards: AE, MC, V.
Very expensive.

Never before has fact become legend as fast as the fact of Le Bernardin. Nothing more need be done. Let the restaurant fall into dysfunction and disrepair, reverence would be the payoff, never mind never an empty table. You half expect, what with the future assured, evidence of the sins of old age here in the establishment's youth, maybe a bit of overbooking, perhaps a dash of scorn for unfamiliar patrons, conceivably a more casual approach to the cooking than obtained during the first years. You will have to look elsewhere for reinforcement of your cynical side. Le Bernardin is not flawless, and it is not exactly as it was when it was new—if nothing else, the nervous excitement is gone —but if you remain capable of being thrilled, the thrill is not gone. And if Le Bernardin seems now to have found a natural slot for itself on the local scene, that has been accomplished by an adjustment of the scene, not of Le Bernardin, for this is that great rarity, a restaurant that redefines, even if only a little, the very notion of a restaurant.

But though this is an imposing physical place, with respect to its looks it redefines nothing at all. It is in fact part of the minor miracle of Le Bernardin that its culinary individuality is not subsumed in the intended monumentality of its architecture, albeit for many who would otherwise fail to grasp what the fuss is about, the grand space serves as a satisfactory explanation. If you see this dining room plain, however, its message is plainly deceptive, for it bespeaks—reverently—the traditional, while within it are served seafood dishes (and almost nothing but seafood dishes) the like of which, a decade ago, would have gone back to the kitchen, after one bite, for more fire.

Here you are, store level of the headquarters building of nothing less than the Equitable Life Assurance Society of the United States (landlords to and backers of Le Bernardin), a corporate entity whose balance sheet tilts with every fourth fatality in the northern half of the western hemisphere, so how come, you wonder, not health food?—instead of, that is, the almost cooked, barely cooked, and uncooked seafood that here obtains, which any life insurance executive of only yesterday readily could have identified as sources of grievous viral, bacterial, and parasitic disorders. Anyway, at Le Bernardin you scorn these hazards in a setting that would persuade even the exec that here he is safe, for it encapsulates (if that is what so spacious a capsule does) all that is most board-chairmanly in executive suite design. Le Bernardin is a great rectangle of a room, high ceilinged and softly lit, all dark blue and stained wood, its front window, which runs the long length of the place, hung with pale curtains of pleated gauze, the well-spaced tables clothed in white linen (a few of them aglow in the light of overhead spots) and surrounded by capacious armchairs and side chairs upholstered in blue cloth of a soft water-lily pattern, the total effect massive and commodious, like the lofty common room of an ancient club. As in all ancient clubs, paintings hang on the walls—these of the sea and seafood, boats and watersides—and they are part of the redemption of these otherwise stolid quarters, for though none of this art is immortal, it is handsome, is part of what humanizes the businesslike interior. No closer to immortality, but an even greater part of what warms this room, is one Maguy Le Coze, mistress of Le Bernardin (and sister of its chef), a smashingly attired presence whose looks and charm quite take your mind off the frumpiness that, by unavoidable comparison, she imposes on those around her at tables other than your own.

Your attention to Maguy is distracted only by the works of the Le Coze in the kitchen, Gilbert, who turns the trick with the likes of this pounded (raw) tuna, a great rosy-pink circle within the rim of your large plate, the fresh, sweet fish, battered almost to a paste, but with its fiber intact, glistening with the oil that enriches it, and strewn with minced chives, which give it tang and sparkle. Raw fish again, this time black bass, a species that has swum in the Atlantic presumably since pre-Columbian times, but which became a common New York restaurant item only after it appeared on this restaurant's first menu. Le Coze fashions it into a tartare to which black caviar has been added, and of which you receive three egg-shaped masses arranged like the points of an asterisk, with them dark-toasted crusts of bread that are soft at the center—you eat the stuff straight or on the bread, and it is notable for its tender stickiness, and for the keen zest of the caviar to the delicate fish. Le Bernardin is not without an occasional comedown, as for example this truffled salad of sea scallops, in which fresh greens in a vibrant vinaigrette are surmounted by thin scallop slivers under a couple of disks of black, nutty truffle—all is well but for those scallops, which are at best of fugitive flavor. But there is no shortage of flavor in the fricassee of shellfish, tiny clams, tiny mussels, oysters, all in their shells, and all bathed in a sauce that, tasted alone, is an herbed and buttery brine, but which does different things to the different mollusks: merges with the oysters, gentles the tender clams without at all undoing them, enriches and heightens the mussels in their shiny black shells. The house obtains Louisiana shrimp that are, of course, devoid of iodine, broils them in their shells, serves them split in a buttery sauce, sweetened by shallots, that is greened by the parsley that makes it fragrant—this is an elemental dish, a clear expression of shrimp flavor underscored by a sauce that is at once rich and light. The house lists clam chowder, and just as this French enterprise on American shores makes do with American seafood solely, so it makes do with chowder as an American dish, does not Gallicize it, tries merely to perfect it, and though the bits of clam in this bowl have been toughened in the making, the nubbly soup is otherwise a model blend of unthickened creaminess, peppery seasoning, tiny nuggets of firm potato, and briny clam flavor.

What is listed as "Lobster and Mashed Potato Pie" would better be given as "Lobster-and-Mashed-Potato-Pie," in which case you might well pass it up in favor of a preparation in which the crustacean is less alloyed. But there is nothing wrong with the rather country dish in this urban setting, a casserole of mashed potatoes, browned and crisped on top and thick with chunks of lobster that are moist, supple, and of vivid lobster flavor in their sturdy tuberous setting. Finfish are most of the main course menu: poached halibut in a vigorous and herbed-green vinaigrette—you may find the snowy white meat obscured by the powerful sauce when you take but a little of the former in much of the latter, but as you go through the dish you note a dazzling, constantly shifting interchange between the components; browned fillets of pompano in a pool of butter that is dappled with green splashes of Italian parsley of heady flavor; that black bass again, a fillet, its attached skin crisped, set in a pool of brick-red lobster sauce of powerful lobster shell flavor, and garnished, stunningly, with a ball of potato-and-fennel purée, the three elements in wondrous contrast to one another; the pavé of codfish, a thick block of the sturdy white fish, its glistening interior rare, almost pink, its top coated with a dense layer of black caviar, the whole set in a pool of briny cream and garnished with a sprig of dill—which, if you consume a bit of it with each bite, leavens and livens the stout seafood; and these thin-cut scallops of salmon in a preparation credited to Troisgros, their barely cooked surfaces whited a little, the rare interiors a glistening coral, the strands of sorrel in their buttery sauce sour and metallic, striking foils to the pink meat.

Fifteen dollars will get you a glass of port and a slice of Roquefort, the blue-veined cheese strong and deep and creamy, and not a bad transition from those seafoods to these sweets: an almost weightless millefeuille of flaky pastry interleaved with thin slices of tart apple and sweet white raisins, set in a pool of sour-apple sauce, and garnished with a ball of icy apple sherbet; another millefeuille, sheets of pastry again, between them an airy pistachio cream, the whole in a chocolate sauce that is black, polished, intense; a dessert that seems at first like something children make in a refrigerator of store-bought crackers and whipped cream, which, when you set aside that impression, is a delicate interplay of crisp, cool chocolate wafers and fluffy banana mousse; the house chocolate cake, light for its richness, thick layers of sticky mousse between thin ones of black cake, their chocolate flavors of liquorlike clarity and strength; a couple of irregularly shaped sheets of crisp coconut meringue, between them browned, acid-sweet chunks of pineapple and a rich pastry cream—a dish of many taste and texture contrasts; and what is given as "a variation of caramel desserts," a fluffy caramel mousse, light floating islands onto which melted caramel has been dribbled, an exceptional flan that is cool and smooth, a caramel ice cream that argues in favor of the proposition that not every flavor is suitable for ice cream—all four arranged in a tangy (you guessed it) caramel sauce.

★ BICE

7 East 54th Street
LUNCH AND DINNER.
Reservations: 688-1999.
Credit cards: AE.
Expensive.

Designed the way it is, Bice (bee-chay) would best be left untouched. But, big but, it is a restaurant, the interests behind it insist on letting people in, they add captains, waiters, busboys, everyone makes noise and moves around, which converts the lively-looking place into an aural and visual circus. It is like the effect you get if, for laughs, while watching an old-time Technicolor production number, you turn way up the volume and brightness on your TV. All of which is too bad, for this is a space niftily fitted out, albeit with so many points of visual focus, and so little provision for the absorption of sound, that the installation succeeds in inverse proportion to the number of people present to enjoy it. Bice's façade is of doors that fold away, so that the softly lit barroom —polished wood, a handsome curved bar, cocktail tables of pink marble, tall wine cabinets, and colorful modern art—is a quasi outdoor café if the weather is balmy, and if you are having your drink at the very front, hard by the zephyrs of East 54th. The dining room farther in is more brightly lit. Its overhead is a modernistic version of a beamed ceiling—it rises to four peaks, each of them rimmed and strutted with metal beams, some pewter colored, some painted white. Glowing light fixtures of polished brass and parchment are mounted on the walls, tasteful prints hang between them in thin black frames. The banquette that encircles the place is upholstered in a striped fabric of muted colors—olive, dull gold, raspberry. And the column that rises through the center of the room is flanked by similar banquettes that extend out from it like wings, and face both to the front and rear—on the shelf that is the top of each wing stands a huge white urn holding a great burst of flowers. The tables are covered with beige linen, the commodious armchairs are of honey-colored wood, the carpeting—the room's one false note—is a blue-and-ivory tartan that looks like a cheerleader's skirt. Like all fashionable spots, Bice is frequented by two crowds, the real crowd, and the crowd that comes to see them. Mostly the two miss each other, for the gawkers are here on weekends, when they encounter mostly one another rather than the midweek set. The latter is made up, in part, of chichi ladies in Miro dresses and wrist clocks, others pleased to be built like snowpeas and to wear their hair pulled back so tight it looks painted on; gents in unpadded double-breasted suits over polo shirts, and others who are more tailored—these latter sport cuff links, handkerchiefs in the breast pockets of their trim-fitting jackets, silken cravats, even the occasional cigarette holder complete with cigarette. This set visits from table to table, they relentlessly agree with one another and smile a lot, then move on.

Whatever you wear, you do well with the swordfish carpaccio, the thin-sliced, translucent, and vaguely pink raw fish applied like a film to the big round plate, moistened with good olive oil, and strewn with strands of carrot and celery, dice of tomato. You do equally well with the lobster-and-arugula salad, the morsels of shellfish, tepid, moist, and of good flavor, garnished with hearts of palm and slices of ripe avocado, and set on a platform of the strong wild greens—a dressing that clings enriches the dish. Have either of those rather than the grilled eggplant, the thin sheets of the vegetable fibrous and of no eggplant character, the bread stuffing mealy, the tomatoed topping of melted cheese not enough to make the dish. One night your waiter assures you that the house does not make half orders of pasta, the next night another fellow winks at you, says that *for you* he will arrange half orders not only of pasta, but of risotto. Anyway, half orders are two-thirds the price of full ones, and the gnocchetti sardi al Gorgonzola, though in a good, parsleyed, and powerfully salty cheese sauce, is of little curls of pasta that insist on reverting to shape; the taglioline primavera are thin strands of noodle in a soupy mushroom-and-vegetable sauce that comes to life only when thickened with an abundance of cheese; and the risotto nero is a watered version of the black squid-and-rice dish that is devoid of sea-gaminess.

Italians do not find halibut in their own waters, but they manage well with the ones they find in New York—this fillet, fluffy and white within its grill-marked surfaces, is of sweet flavor, and it is cleverly garnished with warm chopped tomatoes in warm vinaigrette. A little garlic and much salt and pepper have been applied to the surface of the baby chicken, so when it is grilled, the browned skin becomes a sharp zest to the pale meat. The sometimes available osso buco is undercooked in its sour sauce, so if it is veal you want, have what is listed as rack of veal, the supple meat pale, tender, and of a clear, homey roast veal flavor. The battuta di manzo is pounded-thin beef, oiled and blood-juicy, its vivid flavor emphasized by the garlic, rosemary, and black pepper that have been applied to its surface.

Bice makes much of its gelato, but it is eggy, almost custardy, cloying to the American taste for American-style ice cream. You may have yours with warm apple pie, which is applesauce on a pastry, which reaches you at once and cold (the house is in a hurry, wants to turn you over promptly, means to recover its investment by Labor Day). The cheesecake is of cream cheese on something that, while it looks like a graham cracker crust, tastes like nothing at all—the thing is rich, is served with spooned-on strawberries in syrup. The chocolate cake is a thickness of sweet chocolate under a darker, craggy chocolate top.

• LE BILBOQUET

25 East 63rd Street
LUNCH, DAILY; DINNER, MONDAY TO SATURDAY.
Reservations: 751-3036.
No credit cards.
Medium priced.

This is the one that, when it first appeared, operated without a published phone number. It was assumed the place was about the business of being, how you say, exclusive. But no, that is not this establishment's bag. Rather, it was determining just how much it could get away with, and in the early experimental days it tried to get away without a listed telephone, imagining that spouses, administrative assistants, messengers, et al, would be dispatched in all weathers for purposes of making reservations, cancellations, deposits—who knows, maybe even donations, for no one could tell what sacrifices these Americans would make if the establishment inflicted upon them sufficient contempt. Well, the no-telephone ploy did not produce (when his telephonic cord is severed, an upper East Sider is not cowed, he is addled), but much else did.

First there is your waitress (French) who feels that it is required of her to define for you, item by familiar item, the entire menu, including such puzzlers as le pâté, le steak tartare, and la salade de poulet, which, her beguilingly accented English being what it is, takes her as long as it will take you to eat—your enchantment is such that you do not explain to her that the ordeal is unnecessary, not to say inefficient (inasmuch as the entire floor appears to be under her care), that others are expressing by dramatic gesture their need for her assistance. Then, another time, there is your waiter (French) of the other persuasion, who tells you nothing until it is too late: that at least two (the two you ask for) of the nine still wines on the list are unavailable, that at least two (the two you ask for) of the six listed appetizers are "out." (You may have been plain lucky in choosing two main courses of the seven listed that, in fact, you may have.) All this in a room that could comfortably accommodate a ping-pong table and a couple of close-up players, which instead has been fitted out with a scant score of tables for two (for groups of three or more tables are pushed together), a zinc bar at the back, and art on the yellow walls, the effect of which density, when the place is, as normally, packed, being a concentration of noise heretofore known only to the eating places of the generation just behind the one that eats here. The accompanying background music is ordinarily inaudible, but even when the din is full blast the periodic dumping of dirty dishes into a tub concealed in a corner is punctuation that gets through. In the midst of all of which festivity there suddenly appears a managerial type in a red flannel shirt. He is sleepy, he crawls behind the bar, runs one hand through his tousled hair, lifts the phone with the other, pecks out a number, fails to make a connection, all the while regarding, with somnolent proprietary satisfaction, the scene, forty Americans shouting at one another inaudibly, all of them content.

They are eating the likes of that pâté, a dark, mousselike, livery thing speckled with bits of truffle and framed in dark jelly, moist and powerfully seasoned, and served with a great mound of harshly salty and acidic little pickles and with triangles of, for some reason, toasted whole wheat sandwich bread; or they are at a salade d'haricots verts, the thin green beans at once soggy and tough; or at les endives au Roquefort, the blades of endive arranged like points of an asterisk on the plate, at the center a ball of good Roquefort surmounted by walnuts, the decent ingredients in a distinctly sour pink dressing; or, when it is the soup of the day, at the onion soup, the hot stuff in a little ceramic pot, melted cheese and soaked-in-soup bread at the top, lots of onions at the bottom, the broth between dark and vigorous if utterly without distinction.

Mostly cold main courses, among them a caper-dotted steak tartare, a single anchovy across its top, that, though of fresh-ground beef, is little more than (timidly) seasoned meat, a raw hamburger rather than a steak tartare, much in need of the enrichment of oil or egg yolk or both. The chicken salad, happily, sports real chicken flavor, the walnuts are crunchy, the red and yellow peppers are fresh, and the mayo dressing is the right enrichment. When the poisson du jour is Dover sole, you are served the four imperfectly boned quarters of a fish, floured, browned in butter, firm, moist, and of clear sole flavor. And when lamb chops are the plat du jour, you suffer only for their being overdone— otherwise the three chops are tender and of pungent lamb flavor in their powerfully garlicked sauce.

Your waitress offers, in her puzzling but enchanting English, a plume pie, and you are served a plum tart that is of dull purple fruit on a pastry that tastes like marzipan. The tarte tatin is hot, but the chunks of apple, though dark, are only vaguely caramelized, and the whipped cream is loose. The lemon tart is best, thin disks of lemon over the tangy custard, and a decent pastry.

★★BISTRO BAMBOCHE

1582 York Avenue (near 83rd Street)
DINNER. CLOSED SUNDAY.
Reservations: 249-4002.
Credit cards: AE.
Medium priced.

That ten small tables have been inserted here tightly, where seven or eight larger ones could have been arranged comfortably, you are willing to overlook. A living, after all, must be made, and what with the rents in this neighborhood, etc. An excuse for the paraphernalia, however, you will not find, even if you look under the boldly patterned tablecloths, or within the folds of the napkins that sprout like fans from the large wineglasses, or between the glazed bricks of this one wall, or between the chocolate-brown-painted stones of this other, or tucked under the mattes of these dainty engravings, or behind the tall strips of glass that, wide enough to reflect a child standing sideways, look like salvaged mirror leavings. Nor will you have any luck looking under the red tiles that make up this floor, or over the ceiling's acoustic tiles, which are held in place by black bands that form a bold windowpane pattern—you can't miss them. And if, while looking, you find that you need more light, turn up the lights—they are housed in tulip sconces fastened to the walls. While you are at it, turn up the background music too.

But the price is right, most of the food is good, and this is a cheerful little family operation. So put on your dark glasses, come here, and begin your dinner with, say, a bowl of hot and buttery sorrel soup—it has the good sour edge of that green, and it is

served with crusty croutons. Or begin it with this mousse of scallops, a two-tone semicircular slice cut from a loaf, the pale D-shaped portion the firm and peppery seafood
mousse itself, the green base a contrasting stripe of spinach—the third color is pale pink,
the tomatoed sauce in which the mousse is set. If you attempt to do caviar in a low-price
prix fixe, something has to give—here it is the caviar, which is served, one little black
dollop and two little red ones, on three silver-dollar-size blinis, with crème fraîche. To
paraphrase the wise man, a little bit of caviar is like a little bit of love. Unless, of course,
it is mediocre caviar. Avoid that in favor of the profiterole Bamboche, a nugget of chou
pastry under a mixture of chicken and mushrooms in a creamy sauce that is fragrant of
fresh dill.

The salmon is steamed in paper, with vegetables and dill, and if the process goes on
too long, as it sometimes does here, the fish loses its oil, and thereby its character—but
this is fresh salmon, and fine when fine tuned. The Bistro's menu is a brief one, but its
range of ingredients is even briefer. That first-course combination of scallops and spinach
repeats itself, but much more impressively, here among the main courses. These are sea
scallops, six huge ones that have been sautéed until they are browned and crusted, and
they arrive on a mound of strong spinach that is dotted with pine nuts and black raisins.
Just before the dish is served to you, your waiter pours over it a pitcher of black butter
that sizzles and pops when it hits the food—a good dish, in which each of the disparate
elements is vivid. The Bistro stuffs chicken with chicken, makes a roulade of white meat
around a greened chicken mousse, and serves the big knob of hot stuff in a creamy sauce
of assorted wild mushrooms—including a few black, crinkly morels. There are sweet
green peas and crisp carrots in among the eggy noodles on which the sweetbreads are
served. The thin slices of organ meat are crisp, and the noodles are peppery and creamy
—simple, striking food. The entrecôte is a good steak accurately prepared—it comes
with a couple of crusty little potato pancakes.

For an extra dollar you may have a well-made little soufflé for dessert—the house
flavor is apricot, and the soufflé has a clear fruit taste that is emphasized by a slight acid
edge. The chocolate soufflé cake is weighty, moist, and intense—it comes with whipped
cream. You may have some almond-studded vanilla ice cream—the hot chocolate sauce
is poured on just as it is handed to you.

★ BLUE NILE

103 West 77th Street
LUNCH, TUESDAY TO SUNDAY; DINNER, DAILY.
Reservations: 580-3232.
Credit cards: AE.
Inexpensive.

You descend half a dozen steps to a rambling room, clean and well lighted, its
sanded pale-wood floor sealed and glistening, the walls surfaced with grass cloth and with
Ethiopian art and paraphernalia—musical instruments, household instruments, instruments of unfathomable function: so far, your standard ethnic restaurant. But then you
notice that something is missing. Where, you wonder, are the tables and chairs? And
what, you wonder, are all these *things*? The "things," as well as you can make out, are
elephantine egg cups made of straw, with removable straw lids, and when your hostess/

waitress (she is in what you take to be native Ethiopian costume) invites you to sit, you notice that the straw construct (it is your "table") to which you are assigned is surrounded by foot-high, 12-inches-across, three-legged stools with concave seats—a curled-up cat would fit in one precisely. You, however, do not fit quite so well. Lower yourself onto one of these, and then lean a little, so as to move your center of gravity (you will find it at, roughly, the midpoint between your breastbone and your spine) outside the stool's airspace, and off you topple. It happens here two or three times a night. No one laughs. (Laugh, and you mock a whole culture—and the crowd here is largely academic, both faculty and student.) The victim rights himself with the solemnity of the forcefully evicted temperance ranter picking himself up off the sidewalk outside the saloon door— he is ruffled, but his seriousness of purpose is undiminished. (It is for fear of falling that regulars choose stools that enable them to lean their backs against a wall.) Mere fallers off, however, are the least of the sufferers. Many writhe throughout dinner, for to fold one ample abdomen and two abundant thighs into this low-down geometry effects a compression that pushes dinner back where it came from. Cruelty is it to lure here a certified stout.

The lid is removed from the top of your egg cup, a cloth is spread, and your food is brought on a tray that is lined with the crêpelike Ethiopian bread called injera. In addition, folded sheets of injera, looking much like linen napkins, are provided to each eater. If you and your company have ordered, say, four dishes, each of them—appetizers, salads, main courses, whatever—occupies a space on the single tray, and everyone eats from whichever of the dishes he fancies—but (big but) without benefit of silverware. You tear off a patch of injera, pick up a quantity of food with it, consume the two together. Since almost all the dishes are stews or mushes, after two or three sorties, your fingers are, inevitably, a mess. Dress appropriately. When you have run out of your own injera, you use some of that with which the tray is lined, or you obtain more from your waitress. Many of the dishes are flavored with berberé, a fragrant spice that is much of the character of Ethiopian food. And, happily, the food—some of it spicy-hot—is mostly good.

Among the foods you may have on your tray, there is azefa, a cold and lemon-sour paste, mustardy too, of lentils and onions—very rousing; shuro wot, a hot chickpea mash, touched with ginger and basil, but too lightly—the dish is solid but pallid; yegomen wot, in which the sharp taste and fibrous texture of kale is offset by the plainer taste and texture of the chunks of potato buried in it—the slightly spicy dish is flavored with onions and peppers; doro wot, a very hot chicken item (the house chooses to call it "New York's spiciest dish") in which the chunks of bird, along with a single hard-cooked egg, are buried in a dark, sweet, strong sauce—the chicken is suffused with its flavor; yasa wot, supposedly a fish dish, but one in which the bits of seafood are simply a carrier for a mild berberé-flavored tomato sauce; ye'beg tibs, a dismayingly bony lamb dish in which too little of the pungent meat benefits from a very vibrant sauce that is sharp with black pepper and heady with rosemary; and tibs wot, another red-meat dish, this one much more satisfying, for there are chunks of sturdy beef in the hot, glistening, and garlic-flavored stew.

The desserts are Western, commercial, decent, the likes of carrot cake and pecan pie. Some of them have embarrassing names: "darkest Africa chocolate chip cake"; "the emperor's pumpkin-chiffon cheesecake." With dessert you get a fork.

Beer is best with this food, and Carlsberg, Dos Equis, and many other good brands are available, even Guinness Stout.

★ LA BOHÊME

24 Minetta Lane (near Sixth Avenue)
LUNCH, SUNDAY; DINNER, TUESDAY TO SUNDAY. CLOSED MONDAY.
Reservations: 473-6447.
Credit Cards: AE.
Medium priced.

Note that the restaurant is named for Bohemia (La Bohême), not for the opera about an impoverished girl with a bad cough (*La Bohème*). Note, too, that by its menu, prices, appointments, and situation, it aims itself at that legendary Bohemia, composed of the more-or-less literate more-or-less poor—starving but happy artists, threadbare but secure academics, doing-not-too-badly-thank-you writers temporarily in the advertising business—that once was Greenwich Village. You may have thought, what with all that is new in New York, that that old crowd no longer existed, certainly not here in the Village, which got itself gentrified even before that concept was a dirty word. But no sooner did La Bohême turn up, than the earnest old set dug out its berets, tweed jackets, and baggy pants, its sensible shoes, burlap skirts, and heavy sweaters, and headed here as if this were Stewart's Cafeteria reincarnate. The NYU cells, it seems, have been dormant, not dead, and this is the rallying place they have been waiting for. (The sober gentlemen in suits and ties—with counterparts in matching jackets and skirts—that you see at tables here and there about the dining room, their watchfulness constant but unobserved, are here on duty.)

Blue-collar appointments, of course. A plank floor, walls of rough wood or plain stucco, butcher paper on the densely arranged tables. The wide-open kitchen at the rear is a people's theater in which honest work, complete with sweat, is put on daily except Monday. Particularly moist is he who, at arm's length, tends the pizza oven, the flames of which warm not only him but also the back half of this deep store, which is about ten degrees hotter than the front, an area that, in subtemperate seasons, gets an opposite treatment each time the front door is swung. The thick, shiny wires, red or blue or yellow, that emanate from gray colanders nailed high on the walls and hang in loops from the ceiling, are a designer's joke that the client lacked the self-confidence to laugh at and take down.

Bistro food plus pizza plus pasta, including a perfectly nice artichoke that suffers for being icebox-cold; a gamy and pistachio-studded pâté; slices of saucisson chaud that, though dotted with peppercorns, are a little flat, in need of their hot mustard—they are garnished with disks of new potato in a warm, oily dressing; snails that are plump and tender in their sizzling butter—you wish they were more assertively seasoned. The pizzas are of thin bread (one time crisp, another time mealy), the one known as Minetta a vigorous thing of black olives (beware the pits), strong anchovies, and sour capers on the herbed cheese; the one called Gitane a waste of decent snails, for they are nothing but six textural notes here among the red peppers, garlic, and black olives again—the pies are moistened with olive oil just as they are served. The spaghetti with fresh basil, though the green leaves are in evidence, lacks the herb's fragrance, and the cheese that you permit to be added to the coarse red sauce does little to liven it. The fusilli aux fleurs du jardin is two colors of the corkscrew pasta, several colors of vegetables, and a garlicked tomato sauce in which those elements fail to coalesce.

But then you order a fish of the day, grilled tuna, and the thin crosshatched steak of fresh fish is moist and of vivid tuna flavor in its pale, buttery sauce. Much flavor, too, in the slices and parts of the browned and crusty confit of duck, though the bird is a little dry. Of course there is a steak pommes frites, and the charred beef is tender and accurately done, the big mound of thin French fries crisp and light.

The browned apple tart is of fruit that retains a bit of its tartness on a flaky pastry. The frozen lemon soufflé is icy, acidic, and sweet in its crimson pool of berry puree. Have either of those rather than the marquise, a square of mousselike chocolate cake in a spongecake frame that is low on chocolate strength—its sauce, a Frangelico sabayon, seems only to wet it.

★ LA BOÎTE EN BOIS

75 West 68th Street
DINNER.
Reservations: 874-2705.
No credit cards.
Medium priced.

' The particular accomplishment of this place is that in it are combined innumerable clichés (ilk: French country inn) to an effect almost wholly lacking in hilarity. Also combined in it are an abundance of small tables in a room almost wholly lacking in space, which may be why no one is laughing. So to eat here is to endure thy neighbor and his wife. (When, for example, neighbor forestalls his host from pouring the Côtes du Rhône because, as he puts it, he wants "to breathe it for a while," and when host thereupon nods with accordant solemnity and departs, wife grabs the bottle and pours herself some right off. Explains she, "I don't think they breathe anyway.") La Boîte is a semisubterranean little store that you approach by descent of a couple of steps to a glass-enclosed, lace-curtained alcove. Through that, then down a few more steps, and you are in the low-ceilinged wee cave itself. That ceiling, of course, is of rough plaster, and, as surely, it is beamed, as surely as the floor beneath it is of old wood. The walls all around are surfaced with burlap, except where they are of bare brick or rough timbers. And it hardly needs saying that there are wildflowers on the white-linened tables. What gives rooms of this kind their especial poignance is the lovingly assembled collection of mock mementoes on the walls and shelves. At La Boîte, however, you get not only the common framed prints and mirrors, copper pots and pans, painted pottery, basket, pitchfork, and scythe; but also the quite rare hand iron and wooden shoes; and the virtually unheard-of hatchet, brass bugle, blue-glass syphon, and—the winner—a little loom with a two-inch woof.

Your host is a nervous man within a calm one. He is slight, wears tinted glasses. You can actually see him not wringing his hands. His politesse is so without warmth that you pity him for his felt need to affect it. When he asks you if everything is all right, it is kindness to cut the whole thing short with a smile and a one-word answer. Now and again he escapes to an alcove behind the dining room, where he tranquilizes himself with a cigarette.

If only because it could not possibly be, the food is not as dated as the setting. The little menu even lists a stylish rillettes de saumon, which reaches you as a couple of cool eggs formed of ground salmon, their intense fresh-fish flavor sweet and breezy—the salmon comes with chopped onion, capers, a scallion, lemon. Order poached leeks, and you get three or four big ones at room temperature. They are fibrous, robust in fact, but tender, moist of a vinaigrette that is mostly good oil—the big stalks are strewn with chopped egg and garnished with glistening slices of cool ripe tomato. Saucisson chaud is a virtual inevitability on menus of this sort, and here the three great slices of fatted ground meat are redolent of sweet spice and garnished with a mash of parsleyed lentils —your waiter spoons a dollop of fiery mustard onto your plate. The place even puts forth a good fish soup that it styles "Marseillaise." The dark, saffron-flavored stuff is earthy and has a briny marine edge—it comes with hard crusts of bread and with a mild red-peppered rouille, but not with the pungent garlic sauce often used to fortify this dish.

The salmon is prepared in paper, and it is brought to you in paper, and your waiter tears the paper open for you (thanks), but leaves it on the plate as a kind of shell that you must hold aside with one implement while eating with the other—only to find that though the mustard sauce is not very mustardy, the fish itself is distinctly fishy. So you will prefer to take your chances with the fricassée de poussin à l'ancienne, coq au vin to you, and this is a good stew in which the chicken tastes like chicken, in which the mushrooms and onions and chunks of bacon add a good coarseness, and in which the sauce is smooth and thick and winy. You cannot fault these perfectly nice lamb chops, though the rosemary the menu leads you to expect is not in evidence. For abundance you opt for the kidneys, and you get a huge circle of them, clean and crunchy in their dark, stout sauce, arranged around a mound of buttery rice that is studded with sweet green peas.

A clafouti is a dessert of cherries (usually) baked in a pancake dough, and though it is intended to be a homey, heavy thing, when it is served cool, it can be almost gummy, as this one is—serving it in crème anglaise, as La Boîte does, adds a note of misplaced fanciness. But the sherbet is cleverly served, six spheres of three flavors, orange, pear, and an intense cassis, set in a pale-green pool of pureed honeydew. The so-called salade d'oranges is of cold orange sections, strands of tangy orange rind over them, and a couple of little balls of that orange sherbet, all set in cherry liqueur—sprigs of fresh mint are strewn over the fruit. The place turns out particularly light and firm oeufs à la neige, the great knobs of sweetened egg white—in crème anglaise—adorned with a dark butterscotch sauce that is thick with chopped nuts.

★★LA BONNE BOUFFE

127 East 34th Street
LUNCH, TUESDAY TO FRIDAY; DINNER, MONDAY TO SATURDAY. CLOSED SUNDAY.
Reservations: 679-9309.
Credit cards: AE.
Medium priced.

A shallow, narrow, low-ceilinged little rectangle of a place, noisy and sometimes hectic, with all the comforts of a crosstown bus plus food. At the controls, an animated French pixie. Her safe station is behind the short bar at the front, whereat the press of those waiting for tables, those leaving (they are trying to penetrate the dense little crowd to get their coats), and those entering through the front door combine to form a human gridlock standoff. Madame is calm throughout, exchanging pleasantries in her first language with countrymen of hers who obtained places at the bar early on. But her eye is always on the works, and when a place is free and ready, she plucks from the crowd those up next and hustles them to their table (which is of bare, dark-stained wood, a paper place mat at each place). All tables are along the circumference of the room. The floor is of wood. The ceiling is low. The plaster walls are casually hung with framed art. The place is worked by a couple of ladies who thump through their paces with energy and goodwill. They are French, and they thrive on this occupation, which seems to cheer as it wearies. Many of those who crowd La Bonne Bouffe work or live in the neighborhood. (The others shop there.) They include editorial types from Crown Publishers, medical types from University Hospital. Watch for the inevitable *Gastrointestinal Cookbook*.

The skeletal menu is fleshed out with numerous dishes of the day, among them, often, a splendid endive salad, an abundance of the crisp, yellow-tipped leaves surrounded by mâche, sprinkled with chopped hard-cooked egg and fresh parsley, dressed with good oil. You wish the asparagus had been cooked more briefly, for it is a little limp, but it is fresh, of vivid flavor, and it is livened by a pungent vinaigrette. Something given as "salade de primeurs" is a cold mingling of various marinated vegetables, much like a ratatouille, but crunchy, including such elements as cauliflower and green beans—the rousing concoction is tart, a little sweet, crisp, oily, strongly seasoned. The house pâté is salty, well fatted, strong. The snails surpass the New York bistro norm—they are plump and tender, in an abundantly parsleyed butter that, for all its salt and garlic, is not obvious. Even the onion soup is good—stout, thick with slivered onions, weighted with a chunk of bread, covered over with pully browned cheese.

A great length of snapper, fresh, moist, handsomely browned, is served strewn with sautéed mushrooms, capers, bits of lemon. Chunks of lotte, the French swimmer that calls itself anglerfish at this end of the Atlantic, is served the same way sans the lemon— you squeeze on the citrus yourself. Both these grenobloise preparations have the sparkle of fresh food, alertly prepared, brought to the table at its peak. There is always duck with orange sauce, sometimes duck with honey sauce—the good-tasting birds are well roasted, moist, a little crisp—and the sweetness of the sauces is tamed with vinegar. What the house proudly lists as "Escalope de Veau Bonne Bouffe" is an inelegantly weighty dish of veal, mushrooms, browned cheese—it is heavy but satisfying, perfect if plain hunger is your problem. Sometimes sweetbreads are offered, and the thin slices of organ meat are steamy, hot, fluffy within their crisped exteriors. Two great crescents of liver, sliced thin and then sautéed hot, are at once crusted and rare—the sweet, delicate meat is in a red-wine sauce that is thick with slivered shallots.

The fruit tarts are fresh, and there is a fluffy custard between the fruit and the flaky pastry, but the productions are somewhat unfortunately protected from the environment by a heavy glaze of clear syrup. The crème caramel and ice cream items—peach melba, poire belle hélène—are fine. Sometimes there is offered an almond chocolate torte— this dark and intense sweet is doused with almond liqueur.

The principal irritant is a policy of charging higher prices for daily specials than you are likely to anticipate from the prices of the menu items—that sweetbread special of the day, for example, is about as expensive as a filet mignon; a duck off the menu is higher than the listed one; &c.

★★BOULEY

165 Duane Street (near Hudson Street)
LUNCH, MONDAY TO FRIDAY; DINNER, MONDAY TO SATURDAY. CLOSED SUNDAY.
Reservations: 608-3852.
Credit cards: AE, DC, MC, V.
Very expensive.

Nestled among the TriBeCa warehouses, and hardly a taxi meter click from the Odeon itself, here is a French manor house built to full scale. Thirty gently sloping hectares of cabernet sauvignon around it (the area bounded by Canal Street, West Broadway, Vesey Street, and West Street would do), and an engraving of Château Bouley could go on a wine label. The great front doors could easily serve as the frontispiece for a modest south-of-France cathedral, and once within the anteroom onto which they give, you are surrounded by the massive walls, these the color of pale sandstone, behind which subtropicals keep their cool. In the spacious oblong dining room itself, three great columns are a row down the long axis, their heads the foci around which eight lofty ceiling vaults, four to each side of the room, rise to their peaks. The intended look is Provençale, there are antiques of the region here and there, the doorways and interior windows are in arched frames of dark wood, as are the big front windows—their sills thick with greenery—which are hung with pleated curtains of white gauze. The large linened tables—surrounded by capacious armchairs upholstered with elaborate tapestry cloth—are set with wildflowers in pottery vases, with Limoges china of a gay and fantastical botanic pattern, with little shaded lamps. The room has its false notes—the sophisticated harmless art, the slick swath of mint green that is the banquette along one wall, the functional dull-colored carpeting, all of which suggest that perceived necessity dictated compromises—or that a backer's taste did. It must be concluded that Bouley was installed in this remote corner of the city for reasons of real estate economy, for no one eating here is doing so for having failed to get a table in one of the places on West Broadway—these folks mostly come from uptown in cabs, or from across the waters in sedans, though sprinkled among them are a few who have converted nearby lofts into basketball courts for living. They are attended to by a formal staff in black and white, gents who know the menu and explain it patiently to their moneyed customers.

In its first days Bouley offered certain dishes that, you figured, were on the menu in artistic defiance of popular taste, since the eponymous chef, being also the proprietor, could choose not to pander. Surely no one expected to sell many sea urchin soufflés, or much eel, or even this lobster, being as it was embedded in cold jelly? Anyway, the items were delisted soon enough. The artist discovered that there is little satisfaction of self-expression alone. He found that he wanted also to be loved—and too few loved, for example, that clammy lobster. It was a dish more interesting than winning, experimental work in which chunks of good lobster meat were interred in a cold, brown aspic spread with a thin layer of white sauce, a dollop of black caviar at the center—chilling food at first encounter, also rousing, a poetic dish that yielded pleasure only in repayment of close attention. The smoked-eel millefeuille, on the other hand, was easy to like but, for most, hard to order, the named ingredient not a favorite in these parts, which is too bad, for the dish, a kind of napoleon, had immediate appeal, the shelves of flaky pastry interleaved with the smoky seafood and slivers of firm potato, all in a sauce that was dark and powerfully herbed. The fresh sea urchin and blue crab soufflé attracted little interest because, as food, sea urchins have charms solely for those creatures that are its natural predators—withal the little soufflés tasted like crabmeat, cheese, and not much else. But a word of pasta ensures the acceptance of any dish, and it may well account for the survival of the cherrystone clam ravioli, for though these noodle packages are in a light and creamy sauce that is thick with vegetables and minced clams, the whole clams that fill the ravioli have been rubberized in the preparation. Shrimp, wild mushrooms, and foie gras are the star ingredients in the panaché of three salads, the sautéed mushrooms woodsy on their spiky greens, the charred and crunchy shrimp of clear, sweet flavor in the eggplant wrappers, the blackened slivers of hot liver in striking contrast to the enriched spinach on which they are set. But thicker slabs of that same foie gras, served on their own, will sometimes reach you blood raw, and the so-called "corn blinis" with which they are served materialize not as blinis at all, but as a mound of cornmeal studded with whole kernels—nice, but not what you were sold.

Lobster, to which you responded so coolly when it was cold in jelly, is available warm, au sancerre rouge, that is to say in a red-wine sauce that is smooth and sticky, fruity and faintly sweet, very striking with the firm, moist meat of the crustacean. Plump and succulent sea scallops, lightly browned in the sautéing, are served with a pile of black-olive pasta, the gray strands mingled with slivers of vegetable, everything set in a fragrantly herbed red sauce and strewn with leaves of fresh marjoram. You wish these skin-on fillets of baby snapper were not a bit dried out in the grilling, for their spicy sauce of yellow tomatoes, fragrant of sage, suits the delicate, nutty fish. Ask for pigeon, and you get the whole bird: half of it roasted, browned, glistening, a little rare, and of vivid pigeon flavor—it reaches you on a slice of grilled foie gras; the other half, rolled up in a leaf of cabbage and braised, sports just as much flavor, is juicy and just as rare, its tenderness in nice contrast to the leaf wrapper. Morsels of sweetbread and kidney, the former oleaginous and rich within their crusted surfaces, the latter clean-tasting and crunchy, are arranged on your plate, with sautéed chunks of wild mushroom, in the form of a cutlet, little onions, lengths of green bean, and baby carrots all around, the whole in a sauce of cider vinegar that is herbed, smoky, and a little tart. The lamb, arranged over mashed potatoes, is rare and strong, and the good meat, moist of its juice, is garnished with a nifty zucchini tart: dime-size slivers of zucchini and yellow squash, under a good tomato sauce, on a flaky pastry.

Babas are eggy cakes that are usually moistened with liquor. Here three little ones, very light, form a circle with three eggs of intense, icy tangerine sherbet, all in a pool of light sauce that is tangy of Grand Marnier—a vivifying sweet. The chocolate entry is a trio: rich mousse in a spongecake frame; a fresh, moist, and dark layer cake, pistachio flavored, under a slick black icing; and an almost black sherbet. The soufflés are a mere duet, one of raspberry (whole berries in it), the other a nutted one of chocolate and pear, the two garnished with creamy ice cream, minuscule slivers of blueberry, tiny red grapes. The apple crêpe soufflé is a browned pancake folded around a rich and almost chewy apple sauce—it is garnished with a kind of fruit fantasy of raspberries, blueberries, dice of peach, quartered strawberries, all the fruit ripe and firm. The millefeuille of fig, though well made—layers of flaky pastry, between them a creamy filling dotted with bits of fig—lacks fig flavor, but there is compensation in the acidic citrus ice with which it is garnished.

★ BRANDYWINE

274 Third Avenue (near 22nd Street)
LUNCH, SUNDAY TO FRIDAY; DINNER, DAILY.
Reservations: 353-8190.
Credit cards: AE, MC, V.
Medium priced.

Whether or not she is a member of the Order of the British Empire, here a dame is a dame. The interests behind Brandywine have judged that the Gramercy Park neighborhood, on a fringe of which it is situated, can support a he-man steak house, subspecies horsey. Accordingly, the black-tufted banquettes of simulated leather and the wood-paneled walls are supplemented by a couple of framed equine subjects, horse brasses, and the like. A second, smaller room in the back—which must be called the Tack Room, and the entrance to which is guarded by the statue of a jockey—though it holds only a handful of tables, is stuffed with a truckload of paraphernalia, including bridles, a horse tail on a stick, statuettes, and overhead, on a shallow shelf that encircles the room, hunt country bric-a-brac of every description, English horse prints, a brass boot with spur, the kind of red scarf that trails behind you in the wind when you are riding to hounds. Though many of the crowd here could read the *Racing Form* before they could read a menu, this place flatters them that their interest in the animals is more than the eternal search for overlays. In a place like this guys dinner alone. They read the paper—sometimes not the *Form*—they like the menu, the waiters are polite, and the waitresses are not bad either.

The baked clams, seven little necks, in their shells, are sweet and tender under an oregano-greened breading that is touched with garlic and crisped. The broiled shrimp are rather aswim in their herbed and garlicked oil, but the little crustaceans are crunchy, of vivid flavor, and, rarity, devoid of iodine. The house variant on the tomato-and-onion salad involves a copious crumbling of strong Gorgonzola over the two contestants, and if the tomatoes are not America's vine-ripened juiciest, the red onions are sliced to order and are sharp. Skip the fried zucchini, one-inch-by-two-inch logs, their exteriors a heavy albeit handsomely browned batter, their quite appropriate sauce ketchup.

With respect to the fundamentals: The crusted sirloin steak is accurately grilled of blood-juicy meat that is fibrous, textured, tender. The broiled lobster is truly broiled (not steamed and then finished in the broiler), a demanding method that yields perfect lobsters when carefully executed, though the one you get here may reach you just a little dried and toughened. The grilled chicken seems to have been done in advance and finished to your order, so it is flat. But the tuna steak is impeccable—you are asked how you want it, and the seasoned slab of fresh dark-pink fish is medium rare and positively beefy within its crisped surfaces.

The chocolate cake is, of course, of rich chocolate intensity. The so-called Belgian waffle is merely the platform for a hockey puck of vanilla ice cream under less-than-utterly-ripe strawberries that look red in the strawberry sauce in which they are awash. Eschew the pear and chestnut charlotte, which is one layer of paste on another. When the raspberries are good, they are very good—as is their thick whipped cream.

★ BRAVO GIANNI

230 East 63rd Street
LUNCH, MONDAY TO FRIDAY; DINNER, MONDAY TO SATURDAY. CLOSED SUNDAY.
Reservations: 752-7272.
Credit cards: AE, DC, MC, V.
Expensive.

The exhibitionistic namesake of this foolishly titled place used to be the sideshow at Nadia's, on Second Avenue, now, happily, defunct, and then at Nanni al Valletto, a few blocks from here on 61st Street, now happily bereft of his services. When Gianni worked the door at those places, he made lots of friends, and hordes of them come here nightly for the privilege of getting themselves well done in the glow of his florid hospitality. Gianni is a big fellow, with an aureole of frizzy, graying curls upon his cherubic head. When he first opened this place, he greeted his customers in a chef's hat and white jacket. But now he has settled into an ill-fitting tuxedo from the breast pocket of which sprouts a parti-colored handkerchief. The neck of his ruffled shirtfront is emblazoned with an immense bowtie that looks like funerary bunting. The puckered-lace cuffs of his shirt protrude from the sleeves of his jacket, and resemble strikingly what you find on daintily served lamb chops.

You come here a few times. And then, finally, there is the time you come here and Gianni offers you his hand and grants you an affectionate, congratulatory smile. You have made it, proven yourself. From now on, if it happens that Gianni is not at the door when you arrive, he later apologizes for not having been there. He is sorry, and you understand at once that Gianni knows well how wrong a dinner can go if it gets off to that kind of bad start. When he is not laying on hands and smiles, however, he is his other self, bellowing commands in one direction, pointing in another, marching off in a third. He has so many things to do that it is difficult for anyone not to notice him. When he makes the rounds of tables—Is everything all right? Is everything all right?—his followers lay down their utensils and come alive. Some even stand, do not sit again until he leaves, and then smile at one another. A few words from His Radiance, and the evening's tensions are washed away. A visit from Gianni is the equivalent—at least—of a very good family therapy session.

His clients are from all walks of life. A woman who comes here regularly keeps in shape simply by walking around with all her rings on. Her tan looks like something she got in a tannery. Her black eyes are light blue. Her fingernails are ten ziti, each in a simple tomato sauce. A sign states that gentlemen must wear jackets. But there are gentlemen who come here of whom no questions are asked. A two-day growth and a shirt open to the title under the tattoo—with or without a jacket—command especial respect. At dinner's end these types are served bottles of strega and anisette with their espresso. Groups of marrieds from across the waters come here, the ladies in cotton candy hair of futuristic colors, glinting dresses that seem to be woven of contrasting hues of the same stuff. The function of their gentlemen is to fill their armchairs. In this crowd the disposition of the genders around the table is females next to females, males next to males. Elsewise conversation would be constrained. With this layout, the gents can exchange hindsight wisdom about the stock market, while their counterparts talk about current issues in such fields as shopping, hair care, and illness. But make no mistake. Even East Side uprights come here, and they are as giddily gratified as the next fellow by their host's kindly favor.

Bravo Gianni is where three predecessors rapidly failed, so if you caught portions of the brief lives of Aurelio's, Wally's East, or Pappagallo (Aurelio, himself, sometimes comes back, to see what the place looks like with people in it), you are familiar with the gray suède and charcoal-mirrored walls of this place, the muted velvet stripes of the upholstery on the banquette, the cushy carpeting, and the light that emanates from the contorted glass sconces on the walls. These days the linen is pink, there are trees and bursts of flowers here and there, and people at every table oftentimes, so the place can be cheery.

Regulars here are promptly given a little something to hold them as soon as they sit down: flinty, heady Parmesan cheese; maybe some pungent prosciutto with a few slices of Genoa salami; perhaps some roasted red peppers and anchovies. Unknowns are handed menus. Regulars are plied with elaborate speeches about the special dishes of the day. Come-latelies must ask if there is anything available that is not on the menu. Regulars are constantly stroked by Gianni's aforementioned visits to tableside. Beginners may have to settle for the care of a captain. One of these officials, a mustachioed chap of bored demeanor, is quite capable of walking away from you while answering one of your questions. His manner of asking whether you take pleasure in the food before you has only the purpose of letting you know how little he cares. You answer him anyway. "Yummy," go you, whereupon an unseen force tugs at the ends of his lips while simultaneously lowering his eyelids.

But then there is the food. The varying items that make up the assorted antipasto includes fresh mushrooms, mixed with green olives, black olives, and capers, in a garlic-flavored oil-and-vinegar marinade; and cold marinated frogs' legs in an herbed, spicy, and slightly soured oil. The stuffed eggplant consists of broad, thin slices of the vegetable, lightly browned, wrapped around a hot ricotta cheese filling and covered over with a rich tomato sauce.

Pansôti are plump little ravioli, and they are served here in a thick, oiled, garlic-flavored walnut sauce. Pappardelle are broad, flat, rather thick noodles, and Bravo sometimes offers them in an onion-sweetened red sauce to which dried Italian wild mushrooms have been added—the mushrooms are hard to discern against this background, but when you add this restaurant's good cheese, the foreground ingredients make a pungent sufficiency.

The place had obtained big, fresh Spanish prawns and served them—in their shells —in a red-peppered butter. It has served impeccably fresh red snapper, filleted, lightly browned, and strewn with capers. Slivers and little circles of squid—fresh and tender— and firm chunks of potato are served in a heavily parsleyed and pungently seasoned sauce of white wine and butter. Some kind of game is usually on hand, occasionally venison. It is served as little cutlets (one of yours may be tender, the other not) in a meaty, slightly sweet sauce that is well matched to this somewhat sweet meat. Such standard items as osso buco are also on the menu, and Gianni's is a giant knob of meat clinging to the joint—you wish the veal had been cooked longer, for it is still a little resilient, but it has good, spicy flavor, and its chunky red sauce is a nice moistness with the sturdy veal. There is a straight veal chop, but for a couple of dollars extra, you may sometimes have yours under a small hill of red peppers, mushrooms, artichokes—the chop is huge and, really, too beefy and blood-red for veal, so you will probably prefer the rendition with additives to the plain grilled chop.

If you have barked at that captain long enough to straighten him out, he will retire to the back of the restaurant to make for you some zabaglione—it is hot, frothy, powerfully wined, fine over a handful of fresh strawberries. (He gets even with you by charging $7.50 for that production.) The cheesecake is of cream cheese, and it is nothing special except for its sharp and crunchy walnut crust. The zuppa inglese is anonymous, the chocolate cake the familiar thing of mousse and cake and icing, the almond cake a nice amalgam of pastry cream, nuts, meringue.

★ BRAZILIAN PAVILION

316 East 53rd Street
LUNCH AND DINNER. CLOSED SUNDAY.
Reservations: 758-8129.
Credit cards: AE, DC, MC, V.
Medium priced.

South America, to North Americans whose education about the physical world came from the *National Geographic*, means the tropics, lands where civilization and its amenities are but temporary clearings in a timeless jungle. This civilized clearing, in the jungle that is New York, is itself formed of those disparate elements, for though it is a tidy place, the greenery, broad wood beams, exposed brick, and native art hung throughout are assertive primitive elements among which the white-linened tables, smooth white-plaster walls, and the service of the cordial dark-haired waiters suggest a way of life stubbornly competing with nature. Like all Brazilian restaurants in New York, this is a comparatively inexpensive place, so it is frequented not only by members of the local Brazilian community but by neighborhood people on their lesser nights out, and also by members of those UN delegations (here in UN country), sent by nations for which a UN mission is a government budget item second in magnitude only to maintenance of a standing army.

Mindful of the limitations of their expense accounts, the diplomats begin their dinners with one of the several low-cost soups, among them the vigorous caldo verde, an herbed and pungently salted chicken broth that is thick with collard greens, disks of crisp potato, morsels of strong sausage; or cream of black bean soup, a slightly thin and certainly not creamy substance that is, nevertheless, of vivid bean flavor—you add to the soup, according to your taste, the chopped raw onions served with it. For delegates from oil-producing states, there is the pricier aperitivos brasileiros, a couple of giant hot shrimp, sweet and crunchy, covered with bits of browned garlic, served upon a salad of no distinction that features lengths of canned hearts of palm. Similarly the abacate recheado, in which two other perfectly nice shrimp, these cold, surmount a fresh-made seafood salad, bound in a mayonnaise dressing, that is packed, too bad, into an overripe avocado.

As all the world knows, and as is printed on the menu, and as your waiter tells you anyway, feijoada is the national dish of Brazil. It is perhaps best described by what, more than anything else, it is not. It is not Japanese. It consists of individual plates of many things, among them a deep dish of beans in which are buried slices of fat sausage, lengths of thin sausage, little boulders of stewed beef; another plate of beans, and a gravy thick with onions, either of which you may spoon over the contents of yet another plate, this one laden with buttery rice, all of which you season with the powdery zest—a ground root native to Latin America—called manioc; raw oranges and steamy leaves of metallic-tasting kale complete the array and provide relief. This is a somewhat attenuated version of the genuine article, but it is solid food that will hold you until the holidays. The Pavilion, unfortunately, does not offer the peasanty codfish dishes you find in most local Brazilian places, so for sturdy seafood you opt for the vatapá, a thick and spicy-hot seafood puree that is dotted with nuggets of finfish and shellfish, onions and peppers, and served with the inevitable white rice. In such items as the moqueca de peixas, fish and clams in a sauce of palm oil and coconut milk, you detect a failed effort of fanciness. The big lobster dish goes as logosto catalão, chunks of lobster, removed from and returned to their big shell, in a nutty and creamy mushroom sauce that is browned a little just before it is served. Frango bossa nova is lots of dark-fried chicken, quite crisp and yet a little—pleasantly—greasy, strewn with bits of browned garlic, and served with redded rice that is studded with fresh vegetables. Lots of steak dishes, among them churrasco gaucho, a good slab of beef, tender, fibrous, salty, served with a pitcher of so-called gaucho sauce, a sour and hot-spiced relish of tomatoes, onions, peppers.

What the house calls "marmalade" is a compacture of pureed fruit, sweet, tangy, and dark. The guava shells are like preserves, the chunks of sweet fruit in a dense syrup— they are served with an inelegant Brazilian cheese. The banana cake is layered with ripe fruit. The winner is a dark brown milk pudding, thick and sweet, very nice with the good house coffee.

From the low-priced Brazilian and Spanish list, you order a half bottle of white wine, and it is maderized, must be sent back. Anyway, beer is the right drink with this food— pass up the more familiar Brahma for the brand called Tijuca, which has body, depth, and a touch of fruitiness.

★★★ BRIVE

405 East 58th Street
DINNER. CLOSED SUNDAY.
Reservations: 838-9393.
Credit cards: AE, DC, MC, V.
Very expensive.

Readers who have difficulty understanding *The Waste Land* may make reference to notes T.S. Eliot appended to the poem. No such help from R. Pritsker, poet here. His words, at once evocative and puzzling, scorn, as Eliot did not, the contempt with which the seemingly incomprehensible is met by those whose reputations depend on an appearance of omniscience. Pritsker's critics, confronted with the obsessional remorse of "Rich chicken livers. Rich chicken livers," the defiance of "Mussels in a foaming sea," or the fear, anger, and ultimate release of "Chicken breast steamed over its final outcome," fail to grasp imports that, not solely in the words, can be understood only in the larger context of their denotative objects. For Robert Pritsker, like all poets, is writing of— himself!—of all he has eaten, much of which, clearly (pace, Pritsker), he would prefer to forget (anyway, its consequences). His method, the method of dreams, is to dismantle the ingestions of his past and reassemble them, interethnically into his present menu. (The past menu was that of Dodin-Bouffant, at this site some years back.) In this, the prefootnote stage, antecedents may only be intuited, for the clues, though they mark themselves as such, do not hint of their own meanings. For meaning, one looks elsewhere—to dinner itself. Before that, however, it is essential to establish the background before which the foreground is played out.

You will recall that at Dodin-Bouffant one climbed downstairs from East 58th Street and then, once inside the little house this place occupies, back upstairs to the dining room at street level. The gap has been bridged, and one now enters directly to an anteroom, which precedes a two-part dining room, which precedes a little garden room attached at the back, the four in a row constituting the floor-through. It never quite works, the attempt to make a restaurant seem like someone's, you should pardon the expression, home. The antique sofa in the anteroom, in the absence of the domestic paraphernalia that comprise such an object's natural setting, seems like a misplaced, or lost, antique sofa. Part I of the dining room is pale pink, the lower walls wood paneled, perhaps to simulate the elaborate woodwork that, these days, is being bared and refinished in brownstone renovations all over town. This paneling, however, is of a pattern, ovals of burled wood framed in straight-grained wood, that so ill fits the lengths and turns of the walls that the ovals, quite hilariously, to conform to the spaces they must fill, are here slender and graceful, there overweight, elsewhere obese, the way four children, three adults, or two linebackers fit the backseat of a car. There is a high banquette on one side, upholstered in a handsome, heavy cloth of grays, earth colors, a bit of deep blue; tables and chairs on the other side; and in the aisle between them, a runner on the parquet floor. In Part II, the entire floor is covered by a great Oriental rug. Such rugs, it is said, unify a room, but this one cannot begin to cope with its assignment, for it is surrounded by ivory walls to which has been applied a pattern that is vaguely nursery, less vaguely worms at a Rorschach gathering. At the back are four little tables, under a skylight, in a room that overlooks a prettily greened backyard—a healthy lawn and a couple of glass-topped tables with white wrought-iron chairs—where drinks may be served when the weather is right. Within, there are flowers all about, little lamps on some tables, antique furniture—including the chairs—all of which add up to luxe. Sure enough, the physical place is comfortable, and none of its errors is an enormity, but, finally, the rooms are not informed by a conception, the place does not beguile, just serves.

Back to poetry—well, poultry. "Rich chicken livers. Rich chicken livers," an appetizer in two verses, the first a warm mousse of chicken liver that, but for its smooth texture, is Jewish chopped liver, spicy, fatted, and high, served here, probably for the first time in history, in a particularly bright and garlicky version of the tomato sauce that is a fundament of southern Italian cooking—the disparate characters are in harmony when harmony is imposed upon them; the second a standard French mousse, cool and creamy, garnished with minced jelly, and served with a couple of lightly toasted crusts of buttered French bread. What is given as "meatball hero, deli sauce" is in fact a miniature hero sandwich served hot, disks of a dark forcemeat between halves of a bifurcated little loaf of light, flaky pastry. In its deli sauce, which is mustardy but mild, are set slices of pale sausage with which, presumably, you may augment your sandwich—like all good sandwiches, this one comes with a pickle, in this instance a tiny cornichon. On to Spain, whence the calves' brains, the smooth, cool, slightly tart organ meat served cylindrically, wrapped in a crêpe and cut into short lengths, the construct set in a so-called gazpacho vinaigrette, a redded dressing that is thick with crisp chopped vegetables and strewn with fresh, fragrant coriander. Any New York panethnic menu worthy of the name must at least nod in the direction of India. At Brive, of course, the nod is an oblique one, "sweetbreads and lobster under an unlikely Indian influence," the deep-fried nuggets of the rich sweetbreads arranged around morsels of the lobster that are set on green leaves, the two in a pool of Indian-spiced clarified butter, their garnish lentils, but not a soupy Indian dal—these beans are nubbly. The terrine of salmon roe is a thick square cut from a loaf, its outer ring a cool, firm jelly, within that a thin layer of fresh, pink salmon meat, most of the center a density of the great orange globules themselves, at the very core a nugget of leek—the dish is not a brilliant coming together of flavors, but it is brisk, good with its herbed crème fraîche. "Fish soup as it might appear on Lily Pond Lane" perhaps makes reference to the Suffolk County provenance of its seafood components. It is a finfish soup, and though the name Brive is written on its surface in the stout pink garlic sauce served with it, the soup is a little flat, as if in need of the shellfish and spices that give most seafood soups their assertiveness.

What goes as "Old timer's salmon. Most of what you would have expected twenty years ago" is a reference to those elaborate en-croûte preparations, like beef Wellington, that were the rage back in the first reign of Julia Child. You do not have to travel twenty years to find these dishes—certain New York menus list them today—but no other is as niftily prepared as Brive's, a fillet of fresh, firm, sweet salmon under a layer of earthy duxelles, the two encased in a browned and glowing fish-shaped pastry that is sculptured down to the scales. But, for laughs, the dish is served in the kind of dark oil in which Chinese whole fish are served, and it is garnished with a couple of minuscule poached eggs—quail? pigeon? sparrow?—which is to say, egg droplets. You get with your roast veal what are given as "forgotten stuffings." Forgotten by whom? One of them is a fatted, spiced, and bready substance that is the standard filling of "stuffed derma," a Jewish singularity correctly translated as "packed gut," while the other is a homey rice stuffing that would fill a humble bird. Here they grace a veal chop, no less, the pale and rather refined meat moist and tender in its gravylike sauce. Good roast duck, its joke, if any, obscure, the bird itself served as an abundance of little slices, browned skin attached, the pungent, peppery meat served with its own liver, the pinguid morsels of it wrapped in the green leaves in which they were apparently steamed and set on crusts of bread. In olden days, if you spotted pigeon on the menu of a New York Italian restaurant, you immediately reminded yourself that among local Italians, pigeons were a rooftop hobby; even darker thoughts were entertained, having to do with sidewalk pigeons. (Anyway, you ordered osso buco.) Here there is an Italian pigeon—you know it is Italian because it is listed as "having to do with Milano," and you know it is Italian because at the center of its plate there is a raw fig, broken open to reveal its pink interior and encircled by prosciutto—an Italian image of much meaning. The pigeon itself is good too, the parts and slices, which surround the plate's central floret, of intense game-bird flavor. Middle Eastern restaurants have been on the local scene for generations, but Pritsker's variation on a North African theme is a fantasy less inhibited than some of his other flights. The dish of cold lamb steak is many slices of the rare meat, pungently flavored with Eastern spices—they are served with a so-called couscous salad that is a strongly seasoned mound of the little grains, well oiled, dotted with bits of tomato, bits of black olive, and pine nuts; and with a so-called rosemary pesto that is thick, sharp, and heady. Sometimes, when diverse elements are put on a plate, though each is fine, and does not much argue with the others, the wit falls flat. A tangle of spaetzle and carpaccio surrounded by thin slices of dark, tender sauerbraten, with dollops of spinach here and there and a scent of ginger over all, will amuse you only if farce is your taste.

Salad and cheese are part of your dinner, and the place sometimes has on hand wondrous Parmesan, flinty and sharp, very nice with Brive's warm walnut bread. Perhaps there is an allusion in every dessert, but only one is obvious. The ball of "white collar blueberry sorbet" is polished and wildly fruity, it is set within a circle of breadlike cake that looks like the center cut of a big bagel—and, what do you know, dabs of something like cream cheese (crème fraîche) and dabs of blueberry jam adorn it. The milk-chocolate mousse is rich and creamy, and it is garnished with slivers of candied orange that are at once sweet and sharply acidic. The poached fruits—nectarine, melon, peach—are no more than unimpeachable, but the three-mint ice cream served with them will wake you up. The raspberry tart—plump berries, a bit of custard, a crumbly shortbread pastry—is served in a pool of bright, liquored berry sauce. The strawberry charlotte is a disk of fluffy raspberry mousse on a layer of chocolate cake, the whole—encased in a fence formed of ladyfingers and set in a strawberry sauce that is thick with slivers of the fruit—is adorned with fresh mint leaves.

★ BROOME STREET BAR

363 West Broadway (at Broome Street)
LUNCH AND DINNER.
No reservations (925-2086).
No credit cards.
Inexpensive.

At the Broome Street Bar you can often get a table even when the crowd appears to exceed the Fire Department limit. The habitués are crowded twelve deep at the bar of this tight, gamy joint, disporting themselves. Overt sexuality, overt alienation, overt youth, overt bitterness, overt desperation, overt sinister menace even. Laid back, you understand, does not come here. Thumbs are hooked in the belt loops of tight jeans. Fingers snap and behinds wiggle to the rhythmic jangle and thump of a perpetual tape deck. Whole bodies jiggle like paper dolls controlled by invisible strings. Sullen men pump smoke through their nostrils and stare balefully at the untouchable scene. There are baseball hats on some, leather jackets on others, opaque plastic eyeglasses with thin slits in their lenses over the eyes of those who can stand only so much of the visible world. The bartender regards you from behind bangs that have grown down to his upper eyelashes—when bent forward (a position in which he spends much of his working day), he can see very, very little. Your worldly waitress seems like a naïf in this crowd. And the busboy/sweeper/general aide—a slight gent in a ponytail, chin beard, vest, jeans, and running shoes—scratches the seat of his pants while he chats with the regulars. But when Mayor Koch drops in, everyone wants to shake his hand and grin at him, just like political groupies anywhere.

Those who sit down to eat are largely another set—uptown slummers, NYU and Cooper Union collegiates, suburban gawkers, even leftover flower children, defiantly poor, sharing sandwiches and drinking draft beer, fancying themselves tragic. You may sit in the back room (which is large enough for a double bed and a bureau, but which is furnished, instead, with more than a dozen tables and a suitable number of chairs) or in the front room (which is somewhat larger, and where you get a good view of the action at that famous bar).

Throughout the restaurant the walls are dark, in some places of slate, and pieces of colored chalk are left in the chalk troughs so that customers may express themselves in dull graffiti (e.g., "Perón lives") or in tic-tac-toe. Dim, low-hanging factory lamps light the restaurant, four-bladed fans cool it. The floors are of unfinished wood. Hanging green plants filter the light that comes through the ancient, small-paned windows that look out on West Broadway.

Your board is set with paper napkins, milk in a steel pourer, ketchup in a glass bowl with a glass lid (ketchup in a bottle with a screw-on top would be a collectible). You select your repast from a listing that is chalked, in iridescent colors, high on the walls: such items as blue cheese, pear-and-sprout salad, a serving of food about the size of a major league basketball, the fruit perfect, sweet and crisp, the cheese creamy and sharp, the sprouts fresh, an abundance of peanuts, and an oil-and-lemon dressing that is not bad despite its dried herbs; or the mushroom and watercress salad, the only dish in SoHo (perhaps in all of lower Manhattan) that is served topped with Triscuits—and if that does not make it singular, then the mandarin orange sections do, especially in combination with a clump of watercress that is complete but for its rubber band, enough chopped tomatoes to make a pint of juice, lots of good mushrooms, and sprigs of dill here and there for an unexpected intensity of flavor in every fourth bite or so.

The chili is sprinkled with strong chopped onions and layered over with triangles of an orange cheese that looks stronger than it tastes—the meat and beans that are the bulk of the dish are nubbly, thick and fiery. The hungry and relatively insolvent have been known to make a meal of this chili, augmented with thick slices of the firm, moist, and crusty rye and pumpernickel breads you get here. The burgers are not bad, the best of them served in pita with a slice of tomato, unmelted blue cheese, and a slab of strong onion. The contents of an unfortunate grilled sandwich, unfortunately named pigwhich, are a slice of ham cut from a waterlogged block, Swiss cheese from Brooklyn (or perhaps Austria), slices of tomato, and (for an additional half dollar) that orange cheese—the dish is almost rescued by the toasted brown bread within which it is assembled.

The Broome Street Bar is a busy place, and the desserts are always fresh: moist, honeyed carrot cake; pecan pie with lots of nuts and too much corn syrup; rich, sugary cheesecake; ice creams.

★ BRUNO

240 East 58th Street
LUNCH, MONDAY TO FRIDAY; DINNER, DAILY.
Reservations: 688-4190.
Credit cards: AE, DC, MC, V.
Medium priced.

The fire that closed this place for five months damaged it, apparently, forever. Of the original furnishings, only the plain white bentwood side chairs were saved, and if you are of such a mind, after noting all that is new, you look at them with fond regret. For when the conflagration had done its work, eyes that saw darkly perceived not only damage, but also opportunity. Here was the chance to rip out the straightforward and appealing appointments that were presumably all the house could afford when the place was new, and to replace them with expensive-looking stuff. Of course this attempt to advertise to the world that Bruno is successful will itself prove an instrument of the restaurant's decline, for the new look is of a faceless glitz that only a second fire could warm up. The old appeal of this place, decent food in human surroundings, is gone. Now you enter to an anteroom that is all marble and onyx, in it a sunken little bar and mirrored walls to which are attached torchlike lamps held aloft by bent, leafy arms—each arm combines with its reflection to form what looks like the horns on a Wagnerian helmet. Then it is down a couple of steps to the dining room proper, cushy carpeting, lower walls of maroon velvet, rows of white-linened tables. Here the lighting emanates from glowing blank masks mounted on upright, coffin-shaped mirrors that, at regular intervals, are affixed to the walls. They surround you on all sides, and they may put you in mind of the armed guard that is always present in the generalissimo's office.

You may still eat very well at Bruno, but even in this department you will sometimes fail to experience déjà vu. Happily, however, the mushroom salad is all it has ever been, the many slices threaded with thin strands of onion, their fresh and earthy flavor heightened by the oil and tart vinegar with which they have been dressed. You may have the same good mushrooms hot and stuffed, but the forcemeat they are filled with has been waiting for you, and is flat. The sweet and briny little meats of the baked clams are hot, but not toughened, under a buttered, crisped breading. Bruno uses very thin pasta for its primavera, the mound of it at the center of your plate surrounded by florets of broccoli, sweet green peas, those crunchy mushrooms again, even halves of cherry tomato—the last are notes of striking sourness among the other vegetables, delicate noodles, and hot oil. You get an exceptional carbonara here, the oleaginous sauce of eggs and oil dotted with bacon, thickened with cheese, and served on hefty spaghetti. Order risotto, and the house puts aside domestic in favor of imported—porcini—mushrooms. The hot rice mash and the chunks of darkened fungus are stout food, but the dish lacks the depth and complexity of this stuff at its best—cheese helps, and your waiter spoons some on sparingly. "Don't be bashful," go you. "It's expensive," goes he. He is only kidding.

Occasionally Bruno does an odd thing with striped bass, poaches it and then serves it under thin slices of potato—the potatoes have been very carefully prepared, for though they are crisp, they drape, and cling to the contour of the big fillet. The bass is fresh and firm, and it reaches you in a pool of the good, winy broth in which it was done, but those potatoes do nothing to improve it, come off as just an oddity. Crostacei marinara is the big red seafood production, but it is only a production—in the strident red sauce the lobster and shrimp are low on flavor, the clams are tough, and at least some of the mussels are raucously loud. Prepare a plain grilled chicken, and if, like Bruno, you start out with a tasteless bird, you end up with a tasteless bird. Veal scaloppine may be had as you like it, but the thin slices of veal are short-cut (they are barely browned, on only one side, and then inverted onto your dish)—have them as veal piccata, and the lemon sauce is fine, but the meat is lifeless, warmed through rather than really sautéed. You do not expect sausages in midtown East Side restaurants, but here they are—rough and dull, neither sweet nor spicy in their mushroom sauce. The big winner is the veal paillard, the meat of a big chop, still attached to its bone, pounded thin (until it is the size of a bread-and-butter plate), and then judiciously grilled, so that it is brown-striped and juicy—it arrives sprinkled with parsley, and it is good just the way it is, livelier when you add lemon.

Your otherwise attentive captain relaxes when he prepares, right beside your table, your zabaglione—the whisk work in the copper pot is brief, and the sweetened mixture of egg yolk and wine reaches you tepid and barely frothy. The custard-filled cream puffs are doughy, and they are served in a chocolate sauce that lacks chocolate sharpness. The orange cake is an obvious sweet. And the tirami su is a liquored but dull chocolate cake with a pale cream at the center.

★★BUKHARA

148 East 48th Street
LUNCH AND DINNER.
Reservations: 838-1811.
Credit cards: AE, DC, MC, V.
Medium priced.

Consider, if you will, an otherwise dignified Indian restaurant somehow persuaded to identify its perfectly respectable subcontinental dishes by such titles as "Skewered Salad," "Mellow Cream Chicken," and "Fish du Jour," not to mention "Frontier Dal," and, for dessert, "Crème de la Crème" (the last described as "A classic recipe"). The restaurant's main courses, moreover, occupy a section of the menu headed "Bukhara Sapors*," and, sure enough, follow the asterisk, and you will come to a footnote, to wit, "*'Sapors': A quality perceptible to the sense of taste; flavour. From Latin *sapor*, taste, from *sapere*, to taste." The interests behind the place have apparently been sold the idea that, in New York, such gimmickry is what it takes to make a restaurant go (and that, incidentally, local consultants are masters of the technique of pandering to the barbarians who are the local market). It is both good news and bad that Bukhara will survive its own hype: On one hand, the place is of merit; on the other, some of its success will probably be attributed to the thinkers who vulgarized the place in the supposed service of public relations. The approach was surely conceived and committed at an all-night "creative" meeting, everybody grooving, for the boys even came up with a lofty slogan. Dig it: "Savor the flavor from a place in time." In its favor, it may be said that it will always seem new because it will never be remembered. Lardner! thou should'st be living at this hour. In his absence: "Capture the rapture in a spot real hot." "Down your din din in a manner Indian." "Taste of the best of East of the West of." Readers are dared to do worse. A contest will not be held.

Bukhara is situated in a midtown New York hotel, sees fit to give over part of its space to a "cocktail lounge." Accordingly, you enter between two worlds. The walls to your right are hung with groups of Indian copper trays, elaborately engraved and intricately painted, stunning art in the everyday. But to your left is the bar, presided over by a barman who derides orders for nonalcoholic drinks, and sat at by traveling business guys who exchange ribaldries with him, sedate themselves, manage to make it upstairs before passing out. Most frightening is the baby grand, which, from five to eight too many evenings of the week, is tinkled behind singing that is loud enough to be heard in the dining room. But you have faith, and you keep walking—to a dining room that is relief, both from what this place publicly says about itself and from that first encounter with it. The beamed ceiling is low, the light is soft, and the sound is muted. By way of four thick stucco columns (you could put a sofa along each of their four sides) positioned at the theoretical corners of a smaller square within this square room, the place is subdivided into sections, parts, niches—within them are situated well-spaced, massive unlinened tables of deep-dark wood, most of them at banquettes, the seats and backs of which are plump cushions covered with patterned cloth of earth-red colors. Huge trays and urns of hammered copper—glinting red-gold—are here and there around the room, and clusters of copper lanterns hang from the ceiling. But mostly you are aware of the glorious rugs—of course, Bukhara rugs—that are aglow on the walls. Protruding into the dining room from its west side is the glassed-in enclosure that is the restaurant's kitchen—watch its operation, and you learn nothing of Indian cooking, but the installation does give off a friendly glow.

Much is made of the silverware you do not find at your place, for it is intended that you eat with your fingers (moist hot towels are supplied before and after you eat). If you prefer to use implements, ask for a knife and fork—*not* chopsticks. Before making that request, however, consider that, though the species has come far in fifty millennia, its antecedents include a smiling, ever-present monkey on everybody's back. Like other first experiences, after two minutes of eating with your fingers, it all seems atavistically natural, not to say habitual. Idiotically, the place provides large napkins with strings attached —you are meant to make the napkin into a bib by tying the strings around your neck, as if holding food with your fingers were less secure than using silverware. Of course the reverse is true, so if you wear your prettiest necktie, you may show it off throughout dinner. Just avoid fondling it.

Finger instead the roasted fish of the day, often pomfret (bream), a swimmer of vivid taste, the whole fish, in its skin, spiced, lemoned, and carefully roasted—the flavorings permeate the light, fresh meat. Prawns are roasted in the same oven, from which they emerge crunchy and sweet, their marine flavor potentiated by the citrus, garlic, and spices in which they are done. Lots of chicken on the menu, and though your instincts may steer you off the one encumbered with the name Mellow Cream Chicken, in this instance the dopey title does convey something of the dish, for the morsels of bird are marinated in cheese and cream (with spices) before they are skewered and grilled, and the browned finished product is at once succulent and light. What goes as "Khyber Chicken" is more like what you usually get in Indian restaurants, the lightly floured surfaces of the parts blackened a little, the meat fibrous and tender. Though veal is not a fundament of Indian cookery, it does not follow that veal may not be prepared by Indian methods. Accordingly, "Royal Veal" (it was midnight before they all jubilantly agreed on that one), a couple of chops that, having been soaked in a seasoned mixture of rum and yogurt before grilling, retain more moisture and exhibit more life and flavor than much of the veal you get in local French or Italian places. The "Lamb-è-Chasma" is a kebob item, the chunks of garlicked meat tender, blackened, of clear lamb pungency. Ground beef potently seasoned, then formed into sausagelike cylinders around skewers, then broiled, is given as "Bolan Rolled Beef"—the meat is made pale by the ingredients with which it is combined, but the glistening cylinders are of colorful flavor, tangy, sharp, heady of their spices. Beef of yet another color, "Escalopes Bukhara," consists of very thin sheets of the meat, interleaved with cottage cheese and dried fruits, and baked—each clump you sample differs from the last, now a creamy one, now one that is perfumed of some Indian spice, now one that conceals an exhausted chunk of pineapple.

With those main courses you may select from a brief list of vegetables, among them cauliflower, the crunchy and glistening marinated florets encased in the browned and spicy batter in which they were baked; and stuffed roasted potatoes, the giant tubers skinned, hollowed, blackened, and packed with a fragrant filling dotted with sweet green peas. Many breads, among them "Roomali Roti," which the poets on the account describe as "light as a handkerchief"—presumably much was lost in translation, for this bread has the texture of steamed matzo, though its wheat flavor is not bad. The mint paratha is livened by its sprinkling of the herb, the bharvan kulcha may be had with a thin layer of herbs and vegetables between the two of bread, and the khurmi naan is a bit like a pizza, the circle of bread spread with a light tomato sauce within its raised edges. The cool fruited yogurt is a nice foil to the hot food, and the place produces an exceptionally buttery dal, the thick souplike mash of lentils supplied, happily, with a spoon—theoretically you eat the dal by scooping it up with bread, but hours would be required to dispose of a bowl that way. Much is made of the supposed nonspiciness of this restaurant's food—in fact, much of it is hot, though never searingly. The heady, grassy green sauce on your table, however, is incendiary, and seems only vaguely appropriate to most of the dishes.

"L'Orange Crème" (it was getting toward sunup when the boys got around to naming the desserts) is two-thirds of an orange peel packed with grainy ice cream. Rasmalai, not on the menu, is a good dessert of sweetened cottage cheese in a pool of milk.

Beer is the best drink with this food.

★★CABANA CARIOCA

123 West 45th Street
LUNCH AND DINNER.
Reservations: 581-8088.
Credit cards: AE, DC, MC, V.
Inexpensive.

Life in Brazil is ever gay, or so you may conclude from depictions of it in the brilliantly colored murals that adorn the walls of the stairway leading to this primitive second- and third-story eating place. One flight up, through the parti-colored door, and you are at the pea-green plastic lunch (and dinner) counter and bar, which is lined with stools upholstered in plastic the color of Sunkist oranges. The ancient coffee urn looks like a public triumphal sculpture in stainless steel. The nailed-up wooden shelves suggest the carpentry in a general store in a jungle clearing. Here at the counter New York's Brazilian bachelors eat with dispatch and drink Brazilian beer from the bottle. And nearby, at most times, one or both of this restaurant's bosses—gentlemen in white shirts (sleeves rolled up), neckties, and aprons—are to be found. Either of them is a candidate for mayor of New York's Brazilian community. They know half the customers who walk in (the other half are not Brazilian), but are sweet and hospitable to everyone. The dining room proper has varnished wood walls, garishly colored paintings, a density of tables (most of them occupied most of the time) covered with blue cloths, and steel chairs upholstered with red, white, and green plastic. The front windows are overgrown with greenery, which filters somewhat the overhead view of 45th Street continuing downhill. The third-floor dining room is more of the same, but no counter. Cabana Carioca is not a quiet restaurant. But, happily, much of the noise is the sibilant and singsong sound of the Portuguese language spoken with polite passion. New York's seekers after ethnic curiosity come here too, to broaden themselves by contact with another culture and to fatten up on the immense servings purveyed here at low prices.

Two of you can share a single order of ameijoa à bulhao pato, twelve giant cherry-stone clams (almost as big as full-size quahogs), served in a huge iron pot that holds also three inches of oiled, parsleyed, and briny broth. Clams this big can be chewy, if not tough, and these are such that you may want to have at them with a knife and fork, to eat them in two or three bites. What the Cabana calls a special appetizer of shrimp, you will, on inspection, identify as a lunch and a half. The many shrimp are mingled with black olives, and the dish is singular for the strength of the olive and olive-oil flavors that the hot shrimp have absorbed. The fried sausages are spicy, crusted, and pleasantly greasy, and the lettuce on which they are served is, in effect, dressed—and wilted—by the fat that drains out of the sausages onto the leaves. The caldo verde (green soup) is thick with potato, studded with chunks of strong sausage, laced with sharp kale.

About a quart of black beans and a platter of rice in which you could bury a small mammal are delivered to every table. As an accompaniment to those try the bacalhau à braz, a primitive dish, at once vigorous and homey, of salt cod mingled with black olives, sautéed onions, eggs, and plenty of potatoes. The paella here is not a standout. It is, of course, copious, half a lobster tail and plenty of shrimp, scallops and squid, sections of chicken, sausages, and green peas buried in the rice, but the seasoning does not bring out the individuality of these ingredients, though the chicken, which has absorbed the seafood flavors, is thereby converted into an interesting item. There is an odd lobster dish here—listed as lagosta à cheff—that probably has more allure to those with Brazilian memories than to the rest of you. The decent crustacean is covered over with a seasoned and browned bread paste, giving it an undetectable charm. A menu entry of "carne porco alentejana" is described as "pork bits with clams." Actually the chunks of meat are the size of paving stones, which is to say almost as large as the clams. Both are delivered to you in a pot of sufficient girth to hold a dozen of each, as well as more of those sausages, all in a buttered broth—the meat is tender, the clams fresh, the broth powerful, the entire production adorned with the coarse but good fried potatoes that garnish many of the main courses here. The fried chicken carioca style is a good, moist bird, well crusted, saturated with the flavor of garlic. Of course there is feijoada, which, as all the world knows, is the national dish of Brazil—buried in the black beans are joints of meat, chunks of meat, ribs of meat, sausages. The dish is garnished with slices of raw orange, buttered kale, and manioc, the tangy zest always served with feijoada.

The flan differs from those you get in Spanish restaurants in that it is the color of salmon. The desserts of guava, guava paste, caramelized milk, and hard cheese may well be skipped. The Brazilian coffee, of course, is strong and good.

★ CAFÉ DE BRUXELLES

118 Greenwich Avenue (at 13th Street)
LUNCH, TUESDAY TO FRIDAY AND SUNDAY; DINNER, DAILY.
Reservations: 206-1830.
Credit cards: AE, MC, V.
Medium priced.

Again in new hands, these French, the Café retains a Belgian menu and, of course, its original deviantly configured three-room layout within a Greenwich Village hairpin corner formed by the intersection of skewed Greenwich Avenue with resolutely east-west 13th Street. The skinniest part of the place, at the bend in the pin, is given over to a zinc bar and some bare-topped tables at which those who prefer to remain within sight of the bottles may snack. The restaurant then widens into a center room, to which you enter, this the Café's so called café, which, giving, as it does, on the kitchen, and the entrance from out of doors, and the stairway to the facilities, and both other rooms, and the unregulated traffic attendant thereto, is to be avoided for dinner, though you cannot avoid it when you show up, for it is in the café that you stand—properly awed by the framed photo of the king and queen of Belgium and by the array of good Belgian beers displayed on a high shelf—waiting to be noticed, while staff members float by, each slowing down long enough to promise to be with you in a minute. You do wonder as to the whereabouts of one Patricia, listed on the menu as "your host," but never seen. At its third and widest part the restaurant is a conventional, comfortable dining room, mottled-umber walls, a deep-green banquette along one side, white-topped tables surrounded by black-enameled side chairs, lace curtains on the windows. The place has a sleepy quality to which the sometimes bemused staff seems appropriate (though on occasion you are waited on by individuals who do seem determined to do what they set out to do before they permit themselves to be deflected to something else), and their insouciance, though not contagious, is not infuriating, for they inhabit the world of the twenty-minute hour, which is to say, if you are able to prolong consumption of, say, your pâté over the course of an hour, waiting twenty minutes for the beaujolais you want with it is not so bad. When, however, you ask to have your Beaujolais chilled, and the not cold wine is brought in one of those insulating sleeves in which wine that is already cold is *kept* cold (instead of in an ice bucket, in which wine that is not cold is *made* cold), you realize that suspension of senses other than just your sense of time may be essential if you are fully to appreciate this place.

Very good with your eventually cooled wine is the warm salade Liègeoise, chunks of chewy bacon, sweet sautéed onions, tender green beans, and thin slivers of firm new potato, all in a warm, herbed dressing that is tart of sherry vinegar. An oddity given as gâteau bressan is a block of chicken liver custard, the fluffy and powerfully seasoned meat pureé in a dark mushroom sauce that is sweet of port wine. You get snails here like snails you get nowhere else in town, anyway their setting, for these big, black, plump nuggets are in a pool of melted Roquefort cheese, strong, powerfully salty, enriched with butter and cream, and greened with parsley—you use up a foot of bread mopping up the rich cheese sauce. As a cat washes, so does a Belgian eat mussels. Accordingly the house obtains the good ones devoid of the rank taste you encounter in most New York mussels, serves a dozen of them, in their half shells, under a browned, buttery, and vigorously garlicked breading the aroma of which warms the neighborhood of your table from the moment the dish arrives.

As a Belgian eats mussels, so does a Belgian eat French fries, and during main course time your table is graced with a metal tumbler in which stands a paper-wrapped sheaf of them. They are served with good mayonnaise, but one time in three the fries are greasy, and they are never the crisp, light, vividly potato-flavored article you encounter on Belgian soil. The place makes much of the pallid swimmer called lotte, the fillets of fresh, snowy fish browned, moist, and enriched by a thick and buttery sauce of leeks. Waterzooi is a Belgian national dish. Made in the more usual way, with fish, it is available here on Wednesday, but the chicken version is on the daily menu. For all the complexity of its ingredients, the result is mother's-milk food, a creamy white soup dense with morsels of pallid chicken breast and with strands of vegetable—just the thing, it seems, if you are not well. For those who are up and about, however, there is choucroute (on Sunday), a hillock of astringent sauerkraut overlaid with a slab of ham, slices of gamy sausage, a good frankfurter, and lengths of hefty bacon—you will want also strong mustard and Belgian beer. The house turns out a good carbonnade, the Belgian beef-and-beer stew, this one very dark, thick with chunks of fibrous and tender meat, fragrant of garlic. The steak pommes frites is a not bad sirloin, accurately done, crosshatched and charred by the grill, of decent beef flavor.

Avoid both the café Liègeois, a watery, coffee-doused, vanilla ice cream thing, and the poached pear, also watery in its insipid white-wine syrup. The chocolate cake is intense (Belgians eat chocolate the way they eat mussels and French fries), and the Belgian waffle is light, just a carrier for the good strawberry sauce and fluffy whipped cream.

You will find bottles of suitable wine, but Belgian beer is the better drink with many of these dishes. The remarkable, light-seeming, exceptionally strong beer called Duvel is $4.25 a bottle.

★ CAFÉ DE LA GARE

143 Perry Street (near Washington Street)
DINNER. CLOSED MONDAY.
Reservations: 242-3553.
No credit cards
No liquor.
Medium priced.

A white, rough-plastered cube of a little store, with a stamped-tin ceiling and tables for 30 chairs, to which you bring your own wine—your basic amateur restaurant, but professional enough, which is to say most of the tables do not rock, the linen is linen, not paper, and the food is not only unexperimental, but seems so. With respect to those who wait on you, doing so is their only agenda—their courtesy is such that you are not given to understand that befriending them is part of your responsibility as a customer. And when the place turns unexpectedly busy, as it sometimes does, though a certain slowness may set in, chaos and panic do not. The light is low, there are tiny candles on the tables, and the posters on the walls, including two of Cartier-Bresson photos, undo the starkness of the room. If you find the background music—aimed at the Benny Goodman, Ella Fitzgerald crowd—too loud, the house willingly turns it down.

From a very brief menu that changes every two weeks, and to which a couple of specials are added each night: a hot cream of watercress soup on a potato base, its leafy flavor in nice contrast to the little dollop of curry-flavored crème fraîche with which it is adorned; rillettes of fresh and smoked salmon, the latter adding a good saltiness to the vivid salmon flavor of the cool pink stuff; a sparkling cold salad of rich sea scallops and short lengths of sharp scallion in a tangy dressing made with balsamic vinegar; and a walnut-studded pâté that, because it reaches you cold, conceals the complexity of flavors within it, which are of chicken liver, pork, bacon, brandy.

Perhaps because the restaurant won a lawsuit (though no damages were awarded) having to do with its cassoulet, when the menu otherwise changes every other week, the cassoulet remains. You get something like a half-gallon pot of the stuff—happily, not filled to the top—sizzling around the edges, in which are buried chunks of pork, strong sausage, and preserved, peppery duck, altogether a good cassoulet, for the liveliness of its garlic-flavored sauce, as against the dead-weight white-bean leadenness of many versions. You get good rabbit, the chunks of meat, on the bone, in a tangy apple cider sauce that is thick with black raisins, and with crescents of apple, added late, that are crisp and a little acidic. The poulet chasseur is of a bird that actually tastes like chicken, and its Madeira sauce, with mushrooms and strands of fresh tarragon, is earthy and smoky. Pass up the baked sole with oranges and grapefruit, roulades of the fresh fish stuffed with the fruit and adorned with it, but the dish needs some kind of sauce to make sense of the disparate ingredients.

The problem with the desserts is that they come out of the icebox, under which circumstances this banana coconut tart tastes like a diner item, and the chocolate truffle cake like intense chocolate but like nothing more. The Paris-Brest suffers the treatment better, a rich cream between the two big chou pastries, slivered hazelnuts and much confectioners' sugar across the top. You wish the fruit flavor of the peach bavarian were more vivid, and that it did not need to borrow richness from the whipped cream that adorns it.

No spirits, bring your own wine.

★★CAFÉ DES ARTISTES

1 West 67th Street
LUNCH AND DINNER.
Reservations: 877-3500.
Credit cards: AE, DC, MC, V.
Expensive.

One may eat well here, also not well, but no matter, for the Café is a restaurant that is better than its food, has functions that are quite apart from ingestion. Consider, for example, these three ladies seated at the bar of an evening. None of them is having anything stronger than coffee, the counter before them is spread with linen napkins, each has before her a plate and fork, and they are working their way through the Great Dessert Plate, a compendium of the Café's innumerable sweets arranged, slice by slice, on a giant platter at the center of which stands a silver champagne glass filled with whipped cream, big ripe strawberries on top. The desserts need not be uniformly of merit when their communal consumption this way transforms a just-us-girls evening at the movies into a celebration of life. Calories go unmentioned throughout the rite, and at its end one player announces that "we should do this more often," and the three trisect the bill.

Though the Café attracts the well known, it is a celebrity place in reverse, one in which the famous are their unpublic selves; correlatively, there is not much gaping, as it is the custom of the restaurant's plebes coolly to ignore the elite (though visitors from across the waters may fail to pick up on the code). For both the celebs and the merely prosperous are here (almost no one else is here) for lower-case café comforts that have to do with conversation, down-home cooking (of European dishes usually available at more stylish prices), and surroundings that, for all their spiffy charms, seem well worn. The habitués are happy, too, with the civilized and competent staff, some of whom seem to be habitués of working here, have been at it for many times the normal tenure of a waiter or waitress in any New York restaurant to which he is not indentured.

You enter, from the building lobby, to the principal room, at the center of which stands a great table on an iron base, displayed upon it most of the desserts you saw consumed at the bar in the previous scene. One long side of this room is a windowed wall on 67th Street, and just within it there thrives a jungle of greenery that echoes the plant life aspect of the Café's best known appointments, the murals—of animal life in sylvan settings, most of the animals young and healthy examples of the unclothed human female—that were painted for the café decades ago by Howard Chandler Christy. Where the paintings are not, the walls are mirrored, notes of glinting crystallinity in the otherwise lush room. You go up a few steps to more tables and chairs, more of those Christies, and, a little further along, the three-sided bar, the booths and tables around it under drawings and small paintings that relate to the larger murals, on the bar itself, under low-hanging, soft-glowing halophane lamps, racks of hard-cooked eggs, shelled nuts in cocktail glasses, baskets of salted crackling things—the facility is busy with those waiting for tables, post-Lincoln Center tipplers, even people with no agenda other than maybe one more. Whatever your business, the Café humanizes it, for this is, before anything, a civilized place.

You cannot, however, civilize a herring, which is nevertheless attempted in this tripartite serving of marinated herring, one part the untamed article, sweet and sour and supple, salty and strong, next to which the two variations thereon—the same herring in mustard sauce, and the same mingled with beets—are minor desecrations. But then there is an item that seems always present on the Café's ever-changing menu, salmon four ways (the serving "for one" is first course enough for two), in which neither the cool poached salmon, nor the delicately dill-flavored gravlax, nor the firm and well-salted smoked salmon, nor the herbed and rather obvious salmon tartare need apologize to any of the others. Another collection of which a single order will hold two, the assorted planked cochonnailles (delicatessen to you), on this occasion including jambon persillé, nuggets of dark and chewy ham bound in a firm jelly that is green with fresh parsley; an almost loud sausage lyonnaise, fatty, salty, a little gamy, and very good with the strong mustard that is supplied; a rich, cool, gelatinous sweetbread headcheese; a pâté that was denatured in its overcooking, though it is well seasoned, its chopped walnuts a nice note; slices of decent ham; and a wad of rillettes that lacks the strong seasoning essential to this fatty pounded meat. The sautéed wild mushrooms are fresh, their flavor vivid even in strongly garlicked butter. With respect to pasta, you will never go wrong never going near it here, this fettuccine with bacon, sausage, and broccoli, for example, in which each element is surprised, but not delighted, to meet the others.

Salmon again, smoked again, but this time just enough to flavor it, not to cure or fully cook it, the final cooking a separate step, so the substantial fillet of fresh, pink fish reaches you browned and juicy, its sauce choron (béarnaise pinked with tomato) watery but, happily, dispensable. The scallops are billed as sautéed, but they reach you uncolored and wet, as if stewed tepid in their own juice, and the coriander with which they are done has lost its flavor in the slow preparation. The veal chop is coarse, of veal that is red rather than pink, near beef. The idea of lamb chops in a Parmesan crust reads so bad you figure it must be good. It is bad. Anyway, as all the world knows, selecting meat at the Café des Artistes involves reading the menu thoroughly, considering carefully the possibilities, and then ordering the pot au feu, a kettle of fibrous and tender potted beef that has taken on a deep, complex flavor from the stock and vegetables with which it was done—the good, clear broth, with slabs of turnip and cabbage and potato, plus leeks and whole onions, are part of the act, as is a fat-filled marrow bone, with all of which you are served sharp mustard and a feeble horseradish sauce, though the wondrous dish needs no help.

Order Stilton and fruit, and you are served enough strong cheese for a solid lunch, with walnuts and with half a Granny Smith apple sliced thin. The sweet desserts include a pasty sweet-potato-pecan pie on sallow crust; a so-called joy of bonaparte, a light napoleon of lemon custard, rich whipped cream, and ripe strawberries; a layered mocha dacquoise of good, chewy meringues, mocha cream, and rich whipped cream; and the ilona torte, which has been listed since the beginning, the current version a rich coffee-flavored chocolate cake coated with walnuts—a sumptuous sweet.

The selection changes, but each night there are sixteen wines that you may have brought to your table in baskets, and the waiters and waitresses usually know the best bottles. The proprietor here is George Lang. Sometimes he appears on the premises. Happily, he leaves at home his violin.

★★CAFÉ DU PARC

106 East 19th Street
LUNCH, TUESDAY TO FRIDAY; DINNER, MONDAY TO SATURDAY. CLOSED SUNDAY.
Reservations: 777-7840.
Credit cards: AE, DC, MC, V.
Expensive.

The gentility and propriety that have always been associated with Gramercy Park were much in mind when this place was put together. From the starry white lights strung on the little tree out front, to the background Mozart inside, to the remembrances of things Impressionistic on the walls (here a Renoir, near it a Bonnard, over there an unmistakable Degas—all by the same artist), to the half-inclined head of the (somewhat unconvincingly) deferential host himself, nothing here will offend your Aunt Adelaide (that is, if you ever manage to lure her out of the half-acre apartment—in the Stanford White building overlooking the fenced-in square itself—in which she has holed up ever since that time Hoover lost). And yet, shrewdly, the place is not stuffy. It flatters respectability but is not a slave to it. If your clothes are clean and cover most of you, they will do. For a certain postwar ease has been worked into the Café's old-fashioned formality. The wall of exposed rosy brick down one side of the long, narrow room is part of it, as are the waiters' uniforms—shirtsleeves, four-in-hands, and long white aprons. Accordingly, though there are lace curtains on the front windows, and though you are seated at white-linened tables set with creamy china and glinting crystal, and though the low partitions that subdivide the room are of polished wood surmounted by etched glass, those with whom you share this place do not make up a homogeneous crowd. Most of the diners, it is true, are in cocktail dresses, or long-sleeved silk blouses with bows at the throat, or business suits, or tweeds and flannels—the hair of both genders tonsured trim and locked in place—but here and there you will spot designer jeans, sweaters against skin, unshaven cheeks, even flagrant jewelry. The opposing forces do not fraternize. Neither do they lob shells.

What brings the trucing sides to this place is a taste for dramatic contemporary food, and much of what they find is not only striking, but good to eat. Consider, for example, the Stilton soup, a sometime soup of the day that, happily, is not what you fear (melted cheese), but real food, the weight and the vivid, salty flavor of the cheese compounded with a substantial chicken stock into a thick, sturdy complexity—it is served sprinkled with slivered almonds that, too bad, wilt in the hot setting. What the house calls "arugula, radicchio, and green salad," and subtitles "with warm bay scallops," is a great hillock of the seafood set on but a single leaf of red lettuce, the greens hardly more than stray petals around the perimeter—the leaves are cool, the little scallops rich and warm in their sparkling dressing. More greens are mingled with short lengths of veal-and-duck sausage, the mahogany-colored morsels firm and a little chewy, spicy and meaty, the salad dotted with bits of crisp bacon and dressed with its hot fat. Though the pasta dishes listed as appetizers may be had as main courses, the latter versions, though more expensive, do not appear more copious. Either way, the lobster ravioli are firm little envelopes filled with sweet lobster meat—they glisten with a butter that is of heady shellfish flavor, and they are set on leaves of vibrant spinach. A great tangle of narrow strands of eggy pasta is served with a sauce of veal and artichokes—the dish is more like a meaty stew served with noodles than what you usually think of as a pasta dish, but it is fine for that, the chunks of veal browned and tender, the slivers of artichoke crunchy, but suffused with the olive oil and garlic with which they were sautéed.

100

Monkfish has a taste, but it is a subtle one and easily lost. You can prepare the fish simply and hope its flavor will reveal itself, but that is an uncertain way of dealing with the problem. Here the chance is not taken. Instead, flavor is added. You are served slices of the firm white fish arranged like four points of an eight-point star—the other four are elliptical slices of carrot, each under a single snow pea—with a mound of fresh egg noodles at the center, and small browned onions strewn here and there, everything touched with a smooth, sticky, deep-red sauce of cabernet sauvignon that gives life and unity to the complex dish. The grilled salmon is simpler, the steak of pink meat charred but, unfortunately, dried a bit in the preparation, a condition that is somewhat offset by its pungent sorrel sauce. Order chicken, and you are served thick slices cut from the breast of a large bird. The chicken has been prepared with a fluffy herbed stuffing inserted between the breast and its skin, so that each slice is of two parts—moist white meat and the judiciously seasoned dressing. The slices are arranged over disks of crisp-edged potato, and they are garnished with strong spinach that has been saturated with butter, and with browned shallots, all in a polished red-wine sauce. The grilled steak is of tender and fibrous beef that flashes a bit of real beef flavor—it is accurately prepared, and it is dressed with shallot butter.

The chocolate cappuccino cake is a dark, layered, creamy fantasy, walnuts on top—to be good, such things must be fresh, and this one seems just made. The other desserts are comparatively ascetic: a pear tart that is little more than a flaky pastry under firm slices of the cool, sweet pear; a lemon tart of that good pastry again, this time filmed with a thin layer of light, tangy custard; a passion fruit mousse that is of clear fruit flavor in its pool of crimson raspberry sauce; a tangerine ice (when that is the flavor offered) that has brilliant orange color and a heady, intense flavor.

Prepare to spend time here, for the kitchen does its work slowly, and, on occasion, your host is in no hurry to seat you even when tables are available.

★ CAFÉ GRECO

1390 Second Avenue (near 72nd Street)
LUNCH, SATURDAY AND SUNDAY; DINNER, DAILY.
Reservations: 737-4300.
Credit cards: AE, DC, MC, V.
Medium priced.

Maybe it has something to do with the amplified bouzouki music by way of which, in tavernas that have come and gone from the New York scene, so many unaccustomed local eardrums were reduced to powder; or else it is the Greek habit of doing lamb until the inside looks like the outside; or could it be that the Greek restaurant chromosome is imprinted solely with the coffee shop gene? Anyway, though one or two places thrive, the Greek restaurant is barely a category on Manhattan Island. Comes this place, mindful apparently of that lore, and of the contrasting record of the Italians, with a solution: Make it Greek, but make it also Italian, call it, if necessary, *Mediterranean*, a bit of near-Eastern food will not hurt, and if the mostly French and California wine list abjures entirely the hated word "retsina," then you may take a chance and give the place a name that reveals its Grecian identity.

Tall glass doors framed in honey-colored wood are the foldaway façade before which, when the weather is fine, are placed cocktail tables with tops of false marble (in New York you cannot be too careful, cocktail tables have been known to walk). The marble of the tables just inside is real, and there is a little mural above the bar of goddesses, gods, and multi-species creatures cavorting in, you figure, god's country. The restaurant begins as a narrow place that grows wide as it proceeds down ever lower levels, spreading at the back to a couple of good-size rooms. The interior is all buff colored and putty colored, with brass rails along the descending path and tiny overhead spots that cast soft pools of light here and there. There are prints on the walls, there are flowers on the tables, and the statuary just outside the windowed back wall makes reference to the Greek classical past—cement cherubs doing cherubic things. The tables are covered with white cloths over blue ones, the help wear blue-and-white-striped shirts, the blue-and-white Greek flag is not otherwise on display.

In this setting the strong pink of the salmon carpaccio is very pretty, and the slices of fresh raw fish are sweet, moist, glistening of the good oil that has been poured over them—the fresh basil and chopped pinenuts are nice notes of fragrance and texture. The seafood salad is not exactly what dishes of that name turn out to be in Italian restaurants, for in this the scallops, strands of shrimp, and circles of squid are mingled with lettuce —the bulk of the salad—in a creamy and lemony dressing. The hot spinach pie is the usual thing of spinach, redolent of strong cheese, between layers of flaky pastry—the homey solidity of the dish is in no way undone by the unexpected cucumber salad served with it. A sweet mash of onions, hot and thick, on a pizza pastry is the base of a tart that is topped with thin slices of grilled eggplant, zucchini, tomato, and melted cheese—satisfying, inelegant food.

If you liked that salmon raw, know that Café Greco has more than one way with a salmon. Grilled, the red fish reaches you under an herbed sauce of roasted red peppers and salty black olives—the fish is judiciously done, is moist but cooked through. As is this grilled chicken, a nicely crisped bird that reveals much of its own good flavor and much of the flavor of the grill, though its winy sauce, the pile of nameless couscous served with it, and the garnish of seemingly wood-fibered leeks somewhat undo the effect. A block of ground lamb under pastry that is blackened in spots is served in a pool of tomato sauce that is threaded with onions, herbed, powerfully seasoned—this is the house moussaka, lamb-gamy, weighty, winter food. You figure that maybe the roast lamb is at least autumn food, but this *is* a Greek restaurant, the meat has been rendered bloodless and harsh, and it is garnished with "white beans" like the baked beans you get out of an American can, and with a strong, almost sparkling black-olive tapenade that cannot save the situation.

The raspberry napoleon is assembled long before it is served, so the berries have become limp in their pastry cream. The hazelnut chocolate cake, a layer of praline under the chocolate icing, is intense, but that is all. Happily the baklava is served with a scoop of cold and creamy vanilla, for the thing itself, a sweet-spiced and honey-flavored density of ground walnuts wrapped in pastry, is stiff and dry by evening.

★★CAFÉ LOUP

18 East 13th Street
LUNCH, SUNDAY TO FRIDAY; DINNER, DAILY.
Reservations: 255-4746.
Credit cards: AE, DC, MC, V.
Medium priced.

Here, at lunchtime, comes Village-and-environs publishing, which includes the frankly commercial (*Women's Wear Daily*), the incidentally commercial (*The Village*

Voice), the proudly commercial (*Forbes*), and the commercial (Farrar, Straus and Giroux). Publishing, you understand, is an industry. And if you think you have the knack of distinguishing its various branches from one another by the clothes on the editors' backs, you will have to reserve for lunch well in advance to prove your skill. Publishing brings its credit cards here, to talk business and pleasure at company expense, as if this were a downtown branch of the Four Seasons. At Café Loup, however, lunch will actually set you back something less than the cost of a hard-cover novel.

By night, the Café is quite another thing, a little side-street neighborhood restaurant, the more-or-less private repair of locals who use it for private purposes. NYU professors, for example, bring their most beautiful students here to correct their latest poems. The place is also taken by many as just the spot for starting, ending, or reviewing at midpoint, a romance. Intense conversations à deux—in which neither combatant removes his eyes from his opponent from cocktails through too many brandies—is part of the restaurant's constant theater.

The establishment is down a few steps, low ceilinged, softly lighted. There is a little bar at the front, a few tables at a benchlike banquette opposite it. A small back room, with fewer than a dozen tables more, is the rest of the place. Perhaps mindful of Greenwich Village's past, the proprietor has hung the rooms with framed art, mostly photographs, including examples by Kertész, Brassaï, Berenice Abbott. The serious stuff is augmented by oddments—copper appliances, wooden trains, a pendulum clock, books. The tidy accumulation is readily distinguishable from a decorator's décor.

You sit on pale bentwood chairs before unlinened tables of honey-colored wood. Blackboard menus are situated here and there on a ledge that rims the room. When you want to see a menu close up, one is brought to your vicinity and placed on a nearby chair. It may well strike you as bizarre that though the menu is hand chalked on slates, specials of the day must be announced to you by your waiter.

If he announces oysters, be aware that they may not have slept in salt water the night before, and are not quite revived by their tart and stinging sauce mignonnette. You will have no problem with the smoked trout, however, which, though it is the usual thing, is served with an exceptional horseradish sauce, at once creamy, light, and sharp. The house salad is a glass bowl of fresh greens, good tomatoes, crunchy croutons, and a thick, pink dressing. Of course, there is pâté, and you get a big slab of the pleasantly coarse and pungently seasoned stuff. But if it is meat you want, you will do better with the saucisson, half a dozen disks of fatted, sweet-spiced sausage, hot and glistening, on a layer of buttery potatoes. There are snails, and they are very much a good version of the standard item, with a bit of enriching cheese in the hot butter.

The fish is fresh, sometimes tilefish under a powerful dill-and-mustard sauce that almost overwhelms it, sometimes a slab of swordfish under browned and buttery almonds. If you come when the roast duck is made with green peppercorns, have it, for the sharp pepper is striking against the well-roasted, crisp meat. Pork chops with sautéed mushrooms and cheese may strike you as a rather oleaginous creation, but these are good chops—cooked through but still moist—the mushrooms are fresh and of good flavor, and the lightly applied cheese sharpens the dish without heavying it. You get good lamb chops here, the surfaces of the pink meat crosshatched with grill marks, the rims coated with herbs. And the steak au poivre is tender, beefy, accurately cooked, rather heavily coated with peppercorns, but good in its inelegant way.

Unfortunately the pies and cakes are refrigerated until they are served, which renders them not only cold but flat. Instead have the smooth, rich zabaglione, which is intensely flavored with marsala and served over fine strawberries.

★★CAFÉ LUXEMBOURG

200 West 70th Street
LUNCH, SUNDAY; DINNER, DAILY.
Reservations: 873-7411.
Credit cards: AE, DC, MC, V.
Medium priced.

When executive chef Patrick Clark separated himself from the powers behind TriBeCa's Odeon (their flagship store) and Café Luxembourg (its West Side offshoot), more was lost downtown than up—understandably, for Odeon, the better place, was the tougher act to perpetuate. Not to worry, the loss of Clark resulted in a loss of business to neither establishment. Reputations outlive. And here on the West Side, where most of the Café's competitors are tuned to those whose standard of comparison is the college cafeteria, Luxembourg's share of the grownup market remains safe.

You will recall that, upon a time, American economists discovered that they could get famous only after making inaccurate predictions from high government places. Similarly, today, restaurant architects know that they achieve celebrity status only when—like Sam Lopata and Adam Tihany, for two—their interiors have been home to spectacular bankruptcies. Which calls to mind Café Luxembourg, a whimmy assemblage of parts that do well by one another, it seems, solely by chance, a dining room apparently designed around someone's happenstantial overstock of yellow paint and yellow tiles—the place fills nightly, if not despite the absence of creative visuals, then because of it. The buttery, softly lit room is thick with tables (a carafe of water and a shot glass of toothpicks on each), and you are comfortably seated—albeit, often, hard beside a stranger—on café chairs or on the dark-red banquettes that rim the room here, cut through it there. The aisles are dense with help, waiters in white, waitresses in black, and though their recitation of the day's specials requires a surreptitious glance at a crib sheet, and though one course sometimes arrives before the previous one has been cleared, the staff is available, civil, even cheerful. The crowd they serve cannot be defined by age or income or occupation, for it is made up of those who know that this part of town has little better to offer. In part by way of their multiplicity Café Luxembourg is a convivial neighborhood place.

Since the beginning, the Café has listed this country salad, and it still reaches you in sparkling condition, the greens crisp, the crumbled Roquefort firm and creamy and sharp, the chunks of bacon strong and a little resilient, the whole, overlaid with buttered crusts of bread, in a tangy, mustard-thickened dressing. Bread on the pea soup as well, this time floating croutons on a polished purée that is hot, of earthy flavor, and surprisingly smooth, and lacking the slightly rough texture you may expect in pea soup. Shrimp that reach you right are always noteworthy, and these sautéed crustaceans are sweet, crunchy, devoid of iodine in their shiny pink shells—their lemony sauce, threaded with bits of artichoke, is fragrant of fresh dill. What the house calls chicken liver pâté, you call a rich, almost fluffy mousse—it arrives in a little ramekin, crisp and vividly flavored slivers of almond on top, with slices of toasted rye bread onto which you spread the smooth stuff. Have that any time rather than the carpaccio—you cannot resist the thought that in Clark's day the raw meat would not have been sliced in advance, to reach you discolored and bloodless under its mustard mayonnaise.

Each night there is a pasta of the night, sometimes firm and eggy noodles mingled with substantial chunks of fresh salmon and smoked salmon, moistened with butter, and fragrant of the fresh dill that livens the well seasoned dish. You order a grilled brook trout, and you are dismayed by the infantility of the specimen served—still, the boned fish is fresh and sweet in its crisped skin, and its creole sauce, thick with little shrimp and sweet peppers, is hot and tangy. Order roast chicken, and instead of half a little bird, you get some smaller fraction of a big one—big birds have more flavor than little ones, and this chicken is crisped and juicy as well, is served in a dark, vigorous, and heavily herbed sauce of the roasting juices, which you spoon onto the mashed potatoes that are part of the dish. Cassoulet is another item that has never been dropped from this menu, and, as ever, the density of beans, studded with duck, pork, and chunks of sausage under its handsomely browned bread-crumb crust, is sturdy in its tomato-redded sauce, though the meats have lost some of their distinctiveness in the making. You can get a good steak here, but when you are not so lucky, the beef is chewy, its flavor subsumed in the excess of charcoal on its surface.

Pass up the calvados and apple terrine, a slice of something pale, cold, and wet, cut from a loaf and set in a bit of liquored sauce. Better is the crème brûlée, though you wish the cool custard under the crackling caramel top were fluffier. Under a storm of confectioners' sugar is not quite concealed the apple and prune dartois, a paleness of stewed apples dappled with crushed prunes and wrapped, like the filling of a strudel, in pastry—the item is garnished with rich whipped cream. The big winners are the lemon tart, the citric custard more sour than sweet on its grainy pastry; and the chocolate meringue cake—a chewy meringue and fluffy whipped cream among layers of rich black cake, an abundance of chocolate shavings on top.

★ CAFÉ SAN MARTIN

1458 First Avenue (near 76th Street)
LUNCH, SUNDAY; DINNER, DAILY.
Reservations: 288-0470.
Credit cards: AE, MC, V.
Medium priced.

Almost nothing about this restaurant, except the help and half the food, is Spanish—anyway, not Spanish in the New York manner. There is nary a bullfighter poster on the walls. Black wrought iron is nowhere in evidence. The rooms do not simulate a stone-walled wine cellar in a medieval Castilian castle. The restaurant is, in fact, airy, all white, with greenery standing in the front windows (right next to the piano—which is harmlessly tinkled—and not far from the glittery little bar, and the handful of tables that are arranged in an L around it). There is more greenery hanging from the skylight that is centered over the two-steps-down main dining room at the back. Colorful, ornately framed oils adorn the walls, and handsome cane-and-bentwood chairs surround white-linened tables that are set with painted plates and pale-blue napkins. When the place fills up—with a prosperous but not flashy uptown crowd—it hums and bustles. The hard-working waiters (in white shirts and vests and long, striped aprons) and the captains (in dark suits) are all courtesy, and they keep the place running smoothly.

Café San Martin is not an especially expensive restaurant, but for $14.50 you may discover for yourself that a small plate of baby eels—these are virtually embryonic eels—looks like a small plate of short spaghetti. And with the sizzling oil, browned garlic, and blackened and fiery red peppers in which the creatures are served, they as well could be, for the forthright flavors of the sauce conceal whatever subtle merit this rarity might have to disclose. More of that garlic in the garlic shrimp—but it fails to obscure the iodine that ruins these poorly chosen crustaceans. Opt instead for xangurro, which arrives in the little dish in which it was cooked. The food consists of crabmeat, sherry, and a powerful dose of clove—a substantial patty of the flavored seafood is baked under a breading until the crust is browned. It must be told that this establishment does no better shopping for mussels than it does buying shrimp. The green sauce is good—smooth, creamy, loaded with fresh parsley—but there are, among these mostly lovely mussels, a few that are considerably louder than that piano. Disks of Spanish sausage, with slivers of red and green peppers, are sealed—with seasoned red wine and oil—in a little pillow fashioned of aluminum foil, and then heated. The shiny balloon is placed before you and cut open. Steam pours forth. The morsels of spiced meat are good with the salty wine and vegetables. Of course, there is black bean soup—it may not be as thick as you like it, but it has a deep flavor, and the onions that come with it are recently chopped, so they are strong.

The Café serves one of the best paellas in town—barring the occasional mischance of encountering those less-than-perfect shrimp or mussels. The rice is oiled and red and spicy, studded with chunks of exceptionally sweet and peppery sausage, plump scallops, mussels and shrimp, clams that are sometimes a bit tough for having been cooked too long, red pimentos, green peppers, and glistening sweet green peas. The paella is prepared only for two. If you want lobster in yours, there is a surcharge. All those items of shellfish, as well as a substantial slab of fresh striped bass, make up the zarzuela de mariscos, which—in its broad pottery dish—is immersed in a creamy sauce. Parillada is that same collection again, this time broiled, all the elements of vivid flavor, served with a pitcher of spicy tomato sauce. Hake, a cousin to cod, is a big item in Spanish cookery. Here it is served in a manner given as "à la Vasca," in which the hefty, flaky fish is buried in a thick, green sauce that is both lemony and spicy. The pale meat is garnished with clams and mussels and halves of hard-cooked eggs, all of which are usually fine. But the entire production is served over a few shafts of canned white asparagus, which, perhaps at the sacrifice of some authenticity, could be omitted to excellent effect. A so-called grain-fed chicken is roasted artfully on a spit when you order it (you must allow time). The skin is crisp, the meat is moist, but the flavor of the bird, though a little better than most contemporary chickens, is still shy of the real thing. Much of the rest of the menu is given over to French and Italian dishes—entrecôte au poivre, fettuccine Alfredo, and the like—but that is not what this restaurant is about.

Happily, the deviations from Spanish restraints extend to the dessert menu: a tart of slivers of ripe banana, creamy custard, crumbly crust; a kiwi tart much like it, the green fruit glistening and sweet; a raisin-studded bread pudding that is made tangy by strands of lemon rind; claufouties of cherries or blueberries, in which the stewed fruits are buried in, and stain, the dark cake; an intense and airy chocolate mousse cake; a whole orange, peeled and sliced, served under strands of orange rind that have been marinated in Grand Marnier. None of the sweets is extraordinary, but all of them are more than decent.

• CANASTEL'S

229 Park Avenue South (at 19th Street)
LUNCH, MONDAY TO FRIDAY; DINNER, DAILY.
Reservations: 677-9622.
Credit cards: AE, DC, MC, V.
Expensive.

You wonder where they found him, this perfect host. He has the manner that, even when the restaurant is half empty, lets you know the place is hot. You call ahead because you will be fifteen minutes early, and a sweet voice on the phone assures you, no problem. Host, however, though thirty tables are in disuse, looks at you, then at his watch, then back at you, clearly unable to reconcile your behavior and his imperishable moral standards. Arrive alone, in advance of your other (again there are dozens of places where you could be seated), and he tells you—with obvious distaste for the distasteful demands of his work—that "Your table is not ready. When your guest arrives, your table will be ready." He suggests you make yourself one of the horde at the bar. The fellow is, of course, the complete coin, obverse and tail, and when he deals with those he must please, he is the complete sniveler. The rest of the staff, however, are fine.

Canastel's contributes much toward the goal of providing table space for all of New York all at one time. Where otherwise a mere score of one-bedroom apartments could be installed—to sleep, say, 100 companionable inmates—there is instead this place, with tables, chairs, and bar to accommodate twice that many. This approach to the housing problem comes, moreover, complete with Italian country cooking and uniformed attendants. This commons is high, wide, and long, its pale walls pink in the room's pink light, pink linen on its innumerable tables, each table surrounded by comfortable bentwood armchairs with cushioned seats. Tall foldaway glass doors look out on 19th Street and on Park Avenue South. The easternmost wall is illustrated, and through its painted portals you "see" painted views of old Italy and the Italian sky—the effect manages to be at once undecorative, unrealistic, and untrompe l'oeil. The downtown side of the place is given over to an open kitchen; and, near it, a long table with thirty platters or so of about a dozen appetizers; and, under an awning, within an arc of cocktail tables, wicker chairs, and wicker sofas, the bar, perched on one end of which there is a young lady in summer casuals and shades—she sits there in the lotus position, never smiling, apparently immovable, and though she is attractive, she is clearly jaded and bitter. Someone has taken her temperature and ascertained that she is a mannequin, and now the crowd ignores her.

If you are in luck, the waiter or waitress assigned to your care will be familiar with the relative merits of the items on the antipasto table, and will assemble for you a good collection. More likely, you will get both the bad and the good, including deep-red sun-dried tomatoes that are enriched with, and glistening with, oil; rolled-up browned leaves of sautéed zucchini that retain a bit of crispness, and others of sautéed eggplant that are soft and of strong flavor; crisp and lightly dressed slices of artichoke heart; a seafood salad of mostly shrimp and lobster in a creamy white dressing—the shellfish is a bit mushy; a sweet and crunchy roasted red pepper stuffed with a chopped, pungently seasoned mixture of anchovies and olives; a negligible amount of good smoked salmon; sweet-spiced little clams in their shells; tasteless mussels in theirs. Of course, if you think your eye is keener than your waiter's judgment, you may march up to the display and make your own mistakes.

Like many of the city's new Italian arenas, this one, mindful of the eating habits of its recently undergraduate clientele, has a pizza department. The pies are an extra-large hand-span across, and this one, given as alla napoletana, is of nicely risen, slightly chewy dough, a scant layer of mozzarella, slivers of tomato, anchovies arranged like the spokes of a wheel, and a sprinkling of oregano—it is at once light and satisfying, and though it is also strong (of those anchovies), it comes, like all pizzas here, with a little dish of red-pepper flakes, which you add for incinerative purposes. Add too many, and you may find it necessary to snuff out the inferno under a foothill of pappardelle del pastore, which is composed of broad, thick bands of pasta lightly bound in a sauce of cream and ricotta cheese, with, at the peak, a dollop of tart tomato sauce that is flecked with basil—comforting food, for which the red sauce does little more than set off its pleasant blandness. For pasta that is meant to more than soothe you, there are these orecchiette, dented noodle nickels, the firm disks in a slightly creamy tomato sauce that is thick with ground sausage, crunchy with tiny florets of broccoli, and fragrant of garlic.

The deep-fried squid is not greasy, but it is not light either, and the coarse—and cold—tomato sauce with which it is served helps not at all. The snapper is fresh, the big fillet in an herbed and briny tomato sauce that is slick with good oil—the fish comes with a couple of good clams and several of this establishment's tasteless mussels. What goes as pollo agliato comes off as chunks of tolerable sautéed chicken that are not improved by the wine and garlic with which they were prepared. Similarly the veal chop Milanese, to the listing of which has been added the name, complete with quotation marks, "Canastel's." This is simply a chop that has been pounded beyond the borders of its plate, breaded as if to protect if from the environment, fried as if to dehydrate it, and buried under chopped tomatoes as if to conceal it—the tomatoes are allegedly marinated, but they are dry, and fail to provide the dressing that could partially redeem the meat. The paillard of beef is tan rather than browned—the oil and rosemary help, the promised garlic is absent, and the chopped tomatoes that disappointed you on the veal chop repeat themselves here. With any of these main courses you are advised to avoid the leaden fried zucchini.

The napoleon is of flaky pastry, much rich whipped cream, and an even richer custard. Have that any time instead of the tirami su, the dessert of ladyfingers, cream cheese, coffee, and booze that, in this rendition, is a very sweet goo.

Stick to the first courses, pizzas, and pastas, and you can do well here. After that you are on your own.

★ IL CANTINORI

32 East 10th Street
LUNCH, MONDAY TO FRIDAY; DINNER, DAILY.
Reservations: 673-6044.
Credit cards: AE, DC.
Expensive.

Prosperity has made an honest place of Il Cantinori. It is now possible to dinner here and not find it necessary to put your eyes back in their sockets after a look at the check. Today almost everything offered is listed on the photocopied menu, revised each day, and even the handful of unlisted dishes your waiter describes do not turn out to be notably more expensive than the menu prices lead you to expect. Beware, however, of imported fish—go so far, if you care, as to ask the price before you order it.

Il Cantinori is the air-conditioned farmhouse, rusticity without the bugs, white linen on the tables and straw seats on the chairs. There is a front room, a back room, a bar in the corridor between them. Under the striped canopy, when the weather is fine, three tables are set out on the little porch that becomes an extension of the front dining room when the restaurant's façade—tall glass doors framed in honey-colored wood—is folded back. Inside, the walls are mostly of pebbly stucco, partly of exposed brick, with farm implements (nonmotorized) mounted on them here and there. The unconvincing ceiling beams, of blacked and roughened wood, are massive enough to support this place and everything else on the block. The view through the big back-room skylight is a swatch of sky and the unprepossessing back of the surrounding buildings. The white-shuttered windows on the brick back wall are the one off note of American Federal among the many of Italian Bucolic. Throughout, the handsome floor is of great, square, faded terra-cotta tiles, probably recovered from a demolition, for they look like they have been walked on for centuries. In all, the place is comfortable, part of the reason the good-size tables—even the tables for two are ample.

In the aisles between them rolls the cart, on it a row of white porcelain plates—in each a vegetable—from which you make a selection: broad strands of red and yellow peppers, skinned and roasted, oiled and crunchy; big gray beans, firm and pleasantly gummy, strewn with parsley, well salted, saturated with the flavor of oil; chunks of rich eggplant; blackened mushroom caps filled with chopped red peppers that are pungently seasoned and fragrantly herbed; tomatoes stuffed with rice, the grains firm, polished with oil, the tops of the tomatoes blackened a little. It is likely that if you come here the day the chanterelles come here, the wild mushrooms will be fine, but come a day or two later, and they have lost their earthy flavor—serving them hot over cold bresaola does not help.

Spaghetti in a sauce given as "pirata" is the noodle in a red paste dotted with bits of squid, shrimp, mussel, garlic—you wish the sauce were spicy rather than harsh, that the seafood had as much to do with its impact as the garlic. But then there is this *gray* spaghetti, the strands dyed, in the making, with the ink of squid, and that jet-black ink, thick with slivers and circles of squid meat, is the sauce itself—pungent food, oceanic and rousing. Each day a risotto is listed, sometimes rich with seafood—this is a brusque and briny dish, nubbly and spicy, devoid of finesse and completely satisfying.

The word "dentice" is often used on local Italian menus to represent "snapper." The two are not related, and perhaps to demonstrate the difference, this place sometimes obtains the genuine articles, fish that have swum in the Mediterranean, and serves them—grilled, skinned, and filleted—in this kitchen's version of livornese sauce, a smooth, pale-pink tomato sauce, slightly sour, with a couple of cracked black olives in it. Though carefully done—the fish is firm and moist—this swimmer, anyway this example of it, is of a flavor that is more than subtle, a condition due, perhaps, to meticulous preservation carelessly extended. You get an artfully grilled chicken here, moist meat cooked to the bone within a crusty and well-seasoned skin—the bird itself is not of exceptional flavor, but this is good food, which you liven by squeezing on the lemon that is provided. But if it is a bird you are after, and if it is on the menu, have quail instead. Quail is all dark meat, it is of powerful flavor, and at Il Cantinori it is served cut into small parts (a bone conveniently protruding from each) that are set in soft polenta—the scent of the bay leaves with which the parts are mingled permeates the meat. The rabbit stew is many huge chunks of the pale, tender game in a peppery sauce. The veal chop, oiled and broiled, is done to the perfect point—it is charred, cooked through but pink and juicy, livened a little by the sprigs of sage that adorn it. The lamb stew, with artichokes, is deep and gamy, its mahogany sauce winy and redolent of lamb fat—you either like that kind of thing or you do not.

The salads are not notable for the crispness of their greens. Your waiter suggests "champagne" grapes. You question him. He goes off and returns. Yes, he assures you, they are Pinot Noir. They are tiny, red, firm, sweet, and juicy, but you do wonder what Pinot Noir would not be reserved for wine. Another time the house tries to rescue some dreadful apricots by serving them in white wine—they remain dreadful apricots, green, dry, sour. Good cheeses are on hand, and the Parmesan is fine with fresh figs. The raspberries are ripe under their cool, frothy, well-balanced zabaglione.

★★CANTON

45 Division Street (near Market Street)
LUNCH AND DINNER. CLOSED MONDAY AND TUESDAY.
Reservations: 226-4441.
No credit cards.
Beer.
Medium priced.

Legendary belletrists, architects of international repute, prize-winning playwrights, world-class photographers, literary critics with hyphenated names, potent behind-the-scenes editors, byline journalists, and, even, headliners from the world of sport—all these types get themselves to Canton and, if necessary, wait, along with everybody else, on the street, or in the little alcove just inside the front door, for a turn at a table. Once within, they are at the next table to clusters of gents in jeans and plaid flannel shirts—their leather jackets are draped over the backs of their chairs, and their noses are three inches from their plates when they eat. Pop-eyed, purple-complected fat men come here, sweating and breathing hard, raving eaters, apparently let loose on one-night passes for an oral binge. You see silver-haired academics in rimless spectacles, Hispanics in sunglasses. And when the invading hordes from Queens hit Chinatown on weekend nights, discriminating defectors slip away from the squads of Szechuan addicts for something more subtle here. But what is unique about Canton's clientele is that, invariably, at least a few of the tables are occupied by mixed groups—of Chinese and Occidentals. And thereby depends some lowdown: Though this restaurant has had a menu printed up—complete with such categories as "Soup for One," "Soup for Two," "Chop Suey," "Chow Mein," "Egg Foo Young"—production of this document was clearly just a gesture to the suchness of the situation, for the composition of almost every meal consumed here is determined not by consulting a list but by conversation with the proprietor—a woman whose youthful appearance fails to signal the mature calm and good cheer with which she efficiently governs this place. Her English is as good as yours. But without a satisfactory written summary of the kitchen's real repertoire, white folks and other non-Asians often feel the need for some almond-eyed support during their encounters with the lady of the house. Unless you are unusually persistent, or have been here often and are known, singsong inquiries in native Chinese will yield more information than tuneless, grunting queries in New York English. Still, splendid dinners have been had on first visits by blonds. And if you feel that you must command—rather than ask questions—there are some swell orders in the paragraphs ahead.

Canton is a big, brightly lit, high-ceilinged, boxlike store, a cash register at the front, a stainless-steel coffee urn and some steel shelves at the back, and enough Formica-topped tables—some of them the huge round kind suitable for banquet dinners—to seat around sixty. This place has a Chinatown bare-necessities elementality about it, but it is in no way tattered or ramshackle or improvised. The walls are faced with a cheerful yellow quasicloth covering; the tables do not rock; the waiters are in crisp jackets; everything looks clean; and a lovely stained-glass fish adorns the front window—seafood is Canton's specialty.

But first, the first courses, a number of which your hostess and the regulars refer to, in English, by code names. "The lettuce," for example: one of those dishes consisting of flavored ground meat, which you make into a bundle by rolling a spoonful of it in a lettuce leaf, which package you then hold in your fingers and eat. What particularly distinguishes this version from that available in other restaurants is that the leaves of lettuce are large and unperforated, so the operation can be carried out without spillage. What further distinguishes it is that the meat is mingled with fresh green peas for sweetness, water chestnuts for crispness, strong garlic for flavor. The mixture is light, with a hint of charring in its flavor. Something called "buns" consists of three small slices of meat—lean pork, sweet ham, and tender white chicken, all lightly oiled and a little blackened—impaled on a wooden skewer, the meats accompanied by a two-part muffin of barely baked dough. You make a light, tasty sandwich of the "bun" and the succulent meats. The fried dumplings are fine, but they are much the standard thing, not notably superior to what you get in many places.

Seafood. Pan-fried butterfish: two whole fish, impeccably fresh, each the size of a gentleman's hand, strewn with scallion greens; the skin of the fish—which is crisped to a light, brittle flakiness—is a zest to the light meat within it. This is an easy fish to eat, for the side bones are delicate enough to swallow. The steamed flounder is big; it arrives spread out on a great platter in a pool of oily broth that is so hot the fish continues to cook on the table—you must eat it quickly, while it is fluffy and retains its subtly fibrous texture. The flounder is strewn with scallions and ginger, which are striking against the gentle white meat.

Sturdier seafood. Conch: slightly cartilaginous slices and morsels of the oceanic meat, mingled with ginger and scallions and bits of pepper that you encounter as a surprise every third bite or so, all vibrant in their peppery oil. Squid: the tubular shafts of the fresh, tender meat scored, as if by strokes of a sharp-pointed fork, darkened by a black-bean sauce, made tangy with little disks of scallion and bits of fresh, loud ginger, the whole a dish that is powerful but never weighty.

The roast duck is simple: a half bird cut into slabs that an expert can hold in chopsticks while chewing the crisp skin and moist meat from the bones—an occasional peppercorn adds a touch of fire to the rich meat. The herbed chicken is more complex, the skin coated with herbs that have been blackened in the cooking, the meat moistened with a black sauce that is salty, sweet, a little hard, but hardly too much for this chicken—for Canton obtains chickens that are as flavorful as the chickens of your memory.

Lotus root, that crisp, vaguely perfumed and prettily perforated legume, is mixed with meats here: pork and lotus root, the pork juicy and sweet, with crunchy snow peas, whole cloves of garlic, and ginger in the oily but not heavy dish; beef and lotus root, the slivers of beef medium rare, microcosmic steaks, water chestnuts and snow peas and mushrooms the bulk of the multitextured dish. Canton is capable of turning out such things as roast pork with wide noodles, one of those complicated assemblages the components of which are identifiable only by sight. But one of the simpler noodle dishes is superb, the thin strands of rice noodle moistened with dark oil and dotted here and there with bits of scallion and bits of ginger—as elegant as the most refined Italian pasta. You get terrific string beans: the vegetable barely cooked, crisp and hot and oiled, tossed with slices of red pepper, ground pork, and garlic, all in a gravylike and pungently seasoned dark-brown sauce. Many dishes are not always available. Skip dessert, unless you want some cool canned fruit.

Booze of all nations—Scotch whiskey, Wild Turkey, California rosé, cognac—adorns the tables, for you bring your own.

★★★ LA CARAVELLE

33 West 55th Street
LUNCH, MONDAY TO FRIDAY; DINNER, MONDAY TO SATURDAY. CLOSED SUNDAY.
Reservations: 586-4252.
Credit cards: AE, DC, MC, V.
Very expensive.

In the late sixties and early seventies, La Caravelle was at least a contender, if not a front-runner, in the race for the unofficial title Best Restaurant in New York. Most guidebooks gave it their highest rating. And it had no trouble filling up, lunch and dinner, six days a week, even though eating at La Caravelle was among New York's dearest culinary diversions. Like all French restaurants of that eminence, the place was reputed to be snobbish to all but the upper crust. The dining room was originally overseen by a couple of fellows named Fred Decré and Robert Meyzen, the latter an erect, robust, and barrel-chested gentleman who seemed ferocious to the timid—he was revealed to be an instant pussycat if (a) you answered his faint bark with friendly amusement, or (b) you put him at his ease by addressing him in French. The kitchen was the domain of Roger Fessaguet, whose command of the haute cuisine idiom (if not invariably of its execution) approached perfection—though it never went anywhere near novelty, never mind audacity.

By and by, hard times. Defections from the kitchen staff. Competition from a new, light style of cooking. And, apparently, a severe case of the blahs, as the humdrum business of turning out and delivering the same old style of fancy food lost its charm. In time, one of the original partners, M. Decré, separated himself from the operation. Though everything slipped, the restaurant survived, for much of its bankerly, lawyerly, board-chairmanly clientele never noticed the decline—they figured that if they still ate in the place, it must still be the place to eat. The restaurateurs, however, knew better. The need for change was obvious, and, by a process of odd men in, odd men out, La Caravelle has been reorganized. A new chef in the kitchen, Michael Romano, has bumped Fessaguet—into the dining room. Fessaguet, in turn, has supplanted Meyzen —who has departed altogether, after twenty years as its imposing symbol—and he has been joined by a new partner, one André Jammet.

The shuffle has had a benign effect. You can now eat here about as well as you could when Caravelle was flying high—though, as ever, it is important to know your way around the menu. But, what is more, for the first time in its history, Caravelle has had the nerve to be nervy. While French kitchens all over town have hastened, over the last decade, to update their styles, Caravelle is still talking the language of haute cuisine (albeit a stylish, simplified vernacular thereof). Which is well, for, as you will recall, the cooking that is today condemned for its heaviness and richness was not the joy of its devotees solely for being fattening. The folks loved it because it was yummy.

Caravelle has been in business a quarter of a century now, and though it does not look old—the place is fresh and aglow—its looks are of an old fashion. Murals of Paris are all about, softly lighted, tricolors the tiny accents among the shimmering pastels. Banquettes of lustrous, crimson velvet rim the room, the snowy tables before them set with glinting china and flatware and—in cut-glass tumblers—clutches of flowers. Here and there, mirrored walls are mounted with sconces—pairs of tiny lamps with shades of fluted gauze. Dark-red carpeting, of course, is underfoot. The sound of the place is the comforting murmur of the prosperous at their pleasure, for businessmen and professionals are still the foundation of Caravelle's commerce, though now you do see, at this table or that, a boldly striped shirt, an unshaven cheek, a dress that is not only chic but sexy—you will look high and low, however, for the unpaired earring. But, especially in these days of half-acre, multi-story restaurants, Caravelle seems like a lot of luxe in less than enough space. The low ceiling, especially, hangs heavy, and the plate-glass mirrors, which are meant to open the room, only weigh it down. In its early days, Caravelle was said to be more intimate than its competitors, but these days, seekers after intimacy seek it at home.

M. Fessaguet, the former chef, has taken naturally to his new dining-room tasks, though he does lack M. Meyzen's cosmopolitan style and bearing—you cannot argue with a dark three-piece suit, or with a plain white shirt, but you do earnestly wish the necktie did not match exactly the breast-pocket handkerchief. As ever at Caravelle, tables in the grand aisle that leads into the main dining room are held open for members of the elite (these days they rarely come by), and instead of seating you at one of those, your host may prescribe a short wait at the bar until something elsewhere opens up. That idiocy aside, the known and unknown alike are treated cordially, particularly by the exceptional captains (they know the menu inside and out), who are at once suave and sweet—women, especially, are won over by their Gallic savoir-faire.

Come to Caravelle, and you will not, of course, encounter a New York haute cuisine menu of twenty years ago. But one dish that was available in most of the fancier French places in the seventies is still here today. It is given as la chair de crabe Caravelle, plump nuggets of crabmeat, of immaculate freshness and the most delicate marine sweetness, tossed with fresh parsley and moistened with a light, rich dressing that is heady with cognac—a dish that relies little on technique, much on ingredients, which detracts not at all from the appeal of its perfection. The terrine of scallops—a cool slab of mild seafood garnished with jelly—is lively only by virtue of its well-seasoned herbed mayonnaise. Skip it, and have instead the poached oysters, five fresh Belons set on shallow layers of good, strong spinach in their half-shells, under a rich, honeylike lobster sauce that is browned a moment before the dish is served—the earthy spinach, briny oysters, and sweet sauce make a stunning composition. You cannot much fault the plump snails or the assortment of sautéed wild mushrooms that comes with them, but they are coarsened by the heavily salted green broth in which they are served. Good ingredients again in la salade Caravelle, tender greens, ripe avocado, rich foie gras, a sliver of crunchy black truffle, and a great knob of cool, tender lobster meat, all moistened with an olive-oil dressing of vivid flavor—and yet the dish adds up only to a haphazard assortment. The galantine of duck, a slice cut from a boned, stuffed, and roasted bird, reaches you as a great red circle of seasoned meats with a black core that is a preserve of prunes —the forcemeat's pungency is potentiated by the brandy in which it has been soaked. If it is with rich red meat that you wish to begin, you are commended to l'escalopine de foie gras. The slices of duck liver are artfully sautéed, so that, though deeply browned

113

(actually blackened a bit here and there), they are pink and juicy under the surface—they are set in a pool of a dark and winy sauce that is built on a deep stock, the meat reaches you under slices of ripe peach, and the fruit is remarkably appropriate as the liver's striking foil.

Proceed to lobster—big chunks of the sweet white meat mingled with peas, florets of cauliflower, lengths of zucchini, and slivers of truffle, all of which are bathed in a light and creamy sauce that unifies the elements. Order the soufflé of Dover sole, and you are brought the silver platter on which the whole fish, skinned and boned, is hidden under a just-browned mousse of lobster and pike. The fish and its topping are transferred to a plate and then served to you in a pale and creamy sauce—a plain case of fancy food in the old style, and in perfect form. The salmon is billed as "in parchment," but it reaches you unwrapped, the fresh fillets of deep-pink fish over slivered root vegetables that are moistened by an herbed and buttery sauce.

In the old days, Caravelle was known for a peppered duck it served with a rich sour-cream sauce—sauce smitane. Today, duck does not appear on the dinner menu, but sometimes the bird is offered as a special, and it is well roasted, served with a tangy brandy sauce. Chunks of rich and fluffy sweetbread come with an abundance of woodsy black morels in a sauce that is touched with brandy. You cannot fault the filet mignon, the big fist of meat fibrous and blood-juicy within its seared exterior; its sauce of shallots and cream is thick, almost like a sour-cream sauce, and the meat is accompanied by delicate, browned nockerln—the sauce and those noodles combine to give the dish a slight Central European tone. La noisette d'agneau reaches you as a handful of rare chops cut from the roasted saddle, their edges browned and crisped—their sauce is of the lamb's own juices, and the strong meat is garnished, dramatically, with a stew of fresh artichoke hearts.

Bad enough that the cheeses are a bit flat, worse that the chicory salad, described as "aux lardons," is served not with the nuggets of salt pork that billing may lead you to expect, but with squares of the kind of smoked bacon sold in supermarket packages. But then there are the sweets. Do not think about it: The one to have is the kumquat soufflé, a light, handsomely risen, brown-topped production in which the fruit flavor is a bit elusive—until your captain adds the kumquat sauce, which is intense, almost liquorlike, somehow sweet without being sugary, rousing. The raspberry soufflé, with raspberry sauce, is more the standard thing, though just as artfully prepared. From the cart and from the refrigerator: commendable fruit tarts, kiwi and apple among them; fresh chocolate cakes, a white one and a dark one, the former rich and light, the latter liquored and strong; a so-called frozen soufflé that comes across merely as praline ice cream, whipped cream, and a light mocha sauce; cool sweet mousses, the chocolate intense, the passion fruit tame, the raspberry dark and fruity.

★★CAROLINA

355 West 46th Street
LUNCH, MONDAY TO FRIDAY; DINNER, DAILY.
Reservations: 245-0058.
Credit cards: AE, MC, V.
Medium priced.

Here in America, American food is a novelty. Without half trying, you can go through life without eating any. But even if that is, in fact, what you have so far done, you will recognize the stuff at first bite. Knowing what you know about America, when you encounter American food, you are immediately convinced that, yes, this is what Americans would have eaten in those precosmopolitan times when this country's cookery—like every cookery—derived willy-nilly from what ran, swam, and grew nearby. Of course, you can die not only happy but virtuous never having touched the stuff. There is no moral side to the resurrection of a neglected style of cooking. You do not become a patriot by eating crab cakes instead of quenelles de brochets. But, these days anyway, do it, and you are at least fashionable. For there is, it seems, this little trend: not to so-called nouvelle American cuisine, which is precisely as American as François Mitterrand; but to the very cooking with which, for example, Mary Todd failed to cheer up Abraham Lincoln.

The installers of this place at this address moved into freshly abandoned quarters, and they kept what they found—that certain combination of the rough-hewn and the posh that, for a while there, was the favored look of new New York spots. The front room's soft light illuminates slick, glossy walls of pale gray, within which the tables are set with pale-pink linen. But overhead the beams that stripe the ceiling are coarse and splintery, and you walk on a plain wood floor. The curved bar comes from Paris and sports a well-burnished zinc top. But it is the back dining room that the public has come to prefer, and to reach it you proceed through a narrow, tiled passageway, a windowed wall of which reveals the kitchen—and its staff at their labors. Surely the word "glitz" was in mind when this room was executed. It is small, and the tables form a tight square before the taupe-colored suede banquette with which it is rimmed. The four walls are solidly mirrored up to the skylight ceiling. At the center of the room, under the skylight, a single potted palm stands on the carpeted floor. The mirrors all around reflect and re-reflect the scene, which recedes from you to infinity. The candles become a thousand glittering lights. The couple of dozen diners become a throng. Even the sounds of the room are reflected by the glass, so the cheerful crowd makes a din.

What cheers them is a cup (or bowl) of the house chili, an earthy, spiced stew, thick with little chunks of beef and, in the Texas manner, devoid of beans. The barbecue on lettuce is a big mound of firm but tender sliced meat, mildly spiced by the thick barbecue sauce with which it is coated, served on cool leaves of iceberg, and garnished with a single great circle cut from a red pepper. Carolina offers what it calls "hot smoked sweet sausage," and this is a pleasantly vulgar-tasting, coarsely peppered and abundantly fatted forcemeat, garnished with sautéed green and red peppers and onions, and served with barbecue sauce.

Though much of the food here has a convincingly American character—that is to say, if no backwoodsman ever ate it, he should have—some of the dishes are merely influenced by the influence, which, of course, is not to say they are not yummy. The cool fillet of beef, for example—thin slices of rosy roasted beef, their edges crisp—is very nice, with its sprinkling of capers and strands of red onion and strong, tart mustard-

115

and-caper sauce. The green-chili soufflé, for another example, is a well-risen, hand-somely brown-topped production; the mousse that is its insides is light, glistening with butter, and spicy; and the ramekin in which it is baked and served is lined with hot little green peppers. And then there is the Carolina pizza (named, one supposes, for the restaurant rather than the bi-state region), in which the base of hot, pully, fairly loud cheese is spread with peppers and onions.

In the kitchen there is a wood fire, over which are cooked regular menu items as well as daily specials: a salmon steak, utterly fresh, juicy, and flaky, gloriously charred, and served with a sparkling tartar sauce—but somehow, good as this fish is, you are disap-pointed that it has picked up so little flavor from the fire; what are called "red pepper shrimp," crunchy seafood, deeply flavored by the spice but marred by a touch of iodine; your basic shell steak—it takes well to this fire, which imparts a delicately crackling blackened surface to the beef while drying it not at all. Another section of the menu is headed "Hot Smoke," which a footnote more or less explains as, to paraphrase, meat cooked in a pit by scented wood smoke, the temperature never allowed to rise above 200 degrees, for as long as twenty hours. Ribs get this treatment, and they are tender, very meaty, and come with a red sauce the pungency of which is of flavor, not just strength. And breast of chicken gets the treatment, yielding white meat that is powerfully smoky, moist, livened by its charred surface. Sometimes the house hot-smokes pork—the re-sulting meat is rich and delicate, only slightly smoky, exhibiting mainly the sweet taste of the pork itself.

Here you get genuine strawberry shortcake, a hillock of biscuits, ripe berries, an abundance of whipped cream, and a sweet and tangy berry syrup. Something given as vanilla cream with black-currant sauce is a great, craggy mound of vanilla mousse in a pool of the intense sauce. The apple crisp is a cinnamoned, sugar-crumbed thing of crisp cooked fruit, much like a pie without a crust, and the mud cake is a chocolate cake of a nice coarseness—both are served with good whipped cream.

All the still table wines are American.

★★CEDARS OF LEBANON

39 East 30th Street
LUNCH AND DINNER.
Reservations: 725-9251.
Credit cards: AE, DC, MC, V.
Inexpensive.

The history of the Cedars of Lebanon (on East 30th Street, not in the Levant) is one of repeated redecoration in pursuit of anonymity. Originally a seedy place and then a garish one, in both those incarnations the Cedars threatened to become camp-fashion-able. Now the place is Motel Byzantine, with a Cocktail Lounge barroom, red carpeting, shimmering wallpaper of golden branches on a soft gray ground, paneling of dark, grainy wood, and beige-linened tables softly illuminated by lights recessed in the deep-maroon ceiling. You note also, at one end of the long dining room, a platform, the appliances on which suggest that on occasion players of amplified instruments perform there. Story is that though the $5 lunch is quite an attraction by day, by night this establishment's neighborhood is deserted. To attract the folks it has been necessary to make of the mere restaurant a social scene—anyway on Friday and Saturday nights.

On those evenings rows of tables are shoved together to accommodate great gatherings of clans. Swarthy, black-haired Easterns in three-piece suits bring blond girlfriends here—to show off their culture to their ladies, and to display their conquests to their compatriots. When the ouzo on the rocks has been flowing for a while, the gents remove their neckties. If things are going swimmingly, the giggling ladies put them on. Flashbulbs pop. The waiters move really fast. And promptly at 10:15 the 10 o'clock music starts. The thumping, modal wailing and loud singing get them clapping their hands. One waiter half closes his eyes and sways a little to the music as he delivers a dozen skewers of shish kebab, and the ladies in the party shriek in delirium at the wanton departure from rôle. The real frenzy begins later, when the belly dancing starts.

Between passions the crowd eats kibbee nayeh, chopped raw lamb, lightly oiled and seasoned, mixed with cracked wheat. They eat thick hommus and a smoky and well-oiled baba ghannoush, tabbouleh that is lemoned and fragrant with greens, hot spinach pies, cold grape leaves that are oily and lemony and filled with sweet-spiced rice. They drink a yogurt soup that is minted, soured with lemon, hot. That shish kebab is abundant, two big skewers of broiled marinated lamb, chunks of tomato, onion, pepper. The kaftah kebab is two great logs of ground lamb, spiced and juicy and steamy. The baked kibbee is like a nutted and grainy ground-lamb sandwich, black and crusty, served with warm stuffed grape leaves—a homey and satisfying dish. The place makes a coarse couscous, a hefty lamb stew that is here served in a red sauce with chickpeas, big chunks of root vegetable, and a mound of hot, moist grain. Steaks, chicken dishes, even a couple of seafood dishes, fill out the menu, but lamb is the basis of this food.

The honeyed and nutted pastries are served here in good versions—the baklava, with its brandylike sweetness and thickness of ground walnuts, is much above average. The bird's nest is a flaky little circle of pastry, like a doughnut without a hole, its center filled with honeyed pistachios.

★ CELLAR IN THE SKY

1 World Trade Center
DINNER, ONE SITTING. CLOSED SUNDAY.
Reservations: 938-1111 (deposit required).
Credit cards: AE, DC, MC, V.
Very expensive.

The Cellar lures neurotics and other mildly disturbeds. It offers, after all, what the emotionally unfinished long for—"return" to that perfect childhood that never was, when everything was taken care of. The long, varied menus that ordinary restaurants offer are probably full of promise to you. But to the chronically undecided they are a threat. You see these types everywhere—they read the bill of fare as if it holds an indecipherable secret, look desperately at dishes on nearby tables, ask questions not only of the help, but of one another, want urgently to order the right thing, invariably end up fearing they have not. To them, losing the right to choose is like a reprieve from final exams. All at once, they cannot fail.

Naturally, Cellar in the Sky does not promote itself as respite from the wearies of decision making. Though the menu and the five wines served with it are fixed of an evening (every two weeks, everything changes), this format is ostensibly aimed at perfection—the flawless marriage of foods and boozes—not at escape. And of course those who come here do not admit that they are symbolically seeking the cared-for condition of ideal infancies. Rather, they persuade themselves that a visit to the Cellar is an expression of their connoisseurship (not to mention a conspicuous display of their position in life). You actually see people here closing their eyes and wrinkling their foreheads as they ecstatically inhale the bouquets of wines that are surely embarrassed over all the attention. Which is regrettable, for the Cellar is best used for what it is, an eating place that, given half a chance, is an excellent background for your private purposes, with the succession of foods and wines a series of mild diversions that only occasionally command your attention. Moreover the duration of the dinner and the nature of the setting may be exactly suitable when your goals are interpersonal (persuasion) rather than gastronomic. For you can easily pass three or more hours here over dinner; and the room, a dim aerie set within Windows on the World—away downtown and away up in the sky and with no view of any worldly thing outside its walled confines—seems as remote from New York as the cabin in the sky itself.

You must ride up 107 stories in the elevator with the honeymooners and farm equipment conventioneers and members of the East Cupcake Gourmet Society on their annual field trip—all of them bound for Windows. But once inside the Cellar, you are effectively alone. The physical place is muted, and its frequenters observe library decorum in apparent honor of some of the appointments—racks of esteemed wines on the walls, wine cases with the names of legendary châteaux burned into the wood. The wine-cellar theme is expressed as well in the bare tables—around a dozen of them—and the low archways that straddle the massive pillars. You sit in chairs of wood and leather that are much like director's chairs, except that they do not fold. The place is illuminated by pinpoint spotlights—they cast gentle beams here and there, which are reflected by, among other things, those wine bottles, casting bits and spots of soft light on the polished tables and marble floor. A guitarist strums.

A uniformed gentleman (title: wine steward; function: wine pourer) asks if you would like champagne or kir royale. The kir royale, you understand, is the same champagne (in this instance the Piper Brut of 1980), to which has been added a bit of crème de cassis, an effective method of making wine into soda pop. So much for high oenological seriosity. That particular champagne—like almost all Cellar wine—is nothing special, actually somewhat hard, but worthy of better than dilution with alcoholic syrup.

Champagne is really appropriate to almost no food, but here it lasts through the quasi cocktail hour that is built into the extended dinner, when it is served to you with whole grain crackers and then with individual little leek tarts, two-inch quiches, really, that are just made, quite fluffy, sport a vivid flavor of the vegetable; and through the first course, cool sections cut from a roulade of sliced chicken wrapped around spiced mussels, those garnished with tender asparagus spears that are moistened with a good vinaigrette. The 1981 Puligy-Montrachet Clavoillon of Leflaive is a wine that is perfectly polished, but with more of the maker's finesse in it than fruit. It accompanies a creamy frogs' leg soup that is much like a billi-bi—briny and stout. The same wine is poured with ridiculously oversalted ravioli of snapper and celery—they are otherwise of good flavor and texture in their cream sauce. No amount of exposure to air by pouring and by twirling in the glass can overcome the prematurity of this Freemark Abbey Cabernet Bosché of 1975, which clearly will not be ready for at least three years. To serve it with this venison makes verbal sense (big wine with game) but no other, for this meat is tender and sweet next to its fruit-and-pumpkin garnish, and the next wine, a Léoville Lascases of 1970, all elegance, suits it more than the good cheeses with which it is actually served.

The Cellar of course serves sweet wine with dessert. This is a fine Niersteiner Oelberg Beerenauslese of 1976, fruity but not obvious, heady and fairly intense. It would be great with nothing at all, or with foie gras. But no wine—not sweet wine, not fortified wine, not champagne—makes much sense with sugared food. (Brandy makes some sense, coffee makes more.) To serve this wine with an atrocity called "coffee and chocolate charlotte"—a layer of chocolate pudding over a layer of coffee pudding on a chocolate-snap crust—is a really super boo-boo.

The wines of the evening are listed, with the food menu, on a little sign on each table. You may, if you wish, limit yourself to the best wines of those offered, or have your wines in an order other than the suggested one.

The prix fixe dinner is $70 per person, including wine, plus tax and tip.

★★★ CHALET SUISSE

6 East 48th Street
LUNCH AND DINNER. CLOSED SATURDAY AND SUNDAY.
Reservations: 355-0855.
Credit cards: AE, DC, MC, V.
Expensive.

Chalet Suisse has been in New York for around a half century. A few decades ago it changed hands, and fifteen years ago it moved from its original 52nd Street site to the present one on East 48th. Restaurant guidebooks from the 1930s reveal that some of the dishes served now were served then. But during its long and consistent history, Chalet Suisse has never been the rage. It is, and for years has been, simply a marvelous restaurant, characterized by the most fundamental restaurant virtues. Enough people know about the place to keep it quite humming, but they do not make a lot of noise about their knowledge. Chalet Suisse is not mentioned in the gossip columns. Faces seen on television are not seen here. And the city's culinary avant-garde have never discovered the restaurant's merits (though the hot new places they tout every year cannot, ten times in eleven, warm this one up).

Chalet Suisse has the look of an old-fashioned European country inn. Its comfort derives from its simplicity. Rough plaster walls, the color of aged ivory, are hung here and there with oil paintings and pottery. The ceiling beams are of dark wood. Ironwork and suggestions of arches and pillars divide the room into snug areas, and the banquettes along the sides are fitted into niches. The tables are surrounded by slat-back chairs that have loose cushions on the seats. The restaurant is softly lighted by sconces that give off an amber glow.

Much of the pleasure of eating at Chalet Suisse traces to its civilized service. The standard is set by your host, a gentleman who seems to take pleasure in touring his restaurant floor to fill a glass here, provide a fresh plate there, answer questions, whatever. Happily, the waitresses follow his example. They are dressed in what are, presumably, native Swiss costumes, brightly colored, trimmed with lace, protected by gaily striped aprons. And they attend to their tasks with alertness, intelligence, and goodwill. It is enough to make you cry.

At lunchtime, the most tasteful executives of the least frivolous industries decorously crowd the place to the rafters, filling it with the soft, cheery tinkle of ample coin. At night, vintage New Yorkers, sometimes whole families of them, relax here in a manner most at-home. The Chalet is also well known to visiting European businessmen, Stock-

119

holmers and Amsterdammers and Düsseldorfers, who have found here the little plot of Manhattan Island that is echt home away from Frau.

Swiss food, as all the world knows, derives in large part from German, Italian, and French cooking. It is, however, less ponderous than German, less emotional than Italian, more forthright than haute cuisine, more dramatic than cuisine bourgeoise. So much for eminently destructible generalizations. Whatever its provenance, much of what the Swiss eat is sui generis—like bündnerschinken and bündnerfleisch, the salted-and-dried ham and beef of Switzerland. The ham is pink, smoky, and high, with fiber in its texture, fat around its rim; the beef is a stronger red but a paler flavor, rather gentle for a cured raw meat. Each is served in abundant portions, the rosy slices spread across broad plates. The so-called cervelat salad is humbler stuff, disks of porky sausage adorned with marinated onions and moistened with a light vinaigrette. The meats and the sausage are especially good with the strong, salty breads and the splendid sweet butter served here, and they may be nicely supplemented with an order of mushrooms Ascona, in which the chunks of fresh mushroom are served in an herby and slightly sour sauce that is thick with morsels of tomato.

Among the hot appetizers, the sleeper is the ravioli milanese. It is not like what you get in your neighborhood spaghetti joint. These tender pasta envelopes are filled with fluffy ground meat, greens, and grain; they are bathed in buttery consommé; and they are strewn with just-ground strong cheese and fresh parsley. The dish is airy, it seems to sing a little, and it disappears weightlessly, miraculously. There are wondrous snails, deeply flavored by the stock they were poached in, served in an herbed and well-salted butter; a cheese-and-onion pie that is actually a hefty quiche larded with sautéed onions; and délice d'Emmenthal, crescents of strong Swiss cheese that have been breaded and deep-fried until the cheese is hot, soft, and pully, the crust brown and crisp.

When your enchanting waitress spoons some médaillons de veau aux morilles onto your hot plate, she always asks, "May I keep the rest of this warm for you?" And when she delivers the balance (having observed that you vanished the first helping in a twinkling), she brings a fresh hot plate as well. This second delivery, if you forget to expect it, can render you deliriously happy, for this delicate veal, in its polished brandy sauce, studded with woodsy wild mushrooms, is at once easy, earthy, and rich. Then there is the veal chop sauté au marc du Valais—a large eye of meat on a long bone that is dressed in a little paper pant, the meat white, flecked with glistening brown, and moistened with a dark sauce and dozens of hot, sweet white grapes. There is a crusty rack of lamb, touched with garlic, utterly tender, juicy, and slightly high—racks of lamb are not roasted better within a day's drive of this restaurant. Liver and kidney à la Suisse is composed of bite-size chunks of the meats in a stout, herbed, gravylike sauce. Another dark sauce, this one winier and more polished, is served with slices of tender beef as filet de boeuf à la mode du chef. Whatever you do, do not pass up the rösti, the remarkable Swiss potato dish in which partially cooked potatoes are formed into broad pancakes that are then fried until golden. At Chalet Suisse the pancakes are crusty and tender, and if you are not yet in love with your waitress, you will capitulate completely when she comes around with a second plate.

The outstanding, low-priced main course is a cheese fondue called Neuchâteloise. It is perhaps a bit more work than eating in a restaurant ought to be, but this dish, brought to you bubbling over a flame in an enamel pot, dispels quibbles. The soft, slightly pully, nutmeg-flavored mixture of Emmenthal and Gruyère cheeses, mingled with wine and kirsch and a little garlic, is solid and heady, and it thickens and becomes stronger as it simmers. A basket of bread cubes is supplied, and you eat the dish by dunking the bread in the hot and fragrant stuff.

If you wish to continue dunking, the chocolate fondue (for two) is yet another bubbling pot, this one filled with chocolate that is at once creamy and sharp and sweet, slightly liquored, into which you dip slices of fruit—pineapple, banana, apple—thereby creating your own hot little candies. Chocolate is prominent throughout the dessert list. The chocolate mousse has an emphatic, almost naked chocolate intensity; the coupe chocolat is little more than a perfect sundae: vanilla ice cream and the kind of rich and fluffy, unsugared whipped cream that is just about unobtainable in restaurants these days—you pour a strong, hot, nutted chocolate over the two white creams and eat. The apple tart, a simple pastry filled with crisp fruit, is a good vehicle for more of that whipped cream—as is Aargauer rüblitorte, a lightly liquored carrot-and-almond cake—as is the surprise Valaisanne, a crisp meringue that is mounded over with fresh strawberries that have been cured with Grand Marnier. The dessert menu is long, and all the sweets are pure and fresh.

★★★★ CHANTERELLE

6 Harrison Street (at Hudson Street) (new address)
DINNER. CLOSED SUNDAY AND MONDAY.
Reservations: 966-6960.
Credit cards: AE, MC, V.
Very expensive.

In olden times, a first-class restaurant was a comfortable room, furnished with tables and chairs, in which commendable food was served by a discreet staff. In those days, mealtimes were considered particularly suitable occasions for conversation, for the conduct of human affairs (personal, commercial, political, whatever), for celebration of the day; and it was the business of restaurants to provide the setting, absorb the work, and, at best, to offer food and drink of such quality as to catalyze the proceedings. The tone of the old establishments was set by proprietors who were—necessarily—civilized. And though they often gained the respect of their fellow citizens (customers might well greet their host warmly when they came to his place), celebrity was not intrinsic to the restaurateur's position. He was a merchant like any other, in business to make a living. And though, inevitably, his establishment was to some extent an expression of himself, its prosperity depended mainly on how well it fulfilled the expectations of its community. In that era citizens did not go to restaurants to escape from their day-to-day lives. They were looking, rather, to be themselves.

Today, of course, there are few such restaurants—and properly so, for there are few such citizens. Who, any longer, will settle for being merely who he is, when he can define himself, instead, by where he has been, whom he has seen there, what he has spent there? Nowadays, eating places are built on the calculation that if a place can become (with media help) a hot spot, at least half the restaurant freaks in town will try it at least once—enough to return the investment several times over.

But even the rare restaurateur with traditional intentions is doomed to a modern fate: On the one hand, his place will likely fail; but if it succeeds, it is, willy-nilly, a contemporary success, and therefore in danger of destination status ("Have you been to . . . yet?"), susceptible to lionization of the chef and/or proprietor, and almost assured of an attenuated life—as newer successes replace it. Some restaurants survive their vogue, but few come out of it the way they went in. This place, Chanterelle, did just that. Unscarred by early acclaim, and no longer the talk of the town, of all restaurants in New York, it is not only the closest thing to the primeval model, but a purveyor of superior food as well. If the critics have lately been guarded, albeit favorable, in their assessment of the place, that is in part because the chef's youth makes it temptingly easy to say that he shows talent and promise; and in part because the restaurant's plain trappings are not the sort that provoke enthusiasm in those who crib their judgments from clues.

Though its dining room is simple, almost unadorned, it is neither antiseptic nor merely utilitarian. Whether by design or—more likely—by chance, its cleanness of line is of a distinctly Early American spareness, and though the effect is achieved with little in the way of, say, Colonial or Puritan or Shaker appointments, one look at the place, and you know you are not in the Old World. At the front of the room, there is a little desk, a few extra chairs for those next up, and a tall armoire of honey-colored wood for coats— atop it is a great burst of branches and flowers that, together with another much like it on a small table at the rear, are just about the only nonfunctional components of this installation. The high walls are of pale, pale apricot, with lower walls of dark paneled wood on one side of the room, gray wainscoting on the other. This is an ancient store-front, and despite the many decades of its existence, there has somehow been left intact an elaborately worked ceiling triptych of stamped tin. The current tenants have painted it white, and from the centerpoint of each of the three panels they have hung an airy chandelier of slender brass arms with, at their tips, tiny bulbs that fill the room with soft light.

Because Chanterelle appeared when all the talk was of so-called nouvelle cuisine, the restaurant is usually tagged with that meaningless label. Otherwise, presumably because its proprietors were born here, it is called American. In fact, the kitchen is rooted, and always has been, in what is traditional and French—less modified by what is new than are any number of French places that, because they have been around a long time, are still thought of as old style. If now and then a listed menu item—e.g., salmon with cranberries—suggests that the food is trendy, one dinner will correct the impression. The short menu is revised every two weeks, and from soup to sherbet, here is every item on one edition, plus a couple of special dishes of an evening.

That "soup" is actually lobster consommé, a hot broth, dark and steamy, its sharpness that of lobster shell, its sweetness that of the meat—in the broth you find tiny dice of tomato, filament stands of root vegetable, and little knobs of lobster that are moist and of vivid ocean flavor. Shellfish again, this time an assortment of small nuggets, mingled with pine nuts and packed into a sausage casing that reaches you, browned and crack-ling, in a pool of rich sauce that is of almost brandylike headiness. One night there are oysters, and, technically, they are poached, but just barely, enough to warm them through without actually cooking them, in which state the special quality of oysters, that integration of brininess and succulence, is at its peak. The mollusks are on their half shells, in a concentrated and buttery white-wine sauce, each covered with slivers of white truffle, the earthiness of which is in stunning contrast to the seafood. The cool terrine of duck foie gras is formed of conjoined morsels of the pinguid livers—the strong, seasoned meat seems rich enough to spread like butter on bread, and its striking foils are a cool, dark jelly and a crunchy, tangy slaw of sharp white radish. What the house calls ravioli have the familiar shape, but these pasta envelopes, firm and tender, are filled with a woodsy hash of wild mushrooms and are moistened with a dark sauce built on a sturdy stock—more of those white truffles are grated over the little packages.

Much finfish served here: that salmon with cranberries, the slab of pink meat wrapped in a leaf of lettuce and poached, the moist and flaky fillet then served in a sauce that is slightly acidic of the berry—a latticework of haricots verts surrounds the fish, with eight or ten whole, tart cranberries distributed among the slats; swordfish, the thick steak fibrous but tender, juicy within its crisped surfaces, its sauce a smooth and only slightly fruited lime butter—the fish is strewn, to striking effect, with uncooked leaves of fresh, heady coriander, and it is served with little carrots and crunchy spears of asparagus; and a firm fillet of striped bass in a buttered mustard sauce that is fragrant of dill and nubbly with bits of tomato—the sauce surrounding the fish is adorned with glinting emerald-green snow peas. The breast of Muscovy duck is grilled until its entire surface is crusted and deeply browned, it is sliced before serving, and each slice consists of a rim of that crust, within that a thin ring of pale-pink meat, and within that a glistening oval of meat that is warm but blood-rare—the sauce is a smooth and winy one of sherry vinegar. The rack of lamb reaches you as four thick chops, their edges deep brown and crisp, the meat pink and glistening (if you ordered it medium rare), its dark sauce heady with garlic—for still more garlic there are whole roasted cloves of it, one on each chop. Venison is sweet meat, and here it is served as thick little steaks (noisettes) that are charred, tender, and juicy—their polished sauce is a slightly tart, slightly fruity poivrade.

Hard cheese, creamy cheese, and blue-veined cheese, goats, sheep, and cows, strong ones and mild ones, French and Italian, there is not a better cheese tray in New York, every item at room temperature and in blooming condition. One night they are presented to you with a couple dozen lady apples strewn among them, and the tart and juicy three-bite morsels of fruit set off any cheese strikingly. The sour bread you had with your dinner is fine with this course, as is the walnut-onion bread the house prepares especially for it—it arrives sliced, warm, wrapped in linen. Order salad, and you get a great mound, crisp and vibrant—sharp watercress, crunchy endive, bitter radicchio, tender green lettuce, all in a judiciously seasoned dressing made with an oil of vivid olive flavor.

Crescents of cool, sweet, grainy pear, hard and yet tender, their fruit flavor potentiated by the wine in which they were poached, are served around a dollop of sauternes sabayon, a sweet-wine sauce that is at once thick, rich, and light—the dish is sprinkled with slivers of crisp almond. What goes as "Reine de Saba" (Queen of Sheba) is a rich, velvety, and intense chocolate cake moistened with liquor and touched with citrus rind —it comes with thick whipped cream. More of that cream is served with the gooseberry tart, the tangy fruit on a browned and crumbly pastry. The prune ice cream reaches you in a huge wineglass from which a great cookie protrudes like a sail—the slick cream is dotted with chunks of prune and fortified with Armagnac. The passion fruit and pear sherbets are remarkable concentrations of those fruit flavors, the latter intensified with pear eau de vie. While you are looking twice at your check, someone comes around with a tray of tiny profiteroles, airy pastries about the size of grapes, in each of them a bit of fluffy pastry cream.

Chanterelle is an expensive restaurant, despite which the floor staff is uniformed only in white shirts or blouses—no ties—and white over-the-head aprons. Because of this unexpected informality, it is often reported that the help here is amateurish. In fact they know the menu, are available, and, happily, do not address you in any of this day's more familiar modes—they are neither old pals, wind-up orators, nor food majors. If the clientele strikes you as odd, that is because they appear to consist, in substantial part, of folks with whom you yourself might consider sitting down to dinner.

★ CHELSEA CENTRAL

227 Tenth Avenue (near 23rd Street)
LUNCH, SUNDAY TO FRIDAY; DINNER, DAILY.
Reservations: 620-0230.
Credit cards: AE, MC, V.
Medium priced.

Your basic converted saloon, long bar up front, barbershop-tile floor, 4-bladed fans under the stamped-tin ceiling, jukebox. A joined pair of vintage telephone booths—complete with working phones, folding doors, and little fans that spin—forms the hint of a partition between the barroom and the dining room in the back, which houses rows of white-linened tables, dark bentwood side chairs around them. The standing coat racks are all right, the exposed brick here and there is surely to be expected in a place of this kind, and the posters contribute to the slightly cluttered comfort of the softly lighted place. But even if it were to be established that the construct of mirrors and stained glass that dominates the back wall is the only surviving example of a long lost folk form, no right-thinking landmarks commissioner with any kind of eye could possibly be restrained from smashing the hideous thing if allowed near it.

Styled "An American Bistro," the Café undertakes to ennoble such Americana as the shrimp cocktail. There is no denying the fiery sparkle of this cocktail sauce, nor the excellence of the oil with which the salad at the center of your plate is dressed, and it is always a pleasure not to find the shrimp hanging on as if in a struggle for life to the edge of a glass cup of cracked ice, but the crustaceans themselves, their good texture notwithstanding, are only of the remotest seafood flavor. Each of the five fried oysters is surmounted by a strand of roasted red pepper, and they are all set in a lemony mayonnaise that sparkles a bit, but the oysters are in a batter that outweighs them, overwhelms them, they have been fried too long, at considerable sacrifice of flavor, and the shoestring potatoes with which they are garnished only add to the impression that this is boardwalk food with airs. Happily, this American Bistro is of the melting-pot school, makes immigrant dishes its own, wraps great sheets of grilled eggplant around warm slabs of mozzarella and chunks of roasted red pepper, serves the packages in an herbed and seasoned oil. Nor do difficulties arise if the foreigners are of impure lineage, as is this duck salad, the slices of warm, dark, tender meat of exceptionally vivid flavor against the well-dressed lettuce and tomatoes over which they are strewn—the other side of this item is a couple of crusts of bread, the slices of goat cheese on each surfaced with fresh herbs.

The excess of salt on this salmon suggests it was seasoned by someone, then seasoned by someone else, but that is not enough to undo the fresh, carefully grilled fillet—the fish, and the fresh spinach pasta served with it, are in a thick and creamy sauce that is fragrant of dill and dotted with bits of tomato. Another creamy sauce, this one spicy and threaded with long strands of chive, moistens the thin, thin angel hair pasta, which is tossed with sautéed shrimp that, this time, are full of flavor. The grilled chicken benefits from its charring, for the bird itself is bland, and it is spread with the minced scallions and tomatoes that were stranded on it when the dull sauce of which they were a component was poured over—the muffin of wild leek risotto at the center of your plate has the dried surface of a thing that has been waiting to be called. You get a more than decent grilled sirloin, though its degree of doneness is not exactly what you specified.

The hazelnut mousse tart is just a sticky richness of little hazelnut quality—it is garnished with loose whipped cream. So is the chocolate amaretto cake, which is almost black under its deep-brown icing, of sharp chocolate strength, the amaretto a good note of heady clarity in the rich setting. The deep dish sour cream apple pie is a great thickness of apple slices overlaid with a great thickness of sweet-spiced pecans—a vigorous if obvious dessert. The lemon curd tart is notable for the sourness and smoothness of the custard on the rather dull pastry.

★ CHEZ JACQUELINE

72 MacDougal Street (near Houston Street)
DINNER.
Reservations: 505-0727.
Credit cards: AE.
Medium priced.

The picture side of an old French monochrome postcard has been blown up, framed, and mounted on the wall right next to the short bar that occupies one end of this small restaurant. The fuzzy picture depicts a section of the beach at Nice, circa 1910. In it you see ladies and gentlemen of the era, some with parasols, strolling under the palm trees. Nearby, rowboats have been pulled up onto the sand. Like all old photographs, it reminds you of your mortality. And, like many, it may make you nostalgic for a past you never knew—and, in so doing, cause you to appreciate this place for the little it does preserve. For Chez Jacqueline manages (happily, without the assistance of embarrassing trappings) to recall a bit of subtropical France in the era before it was invaded by the second half of the twentieth century—a function without which the restaurant might be no more than marginally noteworthy. It is the combination of more-or-less down-home French cooking and modest, mildly evocative surroundings that makes this place more than what it is.

What it is is a plain, low-ceilinged rectangle of a store, its length parallel to Mac-Dougal Street. And what it is when the weather is fine is a parallel place, out on the sidewalk, under the long awning that runs from the northern to the southern end of the establishment. For, just as in many eating places along the Riviera, when it is hot outside, it is cooler inside; but when it is at all temperate outside, it is hotter inside. Jacqueline's dining room sports air-conditioning vents, but they do little to stand in your way if what you wish to do is have a good time and sweat. Outside, you get this really terrific view of the little park that extends from MacDougal to Sixth Avenue just above Houston Street—and the gay carousings therein of the neighborhood's aspiring young goons-to-be. Inside, the white-linened tables are in neat rows. The floor is tiled. The walls are vaguely patterned in a way that suggests the very thick walls of houses in hot parts of the world. A palm here and a philodendron there add marginally to the semi-equatorial effect.

To the gruff gentlemen who serve you, learning restaurant ways was not second nature. One chap breathes hard and stares at the ceiling as he itemizes the daily specials. And the boss appears much more at ease when he is pouring himself a glass of wine at a table of his pals than when forcing himself through the motions of proprietorial politesse.

If nothing about the physical restaurant and its style put you in mind of its region of origin, the brandade de morue may. This is a provençale dish of salted codfish, oiled and pounded into a paste, fortified with garlic and flavored with parsley until (in this version) the mash is a brilliant green—the dish is served here in a shallow casserole dish, hot from the oven, and it is very good with cold wine of any color. Jacqueline serves,

125

sometimes, a good octopus salad—cool morsels of the resilient but tender meat, with bits of shallot and much parsley, in a dressing that is little more than good oil. That is much to be preferred to her mussels—their powerfully garlicked tomato broth is fine, but the mussels themselves are rank. The snails here are leathery little morsels, their red sauce at once strong and tasteless. But the cool mixture of potatoes and chunks of garlic sausage in a thick mustard dressing—an occasional dish of the day—is rousing and satisfying. Another daily special is a stuffed suckling pig. The beast is displayed to you—reclining on its side—its rear portion already partially sold off by the slice. His innards and meat have been made into a well-fatted and abundantly sweet-spiced forcemeat, with pistachio nuts, with which its tegument is packed. You are served a round slice, rimmed with pigskin—to the inside of which clings a thin layer of rich meat. This is a good—but pinguid—dish, and strong mustard and bread may be essential to you for its consumption.

When soft-shell crabs are around, this place has been known to get little ones, and to sauté them with lots of garlic and parsley—you wish they were crisper, but that hardly matters when the crabs are this small and delicate. The poulet basquaise consists of substantial sections of chicken in a rather coarse tomato sauce that is thick with onions and green peppers. Once in a while the house offers rabbit—this is a good stew, of well-browned meat simmered in white wine, in which sharp green olives and strong black peppercorns are striking notes. Of the lamb dishes: the herbed and crisped rack—served intact—is simple and unimpeachable; the gigot—served in quarter-inch-thick slices—is a little chewy, its white beans a little soft. Of the beef dishes: the steak is tough in its rather harsh pepper sauce; the daube niçoise, though not of first-rate stew meat—the chunks are tender from long cooking, but have little beef character—is hearty, notable for its strong black olives.

Not a dessert house. An otherwise well-made dacquoise—of layers of meringue and two colors of pastry cream—is robbed of its delicacy by its thick chocolate icing. Something variously given as champagne mousse or champagne cheesecake is a tasteless fluff. The black currant mousse pie is light, cool, pallid.

★ CHEZ JOSEPHINE

414 West 42nd Street
DINNER. CLOSED SUNDAY.
Reservations: 594-1925.
Credit cards: AE, MC, V.
Medium priced.

Josephine Baker was an American singer and dancer who made a big hit in Paris in the twenties and remained in France, most of the rest of her life, as a music-hall entertainer. Though talented, she knew that talent was no surety of success, so she often performed with most of her clothes off, was reportedly sensational when wearing nothing but a G-string and bananas. The elfin Frenchman who runs this place tells you that her hobby was adopting people, not necessarily de jure, and that he was one of her unofficial wards. In this place, his tribute to her, he has theatricalized a long and narrow room with yards of red velvet, much cerulean-blue paint, mirrors, zebra carpeting in the little back room, a piano complete with pianist in a mirrored alcove, and scores of posters, paintings, caricatures, and sepia photos of Josephine herself, wearing very little, or in a fedora and dancing with a guy in a tux, or dancing on a piano, the look in her eye, when you can see it, mischievous and gay. You figure she might have found this place small of scale, but that she rarely found things beneath her; and that she would have been indulgent of, even amused by, a restaurant host who, like her boy here, presses himself on you with more fervor than you wish to share about this, his enterprise. To get away with that, his fervor would have to be like Josephine's itself.

Bistro food and dishes that are its contemporary equivalent: gently warmed, crisped oysters, fresh and plump in their half-shells, touched with lime juice and a bit of fresh fennel; judiciously poached leeks, firm and crunchy, in a warm vinaigrette made with pungent olive oil; a robust salad of assorted fresh greens with crusts of garlicked bread; thin pasta in a buttery sauce, fragrant with basil, that is thick with wild mushrooms and both fresh and sun-dried tomatoes. The main dishes include the oddly named lobster cassoulet, oddly because it is made with scallops and shrimp as well, not to mention a disk of seafood sausage, all those elements, with black beans and chunks of tomato, in a buttered and briny soup; the oddly named chicken Alvara, oddly because fried chicken would describe it better, the parts of moist bird, in a sweet batter that peels away like a tender shell, garnished with dry corn bread (butter helps) and French-fried sweet potatoes (nothing helps); boudin noir, the rich pudding of seasoned blood and fat in charred, crackling casings, with French fries that, on occasion, are limp; a crusted, accurately grilled steak that is a little dry within its almost harsh coating of pink peppercorns, with French fries that, on occasion, are crisp.

The otherwise fine raspberry tart is ice cold. The chocolate cake, though given as "Le Délice Josephine," is an ordinary commercial chocolate item, anyway its equivalent.

★ CHEZ LOUIS

1016 Second Avenue (near 54th Street)
LUNCH, MONDAY TO FRIDAY; DINNER, DAILY.
Reservations: 752-1400.
Credit cards: AE, DC, MC, V.
Expensive.

A mini-bandwagon is heading back to bistros, and the dying Manhattan Market, to save itself, has, with several buckets of saucy red paint, yards of crimson cloth, a carload of garlic, and the new name, hopped on. It is a case, however, of imitation without understanding, the fashionable clothes without the style, the retold joke with the punch line at the beginning. Not that you cannot eat well here, or that to run a bistro you must have grown up in the tradition, rather that a bistro, by its nature, is a community place—though good ones attract folks from all over—one that draws its identity from the harmonious interaction of he who runs it with those he understands how to serve. Chez Louis is an exploitation of the mode without the calling, which is to say, getting in on a good thing. The only vision behind Chez Louis is a vision of a simpler, more profitable, more merchandisable operation than Manhattan Market. There is of course nothing reprehensible in turning an additional dollar, but peddling the imitation as the article, it is hoped, will always be vulgar. The proprietor has been quoted as saying that he is going to keep working at this place until he "gets this perfect," as if running a bistro were a trick that can be mastered by application, like wriggling your ears. His method is to lay on thick certain superficialities (much crimson, much garlic, and himself in a white jacket awkwardly carving roasts in the dining room), while pandering to local taste—an evening's main courses may consist almost exclusively of chicken, lamb, beef, swordfish, salmon. Pig's feet, you understand, are not here. While flattered that this is down-to-earth dinnering, the folks are getting what they always eat anyway.

You still enter to the lofty barroom, the long counter of polished gray stone, behind it a triptych of mirrors framed in carved wood, the floor of white barbershop tiles, the monumental hanging lanterns apparently relics from some torn-down cathedral space— the parts are handsome, but this is a cavernous room, in desperate but usually unsatisfied need of a crowd at the bar to warm it up. The dining room is up a few steps at the back, and looks like a movie set. That is to say, the long walls on each side are of suitably Toulouse-Lautrec scarlet, and the aperitif posters on them are unmistakably French, but the rear wall (gray glass looking out on a gray backyard cityscape), and the floor (dark-gray carpeting), and the ceiling (a sound-baffling mid-tech geometric arrangement of painted boards) look like the unmade-up parts of a room on which the camera will not focus anyway. The effect is, how you say, transient, unpersuasive. You think of La Goulue on East 70th Street, or, in a completely different bistro vein, of Le Relais on Madison Avenue, and you know how shoestring is this version of the genre.

Still, the cost of converting the gray box that was Manhattan Market into the red one that is Chez Louis must be picked up, and so even the prices here scorn bistro precon-ceptions. You are exacted, for example, $5.95 for this admittedly well-made little bowl of customary onion soup, its broth, based on a deep stock, thick with onions that have been sweetened and darkened by slow cooking—and though the melted cheese that seals the contents in their vessel is not of notable flavor, its pulliness is a nice textural note in the steamy context. But the snails (in shells, in dents, in a snail plate), though plump and tender, have not enough flavor of their own to get away with this greened but timidly seasoned butter. You get a giant sheaf of warm, fresh asparagus, the stalks peeled to their tender white cores, with a pitcher of warm chervil vinaigrette that lacks nothing except sparkle. The terrine of foie gras is a couple of cool slices cut from a loaf, a thickness of duck fat along an edge, the tight-packed morsels of rich liver sweet, pinguid, and in good contrast to the toasted slices of warm, eggy brioche with which they are served. What are given as "roast wild mushrooms" are about a dozen fresh shiitakes, whole cloves of garlic among them, the two blackened, hot, and knee-deep in their herbed butter.

You order it (the seafood salad) because you are surprised to find it on this menu, and you regret it, because (a) the cool ingredients—plump sea scallops, sweet mussels, shrimp, the tail of a tiny lobster—though in no way off, have lost their liveliness during the time between their preparation and their consumption, and because (b) their herbed dressing, of good oil, lacks the tanginess that could bring the elements to life. But the grilled salmon is fine, the great side of pink meat, moist under its black-striped top, spread with a piquant sauce of pommery mustard. You order the roast chicken for two, and the two of you are brought a bird that is so fetching in its browned, glistening skin, that is so fragrant of the garlic with which it has been roasted, and that is so small, that each of you (just for a brief, instinctual moment, you understand) resents the presence of the other—moreover, the scrawniness presages a certain thinness of chicken flavor, though the bird is carefully prepared, juicy but cooked through. Much is made of show-ing you what you are presently to eat, and your waiter, as he holds your veal chop in its pan under your nose (before it is taken away and magically transferred to a plate), confides, clearly feeling stupid, "We're supposed to show it to you first." When it returns, unchanged in its new surroundings, you find that the eye of meat, browned and herbed and very handsome at the end of its long bone, is not exactly the plump thing, bursting with moisture, that is a veal chop done to the moment. The chop, garnished with a clump of warm, garlicked watercress, comes also with some of the roasted vegetables that are otherwise available à la carte—a crunchy beet that is metallic and sweet within the blackened skin you peel away, an earthy turnip, cloves of garlic, a single tender carrot (unfortunately cold); comes also with a small version of the potato pie that is served in a double portion with that chicken: The crusty exterior is strewn with chopped raw garlic, and though the interior of the small pie is an abundance of firm little slices of vivid potato flavor, the big one is just mush within its skin. The roast lamb is listed as being served only for two, but your waiter allows as how late at night there is sometimes a rack available for one, and asks how you want it. You want it medium rare. Waiter returns with the nonsense he has been fed, that racks of baby lamb must be cooked to medium if they are to be cooked through at all, when, clearly, the facts are that the lamb has already been roasted, that the house is accepting small orders to facilitate selling off the roast before the end of the night. You get lots of these tender, strong flavored but bloodless little chops, and they are in a slick, blackened coat (which could have been achieved only by long exposure to heat)—the good roasting juices are salty and blood-strong.

Some decent Roquefort may be had with the excellent house bread—it is sour and chewy within its crunchy crust. Cherries, berries, gooseberries, grapes, and other fruits, depending on the season, may be had singly or mixed, with rich whipped cream. The unfortunately titled "chocolate sweetness cake" is a holdover from the Market—it is flourless and of a chocolate intensity exceeded only by that of the black, sticky icing with which it is surfaced.

★ CHEZ PIERRE

170 Waverly Place (at Grove Street)
LUNCH, SATURDAY AND SUNDAY; DINNER, DAILY.
Reservations: 929-7194.
No credit cards.
Medium priced.

A two-small-room corner store with, when the weather is fine, sidewalk tables outside under the red awnings. The eight back-room tables are in a space you would find ample for a sink, WC and stall shower. Of course the tables are small—eating at one is like eating off an upended orange crate—and in certain parts of the room, what with the jigsaw-puzzle furniture arrangement, the cooperation of your neighbors is essential when you must leave your place. In the comparatively wide-open space of the front room, there is actually an ample round table beside the Waverly Place window, with an excellent view of the Northern Dispensary (founded 1827). In the Grove Street window there are flowerpots and bottles of wine, and in the room itself, between an ancient wood floor and a stamped-tin ceiling, the walls are hung with old mirrors, an antique thermometer, and posters—Paris, the Statue of Liberty—including one that obscures all but a thin opening at the bottom of the interior window through which food is passed from the closet-size kitchen to the dining room. There is a rack in one corner, with hangers for coats—it will not hold many in goosedown season. Plain wood chairs surround the white-linened tables, and the place is frequented by types to whom eating in restaurants is not a diversion, but a practical matter—foreign accents and languages are often heard here. The help is never far away, and the absence of pretension yields more comfort than the rather functional appointments take away, against which you must weigh the danger that, when you visit, you will be beset by Edith Piaf, in the background, enumerating her difficulties.

More than in most places, here it is good to know what the house does well, for the lesser dishes—the cold and coarse pâté and, when it is offered, a flat fish mousse—are no clue at all to what the better ones are like: big tender snails in the mild but well-seasoned and heavily parsleyed butter; an abundant salad of crunchy walnuts and crisp endive in a tart and thickened vinaigrette; another salad, this one of fresh romaine, red cabbage, and tomatoes in a brisk red-vinegar dressing—it is served with crusts of bread that have been spread with strong goat cheese. Pass up the roast pork (its tangy mustard sauce fails to rouse it), and do not expect much from the rump steak, a knob of red meat, short on blood-juiciness, that is only as exciting as the black pepper with which it is coated. Opt instead for the poulet chasseur, much good chicken, with mushrooms, in a spicy red sauce; or, when it is offered, the osso buco, the tender and steamy veal moist and lean and peppery—the thing is surrounded by white rice that is dotted with onions and red peppers, and you get the marrow out of the bone by using the other end of your fork; or for one of the fish dishes of the day—one time snapper in a white sauce thick with capers, another time blackfish of such sweet flavor that, happily, it is moistened with nothing but the butter in which it was done.

The desserts are what you expect—eggy crème caramel, rich chocolate cake, and a tarte Tatin notable for apples that, though caramelized, reveal much of their tartness.

• CHIN CHIN

216 East 49th Street
LUNCH, MONDAY TO FRIDAY; DINNER, DAILY.
Reservations: 888-4555.
Credit cards: AE, DC, MC, V.
Inexpensive.

Someone started to build a steakhouse, maybe an across-the-street branch of Smith & Wollensky lacking only a footbridge to that many-chambered beef pavilion, then switched culinary gears—for with its straight lines, wood lower walls, benchlike oxblood banquettes, this is for guys, right down to the waiters, in their black vests over long-sleeved white shirts, white aprons to the ankle. There is even a clubby little room off the bar, like rooms that, in beef-and-potato establishments of yore (and not so yore), used to be set aside for what were coyly referred to as private family gatherings. There is even a row, all around the room, of framed photos that, in a steakhouse, would be glossy black-and-whites of ballplayers and/or movie stars and/or pols, and/or pugs and/or Frank Sinatra. Here they are faded sepia-tinted Chinese family pictures of, at a guess, 60 years ago, none of them taken on these premises, none of them signed, Your pal, with best wishes to the proprietor. Only the few-steps-down rearmost dining room—rows of tables and chairs, Chinese vases in wall niches—suggests unambiguously Chin Chin's Orientality.

As you are served pickles in certain steakhouses, you are served picklings here, a bowl of bean sprouts that, as in any context, taste like string, and a bowl of vegetables, sometimes mostly cauliflower livened with sprigs of coriander, sometimes green beans with strands of red onion, both in rousing hot-spiced sesame marinades. Thereafter you are at the mercy of the menu, though it is no one's responsibility but your own if, despite the description, you go for the thousand-year-old (give or take) eggs. Shelled, quartered, and dusky moss green, they have the flavor of egg yolks mixed with flour and ammonia and a texture you have avoided since you grew teeth—you reward yourself for every unbelieving mouthful with either a pickled shallot or a leaf of fresh ginger, the bright garnishes that redeem a little this familiar Chinese prison staple. The shredded roast duck salad is one of those dishes in which the Chinese reveal their talent for assembling ingredients that neutralize one another—the huge mound of duck and tomatoes and shredded leaves has the flavor of nothing but its cool, vaguely sour dressing. But there is real food here. Whatever the snails were done in, they emerge tasting like salted potted meat, which is not to say they are bad, and they reach you in a garlicky broth that is thick with coriander. But the so-called crispy fried squid tastes like boardwalk food, and the cold chicken soong—packed into pockets carved out of sides of wet iceberg lettuce —is a lot of noodles and a little chicken in a nutted and sugary sauce that is of an insipidity. The first course winner is the vegetable duck pie, mock Peking duck, a vegetable composition that, if it does not taste like duck, is a lively, crackling imitation—your waiter wraps it in pancakes, with a length of cucumber, another of scallion, and a thick, dark plum sauce. As at most contemporary steakhouses, one section of the menu is headed "pasta," albeit even at Smith & Wollensky you cannot always get your very favorite noodle dish. So when you are across the street and get a certain craving, phone Chin Chin for prompt delivery of some crispy pan-fried egg noodles, a garlicky dish in which the great farinaceous tangles are part crispy, part straight al dente, in among them slices of mushroom and slivers of pork, crunchy shrimp that are heady of iodine, emerald-green snowpeas, and more, all the elements of this complexity of clear, if not always good, flavor.

Encouraged by the salmon in black bean sauce—the large fillet of fresh, juicy fish under strands of red and green pepper, and in a broth that is thick with the strong, pleasantly gritty beans—you try the clams in black bean sauce, and the mollusks, leathery in their shells, arrive in a sauce that is little more than thickened, darkened, salted water. The country style chicken is treacly, the red peppers that are in evidence add little fire, though you find no fault with the spinach on which the chunks of fried bird are set. Of the sautéed leg of lamb with leeks it may be said that the lamb flavor is clear, of the crisped orange beef that the marmalade flavor is clear.

Chin Chin offers for dessert ice cream, fruit, a Mandarin rarity called sorbet. You need a beverage that will, how you say, cut this food—saké or whiskey will do.

★★CHRIST CELLA

160 East 46th Street
LUNCH, MONDAY TO FRIDAY; DINNER, MONDAY TO SATURDAY. CLOSED SUNDAY.
Reservations: 697-2479.
Credit cards: AE, DC, MC, V.
Very expensive.

Considering the kind of gross feeding that goes on in this place, its properness is at least odd. Guys wash behind the ears, comb their hair wet, and put on a dark-blue suit to come here and sit themselves down to a lobster the size of a Bedlington terrier. While eating with, at the very best, both hands, they are being tended to by well-trained gentlemen who by their administration of very serious intensive care seem to transform

131

this well-organized gluttony into a solemn pursuit. When you are first seated, one of these white-aproned officials arrives at tableside to recite, with admirable if not perfect completeness, the menu (there is no printed one). He returns later wheeling a serving stand laden with food and paraphernalia. The more senior of the Christ Cella waiters are at ease, their once carefully learned politeness now second nature. The younger members of the staff are less than at home with their schooled demeanor, and sometimes they seethe a little as they respond to your inquiries—with answers that might be taken for short if they were not complete. However, when asked "What's good?" the old and young alike preface their responses with the same aperçu: "This is the best steakhouse in New York," it goes, uttered, always, with a gravity that would be entirely appropriate for the divulgence of a medical diagnosis.

The formalities begin when you arrive and are greeted by an accountant type in one of those dark suits, white shirt, necktie, and 1940 haircut. Though he flashes a bit of camaraderie with people he knows—a thin smile, a clutched shoulder—with most he is very much the church usher, first peering through his Franklin glasses at the book, and then indicating the way with a nod of the head and a half gesture of the hand. If he does not know you, and if you have not made specific arrangements to the contrary, he will probably point you upstairs to the second floor, where are housed the two bleakest of this restaurant's solid, comfortable, but far-from-lovely dining rooms. The upper deck has been gussied up in recent years with grass-paper walls and pale, pleated drapes on the big front window—still, the gloomy seascapes that look out over the spread of well-spaced tables on the old wood floor seem to reflect rather than offset the spartanness of the surroundings.

The five rooms downstairs are smaller, cozier, clubbier. One is the barroom, in which two of the wood-paneled walls are adorned with the front end of one antelope each. One of them is mounted sideways (he is in position to peer *along* his wall), with one shoulder intact—a triumph of the stuffer's art. To the stand-up bar, baskets of hot, crisp-fried matchstick potatoes are delivered from time to time, to help the lined-up gents wash down their drinks. The three barroom tables are choice ones, but they are usually not used on slow nights. The ivory-colored walls of the other downstairs rooms have had a pattern of blue-green squiggles applied by means of an embossed paint roller—the kind of beautification usually found only in apartment-house hallways. The brightly lighted and somewhat turbulent wide-open kitchen abuts on one of these dining rooms—just inside it is that famous single, large table that is available to customers who, perhaps nostalgic for simpler times, enjoy eating in the kitchen. Wherever you sit, you are surrounded by at least 80 percent guys (the spectrum is from successful used-car dealer to successful non-corporate-law lawyer) and 20 percent dolls (the spectrum is from girl-friend to wife). Once in a while you will see a female executive here, in among a gang of male managers of equal rank. The lady's two-piece suit seems designed to get her lost in this crowd, and in fact she does seem lost—somewhere between the genders. Almost all the time everybody in the place is not a feminist.

And *almost* everybody in the place, at one time or another, gets the Caesar salad, a copious mound of crunchy romaine lettuce and crusty croutons in a clinging, egg-thick-ened dressing that is sharpened with anchovy, made fragrant with garlic. A lighter thing is the spinach salad: broad, deep-green leaves of the fresh raw vegetable dotted with chunks of bacon and moistened with a good, tart—almost sour—vinaigrette. The shrimp in the shrimp cocktail are sometimes tasteless, but they are not tainted with iodine. If you must start with shellfish, the crabmeat and lobster cocktails are the only way to go: abundant amounts of cool, fresh, and sweet meat, served with a standard—but very strong and sparkling—cocktail sauce.

Several varieties of finfish are usually on hand, and you get big sides of such as snapper and striped bass. They are almost always moist, fresh, of clear flavor within their darkened surfaces—sometimes, alas, they are a little overcooked. An order of scallops is several score of the plump, rich little morsels, lightly floured and browned. Of course, all this time you have just been doing lobster avoidance. Christ Cella sells large lobsters, very large lobsters, and lobsters that will serve for two or three of you—though you see fellows here dispatching these giants solo. The lobsters are usually perfectly broiled— now and again one is overdone. While you are extracting the big, supple length of ocean-sweet meat from the red carapace, your waiter—at his serving stand beside your table—is extracting the meat from the claws and arranging it for you on a second plate.

As all the world knows, New York steakhouse beef is now only sometimes what it once was. But Christ Cella seems to serve what once was more often than does any of its rivals. You get sirloins that are fibrous, tender, and with that distinctive beef flavor in which succulence and mineral sharpness are combined. At their best, the filets mignons are firm, tender, and velvety—never mushy, as this cut of beef elsewhere often is. The roast beef is good too, the big rib at least an inch thick and tasty. It is a sign of the intelligence that informs this place that though you are asked how you would like your red meat cooked you are not asked that if you are having veal chops, for there is only one right degree of doneness for veal chops, and you usually get your two big ones done that way here—they are bloodless but still juicy, pink but not red. The batter-fried onions are an immense pile of thin strips, crinkly and sweet. The hashed browns are a giant pancake about the dimensions of a professional Frisbee—it is deeply browned, blackened in places, the chunks of good potato firm under the crusty top.

Now the dessert cart is wheeled by, on it three monuments: a slab of cheesecake, a slab of rum cake, a slab of napoleon. The last two are inelegant sweets—and so is the cheesecake, but it is a perfect example of a certain kind of rich, creamy, sugary, lightly lemoned combination of airiness and weight that is integral to a place like this.

★★CINCO DE MAYO

349 West Broadway (near Broome Street)
LUNCH AND DINNER.
Reservations: 226-5255.
Credit cards: AE, DC, MC, V.
Inexpensive.

You enter to a mildly raucous bar, a row of tables across the aisle. If you do not get seated here, you are conducted through the kitchen to the big dining room beyond, which consists of an orchestra and a balcony—there is even a kind of stage, where, when he is not performing in the front room, the Mexican harpist positions himself, passionately plinks, and, sometimes, wails. (It sounds very native, but attention reveals that some of his tunes—though not his style—are contemporary gringo.) When the harpist is performing out front, the jukebox thumps in the back, and when he is working the back, etc. Depending on where you are, your surroundings may consist of rough plaster painted pink, bare brick, whitewashed brick. There may be pipes and conduits crisscrossing the ceiling. You will be within loud shouting distance of lots of tropical plants. The place is lighted by factory lights, track lights, candles. The constant din is dense enough to render harmless the sound of a load of dishes being dropped into a waiting tub. The tables are packed with young people, the aisles with young waiters and waitresses. Sometimes, unpredictably, everyone applauds the harpist. Naturally, he seems surprised, and a brilliant smile radiates from his dark, flat Indian face.

No sooner are you seated than you are brought a basket of chips and a dish of exceptional green sauce—it is not especially hot, as these things go, but hot enough, and it is fresh, polished, heady with cilantro. (Refills cheerfully provided.) Your ceviche comes in a glass, chunks of lime-cured fish buried in a cold, thick, and citrus-sour red sauce. The guacamole is served as "guacamole treat," and many regulars here start their dinners by sharing one of these big bowls (formed of fried tortilla) of about a pint of the avocado mash—its texture is distressingly sticky, but that is offset by its good avocado flavor and by the bits of moist tomato and strong onion with which the paste is dotted. Taquitos de moronga are tortilla tubes filled with bits of blood pudding, leaves of cilantro, raw onions—you pick up the warm bundles with your fingers, and like much of the food here, they are good with beer. The tortilla soup is a nice enough tomato-reddened broth, many slivers of tortilla in it—you add mild grated cheese, and that makes the simple stuff substantial, though not fascinating.

The menu lists two specials for each day of the week. Come on Wednesday, and you may have mejilliones à la Mexicana, a huge glass bowl of fresh mussels—sweet, tender, not claylike—in their shells, mounded up over the hot broth they were steamed in, garnished with redded rice, and served with a short stack of hot tortillas that come wrapped in tinfoil. Any day of the week you may have the alambres à la Mexicana, crisp marinated shrimp that have been grilled with onions, tomatoes, and violently hot green peppers—the dish is served with seasoned rice, of which you will need all, at once, if you bite into one of those jalapeños as if it were an apple. The budin de tortilla is weighty, utterly satisfying, a triangle cut from a great pie of alternating layers of chicken, cornmeal pancakes, and a top layer of melted cheese—you get a pitcher of hot green sauce which is a good foil to the solid dish. The tripe stew (menudo norteno) is a million slivers of the pale, tender, gummy innard and an equal number of white beans, all in a salty and red-peppery broth—you may add chopped onions and/or dried oregano and/or lime juice (three slices of lime are supplied) to modify the hot stuff according to your temperament.

What is called Kahlúa mousse is a fluffy and obvious thing of whipped cream and the liqueur under chocolate shavings. There is flan and little else.

All the familiar Mexican beers are here, and also Negra Modelo, an especially well-balanced dark beer that is at once malty, creamy, and refreshing.

★ LE CIRQUE

58 East 65th Street
LUNCH AND DINNER. CLOSED SUNDAY.
Reservations: 794-9292.
Credit cards: AE, DC.
Very expensive.

Mindful that the privilege of dinner at Le Cirque is not easily earned, you telephone some weeks in advance to reserve a table at 8, or, if that more suits the house, 8:30—even 7:30—some hour that, in the pattern of New York life, is feasible and comfortable. You have identified yourself by a homely name, have mentioned no affiliation, are informed that, on the dates you propose, you may dine either at 6 or at 9:45. You suggest dates weeks later. On those dates, presumably by remarkable coincidence, only 6 is available or, if that is not suitable, 9:45. You begin to mention dates later still, but are interrupted. Though the gentleman with whom you are dealing quite democratically expresses no opinion as to what you should do with your time, he clearly abhors wasting his own. "The date," he carefully explains, "does not matter. You may have a table at 6 or at 9:45." The problem is solved, of course, when, a day later, another voice identifies itself as that of an executive of a major outlet of news and opinion, which voice readily arranges for tables on the very dates and at the very hours you originally proposed. The respect with which you are treated when you, instead, show up is clearly bemused, for, in the event, you look like an ordinary shlub. Sirio Maccioni (proprietor here) smiles at you, sure enough, but in the manner of one who longs for—even, self pityingly, regrets the loss of—a society in which class distinctions are clear and binding. Poor Sirio—with his slicked-down hair and accidental face, in his surely hand-tailored but too tight suit—is not aware that, though the moneyed and powerful are his clientele today, in any reverse revolution, he and they will be separated at the first cut.

It is always somewhat dismaying to enter this fabled place, for no sooner are you in the door than you are upon a table (nary a square inch of Le Cirque's real estate is nonproductive) seated at which, and well within the territory of the front-door traffic, are three or four of the most monumentally downcast faces anywhere above the level of the starving. They came for grandeur, dreamed of seeing a show of pols and party givers, maybe even folks up on felony counts, and, instead, here they are in the theater lobby. They will, in effect, eat, leave, and not have been to Le Cirque. They are unaware that theirs is among the most commodious accommodations in the house, for with respect to the dining room proper, no other in New York, at any price, is more densely tabled and chaired. There are sites at which four tables can share an ice bucket, and each table's wine is within easy reach. The waiters and captains quite by reflex stretch their bodies thin to move about, and regular customers have learned routes to the facilities that, though circuitous, bypass the most thickly obstacled terrain. With respect to the appointments, the framed panels of latticework wallpaper are occupied, as ever, by monkeys engaged in human pursuits, the square columns are mirrored, the deep-rose banquettes match both the chemises on the backs of the chairs and the short skirts on the seats, from under each of which protrude four skinny white fluted period legs. There are flowers on the white-linened tables, and the sconces on the walls, you judge by Sirio's tie, must have been chosen by himself—they are made up of clusters of thin black arms that thrust into the room glowing lights that amount to frowning gargoyles of floral configuration. Half the ladies are in pearl chokers, many a long-sleeved black dress is adorned by mink at the cuffs. Gentlemen are close-tonsured and (by meal's end) flushed over their tight white collars—you see among them liver-spotted sybarites, their noses inches from their plates, shoveling north the fettuccine. Le Cirque's best dressers are in black and white and work the floor, and these days the service is positively human. A captain compliments you on your French; you counter by pointing out that his English is better than Sirio's; he shrugs, so much as to say, "Whose isn't?" With time, it seems, the staff has learned to laugh off Maccioni's way of snapping his fingers and grandly pointing (as a conqueror to distant lands), to underscore a peremptory command.

Why is Sirio not instead pointing out that this marinated tuna ought to be left in its marinade long enough to flavor it and maybe make it tender, for the thick-cut sheet of fish is resilient and lacks seafood—or any other—character, though it is cleverly served over a crunchy mash of tart sorrel. Much more itself is this peasanty terrine of beef shanks and leeks, the thick square, cut from a loaf, a mosaic of the dark, tender, deep-flavored, fibrous meat, which is studded with short lengths of pale-green leek—you moisten the sturdy stuff with a sharp and creamy horseradish sauce. A place like this would not be a place like this without foie gras, and it is usually listed among the daily specials, the pan-sautéed oleaginous meat served, oddly, with a salad of young greens, and, sometimes, with sections of citrus fruit—the garnishes are nifty foils to the extraordinarily rich, browned liver. Never mind that Le Cirque is a French restaurant, Sirio is Italian, and these days he consoles himself for the loss of his former French chef, Alain Sailhac, by listing more than just a token number of Italian dishes—presumably the current Frenchman in the kitchen, Daniel Boulud, has fewer veto rights than his predecessor. Anyway, in black and white are listed fettuccine with truffles—even the truffles are black and (or) white, according to the season—and these are wondrous, eggy noodles, their sauce creamy and cheesy, and when the truffles are black, your captain scrapes the big, dark flakes until you yawn—they flatter, but add only a dim note of nuttiness to the good dish.

Of course you should laugh off simply by virtue of its name the "Homard de Maine au Curry," which may be not so loosely translated as "lobster in college sauce," the sort of thing you made in your school days with any suitable or unsuitable solid protein, curry powder, and any suitable or unsuitable liquid, for example milk—the mound of lobster meat at the center of your plate, every ounce of sustenance to be found in, at a guess, a six-ounce crustacean, tough despite its youth, encircled by little balls of fruit, and seated in a sauce the color of sulfur. Less depressing is the Dover sole, the nicely floured and sautéed fillets browned and moist, overlaid with skinned sections of orange, grapefruit, lime—the fruit is in nice contrast to the heavily salted fish. The lamb stew would be better were the meat better butchered, for instead of the great nuggets of tender, fibrous lamb you hope for, you get misshapen chunks threaded with cartilage—still, the sauce is complex and fragrantly herbed, and the vegetables and elbow macaroni with which the meat is garnished make of the item a lively dish. Italian food to the rescue, the osso buco that, from time to time, appears on this menu, M. Boulud reduced to, but apparently stimulated by, alien responsibilities, the great knuckle of spicy veal tender and juicy on its hefty bone, in which, when you poke about, you find much rich marrow—the veal is in a deep, meaty, onion-sweet sauce that, though livened with tomato, is far from a mere tomato sauce, and it is garnished with fresh noodles and root vegetables.

From among the pastries you do well to select, when it is on hand, the pithiviers, the tart of puff pastry and ground almonds that, when well made, as here, is a dessert that, by its airiness and sweetness ends a weighty dinner lightly. The crème brûlée is good, the fluffy custard under a crackling caramel top. The circular apple tart—skinlike leaves of apple on a skinlike pastry, a ping pong ball of vanilla ice cream at the center—may be admired for its subtlety. The chocolate soufflé (for two) reaches you dry, devoid of chocolate character, in much need of the sugared whipped cream served with it.

★★CLAIRE

156 Seventh Avenue (near 19th Street)
LUNCH AND DINNER.
Reservations: 255-1955.
Credit cards: AE, MC, V.
Medium priced.

There is an eating place in Key West called Claire, and this one derives from that one. The Floridian isle's remote situation—it is the southernmost point of the continental United States, connected only by a causeway to the rest of the world—probably accounts for the community's independent style of culinary development. If Claire's menu fairly represents Key cooking, it may be concluded that the islanders subsist largely on what may be fished from the waters around them. The look of this restaurant suggests that they like to take their catch out of the tropical heat into a cool, dark place to eat it.

This cool, dark place is a couple of stories high, big, two-roomed. Up front is the bar (with an armrest of glossy python skin), under an overhang on which rests a collection of pottery perhaps meant to suggest the fruits of undersea salvage operations in the once pirate-infested waters around the keys. A big trelliswork panel—with built-in, slowly spinning four-bladed fans—lowers the ceiling in this part of the place. More trelliswork separates the front from the back room, in which—in season—three tall palm trees reach to three skylights overhead. Throughout, beams from track lights pierce the dusky atmosphere. The tabletops are covered with gleaming pastel oilcloth and broad criss-crossed bands of white butcher paper. At them are seated, mostly, gentlemen of exceptional neatness, trimness, cleanliness, and posture. The self-conscious among you are invited to come here and feel like a frump. Actually, there are always on hand enough lumpy nuclear-family types for anyone not to feel out of place.

The regulars keep their figures eating the like of these Chincoteague Bay oysters. They are opened to order, are fresh and sparkling. The seviche of tuna is fresh, raw red fish, "cooked" by the acidic lime-juice marinade in which it is served with dill and capers. Claire turns out a good gravlax, the supple cured salmon heady of its dill flavor, served with a rich mustard sauce. And it produces an exceptional squid salad, the slivers and circles of pale, tender seafood in a cool but fiery olive-oil dressing. You get well-chosen mussels here, a rarity these days in New York. They are in their shells, mingled with strands of sharp red onion, and mounded up over the hot broth—of white wine flavored with garlic, herbs, lemon—in which they were steamed. For some reason there is Thai beef salad on this menu, and though some purist somewhere can probably prove that it is no good because it varies from the Oriental recipe, it is nevertheless one of the best in town. But you have to be able to take it, for the warm ground meat and the chopped onions and scallions with which it is mixed are in a spiced lemon dressing that can be numbing if eaten greedily. The Bahamian conch chowder is thick soup, peppery, with a nutlike flavor, laden with conch meat.

Claire is yet another restaurant that essays the New Orleans dish called blackened fish. In this version the panfried fillets reach you with an especially spicy crust—the fish within is said to be redfish, is utterly fresh, falls into tender flakes. One kind of shark or another is usually on the menu, sometimes black-tip shark. This is not the world's tastiest swimmer, but its preparation—it is sautéed with dill, sherry, and mushrooms—turns it into a plate of more than decent food. River catfish is presumably not found in the ocean around the keys, but Claire manages to obtain some anyway—the skinned and boned fish is breaded and fried in a pan, and its delicacy and moistness are startling when you encounter them within the hot, brittle, and greaseless crust. Norwegian salmon is also foreign to the Gulf of Mexico, but this place has figured the species out. The hefty slab of pink fish is broiled to the perfect point, dressed with a light cucumber-and-dill sauce —a superb dish. Tiny bay scallops are served here, lightly floured and sautéed until the surfaces of the plump little morsels are delicately browned and crisp—the scallops reach you in a gentle sauce of butter, white wine, a bit of lemon. Claire often combines meat and fish. It sautés shrimp and chunks of beef with hot peppers and sweet peppers, onions and fresh basil, and creates a dish in which the complexity of flavors is as vivid as its color scheme. With less success, it serves broiled tilefish under crisped strands of ham, with chopped scallions and walnuts—this is well made, but tilefish can be pallid, and the other ingredients do not rescue it.

Though mainly a seafood house, Claire consistently turns out some of the best filets mignons around. As thousands of cookbooks say, but as few restaurants do, these little steaks are rimmed with bacon before they are broiled, which imparts all the flavor the tender meat needs—the beef reaches you with the bacon in place, under a big mushroom cap.

As you surely guessed, there is key lime pie. The citrus flavor of its pale chiffon is vivid, lovely against the graham cracker crust. You wish that the whipped cream with which it is served did not on occasion do this excellent imitation of cream "whipped" by a blowing machine. Something called chocolate chambord is a splendid black layer cake soaked in raspberry liqueur. Chocolate and booze come together yet again in the Mississippi mud cake, in which the cake—of strong chocolate flavor and genuinely mudlike weight and texture—is served in a pool of approximately 60-proof buttered whiskey. The pecan pie is dark, spicy, and rich, topped with crunchy pecans—good with whipped cream when the whipped cream is good. The chocolate walnut pie is sticky, its pastry doughy. The cheesecake is of cream cheese, but it is light.

This is a busy place, but arrive even when there are a dozen empty tables and you may well be asked—quite officiously—to have a drink at the bar before you are seated. The menu informs you that what it refers to as "waitwomen" and "waitmen" are in shirts by J. G. Hook, Inc.

• COACH HOUSE

110 Waverly Place (near Sixth Avenue)
DINNER. CLOSED MONDAY.
Reservations: 777-0303.
Credit cards: AE, DC, MC, V.
Expensive.

Nothing about this restaurant is as remarkable as its reputation. To find something similar, you must go to the great books, the ones nobody reads. Wander through the place of an evening, consider those present, and you will understand at once why this reliquary of Institutional Cuisine, though open to the public, remains almost exempt from any threat of ordinary human assessment. The restaurant is attended principally by the very folks who, in the ritualistic course of their lives, sit through Philharmonic concerts, church sermons, political eulogies, and commencement addresses in states of blank, contented reverence. They do not attend for the message, of course, but for the occasion. And they come to the Coach House for the occasion. They would no more judge this place than they would their own goodness, for the Coach House is truly loved. But it is not loved in the way that, say, a lover is loved. Rather, it is loved forever and unquestioningly, like money.

You arrive to a sign outside, RESERVATIONS ONLY, JACKET AND TIE REQUIRED. This is presumably meant to keep the riffraff out, for Mr. Leon Lianides himself, the proprietor, has been seen seated with the bare necked. As to the reservation "requirement," if you look like you can pay your way, and there is a table, it is yours. You enter to Lianides, a grim presence, who receives you more or less the way the warden receives the recidivist. He looks you up in his book, waves you on your way. Next step is a large lady whose job it is to decide the kind of table you deserve—she transfers you to an escort, to whom she has whispered instructions. He leads you to a table for two that would be fine for sandwiches and coffee but that seems skimpy when you are about to drop $100. You ask for something large, point out a larger, untenanted table that is just like those occupied by other couples. No dice. You settle for something upstairs, in the so-called Hayloft (Siberia), where a table for two is of human proportions. Later, you walk downstairs to see what has become of the table you wanted. It is occupied by two gentlemen only, fellows of more apparent substance than yourself, while what you rejected remains in disuse.

Actually, the upstairs is the more commodious of this restaurant's two dining rooms. The tables have space between them, and the traffic is light. The brown walls are hung with painterly paintings, the ceiling is beamed, and the great, airy, long-limbed chandeliers hang low, within reach of a tall man's antennae. Similar ceiling fixtures illuminate the lower level, a considerably larger high-ceilinged room that glows with the Colonial *Gemütlichkeit* that, to the enduring contentment of Coach House partisans, sets the place apart from the trendy and/or funky and/or foreign restaurants that are 99 percent of this ostensibly American one's local competition. This room glitters with a kind of year-round holiday festiveness, which is the sum of its wood paneling and exposed bricks, beamed ceiling and red carpeting, hunting scenes and still lifes all about in handsome frames. The table linen is pink, and it is set with fresh flowers and cherry-colored napkins.

If you are given a table upstairs, you may very well get seated and nothing else. After a while you must seek out the help—you find them around the corner, arms folded, chatting. Sometimes the house offers one or two special dishes of the day—if you do not ask about them, you may not find out about them. Order a bottle of California Chardonnay (from among the many on the list), and your captain upstairs does not listen to your order, but returns with three or four Chardonnays and word that "these are the ones we have." Downstairs the courtesies are better observed, but in either location the waiters tend to be bizarrely matched to their responsibilities. There are a couple who understand English no better than they speak it, and one who chews gum (or something) throughout dinner, demands your order in the manner of a district attorney, and carries his hands in the position of the forepaws of a dog walking on his hind legs.

Which is not to say that you cannot eat well here. There are the raw oysters, for example, which are opened to order, are cool, sweet, and briny, and come with a standard cocktail sauce. But the smoked turkey seems to have been frozen (or close to it) and thawed, for the pink slices are not so much moist as wet, their smoky flavor is vague, their garnish of horseradish and cream the only life of the dish. Of the hot appetizers the shrimp are the clear winner. You get five big ones in a pool of dark, rich sauce, the former crunchy and of vivid—albeit iodine-tinged—flavor, the latter dominated by good mustard. For years the Coach House has offered its special baked-clam appetizer for two, and during all that time it has never mastered the knack of heating clams without toughening them. Moreover, though these are good, fresh littlenecks, their buttery, heavily seasoned herb sauce is too indelicate for their gentle flavor. Among edible snails there are big, plump, tender ones, and there are little leathery ones. Here you get both kinds in a very green so-called garlic butter that would not sully a baby's breath. These days the famous black bean soup is the best it has ever been—thick, winy, sharply seasoned, dotted with chopped egg, a slice of parsleyed lemon on top.

You are shown the whole roasted bass (for two), and then it is boned and served to you not in its promised dill sauce but in butter and lemon, with chopped dill and parsley strewn over the fish—this is perfectly good food, fresh and not overcooked, but not what the menu leads you to expect. The house sautés big lumps of crabmeat with strands of ham and serves them in lemon and butter—the seafood is first-rate stuff, fresh and sweet, but these days the ham is coarse and salty, so the subtle interplay of the two principal ingredients is lost. The presence of chicken pie on this establishment's menu accounts in part for its reputation for being American. This dish is precisely the chicken in glue you remember from your high school cafeteria, here served over a shingle of tasteless baked dough. The mignonnettes of veal have the dead flavor of something warmed over; they are served with mushrooms that also seem reheated, and with meaty chestnuts. Sometimes the rack of lamb is fine—simple, tender, juicy, accurately prepared, of good flavor. But not infrequently it reaches you incinerated, its exterior like the surface of a marshmallow left too long in the fire. The roast beef gets a place of honor in a box near the center of the menu—the slab of meat is thick, pink, picturesque, has everything but beefiness. The sirloin steak, because it is not well seared, loses much of its blood-juiciness even when cooked only to medium rare. With these treats the restaurant serves good potatoes (baked, sautéed), or carrots so overcooked that a sharp glance turns them to puree, or spinach so plain it seems naked—eating it is much like eating grass.

The Coach House has served Stilton that is not only ripe but senile, having deteriorated into a loud, brown paste. But the chocolate cake—a rich mousse between crusts that are almost black—has a good, intense chocolate flavor. The hot-fudge ice-cream cake is lightly lemoned sponge cake, deeply flavored vanilla ice cream, and warm, thick chocolate fudge—a good adult sundae, which is not to carp. What is called the chef's custard is a kind of bread pudding with a bright raspberry sauce. The apple tart is prettily golden brown and conventionally sweet-spiced—the apples, however, are mushy. The dacquoise—nutted layers of meringue and mocha cream—is good when you get it fresh. But if you come just once, the dessert to have is the pecan pie, the only distinctively American dish the house turns out in an exceptional version: lots of nuts, and the brown-sugar filler has the wonderful complexity of aged, fruity mincemeat. The pie is served with superb whipped cream.

You have to look out for yourself at the Coach House. Order, say, oysters, roast beef with a baked potato, and—at the end of your dinner—chocolate cake, and you may pay $37. You could have paid $29, but when the waiter asks if you would like spinach or carrots with your roast beef, you are being lured over to the more expensive, dinner side of the menu, and you drop $8 for a dreary vegetable. Restaurants with both à la carte and prix fixe menus will usually try to find the cheapest way to charge you, but the Coach House has not perfected this nicety.

A few wines are $12, some are around $15, most are around $20 or higher—up to three figures—despite which you never know what you are getting until it arrives, for the list states no vintage years, and some of the red wines are far from ready.

★★LA COLOMBE D'OR

134 East 26th Street
LUNCH, MONDAY TO FRIDAY; DINNER, DAILY.
Reservations: 689-0666.
Credit cards: AE, DC, MC, V.
Medium priced.

Upon a time, when New York French food was a more-or-less stable commodity of maybe two or three complexions, this place was an oddity. It served neither standard New York bistro food nor standard New York fancy food. It was, rather, just about the only place, among many that so claimed, that produced a fairly convincing version of the cooking of one French region—Provence. It still does, but today the restaurant seems old fashioned, though there never was much of a fashion for restaurants like it. It seems that way, of course, because of how it looks (like an American restaurant trying to look French to Americans) and because of its menu (which, in all but a few dishes, reveals no influence of recent trends).

A Colombe d'Or predates this one, a meritorious restaurant of the name in Provence itself, but this New York borrowing is surely more a tribute than a token of emulation, for the real similarities end with the title. Which is not to suggest that this Dove—La Colombe d'Or is The Golden Dove—wants virtue, rather that if you have been to the original and wish to repeat the experience, you will have to return to France. You enter to a passageway that is hung with reviews and articles that have appeared in the local press, all laudatory and all suitably framed. The passage connects the restaurant's two dining rooms, which also house framed objects, these however works of art or, anyway, reproductions thereof—mostly Légers, including even Léger plates—which make reference to the genuine articles that hang in the establishment overseas. Their presence here does not, however, dominate, for at La Colombe d'Or the artifices of the French country look are in every stick, from the red-tile floor to the bare-brick walls, from the rough old plaster to the cans of wildflowers, from the rough-hewn wood counters to the printed cotton fabric of the banquettes, which is also the fabric of the cushions on the stick-and-straw chairs, also of the curtains on the windows. Here there is a bit of copper cooking-ware, there a string of garlic, elsewhere plaster figurines. The wood tables are bare (except for tan napkins that form diamonds at their centers), and you would happily forego this last rustic note for white linen. Even the help are part of the scene with their musical French accents.

Listed as carpaccio de thon, these thick slices of tuna, though raw at their centers, are browned along the edges, suggesting that they are cut from a large, lightly grilled chunk of fish—the supple pink meat is cool and fresh, and it is livened nicely by its sauce raifort, which is of rich whipped cream and sharp horseradish. So much for dishes you will *not* encounter in the south of France. But look there anywhere, and you will find pissaladière, a baked pastry that, in this version, is of bread dough topped with sautéed onions that have been fortified with anchovies and adorned with slivers of black olive— the dish is at once sweet of the onions, salty and spiced, and it is prettily garnished with a little mound of roasted red peppers. The salade de pois-chiche is an abundance of brown chickpeas mingled with slivers of good, fibrous ham, the two bound in a cold pesto sauce that is heady of fresh basil. The ratatouille is hot in winter, cold in summer, either way the eggplant-dominated vegetable stew is thoroughly oiled and aggressively seasoned, and the various vegetable components retain their separate flavors despite the strong treatment.

141

You are puzzling over your poulet aux olives—how, you wonder, can a chicken be so perfectly separated from chicken flavor?—when your chef wanders by and is collared by the innocents at the next table. They want to know where he gets his yummy chicken, and with such encouragement his confession becomes a proud assertion—from Frank Perdue, he avers, and with no further questioning goes on to explain in more detail than you hope to retain the feather-plucking superiority of a Perdue chicken factory (his word) to all others. (He is a perfectly nice young man, and his problem may well be that he does not remember, never having known, what chicken tastes like, for he is of the generation that prefers frozen juice to the pulpy stuff you squeeze out of orange-colored balls.) Any better bird, and this poulet aux olives would be a good dish, for the chicken is handsomely browned, and it is in a wondrously vibrant olive sauce that is thick with herbs. His salmon, however, is fine, the fillet of pale, rosy fish striped a handsome deep brown where the fresh, moist meat touched the hot grill—the salmon is served with a powerful mustard sauce and with new potatoes, in their skins, that, too bad, are soft. The pale sausages called boudin blanc are solid and just fatty enough in their charred and crackling casings—they come with a thick and enriched applesauce, a crusty potato tart, and with a ramekin of strong, grainy mustard. The big item here is bouillabaisse, and there are those who frequent La Colombe for this alone, a version notable especially for its garlicked, deeply fennel-flavored, and fragrantly saffroned broth. The production reaches you in an iron pan, the abundant seafood (a section of lobster, clams and sweet mussels in their shells, and much fish, all in good condition) piled high over the hot soup and overlaid with crusts of toasted bread, on one of them a garlic sauce of searing strength—you add it to the soup according to your taste. When you have gone through much of the dish, a great lidded bowl is brought to your table from which more of that sturdy stock will, if you wish, be ladled onto what you have left.

Sometimes examples of the evening's desserts are put on a little tray at, at a guess, around 6 p.m. When they are shown to you at, say, 9 p.m., they may well look tired and sullen. What you are served, however, is wide awake: more than decent fruit tarts, a flourless chocolate cake of good intensity that is served with stiff, perfect whipped cream.

★ CONTRAPUNTO

200 East 60th Street
LUNCH AND DINNER.
No reservations (751-8616).
Credit cards: AE, DC, MC, V.
Medium priced.

Of itself Contrapunto says that it serves "unusual pasta dishes not generally found elsewhere," which is so. This fact, together with the fact of some lively first courses, is the only, albeit not inconsiderable, excuse for undergoing the place, for Contrapunto is crowded, noisy, and, in its harsh light, none too lovely to look at either. Here you are in the Yellowfingers/Arizona 206/Arizona 206 Café/Contrapunto complex, and when you pass through the East 60th Street portal at the base of the stairway, your options are open to all four possibilities—until you commit yourself to Contrapunto by embarking on the one-flight climb. At the top of the stairs you find a six-foot-by-six-inch bench on which you must wait your turn (no reservations), but at least this site affords an excellent view of patrons (not only from Contrapunto, but from the lower level as well) on their way to and from the facilities. You may if you wish wait for your table downstairs at the Yellow-fingers bar—around comes your turn, down goes the Contrapunto host, back up with him drags he you. If you are lucky he has for you a windowside table overlooking Bloomie's or, not quite so diverting, a windowside table overlooking East 60th. Other tables have little to offer except yet other tables terribly hard by, and if you note the occupants, you note, too, that some of them, minks tossed over the backs of their chairs, are accompanied by gents in three-piece navy blues, for in addition to the young, the place gets adults who, of an evening, have not available to them any money but their own. The light fixtures on the walls look like inverted World War I helmets attached by wires to dialless telephone torsos. The linen on your table is protected from your indis-cretions by a sheet of glass. The shiny, sealed-in-plastic white menus are blinding when they reflect onto your retina beams from the overhead spots that hang from the oppres-sively low ceiling. This is waiters and waitresses kindergarten (presumably employees who perform well here are graduated to Arizona 206), the staff is young, are cute in their party costumes of long white aprons, white shirts, bowties, and a pair of Daddy's sus-penders.

The phrases "virgin olive oil," "extra virgin olive oil," and "Tuscan olive oil" appear in the descriptions of all but two of the first courses, and, as it happens, the substance, albeit uncredited, is present even in the two: roasted red and yellow peppers of strong, sweet flavor arranged among leaves of endive, strewn with fresh herbs and with slivers of raw, strong garlic, and set in a pool of the ubiquitous oil; big caps of wild mushrooms, each adorned with coarse-chopped Italian parsley and with bits of garlic (this time not quite raw), the earthy fungi in more of the famous oil, this time strongly peppered; braised hearts of radicchio, warm and chewy and pleasantly bitter, garnished with a salad of diced tomato, limp arugula, and little morsels of mozzarella, the ever present oil this time supplemented by balsamic vinegar; and what is given as pinzimonio caprese, a couple of ounces of the famous Tuscan juice, fortified with coarse-ground black pepper, in a ramekin that is surrounded by sliced peppers and tomatoes, smoked and unsmoked mozzarella, hard slices of good fennel, each of which you moisten with the oil.

Pasta. The recipes are fine, the renditions occasionally less so, as this plate of malfatti aragosta, in which the pasta packages, though filled with lobster, scallops, fresh fennel, and leeks, suffer from a flatness of flavor, as if they have been cooked and waiting, and in which the buttery sauce reveals little of the excitement that the listed lemon and chervil promise. But a good version of the capelli marina piccola is worth gambling on, for when the dish is right, the mound of noodles at the center of your plate, threaded with strands of sundried tomato and leeks, is heady of its abundant fresh basil, and it is surrounded by a dozen littlenecks in their shells, warm and fresh and tender—a stun-ning dish. The fettuccine uccelletti is a great tangle of the wide noodles with strands of leeks and chicken, strong and salty ham, and chunks of mushroom, all the flavors clear in the white-wine-and-tomato sauce, particularly that of the fresh oregano that gives the dish its fragrance. You order the tagliarini forte because the title and the jalapeno listed as an ingredient suggest a hot dish on this cold night. You are disappointed as to the heat, detect but a hint of the infamous Mexican pepper, though the garlic is clear enough, the Italian bacon pungent, the arugula with which the noodles are threaded revealing much of its sharp green flavor—the child in suspenders grates on the Parmesan until you tell her to stop, or until her Mouli grater runs dry.

The raspberry tart has become a little dry by late in the evening, the apricot tart is a heavy dried-apricot paste on a leaden dough, the raspberry-mascarpone ice cream is a mistake—especially its icy raspberries and nuggets of unadulterated cream cheese—and the burnt chocolate ice cream is not especially burnt, though it is rich, intense, velvety.

With your ice cream you are served one of those nutted, rusklike biscotti that are flavored with amaretto—it is the best end-of-meal item in the house.

If you want beer with your pasta, be warned, nothing is available but Amstel Light or a thin, flat Italian substance called Raffo. If you want to *share* a pasta, the menu announces "Our dishes are balanced in form and size so that splitting is inadvisable, and we prefer not to do so. However, split orders will be charged $10.00 *extra*." (Emphasis theirs.) You may, however, pass things around at the halfway point—to confirm that the "balance as to form and size" is bushwa. A few non-noodle main courses are offered.

★★★ LA CÔTE BASQUE

5 East 55th Street
LUNCH AND DINNER. CLOSED SUNDAY.
Reservations: 688-6525.
Credit cards: AE, DC, MC, V.
Very expensive.

Though Henry Soulé intended La Côte Basque as casual relief from the solemnity of his legendary Pavillon, New Yorkers have persistently treated the place as a ranking star, complete with all the formality attendant thereto, in the haute cuisine firmament. That is, a distinction is not made between going out to dinner (at, say, La Caravelle) and simply grabbing a bite to eat here. And yet Soulé has had his way, for he seems to have built lightheartedness right into the place. Only under the grim duress of Henriette Spalter—Soulé's close friend, and the establishment's long-term interim proprietor after his demise—was the restaurant in the grip of the kind of ceremonial lockjaw for which New York's most expensive French restaurants are (often unjustly) known. Today, under the seemingly casual care of its present owner, Jean-Jacques Rachou, one gets the impression not so much of a restaurant made cheerful by how it is run, rather that an attitude of benign sanction fosters the conviviality intrinsic to it. La Côte Basque is, of course, the prettiest restaurant in New York, and in its current happy state, it is easy to imagine that the good cheer in which one is here immersed is of its rooms' very textures and palette. The lofty plaster walls are the color of old ivory, the chairs and banquettes are of cherry-red leather, the beams and timbers are the near-black of espresso coffee, and among those there are the foggy or sunlit blues and tans and subtropical greens of Bernard Lamotte's murals, affectionate depictions of seaside towns, their harbors and beaches—and the countryside around them—on the Côte Basque itself.

The present management has enlarged the original place—it is now almost a full circle of rooms, with the bar and the hidden kitchen at the center—but the expansion has been so artfully carried out that it is impossible to fix, without the aid of memory, the borderline between the old part and the big new room just west of the bar. Some of the artwork has been moved, and mirrors have been installed, but the feeling of the place has been preserved—except that the large rear room, with its panoramic view of the harbor of St. Jean de Luz and the views of the town through trompe l'oeil "windows" in three other directions, has now become the closest thing in the place to an intimate corner (it seats around seventy). When Rachou first took over, word got out to the city's well informed that good things were happening here, and during the early years of his regime, the restaurant was frequented by an engaging crowd. Today the place is popular, so you may spot too much makeup on your right, cringe at too much noise on your left, and catch, from across the room on a Saturday night, the judgments of intrepid weekend restaurant samplers. As one such puts it, "This place has it all over La Groonawee" (though he would surely agree that there will always be those for whom nothing will ever match those wonderful days at summer camp).

Generalize, and, promptly, you must list your exceptions. Still, it appears that you do a little better here with special dishes of the day than with menu items. The listed salad of crabmeat and lobster, for example, is perfectly nice seafood and a good thick sauce that is almost emerald green of its fresh herbs, but the shellfish lacks a certain sparkle—it is fresh, but you will not for a moment suspect that it was in the briny this very morning. And the listed gratin de homard aux morilles, for another, is that nice lobster again, this time combined with sweet black morels in a hot sauce of almost liquorlike headiness— and yet you can get a copy of this dish in which the overdose of salt is almost its undoing. The printed menu is not, of course, barren. Consider the quenelle de brocheton, a great sausage-shaped log of fish mousse, solid but not heavy, its brusque pike flavor vivid against a Nantua sauce that is at once honey-sweet and tangy of the flavor of lobster shells. The menu lists a good snail dish as well, the plump morsels mingled with sautéed wild mushrooms, and bound in a red-wine sauce that is concentrated, sticky, and silken. But when your captain informs you that quail is available, you will do well to set aside the printed menu in favor of that little bird, for it is served here filled with a fluffy and well-seasoned dressing that is enriched with sweetbreads, and it reaches you, in the form-fitting pastry in which it was baked, at the center of a pool of concentrated red-wine sauce, surrounded by hot white grapes—the elaborate treatment does nothing to diminish the clarity of the pungent natural flavor of the quail itself. At other times there is fresh duck liver, and the slices of unctuous meat, very rapidly browned, cooked through but retaining much blood-rare flavor, are laid over a mound of chestnut purée, are adorned with a few raspberries, and are moistened with a dark sauce that is touched with fruit— the sauce is fine with the meat, but it is particularly dramatic with the sautéed wild mushrooms that are yet another element on the wide-ranging plate.

You will pass up the bass—fresh fish, nicely prepared, but revealing little or none of its natural flavor—in favor of the grilled Dover sole with mustard sauce. The English swimmer reaches you filleted, the four quarters returned to their original positions, and though the exteriors are done to a glinting copper highlighted by flecks of black, the meat under the surfaces is unsullied milk white, moist, shining, and firm, its delicate flavor intact—the smooth, weighty mustard sauce, sharp but subtle, sets the fish off without obscuring it. Order a roasted chicken, and you are shown the whole big bird (poularde), its skin taut and glazed. It is taken away, and you are brought great slices of the white meat—they are cooked through but have lost none of their moisture, and they have chicken flavor that, by today's standards, is pungent—the bird's earthy sauce is fragrant of tarragon without being obvious. The noisettes of veau may be the most remarkable dish on the menu, for the nutty flavor of the pale, lightly browned and juicy little steaks is of a strength almost never successfully imparted to veal—do not, however, become so engrossed in the meat that you neglect its truffle sauce, the slightly "burnt" flavor of which is its stunning seasoning. When there is venison, sautéed scallops of it are served with matching slices of that duck liver you had as a first course. This is mild venison, but its light, clear, slightly sour sauce poivrade, dense with peppercorns, rouses it smartly. You do not expect cassoulet on the menu of a restaurant of this particular class, but the current management has always offered one. For the clarity of the different meats and sausages, and for the perfect texture of the beans, firm but not hard, this is a flawless version—but it is a bit refined, lacks the coarse edge that you may well think of as an essential element, if not the essence, of cassoulet.

Scores of soufflés stream from this kitchen of an evening, all of them handsomely browned and proudly risen. It is not unusual for a table of, say, eight, to be dealt eight of them. The waiters circle the party, puncture the tops, spoon in the sauce—mostly raspberry sauce into soufflés lightly flavored with Grand Marnier. Other sweets: a tart of thin-sliced apples on parchmentlike pastry, very nice for its austerity, for the bite of its slightly sour fruit; apples again in the tarte Normande, the minced fruit between layers of a light and creamy cake; a flat rice pudding cake not improved by the bits of fruit with which it is studded—it is set in an apricot sauce that helps not enough; a Grand Marnier mousse that is creamy but light, the liquor clear but discreet; a rich, polished chocolate mousse in which, happily, there is intensity but not chocolate overkill.

★★CSARDA

1477 Second Avenue (at 77th Street)
LUNCH, SATURDAY AND SUNDAY; DINNER, DAILY.
Reservations: 472-2892.
Credit cards: AE.
Inexpensive.

In the old days it would have required all your fingers and toes to count the Hungarian restaurants on the Upper East Side. Today only a handful cater to the neighborhood's small but apparently vigorous Hungarian community. Of the scant half dozen, this is the one that, by virtue of its uncompromising Hungarian flavor—of food, of the surroundings in which it is served, of the staff that serves it—and its consistently decent cooking, is the best. Accordingly the place gets a largely Hungarian crowd and a contented one. Of an evening you will spot Second Avenue shopkeepers—gentlemen alone with their newspapers next to couples who sometimes eat just as silently. But there are gayer gatherings, too, in which dramatically made-up ladies with cigarette holders and Gabor hair— or the mahogany-colored hair that one thinks of as gypsy—laugh the evening away in the company of mustachioed Magyars. Sunday is family day, and the place is packed with multigenerational gatherings, over which an elder presides from the head of a row of pushed-together tables.

The site of all this mitteleuropaisch happiness is a foursquare, brightly lighted little cube of a place, with walls of white plaster, a floor of red tiles, a density of tables. The restaurant is hung with old-country pottery, native costumes, boldly patterned little rugs, and framed art, much of it of equine subjects—Hungarians are great horsemen. You are served by waiters in white shirts or by strawberry-blond soubrettes in red blouses—they look sexy, and very likely are, but their ministrations are motherly. Your wants are heard by them with a concerned attentiveness that will, at least a little, intoxicate.

Whatever you order, your dinner begins with the little dish of cool, crisp, sweet-and-sour cucumber salad that is a given in these places. That is the lightest thing you will eat. The marinated herring is more like it—a slab of briny, soured fish under crisp onions in thick cream. The chopped liver is eggy, thick as paste, onioned, polished with fat. A firm lump of seasoned ground meat is the core of the stuffed cabbage, which is buried in mild sauerkraut, moistened with a creamy sauce that is pink with paprika, and garnished with stewed green pepper and disks of strong sausage. Stouter still is the lecsos kolbász, that same good sausage in a spicy, stewlike setting that is thick with onion and peppers. But the first-course big winner is brains and eggs—a peppery hot mush, prettily parsleyed and strewn with hot paprika; it is light and steamy, but rich.

If you come only once, the dish to have is the stuffed roast chicken. You get half a big bird, and its vivid chicken flavor is emphasized by the dark, aggressively seasoned liver dressing that is stuffed between the white meat and the glazed, crisp skin. The roast duck is even crisper, its dark meat even juicier, of stronger flavor. The garlic medallions of veal are of good meat, but the sauce they are served in these days is a pale version of what used to be little more than straight pureed garlic. The roasted veal shank looks like an instrument of violence: a big bone, a great knob of dark meat at one end—you wish it were tastier. Four thick slices of meat make up an order of roast pork—the meat can be a little dry, but this peasanty food is satisfying. Four slabs more are an order of boiled beef, succulent meat, with the sharpness common to this dish—you will notice it not at all if you apply the strong horseradish. The beef goulash is a powerful stew, hefty chunks of fibrous, tender red meat, their surfaces dark, in a thick brown sauce, garnished with the tiny, eggy dumplings called nockerl. More nockerl with the calf's liver paprikash, a giant mound of pleasantly greasy morsels of liver, threaded with strands of onion and green pepper, all moistened with a reddened, peppery oil—weighty food.

Palacsintas may be had filled with chocolate or (the genuine article) with apricot preserves. These are tender pancakes, good when filled with the sweet jam and sprinkled with confectioners' sugar and chopped nuts. The strudels—apple or cherry or cheese— are hot, light, flaky.

Pilsner Urquell from Czechoslovakia is carried, but often a slight residue of detergent in the glasses flattens the good beer.

★★LE CYGNE

55 East 54th Street
LUNCH, MONDAY TO FRIDAY; DINNER, MONDAY TO SATURDAY. CLOSED SUNDAY.
Reservations: 759-5941.
Credit cards: AE, DC, MC, V.
Very expensive.

When this third incarnation of The Swan first appeared, back in the early eighties, the impeccable cool of its physical charms quite bedazzled. Haute cuisine had never gone the laid-back route before. Now, though the bird's muted interior is just as was, its visual day is past. Finally, if subtlety is not *about* something, it is merely coy. Revisit Le Cygne, and you find that its undeniable good taste is good taste and nothing more. It is like a pastel heaven that, after not long, has you quite curious about the other place. Worse, the restaurant has come to resemble itself. You will eat well, about as well as ever, but that is all you will do. Except for some exciting food, Le Cygne is without excitement—a condition that feeds on itself. Just as its inoffensiveness attracts an innocuous set, the climate they create lures only more of the temperate. The place is busy, but nobody makes the scene at Le Cygne anymore.

Installed in the street and one-flight-up levels of a townhouse, the restaurant's two parts are joined at the front by a pair of stairways that curve away to the left and right from the lower landing, converge at the upper. The downstairs room is all pale grays and pale blues, its strongest notes the white linen on the tables, the marine-blue plush banquette all around. In part because the ceiling peaks gently along its length, and in part because the walls, above the banquette, are defined into squares by studs that lean forward at their tops, the room has a vaguely nautical, cabinlike air, a condition not undone by the treatment of the squares—some are mirrored—some are muraled with floral pastels so vague they merge with their surroundings. Upstairs you are under an arched ceiling, and these days the condition of its backlighted translucent panels suggests that their backs are inaccessible, for the light passing through them is dimmed by a gray accretion resembling dirt. That, however, does not diminish the ceiling's superb acoustic qualities. There remain few rooms in New York in which you learn so much you do not want to know. She: "Can't we stop now till after I move out? I just get confused this way." He: "My wife never had that problem."

The members of the very professional staff, on the other hand, exhibit no confusion as they willingly accommodate your needs, delivering from a menu that is one part modern, one part haute cuisine with a light, contemporary touch. There are even a number of dishes here that appeared on New York menus back when excess, so long as you called it by another name, was not a dirty word. There never was anything excessive about a well-prepared version of littlenecks des gourmets. You are served nine of the tiny mollusks, in their half-shells, warmed through but tender, all their sweet and briny marine flavor intact, each tiny morsel adorned with a mildly garlicked puree of mushrooms and white wine, green of its herbs, that emphasizes dramatically the clams' ocean flavor. Oysters the same way, albeit of these you get only six, and the treatment does just as much for the more complex flavor of the bluepoints. With your smoked duck—the slices of dark, rosy, tender meat are smoky and of clear duck flavor—you get a little muffin of rich duck liver mousse and a mound of crisp salad in a dressing made with vibrant olive oil. The sweetbread rillons are very much of these days, crisped slivers of the characteristically gummy and oleaginous organ meat in a tart and sticky sauce of sherry vinegar.

Done to a point a little past that perfect one, the fillet of snapper, though fresh and firm, has lost some of its flavor, really needs the well-seasoned mélange of sautéed mushrooms and tomatoes, with basil, by which it is surmounted. Though the menu refers to them as "petites cuisses," the frogs' legs are of quite ample development in the quadriceps department, which in no way compromises the delicacy of the buttered, garlicked, herbed, and handsomely browned limbs—the great mound of them is garnished with vegetables and a dollop of ratatouille. The Swan braises the pigeon with green olives, cèpes, and artichokes, your waiter shows you the whole bird, takes it away, carves incisions into it, stuffs them with the vegetables, and serves the slightly rare and powerfully flavored bird to you in a sauce of the pungent broth in which it was done. The printed menu lists loin of lamb, but some nights you are offered both loin and saddle—you get two substantial lengths of loin, pink, and glistening, and two rosy little chops, the strong lamb flavor of the tender meat much heightened by garlic.

Another variation on the crème brûlée, this one successful, a handful of ripe raspberries just under the glaze of caramelized sugar with which the fluffy custard is topped. The nougat glacé is a disk of rich ice cream studded with bits of candied nut—the good sweet is set in a crimson pool of raspberry puree. The chocolate roulade is very intense in its Grand Marnier crème anglaise—the light sauce is threaded with strands of orange rind. The chocolate pancakes wrapped around sweet, pale-green cream amount to elaborate after-dinner mints.

★★DARBÁR

44 West 56th Street
LUNCH AND DINNER.
Reservations: 432-7227.
Credit cards: AE, DC, MC, V.
Medium priced.

You will recall that back in the seventies New York had a brief fling with Indian food. Those were the days when Raga, Shezan, the now-defunct Gaylord, and several other restaurants arrived on the scene and revised local notions about eating habits on the Subcontinent. (Until then, Indian restaurants had been perceived as sources of cheap, suspect, stewlike dishes called curries, in which exotic and fiery spices concealed, rather than emphasized, the characteristics of the foods they flavored.)

The fling is over, but it has left its mark. To this day, meritorious Indian restaurants are commonplace in New York, are even well attended, but they are no longer talked about. It is the misfortune of this one, Darbár, that it came to town years after its predecessors, in the early eighties, when a new Indian restaurant could get a favorable reception in the press, as this one did, and yet generate no excitement in the community. Had Darbár been part of the wave—well, ripple—of the seventies, it would today have a past, a history of glory days, a reputation. Instead, though it is among the city's preeminent Indian eating places, arguably the best of them, it is known mainly to the midtowners who work nearby and sometimes fill it for lunch, and to those rare diners-out who do not mind places that have never made it as a scene—their numbers are too few ever to crowd Darbár for dinner, so you may walk in here any evening, without a reservation, and get yourself a choice table at once.

Native artifacts are as inevitable in Indian restaurants as native waiters. Usually these adornments amount to a stringed instrument on one wall, a cooking implement on another, and, somewhere, a carved screen. In a few places, the appointments are in fact diverting. But Darbár, alone among New York Indian restaurants, is more an Indian environment than just a decorated store. Step through the front door, and you are in a small vestibule that, from floor to ceiling, is of burnished hammered copper, glinting red-gold, in a pattern of row upon row of perfectly rounded, tipped hemispheres that closely resemble, visitors always note, ripe examples of the female breast. Through another door, and you are in the two-story anteroom of the restaurant proper, from which a curved stairway ascends to the upper level. On the wall to the left of the stairway hangs a majestic and elaborately patterned rug—all ivory and gold, accented with a deep, vibrant blue, it bridges the two floors, and gleams in the soft light of the overhead spots that play upon it. Just under the rug, at the foot of the stairs, stands a dome-topped ceremonial vessel of polished brass—it is taller than a fire hydrant, and its slender, curved spout, which reaches from the base almost to the top, is balanced by a threadlike handle, almost as tall, that describes in outline a great ear. The walls throughout are of a glowing cocoa-colored velvet, and upstairs and down, the place is hung with wood carvings, paintings on silk, tapestries, elaborately framed mirrors, panels of brilliantly colored cloth or carpeting, and, downstairs at the back, more of that hammered copper, an entire wall of it, this time in a pattern that no stretch of mind will perceive as suggestively representational.

These appointments, you understand, are not merely decorative—they are, to a certain extent, the place itself. They seem to shape and define it—in one instance, quite literally, for the best tables in the house are the handful of semi-private ones along one wall of the lower level, each of them shielded on two sides by tall screens of carved wood that are framed with rods of glinting brass. Withal, you are dismayed to note that in this handsome and exotic place the background silence is mutilated by the same domestic music you endure while holding the phone for the next available service representative.

At Darbár, the service representatives are emissaries from the homeland, and they reveal, through their colorfully accented English, a good familiarity with the menu, and a willingness to discuss it with you cordially. Conversation out of the way, they deliver, from a regularly available selection of three, some of the most stimulating soups in town (this even though soups appear almost not at all in India's cookery, and were developed there, it is said, to accommodate the peculiar preferences—and poor teeth—of the English). Among them is a mulligatawny, in this version a thick, lentil-based puree, touched with tomato, that, despite the complexity of its herb-and-spice flavoring, makes an impact of direct, primitive earthiness. Another is called palak shorba, also a thick soup, but headier and sharper—of the spinach with which it is threaded, and of sweet spices and strong pepper.

Deep-fried vegetable fritters and turnovers are much of the standard Indian first-course menu, and among those available here, there is an exceptional onion bhajia, in which a packed and tangled mass of herbed onion strands is dipped in a flour batter and then fried until crisp. Like all of Darbár's deep-fried dishes, this one is light, crusty, and retains just enough greasiness not to be dry—at its center you find a nugget of onions that is sweet and tender. The anguri samosa is a big pyramidal turnover filled with a great assortment of herbed and seasoned vegetables, much like a hot vegetable salad within a flaky shell. Those are first courses for hunger. There are also some designed for the lack of it, stimulating ones like channe ki chaat, a mound of cold chick-peas mingled with chunks of potato and lengths of onion, all of them made rousing by a tamarind sauce that is at once fruity and spicy. The cold dish called crab Bombay is also meant to waken the palate, but, though this is perfectly good crabmeat, as modified by its sweet and sweet-spiced sauce, it is at best only interesting to the Western palate. There are shrimp pakoras and chicken pakoras, each dish a dozen or so very lightly battered and deep-fried morsels, the shrimp crisp and of notably clear shrimp flavor, the chicken just as beautifully browned, but mushy, and devoid of chicken taste. All the deep-fried appetizers take well to any of the three condiments served with dinner: a cold herbed yogurt, a tamarind sauce, and little chunks of root vegetable that have been marinated and, thereby, made violently spicy.

Indian attitudes toward the preservation and preparation of seafood differ from your own. In Indian restaurants, finfish, especially, may be impeccable one time, inedible the next, and in this respect Darbár has nothing on the competition. Consider the pomfret tandoori, on occasion a perfect dish, on occasion what seems like an oven-baked frozen fish—handsomely reddened and blackened on its scored exterior, but pasty, mealy, and almost raw at the bone, devoid of fish flavor throughout. The lobster tikka, also done in the oven, is the tail meat of a substantial crustacean, out of the shell, carefully baked so that it is moist, tender, and cooked through—still, its lobster flavor, though sweet, is slight, and the impact of the lemon, garlic, and pepper with which it was treated before baking is at best subtle. But the most familiar tandoor dish—chicken tandoori—is always in good form here, the tender, moist young bird dramatically charred and suffused with the pungent spices of its marinade.

Red meat in many forms, among them saag gosht, massive chunks of lamb (or, if you wish, beef) immersed in a hot, black, and buttery mash of spicy spinach—the meat is firm, fibrous, of strong lamb flavor; shahjehani biryani, which is billed as a rice dish, though predominant among the items you find buried in the huge mound of glistening pale-brown grain are chunks of good lamb yet again, plus raisins and nuts, as well as spice seeds that you experience as unexpected bursts of flavor—the food is wondrous for the interplay of diverse elements, and when you add its warm yogurt sauce, you enrich the dish without disguising it; and goat rogan josh, another complex production, this one of almost sugar-sweet goat meat in a yogurt sauce that is textured with bits of ginger and almond—fresh coriander is the heady note in the sturdy stuff.

Vegetarians will find here sustenance requiring no compromise of ingestive proscriptions, for elaborate dinners may be built solely of Darbár's vegetables (offered both à la carte and in an assortment called vegetarian thali) and breads. Among the vegetables: dhal, a thick and creamy mash of lentils, their solidity leavened by their spiciness; bayngan bhurta, an oily and rich eggplant paste perfumed with coriander; a mixture of sliced mushrooms and plump fresh peas called mushroom matar, in which the two main elements are bound in a thick sauce that is fragrant of sweet spices; buttery spinach, dark and pungently seasoned, the lumps of mild cheese buried within it mainly a textural contrast to the fibrous green. Among the breads: poori, the balloonlike wheat bread that is made here in a version of particularly vivid grain flavor; naan, a soft, lightly browned leavened bread with a flavor much like that of matzo; and onion kulcha, a big winner, another unleavened bread, this one filled with—and moistened by—buttery onions.

The appeal of Indian desserts is elusive. The ones that resemble Western desserts usually come off as inferior by comparison. The others resemble candy. Burfi, for instance, described as "almond milk fudge," is, unfortunately, that. And the kulfi (ice cream), as the menu warns you, is "made from thickened milk cooked for several hours." Kheer, a creamy, grainy, cardamom-flavored rice pudding strewn with ground nuts, is the best sweet in the house.

★★★ DA SILVANO

260 Sixth Avenue (near Bleecker Street)
LUNCH, MONDAY TO FRIDAY; DINNER, DAILY.
Reservations: 982-2343.
Credit cards: AE.
Expensive.

After a decade of fighting off the credit card infection, Silvano Marchetto counted his empty chairs one night and (with a scornful aversion of eyes, you may be sure) let American Express in. For the first time, you may now eat at his place and find yourself among folks who, because they declare income, care to document deductions. There are better reasons for coming here, however, than curiosity about such strange types. Marchetto was, after all, among the most talented of the pioneers who, in the seventies, brought to New York undrenched Italian food, and the decline in his restaurant's popularity in recent years did not reflect any slippage in his kitchen's performance, devolved, rather, from a plethora of new competitors cooking in similar style, and from their willingness to do what he would not: pay for the convenience credit of others. It got to the point where you could, on occasion, walk in here and regret it—that is, if half-deserted eating places depress you. Happily, word of Silvano's concession to the bankers has got around, and on occasion the place now bustles again.

The author of that one-man passive resistance movement does not look unlike the part, and if you came here when the place was new (back when Rockefeller was vice-president), you will readily recognize the proud bearing of the short, compact fellow. His stance is unchanged, as is his compactness, though of the latter there is these days half again as much. But his recent willingness to go financially modern is no surprise if you judge him by his forward-looking attire of an evening—tasseled tan loafers, slightly harem trousers of delicately wrinkled muted-gray plaid, a striped shirt open at the neck to the beads, and a black painter's smock to mid-thigh, its collar partly concealed by long hair that, combed back, reveals the jewel in one earlobe. You can't miss him.

His place is a couple of well-lighted, vaguely rustic rooms, the white-linened tables, flowers in tiny copper pots thereon, surrounded by pale-wood chairs with straw seats. You walk on a floor of small quarry tiles. Where the walls are of brick, they are hung with wood-framed mirrors here, coat hooks there; and where they are of ivory-painted plaster, with those dim reproductions of Renaissance art that, in certain Italian restaurants, appear to be stuck up instinctively, as if for purposes talismanic, presumably in the expectation that this devoir to the cultural heritage will provide protections elsewhere secured by a mezuzah on the doorpost, a crucifix over the bed. An espresso machine stands on the service bar in the smaller room (to which you enter), in front of it a display of appetizers, desserts, wine. In both rooms there are hanging and standing flora in the front windows. When the weather is fine you may eat at the marble-topped tables out front, under the blue canopy.

A printed menu exists, and you are handed a copy, but the document is just a gesture to the situation. You glance at it, but at the same time you switch on your tape recorder, for the arrival of the menu signals the beginning of your waiter's spiel, a recitation of the fifteen or so special dishes offered each day—it is from among these that most dinners are assembled here, for your announcer does his best to make them sound yummy. A couple of menu items: panzanella, a bread salad, chunks of wheat bread moistened with vinaigrette and mingled with morsels of tomato and strands of pepper—sometimes with other vegetables as well—the fragrantly herbed and well-seasoned salad cool and stimulating; and scampi in graticola, shrimps that are lightly breaded, judiciously grilled, moist and crunchy, and, too bad, more than a bit touched with iodine. From off the menu: fresh fennel, the almost hard white slices of a sweet and pungent licorice flavor, mingled with bits of tomato and gentled with balsamic vinegar; equally fresh asparagus, the great green shoots peeled down to their tender cores and, though served hot, moistened with a *cool* dressing of velvety olive oil and lemon—the vegetable is garnished with glistening white knobs of almost fluffy buffalo mozzarella.

A handful of well-made pasta dishes are listed on the printed menu, but they are mostly familiar items, and the man standing beside your table suggests you have your spaghetti today's way. You agree, and the firm, supple strands reach you in a creamy and nubbly tomato sauce that is thick with sweet-spiced, fennel-flavored ground sausage—green peas are a pure, green note in the otherwise strong and fragrant dish. Much is made here of spinach: come when rotolo is offered, and you are served slices cut from a log that is formed of a sheet of pasta and a vigorously seasoned filling of spinach and ricotta—strong Parmesan cheese is grated on at the table, and it adds a pungent edge to the hot, rich stuff; but you are in especial luck if you come when the spinach (again with ricotta) has been formed into gnocchi, for the dumplings are at once well bound but light, pleasantly sticky, and their vivid spinach flavor is potentiated by a mild admixture of sweet spice—moistened with hot, clear black butter, the gnocchi too may be advantageously fortified with grated-on cheese.

Orata, a distant relative of the snapper, is flown to Silvano from the Mediterranean, so that he may marinate it in herbs and olive oil, grill it whole, and serve it as four great-flaked filleted quarters—the marinade enriches the fish and invigorates its remarkably vivid ocean flavor. He also gets local seafood, prepares it a local way—the sautéed shad roe is grainy but moist, its nutlike taste potentiated by the butter in which it is done, by fresh parsley, by the lemon you squeeze on. Your waiter informs you that the squab is spicy and well done, meaning that it is coated with mildly hot red pepper and cooked through—this bird is all dark meat, of powerful flavor, and though its fat has largely been lost in the roasting, it is moist of the olive oil with which it is slicked. You get an abundance of rabbit, on the bone, in a winy sauce that is fragrant of herbs, the firm chunks of pale meat peppered and darkened on the surface, their sauce thick with bits of organ meat. You depart from the off-the-menu specials in favor of the listed veal chop, and you are a bit disappointed that, though not dry, the big chop is not bursting with moisture either—it is just about redeemed by a tomatoed sauce that is fortified with bits of chicken liver, livened by sweet peas. Back to the specials, a steak styled "Robespierre," marinated in olive oil, rosemary, black pepper, grilled, served sliced, the blood of the meat and the marinade forming a "sauce" of heady strength—this dish takes especially well to the handsomely browned roasted potatoes and sautéed zucchini that are the usual vegetable garnishes here.

The good Parmesan you had grated onto this dish or that may also be had straight, if you wish, with one of the brightly dressed house salads. Ricotta ice cream, you will be fascinated to note, is vanilla ice cream with a slight ricotta flavor. Torta de la nonna (Gramma's cake) is a fluffy white cake, lightly lemoned. The grape pie is an abundance of plump, white, seedless grapes in a nicely browned pastry with a latticework top.

★★★ DA UMBERTO

107 West 17th Street
LUNCH, MONDAY TO FRIDAY; DINNER, MONDAY TO SATURDAY. CLOSED SUNDAY.
Reservations: 989-0303.
Credit cards: AE.
Medium priced.

You may recall Umberto Assante from the restaurant Cent'Anni. It was he who, in that restaurant's first years, kissed hands at the door, sat down at your table but kept his eye ferociously on the visible and, probably, invisible staff's every gesture, presided over the establishment's then ascendancy to a rarefied position among the city's Italian eating places. Recall him or not, others do. No sooner were his name and this address announced than the obscure site became a hot repair. Da Umberto is that familiar myth but real rarity, the warm, lighted place on a block that otherwise goes to sleep when the sun goes down, a destination to which the knowing alone are privy. This, however, is burgeoning Chelsea, Da Umberto is after all but one avenue block from Barney's, another from Lower Fifth, is thus ideally situated to become the fulcrum around which the Joyce Theater to the west, the Union Square Green Market and Zeckendorf Towers to the east, the Flatiron District to the north, seething Fourteenth Street to the south, and all within their orbit, merge, spin, and take off together in a riotous new birth of free-wheeling cultural and commercial urban efflorescence! Barring that, it will have to settle for being the primary source of a hot meal north of the Village and south of the Shuttle. And, yes, food tastes better where you least expect it.

Da Umberto is a deep high-ceilinged room that, by partitions extending into it a little from each side, has been divided into a suggestion of three rooms, one behind another.

You enter to the barroom, on your right the green-marble bar, behind it the bottles before a mirrored wall, across from it a display of foodstuffs and wines, next to that a large white-linened table, black bentwood side chairs around it. In the second room the tables and chairs are well spaced, and beside a glistening white-tiled wall, on a high marble counter, under overhanging hams, salamis, strings of garlic, and copper pots and pans, are displayed the salads, grilled vegetables, and meats that comprise Umberto's cold first courses and slightly less than encyclopedic antipasto. In room three your diversion is the kitchen at the back, visible through glass, and spiffy. Throughout the restaurant the walls are of the mottled umber that Italian places have recently taken to, the floor is of hardwood up front, big red tiles at the back, the light is ample, and if the treatment is a bit stark, the crowd that crowds the place adds color.

From that marble counter: a garlicky seafood salad, squid and scallops and little shrimp, their character distinct, moistened with velvety olive oil; firm chunks of artichoke accented with the flavor of the grill; Genoa salami strong enough to bring you to attention; grilled red lettuce, crunchy and a little bitter; dark-skinned baby eggplants that are soured and rousing; gamy cured beef; pale and tender veal in a thick, caper-dotted tuna purée; a salty and thoroughly oiled caponata, eggplant and olives and more in a thick tomato sauce; disks of sautéed zucchini, oiled and charred: all these things are fresher, more vivid, more alive than their counterparts almost anywhere else in town.

Pasta et al: rigatoni fagiolata, hefty tubes in a vigorous red sauce that is crunchy with white beans—a stout, peasanty dish; another tomato sauce, this one frankly and fragrantly garlicked, on soft but firm little gnocchi; red again, the remarkable capellini con aragosta, filament-thin strands of pasta in a lobster sauce that is briny, stout, thick with moist chunks of the sweet white meat; panzoti, a white entry among the reds, pasta envelopes stuffed with spinach and served in a buttery sauce, at once rich and light, that is nubbly of walnuts and strong Parmesan; a rice dish, risotto con porcini, the brown and stocky meal earthy of the wild mushrooms with which it is studded.

It is perhaps not exactly what you expect, but when there is salmon on hand, you get an impeccably fresh fillet, browned a little, that is as rare and rosy as the latest French article in its piquant mustard sauce. Da Umberto styles itself a Florentine restaurant, so you opt for the tripe because it is listed as trippe Fiorentina. Were it not named for a city, you would call it a country stew, the lengths of innard resilient but tender in their well-seasoned red sauce, which is thick with strong black olives and strands of root vegetable. Order quails, and you get four halves, their dark meat of intense flavor, their stuffing vigorously seasoned, nicely garnished with blocks of browned polenta. One dish bears your host's own name, scaloppine all'Umberto, the browned veal, pale and juicy, mingled with slices of artichoke in an herbed and winy sauce that is tinctured with a bit of tomato—the thin slices of delicate meat take on the flavor of the bay leaves that cling to their surfaces. Sometimes the house offers suckling pig, boned, packed with a garlicky stuffing that is redolent of rosemary, formed into a roulade, and roasted—you get a couple of thick slices cut from the great log, the tender, abundantly rich meat glistening of fat within the rims of crisped skin.

Though the Parmesan is hard, flinty, vivifying, the Gorgonzola both creamy and gamy, if you limit yourself to but a single cheese, you will do well with the Sardinian ricotta—it tastes like earthy butter, you have it moistened with olive oil, seasoned with fresh-ground pepper, and you eat it with a salad of arugula in a tart red-vinegar dressing. You wish there were less sugar in the well poached and sweet-spiced pear in red wine, and that the almond cake were livelier, but you have no quarrel with the cheesecake, which is cool, wet, weighty, touched with orange under its browned and white-sugared top.

★★DAWAT

210 East 58th Street
LUNCH, MONDAY TO FRIDAY; DINNER, DAILY.
Reservations: 355-7555.
Credit cards: AE, DC, MC, V.
Medium priced.

The subcontinental mind, alas, judges Western courtesy quantitatively. The more, it judges, the better, The New Yorker, on the other hand, when up to his ears in salaams, takes it that he is the victim of rudeness; or, if he is of psychoanalytic bent, of hostility; or, at least, that he is the victim of a bore. It is decades now since the imperial yoke was lifted from the Indian back. Are not Indians now taught in school that it is unnecessary —never mind risible—to fawn on Occidentals? On anyone? Does your host really imagine that if he doubles over, clasps his hands, and inquires after your well-being maybe thirty times during dinner, you will ever return? You figure that "the treatment" (as the treatment may well be called) is intended to elicit an expression of your hostility to the foreigner, thus confirming the foreigner's suspicion of your prejudice, thus justifying his administration of the treatment in the first place. You figure, too, that if you tell the smiling groveler to go away please, he will go away mad; that if you do not tell him to go away please, he will not go away; that, ergo, you cannot win; that, as you cannot win, you may as well tell him to go away please.

At the front door a turbaned giant in ceremonial dress bows you in, as a warm, fragrant breeze of Indian spices enwraps you on its way out. The rooms, however, do not deliver on the exoticism of that promise, for Dawat avoids the trappings of New York Indian restaurants as you usually know them. It is open and sunny, all pink and pale green, modern Western chairs around pink-linened tables that are set with copper service plates, nothing notably Indian about the pink-and-turquoise plaid cloth on the banquettes that rim the room, or about the few tropical trees. There are, however, these carved wooden heads, clusters of them here and there on the walls, their left sides painted one way, their rights another, giving them a queer one-eyed look. Their significance is lost on locals, which is not to say they are not decorative, but take them down, hang a curtain over the interior window that, at the back of the restaurant, provides a view of the spiffy kitchen, and this could be a place of any nationality or none. Conceivably as a corrective to the thinness of visual flavor, Dawat is patrolled by a handful of ladies in saris, hostesses, it seems, without portfolio. Signal one of them, and perhaps she will come by and ask if everything is satisfactory.

If, however, you have mastered, and are comfortable with, snapping your fingers for attention and flicking them to be let alone, you will do well at Dawat, for the food, unlike some of the help, is self-respectingly assertive: four shrimp that go as "Madhur Jaffrey's Baghari Jhinga" (her name is all over this menu), the little crustaceans in a heady and wondrously complex sauce dominated by garlic and mustard; MJ's "Bhaja," deep-fried leaves of spicy spinach in a nubbly batter garnished with slices of potato that, though of clear flavor, are mealy; keema samosa, triangular turnovers of light, flaky pastry filled with warm and gently seasoned ground lamb and garnished with strong redded onions; and dahi aloo poori, which is served from what is given as MJ's "Snack Cart," a vehicle adorned with more of those wooden heads, from which you are served bread crisps the size of half-dollars, those strewn with chickpeas and nuggets of potato, those dribbled with yogurt and with a fruity tamarind sauce, everything then sprinkled (from shakers) with spices—judiciously, so that none of the many flavors is obscured.

A principal appeal of Dawat is in the dishes it offers that you do not find elsewhere, notable among them the Parsi-style patra-ni-machhi, in which a fillet of fish, sometimes salmon, in a coriander chutney is wrapped in a banana leaf and steamed—the seafood is fresh, firm, moist, and the spiced density of green coriander in which it is buried imparts to it a wild herb flavor. Of course there is tandoori chicken, and this one is red, blackened, suffused with the moisture and spices of its marinade, nicely garnished with onions that are oiled and hot. Many other chicken dishes, among them chicken sag, the lengths of white meat in a pungent, sweet-spiced spinach puree. Though tiny, the lamb chops masala have an almost muttony meat strength, and though the lamb is cooked through, it is utterly tender in its tart, spicy, gravylike yogurt sauce. The meat in the goat biryani is milder and sweeter than that lamb, the nuggets of fibrous goat buried in fluffy saffroned rice that is studded with nuts and raisins. Mostly good vegetables: thin, darkened slices of eggplant that lose none of their powerful eggplant flavor to the fruity tamarind sauce in which they are done; mustard greens, the hot mash a little spicy, a little bitter; crunchy chickpeas in a hot-spiced sauce that has been made fragrant with coarse-chopped coriander. The somewhat heavy wheat bread called paratha is prepared here in a version flavored with mint—the lively herb leavens the bread's weightiness.

Carrot halva is a hot carrot mash studded with pistachios and white raisins and topped with a bit of whipped cream—good, though perhaps not what you think of when you think of dessert. The sweet-spiced rice pudding, though thick, is rousing. Ice creams and sherbets are available.

Beer is good with some of this food, wine with none of it.

★ EAMONN DORAN

988 Second Avenue (near 53rd Street)
LUNCH AND DINNER.
Reservations: 752-8088.
Credit cards: AE, DC, MC, V.
Medium priced.

Primarily a drinkery, complete with such legendary beverages on tap as Guinness Stout and Bass Ale, sold by the pint or half pint no less, this very American-accented Irish bar serves not only booze until the usual all hours of the morning, but food until then too. If things get bad you can summon an ambulance and have yourself delivered here. It is said that there was a time when English spirits were not handled at this place—no Beefeater's gin or the like—but today, if you have the nerve to order such things here, the house will make the most of your impertinence by selling them to you. Suddenly the phrase "selling out" takes on fresh meaning.

Do not judge Eamonn Doran by the occasional condition of its barroom, crowded, as it sometimes is, by folks who brandish the belligerent conviviality of the oiled insecure in a place where they fancy themselves welcome. Mostly this front room is filled with talkers, people who find their own banal conversations preferable to Johnny Carson's. In addition to the hammered-copper bar, Eamonn Doran has all the required paraphernalia: a beamed ceiling, maps and insignia on the walls, scenes of old Ireland, much wood, golden lantern light, a shamrock of stained glass, pottery models of country cottages, a jukebox, and, downstairs, near the facilities, a framed list of Irish poets and playwrights, and a poster on which are printed the words to certain Irish songs. The dining room at the back is surprisingly spiffy, if you anticipate it by the pubby saloon up front. There are mirrored walls, tufted "leather" banquettes, beige linen, elaborately folded napkins at each place. In this back room you will do well to get waited on by one of the waitresses —their Irish English is like music, and cordiality is their method. The waiters must be occasionals, locals hired for lack of the real thing, and they are sometimes mechanical and/or resentful.

If your received opinion has been that Irish cooking is narrow and dull, be prepared not to have your prejudice revised. There are, however, a few good reasons for eating here, not the least of them the crusty, floury, white soda bread, studded with black raisins, with which you are copiously supplied. Perhaps the most of them is the superb Irish smoked salmon, which is pale and airy, powerfully salted but somehow not excessively salty, garnished with strong onion, capers, lemon. The place turns out decent baked clams, littlenecks, fresh and sweet and tender, their browned breading oiled but not greasy. Rock shrimp, which are showing up all over town presumably as a substitute for real shrimp, have reached Eamonn Doran, tasting as little like shrimp here as anywhere else. The rumor that they taste like lobster was put forth by the Rock Shrimp lobby. Anyway, they are pallid little crustaceans, much improved by being dipped in melted butter. To their credit, they never taste of iodine.

Steak and kidney pie does what it is supposed to do here—when you break into the pastry that seals the stew within its pottery pot, a great cloud of steam is released. The pastry is nicely browned, and the chunky hot stew is gamy and strong. In game season the same format is used for the venison pie—in this the stew is of meat and mushrooms, with onions and leeks and red peppers. The dish lacks venison individuality, but it is solid and satisfying food. When Muscovy duck is on hand, you get a big section of the big bird, roasted until crisp, blackened here and there at the corners. But the meat is not dry, and its black-currant sauce is fruity, only a little sweet. The rack of lamb is the big winner, roasted and then cut into chops, their edges seasoned and crusty, the pink meat of the eyes juicy and of good lamb flavor.

The Irish sherry trifle is horrible. The chocolate cake is of such extreme chocolate strength as to make the good whipped cream with which it is served essential for dilution. You can get good ice cream, ordinary chocolate mousse.

The Bass Ale is colder than it should be, but the pipes here are clean, the glasses are clean, the draft beers hold their heads. A pint of Bass is $3.25, two are $6.50, three are $9.75, and so on.

★★ECCO

124 Chambers Street (near West Broadway)
LUNCH, MONDAY TO FRIDAY; DINNER, DAILY.
Reservations: 227-7074.
Credit cards: AE.
Expensive.

In this converted old space the age has been left in, the downtown style left out. In fact what you have here is an Italian restaurant in what must once have been a baronial two-story-high Teutonic beer hall, and the place is crowded with money managers in three-piece suits, art hustlers in zippered leather, and scores—it seems—of waiters and functionaries coursing through the aisles in a hurry. On first encounter the effect is of a swarming old oyster-and-chop house (you assume such places once existed), but then you spot, for example, this lady in the vented cowboy hat and mirrored sunglasses, and you are back in your own era.

Ecco's nineteenth-century flavors is a function, in part, of the soaring edifices of carved mahogany and glass that, stocked with crystal and liquor, rise almost to the ceiling behind the long bar up front; of the ancient tile floor; of the glowing white globes that hang on wires from the distant stamped-tin ceiling; of the old wood paneling, inset with big beveled mirrors, with which much of the room is rimmed. The red-leather banquette opposite the bar is where you sit for a good view of the comings and goings and millings of the Ecco crowd. Farther back—just beyond the big table on which are displayed bowls and platters of the restaurant's cold appetizers—is the dining room proper, a great spread of white-linened tables, mostly large ones, many of them surrounded by gangs of just folks, in shirt-sleeves and jeans, getting fat and happy celebrating (you like to imagine) life; at others you spot teams of big-time operators from the Street, clean-shaven gents and smartly coiffed ladies, gloating over (again you like to imagine) the consummation of a particularly cynical distribution. A handful of old booths—carved wood and red leather—is along one wall, and for some reason, the tables within them are shaped like ironing boards. Of the gentleman who has just shown you to one such, you ask why. Goes he, as if, clearly, he has gone this way before, "Because to make the ladies to feel at home."

Comes your captain. For that which he cannot give you in height, he substitutes delivery, which is basso resonanto, puncho, and boffo. His spiky mustache draws attention to the big white tiles with which he bites off the last syllable of each special of the day. Then he chews into the next one. Choose to send him to that collection of antipasti for to make you a plate of a little of this and a little of that. He returns with nuggets of fresh mozzarella cheese, soft but not without a nice resilience, under chunks of tomato that are soured by their vinegar dressing; crunchy little marinated mushrooms, fragrant of fresh herbs and polished with oil; thin leaves of sliced zucchini that have been just briefly sautéed—but in proximity to enough garlic to imbue them with that flavor; similar leaves of eggplant, also sautéed, and, despite their filminess, weighty with the good oil in which they were done; cool hearts of artichoke, firm, browned here and there, which heightens their subtle taste; a salty caponata of capers, onions, and olives in a thick and spicy oil; the half of a roasted red pepper, stuffed with anchovies and cherry tomatoes; a seafood salad of little scallops, chunks and strands of octopus, circles of squid, and crisp shrimp, all fresh and all gently oiled. If you wish to begin with red meat, there is of course carpaccio, the thin sheets of raw beef distributed across the entire surface of a good-size plate, moistened with oil and dotted with capers—it hurts that the beef is icy; it helps that your waiter, turning to the coarsest face of his four-sided grater, blankets it with shreds of sharp Parmesan cheese.

He selects a finer screen to cheese your tortellini della nonna, little meat-filled pasta dumplings, sweet spiced and nutty, in a creamy sauce that is thick with slivers of ham, plump green peas, and wildly woodsy wild mushrooms. You may have that cheese yet again on the green fettuccine amatriciana, the firm, tender noodles in a dense and spicy red sauce that is smoky with prosciutto and sweet with sautéed onions.

The food being flown to local airports these days from all over both hemispheres is even getting through to Manhattan's extremities. On occasion Ecco receives big Hawaiian prawns and serves them to you in their shells, complete with dark, beady, staring eyes, and long feelers waving about. They come with nutcrackers, but these carapaces are flimsy, and you will need only a small fork to extract the meat. There is not much of it, after all, but it is supple, and has a mild but sweet marine flavor. The fish of the day may be had in any of three listed preparations. Sometimes the fish is snapper, and you may have yours "brodetto," in a peppery white-wine broth with a couple of lovely little clams in their shells and several slightly loud mussels in theirs. That snapper is firm and fresh, skinned and boned and (partly as a result) of rather mild flavor—with it you are served disks of sautéed zucchini, browned and crisp, in a tomatoed oil that is dotted with cloves of garlic. The zuppa di pesce is a mammoth collection of clams and mussels (the latter again loud), slabs of swordfish, crisp shrimp, and lots of scallops and squid, all mingled with chunks of garlic in a particularly vibrant red soup to which sprigs of rosemary add their fragrance. The so-called chicken Vanessa is a simple thing, half a little chicken, nicely browned in the broiling, served with cool chunks of marinated tomato, the juices of which are a striking zest to the delicate bird. All that may be beside the point, for if you come here only once, you will have the sense to order the veal chop valdostana, a version of this familiar item that is surpassed nowhere in town. The hefty chop is laterally bifurcated to the bone, stuffed with fontina and good ham, handsomely browned, and then served in a sauce that is thick with sautéed wild mushrooms—the meat is pale and juicy, the cheese pully and pungent, the ham of a nice sharpness, the winy mushroom sauce almost overwhelmingly earthy. The baby lamb chops are simpler things. They arrive considerably rarer than ordered, but the tender meat is of powerful lamb flavor, and the chops are heady with rosemary and garlic.

Aged Parmesan cheese is served in substantial chunks, and it is strong enough to clear your ears. You will do well to have yours with the house salad—slices of dark-red tomato, sprigs of arugula, deep-red radicchio, and tender little leaves of endives, all in a spanking wine-vinegar dressing. The sweet desserts include a cloudlike napoleon of almost ephemerally flaky pastry and fluffy whipped cream; and a good ricotta cheesecake that is plain and a little grainy, sugared, abundantly liquored. The zabaglione sauce is thick, dark and winy and sweet, sticky enough to cling heavily to the berries with which it is served; you may have a great pile of deep-purple raspberries, ripe and bursting with juice; or a handful of strawberries, each of them the size of a plum, ripe-red and glistening.

Do not be discouraged. There is plenty to complain about. The house will not, for example, prepare half orders of pasta. Divide a full order, and you will find yourself assessed an unannounced $2 for your effrontery. In fact if two of you elect to eat serially, one dish at a time, though the sum of your consumption is easily two complete dinners, your bill will carry that $2 penalty for each dish so shared. Order an off-the-menu special, say the fish of the day, and you are charged $18.95, which may well surprise you, for on the printed menu only the 20-ounce T-bone steak and the double veal chop are that much or more.

★★ELIO'S

1621 Second Avenue (near 84th Street)
DINNER.
Reservations: 772-2242.
Credit cards: AE, MC, V.
Medium priced.

The craze for clubby restaurant-saloons has subsided, which is to say knockoffs of this place now materialize on New York's Upper East Side with less frequency than ethnic parades. Now more than five years old, Elio's has survived both its initial hot popularity and the hasty competition of its imitators, is today a sturdy—not yet a stodgy —landmark in the flux that is this neighborhood's restaurant scene. Elio's derives from its scruffy neighbor, Elaine's, a media hangout with which this restaurant's eponymous godfather was associated before he went straight. Faces seen in one place are sometimes seen in the other, but at Elio's it is not required of these stars that they show up with a three-day beard and a despondent air, or with a drunken strut, or with a lubriciously chattelistic posture, brazenly brandished, toward their biped of the evening. Here you find quite another scene.

Echt Elio's is Sunday night, when gangs of *Times* guys, trim-tonsured and in suits and glasses, having spent the day at home with their own paper, re-bond—for best results with pasta and cheese—in preparation for the solemn work of the week ahead. Today's *Times*man is responsible to a competitive degree, and it is not till most of the wine has been drunk that anyone is bold enough to switch the talk from local, national, and international affairs to office politics. Mondays to Thursdays are professionals' nights, and the at-home ease with which these doctors, lawyers, and Wall Street bankers take their $50 dinners—the way others grab a sandwich and coffee between the subway stop and the fourth-floor walk-up—will put your social conscience in mind of the sharp economic stratification of American society today. Or else it will not. Friday and then Saturday are, well, Saturday right after Friday. The point most carefully demonstrated by certain of the guests these evenings is that the ladies, being supported by the gentlemen, no longer type for a living. This to establish, fingernails are permitted to grow until, at a point an inch or so from fingertip, they take right turns, as if lost, go off in a new direction in search of home base. (So adorned, a lady must grip her steak knife like a golf club.) All this in a handsome, well-lit, wood-paneled room, a bar up front on the left, a handful of linened tables on the right, most of the tables in the back, under six great white hanging globes. Elio's is noisy, but not painfully. The floor is worked by white-shirted, white-aproned gents who have confidence and aplomb, but do not violate the no-nonsense tenor of this place with any excess, in carriage or speech, of finesse. They do, however, all they have to do.

Ask one of them, and he will bring you an order of raw mushrooms, a great pile of the almond-colored slivers, crunchy and earthy, slices of crisp fennel mixed in, sheets of Parmesan, hard and sharp, on top—the salad is good straight, is better when your waiter pours over it, from a tall spouted bottle, the strong-flavored olive oil served here. Suggest to your companion the clams oreganate, an exceptional version of the familiar dish, the tiny littlenecks, in their shells, fresh and tender and sweet, their lightly oiled breading, judiciously seasoned and delicately browned, just touched with oregano. The spaghetti in its nubbly meat sauce has possibilities that are not apparent when you sample it as is, for though honest, the dish is of a plainness—but add an amplitude of Elio's good ground cheese, and it is transformed, becomes at once sharp and deep. There is spaghetti also with seafood, a good dish that would be even better if the iodine were subtracted from the shrimp (or the shrimp from the dish), for the simple red sauce is thick with scallops (their rich pink roes attached), sweet little clams, and chunks of firm clear-tasting fish—the added parsley is chopped coarse, and little sprigs of it you encounter in this bite or that are sudden, unexpected bursts of fresh green flavor. A couple of rice dishes are listed, including risotto with porcini, the buttery grain (it is almost, but not quite, hard), black dotted with chunks of the wild mushroom—the very sturdy stuff is marred one time by sand imperfectly washed from the parsley.

Each day there is a fish of the day, and when it is salmon, you get a thick slab of it, sometimes with green peppercorns, the dark dots of pepper, in their creamy sauce, very pretty on the surface of the moist and sweet pink meat. Elio's zuppa di pesce is distinguished by the great chunk of lobster, supple and tender, among the tender scallops, morsels of firm fish, and fresh clams and mussels in their shells—the briny, saffron-flavored broth is thick with chunks of tomato. The chicken ortolana is a boned, sautéed breast, often not a good beginning, but this one is in a light tincture-of-tomato sauce, and it is overlaid with good mushrooms and, striking notes, with red peppers and black olives, which make for a vibrant, vigorous dish. There are places around town that, in recent years, have demonstrated that hot meat and cold salad may be artfully combined. Elio's attempts it in what they give as "milanese capricciosa," a pounded veal chop, lightly breaded and sautéed, that is covered over with a dressed salad of tomatoes and red onions, but the drama of such dishes is barely in evidence here, for the dressing is mild and the veal, of course, has little flavor of its own. The lamb chops are apparently sautéed rather than grilled, so they are of a succulence rather than of a browned strength —their slightly redded sauce is thick with slivers of garlic.

A loud and creamy Gorgonzola and that strong Parmesan you had with your raw mushrooms are fine with the house salads, which are of crisp greens—the salad and cheese benefit from Elio's terrific bread, which is fresh, grainy, chewy, crusty. You wish that, under its glassy surface of caramelized sugar, the crème brûlée's cool and creamy custard were lighter. The black and white layers of the hazelnut cake are subtly nutted— the cake is surfaced with a slick black icing. You may have fresh strawberries or raspberries with a rich zabaglione that is cold and winy.

★★ERMINIA

250 East 83rd Street
DINNER. CLOSED SUNDAY.
Reservations: 879-4284.
Credit cards: AE.
Beer and wine.
Expensive.

A dozen white-linened tables, a flickering taper on each of them (they poke feebly into the dimness, painfully onto your retina), and about a carload of rusticity are the principal ingredients of this place. The recipe is a familiar one, for this is yet another enterprise of the family that brought you, first, Trastevere, and then, Trastevere 84. With a couple of winners already to their credit, and, one assumes, more confidence than ever, they have risked in this enterprise a deviation from the menu that worked so well the first two times around. But it is really a cooking method, more than the character of the food, that distinguishes this place not only from its predecessors but from most restaurants on earth, for at Erminia, as the menu has it, "All entrées are grilled in Wooden Fire."

Unfinished, splintery beams cross the ceiling. The walls—of brick, or of dark, knotty planks—are hung with primitive pottery and with street lanterns that glow dully. The dried flora all about are, of course, wildflowers and grasses. The two little windows at the front are bedecked with potted greenery. At the back of the room, bottles of wine are displayed on an upended old barrel. These snug quarters accommodate you fairly well —you can actually get comfortable once you have wriggled into the chair that is wedged into the space between the wall and your table. But if you arrive a few minutes early for your reservation, or if the people you are scheduled to succeed have no further plans and are lingering, the only place for you to wait is out on the street.

So come here when the weather is clement. And if your host comes outside to commiserate for your delay, tell him to go back and arrange for some vongole alla Erminia to be served as soon as you are seated. You get eight fresh, hot, tiny, and tender littlenecks, in their shells, moistened with a winy sauce that is fragrant with wild mushrooms and shallots. You get an artichoke dish here unlike any other in town. It is described as "artichokes completely cooked in olive oil, garlic, in earthenware pan," and the strands of crunchy heart, though strongly salted and weighty with the garlic-flavored oil in which they were cooked, have a vividness of artichoke flavor that is not obscured at all, but only potentiated, by this preparation. What is given as bruschetta alla Erminia is a slab of toasted bread—brushed with oil, herbs, and slivers of onion—baked under mozzarella cheese until the cheese is hot, browned, pully, and loud. The dish is garnished with dressed tomatoes, and when their vinaigrette drifts across the plate, it adds a striking tartness to the weighty open-face sandwich.

Pasta. Pappardelle alla ricotta, a mound of long strips of broad noodle, quite firm, in a sauce of herbed, creamy cheese, served with a dollop of pungent tomato sauce on top—the dish is homey, elemental. Bucatini alla pescatora, very thick spaghetti, surrounded by shrimps and baked clams and mussels in their shells, the pasta in a well-oiled, fragrantly herbed and almost excessively salted thick red sauce. Orecchiette alla Erminia, little pasta morsels shaped like ears, moistened with oil, flavored with garlic, mingled with bits of broccoli and sausage, and adorned with a few spoons of light tomato sauce—a rare dish, in which all the elements work and none dominates. Gnocchi di patate, a simple item of firm little potato dumplings—their slight gumminess is the right texture with this deep, thick, and spicy tomato sauce.

Though some of the help here worked at the Trastevere restaurants, a member or two of the staff are apparently new to this territory and have not yet cracked their English texts. One of these informs you that the fish of the day is "malibu fish," which he describes as "like sole fish." Rather than never know what he is talking about, you order it, and receive a great long steak of—halibut! The firm fish does well in the low temperature of a wood fire, and the flavor of its charred surface is a good zest to the juicy white meat. The fish is garnished with baked clams and oysters in their shells. That fire also does well by chicken—the bird is oiled and herbed (much rosemary), lightly lemoned and abundantly garlicked, and it is garnished with sweet roasted peppers and hefty shafts of roasted potato. Even the steak is well served by that fire—with low temperature cooking, the good beef retains all its tenderness. The sirloin is garnished with a skewer of good grilled mushrooms.

The deep-fried apples are three disks of crisped hot fruit, much like sweet fritters, sprinkled with confectioners' sugar. There are ice cream items of intense Italian ice cream sweetness.

No hard liquor. What the menu refers to as "caraffa wine" is available by the caraffa.

★★EZE

254 West 23rd Street
DINNER. CLOSED SUNDAY AND MONDAY.
Reservations: 691-1140.
Credit cards: AE, MC, V.
Expensive.

Rhymes with fez. Is a town on the Riviera between Nice and Cannes. Makes an odd name for this place, the menu of which is only fractionally Provençale, the physical appointments suggesting the south of France not at all (though whoever put them together may think otherwise).

A flashing neon arrow would help, for the signs out front have you heading downstairs in search of the entrance when the right direction is up the stoop to the parlor floor of this old house, within which the high ceiling provides just the note of emptiness needed to cap the austere installation. Simplicity was sought, nakedness was found, and it will take a boisterous crowd to liven this place, a full house anyway. Blindfolded, however, you are entirely comfortable here, for the straightforward layout of the L-shaped place—15 tables or so, chairs around them, plenty of room between them, a small bar with a handful of stools—is noncontroversial. But you do wish something could be done to warm the pallor of the upper walls (which are separated from the lower walls by a chair rail of cream-of-split-pea green), to liven the gray industrial carpeting, to simplify and dignify the patterned and pleated and busy lace curtains in the windows. With respect to the chairs, it would be best to start over, for they are upholstered in a fabric that means to be bold and manages to be murky, even lugubrious in the deathly-white frames. For some reason a khaki-colored ceiling was chosen, and from it hang chandeliers of real or simulated green-oxidized copper, which are matched by sconces mounted on the walls. Eze has managed just to catch the new manic-depressive chic at the very nadir of its swing.

So dry your eyes, smile bravely, and address the carpaccio of sea scallops, the thin-sliced mollusk meats formed into a sheet across your plate, delicately dressed, and adorned with splashes of heady, fresh coriander, dabs of crushed black olive, and lengths of strong-flavored roasted red pepper—a wonderful array of tastes, which is a bonus, for in this room the colors alone are worth the price. The herbed salmon, though listed as a salad, turns out warm, four substantial nuggets of the browned and well-seasoned fresh fish set, surprisingly, among cold beets and arugula. On the weekly changing menu there is always pasta among the appetizers, on occasion this fettuccine in an herbed sauce of anchovies and garlic, a dish that, though obvious, fails as an expression of its listed ingredients; and on occasion these ravioli, in which the tender packets, filled with a green mash of Swiss chard, are in a creamy and nubbly anchovy sauce, the lively, satisfying dish redolent of Eastern spices.

The blue prawns, shrimp to you, are crunchy, free of iodine, and of vivid shrimp flavor in their creamy and well-herbed leek-and-tomato sauce—the crustaceans are nicely garnished with a new potato and a mound of strong spinach. Order swordfish, and you are delivered a thick slab, impeccably fresh, charred a little under its heady sauce of lemon and rosemary. Order the rack of lamb, and, perhaps intentionally, you are not asked how you want it. Turns out you want it the way the kitchen wants to turn it out, the three little chops blood pink, and garnished with a dollop of sweet onion-garlic jam that is set in the meat's dark, slightly acidic, rich sauce. You will recognize that the

163

cassoulet is cassoulet by way of the meats buried among the beans, but this is a leaden version, all the parts subsumed in the heaviness.

For a boutique restaurant, one in which it is meant that a few unusual things will be done well, and in which very little else is meant to be done, you do wonder how it goes unnoticed that the grapes served with the perfectly nice Stilton are wilted. The crème brûlée is cool and fluffy under its crackling paper-thin caramel crust. The profiterole is notable for the intensity of its espresso ice cream flavor, the strength of its chocolate sauce. A ball of rousing grapefruit sherbet garnishes the grapefruit tart, which is a simple thing of peeled grapefruit sections (a bit of their sourness gone), thick cream, a crumbly pastry. The praline ice cream cake, a slice cut from a roulade, is cold and sweet and densely nutted in its pool of chocolate.

The menu changes weekly.

★★EL FARO

823 Greenwich Street (at Horatio Street)
LUNCH AND DINNER.
No reservations (929-8210).
Credit cards: AE, MC, V.
Medium priced.

Some years ago new plastic-topped tables were substituted for the old ones, which were retired after a generation of loyal, wobbly service. And the prices do creep up, but no faster than the rising cost of, say, newspapers. The place is even painted from time to time, though of course nothing is ever applied to the surfaces of the murals and bullfight posters with which the restaurant is, as they say, adorned. In fact, it will not be long now before the ladies with fans and the gentlemen with red capes—the subjects of said art—will be discernible only to veterans of the place, those who will be able to flesh out the murky outlines with the aid of memory. Nobody alive remembers when this four-square establishment first materialized on this remote corner, but the policy has always been the same: Place a large number of customers in the bar, where they will happily drink, make noise, and patiently wait for tables; when their turns come up, seat them at tables at the back of the barroom, or in the dining room at the rear, where they will happily drink, make noise, incidentally eat like pigs, and wobble out euphoric. Any Greenwich Villager who does not go through this bacchanalia once or twice a year is just one of those fellows who will go to the grave never having crossed against the light blindfolded. The lure of the place is in its low prices and in the solidity and abundance of its food. But cheap Spanish eats of commendable quality are not rare, while a popularity like El Faro's is. The secret, of course, is the popularity itself, which is self-perpetuating—lots of people come here to be where lots of people come.

As in all Spanish restaurants of this ilk, you are provided with a dog bowl of salad with which to divert yourself while waiting for what you ordered. This item, of chopped iceberg in a thick, red-peppered dressing, though edible, is not so much one of the courses of your dinner as it is a tradition, part of the ritual of eating at a Spanish restaurant in New York—like standing up for the Hallelujah Chorus. That "salad" out of the way, you proceed to an order of salpicon, a cool and lemony seafood salad, mingled with herbs and chopped egg whites. Or to a bowl of gazpacho, the cold red vegetable soup frankly sour, deeply oiled, garlicked, but lacking the croutons and chopped vegeta-

164

bles that can make the dish striking. The shrimp ajillo consists of lots of little shrimp, garlicked and spicy, covered over with hot oil and bread crumbs, which form a crackling topping when browned. The fried calamari are circles of resilient but tender squid, artfully deep fried, so that the good batter is crisp and not greasy—you squeeze on lemon to make the dish sparkle.

The minuscularity of a number of this restaurant's tables becomes especially evident when main-course time comes around, for you are provided not only with a large dinner plate from which to eat but also, in most instances, with a great iron pot from which you fill and replenish it. If you have ordered the lobster in green sauce, the pot is filled with a thick, emerald-green broth in which the parts of your lobster are immersed. The green soup is winy, briny, pungently seasoned, fragrant with parsley, and the chunks of lobster meat in their red shell, though perhaps a little overcooked and chewy, seem particularly sweet in this setting. El Faro makes good paellas, the one called Valenciana of disks of sharp and fatty sausage, big sections of moist chicken, shrimp and mussels, fresh (though toughened) clams, sweet green peas, all buried in moist, sweet-spiced rice. This place has always put out an exceptional chicken villaroy, that odd dish that, though it seems like an anomaly on Spanish menus, turns up on almost all of them in New York. The unlikely item consists of chicken white meat coated with béchamel sauce, battered, and deep fried. In the version made here, the chicken is moist, the sauce airy, the outer crust crisp and light. What El Faro unashamedly calls "Duckling Bar B.Q." of course easily transcends its title. The big slabs of bird are formed by cutting right through the ribs, as if the duck were a loaf of bread—the mahogany-colored slices are moist of their fat without being fatty; the skin is almost black without being burnt or dried out; and the whole is sprinkled with crisp almonds. If you squeeze on juice from the quarters of orange with which the bird is garnished, the meat becomes tangy without losing any of its richness. But enough of all this fancy food. No dish on the menu is so much at one with this place as the Spanish omelet, a great pancake of lightly browned egg almost as big as the dinner plate itself, thick with chunks of potato, with strands of pale and sweet sautéed onion, and with little nuggets of smoky Spanish ham, the whole vigorously peppered. This tortilla, as it is called, with some of this establishment's fried potatoes—much like fresh, hot potato chips — will put you in mind of Western omelets and fries raised to a high order. A Spanish omelet is very good with cold red wine.

The desserts—flan, natilla, guava with cream cheese—replicate precisely the versions of those things that have been served for decades in Spanish restaurants all over Manhattan.

★★FELIDIA

243 East 58th Street
LUNCH, MONDAY TO FRIDAY; DINNER, MONDAY TO SATURDAY. CLOSED SUNDAY.
Reservations: 758-1479.
Credit cards: AE, DC, MC, V.
Very expensive.

You enter to a display, on a sturdy old sideboard, of weighty Italian red wines in bottles the size of fire hydrants. Nearby, in tall cabinets with glass doors, innumerable brandies, liqueurs, eaux de vie, in bottles adorned with labels of every pretension. The furnishings are old and weighty, and though Felidia dates from this decade, its appointments are dictated by an ancient restaurant formula: more or less equal parts of rusticity and posh. You proceed, in the dimness, under the low ceiling, past a massive brass-topped bar to yet another display, this one on tiers of green marble: plates and platters of cold shellfish, meats, vegetables, ripe fruits, at the top a great burst of flowers. At this point you are at the dining room proper, all chalky stucco, wood paneling, and fancy brickwork, a floor of red tiles, the white-linened tables surrounded by high-backed chairs, their padded seats of elaborately woven tapestry cloth. A brass-railed stairway (a potted plant at the end of each step) leads to the upstairs dining room: white walls, skylights, much greenery—a bit of crowdedness too, this the slightly less commodious of the two floors. The staff is in formals, but the clothing on the prosperous crowd varies: wizened tycoons in loose-fitting size 36 suits accompanied by pinched ladies in silks and pearls; big fellows who, though in the required jackets, wear their shirts open at the collar (the upper alimentary canal thus stripped for the action of feeding the massive frames); bejeweled visitors from across the East River (the owners of Felidia once ran a restaurant in Queens, and some of the friends they made there visit them here); and many a uniformed East Sider—the gents in suits, the ladies in impeccable little numbers out of Bendel's or Bonwit's, for this is one of the city's most revered Italian restaurants. It *is* good, and when it was new, it seemed likely to become superb—it did not, but it would be idiotic to fault the place for the failure of that eventuality.

You unavoidably pass that fetching display of food on the way to your table, and so you are tempted to sample the cold appetizers, of which your waiter will prepare an extensive assortment. Though the dishes have clarity and freshness, some of them lack the vigor their lively appearance leads you to expect. But, happily, while you are waiting to learn that from experience, you may be brought a plate of the house garlic bread, of which, says the Texan at the next table, to his awed guests, "You can't get this stuff anywhere else on earth." It is good garlic bread, crusty, buttery, laden with powerful, vibrant garlic, and it becomes the foreground, when you eat it with the (background of) cold appetizers: long, delicately sautéed tongues of eggplant rolled into roulades; roasted yellow peppers, skinned, succulent, very sweet, suffused with the oil in which they were done; firm white beans mingled with strands of red onion; slices of fennel that are fresh, crunchy, almost hard; crisp, nicely cooked shrimp that are, unfortunately, of only vague seafood flavor; circles of tender squid; and strands of rather cartilaginous tripe—these last especially, but some of the other items as well, in need of a dressing more vigorous than the velvety oil with which they are polished. Hot appetizers too, sometimes sautéed porcini mushrooms, the flavor of the slices earthy and also rooty, vigorously but judiciously salted, strewn with fresh parsley.

An occasional oddity among the specials of the day is risotto nero con seppia, rice with squid and its ink, the mound of firm grains glinting, pitchy, threaded with slivers of squid, the flavor of the dish oceanic and sea-gamy, and yet, like much of the food here, a bit timid about itself—still, good food, the like of which you do not encounter daily. Capital pasta: occhio (heavy pasta tubes) in a pink and creamy tomato sauce that is thickened with cheese, weighted with ground peppery sausage, sweetened and brightened with green peas and strands of red pepper; firm, hot, light gnocchi, the little morsels in a well-oiled pesto sauce that is of almost winy basil fragrance—strong cheese grated on at the table adds sharpness to the heady dish; fuzi alla fortuna del cacciatore, which is to say, two-inch tubelike lengths of pasta with one kind of game or another—when the game is quail, the sauce of the bird's meat is a dark and rich one, touched with tomato, and you get chunks of the bird as well, the meat pungent of the distinctive, almost chocolate flavor of quail.

You may, if you wish, eat simply here, by way, for example, of this grilled snapper, the utterly fresh fish nicely browned, moist, just beginning to flake, all its nutlike flavor intact. Not much fancier and just as carefully timed is the chicken roasted with rosemary and brandy—the moist sections of bird reach you encased in their lightly crisped skin, and they have real chicken flavor that has been made woodsy by the herb, stout by the brandy. New York is no city in which to serve a less-than-first-class osso buco, for folks hereabouts have been at the dish since the days when Little Italy was one block of tenements and half a dozen restaurants. Here the big knuckle of meat is tender but dry, and lacks both the succulence and the spiciness of the dish at its best, though its rather tart red sauce helps. An order of roast baby lamb is a couple of tiny chops, the eyes of pink meat of almost fluffy tenderness, and a few slices of loin, these distinctly resilient— the sauce that moistens the strong-flavored meat is redolent of fresh rosemary. You do not often run into elk, but in season here they are—anyway, medallions thereof, the tender, blood-dark, and somewhat livery meat handsomely charred in its heavily seasoned red-wine sauce.

It is likely that at this point you will want, rather than a weighty dessert, something lively, and the Felidia salads are crisp and sparkling in their smooth, subtly seasoned oil. With them you may have Parmesan cheese that makes you sit up straight—it is hard, flinty, rousing. The zuccotto, a roulade of sponge cake, chocolate, and whipped cream, is astonishingly light for its richness. The chocolate mousse cake is not.

Good service, though the upstairs crew seems to be a distinctly second team, including a captain who is always around when you want him least. He just about butters your bread. Order a bottle of rather young and perfectly clear sfurzàt, and you have to stop him from demonstrating the art of decanting.

★★LE FESTIVAL (now closed)

134 East 61st Street
LUNCH AND DINNER. CLOSED SUNDAY.
Reservations: 838-7987.
Credit cards: AE, DC, MC, V.
Very expensive.

Once again Jean-Jacques Rachou, master of La Côte Basque, takes note of his East 61st Street satellite store, experiences dissatisfaction, considers the marketplace, undertakes a revision tuned to prevailing conditions as he sees them. Apparently, however, Rachou is not certain he has read the market right, for in physically remodeling Café Lavandou (the five-and-ten version of La Côte Basque that was) into Le Festival, he has kept, as they say, his options open, that is, his funds in reserve, for in this light renovation, in which south-of-France rusticity has been supplanted by geographically indeterminate swank, so many of the old appointments were thriftily retained that the incomplete new outfit looks like a masquerade costume not meant really to deceive. The anomalous room thus yielded juxtaposes costume-jewelry light fixtures with rustic timbers of dark, rough-hewn wood, banquette upholstery of Howard Johnson's orange with a cloth wall covering of dressy dove-gray. The high shelf that rimmed the room when this was the Café is in place, its country kitchen implements and crockery now exchanged for plates bearing nautical or marine-life illustrations—Le Festival is a seafood restaurant. And while the beveled mirroring of the front and back walls is more at home in this than in the previous room, the many-colored clutches of flowers on the tables are more casually gay than the intended cool of this setting wants. The halfheartedness of the redesign reflects, of course, the establishment itself. Though the food is very good, occasionally superb, undeniably out of water, Le Festival, like its name, is anonymous, lacks flavor of its own, fails to persuade you that behind it there is, rather than just a calculated business judgment, an urgent human involvement in things finny.

Overall impressions, however, though they will inform your recollection of Le Festival, need not distract while you are here. Attend, rather, for example, to the raw first courses: sea scallops with olive oil and basil, an abundance of the rich, iridescent slivers of supple white meat moistened with good olive oil and a bit of lemon, strewn with strands of fresh basil, adorned with a dollop of red caviar; snapper and salmon, a stripe of the thin-sliced pink meat between two of the white, both fish fresh and utterly sweet, but salted and thereby "cooked" a little, filmed with more of that smooth oil, and, around the dot of black caviar at the center of the plate, sprinkled with fresh coriander; three tartares of fish, each a sticky egg-shaped mass, the white one of snapper, the pink of tuna, the darkest of salmon, the last flashing the clearest fish flavor, but all herbed, lemoned, lively. Red meat—duck liver—appears but once on the printed menu, as one item in a three-part dish, scallops and lobster the other two, each shellfish in its own pale sauce, the slices of sautéed liver mingled with wild mushrooms of a notably earthy fragrance in a sauce that is winy, well seasoned, dark. On occasion the warm lobster salad is of toughened meat, and its gentling vinaigrette is not enough to save it. There are ravioli, they are firm, tender, filled with seafood and wild mushrooms, and their buttery white sauce, thick with slivers of zucchini, is touched with herbs of Provence.

Eight varieties of finfish appear among the main-course listings, skate, a French favorite, for years a discard on this side of the Atlantic, the comparative rarity among them. The flat fish is a semicircle occupying half your plate, the delicate but firm white meat moistened with black butter (pale brown), dotted with capers (suitably tart), garnished with buttered noodles (heady of tarragon). Other finfish: pompano, its intense flavor not at all obscured by the paste of green herbs and the layer of wild mushrooms that cover it; halibut, the snowy meat of fluffy lightness, strands of sautéed tomato and eggplant on it, in a pink sauce threaded with lengths of chive; thin scallops of salmon, fresh, firm, and of clear flavor, over a mound of noodles that are moistened and enriched with an herbed and creamy sauce; red snapper, the huge fillet, in a skin formed of thin slivers of zucchini, in an aioli sauce of much garlic pungency, though the fish itself, one time, is a little flat. Order sea scallops, and you get a half dozen of the big knobs, rich and silky within their handsomely browned surfaces, arranged in a circle in a pool of tart vinegar sauce—snow peas, a couple of sweet mussels, and a mound of strong spinach occupy the rest of the plate.

The crème brûlée is prepared in, and fills, a deep soup plate, the custard just a little weighty under its brown-sugar skin. The trio of chocolate desserts—an intense ice cream, an overwhelmingly rich white mousse, and a weighty chocolate mousse cake—reach you in a pool of light, pale-green mint sauce. What is given as "croustillant" is a stack of three circles of flaky pastry, rich whipped cream and wild strawberries in among them, all in a melony fruit sauce—the perfume of the berries wins you before the first bite. Thin, browned slices of apple and a good shortbread pastry make up the individual apple tart—it is garnished with a dollop of apricot puree and with two eggs of cinnamon ice cream, a cinnamon stick protruding from each.

★★FLAMAND

349 East 86th Street
DINNER.
Reservations: 722-4610.
Credit cards: AE, DC, MC, V.
Medium priced.

This could have been a neat, clean, harmless, nondescript room. You could have found yourself judging the place by its good food and whimsical service alone. But, no, someone had to go and improve it in a manner that misses utterly the intended bistro mark. You really cannot find much fault with the tweedy brown rug, and you would never notice the ceiling of acoustic tiles were there not hanging from it mammate chandeliers that glow the color of sallow Caucasian skin. Even the walls, dark pink with brown columns, the colors, more or less, of rare meat and milk chocolate, will probably fade well with time, though for the present much attention is called to them by the prints and travel posters stuck up, apparently, wherever there was a helpless empty space. Still, the winners are the stained glass scenic (you know—trees, rocks, water, sky, each its own color of glass) installed in the rear wall, and backlighted by the kitchen behind it; and, in the front window, the flowers that, in a foot-high scallop shell of black enamel, stand on a knee-high pedestal of mock marble, the unique composition framed in tied-back curtains of snowy gauze. Almost, but not quite, is this taste redeemed by its innocence. Meanwhile, in the background, there is Edith Piaf, failing yet again to ennoble self-pity.

You know from the title this place purveys, as the house puts it, "cuisine belge," which is to say, weighty food. It is therefore perhaps wise to begin with the like of this salade d'endives au jambon, scores of strands of the yellow-tipped leaves arranged on your plate like the spokes of a wheel, at the hub a dollop of good mayonnaise that is laced with little slivers of pungent ham—a lively salad, but you do wish the ratio were reconsidered, for you run out of dressing long before you are out of endives. You suffer from no such ham deprivation when you have the meat served to you in large rolled slices with ripe pear. What is given as "gratin Ostendais" benefits particularly from the clear sweet seafood flavor of its shrimp and scallops, which reach you buried in a small soup bowl of thick, herbed cheese sauce that has been browned before serving. The solidity of that stuff has nothing on the sweetbread-filled pannequet aux ris de veau, a thin, nicely browned, vaguely sweet pancake wrapped around great chunks of sweetbread, the rich organ meat in a spicy white sauce that is parsleyed just before it is served.

No restaurant is Belgian, of course, unless it lists waterzooi, and of the versions offered in the few Belgian restaurants that have come and gone on the local scene, Flamand's seafood waterzooi is the first to give any idea of why it is any nation's national dish. This is a briny white broth, creamy but not thick, peppery but in no way harsh, in which you find strands of fresh vegetables and seafood that, though part of a stew, have been judiciously done, so that these morsels of salmon are firm and of clear flavor, and these scallops, while they take on the creaminess, retain all their own richness of taste. Order quails, and you get three of the little birds, browned and moist and strong, set in a sauce that is thick with bits of endive. Flamand's blanquette de veau is in a thick sauce of Duvel beer (one of the world's most remarkable liquids), the big chunks of tender meat mingled with fresh mushrooms in the tart gravy—you do well to drink Duvel with the dish, but be aware that its polished and creamy texture conceals an almost violent level of alcohol. For some reason Belgians cannot leave well-enough alone, they produce such things as cherry-flavored beer, and though it is not suggested you drink the stuff, it

169

is the basis here of an excellent sauce (thick, spicy, tangy, and with just a touch of fruit), in which Flamand serves huge logs of tender rabbit.

Belgium is chocolate country, and sure enough, its chocolate cake is wonderfully intense—too bad it reaches you cool. The marjolaine is a layer cake of chocolate, nuts, good chewey meringue. It seems that the dearth of hazelnut flavor in the hazelnut cake is a function of a day-old state. Anyway, come to Flamand once, and the croustillant aux pommes is the dessert to have, a great construct of pastry leaves, like the petals of some grandiose flower, under them a mound of sweet and sour and tangy stewed apples—on occasion, the thing takes forever to make, but you get it in sparkling, just-made condition.

★ FLORENT

69 Gansevoort Street (near Washington Street)
LUNCH AND DINNER.
Reservations: 989-5779.
No credit cards.
Inexpensive.

Though once an old diner that catered to the meat-packing and warehousing industries in this grim waterfront neighborhood, Florent gets its lunch-counter looks as much by design as inheritance. The plastic and stainless steel are where they always were, but look closely by the room's bright light, and you see that they are largely new plastic, new steel. There is a coffee maker behind the counter, display cases—with sliding glass doors—for desserts, a slicing machine. The floors are of (probably the original) terrazzo, fluorescent-light fixtures are on the ceiling, chrome pipe chairs surround the tables. The working-class crowd that once frequented the old place is not, however, fooled. They do not constitute even a discernible fraction of the current clientele. Perhaps they have come in but gone elsewhere after reading what they thought was the posted menu, for high up over the counter are mounted three panels of black signboard with white lettering stuck on, the kind of fixtures that usually carry such advice as "bacon w egg .75 w 2 eGg $.95¢." Here, however, the signs offer only the day's weather report, the latest pollen count and reservoir levels, and the fares of various airlines to major American and European cities. Imagine, if you will, a longshoreman with too many drinks in him coming here for a bite to eat, looking at the sign, and finding that nothing is under $49. He leaves, of course, vowing to go a little easier, hereafter, on the juice.

Jet-set whimsy in a proletarian environment is aimed, of course, at the intercontinental youth crowd, chaps who talk four languages, shave three times a month, dress like automobile mechanics—the occasional beret does show up—and have with them willowy, lofty-cheekboned models who are sheathed in black rubber and wear doughnut-shaped earrings, of silver or gold, that hang to their photogenic shoulders. But that crowd has not managed to keep Florent to itself. Word has got around. You find here, mixed in with the world travelers, recently baccalaureated New Yorkers who, though they are going places in quite another world, wish to keep up with this one. Answers one of these to her suited-and-tied escort: "I *happen* to know you're wrong. Le Zinc is *definitely* Eurotrash. I'm surprised at *you*, David." David is crushed.

David attempts to pump himself back up with some invigorating fish soup Provençale—a dark, saffrony, but slightly thin broth that is dense with strands of vegetable and

170

bits of seafood, while his overseer gives 100 percent of her attention to an appetizer portion of "Alex's Mussels Provençales"—a score or more of the local mollusks (some of them, unfortunately, a little loud) mounded up, in a great glass bowl, over several inches of the redded, spicy, and oceanic broth in which they were done. Meanwhile, their companions pretend nothing has happened, attend to a rather scant portion of leeks, the cool strands in an herbed and mustard-thickened vinaigrette; and a plentiful salad of strong arugula that is mingled with walnut halves and dressed with walnut oil. The smoked chicken is good—you get many thick slices of the white meat, they are tender, mildly smoky, of clear chicken flavor, and they are garnished with small black olives that are oily and strong. The red-meat first courses disappoint; the pâté is cold and rather grossly liverish; the rillettes, the fatted dish of pounded, seasoned pork, also suffers from the cold—it is clammy at this temperature; only the hard slices of purple garlic sausage survive the chilling.

The fish are of the day, sometimes a misnomered tuna "steak" allegedly marinated in wasabi, which arrives as half a dozen little shafts of the fish, nicely grilled, touched with citrus, but not, detectably, with the listed Japanese radish; and sometimes grilled bluefish with rosemary and garlic, the fresh fillet artfully browned and crisped, the oil-rich meat moist within its crusty exterior, the promised flavorings only subtly present. You no longer find tête de veau on many local French menus, but Florent sometimes offers it. "Tête de veau," you understand, is "head of calf." But not to worry, you are served only a cross-sectional slice—sans staring eyes—its rim a ribbon of leathery but tender skin, within it a mosaic of glutinous sections, cartilaginous ones, meaty ones, the gummy and gamy stuff in a hot, creamy, thick, and fragrantly herbed vinaigrette. The plump blood sausages are deep brown and rich—but not particularly tasty—in their crackling wrappers, and they are served over sautéed onions and apples that are moist, sweet, and powerfully flavored of thyme. The medallions of veal are hefty charred slices of grilled meat, but this is coarse veal of little flavor, and it needs a sauce—you are offered a choice of them, and you pass up the pallid mustard sauce for the sharper and deeper one of shallots and wine. The same wine sauce helps but does not cure the tough and sinewy sirloin steak. Most of the main courses are served with French fries that, often, are thin, crisp, and of real potato flavor.

The crème caramel is eggy and light in its lively syrup of browned sugar. The zuppa inglese is many chunks of liquored cake and candied fruit under good whipped cream. And the lemon tart is a thin layer of tangy citrus custard on shortbread pastry. Plums that have been cooked in sugared, gingered vinegar are served under whipped cream—lively food. There are ripe berries, but sometimes they have been ripe since at least the other day.

You can arrive at 8 o'clock and find yourself alone in the place—the planes are late. But when you leave a couple of hours later, there may be a horde waiting for tables.

• FOUR SEASONS

99 East 52nd Street
LUNCH AND DINNER. CLOSED SUNDAY.
Reservations: 754-9494.
Credit cards: AE, DC, MC, V.
Very expensive.

Cocktail time, and it is easier to order another drink than to get off your stool and push through the four-deep crowd of middle-level businessmen who press around the famous square bar. Above your head, the larger part of the two-part Richard Lippold sculpture threatens, as it has for more than a quarter century, each of its innumerable thin brass rods—they form a kind of futuristic cloud—vertically suspended by two almost invisible threadlike wires. That is, most hang by two, a few by one, their second wires having snapped, these rods of course askew. Yes, the Four Seasons is coming apart. And though, as the bartender assures you (with a nervous upward glance), repairs on the Lippold will be made soon, millions of jokes over the decades about the imminence of cranial perforation are, all at once, less funny even than they used to be.

The big bar, under its overhead hardware, occupies acreage in a corner of the Bar Room, one of the restaurant's two spacious, blocklike, three-story-high dining rooms, this the one you attain when you have climbed the grand stairway from the street-level lobby. Lippold's smaller cloud is diagonally across from its mate, and it is here in the Bar Room, under these works of elevated art, that, at lunchtime, higher-ups in New York's publishing industry negotiate affairs. Many have "their own" tables, at which, by appointment, they receive, as on visiting day. The inner walls are of broad, to-the-ceiling matching panels of dark, black-grained wood, the outer ones of lofty windows, innumerable thin chains of brass and copper looped across each of them, each chain just above another—the chains ripple and flow, collectively, with the currents of air just inside the tall sheets of tinted glass. In this cavernous setting, even these large tables—they are covered with pale linen—seem drawn to half scale. You are seated on banquettes of deep-brown leather, or on wide leather chairs with steel frames, and though you are vaguely segregated from the celebrants at the bar by low partitions of dark glass, the noise of the tipplers makes its way to the dining room proper, and during dinner the calm otherwise imposed by this room's grand spaciousness is undone by the boys' bibulous jubilations. The Bar Room is presumably that half of the Four Seasons set aside for real New Yorkers (as distinguished, presumably, from the tourists attracted to the more pretentious Pool Room), and its brief menu flatters a local's no-nonsense image of himself by accentuating the kind of cooking—grilled meats, grilled fish, crab cakes, pasta—that is fancied by those who refuse to make the switch to filter tips or zippered flies. Actually, frequenters of this room are just squares with local addresses, folks who are as tickled to eat in the legendary Four Seasons as anyone, but like to be cool about it. "Grabbed one of the girls from the office last night, and went over to the Four Seasons for drinks and a couple of steaks—not a bad spot, and you don't have to wait for a table like at the Palm." Etc. In the Bar Room you may also order from the more extensive Pool Room menu, excluding only those dishes that, in the Pool Room, are finished on serving stands equipped with Sterno burners—that fancy stuff just don't go here in the Bar Room. In shape and size, the Pool Room (which you reach by way of a long corridor) is almost the Bar Room's twin—except that instead of a bar in the corner, there is a gurgling white-marble pool, brightly illuminated, at the center, bottom-lighted rubber trees in tortured postures at each of its corners. The trees, taken together with the pots of greenery that, along the windowed walls, hang from the ceiling on long wires, do much to queer the room's grandeur—in this respect the trees take second place only to the overfeds who, in outfits that transform them into pictures from the Sears catalog, come to this place in order, solely, to have been in it.

The Seasons is pushing so-called Spa Cuisine (low calorie) these days, very American, you can tell how good for you it must be by how little you want it. Consider, for example, the squid salad with black beans, a pile of squid, a pile of beans, cold. Were it known widely that such exotic ingredients could be this flat, they would be staples, all across the contiguous forty-eight, at boarding schools and prisons. You desert the Spa section of the menu for the breast of pigeon with figs, only to learn that in addition to

172

Spa Cuisine, there is also the *influence* of Spa Cuisine, for the dish is made up of four small slices of not bad squab arranged like the quarter-hour points on a clock around a not yet ripe fig at the center of the plate, the two upon a film of cranberry puree. The merits of this fruit with this meat are difficult to gauge when the fig is favorless, but the sauce is lively with the squab. Nor will you bloat up on an order of what is given as "crisped shrimp filled with mustard fruits," nicely battered deep-fried shrimp that are filled with nothing, least of all shrimp flavor, garnished with a single morsel of nameless fruit in the mustard sauce. Grilled gravlax sounds like a promising idea, but it involves cooking the salmon twice, by marination and then by fire, which accounts for its denatured quality—that is somewhat offset by the fresh dill that adorns the grill-marked slab, but finally its harsh saltiness, simply too much sodium chloride, renders the article almost inedible. Relative safety in pasta: lobster ravioli, the firm sheets of noodle mingled with sweet peas in a lobster sauce that is vibrant of concentrated lobster flavor, though the chunks of lobster, apparently added at the end, are cold at their centers; and pappardelle with chanterelles, the broad, hefty ribbons of eggy noodle mingled with wild mushrooms that are fresh, crunchy, earthy.

Apparently when the crabmeat that goes into the crab cocktail is getting on, it goes into the crab cakes, for these have the unmistakable air of decomposition, and you are tempted to leave them where they are and move yourself to a table across the room. Well bred, you instead exchange them for blackened redfish, two lengths of firm, fresh white meat, their surfaces a rough skin of charred spices, the fish garnished with fiery black beans that are overlaid with strips of red pepper—a nice plate of food. What started out as fresh, sweet snapper is grilled until dry—it is served with a sauce choron (béarnaise pinked with tomato) that is cold. It is not, however, your now diminished level of expectation that accounts for the seeming excellence of this duck, for the crisped bird's succulent meat is in fact of strong, clear duck flavor, and its peach sauce, which is dark and sticky, is of brandylike intensity—the bird is garnished with a great half of poached peach, firm, glistening pink, of vivid fruit flavor. Around town, what goes as beef paillard is something pounded thin, rapidly grilled, at once browned and juicy. Here it is thicker than the usual thing, of necessity done more slowly, yielding but little of the dramatic contrast between a crusty surface and a blood-pink interior—its diablo sauce duplicates bottled steak sauce. You are better served by the skillet steak, for though its smothered onions seem sugar sweetened, the thick slab of fibrous, tender meat has real beef flavor.

When you select from the good cheese tray offered in the Bar Room, you are offered also a variety of fresh fruit—the cheese is served with a chewy, nutty walnut bread. The chocolate soufflé is a well-made example of the standard thing, fluffy and of a strong chocolate flavor, in this instance enriched by the milk-chocolate sauce your waiter spoons on. The chocolate velvet cake is, no doubt, technically a cake, but seems more like solid chocolate. Blackened edges are a zest to the slightly sour Italian prune tart. The baba is a firm sweet cake soaked in rum—the inserted layer of cooked peaches is a nice note. An abundance of sweet spice accounts for the distinctly American cast of the crisp and nutty blackberry-pine-nut pie.

Four American states and five other nations are represented on the long wine list.

★ FRANK'S

431 West 14th Street
LUNCH, MONDAY TO FRIDAY; DINNER, MONDAY TO SATURDAY. CLOSED SUNDAY.
Reservations: 243-1349
Credit cards: AE, DC, MC, V.
Medium priced.

Put this place in the middle of town, and no one would seek it out. Put it where it is, way out west on West 14th Street—virtually in New Jersey—and when the critics find it, they write about it as if they have turned up a new continent. It is not solely the restaurant's remoteness, however, that has addled the acuity of its admirers. You see, the place has sawdust on the floor, and if you tell the world you like it here, you are announcing that though you have gone a long way in said world (dine on turtle soup six nights a week), you honor more than ever the honest values of your origins—big cars, red meat, and a shotgun in every broom closet. Still, you better get a taxi right to Frank's door, for walking the last couple of blocks to this outskirt at night—anyway, without your shotgun—is spooky if not mad. Once inside, however, and you are in the security of the past, especially on weekend nights, when half the customers look like cops, the other half like their wives. The kids come too, to ruin the arithmetic.

This is a big old store, fairly wide and very deep, with sawdust on a barbershop-tile floor, dark paint on the high, stamped-tin ceiling. Down the right-hand side and down the center run two long rows of white-linened tables. Down the left-hand side, partway, runs the bar; beyond it the kitchen, behind a floor-to-ceiling curtain. The place is painted a weighty shade of deep-salmon (sockeye) pink, with lower walls of brown-stained wood.

Your host, a misplaced undertaker's assistant in a suit that just about gets around him, returns to your table a few minutes after leading you to it. He has with him a slate, which he holds under his chin like an identifying sign, as when one relative is meeting another at a train station, the two having never seen each other before. SAM GROB, the sign might read, and under that, quite unnecessarily, MEETING HILDA GROB. Host's expression, as he looks at you over the blackboard, is just as uncertain as Sam's, which is odd, for he performs this trick, of showing you the blackboard while at the same time reciting its contents—the evening's special dishes—dozens of times a night. Moreover, many of the supposed blackboard specials are identical to items on the printed menu. Still, he has to sneak a peek every third item or so to remind himself what comes next. The short recitation takes a long time—his delivery is that of someone orating in a language he has learned to pronounce, but not to understand.

Once you get past well-meaning Sam, however, you are in the hands of help that will not get you down. The waiters are, in fact, cheerful and efficient, greet you with a freebie of rather coarsely pickled mushrooms and red peppers, hot green peppers, and nuggets of blue cheese (the variety varies from time to time). And if you know your way around the menu, you will actually eat quite decently. You will, for example, eschew the snails, which are leathery, though their greened and garlicked butter is very much the usual thing. And you will bear in mind, when you go for the sometimes available wild mushrooms, that they may be sautéed in butter that is not as hot as it should be, which makes them a little greasy—still they have a woodsy flavor. A first course listed simply as "tripe" consists of a round casserole dish, fiery-hot from the oven, filled with a spicy red sauce that is thick with lengths of the pale, gelatinous innard—good food. The fettuccine alla panna is a dish that longs to be made of fresh pasta—these wide noodles lack egginess and are slightly more resilient than even your broadest idea of al dente, but they are in a suitably rich and sweet-spiced cream sauce. The tagliarini (thick spaghetti) is also somewhat recalcitrant, but its salty anchovy-and-tomato sauce, thick with olives and capers, is stout and vibrant.

The scampi are good shrimp moistened with a lightly parsleyed tomato sauce. The fish of the day is fresh, sometimes carefully prepared snapper, flaky and moist and of clear snapper flavor, in a sauce livornaise that is just a light tomato sauce sharpened with capers and bits of olive. Frank's has been known to ruin a perfectly good veal chop by overcooking it until it is gray and dry. And though the restaurant is in New York's beef district, its shell steak, though perfectly well prepared—charred and blood-juicy—will certainly not put you in mind of the beef of yesteryear, though it is no worse than most beef of today. The house sometimes offers roast ribs of beef—once again the meat is tender but otherwise not of anachronistic beefiness; if quantity moves you, know that a single Frank's rib will feed you today and then tomorrow for lunch.

The pecan pie is 90 percent filler, but order it hot, and it reaches you heated through (which helps)—the nuts are fine, and the whipped cream is the real thing, albeit sugary. There is more of that whipped cream on the key lime pie, which is tangy and comes on a good graham cracker crust.

o **FU'S**

1395 Second Avenue (near 72nd Street)
LUNCH AND DINNER.
Reservations: 517-9670.
Credit cards: AE, DC, MC, V.
Medium priced.

It is your lucky night, so you get seated at a table right beside (almost all the tables are right beside) a table at which the lady who is mistress of this place is visiting. She is explaining to her honored customers the special lengths to which she goes to train her staff—or, as she calls them, her boys. "You know what I call them?" she asks. "I call them *my boys!*" She laughs. "You know, every Friday I hold a special class for them. You know what I teach them? I teach them to say madame, sir, good evening, thank you. You know where I take my chef, my captain? I take them to Lutèce, to the Four Seasons, to Le Bernardin. I want them to know there is something else." It is more as if she wants them to know that something else is all there is, for Fu's is denatured Chinese, the enterprise of one who wishes, at once, to capitalize on her background and get as far from it as possible. The restaurant is built on the notion that the trappings of successful Western restaurants are what those places are about, and that those devices will work the wonders for Fu's that they did for, say, Lutèce, the Four Seasons, Le Bernardin. Of course she is right. This place hops—with customers who, like her, judge restaurants by whether there are captains in tuxedos, never mind that the civilities they murmur have been memorized phonetically.

You enter to what the house surely thinks of as its cocktail lounge, though it is tiny for the classification, a slick little black-topped bar, a gleaming steel rail for your elbows, another for your shoe. Behind the bar, wine is stored in a diamond pattern of racks to which your attention is called by the rods of glowing light that are the edges of each bin. The floor is of marble, the wall is a black mirror, potted palms stand in the corners. The bar is tended by, presumably, one of the lady's boys, this one, somehow, a girl. She must handle not only the bar before her but also, through a window in the wall behind her, the dining room. With the dining room she has only the trouble that results from there being more to do than she can handle. With the bar her problem is that she and her customers speak different languages, and she has no time for slow talk or slow listening. You ask what beers are on hand. She answers, but the only brand she can pronounce clearly is Tsingtao. (As it happens, the menu deals with this subject: "Our subtly and artfully blended drinks and the personable responsiveness of our staff are the ingredients with which we hope to transport you into the spirit of Fu's welcome.") Your wait for a table is rarely long (Fu's, though in certain other respects modeled after fancy midtown places, does not encourage those seated ahead of you—or anyone else—to hang around once the check and fortune cookies are delivered), and presently you make it to the nightclubby dining room, much charcoal-gray, pink, black mirrors, all softly lighted, at the center of the room a massive rectangular column—black glass yet again—hung with glowing strands of light. The banquettes are red velvet and cushy, but the chairs do not fit the tables— the legs of the former collide with the bases of the latter, so you can get only so close to dinner.

Your hostess has observed that non-Chinese restaurants offer special dishes of the day. Accordingly, she offers them too. But she has failed to note that such dishes are, often, either seasonal foods that cannot be listed on printed menus all year round, or dishes chosen for the variety they add to an otherwise limited menu. At Fu's, the menu in-cludes more than forty main courses, and the ingredients of the specials simply duplicate those of the listed items. But you figure out the thinking behind the practice quickly enough when the captain tells you that today's featured dish is shrimp in Grand Marnier sauce.

In search of safety, you repair to the printed menu, send for tangy spicy shrimp, not bad, the cool morsels in a nutty and slightly spicy sauce that is threaded with citrus rind. But the hacked chicken and sesame noodles are dreary versions of those familiarities, their usual drama lost because they are premixed and waiting for you—you even find a few strands of chicken among the noodles, as if the two items occupy adjacent tubs and visit each other. The fried dumplings are of normal flavor but of abnormal greasiness. The shu mei—little noodle dumplings filled with pork—are, for some reason, fishy, and are apparently glued together (your captain must pull them apart to divide an order). An order of steamed stuffed mushrooms consists of two mushroom caps, a shrimp on each.

You give the house the benefit of your now considerable doubt, choose your main courses from among the "chef's specialties," fail to regret it with respect only to the home-style chicken (though it is marked with the "hot & spicy" asterisk, it is not espe-cially), nicely battered and crisped morsels of chicken in among a ginger-flavored assort-ment of sautéed vegetables. The jumbo shrimp Fu's style are utterly without shrimp flavor, though it is probably a decent dish—the shrimp are mingled with water chestnuts and snow peas in a clear and sticky sauce—when the seafood element is itself. The crispy sea bass Hunan style tastes like candy. Fu's (sliced) steak is finished, on a side stand beside your table, by pouring over it a vegetable stew—a way of giving the customers the steak they want while permitting them to think they are eating Chinese. Of dishes not among the so-called specialties, the "banana chicken" (that is the concoction's title) is exactly what you think it is. In the crispy beef Hunan style, the shreds of meat are suitably crisped and chewy but utterly devoid of beefiness—bean sprouts, scallion greens, carrots, and a lot of salt complete the dish.

For dessert, pineapple is recommended. That the place does not offer cherries jubilee or crepes suzette is a function, surely, of the time it takes to prepare them, for Fu's likes to turn you over in forty-five minutes flat.

• GEORGINE CARMELLA

165 Mulberry Street (near Grand Street)
DINNER. CLOSED MONDAY.
Reservations: 226-3999.
Credit cards: AE.
Expensive.

Once the bold advance guard of restrained Italian cookery here in brash Little Italy (where the definition of just right is too much), this is now a lonely enclave. Georgine Carmella saw the light and brought the word, but Little Italy hardly noticed, not to say laughed. All of which is not, however, the opening chapter of a morality tale, for the restaurant is not quite up to scorning the scorn of its lessers, and though it has not taken on the customs of its alien host, it no longer asserts its own ways with anything like its original vigor. You can still get a good anti-Neopolitan dinner here, but the menu is skimpy, the daily specials are few, and the preparation of the dishes only sometimes flashes the talent that informed the cooking when the place was new. Georgine Carmella has proven a point pointlessly, that a non-Little-Italy Italian restaurant can make it in Little Italy. This is like proving that by taking off your clothes and lying on the beach, you can get a suntan in the wintertime. Neighborhood types are never seen here, and throngs of visitors from the outer boroughs—they occupy most of Little Italy's restaurant chairs of an evening—pass it by as if it were picketed by certain local authorities. The establishment's commerce derives in principal measure from those who are persuaded that Georgine Carmella is your basic oasis, an out-of-the-way secret of the few. Put it in a neighborhood where you would expect to find it—that is, take away what makes it special, its location—and it would either shape up or file for protection.

The restaurant is a cube of an old storefront painted dark pink, with a stamped-tin ceiling and a white, barbershop-tile floor. A fern occupies each of the two front windows that flank the front door. Within, the walls are unadorned, one of them surfaced with a tinted mirror under which a banquette runs along that side of the room, a handful of this restaurant's dozen or so white-linened tables before it. The softly lighted room is illuminated by eight school lamps that hang from the ceiling. The waiters are in black trousers, white shirts, black four-in-hands. Nothing could be simpler, and the tasteful, unselfconscious restraint is much of what makes the restaurant convincing to those it convinces.

You will not be convinced by the mellanzane alla griglia, thin slices of charred eggplant, shaved Parmesan over them, fresh arugula in a tart dressing under them, everything fine except that the eggplant itself is dry and of little flavor—ask for, and moisten it with, olive oil, and you improve things considerably. Better yet, start your dinner with the vongole gratinate, littleneck clams, in their shells, grilled with lemon and garlic, touched with parsley, the livened mollusks tender, fresh, and sweet. The circular ravioli are packed with a fluffy herbed-ricotta filling and they are served on a layer of vibrant spinach. And each day there is a risotto of the day, and sometimes the moist rice is dotted with bits of ham, sweet peas, snap peas—good food that becomes better when the grated cheese is spooned on, though on occasion the rice is a little undercooked, some of the grains hard rather than firm. All pastas, the risotto as well, are available in half orders.

177

Your waiter pushes the sole in what he describes as a sweet-and-sour sauce, made with carrots, pine nuts, raisins. It is a miracle of your palate's discernment that it can detect the sauce's quality when it is in the presence of fish that is rank and inedible. The chickens on this menu are identified as "free range," but the grilled baby chicken is still too much the baby to taste much like chicken—the juicy bird, moistened with olive oil and lemon, is nicely grilled, however, the charring most of its flavor. The crusted sautéed veal chop has been dried out a little in the pan—still, it is not bad, though the salad of mozzarella, sun-dried tomatoes, and basil with which it is garnished is the real life of the plate. Although, as the menu leads you to expect, the shell steak is coated with coarse-ground black pepper, there is little pepper flavor to this dish—the steak reaches you, moreover, vastly underdone, raw at the center, and its sauce, of blood and the grappa in which the meat was flamed, must serve to gentle the inelegant slab.

If you have left more on your plate than is your habit, you may opt for cheese before dessert—the place serves good Parmesan, flinty and pungent, but you will need two of these skimpy orders to dispatch much of your lingering hunger. On the other hand, an order of fresh berries with this establishment's cold, very rich zabaglione may well take care of the rest. The chocolate cappuccino mousse is vibrant under the good whipped cream. A couple of the crunchy pastry tubes called cannoli come packed with a creamy custard that is coated with ground nuts where it protrudes from the ends.

★ GIBBON

24 East 80th Street
LUNCH, MONDAY TO FRIDAY; DINNER, MONDAY TO SATURDAY. CLOSED SUNDAY.
Reservations: 861-4001.
Credit cards: AE, DC, MC, V.
Very expensive.

Not far from the Whitney, hard by the Met, and on the very flank of Madison Avenue's gallery row, Gibbon caters to a world of curators and donors, dealers and collectors, even artists. That set eats elsewhere, too, of course, but of all its uptown hangouts, only this one provides a setting that is sufficiently reliquary for the conduct of affairs that involve both high culture and high finance. The restaurant occupies the ground floor and second story of a venerable townhouse, and though the appointments are mostly Japanese, the rooms in which they have been installed suggest the insular mansion of some old New York family—the kind of place occupied by the dowager, the butler, and the matched pair of snarling mastiffs.

Down a couple of steps to the lower, more commodious of the two levels—softly lit and brick-walled, at the front a bar and a fireplace, at the back a number of tables formed into groups by partitions of elaborately woven and tied bamboo. Up a flight of stairs to the stark parlor floor, high-ceilinged and harshly lit, the walls covered with raw silk of an indeterminate color, the tieback curtains on the huge windows a somewhat more straightforward dirty beige. The four-panel painted screen hung high on one side of the room is probably a masterpiece, but to the untutored eye it is an essay in faded gray on faded silk. But none of that matters. Those who frequent the Gibbon are past caring about superficialities. There is well-bred old money here, in old clothes: well-worn tweeds and flannels, button-down shirts and club ties, calf-length dresses and sensible shoes—and yards of pearls. When high-level salesmanship is going on, you see mixed groups consisting of the moneyed, the middlemen, and the artist—the last distinguished from his companions by his taciturnity and open collar.

One of Gibbon's more successful ecumenical creations is a shrimp appetizer in which four crunchy, sweet crustaceans and a couple of disks of crisp lotus root are served in a crimson sauce the house calls strawberry vinaigrette—it is more like a fortified purée of the ripe fruit, but that brilliantly chosen dressing is the making of the dramatic dish. Most of the food here is strikingly presented, including an item in which two chimneys formed of peeled and seeded lengths of cucumber stand side by side on a handsome square blue plate. The columns are filled with and surrounded by chunks of good, cool lobster meat, which are coated with a thick mayonnaise.

The Gibbon has one flaw that, particularly in Japanese restaurants, is deadly—its fish sometimes tastes less than fresh. The knowing therefore eschew the first course of assorted sashimi, for that defect is utterly off-putting in fish served raw. But there is another sashimi item on the menu—it is called usuzukuri—that, for some reason, never seems off. The dish consists of innumerable slices of white fish, each of them paper thin and translucent, arranged on a plate like the filmy, smoky-white petals of a huge white flower, a mound of shredded scallion at the center, on that a smaller mound of strong grated radish. You add the radish, according to your tolerance for fire, to a little dish of citrus-flavored soy sauce, dip the fish in the sauce, and eat—the flavor of the fish is clear despite the pungency of the sauce. There are hot first courses as well, among them minced cherrystone clams mingled with chopped mushrooms and served, in three big clam shells, on buttery spinach and under a browned breading—spicy, earthy, bracing food. A dish called tataki is billed as "charred filet mignon delicately raw inside." It turns out, to your surprise, to be cold, the strands of meat not charred at all, in fact barely browned. Still, this is good food, the thin red strips of rare and tender beef strewn with curls of shredded scallion and garnished with caviar and grated radish—you dip the meat in what the house calls "sauce Gibbon," a salty soy sauce dotted with sesame seeds.

The meat of a lobster is taken from its shell, sautéed, piled back into the shell, and served in a soy sauce made nutty by sesame—the carefully prepared lobster is firm and sweet, that sauce a fine foil to it. But the steamed pompano sometimes suffers for being a little over the hill. So if you wish to take no chances when you try this place, opt for the main courses of meat: sautéed scallops of pale, juicy veal, nicely browned, in a complex soy-based sauce that is sweet, salty, thick with leaves of watercress; or the six-rib rack of lamb, brought to you intact, its surface handsomely browned, the meat pink and of strong lamb flavor, the sauce of roasting juices given a slight Japanese accent with a bit of soy sauce.

All the desserts are Western ones, among them an intense, black-frosted chocolate cake that seems to call for a glass of milk; a lemony, lemon-rindy, creamy, and polished lemon mousse—fluffy whipped cream comes with it; and a rich banana ice cream of vivid flavor.

★ GIJO'S

1574 Second Avenue (near 81st Street)
DINNER.
Reservations: 772-0752.
Credit cards: DC, MC, V.
Medium priced.

Pronounced "G-Joe's," the title of this one is a neologism composed of the first syllables of the given names of the Italian-American gentlemen who are its proprietors.

This artless, almost childlike approach is clue to the whole place, for Gijo's is an innocent, seemingly uncomprehending imitation of certain Upper East Side Italian restaurant/saloons. It is Elio's and Dieci and any number of many other such places, but done on a budget and coming off about as convincingly as a rubber chicken. And yet, it is precisely this quality—of being the almost comically poor relation—that makes Gijo's the only one of this neighborhood's Italian restaurants that could be called endearing. When, for example, your host himself comes to your table to announce to you the specials of the evening, scratches the back of his neck, looks to the ceiling for help, and finally asks you for the hard-to-remember name of that red sauce with olives, capers, and anchovies in it, you close your eyes, put your hands to your head, and struggle to recall it, in your eagerness to help him out.

Gijo's is a horseshoe-shaped place, one leg given over to the restaurant, the other to its bar. It is to the bar that you enter, and here your surroundings are principally what was abandoned by the saloon that was the site's previous occupant. A coat of glinting varnish now seals in the decades of scars on the long bar. The walls are of oak flooring, a sight gag the current proprietors found here, liked, and kept. A television set threatens from its position high up at the front of the room, directly over the jukebox. But head to the back, make a U-turn at the espresso machine, and you are in the restaurant proper, wherein Gi and Jo give you their version of Lusardi's and Parma. The cushy masculinity of those places—massive buff-colored walls trimmed with heavily grained, honey-colored woods—is rendered here in tan and dark-tan paint, a ragged edge between them. And the unadorned, spare solidity of the prototypes is here improved upon with five-and-dime scenics all over the walls. But the white linen on the tables is real, as are the simple side chairs around them, and if you miss the substantiality and swank of the places this place emulates, you will certainly not rue the absence of their cliquishness and favoritism.

You are granted, gratis, a small portion of fried zucchini, on which you nibble while you consider what next, and those fries reach you hot and juicy within their crisped batter. But then there is this seafood salad, in which the crisp shrimp are a little bland, the fresh squid a bit tough, the bay scallops minus some of their plump richness. Those elements are mingled with celery, much parsley, and a tart vinaigrette, but you miss the garlic that might just rescue the dish. Gijo's carpaccio, however, is first-class, the thin slices of just-cut raw beef covered over with a thick, emerald-green dressing of good oil and much parsley, which is in turn strewn with slivers of fresh raw mushroom and with small chunks of sharp Parmesan cheese. The vitello tonnato is almost that dish's equal, the many thin slices of cool, tender veal piled up like a stack of pancakes, the sauce under which they are buried a thick purée of tuna that is enriched with oil, soured with lemon, dotted with strong, salty capers.

You may have a half order of pasta as a first course—unless the one you want is the spaghetti with seafood, of which you may well be able to handle a full-size allotment unaided, for its briny and pungently garlicked red sauce is thick with scallops, shrimp, chunks of swordfish—all fresh tasting—and the dish is adorned with a couple of good hot clams in their shells. The seafood is not of especially vivid flavor, but the vibrant red sauce easily carries the dish. Gijo's makes a good sauce bolognese (meat sauce)—thick and nubbly, dotted with bits of tomato, strongly seasoned—and serves it on green noodles that could as well be white ones, for these are dried green noodles, have no quality of the vegetable of which they are colored, are just a neutral carrier for that more-than-decent sauce.

Each day there is broiled swordfish, sometimes with one kind of sauce, sometimes with another. When it is offered with the sauce the name of which your host could not remember, have it, for you get a substantial slab of the fresh fish, it is firm and fibrous and juicy, and that sauce livornese—thick with capers and olives, subtly sharpened with anchovies—is a terrific foil to the sturdy white meat. What the house calls broiled chicken would more accurately be called chicken paillard. The breast meat is skinned, boned, flattened, grilled in lots of butter, and served strewn with parsley—the flavor of the bird is vivid, potentiated by that butter, and it all adds up to a simple, satisfying dish. The same treatment works less well on veal that *is* called veal paillard, for veal must be well browned if it is to have much flavor, and this meat reaches you pale—you squeeze on lemon, which helps a little. Better yet, you may have your veal and lemon combined for you, in Gijo's version of veal francese, in which the lightly egg-battered meat is served in a deep, dark sauce that is powerfully citrus flavored. The restaurant makes good lamb chops—they are accurately broiled, tender, of heady lamb flavor.

For dessert there are ice-cream things, and a cheesecake that, though made on these Italian premises, is of cream cheese rather than ricotta—the cake has good flavor, but it is cold and, inevitably, claylike. The best conclusion to dinner here is a salad of fresh greens and some strong Parmesan cheese.

When the air-conditioning is on, it can be quite cold here, when off, quite warm. When the back door is opened, it can be just right, but noisy of the sounds of the street. None of this does anybody seem to mind.

★★GOTHAM

12 East 12th Street
LUNCH, MONDAY TO FRIDAY; DINNER, DAILY.
Reservations: 620-4020.
Credit cards: AE, DC, MC, V.
Expensive.

In this, the Age of Ego, mere success is contemptible. Any fool can follow the rules to make an enterprise work. The trick is to make a trap at which even the dullest mouse would sneer and still get the world to beat a path to your door. In the restaurant business, attempts to work such magic are usually the essays of those who, how you say, do not need the money anyway, and it was presumably with just such wizardry in mind that Lindsay-Administration-politico-turned-realtor Jerome Kretchmer, a few years ago, set this trap on East 12th Street. During the restaurant's early days, you often saw Kretchmer on hand, business-suited and nervous, clearly a dynamo, and, equally clearly, one who, given all the freedom and encouragement in the world, would still construct a terribly functional mousetrap indeed. No complete fool Kretchmer, he knew that if his restaurant were built along lines he himself could envision, though it might well succeed, it would do so not even slightly in spite of itself. What, what to do. To the rescue surrogate egos, two so high on their success, they look up the rules only to be sure of leaving none unbroken. Considerations as to the taste of the community, the condition of the marketplace, and common (or any other kind of) sense are by such types grandly scorned. It is not known which of the experts—who, respectively, designed this place and wrote its first menu—hit on the concept of the Near East as a point of uncertain departure (or even if they ever spoke to each other), but at the outset, the menu here was sure-enough Nouvelle Moroccan, the dining room an equally authentic example of Ottoman Deco Revival.

Hiring a menu consultant to devise a menu to be executed by a chef is like hiring an art consultant to hire an artist to paint by numbers. That first menu was just an advertisement for the supposed creativity of the mind behind it, and like a burglar's calling card, it served mainly to underscore the perpetrator's contempt for the victim. Happily, it flopped. Today's menu is the work of today's chef, and if neither it nor its execution is invariably inspired, eating here is at least an encounter with the work of an individual with an individual's style.

The Gotham's looks, however, are as they were when the restaurant was new, the big space distorted, as if by whimsy gone amok, into a bad dream of inexplicable parapets, misplaced towers, and hulking columns of, variously, faux malachite, mock marble, and genuine cement. The walls and linen are desert tan, the chairs are green, and a long banquette, upholstered in a dark tapestry cloth, cuts through the room diagonally like a geologic fault. The front of the restaurant has been raised, so you must climb up to it, and then down into the dining room. Elsewhere, too, there are meaningless shifts of level—the bar, for example, is pointlessly on a raised plateau to which almost no one ascends. Overhead, track lights play onto huge cloth cups that are suspended from the distant ceiling—meant as fey lampshades, they look like underpants for some species of legless behemoth. The total effect here is of noticeability, distraction. The room fails utterly as a civilized setting for dinner, competing, as it noisily does, for attention you would ordinarily direct to your food and conversation.

So don your dark glasses, come here, and order the seafood salad, fresh, clean mussels, chunks of lobster, and slices of squid and octopus in among crisp leaves of red and green lettuce, the assortment garnished with a section of fresh avocado, and moistened with a lively dressing. The duck breast carpaccio is a thin layer of the raw, dark-pink meat spread across a great black plate—it is painted with an exceptionally vibrant pesto sauce, and it is garnished with crunchy marinated beans and a bit of green salad. Terrines of chicken are usually tasteless, but the one you get here is suffused with the strong, sweet flavor of chicken fat—the fat almost obscures the woodsiness of the dark morels that marble the terrine, but not at all the crunchiness of its many pistachios. Morels again, this time in the earthy company of shiitakes and chanterelles, the three mushrooms being most of the sauce for a mound of firm but tender fettuccine—leaves of basil add fragrance, and crisp pine nuts and bits of cool chopped tomato adorn the top. Withal, the winner is what is given as "roasted quail salad," an English-muffin-size patty of cool minced salad—greens and wild mushrooms in a walnut oil dressing—surmounted by the nicely roasted eponymous bird, moist and cooked through, its dark flavor intense.

Many fish, the salmon a bit fishier than the others, the artfully sautéed fillets prettily browned and arranged on a mound of sweet-spiced spinach dotted with pungent Mediterranean olives—probably lovely food when the salmon is fresh. The swordfish, however, is, and it is adorned with crosshatched grill marks—but it is rare, and underdone swordfish is tough. Steamed whitefish is the surprise top swimmer, the fluffy white fillets gilded with a silken purée of sweet yellow peppers. What the house calls lobster pasta you will call one mound of buttery lobster meat, another of eggy noodles—the dish is made picturesque by the presence of the head and tail of the lobster shell, but that cannot undo the fact that the two edible elements do not add up. The striking veal dish is of many thin slices of the pale-pink meat arranged around a mound of pungent ratatouille that is suffused with the flavor of strong olive oil—by some miracle, the delicate meat is not overwhelmed in this setting, and the two components set each other off dramatically. Chunks of rare roast lamb are arranged on a sheet of crisp, thin-sliced potatoes—

crunchy root vegetables, dark roasted shallots, and quartered artichoke hearts are the other elements of the well-balanced dish.

The custard of the crème brûlée lacks fluffiness. The poached pear arrives in a long-stemmed wineglass that you must nail to the table to eat safely from its bowl—the pear is icy and is set in icy raspberry syrup, which makes for a cloying, candylike dessert. The apple apricot charlotte is of those stewed fruits and raisins—it arrives, under whipped cream, surrounded by tiny walls of bread, moistened with a liquored butterscotch sauce, and garnished with a honey-flavored ice cream. The chocolate cake is a good, rich one, and you wish it were at room temperature.

★★LA GOULUE

28 East 70th Street
LUNCH AND DINNER. CLOSED SUNDAY.
Reservations: 988-8169.
Credit cards: AE, DC, MC, V.
Medium priced.

To survive, this establishment had to be transformed, for it began (in the early seventies) as one of the principal destinations in New York of what was then called the jet set; and it became, less than a decade later, just a neighborhood place, one at which the habitués usually arrive on foot. The change was effected, however, without the alteration of so much as a physical—or conceptual—stick of the place. So if you have not been here in some time, prepare yourself for a double déjà vu: the restaurant is still what it was in the beginning; and it is still a startlingly clear memory of Paris.

You will recall that La Goulue is an entrance room and two vaguely separated dining rooms; that up front there is a tiny zinc bar and a few cocktail tables with brass-framed marble tops; that, under a deep-brown stamped-tin ceiling, the walls are of dark wood, except where they are inset with the big plate-glass mirrors that, even when this place was new, looked as if they were losing their silver in random streaks and patches; that the floors are of broad wooden planks, the curtains of lace; that the dining rooms are rimmed with high-backed banquettes of caramel-colored leather; that the rooms are lighted by sinuous Art Nouveau wall sconces; and that the tables are set with white linen, glinting crystal and china and flatware, and flowers in slender vases. If you are still having difficulty dispelling the notion that, this setting notwithstanding, you are in the same old Big Apple, consider the serving staff in their black-and-whites and long white aprons. Most of them are those businesslike French professionals for whom discussions between consenting adults on the subject of food are serious matters but never solemn ones. Even the few non-Gallic members of the staff have picked up the habit of straight talk, if not yet easy conversance with their subject. And now that La Goulue no longer gets the crowd that used to come here only because the place was fashionable, you find yourself surrounded by folk with whom even you yourself might consider having dinner. They are here for the restaurant's comfort, for its more than decent traditional food, for the pleasure of being among others whose minds are as sound as their own. And in summer, some of them are here for the breezes. For when the weather is fine, tables are set out on the sidewalk under the awning, a stand of greenery at each end of the row. Some even come with their dogs, tie them to a nearby tree, blow them kisses during dinner, deliver snacks. The view is only of East 70th, but when you consider the places into which much of New York is clamoring to get, you realize that a two-hour dinner on this quiet street is actually a month in the country.

You do not expect, in these times, the bistro food of forty years ago (though you would not complain if it were offered). You are content, even happy, to settle for the traditional New York bistro menu in contemporary terms, for actually, with respect to many dishes, that is simply the old item upgraded. This smoked salmon, for example, is far from the salted and oily red meat that was once a staple in New York French restaurants a rung or more below the caliber of haute cuisine. It is, in fact, a great sheet of rosy, velvety seafood, of light texture and of a sweet, only vaguely smoky flavor, served to you with good olive oil, lemon, capers, and sharp and crunchy chopped onions. You are disappointed to find that the so-called haricots verts are not at all the tiny, almost thread-like green beans the name suggests, but, rather, everyday green beans, albeit young and tender ones—still, this is nice light food, the cool green shafts mingled with slices of fresh mushroom in their tangy, mustard-flavored dressing. The duck pâté is distressingly dark and dry, a function of an overextended stay in the oven, but the peppercorns with which it is studded and the pungent mustard with which it is served help. Why tomatoes and mozzarella are on this French menu is a mystery, more of one when you find that the cheese is crumbly, a little loud, not at all like the smooth and milky Italian article. The plump snails are a decent version of the standard item in their parsleyed, garlicked, and strongly seasoned hot butter. And the onion soup, under browned cheese that has a crust of bread concealed beneath it, is dark and sweet, thick with onions.

If it seems to you that outdoor eating calls for picnic food, consider this cool (but not cold) lobster, which arrives with the meat of the tail still encased in the split carapace, that of the claws out of its shells, all of it firm and of a fresh ocean flavor, garnished with cool vegetables, and served with a big dollop of rich mayonnaise—very nice with cold white wine. But in the right season you may gladly forgo the illusion of a picnic for the reality of soft-shell crabs, for La Goulue obtains little ones, flours them, sautés them rapidly in hot butter, and delivers them in tender, delicately crackling condition. Swordfish is often the finfish of the day, the big steak fresh and fibrous and juicy, served under a strongly tarragon-flavored sauce béarnaise that seems actually to combine with and enrich the juicy fish. That swordfish is quite sound, but this salmon is striking, the side of fresh fish firm and flaky under a sorrel sauce that is a slightly sour, distinctly earthy, and vaguely metallic deep-green purée, which contrasts dramatically with the pink meat. The suprême de volaille is a boned and nicely browned breast of chicken in a tart vinegar sauce that is hot and smooth, as if the sauce was finished just a moment before it was served. Only a few red-meat dishes on the menu, among them a tournedos à l'estragon, in which the two-inch thick filet mignon—its silken meat tender, but not especially tasty—is provided with plenty of flavor by the winy tarragon sauce in which it is served. Light, crisp French fries and grilled tomatoes come with the steak.

You inquire of your waiter the condition of the Brie. He is frank with you. But come on a night when it is in good condition, and you get lovely cheese, its chalk-white shell a nice bit of texture against the soft, buttery center. Ripe berries are served with whipped cream that is very sugary but otherwise fine. The raspberry mousse cake consists of the mousse, a jellylike icing on top, chocolate at the base—a fun sweet. What the house gives as "orange napoleon" is nothing like what you think of as a napoleon. It consists of sections of orange and strips of rind that have been steeped, with whole cloves, in cognac—a cold, rousing dessert.

★★★ LA GRENOUILLE

3 East 52nd Street
LUNCH AND DINNER. CLOSED SUNDAY AND MONDAY.
Reservations: 752-1495.
Credit cards: AE, DC, MC, V.
Very expensive.

Here is well enough not left alone. La Grenouille, where once panache, prettiness, and sparkle were all the more dramatic for their simple setting, has been "done" down to the final square inch. The changes seem minor, are only background—the once painted-green walls are now padded and covered with a pale fabric that simulates grass cloth, and the once plain ceiling is now surfaced with grainy wood veneers. The perhaps intended net effect is a quieter Grenouille, but a presumably unintended additional effect is that the revised surroundings never quite leave off pointing themselves out to you. Lift up your eyes, and there is no place to rest them.

La Frog is in two parts, preferred seating in the smaller front room, most of the tables in the somewhat wider, deeper room just behind it, the areas separated by little more than turns toward the center, from the left and right, of the great banquette that is a brilliant swath of crimson velour rimming the entire place. Where the walls are not padded, they are surfaced with mirrored glass, the floral carpeting underfoot is dark and cushy, painterly paintings hang in carved and gilded frames, and the little lamps on the walls and tables glow softly in their silk shades. Then there are the famous flowers, in great bursts here and there all around the rooms, in dense, luxuriant bouquets on every table. By their freshness, beauty, and especially by their audacious abundance, they set this place apart—too bad that their power has been mitigated by fussy changes in the surroundings.

If you are famous or infamous, a friend of the house or a darling of the press, a lord, a leader, a mogul in a glamour industry, you will be seated in the front room; otherwise in back, even if you must wait for a back-room table while tables up front are in disuse. (And if there are just two of you unknowns, you will be taken—unless someone else is already stuck with it—to the only really small table for two, which is against the rear wall, even when more comfortable tables are all about. But no fuss is made when you reject that accommodation, and you are at once shown to a better one. Still no one has been able to figure out why that table is not filled last, since no one can reasonably object to it if nothing else is open.) When you are seated, happily, you are treated sweetly by captains who know well the (rather limited, these days) menu and by diligent waiters. The place is manned also by the Massons, mother and son, proprietors. Obviously they sanction the two-tier system, even its excesses, for it is the essence of their place. But it is nice to think they do so reluctantly, out of perceived necessity rather than in scorn of the lower orders. Surely the beautiful Mme. Masson, now silver haired and gracious as ever, though she does go unseeing through the back of her restaurant, where after all she does not know by sight those present, turns out to be more shy than aloof, for she does light up a little if you catch her eye and smile at her, inquires right away, with a show of interest that is at once aristocratic and motherly, after your contentment. Similarly Masson the Younger, his good looks at once princely and collegiate, whose agreeability is unvarying from one end of his store to the other.

Upon a time this restaurant's culinary reputation owed something to the dazzling selection of cold items from which were assembled plates of assorted hors d'oeuvres. There is still the display just inside the second front door, its components as lively as ever: crunchy, almost hard celery root, the long strands in a remoulade that is at once polished and acidic; great stalks of asparagus peeled down to their tender white cores; ratatouille, the individual oil-enriched vegetable morsels firm and discrete in their well-garlicked sauce; shrimp of clear, sweet ocean flavor in a rich pink dressing; mushrooms à la grecque that, too bad, are sour rather than tart; a bracing salad of cucumbers; poached salmon, the fish impeccable under its herbed mayonnaise. Still, when you want a cool first course, you will find more diversion in the salade de foie gras à l'aile de poulet, in which slices of foie gras, smooth and rich, and shafts of chicken, of memorably deep chicken flavor, are arranged on a mound of tender, deep-green haricots verts, wild greens and bits of diced tomato all about, white raisins as well—a nice note—everything glistening in a silken walnut-oil dressing. You will do well to pass up the pannequet de fruits de mer, for the rarity of seafood in a vanilla sauce does not offset the undistinguished seafood mash that fills this pancake. Have instead the quenelle de brochet, a fluffy dumpling, of bright pike flavor, set on an earthy mushroom duxelles and covered with a rich white sauce that, just before serving, is browned on its plate. Two may strike you as a small number of ravioli, but those served here arrive in a shallow silver casserole, are formed of particularly delicate pasta, are filled with a mix of leeks and truffles, and are in a dark morel sauce that is at once profoundly earthy and polished.

The lobster is a small one, supple and sweet, the tail, out of its shell, and set over a gentle hash of red cabbage, is flanked by the delicate claws, all in a pale, sweet sauce that is touched with saffron. Your grilled Dover sole is shown to you whole (its skinned surface coppered in butter), is taken away, returned to you as four filleted quarters, firm and fresh, which you consume with a sauce that, though of vivid mustard flavor, does not obscure the good fish. The thin slices of salmon are fresh and a little rare, accordingly their flavor is clear, and they are arranged over a thick, dark, grainy pancake that is juicy with the white sauce, dotted with black caviar, that moistens this dish—little sprigs of parsley and a dollop of caviar adorn the pink salmon. Inevitably there are frogs' legs, and perhaps to hint at how they are eaten, a finger bowl arrives when the legs arrive. Sure enough, though the delicate thighs are browned and glistening, when you do this dish digitally, your fingers pick up only a little oil—also garlic and lemon (the presence of lemon seeds suggests the kitchen is out of cheesecloth). The roasted poularde paysanne is peasant food indeed, the huge half chicken garnished with chestnuts and with a dressing that is thick with lengths of gamy sausage—the bird is notable for the strength of its chicken flavor. You wish the braised beef had spent more time in the stock, for the good meat is still a bit dry and resilient, while its sauce (of the cooking liquid) is earthy and strong of its vegetables—and of spices that, surprise, have an Eastern accent.

Soufflés that are light, triumphantly risen, handsomely browned, and prettily sugared, among them one of deep chocolate strength, the sharp edge of which is the slightly burnt flavor of the top—you enrich it with whipped cream or with a thick and tangy Grand Marnier sabayon. The hot roasted pear, firm, fruity, and sweet spiced, is set on a patty of ground almonds in a pool of chocolate sauce. The warm, cinnamon-flavored apple tart—its pastry is light and flaky—is topped with a ball of rich pecan ice cream. From the pastry cart you do better with the Paris Brest—the airy cake is surfaced with almonds and filled with a rich hazelnut butter—than with the mousse-of-rhubarb tart, which is well made but comes across as something to do when you find you have on hand lots of rhubarb.

• GROVE STREET CAFÉ

53 Grove Street (near Sheridan Square)
DINNER. CLOSED SUNDAY AND MONDAY.
Reservations: 924-9501.
No credit cards.
No liquor.
Expensive.

Supposedly there are, around town, cozy neighborhood restaurants in which more-than-decent food is prepared and served, by amateur but dedicated crews, in unpretentious surroundings. The discomforts that necessarily obtain in such places, it is thought, are trade-offs for economy—maybe you bring your own wine, obtained at liquor-store cost, and presumably the menu prices are low. Of course no such places exist. Any establishment taken to fit the description is really a cooperative fantasy—between a clientele that likes to believe it is in on a good, private thing, and a management that, in fact, is.

What distinguishes this Village example of the genre from most of the others is that the collection of recipes from which the kitchen works includes some real winners. The house, however, knows not which those are, alternates the good with the dreary. And though you do bring your own wine, you may find a disaccord between the food prices and, say, a tiny table hard by the radiator. The cubical store is wee, the brown fabric on the walls is adorned with a tiny floral print, the four-bladed fan hangs from a dark-red ceiling, and you walk on a dark-red rug. The bentwood side chairs that surround the white-linened tables are, in some places, back to back. The waiters are eccentric, but, of course, each in his own way. Your host is short—not in stature. You arrive, spot an emptying table by the window, ask if you may have it. Goes he, "Do you *mind* if we set it up first?" Oh, the disturbances.

Have: the grilled seafood sausage (the milky-white forcemeat is firm and well seasoned within its handsomely browned casing—you do wish the pinked beurre blanc were warm) and the smoked quail (the cool halves of the little bird are tender and of strong flavor—you do wish that the chutney garnish were at something higher than icebox temperature). Eschew: the "jumbo lump crabmeat gratinée" (crab fibers under a darkened topping, a shellfish imitation of macaroni and cheese) and the sautéed garlic lamb (a meat gruel that would constitute an accomplishment if made from leftovers). Have: the fillet of Norwegian salmon (handsomely browned, medium rare, and of perfect freshness, firm texture, and clear flavor in its smooth beurre blanc) and the roast duck (a decently roasted bird with a tart red-cabbage garnish that is its excellent foil) and the roast pork (supple meat in a thick and fruity sauce of apricots and prunes). Eschew: the fusilli in three-meat bolognese (bland and wet, like something made from the contents of two poorly drained cans). Have: the walnut ice cream (gritty of ground nuts and of deep walnut flavor under its strong chocolate sauce) and the chocolate roulade (intense but light chocolate cake and rich whipped cream). Eschew: the raspberry mousse (the pallid stuff is rescued neither by the whipped cream on top nor by the few berries under the cream nor by the brownie on the side) and the lemon curd tart (the custard is harshly acidic on its burnt pastry).

You bring your own wine.

★ GULF COAST

489 West Street (at 12th Street)
LUNCH, SUNDAY TO FRIDAY; DINNER, DAILY.
No reservations (206-8790).
No credit cards.
Inexpensive.

It is Saturday night, and the chap at the door—he is in jeans and plaid shirt—informs all comers that there will be a two-hour wait to eat. Nobody pays him any mind. It is not that no one believes him, rather that no one cares. You give him your name, affix yourself to the back edge of the crowd along the bar, and eventually get a drink from one of two bartenders—their perpetual motion is interrupted only to light cigarettes (their own). Called Gulf Coast, this place is in fact Fort Lauderdale-on-Hudson (you can see the river from the West Street window), and it constitutes the eternal spring vacation that, by its frequenters' lights, is the natural consequence and reward of their recently earned bachelor degrees.

Gulf Coast is a brightly lighted two-room saloon with an ancient bar in the front room and with a corrugated-aluminum ceiling and an old wooden floor throughout. The plastic-top tables are stocked with sugar in sugar pourers, bottles of hot sauce, stacks of paper napkins. Most of everything else about Gulf Coast has been chosen to satisfy its clientele's addictive nostalgia for the present. The tape deck, for example—it is ever on, and only at full volume—produces the very sounds with which, ever since their parents learned to sedate them with electronic audio and/or visual devices, these children have obliterated their inherited cultural past. Many who come here do not disconnect their Walkmans until they are safely inside the door. (Look around, and you see a suspicious abundance of a kind of bliss that owes nothing to controlled substances.) The back bar is festooned with snapshots and picture postcards, lots of them from Florida. The inside neon signs include one that advertises Ford trucks, another that welcomes tourists, yet another that advises of the availability of hot plates and sandwiches. The principal difference between the help and the customers is that the former, as they suddenly, impulsively, jiggle and shuffle to the irresistible background beat, are likely to do so while in the very act of handing you your dinner. Meanwhile, at the next table, a young lady in jeans and sweatshirt, her left ear bejeweled, rises slowly, like a cobra, from her chair, writhes to the music as she does so, gyrates for a while, and gradually subsides back into her place. Her friends seem not to notice. The central figure here, most nights, is the gallant young lady whose job it is to extract from the crowd the customers scheduled to occupy the next table. Her straightforward method is to shout out names while wandering among the multitude. Occasionally she hollers from behind the bar. Other times she bellows while standing on a chair. Mostly she goes unheard and gets no response—still, she remains cheerful. About every ten minutes, the competition she gets from the tape deck is augmented by the roar of the 60-horsepower cement mixer in which half-gallon batches of blue margaritas are whipped up. The blue margarita is the big drink here. Order one and you get a glass of pale-turquoise foam adorned with a slice of lime and a plastic fish. After a while the drink separates out into its component parts: Windex on the bottom, suds on top.

The "two-hour" wait for a table rarely exceeds sixty minutes, but if even that seems long, and if you have worked your way to the physical bar itself—have the use of a square foot of its actual surface—you will do well to get yourself some tamales (three for $1.95, six for $3.50) while you wait. The steamed, string-tied cornhusk packages are filled with ground meat that is coated with cornmeal. You untie, unwrap, and, with gingerly care, lift out the thumb-size contents with your fingers—the fragile, sausagelike constructs are mildly spiced, very light, and their clarity of flavor suggests that the force-meat was made fresh not long before you ordered it. Nibble slowly, and you may be seated by the time you dispatch your last tamale, in which case you may proceed to a plate of chilled shrimp, a couple dozen small crustaceans (a half pound, according to the menu) in their shells, distributed over a plate at the center of which stands a double-shot glass of red sauce—the shrimp have been cooked with celery salt, which heightens their sweet flavor, and that cold sauce is nubbly and spicy-hot. You get the same cold sauce with hot food too, including the lightly battered and deep-fried crab claws, yet another two dozen lengths of good seafood, these crisped in a fryer that, evidently, is regularly replenished with good fresh oil. Considerably more batter encases the fried and stuffed jalapeños, which reach you looking like three harmless fritters—their contents, however, are searingly hot green peppers filled with mild and pully cheese that can only begin to mitigate their impact.

Blackened redfish (here called "peppered redfish"), though not on the printed menu, is usually among the specials listed on the blackboard. The big fillet is fresh, cooked through but moist, and its gleaming mahogany-colored coat of herbs and spices is of a strikingly complex flavor that does nothing to hide the sweetness of the fish itself. Order catfish and you get the entire beast, battered and fried, the delicate meat fresh and steamy within its crust. The grilled chicken, though well made—handsomely browned and crisped, cooked through but not dried out—suffers from the tastelessness of the bird itself. A bigger and tastier chicken supplies the meat for the chicken and dumplings, a homey and utterly satisfying item that is just a bowl of a weighty, well-seasoned chicken gravy that is thick with slices of dumpling and hefty chunks of meat. What is listed as "red beans, rice, and sausage" is many of the first, much of the second, and a big, strong and somewhat fatty example of the third—inelegance in abundance, the red beans in a gravy that is thick with shreds of meat.

The desserts include treacly bread pudding, a buttermilk pie that is much like the kind of custard pie that used to be sold in glassine envelopes, a lime cream pie that is sticky and sweet (albeit of tangy lime flavor).

★★HASAKI

210 East 9th Street
DINNER.
Reservations: 473-3327.
Credit cards: AE, MC, V.
Medium priced.

The East Village suffers from cancer in reverse, here and there a few healthy cells multiplying in, and slowly taking charge of, a malignant environment. The regeneration is most visible along the broad avenues, but new life may be found also on the side streets, even, as in the instance of Hasaki, at their extremities. The change of scene is abrupt. Down a few steps from the grimness that is this stretch of East 9th Street, past a bit of greenery and a tiny stone wall, and through the door to a little vestibule in which, when this place is busy, the patient locals, mostly young, wait, in faded well-washed cottons, or in jeans and oversize sweaters, in sandals or in sneakers, much of their attire by way of disguise, for the current cost of living in this part of town is such that many of its citizens spend the better part of their days away from it, in straight clothes, earning the rent. When there is a little something left over, the more discerning of them repair here, for Hasaki is one of very few eating places in this arrondissement in which the food equals food of the same kind in other neighborhoods. Similarly the physical plant, which not only equals but is indistinguishable from a thousand other Japanese establishments on Manhattan Island. Hasaki is spick-and-span and well lighted. The sushi bar, the tables and chairs, and the whimsical partition that divides the dining room into two parts are all of pale wood. The young Japanese who wait on you—including this waitress in red sneakers, spiky brush cut, and boldly patterned tunic and shorts—are working hard on their English. As in most of these places, the sushi bar, wherever it is situated, is the focal center, and this one, with seats for about a dozen, and more brightly lighted than the rest of the place, is manned by three young men who perform their sculptural tasks deftly, cheerfully, tirelessly—if you have little else on your mind, and you sit at the bar or at a nearby table, they may be all the diversion you need. Other possible diversions, besides your own company: the sky—a handful of tables have been set up in the unimproved backyard, though only for drinks and a limited menu; and gray East 9th—a few tables situated just inside the glass façade look out on the street.

At one of those front tables you also get a view of the sushi bar from behind, albeit off to one side, and you may observe the assemblage of your kinutamaki unagi, a broad coil of cucumber that, with a sheet of seaweed, and with a swatch of eel warmed at the last minute in a toaster-broiler, is wound with those contents into a roulade, cut into disks, and served sprinkled with sesame seeds—the complexity of flavors and textures, and the contrast of the warm and oily eel with the cool and crisp cucumber, make this a rousing and yet subtle first course. Watch closely, and you may learn also how to prepare the tiger's eye—you pack the body of a hefty squid with salmon, then slice the construct into oval-shaped sheets that are a red iris within an iridescent white, and if they do not exactly call to mind the cat's orb, the fresh red fish and its frame of slightly chewy squid sparkle when you moisten them with soy sauce. Some of the first courses emerge from an out-of-sight kitchen, among them the shrimp dumplings, steamed or fried, the former in noodle wrappers that glisten, the latter in noodle wrappers that are browned and crisp— if you prefer the fried to the steamed, you prefer an assertion to a suggestion, but both are good, the shrimp fillings very sweet. Something given as chicken yasaimaki will probably strike you as Western, for it is a kind of chicken sausage studded with pink and green vegetables—the cool slices are delicately seasoned, sport real chicken flavor, come with a dollop of something akin to mayonnaise, on a slice of lemon, at the center of your plate. It is well to buffer these sprightly first courses with broiled fish, specifically tilefish, the great chunks of it fresh, moist, lightly filmed with oil, done so judiciously that even this rather pallid species reveals a clear marine flavor.

Sushi, sashimi, and the related maki rolls and hand rolls are here prepared of fresh seafood, crisp vegetables, and crackling sheets of seaweed, and they are served with sparkling fresh ginger, and with a particularly vibrant example of the green radish paste called wasabi, which you add to the soy sauce that seasons them. In addition to the usual components, Hasaki offers a few items you do not encounter everywhere, among them what is given as "sweet raw shrimp," which is exactly that, the little gray morsel cold and almost candylike; and a maki roll of salmon skin, prepared with the rice outside, salmon meat one of the components as well, though it is the crisped skin that accounts for this item's special piquancy.

One section of the menu is headed, perhaps uniquely, "tempura à la carte." For small amounts of money ($1 for vegetables, $1.75 to $2.25 for seafood), you obtain small amounts of what you want. A dollar gets you a single shiitake mushroom, hot and earthy in the cloud of delicate, almost fugitive batter that is characteristic of all the tempura here—or it gets you several crescents of butternut squash, or as many rich, well-oiled chunks of eggplant. For a little more, you may have a single shrimp with nuts, the body of the sweet pink-and-white crustacean surfaced with slivers of a crisp green nut within the rarefied batter. A single order of scallops or squid is a mass of several morsels of the seafood—assembled on a sheet of seaweed—bound in the light batter.

Beer and sake are the drinks with this food.

★★HATSUHANA

17 East 48th Street, 237 Park Avenue
LUNCH AND DINNER. CLOSED SUNDAY. PARK AVENUE STORE CLOSED SATURDAY AND SUNDAY.
Reservations: 355-3345, 661-3400.
Credit cards: AE, DC, MC, V.
Medium priced.

Japanese morsel food focuses the attention. Not only does it do away with certain of the distracting mechanics of eating—particularly for maladroit chopstick manipulators —it also concentrates a more or less complex culinary thought in a single mouthful. Eating Japanese is to eating Western as the haiku is to a fat novel. Consuming, for example, a single nugget of sushi is not one of a series of scenes of cumulative power (as is, for example, one of twenty forkloads of spaghetti bolognese). It is, rather, the entire act, and not much altered by repeating it. At the two restaurants called Hatsuhana, a single meal often consists of many small acts.

The restaurants are known especially for their sushi, and in sushi basics, they cannot be faulted: vinegared rice in which the sweetness and tartness are nicely balanced, as are the stickiness of the rice and the firmness of the individual grains; seaweed wrappers that are tender and a little sea-gamy; wondrously heady thin-sliced fresh ginger; and an especially potent wasabi, the searing radish with which you fortify the good house soy sauce. Beefy tuna, delicate yellowtail, and soothing fluke are among the impeccably fresh finfish you may have mounted on that rice, the last named prepared with bits of wasabi tucked under the little fillet. Other rice-bottomed packages in this department: shafts of shrimp—very crunchy, but of rather mild flavor; sweet pink crabmeat belted to the rice with a ribbon of deep green seaweed; orange fish roe, the glistening globules and rice packed into a squat seaweed tube; and this establishment's excellent California roll, in which the cylindrical constructs are built with the seaweed near the center, the outer walls of sticky rice dotted with clinging sesame seeds.

More morsels: Hatsuhana dumplings, the firm (not tough) noodle wrappers packed with mildly seasoned meat—you liven the nuggets by dipping them in a dark and salty sauce; unagikyuri maki, thin, cool disks of eel, dark and oily, enclosed in circles of crisp cucumber; Japanese fried chicken, the remarkable little chunks of deep-fried but greaseless bird well browned and of an almost airy delicacy—you may dip them in soy sauce, but that overpowers them, so you squeeze on the supplied lemon instead, which livens the chicken without obscuring its flavor; Japanese fried tiny crabs (the largest of them less than an inch across from claw tip to opposite claw tip), which you dip in soy sauce and eat whole—they are hot-oiled, almost as hard as walnut shells, have a fugitive flavor that is at once nutty and slightly oceanic, are noisy to chew, and may, like the pebbles certain creatures swallow, aid digestion; what goes as "avocado salad," two quarters of firm but utterly ripe avocado topped with mounds of glinting salmon roe and set in a cloud of seaweed—you are proffered a spoon and told, "You eat this with a spoon"; broiled duck and scallion, the warm slices of rich meat, bone and skin still attached, in a gentle sauce—sharp bits of scallion green are a nice contrast to the oleaginous bird; boiled beef with ginger, the thin slices of tender meat suffused with ginger flavor—sesame seeds add a bit of texture; eggplant with miso sauce, the sharp peanut- and sesame-flavored sauce a good foil to the hot and meaty vegetable.

Very little in the way of desserts—you try some papaya, and it is not really ripe.

Both stores are clean, well lighted, somewhat antiseptic places: the one on 48th Street is an upstairs and a downstairs, a sushi bar on each level; the "Park Avenue" location (it is not really on Park, but is connected to the Park Avenue Atrium, which is on Lexington) is a sleeker, slicker one-level place with glass walls looking onto an open arcade between the cross streets.

★★L'HOSTARIA DEL BONGUSTAIO

108 East 60th Street
LUNCH, MONDAY TO FRIDAY; DINNER, MONDAY TO SATURDAY. CLOSED SUNDAY.
Reservations: 751-3530.
Credit cards: AE, DC, MC, V.
Expensive.

Driven from 55th Street hardly a year after its opening, L'Hostaria promptly brought its remarkably variegated menu of unfamiliar dishes here to East 60th—and had the good sense, in the act, to leave its failings and confusions behind. You can now come here, order a multicourse dinner of dishes you never heard of, and, with no further effort on your part, get what you asked for and, moreover, probably like it. Which is as it especially should be in this place, for L'Hostaria is very much the repair of prosperous and/or upper-class Italians in New York. And what fun is there, after all, in being highborn and well-to-do, if you must give your own attention to your needs.

Like the old one, the new Hostaria calls to mind a house in the Italian subtropics. The archways and pastel-painted plaster, the crockery on the walls and the ornamental tiles, the floral upholstery on the chairs and banquettes, and the sunny light all combine to suggest summer and a Mediterranean villa. And it is because of the looks of the place that, though these silver-haired Italian diplomats and businessmen, with their manicured fingernails and manicured wives, look very much at home here, the polo-shirted playboys, gold watchbands glinting on their bronzed arms, their beautiful companions admiring them from behind saucer-size sunglasses, seem more of a piece with the place.

All these types, and a good many non-Italian New Yorkers as well, settle in comfortably here for the likes of this insalate mare, in which fresh conch (a little resilient, as it is in its natural state), fresh octopus (a little rubbery, as it is in its natural state), tiny shrimp, and rings of tender squid are moistened with lovely oil—you may add lemon for a bit more sparkle. Have that any day rather than the raw beef with truffles—the meat is pallid, the ornamental truffles accomplish nothing when used this way, and even the good house oil, poured on right before your eyes, cannot bring it to life.

Of the nineteen pasta dishes on the menu, few are more than even vaguely familiar. Penne, a thick, tubular noodle, is served all'arancia, the hefty shafts in a fruity, but not sweet, orange sauce that is fortified with orange liqueur, made fragrant with herbs, and sharpened with coarse-ground black pepper. You have often had trenette (same as linguine) in pesto, but here the heady and creamy basil sauce is dotted with tiny dice of potato as well—the little morsels of tuber are cooked through but retain a bit of crispness, and they are a good textural note in the rich dish. Add some of this restaurant's good ground Parmesan cheese, and everything goes up about an octave. Pasta in the shape of little lenses is called orrechiette (little ears), and this place serves it in a tomato sauce that is threaded with arugula—the slightly creamy sauce really does not need help, but it takes on a striking complexity with the slightly bitter accent of the green. You may have pasta dishes by the half order, but not so the risotto dishes—which, moreover, take around twenty-five minutes to prepare. When you have time, give some of it to this rice section of the menu, for, though it consists of only ten items, it constitutes a greater diversity than H. Johnson's twenty-seven flavors. The house specialty (anyway, it is called risotto "alla bongustaio") is a great mound of the nubbly grounds, copper tinted by the saffron with which it is so pungently flavored, the rice in stunning contrast to the firm shafts of bright-green asparagus with which it is dotted.

A whole red snapper is baked with bay leaves—the fish is fresh, snowy, moist—and the flavor of the strong herb suffuses the white meat. A breast of chicken, though not from one of the tastiest birds, is redeemed by the thick, piquant walnut sauce under which it is served. When artichokes are out of season, have your scaloppine di vitello con piselli e carciofi without carciofi—the buttery meat, nicely browned, is moistened with a delicate tomato sauce that is studded with sweet, green peas. Sometimes the house offers a veal chop with sautéed mushrooms in a carefully seasoned sauce that is mostly the juice of the meat itself—the chop is craggy, crusty, tender. There is one rabbit dish on the menu—big chunks of the firm meat, on the bone, in a sauce that is sweet-spiced, a little sour, sturdy. And there is one sausage dish—three husky, almost hard cylinders of well-fatted forcemeat, powerfully seasoned, primitive. It is served with a mound of the bitter green called wild broccoli, its chewy leaves hot, thick with slivers of garlic. You may think that $7.50 for braised radicchio is steep, but this red lettuce, wilted a little by hot oil, is still resilient, pungently flavored by the chunks of garlic in among the tart pink leaves. And the house turns out stunning salads, among them a mixture of fresh, ivory-white mushrooms, slivers of crisp celery, and curled shavings of strong Parmesan cheese, all dressed with lemon and good olive oil.

You may also have that Parmesan in big slices—it is the color of sandalwood, its sharpness a little worn down by its great age. The Gorgonzola is good too, creamy and biting. The cheesecake is dreary, but you can get good berries, with or without the cool, whipped-cream-enriched zabaglione sauce.

★★★ HUBERTS

575 Park Avenue (entrance on 63rd Street)
LUNCH, MONDAY TO FRIDAY; DINNER, MONDAY TO SATURDAY. CLOSED SUNDAY.
Reservations: 826-5911.
Credit cards: AE, MC, V.
Very Expensive.

Though born in the legendary borough of Brooklyn, and raised in the old neighborhood around Gramercy Park, Huberts has chosen to shrug off its historic past, has removed to Park Avenue—the *real* Park Avenue, Upper East Side Park Avenue—and, in the grand tradition of millions before who worked their way uptown as they climbed the economic ladder, no nostalgic signs of humbler days are on display in the new digs. There, however, the parallels part, for when Huberts acquired the new money to make its move, it revealed that, somewhere along the way, it had acquired a style usually associated with older coin. The new Huberts is that rarity, a dining room that, though indubitably luxurious, panders not at all to the common taste for common denominator posh. This is luxury, you understand, but you know it not by any resemblance to upper-middle-class living rooms or three-hundred-dollar-a-night-hotel lobbies. You know it, rather, because you are instantly comfortable, and because the creation of this commodious environment was in the hands, clearly, of an imagination both practical and free. While the place fills all the usual needs, it ignores innumerable conventions.

Moreover, it achieves its dramatic effect within a seemingly narrow range of tones. Huberts is all the so-called earth colors, beiges and browns and tans, darkened reds and dusty pinks and bronzes, to which the strongest contrasts are a bit of black (the armchair frames) and a good bit more of honey-stained oak varnished to a glass finish. You enter to a large anteroom, its focus the glinting semicircle of polished wood that is this establishment's snappy bar. To your left are subsidiary rooms, the restaurant's smaller dining room and a clubby lounge with black leather sofas. To your right is the main dining room, which you enter through a portal that, flanked by freestanding, high, arched, oaken fences, is like a gateway with its golden gates opened wide. The room itself, oblong and high ceilinged, seems, by architectural sleight of hand, to be windowed on three sides, though one of the sides is an interior wall, and none of the windows—all backlighted—can be seen through. The windows (and "windows") are broad, reach to the ceiling, and their panes, of various sizes and shapes, are of smoked glass or vaguely pink silk, are framed and divided by that handsome, grainy oak, are set in walls that, though they mock weathered masonry, by way of their intricately mottled coloring—which incorporates an almost invisible patina of pale gold—make an impact that is at once granitic and warm. A cushy banquette runs along the room's rear wall, its back a delicate geometric pattern of dark claret on a pale ground, its seat a glowing velvet of coppery brown. The velvet appears again on the seats of the black-wood armchairs, and the floor is covered with plush carpeting, the stripes of which—sand and deep raspberry—seem to shimmer. There are flowers in each corner of the room, and their primary colors are brilliant in this setting. Only the uniforms on the help—Cambridge-gray pleated trousers, gun-metal-gray shirts, and white wing collars with black bowties—seem to have been chosen in disregard of the looks of the rest of the place. Ladies, of course, will wear black dresses or red ones, but gents will have to give up the whole game, for every business suit in the house looks tepid in the glow and umbered solidity of these surroundings.

It is not any comparison with the setting, however, that makes for your disappointment with these crabmeat pirogi, rather that the pouchlike pastries are of that cakey dullness you know so well from certain lesser fortune cookies, which is too bad, for their crabmeat filling is fresh and sweet, and the greened butter in which the constructs are set enriches and livens them. With respect to this fettuccine, however, you may find that you forget your surroundings entirely, for the good broad noodles, threaded with bits of spinach, are mingled with crisped, browned, sticky-rich morsels of sweetbread, and with plump oysters that, though warmed through, retain all their raw ocean flavor—the dish is moistened with a bit of sauce that is herbed, light, and creamy. At this point in culinary time, you must do something striking for notice to be taken of a cheese soufflé, and making it of Roquefort is hardly enough, for that kind of variant has been around almost as long as the basic soufflé itself. Still, this browned, fluffy, and moist little column, of restrained but vivid Roquefort flavor, is so well balanced as to its solidity and lightness, the acidic apple-flavored sauce in which it is set so much its nifty flavor foil, and the strands of pickled cabbage in the sauce so striking a contrast of texture, that the old soufflé is almost a new dish. There are those for whom the particular appeal of this establishment's rabbit sausage is the garnish of two little rabbits sculpted out of green apples—white bodies, apple-green ears, tiny red spots for eyes. You, however, will note that the sausage is solid but not heavy, peppery and juicy, and that the thick, dark molé sauce in which it is set, which sports a strong chocolate edge, is vibrant of its hot spice.

The grilled lobster reaches you out of its shell in a complex poblano pepper sauce that is smoky, nubbly, a little rich—there is much of this tender lobster meat, and it is nicely garnished with asparagus spears and with broad noodles, and its sauce is dark and earthy. Within a browned surface of such evenness that it appears painted on, your utterly fresh salmon is pale pink, glistening with moisture—the good fish is garnished with a cucumber-and-melon relish, heady with coriander, from which a delicately fruity moisture forms a pool around the seafood. With respect to the bird, the roast duck is a simple affair, except for the striking treatment of its skin, which is a deep, crisped brown (almost, but not, black) under which is the layer of fat responsible for the juiciness and strong duck flavor of the meat—a good cinnamoned, cinnamon-colored poached pear is the gesture to the fruit-with-duck-tradition, but the principal garnish is a vegetable strudel that, roused with ginger, converts this compacture of bits and pieces, within its flaky pastry, into a memorable eggroll. The rack of lamb, cut into four chops, is wondrous meat, tender, blood-juicy and of potent lamb flavor, but its garnish of goat-cheese lasagne is from another—macaroni-and-cheese—world.

What the house calls a sugar cone looks like a flower—with assorted petals of crisp, sugared pastry—mounted on a large white-wine glass. The thing is packed with a prune fool, which is to say whipped cream mixed with a mash of the fruit and, in this instance, Armagnac, the fool in turn adorned with prune halves, and with straight whipped cream on top. While the fool is poised to fly off, the plum strudel is firmly planted on its plate in a film of buttery plum sauce, the delicate, sugar-whited sleeve of pastry packed with a chunky, sweet-spiced mix of fruit and nuts, on the side that good house whipped cream again. You may consider "strawberry roulade" a misnomer for these three ovoids of white cake, for though they are clearly cut from a roulade, the pink and tan creams (strawberry and chocolate) with which the cake was painted before it was rolled up have little impact other than that of a moistness—the garnishes, spiced figs and delicately basil-flavored ice cream, are the life of the plate. Another unlikely ice cream, this one tinctured with nasturtium, accompanies the blood-orange tartlets, three crackling little pastry cups, a dab of custard in each, and sweet, juicy sections of the red citrus.

★ HULOT'S

1007 Lexington Avenue (near 72nd Street)
LUNCH AND DINNER. CLOSED SUNDAY.
Reservations: 794-9800.
Credit cards: AE, MC, V.
Expensive.

As all the world knows, the so-called New American Cooking is French. In some of its forms it reveals other influences as well, Mexican, Japanese, and Italian among them.

But in none of its guises is it domestic. Everything about it, in fact, is imaginable without American, how you say, input. Were the continental forty-eight still unexplored, the nonexistence of this cookery would be attributable solely to a shortage of Americans willing to pay for it. Now, the interests behind two of New York's preeminent NAC restaurants have dropped their masks and revealed their true identities, have opened a bistro wherein they purvey what they have always purveyed: French food, but this time sans New American trappings. The establishment's success suggests that locals would have settled for the undisguised article all along.

Perhaps to exaggerate the French vs. American differences between Hulot's and its predecessors, the combine has taken on, for this place, a French associate, complete with French accent, apparently with the understanding that the fellow will make himself highly visible here in ways that Americans think of, rightly or wrongly, as French. Like the constant husband of the jealous wife who, having been falsely called adulterer one time too often, decides, since he has been convicted, to perform the crime, M. Oliver (for that is your host's name), standing in for the French as a race, has elected to assume the superciliousness with which his countrymen have often been charged. You have, say, reserved a table, and you arrive, say, at seven, to a restaurant only a third full. Oliver checks your name against his book and, with a curt nod of the head, suggests you follow him. He leads you to a table that comfortably accommodates two plates, salt, pepper, and perhaps an elbow, a table that, moreover, is not only convenient to the men's room, but, being hard by the wide-open kitchen, is fanned throughout dinner by the scents and warmth of that operation. You object, point out that other quite unoccupied tables are less divertingly situated. The man does not disagree with you, you understand, for that would honor your position. Rather, by an exasperated aversion of the eyes, he makes it clear that, once he has decided where you are to sit, elsewhere is, willy-nilly, unthinkable. His pained last glance and unconvincing "I'm sorry, monsieur" make it clear that at the moment his dearest wish in life is for your instant disappearance. And his studiedly indifferent shrug when you offer an impossible suggestion indicates he has received that advice before.

Remain for dinner, and get a central table, and you are certain to spot him in at least two or three altercations, of an evening, with soon-to-be-former customers. It is not that his position is invariably without merit, rather that his apparent inexperience with anything other than complaisance has the poor fellow constantly dyspeptic with ill-processed frustration. Naturally his outlets are his underlings. "Check on table nineteen!" he barks, the angle from horizontal of his extended stiff right arm in need of but five more degrees of elevation for the gesture to take on political significance. That emergency out of the way, he proceeds to make a great show of getting the floor staff caught up, picking up orders from the kitchen counter and marching them to their destinations with a thumping stride that, somehow, echoes the outstretched arm. Find yourself in his path, and you get glared at. The fellow even has a black mustache. Hulot's is a front room and a back room, the corridor between them the site of the kitchen and, across a narrow aisle—often crowded with waiters and waitresses at their tasks—five marvelously tiny tables for two. Such accommodations may be suitable for folks who walk in off the street without reservations, who can then either take or leave what is available; but when those who reserve ahead discover that what they have reserved is one of these, enraged disbelief is sometimes the reaction, even from the easygoing. The front room is a row of tables for four opposite the bar, the back room, under its skylight, a banquette around three sides and a few tables at the center.

Throughout, the tables are covered with white linen, the non-banquette seating is on Paris café chairs, the floor is of red tiles, and the lighting is soft but not low. A few old

Jacques Tati movie posters are the only distractions, though observers who get tables in the narrows learn, before the evening is out, that tossing a salad with the fingers is standard restaurant-kitchen practice, and that the chicken on a plate is very likely nudged into its position by caressing hands. But be assured that this observed kitchen is a tidier operation than thousands of the unobserved. Some of the waiters and waitresses are French—mostly they demonstrate that Oliver's choice of manner is a personal, not a national, preference, though on occasion one of them will become impatient with customers who have neglected to master bistro French before coming here, for nary a word of English sullies the menu.

That kitchen accommodates a staff of only three, so the menu is brief—on occasion the first and main courses amount to fewer than a dozen dishes all told, most of them elementary items: a cold mound of crunchy green beans and slivers of fresh mushroom over leaves of endive, the creamy, slightly acidic dressing dotted with fresh herbs; a couple of fat disks of warm goat cheese on crusts of toasted French bread, those in turn set on fresh greens dressed with excellent olive oil; pencil-thin shafts of tepid asparagus, lots of them, strewn with fresh parsley, and dressed to excellent effect with walnut oil; pissaladière, the rectangle of breadlike pastry overlaid with sautéed onions and tomatoes, those in turn sprinkled with parsley and dotted with bits of black olive, the whole surrounded by leaves of crisp, fresh, sharp arugula.

Come when both lotte and halibut are offered, and you will do well to pass up the former (it is strewn with lemon thyme, but that does not alter the blandness of the fish itself) in favor of the halibut meunière, the sweet oceanic flavor of the delicately crisped fillets livened by the browned butter in which they are done. The grilled half chicken has a good bit of chicken flavor for so small a bird, and though it is moist, it is handsomely browned and cooked through—it comes with scalloped potatoes that, though they could be creamier, have crusty edges and vivid potato flavor. The huge slice of gigot d'agneau just about covers its plate—the tender pink meat is of strong lamb flavor, the homey dish completed with an assortment of vegetables that, like all the vegetable garnishes here, are cooked through but not overdone.

The tarte Tatin is dark and mushy, conditions for which the dollop of crème fraîche served with it does not compensate. Big chunks of charred red plum form a kind of lunar surface on the plum tart—the fruit is a little sour, the dessert rousing. When blackberries are in season, this place gets good ones—neither gritty nor soft nor sour—and serves them as little individual tarts, much smooth custard between the fruit and the dark pastry. Order the mousse, and you get a small ramekin filled with a pale and cool, sticky and creamy milk-chocolate goo—it is at once rich and lively.

The place is popular—most folks simply overlook Oliver's tics.

★ INDOCHINE

430 Lafayette Street (near Astor Place)
DINNER.
Reservations: 505-5111.
Credit cards: AE.
Medium priced.

Myths have attached themselves to this place, mainly to the effect that it is hard to get into, is insular, caters to an artsy crowd, gives the back of its hand to interlopers who are not regulars on its scene. The facts are that to get a reservation here you need only telephone, though calling late in the day may be too late; that you will be seated (once your group is complete) in turn; that the crowd is more of business than of the arts, more before and after the Public Theater (across the street) than from the East Village or SoHo or NoHo, mostly go unrecognized by the management, are all treated about as well as the utterly casual staff knows how—though the young waitresses in their assorted outfits do direct more breathless attention to gentlemen in carefully unmatched clothing than to squares in suits and ties. The appeal of the place is plain: The prices are not high, the food is not bad (though not what it was when Indochine was new), the accommodations are comfortable, relaxation reigns. All you have to know is your way around the menu.

Indochine is a big, rectangular place, up front yellow-tile window seats under the two windows, tables and wicker chairs near them where you may sit while waiting to be seated, a short bar—you may wait there instead—and a lectern on which rests the book in which reservations are recorded. Your name is found there by a young chap, in a shirt buttoned to the neck, the collar turned up, who scratches his head while he looks, finds, and hands you over to the slender giantess—in two-inch platform sandals, modest over-the-knee stockings, white shorts that appear to have been angrily ripped from the legs of pajama bottoms, and a buffalo plaid shirt—who will lead you (she is easy to follow) to your table. The dining room is a rectangle rimmed with a green banquette that, along the long north wall, is formed into the big semicircular booths that are this room's choice seating. The place has been made to seem vaguely subtropical-Asian by the big green fronds painted on the walls, by the palms that stand here and there, by the exotic flowers on the tables. But a single coat of paint, and this mostly Vietnamese (but also Thai and Cambodian) restaurant could be any brand of eating place at all. The early crowd is here after the office. You do not get the tattoos and shaved heads, the illustrated sweatshirts and bared navels until, when no one is looking, the folks who clean the offices after the first shift has departed, duck into phone booths, switch out of their uniforms into their civvies, and, from towers all over town, head for Lafayette Street.

Be it understood, no one who serves you speaks the language of this menu. Try to order, say, moine chha khnay phonetically, and your waitress comes around to stand beside you and suggest that you point at the menu entry to which you refer. Happily, the dishes are numbered, and ordering by the numbers is the custom. Nhom lor hong, for example, is better known as Number 10, thin-sliced shrimp over a mound of what the menu calls green papaya, which seems like shredded cabbage to you, the interleaved fresh basil and the chopped peanuts on top the principal interest of the dish. Number 13 is another shrimp dish, this one livelier, the seafood mingled with mint and red peppers in its sharp and sweet lemon-grass dressing. If you liked 13, you will like 14 even more, the same dish, but with pearly sheets of squid in place of the shrimp. A dish that goes as goi ga, Number 11, is yet another cold salad, this one of shredded chicken on greens, the chicken of good flavor, the greens of good texture—a bit of basil livens the item. If you favor the spicy-hot beef salads served in Thai restaurants, its relative is here, going as Number 12, nhom sath ko, the cold and tender beef in a fiery marinade, with lemon grass and strands of red pepper—the spiciness of this dish accumulates in your mouth, mounts in intensity as you eat it. Still, for many there is but one first course at Indo-chine, what is given as steamed Vietnamese ravioli—Number 16, banh coun—which arrives in a lidded bamboo basket, the contents four square packets formed of a kind of doughy noodle, each stuffed with a moist and well seasoned filling of vegetables and mushrooms, all of which you moisten with a bit of the pink, fruity, mildly spicy sauce—the degree of hotness varies from time to time—that is served with this and many other dishes here.

It is well to know that at Indochine there is safety in finfish, danger in anything fried.

Come here just once, and you will do well to consider nothing but Number 25, amok cambodgien, fillets of fresh fish steamed in a banana leaf, a dish that reaches you as a tentlike package formed of the great leaf, within it the meat of the fish, firm and juicy and permeated with the flavors of the coconut milk and lemon grass in which it was done. Barring that, you will do almost as well with Number 27, trei chom huy khnay, a steamed whole fish that, on lucky days, is a sweetwater trout, the swimmer overlaid with strands of ginger and set in a pool of the strongly seasoned and oily broth in which it was done—the fish is fresh, firm, juicy, of vivid trout flavor. The menu does not so state, but Number 31, annkep chha kroeung, frogs' legs in coconut milk and lemon grass, is fried—anyway, the lightly battered surfaces of the legs are greasy, which is too bad, for they are otherwise plump and meaty. Similarly Number 28, the stuffed boneless chicken wings (you are served legs, not wings), the handsomely browned constructs packed with a lively herbed forcemeat of ground chicken, lemon grass, rice noodles—but, once again, greasy. You will do well to avoid also the roast chicken and roast duck, which seem to have been roasted in advance, are tired. Your waitress has been trained to ask if you want rice. You do not want the sticky rice, Number 44, which tastes like sweet cake, but you will do all right with Number 55, plain rice dotted with peas, bits of ham, egg.

Among the (Western) desserts, the key lime pie and lemon tart are lively of their respective citrus fruits, the berry tarts are of good berries on a somewhat doughy pastry, the hazelnut mousse an excess of richness not quite corrected by the good chopped nuts buried in it.

★ JACQUELINE'S

132 East 61st Street
LUNCH, MONDAY TO FRIDAY; DINNER, MONDAY TO SATURDAY. CLOSED SUNDAY.
Reservations: 838-4559.
Credit cards: AE, DC, MC, V.
Expensive.

Jacqueline gets into something comfortable before she comes to work, for she, herself, is going to initiate you into the romantic mood of her place. She is in light, white, loose-fitting trousers and tunic, there is a colorful scarf draped casually around her neck, and you know from her manner that at any moment she may flick it at you and then smile coyly. Jacqueline has excellent English that becomes music under the influence of her French accent, and as she leads you—nay, coaxes you—toward a corner table at the black banquette opposite her bar, she tells you about her restaurant, that it is a *champagne* restaurant, that in addition to bottled champagne, she sells half a dozen bubblies by the glass, that she also sells so-called elixirs, which are champagne cocktails, e.g., champagne with peach liqueur ("Renoir"), with strawberry liqueur ("ruby"), with raspberry liqueur ("infatuation"). When Jacquie gets you seated, she more or less tucks you in with loose cushions she tosses into your general vicinity, presumably for purposes of your swooning onto. Her place is, of course, dimly lit, consists of that bar (the long-stemmed flowers at intervals along its length are dramatically illuminated by pin-point spotlights overhead), the snug row of tables along the banquette across the aisle, and a slightly curtained-off little square room just to the rear—it is furnished with a banquette all around, before it a handful of side-by-side tables for two, plus a couple of corner tables, also for two. The background music is soft and jazzy, the crowd is here for the atmosphere, and the food, billed as "Swiss/French," is nothing of the kind—still, it is mostly good.

Jacqueline does move a lot of champagne, and the worldly and good-humored young women who are her floor staff are expected to convert service of the stuff into something of a rite. The cork is removed noiselessly, and, when pouring, your waitress must hold the bottle by its bottom, thumb up its punt. If you are spotted about to pour your own, choking the bottle rather than violating it, a staffer hastens by to take over the task and do it right. Put aside received ideas, confront the evidence of your palate, and you will realize that champagne, for all its charms, is poor wine for most food. But its capacity to make an event celebratory is such that it always seems right with foods that are themselves luxe, as, for example, this terrine of foie gras, the smooth, pink, and buttery slices of cool and fatted meat served on fresh greens in a tart dressing—you will probably find that you are simply uninterested in judging whether champagne and that compacture of rich livers are meant for each other. But then there are dishes not so readily reconciled to your blanc de blancs: Louisiana shrimp that are sweet, blackened in the pan, very nice with the warm, spicy, and cilantro flavored chopped tomatoes on which they are served; so-called "cremini" mushrooms, very fresh and very charred, mingled with red peppers and with minced jalapeño peppers, both nice foils to the mushrooms' woodsiness; a more than decent pasta dish in which the firm linguine are in a red seafood sauce—shrimp and scallops—that is sweetened with onions, made nubbly with minced zucchini.

Each day there are a couple of fish of the day, sometimes halibut, the poached fillet fresh, a little overcooked, a little underflavored, and in a pale, winy sauce that is thick with vegetables. The sautéed sea scallops are browned and rich, but the sea urchin that is a billed element of their otherwise decent red sauce is a remote element at best. The roasted poussin sports lots of chicken flavor for such a little bird. And the mildly garlicked sautéed rabbit is much pale and tender meat, nicely browned on the bone, the warm salad greens served with it a sharp contrast to the solid game.

You will find a bit more sugar than you want in the smooth, intensely chocolate flavored pot au crème. A warm berry sauce does not quite rescue the cold lemon soufflé, which is rubbery. The cherry-blueberry tart is an absence of cherries, a presence of many fresh, firm, ripe blueberries, a dull pastry.

The menu is a champagne list on the left, a food list on the right.

★★JANE STREET SEAFOOD CAFÉ

31 Eighth Avenue (at Jane Street)
DINNER.
No reservations (243-9237).
Credit cards: AE, MC, V.
Medium priced.

This place has something of New England about it, or, anyway, elements that go to make up a romantic imagining of a snug tavern—complete with fireplace—in an old fishing village by the sea. The curtains that hang over the two small front windows are tied to the side. The floor is of old wood, the walls of brick or pale plaster. The ceiling is low. There are candles on the bare wooden tables. The café is not, however, pure nineteenth century. A four-bladed fan depends from the ceiling. Electric fans that swivel are mounted on the walls. (When needed, there is even air conditioning.) And it is mostly modern art that hangs here and there. Certainly the fish is timely. For of the seafood restaurants that have sprung up around town in recent years, in response to the fashion away from red meat to white, none serves fresher seafood than this one. Your ever-present shirt-sleeved host remains in the background while keeping his eye on everything. This has the splendid effect of bringing out the best in his waiters and waitresses, who treat you with a courtesy that thrives on the extra appreciation it receives from the boss. The folks they are treating so well are a Greenwich Village crowd (cabs do not draw up), all the classes, from those in sneakers to those in pin-striped suits.

They sit down to some of the best bread in New York, crusty and resilient and profoundly grainy, and to a bowl of coleslaw that is of coarsely chopped cabbage so crisp you will conclude that its creamy dressing, sharpened with celery seeds, was just added —the bowl is refilled as promptly as it is emptied. You will have very likely emptied it again by the time you have ordered and received your steamed mussels. Two dozen of them, and the deep bowl in which they are mounded up, arrive encased in a clear plastic wrapper. The film is removed when the dish is before you, and you are at once engulfed in the fragrances of garlic, wine, herbs, and the fresh hot mollusks. The mussels stand in an inch of broth at the center of which you will find a slice of wine-soaked bread. The steamed littlenecks are just as good, though you get only a dozen and a half, and no polyethylene. Though they are hot, they are tender, which means that their steaming was carefully kept brief, and they are served with a little dish of garlicky and buttery brine, into which you dip them. The deep-fried oysters and deep-fried soft-shell clams are fresh, tender, lightly battered, and delicately crisped, and you may enliven them with a tangy and creamy tartar sauce—but good as they are, they have little seafood character. The baked clams are made with chopped clams, a manner of preparation that is yet to be justified—the dish is little more than a vaguely oceanic breading. The Manhattan clam chowder is fine, the lobster bisque rather special for its creaminess and for the intensity of its lobster-meat flavor.

There is an everyday menu (photocopied and supplied to you in a clear vinyl holder) and a listing of specials of the day (handwritten on a five-by-eight ruled card). It is from the former that you will choose the fluffy broiled fillet of gray sole—it is fresh and moist, and it is sprinkled with paprika, so you can differentiate the white meat from its white plate. But the index card is the source of the most interesting main courses: an inch-thick swordfish steak that is intensified by its enrichment with butter and its flavoring of wine and herbs; snowy, flaky red snapper surmounted by thick, crunchy strands of sautéed potato and by sautéed onion that retains much of its bite; fried whole smelts, crisp and light, which you dip in tartar sauce and eat from head to tail. Fresh flounder is served whole, carefully broiled. The bluefish has all its natural oiliness and strong flavor. The so-called broiled lobster is really steamed and then broiled—a poorly conceived method that dilutes the lobster's natural juice by steaming, while failing to add the special charring flavor that broiling all the way imparts. But the lobster is fresh, and you can have yours just steamed. Once in a rare while you will detect the flavor of butter that has been kept around the kitchen too long. It is excellent butter from your table, however, that you insert in perfect baked potatoes.

The walnut pie is all hot, spicy nuts and cool whipped cream. When the pumpkin pie has been refrigerated, it is a little clammy. The key lime pie has a clear citrus flavor and a good graham cracker crust, but it is more gelatinous than you want it. A rich and sticky chocolate mousse is tinctured with amaretto liqueur—not a bad note.

People stand in line to get in here at the peak of the dinner hour on weekend nights.

★ JEAN LAFITTE

68 West 58th Street
LUNCH, MONDAY TO FRIDAY; DINNER, DAILY.
Reservations: 751-2323.
Credit cards: AE, DC, MC, V.
Medium priced.

Another evocation of old Paris, all dark-honey-colored wood trimmed with brass, sconces and chandeliers in the gracefully curving Art Nouveau manner, here and there handsomely framed posters and great, plain rectangular mirrors on the walls. Before the deep-red banquette that rims the big room, the tables are set with snowy linen and with simple, glinting crystal, china, flatware. Naturally the place is patrolled by gentlemen in black and white, and happily, they croak at you, intelligently and politely, in the guttural French of genuine bistro waiters imported from the old country, which means that they neither introduce themselves by name, nor in any other way betray the assumption that citizens go to restaurants to meet waiters.

The original Jean Lafitte was the French pirate who, in return for his cooperation against the British during the War of 1812, was pardoned by President Madison for his prior sins. The significance of this, of course, will not be lost on you.

Jean Lafitte (the restaurant) was apparently intended to fill a gap in its chosen neighborhood, for the area is one in which no magnet for fashionable folk has taken hold. You do see some dressy types here, especially at cocktail time, when the little marble tables just across the aisle from the short bar up front are choked with depressed ladies who are resting their tired tootsies after hours of frustrating Fifth Avenue shopping. (In this crowd, it is a wasted day when Bonwit's has left them with enough change for an icy, revivifying Lillet—over which, you may be sure, they muster fresh determination to go forth again tomorrow.) But mostly the place draws folk from nearby office buildings grabbing a bite after working late; music lovers before and after Carnegie Hall; and residents of Central Park South who have discovered that this place, whatever its high-toned intentions, is actually more straightforward than any of those on their own famous thoroughfare.

You will not, for example, find herring on Central Park South, but Lafitte offers great firm strands of the soured seafood, served with a plain salad of potatoes in vinaigrette. The gravlax here is simple and impeccable—gentle, supple, cured salmon, a little sweetness and a clear dill flavor imparted by its delicate marinade, served without a sauce. Sometimes the house offers what it calls a cassolette of oysters—the fresh mollusks, out of their shells, are warmed and mellowed in a buttery saffron sauce that is threaded with thin strands of green beans. The good pâté is rimmed with white fat, dotted with pistachio nuts, garnished with sharp-tasting sprigs of mâche and with firm, curly leaves of red lettuce. What is given as crottin de chavignol roti is a big knob of hot, baked goat cheese, brought to you on a slab of warm, slightly toasted buttered bread—a first course that manages to be both satisfying and stimulating. When it comes to the pasta of the day, your French waiter, determined not to commit to memory information about foods from the lands outside his native borders, must consult his notes to tell you that today the pasta is fusilli in an anchovy sauce. You, too, will do well to forget it, for the noodle is tough, the red sauce—despite its anchovies, capers, olives—flat.

The place obtains Dover sole, poaches the fresh-tasting fillets, serves them in two sauces—one pink with red pepper, the other green with fresh herbs. The quite nice shrimp are crunchy, free of iodine, and they are served in a creamy sauce that is thick with fragrant dill. Virtually anything on the menu is a good reason to avoid the house chicken. The bird is well roasted, but it started out and ended up tasteless. Have instead, for example, these two little crescents of sautéed liver in a mustard sauce that clings to the pink meat. Or have gigot, the three slabs of strong roasted lamb, rare at the center, in a dark sauce that is mostly the blood of the meat, with firm but tender white beans. One dish has the house name on it—Boeuf Jean Lafitte. The help has been trained to tell the Americans that this is beef "prepared like pot au feu, but it is not pot au feu." Anyway, it is boiled beef, it has been simmered in a strong stock, it has a pungent flavor, it is garnished with little mounds of well-prepared vegetables of various hues, and it is served with one dish of horseradish and another of herbed mayonnaise—which sauce you choose says a great deal about you.

The waiter who says the boiled beef is like pot au feu also says the roulade de pommes is like strudel. He is right. In fact, it *is* strudel, but not a special one, just hot, dull apples in a flaky, sugar-strewn pastry, served mit schlag. The praline cake is a jellied, layered thing of cloying sweetness. The chocolate cake is the familiar sweet of these days—thick mousse between layers of deep, dark cake, whipped cream on the side. The pear tart— slivers of pear on a cakelike pastry—has a fruity liveliness, to which the rich whipped cream garnish is a good foil.

• J. G. MELON

1291 Third Avenue (at 74th Street)
LUNCH AND DINNER.
No reservations (650-1310).
No credit cards.
Inexpensive.

This place is adorned, if that is the correct word, with melons. There is a neon melon and a melon clock. There are melon paintings—a surreal melon in a de Chirico wasteland, a painted balloon melon pulling upward on a painted string, an endless slice of watermelon cut off at the ends only by the picture frame. There are melon photographs, models of melons, a melon bas-relief, a papier-mâché melon. Contrary to what you might expect, the effect is meloncholia. Midweek cocktail time, and the bar is lined with losers drinking and smoking their lives away, truculently pretending they have the world by the olives in their martinis. Sad and lonely women at the bar giggle deliriously as soon as someone recognizes them. On occasion these folks' affected camaraderie is so well rendered that the place takes on a beery jollity. Melon's is not, however, what it was. It used to be atmospheric. But one of those smoke-eaters has been attached to the ceiling, and these days there is an unreal clarity in the Melon air, as in a color transparency from which the haze has been filtered out.

Here no one tends bar. Instead one woiks behighnastick. Leave the stick-tender a tip, and he does not say thank you. He says, "God love ya, m' darlin'." The place is ramshackle and cozy, popular and insular. Anybody may walk in, have a drink, something to eat, be treated all right. But to the crowds that overflow this place, it is knowing the bartenders, the waiters and waitresses, the host and half the other customers by name that is the lure. Many come here straight from the office and do not leave until bedtime.

Melon's is a barroom with a handful of tables, a closet-size kitchen built in, ten tables more at the back. The tables are covered with green-and-white gingham, equipped with a sheaf of paper napkins and a bottle of Heinz ketchup. The menu is painted on a slate on the wall. The food is what you expect.

The chili, peculiarly, tastes of commercial preground black pepper, and it is adorned with onions that, chopped in advance, are devoid of strength. Still, the beans are firm, the concoction sturdy, and it will handle your hunger. The spinach salad is a bowl of wet food. Beef is probably brought in already ground, and it is bloodless by the time it is converted into burgers or chopped steaks. The unchopped steaks are a good bet—they are of decent, tender meat, accurately broiled, though the potatoes you get with them are those corrugated-looking frozen things that do dishonor to the name of pulp. The omelets are not really omelets, for instead of being turned in a pan, they are cooked—or overcooked—on a grill and then folded, so the inside is as dry as the outside. A surprise winner is the chicken salad—a big dollop of tasty chunks of chicken and crisp celery in a mayonnaise dressing, garnished with slightly tired raw vegetables and a hard-cooked egg. The desserts—including a lemon mousse pie that tastes like a lollipop—are uninspired.

★ JOCKEY CLUB

112 Central Park South
LUNCH AND DINNER.
Reservations: 664-7700.
Credit cards: AE, DC, MC, V.
Very expensive.

Here is haute cuisine in a British pub. The food is mostly good, and the rooms are entirely comfortable, but the disconsonance of styles reflects the absence of a point of view. The restaurant is less than the sum of its estimable parts because you are in a hotel, one of a chain, and the products of corporate managerial compromise cannot compete with those of human imagination—or, as in restaurants, human fantasy.

You enter to what is presumably the taproom, one room of five, and seeing one, you have seen the five. The walls of the place, every inch, are surfaced with knotted wood, and they are hung with a truckload of English oils, very horsey and doggy, but with here and there the depiction of a little flock of sheep, or hale gentlemen around a tavern table, or a bare-fisted prizefighter, his dukes up, posing for his portrait. Some member of the committee insisted on flowers and pink linen on the tables. The stiff side chairs, inevitably, are done in "leather" that is held in place by upholstery nails with big brass heads. The best seating is on the banquettes, which, though also of "leather," are cushy as down.

The menu, too, is a distinct comfort—to those who long for culinary yesteryear (and the place does get more than its share of those, from this neighborhood, whose families have been occupying apartments overlooking lower Central Park since the days when Frederick Olmsted himself used to revisit the place to rant at rocks and boulders no longer in their assigned positions). They are very content with the assortment of hors d'oeuvres: cool, fresh poached salmon of vivid salmon flavor; crisp cucumber salad, sweet, sour, and touched with dill; crunchy shrimp in a pinked mayonnaise dressing; and asparagus and haricots verts, both of which have become limp and lifeless in the hours since they were done. And they are much at home with the smoked salmon, a great sheet of it, pale pink and delicate, across a big plate. What are listed as "terrines & pâtés" turn out to be one country pâté and one game pâté, the former chunky and studded with pistachios, the latter strong and marbled with fat, both well made, not overbaked, pink —you are offered with them four little dishes of condiment, hot mustard, grainy mustard, and, presumably in anticipation of odd requests from transient residents upstairs, ketchup and horseradish. The ravioli are a big winner—they are filled with a red force-meat of ground lobster, and they are served in a pale sauce, rich and light, that has been sharpened with the flavor of lobster shell.

Black grill marks adorn the firm, moist salmon steak, which is served with a sauce béarnaise that is powerful of fresh tarragon, and with boiled potatoes that have the texture of wet snowballs. The quenelles of pike are as fluffy as fish dumplings ever are, but they have very little of the distinctive pike flavor that characterizes this dish at its best—they reach you set in a rich white sauce that has been browned under the broiler, and with a mound of white rice. The roast chicken is half a big bird, the skin browned, the meat of exceptionally clear chicken flavor, the whole slicked with yet another fragrantly tarragoned sauce. Good steaks and chops, including lamb chops (two doubles, in case you are counting) that are blackened, blood-pink at the core, served without a sauce.

The cheese, your waiter lets you know, is in the refrigerator and should remain there. He allows as how the hot soufflés are good, but is sorry to inform you that they are prepared neither on Sundays nor Mondays. You opt for the frozen raspberry soufflé instead, and you get a cold pink disk the size of a hockey puck—it is richer than mere ice cream, stands in an intense raspberry sauce, is surrounded by ripe berries. You may have those berries separately—with loose whipped cream. The floating island is airy, its crème anglaise watery. Avoid the almond meringue cake, a sugary layered affair of pastry creams and meringue encased in leathery slivered almonds.

★ JOHN CLANCY'S

181 West 10th Street
DINNER.
Reservations: 242-7350.
Credit cards: AE, DC, MC, V.
Expensive.

"Certitude," explained Holmes, "is not the test of certainty." But for those who make this a regular repair, it is certitude, established and repeatedly reinforced by the critics' near unanimity in praise, that accounts for the self-satisfied contentment with which they settle into their chairs. You, however, begin to have your doubts when your waiter, after taking your order, puts the question. Puts he, "Will we be enjoying wine with our dinner tonight?" He puts it, however, in a manner so insinuating that, happily, you are free to punctuate your conversation for the rest of the evening with speculations as to what, exactly, was insinuated. John Clancy's reputation and style were made, of course, in the days when it was owned in part by John Clancy, whose connections to the food world's opinion makers did not, how you say, hurt. With his departure, the place is, if anything, somewhat more reliable than it was under his offhand guidance, and on a good night you now do well here. But the establishment continues to prosper mainly on the commerce of those who were taught to admire it in the years when Clancy was often a bumbling presence somewhere in the vicinity of the front door.

Occupying two low-ceilinged floors of an old Village house, Clancy's is all pale gray and off white, white chairs around white-linened tables, soft light, posters on the walls, a bar at the front downstairs, a fireplace unlighted upstairs, the rooms somewhat more crowded than cozy. There are flowers here and there, which are nice, but also figurines of oceangoing creatures that look like wacky characters from an underwater sitcom aimed at drugged children. Those who believe this is the best seafood restaurant in New York are capable of believing also that these objects are decorative.

Past a point, pickled shrimp are not shrimp—they are marinated nameless protein, have all the seafood character of gherkins. It could be that if you come here the day the shrimp are prepared, you get soured rather than denatured crustaceans, but these seem to have been stored in their marinade until whenever sold. Similarly, albeit to a comparatively trivial degree, the Maryland crabmeat, which is obviously purchased fresh, but not necessarily the day it is purchased by you—nice crabmeat, in great, firm lumps, but some of its sweetness has been lost to time, and though the cocktail sauce served with it is winier and more complex than the usual thing, good crabmeat calls for little more than lemon. Pass up the broiled oysters, for though they are delicately breaded in their half shells, and in their herbed butter, they have given up any flavor that identifies them as those bivalves. Opt instead for the clams in black bean sauce, many, many of the little mollusks, in their whole shells, and though they are toughened a bit in the making, their flavor is intact, and the dark sauce is nubbly and vigorous. And there is no denying this gravlax, a great swath of cool, thin-sliced salmon, the supple pink meat, delicately seasoned in the curing, striped with a lively mustard sauce adorned with sprigs of dill. You may not respond at once to the lobster bisque, for unlike most, it tastes more of lobster meat than shell—this is good soup, dense of that meat, though it seems thickened, as if with gelatin.

Maybe it was not the pickling that undid those shrimp, for they are just as tasteless when sautéed with jalapeño peppers—in this setting, however, their crunchy texture is preserved, and they are a suitable carrier for the rich and fiery sauce. Clancy's was among the earliest of the mesquite grillers, now does great big sea scallops on a skewer on the grill, and they are succulent within their browned surfaces. Also from that grill: a great knob of fresh halibut, heavily grilled on one side, lightly on the other, the snowy meat toughened near the black surface, fluffy near the tan one; and a boned, skin-on trout (your waiter beheads it for you) in a tarragon sauce that is powerfully fragrant of the herb. Occupying their own boxed-in section of the menu are a half dozen "specialties of the house" (presumably there is nothing special about the rest of the menu), among them lobster Américaine. At its best, this is a wonderful dish, the lobster and the sauce the product of an assemblage, in the sauté pan, that takes place just before it is served, and in which all the elements—lobster, wine, tomatoes, herbs, occasionally brandy—are at once distinct and part of the whole. This version seems to be a pre-prepared sauce poured over lobster when the dish is ordered, and though it has decent flavor, it lacks the life of the real thing. Your waiter, unasked, ties a bib around your neck when you order the fisherman's stew, this another "specialty," sturdy stuff, a garlicky tomato sauce, thick with shellfish (shrimp, scallops, and overcooked clams), in which you find also a finfish devoid of identity in this setting—withal, hearty food.

Dessert time, a team of waiters assembles itself, parades the dishes past you for your inspection. Among them is an English trifle, and you are shown a whole one packed into a cylindrical glass container that looks like something in a pharmacist's window—which is quite enough exposure, for what you are served of it amounts to lumps of fruit, lumps of spongecake, a rather sugary binder, good whipped cream on top. You wish the crème brûlée were fluffier, that the pecans of the pecan pie were not soft, that the individual lemon meringue tart had a bit of citrus bite. Better are this mildly liquored roulade formed of nutty carrot cake and whipped crème fraîche; and another roulade, this one of fresh spongecake and the crème fraîche again—this time thick with slivers of strawberry —whole ripe berries on top.

★★LAFAYETTE

65 East 56th Street
LUNCH, MONDAY TO FRIDAY; DINNER, MONDAY TO SATURDAY. CLOSED SUNDAY.
Reservations: 832-1565.
Credit cards: AE, DC, MC, V.
Very expensive.

As much as could be done safely has been done to infuse with life this formally-laid-out dining room. But this is, after all, the Drake, and though the hotel has been refurbished by new Swiss owners, care has been taken not to offend the sensibilities of the establishment's traditionally sedate clientele. Your grandmother will find Lafayette lovely. All possibility of spaciousness is undone by four columns that, presumably out of structural necessity, rise from the room's carpeted floor to a less than lofty ceiling, from the center of which hangs a crystal chandelier—it is reflected in mirrored niches that have been carved into the ceiling overhead, and it illuminates a huge burst of flowers on a platform just below it. The walls are faced with rust-colored raw silk between painted surfaces of beige or ivory, the snowy tables are surrounded by wood-framed armchairs upholstered in deep-rose plush, and the room is brightly but softly lit. Lafayette is all one big warm glow, luxe for the sake of luxe. But for those who require at least a bit of diversion, there is pantomime, the kitchen, seemingly at hushed work, visible through panels of soundproof glass cut into one wall. The vision is dreamlike not only for its silence but also for the clean, silvery glow of the installation, as well as for the seeming innocence of the staff, for they are all young, their fresh faces now earnest now grinning under their bobbing toques blanches.

What they are about is their Master's work, he Louis Outhier, renowned chef at L'Oasis, La Napoule, French Riviera. Here he is listed as "master chef," the supertitle denoting that he does not cook, rather that the establishment is under his, how you say, influence, which of course is all pervasive, so that there may be, as there are, seven (7) restaurants around the world that benefit from his south-of-France emissions. You do imagine the chefs de cuisine, at their respective links in the worldwide chain, stepping out onto the street or roadway before each day's work, and lifting their eyes and arms to heaven to receive the daily charge. But, what with interference from intercontinental and satellite-to-earth communications, something is often lost in transmission. From time to time you get a dish here and you say to yourself, What was this supposed to be?

You are not certain, for example, about l'oeuf au caviar, which the menu describes, in part, as a "shirred egg in its shell," which it may well be, though an egg soft-boiled would do as well. The dish is an eggshell with its head cut off, in it, to the waist, about half a warmed egg, around the open neck a tiny collar of whipped cream that has been roused with vodka and dotted with black caviar. If as served it is what was intended, it is an item that makes sense not as sustenance, but as a display of the master's hand, and though you may well ooh and aah at the surprising harmony of the ingredients, for home consumption you will want the six-egg version, in a bowl. The airwaves were free of interference when fricassée de homard et pamplemousse was sent, so you are given an ample pile of the cool lobster meat, sections of grapefruit laid upon it, the two in a pink and creamy lobster sauce that is threaded with fragrant mint. Warm crustaceans too: artfully steamed shrimp, their flavor close to that of the raw article, for they have been judiciously done, not a moment too long—they are served on delicate greens in a light dressing; and the tiny meats of crayfish, lots of them, packed together side by side on a couple of wood skewers, the rectangular constructs so formed lightly browned and set in a white sauce, thick with bits of oyster, that enriches them and potentiates their ocean flavor. Much is made of foie gras. You may have it as a square cut from a terrine, the tightly juxtaposed morsels of nutty, rich, almost creamy meat bound around the edges by a jelly that is hot with green pepper. Or you may have it as the mock chocolate truffle (that is, a mock mock truffle) given as "truffle surprise," which reaches you as a glistening black ball that is a sphere of coarse-ground goose liver coated with a thick layer of powdered truffle, and filmed with shiny jelly. The thing is set in a ring of minced, almost colorless jelly, like a dark stone surrounded by tiny diamonds, and the truffle treatment does intensify and dramatize the high flavor of the rich meat.

Lobster again, out of its shell again, this time warm, its sweet flavor made complex, though not disguised, by the winy broth in which it is steamed, the firm, tender, red-flecked meat mingled with strands of vegetable that are notes principally of texture—the dish is moistened with a sauce that is herbed and a little spicy. The turbot is a dish that depends for its impact on a diversity of elements, in this instance the fresh but rather mild braised fish, good red-wine and white-wine sauces made into a geography on the plate, and the particularly pungent spinach on which the fish is placed. If you must select a finfish, however, opt for the salmon, very thin slices of the pale-pink fish inter-mingled with layers of a delicate and flaky pastry, the two forming a kind of napoleon. The salmon is barely cooked through, so its texture is like that of fruit that is ripe but not soft, and the pale sauce with which the object is moistened and enriched is judiciously seasoned, piquant, thick with chervil. Gourmand de volaille is chicken that has been formed into a tube, lined with lettuce, packed with a pungently seasoned sweetbread forcemeat, cut into half-inch lengths, and served in a strong dark sauce in which you discover sweet peas, crisp ears of baby corn, woodsy morels—with all those, it matters less than it could that the bulk of the dish, the chicken, has little flavor of its own. Lafayette's duck is the better bird, thick slices of the dark meat arranged like spokes of a wheel on half the plate, on the other half hefty crescents of hot apple, at the center a mass of fresh vegetables, in shreds and little chunks, bound in a fluffy custard, all the elements set in a dark and polished sauce that is powerfully flavored of brandy. The lamb is configured the way the chicken is, morsels of the strong-flavored tenderloin packed with a mushroom stuffing and served in a sticky port-wine sauce that is dense with baby vegetables and wild mushrooms—a dish that is at once weighty and spirited.

To adulterate Brie is usually a mistake, but Outhier has devised a treatment—le brie aux truffes—well rendered here, that is a useful variation. It is made by removing the tops of two Bries, spreading one with a rich cream cheese that is dotted with chopped truffles, inverting the other over it. Triangular sandwiches cut from this pie do come off as Brie that is somehow more than Brie, very useful here in the U.S., where Brie is less than Brie. The sweets on the cart are fresh, nifty, even perfect, never surprising; a tangy lemon mousse cake with browned meringue on top that looks like, and comes across as, a first-class lemon meringue pie; an orange mousse, adorned with strands of acidic orange rind, set in a pool of crimson berry sauce; a nut-flecked layered affair, chocolate at one level, white cream at another, the whole moistened with anisette; others.

★★LATTANZI

361 West 46th Street
LUNCH, MONDAY TO FRIDAY; DINNER, MONDAY TO SATURDAY. CLOSED SUNDAY.
Reservations: 315-0980.
Credit cards: AE.
Expensive.

Eight P.M., the dozen-and-a-half eating places along this so-called Restaurant Row have emptied of their pretheater customers, the drearies have set in, and most of the dining rooms will be semideserted until closing. When the resourceful entrepreneurs who are the Lattanzi family (they of Trastevere, Trastevere 84, and Erminia, all on the Upper East Side, all successful) initiated this theater district store, they were confronted with the depressing prospect of operating a restaurant in which little or no business would be done during the dinner hours that, everywhere else on Manhattan Island, are the busiest. For generations, restaurants in this neighborhood have suffered this situation, and for just as long, only the cheap places and tourist traps have overcome it. It took this family of minor commercial geniuses to note the big fat fact that New York's Jewish population has little in the way of serious eating places to call its own. (Much of the reason, of course, is that Central European cooking, Jewish or otherwise, is mostly dull stuff, cannot compete with the magic that is, for examples, French, Italian, Japanese, and Indian cooking.) The Lattanzis calculated—as it turns out, correctly—that any food that could legitimately be called Jewish, if it also tasted good, would appeal to that large market. And since the problem they were solving was an after-eight problem, the supplemental menu they initiated to deal with it—of food from the Roman ghetto —is offered only from that hour on. Sure enough, Lattanzi today is the only spot on the block in which it is sometimes hard to get a table even after the crowds have moved into the theaters. But it is clear that when they introduced the new cooking, the Lattanzis were not so sure it would succeed, and presumably meaning to leave nothing to chance, the food is identified—in a brief introduction that appears on the special printed menu —as "nouvelle Jewish-Roman." Not to worry. Except that it is not kosher, it is the real thing.

Physically, Lattanzi is what it was before the integration, low ceilinged, brick walled, dimly lit—except for the half dozen white-linened tables that, situated just under napkin-draped hanging lamps, are aglow. The restaurant is hung with Italian engravings and, on one side of the room, with a quasi-Pompeiian painting of ladies of an ancient time serenely about their domestic tasks. If none of that strikes you as distracting, there is Luciano Pavarotti, who, imprisoned in the kitchen, sings out for his release, sometimes all through dinner.

Of Roman-Jewish dishes, only one has gained currency in foreign parts, carciofi alla giudia, in which trimmed and seasoned artichokes are boiled in olive oil with garlic— they reach you quartered, saturated with oil and yet not really oily, the tips of the tender, edible leaves browned and crisp, the garlic vivid but to no loss of the artichoke's own clear flavor. Artichokes again—they are a big item in this cookery—but this time just as a garnish to the crostini di fegatini, in which chicken livers that have been coarse ground and sautéed in olive oil with onions reach you as a well-seasoned paste on crusts of fried bread. The crostini are garnished with an exceptional caponata, cool, tart, sweet—the oily eggplant and peppers, the crunchy celery, the zucchini and the sour capers all retain their character in the herbed and spicy liquid. The caponata appears also as the one cool item in a three-part first course. The other items: a rather dreary rice ball pinked with tomato and weighted with cheese—it is the kind of dish you must grow up with to love; and a version of mozzarella in carrozza in which the breaded and deep-fried slab of pully cheese is covered over with hot capers. Orecchiette are disks of pasta shaped like little battered coins. Here they are served "al tonno," in a Jewish tuna-fish sauce that, though you may take it as a kind of meat sauce in which fish has been substituted for beef, is not that at all. Its character is its own, the spicy, fragrantly herbed, and dense tomato sauce thick with the fish and dominated by its flavor. The green lasagne are interleaved with, yet again, artichokes, the two in a bright tomato sauce that is peppery and sweet.

What distinguishes the Jewish roast chicken from others is what is absent from it—butter, as well as most of its own fat. Roasted this way—with seasoning, garlic, and rosemary—the bird takes on an aromatic but somewhat dry quality peculiar to Jewish roast birds. You may like it—you may not. Which may be said also of the red snapper, which the menu refers to—with license—as "orata" (quite another fish). In this preparation the fish is baked in oil and vinegar with raisins and pine nuts until it is at once rich and vigorously sour—it is the kind of food you instinctively eat with bread. The agnello al rosmarino is a row of connected rib lamb chops, the unsevered eyes peeled away from the bones before grilling. This beats grilling the chops individually, for a substantial crust can be built up while the meat inside remains blood-juicy. The good lamb, flavored with garlic and rosemary, is served with a great hillock of sautéed mushrooms.

From the regular menu: fettuccine Lattanzi, the broad noodles in a creamy sauce thick with wild mushrooms, all very nice, but you do miss the peas that are listed as an element of the dish; bucatini amatriciana, the hefty tubes of pasta—judiciously cooked, just this side of tough—in a tomato sauce, thick with sweet onions, that is permeated with the flavor of good Italian bacon; calamari Lattanzi, the fresh and tender squid in a spicy red sauce dotted with chunks of pungent garlic and (this time they do show up) sweet green peas that, in this setting, manage to be little more than decorative—the strong, brash stuff is served with thick crusts of well-oiled garlic bread; zuppa di pesce, mussels and cherrystone clams in their half-shells, at the center of the plate a mound of crunchy shrimp and that good squid again, those two on a fillet of fish, the entire variegated abundance in a deep pool of red, briny, winy sauce; pollo capriccioso, chunks of chicken, great slabs of red pepper, sharp-flavored little capers, all in a deep and deep-red marinara sauce; and a veal chop "al funghi" that, too bad, was done until flat before it was buried under sautéed mushrooms.

The ricotta cheesecake is eggy and light—and, surprise, warm. You may have fresh strawberries under a cool zabaglione made with much marsala. The napoleon is the big winner, the layers of pastry so flaky, the layers of cream so rich and stiff, that you take it the thing was assembled moments before it was served.

★★LUSARDI'S

1494 Second Avenue (near 78th Street)
LUNCH, MONDAY TO FRIDAY; DINNER, DAILY.
Reservations: 249-2020.
Credit cards: AE, DC, MC, V.
Medium priced.

Lusardi and Lusardi, the handsome, dapper, mustachioed, and almost twinlike brothers who run this place, are the not so secret secret of its popularity, for theirs is the most genuine cordiality, the kind that has been fixed by reward. Waiters who do not emulate the brothers' benevolent dispositions do not last, so the gents you deal with once you are seated are almost invariably patient and helpful, as if they want to make you happy. The effect of this is to make you happy. Sufficiently so, in fact, that you are willing to overlook the occasional humdrum dish, and surroundings that, originally straightforward, have been somewhat undone. Lusardi's is one of the many clubby Italian restaurants that invaded Manhattan's Upper East Side in the early eighties, almost all of them simple installations of painted-plaster walls and wood trim furnished with rows of linened tables. In them bluff guys, in white shirts and white aprons, handed you the menu, told you the specials of the day, took your order, promptly delivered, their brusqueness part of the style—which was set, often, by proprietors who did not waste their limited respects on strangers. But while this place took a turn for the better by deviating from the usual short manner, it got lost in its effort to improve on the standard look. Lusardi's has been prettied with framed prints; they are hung at stubbornly regular intervals all around, turning the once direct room into yet another poster gallery with kitchen.

Your waiter's good manners, of course, do not forbid consideration of the profit motive. He suggests that instead of Lusardi's ordinary bread, you order the bruschetta toscana, a plate of many crusty bread slices, each of them piled high with a fragrantly herbed mix of chopped tomatoes in a lively vinaigrette. Of the other cool first courses, pass up the seafood salad—loud mussels, and a rather sour dressing that expresses nothing of oil—in favor of a carpaccio: the one of salmon is a great spread of raw pink fish, fresh and supple, covered with a density of chopped parsley, oil, lemon; the one of beef is moistened with oil, is mounded over with woodsy mushrooms and short sticks of sharp Parmesan. Sometimes there is polenta, the hot toasted slices of packed grain under more of those porcini mushrooms, these sautéed, and moistened with a good tomato sauce. Each day there is a pappardelle of the day, the wide, weighty noodles sometimes in a deep and meaty quail sauce that you fortify with cheese.

Branzino, a basslike fish of the Mediterranean, is served in a slightly enriched white-wine broth—too bad that overcooking has softened the fish and diminished its flavor. Similarly the swordfish, the thin steak fresh but of little swordfish character—it is served in a puréed version of sauce livornese, red and garlicky, but lacking the whole capers and chunks of olive that are usually the life of that preparation. An order of fried calamari is a pile of deep-fried circles, tender and virtually greaseless, that you liven with lemon—if you wish, you will be served also a pitcher of simple and vigorous tomato sauce. A good chicken dish: pollo castelli romani, the whole breast, skin on and delicately browned, in a creamy sauce that is thick with mushrooms and slivers of artichoke. A good veal dish: veal martini, the thin cutlets of meat dipped in ground cheese, sautéed until crisp, moistened with a sauce that is smooth and lemony. And a good chop: veal chop salvia, the browned and blackened meat slicked with oil and suffused with the wild flavor of sage.

Lusardi's tiramisù is better than most, this puddinglike version grainy, of real coffee flavor, and of considerable cheese richness. You may have your zabaglione on ripe, fresh berries. And of course there is heady Parmesan cheese.

★★★★ LUTÈCE

249 East 50th Street
LUNCH, TUESDAY TO FRIDAY; DINNER, MONDAY TO SATURDAY. CLOSED SUNDAY.
Reservations: 752-2225.
Credit cards: AE, DC, MC, V.
Very expensive.

Lutèce the hundredth time is like Lutèce the first time, the place is such an astonishment. The shock is only in part a function of the disparity between the restaurant's grand reputation and its unassuming style. The style alone could do it, for New York life simply does not prepare you for this lost charm and forgotten grace. Unlike the other local restaurants usually ranked with it, Lutèce is not a product tailored to a market, has not been programmed to push all your buttons. It simply exists, the distillate of a civilized, appreciative way of life. Today, when more than ever there are other restaurants in which you will regularly get a first-class dinner, Lutèce is not comparable to them, remains apart, is only peripherally a place of public accommodation. It is more nearly a natural resource, the one spot in town that is not in this town at all, if it is even in this century. Lutèce does not merely take you in, it restores you—to the manners, gay and clement, of your inherited past, which are its province. Enter in tune, and you will find that you are not really in a restaurant, but in a time that is forgotten, but part of you. As sole present occupant of that era, the management here, though hard at work, is notably self-assured. It is as if a higher being whispered in the proprietor's ear: All you must do, whispered the being, is please yourself—you will thereby please those you would have as customers, and you will prosper. At Lutèce the secure receive the tasteful, and neither has anything to prove.

All of which is not to suggest Lutèce is complacent. In fact, it is always changing, at least to the extent of new dishes regularly dreamed up by André Soltner, chef-owner. Recently, moreover, he has undertaken to revise the physical plant itself, a risky business when the subject is that rarity, a true institution, and situated in this landmark-mad borough. But Soltner is his own watchdog committee, and though the notorious French restaurant architect Sam Lopata advised, nothing done has altered this establishment's well-known French charm, which has always seemed especially evanescent here on alien ground. No chances were taken. Despite North America's diverse geology, the new façade is of French stone, and it is not emblazoned with the great bold letters that announced Lutèce to its New York street during the first quarter century of its existence, only with a small sign near the front door, gold on black, all discretion. In a misty twilight, when you yourself are perhaps a bit misty, it is possible to imagine that you are seeing the place by the silver light of Paris itself.

As ever, you enter to a tiny foyer that gives onto a minuscule barroom, its space quite occupied by a short zinc bar and a handful of small tables with brass-rimmed marble tops, café chairs around them. The walls are casually adorned, here a small mural of Paris, there a Paris street sign, you should not forget this is France. The foyer gives also onto a narrow stairway leading to a couple of relatively formal dining rooms one flight up, crystal chandeliers and all that. But changes up here are beginning to soften things —the rearmost of the two rooms is now faced with a nubbly beige cloth woven with spice-brown florets among a network of stylized branches, its effect, at once autumnal and cozy, very much of a piece with this room's fireplace (inactive), a pair of Florentine oils, now cleaned and restored, their bold flowers revealed to be of warm, vivid colors, the ancient dusky tapestry that has covered one wall of this room ever since Lutèce was new, the tall white tapers on the larger tables, and the chandelier's golden light. Bypass the stairway, however, and a corridor takes you by the long kitchen, into which you peer, through the aperture that runs its length, to observe a squad in white firing to order, Soltner himself often among them. On occasion he steps out when familiar customers go by, his now famous face a smiling sun. It is the downstairs dining rooms beyond the kitchen that you probably think of when you think "Lutèce," and you will likely be relieved to learn that the first of them has been pruned of the rampant green fronds that, on a succession of wallpapers over the years, added a note of the riotous to this otherwise serene area. The room is square, a good-size table in each corner, each well apart from the others, the new treatment (making remote reference to the old), of delicate trailing vines painted as airy frames on a vaporous ground of mottled green, a bit of hazy countryside, from which you enter the enclosed garden room onto which it gives. As you were pleased by the changes, so will you be content with what has been left as was, for the garden remains an airy fantasy—made up, without regard to any syntax of meaning, of light, space, and whimsy. On a floor of forest-green flagstones, and within slightly fantastical surroundings—white latticework set before pink walls, palms sprouting from gleaming brass pots that stand atop stubby columns of whitewashed brick—are set two rows of white-linened tables that, despite their situation in this particular neighborhood of fairyland, are surrounded by the colorful wicker chairs you know from Paris cafés. The sky overhead is a translucent dome, faced with pale-green blinds, that at its highest point is two stories above ground. The room is weightless, like a mirage. And though restaurant functions take place within it—Madame Soltner (this establishment's down-home version of a maître d') conducting like a good shepherd the happy sheep to their tables, gentlemen in black and white explaining and scribbling, others hastening and serving— the business of the place, leavened by the place itself, is to business as love is to politics. Only Soltner seems entirely of this, his unreal world, aglow in kitchen whites, beaming under his toque blanche. He materializes often during dinner, takes an order here, confers a blessing there, and near the end of the evening goes from table to table, always a little radiant, like—a benevolent host.

Yes, there is a printed menu. But listen to the captains or, especially, to Soltner himself, and you may conclude that the document is beside the point, for most of the enthusiasm, love, and attention go to the newest babies, the special dishes Soltner has most recently sired. Of course you may refer to the menu, order the truite fraîche grillée, and be content with an entire trout that, boned, its dark, crisped skin still encasing the pale, firm, and supple meat, is bathed in a light and creamy sauce that is alive with morsels and strands of fresh vegetable. But if you eat here regularly, the trout is not new to you, and you will be tempted instead by the likes of: cultivated freshwater gambas from Puerto Rico, shrimplike creatures, bifurcated, sautéed, and served in their carapaces, the sweet and crunchy meats touched with the flavor of their slightly charred shells and moistened with a gentle herbed butter; a pungent version of ratatouille, crunchy, tart of capers, accented with bits of black olive, the mound of it at the center of your plate surrounded by dice of sautéed tuna fish in a pinked and buttery sauce that is accented with minced chives; a thin fillet of fresh turbot that is cooked, on its plate, only when the fluffy and creamy sauce, dotted with bits of vegetable, under which it is buried is browned in the broiler—Provençale herbs and the blackened edges of the sauce are the striking accents of the dish; hat-shaped ravioli of paper-thin pasta, the crown filled with a sweet, oceanic stuffing of crabmeat and lobster; tiny morsels of fresh frogs' legs accompanied, in a little tin-lined copper pot, by slivers of mushroom and dumplings (of ground frogs' legs and pike) that are the size of peas and the density of air, all in a rich, creamy, browned sauce that is alive with coarse-chopped herbs; in another such copper pot, fresh

American snails, plump, resilient but not tough, mingled with chunks of cèpe in a winy, creamy, and well-parsleyed sauce, under a lid of flaky pastry; a slice cut from a loaf of a terrine of duck confit and foie gras, the strong and spicy dark meat that is the center layer gentled by the richer pale meat that is the outer ones; a salad in which minuscule slivers of delicately crisped sweetbread and a sheaf of tender, nutty, deep-green haricots verts are mingled with crisp chicory in a warm dressing.

All of which may lead you to conclude that M. Soltner has cut himself from his roots, a notion you drop when you have sampled the listed poussin rôti aux herbes, roast chicken to you, and elemental. The whole bird, in its deep-bronzed skin, is shown, taken away, carved, served as hefty slices of meat in a brown sauce that is heady with fresh tarragon—the chicken has a depth of flavor that these days is usually just a memory. With such a chicken, who needs a pheasant? Still, this place is at home also with the game bird, the sliced breast and whole parts sturdy in a dark sauce that is dense with diced vegetables—a hearty, vivid dish. More unfancy food, a veal shank that has been braised, removed from its braising liquid and browned, the meat taken from its bone, sliced, and served to you in a deep sauce of the liquid, to which have been added onions, potatoes, wild mushrooms—the power of the dish is in the vigorous flavor the supple meat has taken on from being cooked on its bone in a powerful stock. When venison chops are on hand, it is well to know that at Lutèce the plump eyes of blood-juicy meat sport venison's characteristic liver richness at its most intense—the game is served, in its dark sauce, with herbed, eggy spaetzle, whole chestnuts, and strands of crisp, tangy celeriac.

Among desserts, too, both the traditional and the original are available, hot soufflés notable among the former. If the flavor you choose is Grand Marnier, you are presented with a monument loftily risen above the white porcelain pot in which it was baked, on its tawny plateau top, in deep-brown letters, the word "Lutèce." The soufflé itself is light and moist, shot through with bits of orange rind, and it is much enriched by the hot Grand Marnier sauce your waiter spoons on. Unlisted desserts you will sometimes be offered: a frozen lemon soufflé, two white disks—cold, creamy, sweet, and citrus sharp —with a sheet of chewy almond meringue between them; a homey pear cake, nutted and dark, served with an eggy sauce sabayon that is tangy of its fruit brandy; sweet sections of marinated orange in a pool of liquored white sauce that is browned just before it is served; tiny poached pears, firm and fruity, with vanilla ice cream of stunning polish, in a crisp and lacy pastry cup set in a black chocolate sauce.

★ LE MADELEINE

405 West 43rd Street
LUNCH AND DINNER.
Reservations: 246-2993.
Credit cards: AE, MC, V.
Inexpensive.

When new, this place sold sandwiches and salads, desserts and coffee, &c. It was a café, and folks came here to eat a little, to drink a little, and to sit around a lot. Such casual revenues probably cannot support a New York store. Anyway, for whatever reason, the ex-café is now a bistro, complete with kitchen. But only the menu has changed. The place looks the way it has from the start, and young dancers and actors between assignments still make up the staff. Nowadays the restaurant has a price-conscious pretheater dinner following, so if you get here just before curtain time, your ingress is against the current of a small crowd off to balcony seats. Ten minutes later the place may well be empty, but from then on it is neighborhood territory, may even fill again with the new locals—many of them theatricals—in this blooming part of town. Le Madeleine is a brightly lighted, high-ceilinged room with big windows—hung with gauzy half curtains —that look out on 43rd Street. A zinc-topped bar is near the entrance, the brick walls have been muraled with art that looks like old sun-bleached advertisements, and the rows of tables are covered with white butcher paper, additional sheets of which are tacked up here and there around the room, the special dishes of the day scrawled thereon. The background music, it appears, is always jazz.

The mostly vigorous food of this straightforward place includes a soupe au pistou that is a loudly garlicked and fragrantly herbed broth thick with chunks of root vegetable and clumps of greens; smoked trout that is exceptional for its freshness and for the subtlety of its smoky flavor, served with a good sauce that is little more than thick whipped cream touched with horseradish; smoked goose, the slices of dark-red meat tasting (try the blindfold test) very much like mild pastrami, though fine for that, and served, appropriately, with strong mustard; and a duck liver mousse, the jelly-edged slice cut from a loaf of—unfortunately—a flat and pasty amalgam too lacking in fluffiness or air to satisfy your anticipation of a "mousse." You may begin your dinner with an ordinary salad— the one listed as "four greens" arrives with only two, but the unexpected onions, slices of tomato, and celery, all in the strong and thick house dressing, make up for the deficit; or with one of several composed salads, among them one of endive, walnuts, and Roquefort, each of the elements occupying a separate section on your plate (crescents of sliced cucumber and slices of tomato present too), that sturdy house dressing in a little pitcher, should you want it on, say, your endive but not your walnuts.

It was only a matter of time before New York came up with an answer to the New Orleans blackened redfish. The challenger is called, of course, blackened bluefish (which, with any etymological luck, will be black-and-blue fish by the turn of the century). The item has, moreover, more to recommend it than a cute future, is good to eat, consisting, as it does, of a substantial fillet of fresh fish that is hot, juicy, and of vivid flavor within its dark and crusty skin of Cajun seasonings. But you will not always be so lucky with Le Madeleine's fish, for another time you choose tuna, and you get a thin grilled steak that comes off as little more than neutral protein under a pallid mustard sauce. Each day there is a pasta of the day, sometimes a spaghetti dish in which the three elements of the sauce—cream, smoked salmon, dill—are strong, distinct, and utterly at home with one another. The suprême de volaille is the breast of a not particularly tasty chicken, but the browned herb-and-anchovy coating converts it into fun food. The thin-sliced liver is nicely crisped in the sautéing and it takes very well to its buttered, polished sauce of raspberry vinegar, but the mushrooms under which the liver is buried, though perfectly decent, overwhelm the meat. Le Madeleine's steaks are not of America's best beef, so they are sometimes gristly—and sometimes inaccurately done.

Come on Sunday, and you get Saturday's desserts, among them tired apple and pecan pies. But the Mississippi mudcake, when it is fresh, is an overwhelmingly rich chocolate item, lightly flavored of coffee, and of a strong molasses sweetness—big crumbs of chocolate are the rugged terrain on top. The fruit tarts are like clafouties, the plums or cranberries or whatever embedded in the shortbread pastry. Good whipped cream is available with the desserts.

When the weather is fine, you may eat here out of doors: about a dozen tables—covered with that snowy white paper and surrounded by folding chairs and white-painted benches—are set out in a small backyard in which a single tree is strung with little white lights.

★ MALAGA

406 East 73rd Street
LUNCH AND DINNER.
Reservations: 737-7659.
Credit cards: AE, DC, MC, V.
Medium priced.

Bullfight posters, unspeakable oils, framed moments (on linen) in the life of Don Quixote, red lights on the gaudy chandeliers, sexy Spanish ladies painted onto the big barrel bottoms that are mounted on the wall behind the little bar (just under the wine baskets that hang from the tiled, sloped mock roof); not to mention the black-and-white television set that is occasionally turned on, nor the tall gray Model-T air-conditioning monster, the coats that are on display on the attended plain pipe rack just inside the front door; never mind the crowds that come, young marrieds escaping the kitchen on weekday and weekend nights, whole families escaping it on Sundays, slummers in suits and ties and perms any old time. It is remarkable how so much paraphernalia and activity can fail to make a place look other than gaunt and spare. That, of course, is the front room. The back room lacks even the paraphernalia, except for its own unspeakable oils and monster.

On the Upper East Side, Malaga is the only establishment of its exact type, sporting the standard menu that was set as New York's version of Spanish cooking as long ago as the 1930s and 1940s, in the couple of dozen Spanish restaurants that were then around town. The type has not died out, but now most such places are downtown, and Malaga has itself a little monopoly here. Perhaps for that reason the place does not try too hard. This is a decent restaurant, but you love it more when you know it better, for some of the food is good, and some is not.

Not the Spanish ham and olives, for the ham is coarse, even coarsely sliced, though the green olives are strong and sharp. Far better are the cold Malaga mussels, sweet and fresh in their shells, spread with a bright dressing of chopped tomato and onion and parsley. This place makes a good salpicon and sells it in a $5 serving big enough for two—it is a cool chopped salad of crabmeat, hard-cooked eggs and greens, the strong parsley called cilantro, and chopped tomatoes, all in a sharp and refreshing dressing.

You can get lots of hot crunchy shrimp in a bubbling sauce of oil and garlic; a small beach of chorizos, discs of Spanish sausage, that are grilled until they are crusty; a garlic soup that is red with red pepper, thick with chunks of bread and with egg that is cooked in the broth—the soup is homey, but not tasty.

Main courses arrive on a cart in big iron pots, and a huge platter of good red-peppered rice is served with all of them. But the egg sauce that is served on the mixed seafood (mariscada) is thin, hardly eggy at all. And the paella—the biggest pot on the wagon—contains a lobster that is little more than an empty shell, and a lot of other ingredients that are mostly overcooked. Choose instead the crabmeat in green sauce, for it has texture and resilience, and its sauce is fragrant with abundant parsley. Or the shrimp diablo, those good shrimp again, very crisp, in a spicy sauce that is thick with green peppers. The veal extramena is of tender little morsels of meat, but its sauce, allegedly of onions, sausage and peppers, is notable mainly for its good garlic intensity. Eschew the pork with almond sauce—which is flat-out of no interest—in favor of the chicken villaroy, the two halves of a breast of chicken, artfully prepared, coated with béchamel, breaded, and crisped. Remarkably, the dish is light.

As everyone knows, the desserts in Spanish restaurants vary not at all from restaurant to restaurant, only a little from dessert to dessert. Malaga has added a standard New York cheesecake to the standard list, and it is not bad if you like that kind of thing. The best of the Spanish desserts is the guava with cream cheese—the fruit is candied but seems brandied, for it is sweet and sharp, and the block of cheese that comes with it is solid. The dish arrives with a couple of saltines standing in it, like a couple of sails.

★ MANHATTAN OCEAN CLUB

57 West 58th Street
LUNCH, MONDAY TO FRIDAY; DINNER, DAILY.
Reservations: 371-7777.
Credit cards: AE, DC, MC, V.
Very expensive.

Through the two-level dining room rise massive square white columns, and to each of their faces a dark and skinny half column, fluted and with an elaborate finial, has been grafted, forming constructs that may be taken as failed attempts by posts to become pillars. In glass-covered green niches carved into the walls, handsome Picasso ceramics are on display (not for sale). And on the south wall of the lower level there is, for some reason, fruit, shiny red apples one time, oranges another, row upon row of the bright-colored orbs, a display like those at a fruiterer. This seafood restaurant is an enterprise of the interests behind Smith & Wollensky and the Post House, relentlessly bluff and hearty steakhouses bedecked with whimsical assortments of paraphernalia that, by their insouciant irrelevance, underscore the rumpus-room masculinity of those repairs. The Club, however, styles itself "A Classic Seafood Restaurant," and though you may find the slogan (a) meaningless or (b) false, the physical place does have an underlying nautical trimness. Unfortunately, far from being underscored by its accessories, it is almost undone by them. The rooms are perfectly comfortable, you understand, but they have been sacrificed to the simpleminded notion that what worked in one place would work in another.

Qua eating place, on the other hand, the eating place has stabilized to a point at which the piscivore may, by astuteness, eat well at it. To eat well, you pray for your raw oysters, for one time they are sparkling, another time flat—a day too long out of their water and much in need of lemon. But most of the shellfish appetizers are fine: lump crabmeat that is supple and sweet; baked clams in a nutted pesto that is a striking setting for the tender littlenecks; steamed cultivated mussels that, a miracle for these days, are of clear, stout mussel flavor, a couple dozen of them, in their shells, mounded over the briny broth—thick with chopped peppers and tomatoes—in which they were done. The clam chowder is spicy, thick with potato, hearty, though its clam meat is of a toughness.

Finfish—the rules for keeping it, and the theory and hang of preparing it—eludes this place. The swordfish au poivre, for example, is a chunk of fish the size and shape of a double filet mignon, so the thing reaches you overcooked on the surface, almost raw at the center, both conditions deadly to this variety. Snapper, probably broiled as long as

217

that swordfish, though less than an inch at its thickest point, has lost most of its flavor to the overtreatment. Some nicely prepared halibut is a bit fishy around the edges. But then, on a lucky night, you get this salmon steak, handsomely browned, cooked through but moist, all its flavor intact. The so-called broiled lobster is steamed first, and as its exposure to the broiler is brief—just enough to make it *look* broiled—the sweet meat is moist and tender. The crab cakes are a big winner, two hamburger-size patties, almost solid crabmeat of vivid flavor, pungently spiced, handsomely browned, nicely livened by lemon, so in no need at all of the obvious mustard sauce served with them. The baked potato is the size of a watermelon, and it is firm within its crusty skin. In this city of innumerable Italian restaurants, in which threadlike fried zucchini, crisp, airy, and weightless, is served in dozens of places, the Ocean Club is bold enough to send out baskets of soggy logs.

What your waiter calls a pistachio bombe tart is an acid-green, marzipanlike slab in two sauces, vanilla and raspberry—the garish looks of the dish prepare you perfectly for its taste and texture. An assortment of little fruit tarts are of a sugary sweetness that defeats the fruit. The poached fresh fig, with whipped cream and custard in a cassis sauce, is a collection of good ingredients that add up to an adult sundae. The hot plum tart is a winner, the browned slices of fruit on a crunchy pastry of ground nuts.

On your table you find a printed vintage chart. By reference to this, how you say, debatable document, you learn that virtually anything on this restaurant's wine list is worth ordering.

★ MAN RAY

169 Eighth Avenue (near 18th Street)
LUNCH AND DINNER.
Reservations, 627-4220.
Credit cards: AE.
Medium priced.

Named for an American painter, photographer, and film maker who spent time in Paris, this place integrates that geography and some of the biography, for it is hung with movie stills and photos by the artist, and it is installed in the premises of the blessedly demised L'Express—which was fitted out with appointments from the Paris Métro, and which enjoyed a decibel level that rivaled an IRT local stop with express trains screaming through in both directions. The clangor was a function of the marble surfaces underfoot and all around, but, with very little sacrifice of the interior's original look, the sound has been moderated by installation of moiré-surfaced pads that, though they do not simulate the marble they hide, manage not to look like anything else either. The dim blue fluorescence of the light fixtures behind the often busy bar give off a suitably murky subway luminance, and you take it that the varnished wood-slat benches that form the row of booths across the way are well-preserved relics from old underground cars. The black-and-white photos just above the booths are Man Ray portraits, complete with name tags, among the subjects Cocteau, Berenice Abbot, Marcel Duchamp, Giacometti, Picasso, Nude. The brass railings all about, the shiny black tabletops, the Deco wall sconces, and the two-dimensional cut-metal sculpture (a human figure silhouetted before a wall of glinting glass blocks) all contribute to this bistro-brasserie's hard-edged, somewhat glitzy flavor, which is of a time and of a place—the years between the wars, the world below the ground. The customers and staff are young, brisk, and, except that the latter are in white shirts and aprons, interchangeable.

A lot to eat is part of Man Ray's appeal, this plate of smoked fish, for example, much trout, much salmon, both in firm, moist, supple condition, and, oddity, smoked mackerel, the strong dark fish crusted and salty, the three served with a sauce raifort that is of fluffy whipped cream and pungent horseradish. Similarly the bay scallops, which just about cover a good-size plate, but which you wish were browned in the sautéing rather than just warmed in butter—still, they are not bad, benefit from the sprigs and leaves of cilantro and escarole tangled among them. Meat: merguez, the blackened lamb sausages sweet- and hot-spiced, a little dry, served with chickpeas that are redolent of Eastern spices; a terrine, gamy and nutted, rimmed with white fat, served with a hot mustard and a mild one. Salads: one called "crudité," five separate elements on your plate, fennel, endive, slivers of avocado, crunchy red beets, and a well-oiled mingling of sautéed red peppers with anchovies and black olives, everything in a tart dressing; and winter greens with duck cracklings, the great mound of coarse lettuce and chicory dotted with large croutons and bits of crisp duck fat that taste like bacon, all in a warm and tangy vinaigrette.

Salsify is a vegetable much like asparagus, except that it is not asparagus, it is salsify —its crunchiness and homey flavor redeem this fettucine carbonara, for the noodles are a little tough in their creamy, bacon-dotted sauce. As the world knows, the firm white fish called lotte is nearly flavorless, but it does respond well to such outside influences as the garlicked sea urchin sauce that invigorates the great slices of prettily browned fish served here. Experienced readers of New York menus take a look at the entry "grilled chicken with calamata olives," and figure "a chicken and some olives." This bird, however, is literally coated with a glistening black mash of the salty calamatas, despite which the flavor of the pale meat itself is vivid. The steak is of fibrous and tender meat, but so blackened that all you taste is charcoal, which is too bad, for it is served with thin, crisp French fries, and with a pitcher of more than decent sauce béarnaise. The cassoulet is a substantial bowl of firm beans, the top blackened, in which are buried chunks of sausage, lamb, fowl, and though the last two are cooked to a point of unidentifiability, this is altogether a surfeit of sound and satisfying food. Sometimes choucroute is offered, and if the sour cabbage is a little sodden, it is livened by its black juniper berries, and all that cabbage, taken together with the three whole sausages, slab of pork, and boiled potatoes that adorn it, will anchor you to your seat until the arrival of dessert.

You do well with the simple sweets—good ice cream and sherbet, and a crème caramel that is light, almost fluffy, in its dark and tangy caramel sauce. The chocolate roll is a rather dull cake wrapped around nice whipped cream. Slivers of hot pear are served between blocks of flaky puff pastry, the two, in a thick and fruity sauce, garnished with the good house whipped cream.

★★MARCELLO

1354 First Avenue (near 73rd Street)
DINNER.
Reservations: 744-4400.
Credit cards: AE, DC, MC, V.
Expensive.

Marcello, the restaurant, is named for Marcello, your tuxedoed host. Note that it is not named John, though your other host, in civvies, is television news reader John Roland, miniceleb. Folks do come just to shake the fleshly hand that goes with the flickering Channel 5 visage, but still, "Marcello" is the right title here, for the hulking smiler of that name is the real draw. Marcello is that rare thing, a man born at the right time who emigrated to the right place. For only in twentieth-century America has taste developed for the form of mindless sodality that revels in the very contempt in which it is held by those not susceptible to its queer allure. Marcello is one who, when you assure him that your affection for his restaurant is in inverse proportion to the jolly attentions he afflicts upon you, *knows* that the appropriate response is a lengthy inquiry into why that should be so—no matter that you are groaning, staring at your drink on the bar, shaking your head as if to break free of a pain. Marcello is not, however, all insensitivity. He drops the subject when he catches you eyeing the door, concludes correctly that you await the arrival of a guest, recalls the companion of your previous visit, compliments you on your preference for slender women. How ardently you regret that tonight's guest soon to arrive is not fat. Of course you cannot blame the man for his ways. They work. Take, for example, this 88-pound great grandmother, who, as greeting, is embraced by Marcello like a milkmaid by her plowhand lover. The elderly lady is seen favoring the lout with a smile of adoring gratitude even before she is certain ever to recover her breath. It would be well if it could be said that once past the front-door amenities, you are safe from further visitations. But to hide, there is no place. Marcello, all six smiling feet plus of him, patrols the dining room like the proctor at your state bar exam. Just let him catch you and a friend (a) laughing gaily, or (b) hissing and snapping at each other, or especially (c) whispering together, urgently and purposefully, and the punishment is immediate: He is at your shoulder, pouring wine into your already half-full glass, assuring you that the bottle you have chosen is an excellent one and recounting how it came to pass that after tours of duty with scores of Italian restaurants around town and a particularly unsatisfactory relationship at the last place he is at last permanently connected to an establishment in which he is truly a full partner and proud to be here how fascinating. He knows not the boon hidden in this: Now, for the first time, you may set out for an Italian dinner in New York, and by a simple expedient—avoidance of this place—be certain Marcello will not be grinning at you just inside the front door of the restaurant you select.

His share is in a nifty-looking spot, the lengthy dining room sleek and softly lighted, here and there a bit of art, planters built into the long walls, the back wall given over to a sepia photo-mural of an Italian street scene. You walk on a handsome floor of red and blue tiles, sit on high-backed chairs around prettily set white-linened tables, are waited on by a crew of those itinerant Upper East Side Italian waiters whose faces you will recall having seen at dozens of other uptown places they have worked. (Brief) adaptability is their talent. One young captain, who apparently considers it politic to model himself after the boss, claps you affectionately on the shoulder as you are handed into his care. In his favor it may be said that he understands better than Big M the meaning of a blank, unresponsive glare, upon receipt of which he turns his attention to business and hands you a menu. Know that while you are considering that document, you may have brought to you an order of exceptional fried zucchini, the great tangle of filament strands—barely touched with batter—hot, crisp, and dry, very lively when you squeeze on the lemon that (in a cheesecloth pant) is supplied. Work your way through that thicket until your first course arrives: pearly slices of sweet shrimp surmounted by sections of tart orange, a pile of pungent little black olives at the center of the plate, sprigs of basil all about, everything moistened with olive oil of vivid flavor; or veal carpaccio, the film of pale meat, adorned with sprigs of mint, clinging to its plate—your waiter pours on more of that good oil, and you apply the lemon; or sautéed wild mushrooms, great meaty slices of porcini, their woodsiness potentiated by vigorous seasoning, nicely offset by the crescents of toasted polenta with which they are garnished.

To hit a bad pasta dish here is simply bad pasta luck, for the noodle is the strongest part of the menu. Still, it is well to aid your chances, and skipping the ziti alla fava will do it, there being little excitement in a tomato sauce cut with puréed beans. But then there is the spaghetti calabrese, its vigorous sauce, of oil and anchovies, greened with parsley and studded with chunks of fresh garlic; and fedelini (very thin spaghetti) with shrimp and radicchio, the oceanic flavor of the crunchy seafood stunning in a salty sauce built around blackened and bitter red lettuce; and farfallette al salmone, the bowties in an intense and creamy sauce of smoked salmon threaded with slivers of black truffle.

Salmon again, this time a fresh, moist sautéed fillet of the pink meat, enriched by the many strands of buttery leek spread over it, and by the pool of pale, winy sauce in which it is set. Though the calamari are given as "baby squids," you will take their age on faith, for they reach you cut into strands, circles, and clumps, they are mingled with pungent black olives and chunks of artichoke, and they are moistened with a stout liquid composed of the ingredients' juices and the oil in which they are sautéed—a powerful mound of food. The scaloppine castellana is of nicely sautéed veal—it is juicy and lightly crisped—but though the veal and the wine-and-chestnut sauce are on the same plate, they refuse to integrate. Good chops: The veal chop is plump, its charred exterior a zest to the moist, fibrous, tender meat; and the baby lamb chops provide you with four eyes of meat that are both delicate and of strong lamb flavor—the crisped edges are touched with rosemary and garlic.

The salad here is of fresh greens in a dressing made with good olive oil. The Parmesan cheese you may have with it cannot be faulted, but it is not Parmesan at its sharp, heady best. One night the melon-and-raspberry tart is positively treacly within its congealed syrup, but then there is this apple tart, the sweet-spiced fruit lively within its dark shortbread pastry. The tartufo, though little more than a sundae—three colors of ice cream encased in chocolate—is preferable to the sugary-sweet chocolate-chestnut cake.

★ MARIE-MICHELLE

57 West 56th Street
LUNCH, MONDAY TO FRIDAY; DINNER, DAILY.
Reservations: 315-2444.
Credit cards: AE, DC, MC, V.
Medium priced.

Beware realization of your fantasies. Dreams that excite you may survive only in their natural environment—your imagination. Wishes are, of course, translatable into tangibility—it is only their magic that is not. Here, clearly, is a fond dream, for the lady of the title was, for something like decades, associated with the now defunct Georges Rey (the restaurant was the namesake of her spouse), an animated, sprawling bistro on West 55th. In this place of her own, you read her attitude toward that place of her husband's —this is its opposite. Marie-Michelle is, how you say, feminine. Old rose, taupe, mauve, and off-pink are here set off by contrasting shades of beige, greige, and warm skin (Caucasian). If, in the course of wear and tear, the place develops blemishes, you imagine that Marie-Michelle (the name of the restaurant is the name also of its owner) will go around touching them up with her trusty powder puff. The restaurant is a long room, not very wide, the mirrored wall down one side tinted the color of rose dust. The tables are set with sand-colored linen, and they are surrounded by bentwood side chairs that have been painted a smashing shade of coral mist. There are, however, notes of vivid color: The tables are set with service plates, painted on each of them a coy, highly stylized flapper, a different flapper on each plate; and there is your hostess herself, a tall, dark-haired lady who dresses to stand out from her chosen environment. Her long experience in the restaurant business surely serves her well in some respects. But her politesse has become singsong and mechanical over the years (you assume it was once genuine), and her mastery of restaurant logistics has apparently been accomplished at the expense of sweet reason, for when you arrive to a restaurant that has emptied of its pretheater crowd, and there are any number of tables at which you could be comfortably seated, you are nevertheless required to wait at the tiny, rather crowded bar until your companion arrives. (There will always be among us those whose devotion to order transcends mere purpose.) Her peculiarities notwithstanding, the friends she made at Georges Rey visit her here in numbers, with, on arrival, much kissing of cheeks and, on departure, more kisses—and promises to be back. In fact, they will be back, for her place is a useful one.

Between bouts of kissing, they have dinnered decently on the likes of this gravlax, a delicate version, the pale-pink meat not at all oily, each slice edged with a black and green strip of the layer of herbs and spices under which the salmon marinated—this is more a French than a Scandinavian gravlax, and its sauce is a creamy one that is thick with fresh dill. Thin lengths of asparagus, an abundance of them, are served between light pastries—the two are set in a lemony butter. Order snails, and you are presented with a little copper pot, lid on. Remove the lid, and you find that the implement is tin lined, that it is filled with a thick, winy, lightly tomatoed, and vigorously seasoned sauce, and with plump snails and chunks of wild mushroom—a potent dish. The pasta with shrimp suffers from a paucity of the crustaceans (you get three of them) and from the iodine of which they taste.

Perhaps shrimp, or their shells, are used in the preparation of this so-called lobster stew, for it, too, is touched with iodine—which is too bad, for the morsels of lobster are sweet, and their pink and creamy sauce, sharpened by the flavor of lobster shell and touched with herbs, has much depth. The roasted baby chicken is a fine version of a simple thing. But the medallions of veal—three slices of meat surmounted by three slices of apple, all in a vaguely fruited sauce—could as well be three slices of nameless protein. If you make it to this place just once, do not think about it, but order the rack of lamb. Three not large chops are perhaps less than what you want for dinner, but this is good meat, and the eye of each chop is mounded over with a little cloud of browned and garlicked bread crumbs that is studded with minced vegetables.

The crème caramel is unexceptionable, the cassis cake cloying, the chocolate cake liquored and rich—it comes with good whipped cream. In this fancified bistro, the dessert to have is the chocolate mousse, the big scoop of it buttery and almost black, touched with orange flavor—its texture is like that of ice cream, but its concentration of chocolate flavor is its own.

★★★ MAURICE

119 West 56th Street
LUNCH, MONDAY TO FRIDAY; DINNER, DAILY.
Reservations: 245-7788.
Credit cards: AE, DC, MC, V.
Very expensive.

Engrossed in a book, the attentive reader is carried away, experiences foreign places, alien passions, who knows what. Food, unfortunately, though it has powers, exerts none that equal those of the written word. So, well as you may eat in this place, you never forget where you are: in a hotel dining room, one apparently designed, moreover, by a nonreader, the possessor of a virgin imagination that, having never been provoked, provokes not. Two hours' work by the moving men, and this could be the reading room of your neighborhood branch of the public library. Maurice is in no way ugly, you understand, it is simply that no one will ever especially want to be in this room except in preference to some lesser room.

The difficulty begins at the beginning, when you enter the dining room from the hotel lobby, no door between them, so that at once Maurice fails to create the essential restaurant illusion: that you are leaving one world and entering another. This is a cube of a place, high ceilinged and low lit, its walls sadly paneled with big murals, stillborn still lifes on black grounds, wood columns between them, faced with mirrored strips, that rise to the ceiling and extend across it, where they meet identical columns on the room's other side. There is broadloom on the floor, pale-pink linen on the tables, and the place is rimmed by a dark-blue banquette, across from which the comfortable chairs are of amber-colored plush with black-enameled arms. The huge spotlit burst of flowers at the center of the room helps, as do the two palms, one in front, one behind, with which the flowers form a straight line along the room's axis. You are comfortable here, well and professionally taken care of, but Maurice is to be avoided for such purposes as celebration or seduction or consolation.

On the other hand, it may well be sought out for such purposes as these oysters, each of the warm, plump mollusks, in their big shells, encased in a judiciously seasoned and buttery mash of shredded leeks—a stunning dish; or for this warm seafood salad of sweet shrimp, browned sea scallops, lengths of crisped red snapper, those ingredients arranged separately among tender little asparagus spears, leaves of endive, and—a strong, striking accent—dabs of minced sundried tomato. The word "ravioli" is perhaps misleading, albeit accurate, with respect to the ones served here, for the delicacy of these buttered, glistening little packages is not what you think of when you think of pasta, and their filling is of sweet scallops that are heady with fresh thyme. On occasion the house offers a feuilletée of wild mushrooms, a sandwich formed of two great triangles of flaky puff pastry, the top one browned and glistening, the filling between them, which pours out the sides, a mingling of earthy wild mushrooms, powerfully salted, the entire production in a dark sauce that is rich with cream. Order the combination of snails and frogs' legs, and you find one of each in each of the three bundles—formed of browned, delicate pastry—on your plate, the bundles set in a rich sauce that is adorned with X's formed by one strand of cèpe and one of morel. Within the packages the snails are plump, black, of deep flavor, and the legs are delicate—which accounts for the fact that, good as this dish is, the frogs' legs are lost in it. No such difficulty with this assemblage of foie gras (the thin slices intensely rich and strongly flavored by the grilling), duck (the strands of medium-rare meat of clear duck flavor), and a lively green salad in which is buried a ragoût of wild mushrooms and slivers of sweet artichoke.

A fuss is made over salmon. You are shown the fish within the clay shell in which it is done, a panel of the clay cut away so that a side of the pink meat is visible. Sure enough, this is juicy fish, very well served by the dilled butter poured over it, but, on occasion, the salmon is a day past its peak, a particular comedown in consideration of the fact that the item must be ordered for two. Seek safety in the smaller number one, a fillet of striped bass, the great slab of utterly fresh fish under a whimsical sheet formed of thin potato slices, crisped, deeply browned, and arranged to resemble a fish's scales—the construct is in a smooth and winy sauce that has in it a good note of sweetness. The roast squab is browned and shiny, its meat moist and strong, a mound of softened strands of cabbage and carrot its well seasoned garnish. The roasted saddle of venison reaches you sliced, and a good bit rarer than how you ordered it, but the blood-juicy meat is supple in its thick, fruity, and tart raspberry-vinegar sauce. That is nice venison, but the beef is offered in a more interesting preparation—potted beef, mingled with mushrooms, surrounded by slices of roasted tenderloin, the former done in a stock of such depth that the meat is imbued with an earthy essence of roots and bones against which the blushing slices of loin, on their individual pancakes, amount to a delicacy.

Almost all the desserts are based on fruit: a raspberry napoleon in which the ripe, plump berries are arranged in ranks, with a polished cream, among crisp layers of pastry, the whole set in an intense berry purée; a pineapple fritter in which warm and juicy morsels of the ripe fruit, wrapped in a browned pancake, are set in a cool berry sauce and garnished with a ball of citrus ice; a lemon tart that is notable for the exceptional lightness of its custard; and an orange tart that is overlaid with thin sheets of orange rind and garnished with bitter-chocolate ice. Soufflés must be ordered for two, and the one of chocolate is deep, rich, almost black—and strikingly garnished with good pistachio ice cream.

A few wines are as low as $22, but if Roger, your gentle wine steward, suggests a more expensive bottle, it is a good one.

★★MELROSE

48 Barrow Street (near Bedford Street)
DINNER.
Reservations: 691-6800.
Credit cards: AE, DC, MC, V.
Expensive.

By way of little more than fresh paint, upholstery, carpeting, an old Village den—anciently the Finale, subsequently the Paris Bistro, most recently a nameless failure or two that fled before they were noted—has been cut away from the past and set adrift. Your host (the fellow in the garments that are difficult to distinguish with respect to where one leaves off and another begins) shows you around: a dining room in the back that is a peaked tent, another up front that is higher-ceilinged than a crawl space, and a white-lighted cubicle that is both the passage between them and the city's most trafficked kitchen—one wrong turn, and your spike heels are caught in the duckboards. Except for those works, the place is all misty gray and green, the floor of the tent faux astroturf, the canvas top the color of dark clouds, the linened tables surrounded by little black-painted side chairs built of kindling, the light low, the intensity of sound numbing when feelings are high among the members of what you take to be the powdery crowd that has taken this place up. Green carpeting up front too, but it does not glint in the manner of roll-up lawn, albeit the green banquettes that run the length of this room along each side certainly shine like real vinyl, and the glowing little bar at one end, under its Deco light fixture, must be a genuine mirage that will vanish when you approach it from within the depths of this dim room. It has been reported that Melrose was put together with limited funds, which probably accounts for the singular spirit of the installation—it is at once somber, whimsical, and jauntily defiant, and the staff are dressed to help carry it off in their black pants and ties, white over-the-head aprons, merry shirts of authentic mattress ticking.

The proprietor's restaurant lineage traces to Ma Maison, an eating place late of Los Angeles, here memorialized with what is billed as "warm Ma Maison lobster salad, in which chunks of sweet lobster meat are strikingly set off by the excellent greens on which they are set—tender beans, dice of tomato, and a little clutch of enoki mushrooms are the other elements of the dish, which is moistened with a rich dressing given as truffle butter. His lineage traces more recently to Batons, a defunct New York madhouse, and here are the good, crackling potato pancakes he used to make there, on each of them three dabs of caviar and one of crème fraîche, one of the caviars on occasion less than impeccable, the shredded radish garnish misplaced, but the pancakes themselves of strong fried-potato flavor. What the house calls "California baby greens" sport powerfully fragrant flavors, though you may find some of them a little grassy—the salad is served with hefty disks of potato, like potato chips, onto which chunks of stout Gorgonzola have been melted. Pass up the lamb carpaccio, for the raw meat, intertwined with greens, exhibits little lamb character, and the other ingredients—sun-dried tomatoes, enoki mushrooms, Parmesan, do not correct for the error. Opt instead for the herbed and peppery oblongs of blood-juicy charred beef on skewers, in a dark and polished so-called oyster sauce, which are served with Chinese greens that, though stir-fried and hot, retain their "raw" crispness and flavor. The tarragon pasta is heady of the herb in its pink and creamy lobster sauce, the lengths of crunchy artichoke in nice contrast to the noodles, as are the crisped and handsomely browned slices of sweetbread on top.

The big scallops—great morsels of silken white seafood charred in the sautéing—are

225

livened by the cool vinaigrette that dresses the tomatoes served beside them. A rare-cooked utterly fresh fillet of salmon, its skin crisped, reaches you on a vibrant green sauce of miso (Japanese fermented soy bean paste) and green onions—for its purity, the dish could easily be left as is, but the man in the kitchen gets away quite well with this garnish of "black and gold pasta," in which the firm strands are mingled with mushrooms and root vegetables in a gentle sauce. The grilled chicken is billed "with double blanched garlic shallot purée and Italian parsley," which is all very well, but it is the real chicken flavor of the bird and the crisp skin that are the making of the dish. That chicken is good, but this marinated squab is a rarity, the grilled bird served in parts and slices, the skin blackened a little and crackling, the glistening dark meat of deep squab flavor, the sauce fruited and tangy. The roast veal is another rarity, for restaurant roast veal tends toward the arid and pallid, whereas these slices of pale, barely pink meat are juicy, delicately fibrous, take on the life of their creamy port-wine sauce. But there is nothing rare about this grilled beef tenderloin except its near perfection—the meat is beefy, bloody, tender, and for that kind of thing this red-wine sauce with herbs and shallots is, how you say, basic.

Some nights it seems that half the dining room goes for the caramel apples—you see them streaming out of the kitchen in the direction of every other table. Despite its popularity, this is a good dessert, the crisp, cold fruit covered with a mixture of nuts, caramel, and white chocolate. The orange ricotta torte is simply cheesecake roused with the flavor of orange rind, nicely garnished with apples and liquored black cherries. The rice pudding, dotted with bits of "Michigan tart cherries," is just an oddity, the cherries unidentifiable as such, and anyway quite obscured by the cranberry-orange sauce poured over. Come here just once, and the dessert to have is the raspberry tart, firm ripe fruit, a thin layer of nuts under it, a buttery pastry of particularly good grain flavor, and real whipped cream, stiff and rich.

• MÉNAGE À TROIS

511 Lexington Avenue (on 48th Street)
LUNCH, MONDAY TO FRIDAY; DINNER, MONDAY TO SATURDAY. CLOSED SUNDAY.
Reservations: 593-8242.
Credit cards: AE, DC, MC, V.
Medium priced.

It is the essence of Ménage à Trois that with your bread you are served four butters (herb butter, Roquefort butter, anchovy butter, butter butter), the kind of seeming culinary virtuosity that MàT's British backers (the London original is très successful) have brought to a New York hotel to wow travelers from west of the Hudson passing through. Locals, however, will respond to the place with, at best, mild nostalgia very amused, for it calls to mind the time when, in this country, new "gourmet" cooking, like new music, was recognized as such by its dissonances, by combinations of elements theretofore considered, if considered at all, unthinkable. You could simply dismiss this place as antediluvian, but British climate permits only a slow-paced ontology, so you are inclined to be indulgent at listings like "Poached Quail Eggs served on the Base of an Artichoke, topped with Smoked Salmon, Oyster, Scallop, Lobster and Russian Caviar on a Red Pepper Sauce," or "Breast of Chicken filled with Lobster and Asparagus, wrapped in Spinach and served with Lobster Cream" (Capitalization Theirs). But your indulgence deserts you when you consider the promotional copy at the front of the menu, which, in reference to "nouvelle cuisine," reads in part, ". . . we saw 'cowboys' jumping on the bandwagon garnishing everything with kiwifruit and crayfish heads . . . what must remain from the 'new-wave' is the lighter sauces, uncluttered plates, respect of high quality products, and excellent presentation. . . ." The self-paean is signed by "Antony," the chef, but one dinner here, and you figure the prose is the work of some American flack who never saw the menu, for aside from a group of items listed as "Traditional," not one dish in five leaves itself alone—which is not to say that none of them has merit.

You enter, from the street, through a revolving door that gives directly onto the dining room, as if it were a lobby; or, from the lobby itself, through an open portal that, by its visual access to the hotel's traffic center, adds to the impression that here one is just passing through. The transatlantic provenance of MàT notwithstanding, the physical place and its appointments are pure anonymous American hotel, what with institutional broadloom on the floor, cut-glass mirrored walls, oval-backed period chairs, and wall sconces and chandeliers whose lights are shielded by big, leaf-shaped plates of whited glass that look like the things your mother got out when company came, and were called nut dishes. Tables by the window are small relief, for the view, under the raised Roman shades, is of East 48th, dumpsters at curbside.

Today's restaurant talk is of "grazing," a couple of small dishes in one place, a few more at another, maybe dessert at a third. Almost no one actually eats this way, but by the pretense the citizens flatter themselves that they live on-the-go lives. MàT caters to the imagined trend, offers a menu dominated by appetizers (though the word nowhere appears), albeit dishes listed as "Fish and Shellfish" or "Meat, Poultry and Game" are mostly main courses priced as such. Anyway, grazers are lighthearted types, no more fixed in time than place, are not bound by mealtime conventions, gaily breakfast before a midnight movie on soft and creamy scrambled eggs, two dollops of the yellow stuff, on one a dab of sour cream the size of a nickel, grains you can count of black caviar thereon, on the other, which is in a circular frame of smoked salmon, a sprinkling of chopped tomato—a good dish, especially the familiar but unfailing combination of gentle eggs and sharp cured salmon. When it is neither breakfast nor movie time, it is perhaps orgy time, time for one of the "Orgies of Salad Leaves" that, with various combinations of additional ingredients, make up the salad menu. The salad called "Sauvage" is a complexity of rabbit and snails, mushrooms and croutons, morsels of bacon and tender little haricots verts, all arranged over chicory and endive in a thick, lively dressing. Several three-part items are themselves called Ménages à Trois, including these three warm cheese packages in carpetbags formed of thin, crisp pastry, Camembert and cranberries in one, Roquefort and leeks in another, boursin and spinach in the third, none of the combinations inspired, but all of good ingredients. Each day a single pasta shape and a single pasta sauce (from a list of four) are offered, sometimes green and white fettuccine with wild mushrooms, truffle, duck foie gras, and what is given as "Truffle Sauce," an assemblage of decent ingredients that, on pasta, rival meatballs. Two of the seafood items—a gelatinous scallop mousse with morsels of fish and shellfish in a so-called bouillabaisse sauce, and a stir-fried lobster with noodles and baby vegetables in a "Thai-inspired sauce"—suffer for their complexity, and the first is no more a reminder of bouillabaisse than is the second of Thailand. But the boned quail works—it is packed with an appropriate stuffing, of game mousse and foie gras, and set in a strong and sticky sauce of port wine that is adorned with slices of orange.

Dessert trios as well, among them three "Pastry Parcels," rather greasy, of three fruit fillings, all set in a red-berry sauce and served with a jigger of nutted pastry cream. The terrine of chocolate and black cherries is icy, candylike, cloying. The strawberry fritters are doughy little dumplings that you dip in a sugary Grand Marnier sauce.

227

★★LA MÉTAIRIE

1442 Third Avenue (near 82nd Street)
LUNCH AND DINNER.
Reservations: 988-1800.
Credit cards: AE, MC, V.
Expensive.

As more is better, this namesake offshoot of a rustic twenty-chair French restaurant in Greenwich Village is not only many times the progenitor's size, but outrusticates it exponentially. The intent, clearly, is to make of this example of Gallic yokeldom the last word, and in fact it is impossible to imagine what after this can follow—except crowds, which, sure enough, found this place early on, wallow in its kitsch. You enter to sheep, anyway plaster ones, white, life size, chocolate-colored horns on their heads, woolly white blankets attached to their backs, which you may easily pet, for they form, conveniently, the arms of the sofas in which you wait, on a raised platform up front, for your table, its availability delayed by occupants so enchanted with the setting that they proceed through their courses mesmerized by the contents of this jungle of bucolic paraphernalia. Consider, for example, the lighting, which consists in part of wagon wheel chandeliers hanging among the rafters, mock kerosene lamps on the ceiling, brass brackets holding pairs of candlesticks on the walls, squat table lamps (on tables that, in some instances, are too small to accommodate the huge dinner plates as well) that are candles among wildflowers under perforated brass shades, and a genuine fire (wood stacked beside the fireplace) even in warm weather. On tables and counters fruits and vegetables are displayed, also great fish, their scales gleaming. And of course there are the little shelves with homey artifacts, a milk can, a cruet, an iron, scales, copperware, a set of graduated canisters. The cushions on the ladderback chairs are covered with the same French cotton print as the bolsters on the benchlike banquettes that occupy each side of the rear part of the dining room—the banquettes are overhung, of course, by frame troughs of dried grasses and grains. None of these elements is in itself offensive, but that condition is corrected by the two backlighted paintings on glass that occupy the rear wall—Van Gogh-Millet derivatives, you expect them to change from moment to moment, as if they were part of a slide show flashed by recent returnees from a nineteenth century French vacation. It is not necessary actually to enter this place to suffer the visual experience, for its façade is paned glass, floor to ceiling, and no further proof is needed of a normal New Yorker's sangfroid than that not every pane is occupied by the face of a passerby looking through in disbelief.

Oh, yes, there is also a hanging cage in which dwell a pair of cooing love birds, reference to a cage like it in the downtown Métairie. But it is principally in such trappings that this place makes reference to the other, for here there is no North African accent to the French cooking, the famous couscous of the Village store does not even appear on this menu—this place, its bucolic appointments notwithstanding, compromises not at all its high-tone cooking. It is, for example, the rare farmhouse family that sits itself down to a salad in which a small mound of fresh raw oysters, out of their shells, arranged over leaves of mâche, and adorned with strands of tomato, is garnished with lengths of endives and red beet, everything moistened with a tangy lime-juice dressing. Even less likely down on the farm is this mousse d'oursins, a little chimney of the puréed sea urchin—of all seafood the gamiest when fresh—in a creamy pool of a sauce of sweet red peppers. Another pungent mousse, this one milder even though it is of garlic—and of vivid garlic flavor—the disk of it set within a ring of wild mushrooms that, well sautéed with still more garlic, are earthy and strong. The terrine of artichoke hearts suffers for a certain paucity of artichoke flavor, so it is too bad that the lobster sauce in which it is served is of sufficient blandness not to overpower it.

Your whole lobster, however, is nicely grilled, has lost none of its juiciness, retains all its flavor, is mottled with leaves of basil, is served with a pitcher of fragrant, buttery watercress sauce. La Métairie undertakes the demanding task of grilling a *thin* slice of swordfish, does it well, drying it out not at all—the huge steak, handsomely cross-hatched and strongly flavored by the grilling, reaches you with a red pepper sauce that suits it well, though the fish is fine straight. The sautéed veal chop is pink, fibrous, tender, and juicy within its seared surfaces, the eye topped with strips of ham, vegetables, and cheese, the sauce winy and garlicky, with fresh rosemary much in evidence. Still, the entrecôte de boeuf marchand de vin is better, the beefy, blood-juicy steak, under slices of rich bone marrow, in a polished and vigorous rendition of the dark, earthy, red-wine sauce.

What the house calls dacquoise is an interleaving of crisp meringues with light and dark mousses that are studded with blueberries, the whole thing set in a fruity sauce populated with more of those berries and with slivers of sweet, acidic kumquat. What is called honey crisp is a stack of crackling pancakes, rich whipped cream and ripe raspberries between them. The tart tatin is notable for the three-way contrast among firm and slightly sour chunks of apple, caramelized sugar, and rich crème fraîche. The five egg-shaped dollops of sherbet are arranged like the points of an asterisk in a pool of raspberry pureé, four of them intensely fruity, the fifth intensely chocolate.

★★★ METRO

23 East 74th Street
LUNCH, SUNDAY TO FRIDAY; DINNER, MONDAY TO SATURDAY.
Reservations: 249-3030.
Credit cards: AE, MC, V.
Expensive.

The name of this place makes reference to chef-proprietor Patrick Clark's former affiliation with TriBeCa's Odeon and the West Side's Café Luxembourg, but otherwise tells nothing of what this place is like—the Paris subway, you will recall, being in no way a clubby men's club. Which is to say that this installation gives more weight to the assumed tastes of the East Side than to those of the friends Clark made at the aforementioned establishments. Not to worry. Metro's near-stuffy look is no harbinger of any shift to the right in Clark's cookery. Odeon's loss is exactly Metro's gain. You even see rebels in distressed denim, up from the deep south-of-Canal, here on nostalgia trips, recalling what once was theirs.

The sedate bar to which you enter will never, be sure, make it as a scene, and the arched tunnel that leads to the dining room, an Oriental runner along its polished-wood floor, its upper walls and ceiling stenciled in a handsome geometric pattern of warm pastels, is hung with small, colorful, baubled chandeliers that, on West Broadway, would come off merely as somewhat larger-than-average earrings. At the end of the tunnel, on your left, is a small dining room for smokers, directly before you the main dining room, for non-, this room all walnut-colored wood paneling, glinting mirrors, a bit of inoffensive modern art, a deep-green banquette around the sides, and about as many white-linened tables as the place can comfortably hold. Only the floor staff recalls Clark's former days—a number of them worked at Odeon and/or Café Luxembourg, and their casual uniforms, of striped shirts, red ties, and short aprons, with pockets for order pads and such, make clear that Metro is more at ease than it looks.

From a menu that changes at least a little every day, you opt for the buckwheat crêpes, of which you receive two: they are dark, thin, of vivid grain flavor, and they form a circular sandwich of which the filling is a dollop of black American caviar, a dollop of crème fraîche, and a poached egg, the whole surrounded by a delicately seasoned sauce that is little more than melted butter and chives—the dish is at once rich and of almost airy lightness, the caviar has exceptionally clear taste for the domestic article, and all the flavors are dazzlingly at home with one another. For comparative simplicity there are these Louisiana shrimp, six of them, sweet and crunchy and strewn with tarragon, their surfaces seasoned and crisped, their buttery mustard sauce thick with herbs. The squab salad is notable for the warm squab—a crisped leg, and slices of the dark breast meat, rare and glistening; and for the cool salad it is on—delicate greens, tender haricots verts, thin strands of red cabbage, their dressing a velvety oil. It is called a napoleon of foie gras, but the two meaty layers within the three of pastry have a buttery richness like that of chocolate mousse, though there is no mistaking the intense liver flavor—the napoleon is ringed by a dark jelly that is fruity of its port wine.

You do wonder how so much saffron flavor is incorporated in the meat of this lobster fricassee without obscuring at all the flavor of the lobster itself—the meat is out of its shell, is tender and juicy, is mingled with wild mushrooms that are in striking, earthy contrast to the sweet crustacean, and it is set in a light whiskey sauce that is threaded with that saffron. The grilled Norwegian salmon is utterly fresh and just a little rare within its crisped, crackling skin—the good fish is garnished with baby leeks, thin spears of firm asparagus, minced tomatoes, and sprigs of dill in its sauce of lemoned oil. You get a chicken here that, by way of its method of preparation (it has been roasted in a clay pot), has an unmatched depth of chicken and chicken-fat flavor, the cooked-through bird juicy and tender, its skin crisped (presumably by a bit of firing after the roasting), the whole garnished with cloves of garlic (you chew the tamed pulp out of the hulls) and with browned potato pancakes that, though wet with butter, are utterly without greasiness—the remarkable and abundant plate of food is adorned with great sprigs of various fresh herbs. You may want to order the loin of lamb just for the fried onions that go with it, for their batter is herbed and a little heady, in its frying it has seemingly absorbed air instead of grease, and the thin rings of onion within the batter, though sweet, retain just a bit of their strength. But the lamb is not bad either, the thick slices of medium-rare roasted meat blood-red and tender within the browned rims, strewn with almond slivers, and moistened with a dark sauce that is touched with Indian spices.

Seemingly weightless desserts: a blood-orange tart in which the sections of citrus are tightly arranged like the spokes of a wheel, a clump of pine nuts at the hub, within a little dish, formed of flaky pastry, that is set in a crimson strawberry sauce; a similar tart, this one of fresh, browned pineapple, fibrous and acidic and sweet, garnished with whole, crunchy, candied almonds; a vanilla crisp in which three circular pastries—of almost fugitive delicacy, the top one under a storm of confectioners' sugar—are interleaved with a light lemon cream and fresh strawberries in their pool of red berry sauce, the tiered item garnished with a little egg of concentrated strawberry sherbet; a chocolate and banana puff pastry that is hardly more than thin discs of ripe fruit among the brown and flaky chocolate layers—this time it is a banana sherbet that garnishes the sweet.

★ MIKE'S

650 Tenth Avenue (near 46th Street)
LUNCH, MONDAY TO FRIDAY; DINNER, DAILY.
Reservations: 246-4115.
Credit cards: AE, DC.
Inexpensive.

In the era between the wars (the Civil War and World War I) the part of Manhattan known as Hell's Kitchen—30th Street to 59th Street, west of Eighth Avenue—was watched over by such neighborhood civic organizations as the Gorillas, the Hudson Dusters, the Tenth Avenue Gang, and, most notably, the Gophers. When, early in this century, the New York Central Railroad, which maintained substantial facilities there, decided to usurp the influence of these local voluntary groups, it easily gained the support of City Hall, which was always responsive to the pleadings of special interest groups. Soon, some of the area's most respected leaders—Goo Goo Knox, Stumpy Malarkey, and One Lung Curran among them—were removed from their posts. The greed of Big Business had once again been rewarded at the expense of the little people, and the area went into a decline from which it is only now beginning to recover. Today's revival is spearheaded by a group of young restaurateurs. They have banded together to form an organization called The Cookers. Their stationery is emblazoned with the motto, Let's Put the Kitchen Back in Hell's Kitchen.

From the outside, Mike's looks as if it has been on this uninviting block, untended and exposed to the weather, since the days of Goo Goo himself. Taxis delivering passengers here (folks who learned about the place in the press) have been seen to drive up—and then drive off. But a few minutes after you have gained entrance, you find that the inside of the restaurant has been appointed almost as daintily as a nursery. The woodstrip walls have been painted yellow, the table linen is actually prettily striped wrapping paper, and the ancient bar, which runs the full length of the narrow front part of the store, is right at home under its old, bright-red-plastic top. This child's room has the kid's art on the walls. The loving parents have even framed the things and put them up for sale. The tile floor is easy to keep clean. And, so that mama may keep an eye on her charge, the portal to the kitchen is wide open. Tables and chairs are wherever they can fit—a couple under the front window, a few opposite the bar, a density of them in the back—and they are occupied mostly by the young people who are beginning to change the complexion of this part of town. Males among them wear no neckties, but atop the females there is many a fedora. You need not refer to the garb, however, to determine the genders, for makeup is back in, and so far only the ladies have picked up on it. The help wear name tags, all of which read "Mike." New customers unfamiliar with the practice get the attention of their waitress by calling out, "Mike." She comes by to see what is wanted.

The menu is in two parts, "From Mike's Mexican Bar," and "From Mike's American Grill." On the Mexican side, there is cilantro-cured salmon, four substantial slices of the firm, dark pink meat, tangy with lime and heady with the flavor and fragrance of the herb; a guacamole that is fresh-made, but not of first-rate avocados (they may even be Florida avocados)—and though the dish is spicy and well garlicked, it lacks moisture; taco salad, a great dollop of spicy and meaty no-bean chili, a mound of shredded cheese, sour cream, red and green peppers, and onions, all served with crisp chips; bean-and-cheese nachos, sturdy beans and weighty melted cheese, fiery green peppers their foil; Mexican chicken salad, big chunks of the meat of the bird mingled with celery, onions,

231

red beans, and chickpeas, all in a spicy dressing, and garnished with red peppers and tomatoes. On the American side, you find these charred seafood sausages, smoky and vaguely anise-flavored, but lacking seafood quality—they reach you in adjacent pools of red-pepper sauce and green-tomato sauce; grilled Cornish hen, the whole bird, handsomely charred, cooked through but still moist, but still a Cornish hen and therefore low on flavor—it comes with a cool assortment of dressed vegetables called "gazpacho salad"; "Mike's own" meat sausages, big, blackened, and of good lamb flavor—but they are dry, and you do expect fattiness and richness in this kind of thing; and marinated leg of lamb, a winner, many slices cut from the grilled leg, rare and with charred edges, tender and of good flavor—like a number of the dishes here, it is served with corn salad, the cool yellow kernels in a peppery dressing.

The dark apple-spice cake is dense with chunks of apple and powerfully flavored of clove—lots of it is sold here, and it is always fresh, moist, fluffy. The sweet-spiced walnut pie is heavier on the nuts than on the filler, but its side of whipped cream is a little loose. You order something called S-mores because you cannot believe the description on the menu: "toasted marshamallows on graham crackers with melted bittersweet chocolate." The description, it turns out, is correct. Elements hostile to liberation have attributed the concoction to the Girl Scouts.

★★MISS RUBY'S CAFÉ

135 Eighth Avenue (near 17th Street)
LUNCH AND DINNER.
Reservations: 620-4055.
Credit cards: AE, MC, V.
Medium priced.

Every other Tuesday the menu at Miss Ruby's changes—from the cookery of one part of the United States to that of another. The customers come back anyway, apparently confident that if they liked, say, the Yankee Pot Roast one time around, they will be happy with Confederate Pudding the next. If the food of America's regions gets you thinking of the great outdoors, of endless plains, prairies, and deserts, of the young nation's epic march to the Pacific (the primal eviction plan), know that you will get a taste at Miss Ruby's not only of the country's food, but also of its customs and vastness. There is, for example, the campfire in the open kitchen: the flames leap up, radiating light, warmth, and danger—the waiter getting your dinner is within easy reach of the fractious blaze; and there is the ranch-hands'-breakfast style of service, with a member of the staff cruising the tables every ten minutes or so to distribute cornbread or biscuits just out of the oven and steaming. The physical place itself is well lighted, wide open, and painted a red-hot shade of Great Southwest terra-cotta flowerpot. The Café is also, however, distinctly of the present. The young, willing, and cheerful help are in jeans or chinos, sweatshirts or polo shirts. And the folks at the tables are in the casuals they would wear in front of their television sets, did not Miss Ruby's offer comforts like those of home.

It is in the nature of this place that what it has served before it may never serve again. But if Miss Ruby someday elects to repeat its Texas Country menu, you will be able to sample cornmeal-fried green tomatoes, thick disks encased in a grease-free cornmeal batter, the tart, firm—almost hard—tomato slices vigorous and rousing in their crisp casings. On the same menu you will find a crabmeat item credited to Helen Corbitt, a late popularizer and refiner of Texas cooking. Sure enough, the dish is both homey and fancy, the abundance of delicately seasoned crabmeat browned, crisped, and lightly bound by the mild cheese with which it is prepared—it reaches you, in its little casserole dish, in a shallow pool of hot cream. The barbecued chicken is half of a big tasty bird in a slick black gravy that is thick with beans—a cool, creamy, and firm potato salad dotted with bits of crisp onion is its perfect foil. When the subject is Texas, naturally there is chili. You, of course, opt to have yours the beanless Texas way, and the nubbly ground beef comes to you in a dark-brown sauce that is weighty, sharp—almost bitter—pungently spiced, and topped with strong chopped onions, pully cheese, and cool sour cream.

Compared with the earthiness of its Texas fortnight, the Ruby menu is positively recherché when it is Contemporary California. Something listed under "soup" is actually a semicircular orange pool of cold carrot puree adjacent to a semicircular dark-red pool of cold beet puree, the two halves forming a round in a deep soup plate, each an intense expression of the pure vegetable. The duck taco is a folded and crisp-fried tortilla filled with tender shredded duck meat in a dark sauce—you find a dab of spicy salsa verde on your plate as well, sprigs of coriander, bits of fruit, sour cream. Order the squid stuffed with shrimp, and you receive four pearly bodies, each of them the size of a big thumb, packed with a delicate shrimp forcemeat that is dotted with green peas—the constructs are served in a lime-flavored cream sauce dotted with more of those sweet peas. What is listed as "rabbit with vermouth, summer savory and lemon" adds up to a rabbit stew in a sticky and peppery sauce—good food, if not the exotic item the wording leads you to expect.

As part of that California menu, you may have a fresh, firm, and headily perfumed peach that has been blanched, peeled, and sliced—it is served with a great dollop of crème fraîche and a chewy oatmeal cookie; or a great nugget of ginger-flavored pound cake, its dark-brown exterior a good zest to the pale, moist cake—it reaches you under rich whipped cream, and it is served with a glass of sweet and spicy muscat wine. The Texas desserts include a pecan pie that is dense with crunchy nuts.

Yes, there is a Miss Ruby, and most nights she is there in the open kitchen, preparing and dishing out. At late night she sometimes deserts her post, traverses the dining room to the bar, picks up refreshments for the kitchen crew, and returns. Other times, when a menu is nearing the end of its two weeks, she goes among the tables offering samples of something from the one coming up.

A little sign in a plastic holder on each table lists special drinks like "Texas Hot-Pepper Vodka"; it offers wine advice as well, suggesting, for example, that the Montepulciano d'Abruzzi of 1981 is "great with chicken-fried steak."

★ MOCCA ROYALE

1584 Second Avenue (at 82nd Street)
DINNER. CLOSED MONDAY.
Reservations: 737-2322.
Credit cards: AE, DC, MC, V.
Medium priced.

What the advertising refers to as "Romantic Gypsy Music with Strolling Violinists" is a lady at an out-of-tune upright, a gentleman each on the double bass and cembalom (a Hungarian dulcimer), and a strolling, nonplural fiddler, all of them in embroidered vests, their gypsy music leaning heavily to the likes of "Bésame Mucho," "Green Eyes," and "My Prayer." They come closer with "Ochi Chornya." And they actually get the brand of house cooking into a title with a snippet from one of Brahms's "Ungarische Tanze," the ostensible style of the house music into another with a snatch of "Zigeunerweisen" (by the gypsy violinist Pablo de Sarasate). You take it on faith that the numbers you do not recognize are the genuine article. Yes, there is charm here. When the leader goes among the tables with his instrument (his colleagues are anchored to their corner by the unwieldiness of theirs), an occasional couple does nod acquiescence to the private tableside concert he subtly suggests—they even hold hands, clasp them tighter during the suggestive ritards, and slip the man a bank note after three or four numbers (one or two requests usually among them). He can actually fiddle, but does his best only when a good number of his countrymen are on hand to hear him. His name will not be recorded in any history of violin performance, but at least he can play rings around George Lang.

All this takes place in what looks like only the framework of a Budapest café, a square room with rows of tables and chairs, a bar off to one side, dark, wood-paneled lower walls, muted wallpaper above, dim light from chandeliers and sconces—tiny bulbs housed in glinting fixtures of cut glass and brass. But all the place needs is some history, evidence of long use, to make it the real thing. It helps a little that your host is a diminutive and proboscidean fellow with padded shoulders that give him a width to compete with his height, and that his broad but thin smile is subject to as much interpretation as a line of contemporary poetry.

With this music goes stuffed cabbage, an egg-shaped mass of spicy forcemeat, stout but light, wrapped in leaves and buried in a hot sauerkraut that is touched with caraway, the entire production strewn with discs of pungent sausage. You will not be surprised to find herring on this menu, not because it is Hungarian—it is not—but because New Yorkers expect it in Middle European places, and the restaurants do not wish to disappoint. The herring, however, may disappoint, as does this one—it is not what you call spanking, and its onions have gone flat after their long stay in sour cream. Which is of no consequence, because the way to start your dinner here is by sharing one of the four soups that are listed as main courses. They are served, as the menu puts it, "in bogracs," which is to say, in a kettle—this one is more like what you call a pot, it is silvery, has a handle like that on a pail, and from it your waiter ladles out its contents into deep plates. If you have chosen the goulash soup, you get a stout, paprika-redded broth that is populous with great knobs of beef, tiny, shapeless little egg dumplings, and chunks of root vegetable. There is also a fish soup in this category, which the house sometimes prepares with carp—this means that, even with a carefully filleted fish, you will still have to deal with bones; but the fish is fresh, and its spicy and well-oiled broth is at once sweet and sharp—of onions and root vegetables—and fragrant of caraway.

The chicken paprikash is the breast of a good chicken in a creamy sauce that is pink and spicy with paprika—the sauce clings to and enriches the pale meat. The roast duck has been nicely crisped but, in the same process, dried—it comes, however, with chopped red cabbage that is sweet, sour, and vividly flavored of the caraway you encounter in many dishes here. One orders the garlic medallions of veal to satisfy a desire for garlic, not for veal—the meat is pale and tender, but you may well fail to appreciate those niceties in the context of a thick sauce that seems to be no more than an enriched purée of straight garlic. The veal shank, on the other hand, is all veal (except for the bone, which is the size and shape of the grip end of a Louisville Slugger), big overlapping sinews of it formed into a great mass at one end of the club, the seasoned meat blackened and crisp—a weighty dish rather than a tasty one, daunting if you are not

234

forewarned. A few items are listed as specialties, among them what is given as "peasant tidbits as in Brasov," which reaches you as a dune of cubed potatoes and pork, the meat firm but tender, the potatoes handsomely browned, the entire dish vibrantly seasoned. Only on a day when you have not had that goulash soup will you have the beef goulash —this is your basic dark-brown stew, in some respects sturdier than you want it (some of the meat is tough), and though the dish is hearty, it lacks the complexity of stews at their best.

Pancakes are a fundament of the Hungarian dessert menu, but to appreciate them you must forswear the prejudice that associates delicacy with dessert pancakes. In the natural state, the Hungarian pancake cannot be twirled on a fork, is opaque, holds water. But, contrary to what you may have heard, only the occasional one makes a really first-class sink stopper. Here, be assured, the pancakes may be cut with a fork—whether you have them as gundel palacsinta, in which they are filled with walnuts, buried in a sauce of chocolate and rum, and flamed; or as plain palacsinta, in which they are filled—most traditionally—with apricot preserves (here an intensely sugared, almost syrupy jam) and sprinkled with ground nuts that have been tossed with confectioner's sugar. Both versions are good if somewhat indelicate sweets. The cherry strudel is of tart fruit in flaky pastry. And the chestnut purée is a million strands of the airy stuff, under whipped cream, over whipped cream, surrounded by whipped cream—you go on eating it, and you go on wondering why.

• MOE'S

112 Duane Street (near Trimble Place)
LUNCH, MONDAY TO FRIDAY; DINNER, MONDAY TO SATURDAY. CLOSED SUNDAY.
Reservations: 406-1043.
Credit cards: AE.
Medium priced.

You are greeted by Moe himself. Moe wears a pearl gray suit, pearl gray shirt, pearl gray necktie, a silken handkerchief garnishes his lapel. Bespectacled Moe is pudgy-faced, gray-haired, portly, and as he identifies himself ("Om Moe"), he offers his hand at waist level, palm up, close to the belt, as if flashing a dirty postcard for your consideration. Come for dinner any night Wednesday through Saturday, and you are greeted also by the sounds of Moe's singer-pianist, a gent of frayed voice and antique repertoire at a tinny upright just inside the front door, upon his instrument a brandy snifter as big as a pumpkin, protruding from it a $10 bill the size of a newsmagazine. (Tipping, you understand, is permitted.) This rhapsodist has his fans, among them this blond lady, who has attempted to reverse the effects of the years on her skin—by filling it full. She is seated at the end of the long bar, almost right upon the player, and, her worldly mien notwithstanding, she is thrilled by proximity to a living, wheezing public performer, at whom she stares as if dazzled. All the while, the gentleman friend beside her puffs his panatella, arranges for regular refillment of her glass, and, at the end of the evening, you may be sure, makes a donation to that pumpkin.

Moe's has been installed in the quarters originally fitted out for restaurant purposes by Le Saint Jean des Prés, a Belgian restaurant ill-tuned to TriBeCa's taste. Though a couple of subsequent tenants have failed here as well, Moe's has emulated them in trying to make it on the cheap, for the appointments today, complete with whimsical murals of

Brussels and environs that, surreally, enwrap this New York steak house on three sides, are much as was. The huge room, a couple of stories high, is enameled a deep burgundy red, its ancient stamped-tin ceiling is creamy white, there is tan carpeting on the floor, and the shallow cushioned benches that once were the seating have been replaced with comfortable, albeit hideous, upholstered banquettes. Moe has his friends and connections, they come to his place from nowhere near here, guys and dolls, bejeweled widows, gents in bookie suits, all as alien to this neighborhood as this Jewish-accented Italian steakhouse to its found appointments.

The Jewish accent consists in large measure of freebies, these potato pancakes, for example, on your table as soon as you sit down, exact replicas of the egged impedimenta with which Jewish family dinners were once traditionally made weighty. If they reach you hot, as sometimes, they are of a bit more than archeological interest, but you learn nothing from the tepid, greasy ones that on occasion obtain. Show your sincerity by actually ordering dinner, and you are brought a plate of firm, sharp, briny pickles, marinated red peppers that are brisk and sweet and sour, and sauerkraut that is fresh made, the slender strands of cabbage resilient and only delicately flavored of their vinegar. For the money you select the smoked salmon, and this is decent fish, supple and sweet, and though it is not utterly delicate, have it any time rather than these raw clams, which are past due, a condition not susceptible to concealment by their cocktail sauce. A couple of the best first courses are compendia of salad ingredients: three thick slabs of crimson-ripe tomato, each under a slice of red onion, the six disks in a tangy red-wine vinaigrette; and what is given as "Jesse's tomato," two more red slabs, strong anchovies and strands of onion over them, circles of mozzarella on top, leaves of lettuce underneath, sprigs of parsley in between, that forthright vinaigrette again. But skip the salad of string beans and onions, for the beans are of a suspiciously emerald hue, plastic texture. And be aware that Moe's is not a pasta house, the linguine with clams is in a turgid sauce, and the clams themselves—great hunks carved from grandfather quahogs—are capable of doing in the tired jaw.

Each night lobsters are listed, and each night you are told "not tonight." And each night there are fish of the night, sometimes, happily, this broiled salmon, which is fresh and judiciously done, browned a little, moist, and of clear salmon flavor, albeit served with a flat hollandaise. The chicken scarpariello suffers for its mushrooms, which are flat and soggy, probably done in advance and reheated for the occasion, though the strongly seasoned chunks of bird are of decent flavor. The sirloin is served, you figure, the way Moe's mother served his, for the accurately done charred meat, tender and of real beef flavor, is cut into strips, the end of each strip still attached to the bone, the row of strips a fringe—fun, easy to eat, and if you are a good boy, you may have candy for dessert. The Jewish oddity known as Roumanian steak is here, the giant length of meat, about fourteen inches by three and folded upon itself, like some nameless organ meat, a condition not undone by the few bits of garlic with which it is sprinkled. The veal chop is handsomely browned and utterly dry. And when was the last time your lamb chops were served with a little dish of emerald green jelly? Here it is, and here the chops are, each a great coil of fat still attached to the little eye of meat, which is, no surprise, of coarsely fatty flavor. The vigorous hashed brown potatoes are crusty and salty and about as greasy as they can get away with—you do not mind that they have little potato flavor.

You *have* been a good boy, and here is your candy—cubes of halvah, marshmallow twists, the former the singular nut-and-sesame paste of the near east, the latter something like chocolate covered bubble gum—the favorite sweets, when you were a lad, of children who were graduated to them directly from the pacifier. The cheesecake has the texture of wet, rubbery bread. The bread pudding, dotted with raisins, is just a bland custard.

At the end of the night, Moe himself may wander into the vicinity of the piano, remove the cigar from between his teeth, sing along. Way to go, Moe.

★★★ MONTRACHET

239 West Broadway (near White Street)
LUNCH, FRIDAY; DINNER, MONDAY TO SATURDAY. CLOSED SUNDAY.
Reservations: 219-2777.
Credit cards: AE.
Expensive.

Timeworn store space has been gutted, smoothed, painted, furnished plainly with little more than tables and chairs, and opened for restaurant business at scores of SoHo and TriBeCa sites during the past ten years. Though the spare style is dictated at least in part by economics, and surely in part by fashion, it is nevertheless susceptible of individual interpretation, may be rendered expressively. You can go into a project like this and come out with the grandeur stark, the humble cozy, the slick, the sleek, the bold. Some of these installations suggest the straightforward, bustling eating places that, one imagines, were common in New York in its early days. Others, by more or less imaginative use of found-on-premises appointments—brick, ancient wood floors, antique light fixtures, whatever—permit the old site to be reborn, are restorations as much as renovations. Montrachet, too bad, is the downtown style but little else. Nothing terribly wrong with it, you understand, rather that when you walk into this place, almost immediately, nothing happens.

You enter to the first of three rooms, its small dark-wood bar, faced with panels of marble and backed by wine racks to the ceiling, the restaurant's one handsome object. Across from it, a banquette of raspberry-colored plush, white-linened tables before it, skirts the room on three sides. The second and third rooms are furnished with little more than tables and chairs. The walls throughout are milky pastels—baby blue (or is it green?), faded pink (or is it coral?)—with, in the third room, some vaguely patterned wallpaper. The carpeted floors are gray, the stamped-tin ceiling—wavy here, scarred there—is white, as are the exposed pipes just under it. In this setting, you welcome the staff uniform—black shirts and black pants—for being at least a mannerism.

One of the gentlemen in black informs you that the regularly listed scallop soup is this evening replaced by lobster soup, a pale-pink liquid that, though creamy, is light rather than rich, the white at its center a dollop of crème frâiche, the soup's gentle lobster flavor set off by the bits of vegetable with which it is dotted, the many kernels of yellow corn among them of an intense sweetness that competes with the shellfish as the soup's dominant flavor. Do the soup any day rather than this terrine of smoked salmon and eel, a square cut from a loaf, its striped face pink (salmon), brown (eel), and green (greens), and though the ingredients are fine, you find yourself picking them apart to consume them separately, for they do nothing for one another—the dish seems to need a sauce to make it add up. But then there is this oyster tart, a circle of pastry, its circumference raised, upon it four tender oysters, warm but with all their "raw" flavor intact, among them slivers of crunchy fennel, almost hard, and bits of strong Italian bacon, all in a pink and creamy sauce, chives and fragrant dill sprinkled on. Start your dinner with pigeon, and you are served a mound of warm salad, herbed and crunchy, leaning against its sides a half dozen parts and slices of the bird, the dark, moist meat intense of pigeon's characteristically almost chocolate flavor. Even more intense, and considerably richer, are these blackened slices of fresh duck liver, the charred, pinguid meat served on a hot and glistening mass of sweet, slivered shallots.

Black sea bass is beginning to appear frequently on local menus. Its firm, white-to-pink flesh has a delicate but clear marine flavor, and these fresh fillets, served under a tomato hash with strands of green vegetable in a tart vinaigrette, reveal all their flavor in the setting. The place makes a homey roast chicken, the trifurcated breast, moist but cooked through under its delicately browned skin, arranged over mashed potatoes—judiciously seasoned and enriched—that have real texture. The flavor of the chicken, though not strong, is potentiated by the cloves of sweet garlic with which it is roasted (you chew the softened garlic from its hulls), and the bird is, in a sense, garnished with itself, for beside the breast are placed three nuggets of a leg that has been boned, stuffed with spinach, and roasted with the rest of the bird—a wondrous chicken dish. More birds: a duck of deep flavor, thin strands of ginger strewn over its browned skin, the dark roasting juices tangy and a little sweet of the spice; and baby pheasant, redolent of its own fat within its crisped tegument, in a winy sauce threaded with slivers of strong, black olive. The two tournedos of veal loin, though supple and handsomely browned, gain much that they need from the sautéed wild mushrooms with which they are spread, for the meat itself has not been brought to life—the garnish of browned potatoes, strewn with fresh rosemary, helps too. No such problem with the loin of lamb, the four chunks of rare meat—suffused with garlic flavor—arranged prettily among halves of baby artichoke, a bit of vegetable stuffing in each, a clump of strong spinach at the center of the plate. The lamb is served with a baked casserole of butternut squash, the earthy mash, at once creamy and crunchy, threaded with sweet onions.

The crème brûlée is less than fluffy under its caramelized, crystallized top. Though the word "dacquoise" will probably suggest to you a layered thing of crunchy meringues, something creamy between them, when you order it here, you get two slices of an intense chocolate confection in a cool white sauce that is studded with nuts. Much is made of soufflés. The crêpe soufflé is a mass of the fluffy stuff (sometimes flavored with Grand Marnier) within a delicate crêpe—it is garnished with fruits, an egg of passion-fruit sherbet, mint leaves, a cookie. Most, however, go for the pair of small soufflés, one intensely chocolate, the other tangy of raspberry, dots of chocolate in the pool of raspberry sauce in which they are served, a bit of rich vanilla ice cream a nice foil to the hot sweets.

★★IL MULINO

86 West 3rd Street
LUNCH, MONDAY TO FRIDAY; DINNER, MONDAY TO SATURDAY. CLOSED SUNDAY.
Reservations: 673-3783.
Credit cards: AE.
Expensive.

At Il Mulino, as in any singular institution, the tone is set at the top. At Il Mulino's top there is Fernando, a dark and cherubic gentleman whose manner is unfailingly earnest. Accordingly, everyone here is unfailingly earnest. Whether you are dealing with Fernando himself or with one of his men, the issue of you and your dinner is addressed in the manner of the man at your bedside discussing you and tomorrow's surgery. And just as the wig and robe worn by every member of an English court serve to remind each wearer of his commitment to the proceedings, so is the staff at Il Mulino—unlike that of any other Greenwich Village Italian restaurant—attired in formal black-and-whites, with starched collar and bowtie. This is not, you understand, the false formality that is adjunct to the smirking politesse of certain posh spaghetti joints uptown. Fernando and his staff are not competing with you. They have put on their tuxedos for the same reason they attend to you so fervently. What you are dealing with is propitiation. The house is attempting to please you—albeit in ways that seem quaint. It is desired that you come back. For, as Fernando will tell you if you give him a narrow opening, he is from a very small town in Italy—a place, presumably, where the middle class does not seek thrills by shopping around for the latest thing in contempt.

The restaurant is on a grim block, so it is something of a startlement to enter to the cool, oaseal comfort of its cushy darkness. The front room gets only very soft light through the north-exposed gauze curtains that cover its 3rd Street windows. Here you find the crowded bar at which the devoted patiently wait—sometimes they fill the entire room. And here you find the big display of appetizers, cheeses, desserts. Usually the spread is merely admired, but on Saturday nights, when this place gets a certain transriverine crowd, nibblers may be seen plucking a tidbit here, licking their fingers, plucking another there. Mostly, however, the restaurant gets a civilized set. Two stands of palms at the back of this room separate it from the dining room proper—you pass between them on your way to dinner. In the dining room, in the even deeper darkness, the walls that are not of glazed brick are inexplicably covered with a vaguely Oriental wallpaper. The massive low-hanging light fixtures are equipped with five-watt bulbs, and on the rows of white-linened tables the little candles glow, in this setting, like flares. When you get accustomed to the dimness, you note that on one wall there is a big black-on-white painting of a water wheel and attached shed—"Il Mulino" is "the mill."

The place is contentedly occupied by, mostly, groups and large groups, pairs of couples and whole families, and hardly are they folded into their chairs—menus have not yet been handed around, no one has come by to recite the special dishes of the day— and already plates of food are being set on their tables. You are given something to eat even before you are asked if you would like "something from the bar." And if you go at the freebies greedily you will be ready for coffee before you have asked for the wine list. You will not be proffered the entire selection at one dinner, but come here often enough, and you will sample: thin disks of sautéed zucchini, delicately browned, vividly garlicked, abundantly oiled; salami, the hard slices of purple meat fatted and peppered and gamy; chunks of Parmesan cheese—sometimes the wheel itself, or a large section of it, is placed on your table, and you help yourself; cool little mussels, in their shells, sweet and salty in their light dressing; bruschetta, crusts of toasted bread buried under chopped tomatoes, in a garlicky dressing that is threaded with fresh basil.

One pasta dish carries the restaurant name: capellini Il Mulino, thin spaghetti in a sauce, thick with cheese, that is of exceptionally nutty wild-mushroom flavor—fresh peas are the other component, and in this setting they are strikingly sweet. That same thin spaghetti is served also all'arrabbiata, the great tangle of filaments in a spicy and weighty red sauce that is dotted with capers and laced with slivers of black olive. Sometimes the house offers a linguine primavera, and this is an odd version, really a collection of vegetables (snowpeas, zucchini, mushrooms, little florets of broccoli, even a great slice of tomato) augmented by slivers of meat and bits of shellfish, the thin pasta that is threaded among them in a seemingly secondary role—the dish is stout and good to eat, but not exactly what you expected when you ordered linguine primavera.

It is the style of this place to apply sauces to fish, fowl, meat in a voluptuous super-abundance that may well be off-putting, especially if you have done well by what went before. Occasionally, for example, the fish of the day is Norwegian salmon, of which you are served a steak the size of an art book. It is lovely fish, fresh, firm, falling easily into moist flakes, but it is buried under mushrooms and onions that are not only copious, but awash in the oil in which they were sautéed—they are fine, but you wish they had spent time in a slotted spoon before being spread over the pink meat. The clams posillipo are a small mountain of bivalves in their shells, a pungent red sauce over them, an inch of briny red broth under them. The scampi fra diavolo are big and crunchy shrimp (a handful of those good clams as well) in a spicy red sauce that will film your brow—you do wish the shrimp were not touched with iodine. The spezzatino di pollo is many huge chunks of clear-flavored chicken in a dense and winy sauce that is thick with slices of artichoke. What are given as uccelletti alla fiorentina are hefty roulades of browned veal in a rich and creamy sauce that is dense with slices of porcini mushroom and dotted with sweet peas. Those mushrooms yet again, this time in a sauce under which is buried a veal chop valdostana of gargantuan impact. The browned mammoth chop (its giant rib reaches out well beyond the circumference of its plate) is latitudinally bifurcated to the bone, in the interstice a sheet of ham and a layer of pully cheese. There are even steaks, but they are not the usual thing. Consider, for example, this six-inch two-by-four of fibrous and supple beef—it is served in a spicy sauce of capers and mushrooms that is a dramatic foil to the blood-juicy meat.

Order the marinated orange—the whole peeled fruits have been spending time in cognac and Grand Marnier—and your waiter comes to your table and dexterously carves the sections from the body, arranges them in a circle around the edge of your plate, spoons strands of marinated rind over the center. When he has done your orange, he quarters for your companion a nicely poached pear—it is done in white wine—and, before serving it, livens it with pear brandy. There are always berries, and you may have yours under a big dollop of cool, winy zabaglione that is enriched with whipped cream —the crumbled macaroons on top add a nice bit of texture.

★★NANNI

146 East 46th Street
LUNCH, MONDAY TO FRIDAY; DINNER, MONDAY TO SATURDAY. CLOSED SUNDAY.
Reservations: 697-4161.
Credit cards: AE, DC, MC, V.
Very expensive.

If you think that New York's side streets are dotted with little old Italian restaurants to which the salt of the city repair for sturdy food in colorful, convivial surroundings, be informed that the type you have in mind exists, mainly, in the mind. Once, such places were all over the place, but most of the midtown ones disappeared when the buildings that housed them were torn down to make way for very large stalagmites. Among today's midtown restaurants, the one that best exemplifies the old style is this one, which is, in fact, a relative newcomer. It showed up in the late sixties, when most of its predecessors had already shuffled off. One reason Nanni carries on as steadily as it now does—deviating hardly at all from the Italian-bistro formula—is that its proprietor opened a big, fancy joint uptown several years after the successful inauguration of this one, and since he spends much of his time up there, he lets this place run along in an old-fashioned way that, most nights, packs them in.

You enter to a wall, on your left, that is bedecked with reviews of the restaurant, articles about Nanni himself, and photographs of him in the company of his food. On your right is the small, glass-enclosed, second-string dining room, with a handful of tables and twelve chairs, into which that many diners may be folded plus one upright slender waiter. Past that noise box, and you are at the "bar," which stands five comfortably, ten frequently. But things open up farther on. Down a few steps, and you are in the dining room proper, comparatively wide-open spaces—though even back here, whispered conversations at adjacent tables may be your principal entertainment. The simple, rectangular room has an oak floor, travel posters are affixed to its white walls, a shelf of wine bottles rims it a little overhead, and small lamps with red shades stand on its white-linened tables. This particular Italian restaurant gets a steakhouse crowd—pairs of guys and gangs of guys. It also gets a number of couples who have recently met—middle-aged gents in town for the annual convention and ladies to whom they have been introduced, and whom they have invited to dinner at Nanni in order to get better acquainted. She: "Are you married?" He: "Well, it's a long story."

There are a few first courses and soups, including fresh clams that are sometimes as large as quahogs and quite resilient, and a hefty minestrone of pasta, root vegetables, and strong greens in a deep, well-herbed stock. But Nanni will make half orders of any of its good pasta dishes, and for greatest contentment, it is with the noodle that you should start your dinner here. When those clams are chopped up for use with pasta, they become part of a good, standard version of linguine with white clams, in which the sauce is briny and strong, the clams abundant—the dish is adorned with a couple of hot clams, whole and in their shells. You may have that same pasta with a pesto sauce that is dense, fragrant of basil, glistening with oil—you permit your waiter to add a good bit of cheese. The fettuccine is billed as "alla Nanni," and what himself elects to give his name to is rather light, creamy tomato sauce dotted with peas—it makes a homey and satisfying dish. But good as those are, the big pasta winner is the spaghetti all'amatriciana, in which a thick, rich, potently seasoned red sauce is sweetened with onions and fortified with slivers of Italian bacon.

A fillet of sea bass marechiaro, about the size of your forearm, is served in a peppery and garlicky red sauce—the utterly fresh fish is firm, perfectly cooked, glossy with moisture. Big chunks of sautéed chicken on the bone are served as chicken scarpariello—the browned and shiny nuggets, of clear chicken flavor, are moistened with a garlicked wine sauce and strewn with parsley.

The veal francese is pearly meat in a delicately crisped egg-and-flour crust—the bits of prosciutto on top are a nice note, but the lemon sauce is disastrously soupy, and just wets the dish. Try instead the scaloppine alla zingara, in which that same meat, artfully browned, is buried under sautéed mushrooms, onions, strands of prosciutto—the stout food is strongly but not excessively salted. The great eye of meat in the thick veal chop sorpresa is horizontally incised halfway down and stuffed with prosciutto and hot, pully fontina cheese—the production is covered over with mushrooms in a winy sauce, making for a dish of such substantiality that some may call it heavy. The sweetbreads are notable for the fluffiness of the rich organ meat within the nicely crisped surfaces of the many slices—they come in a good mushroom sauce that is flavored with Madeira wine. The medaglioni di filetto alla Nanni consists of two thick rounds of tender steak, rare as you want them, in yet another winy mushroom sauce, this one a little creamy as well.

If you remember to think ahead, you inform your waiter early on that you want your salad after your main course (it is part of the deal). The greens are crisp, and they come in a tart dressing that is vividly garlicked; with them you may order some Parmesan cheese, which is hard, heady, and sharp. The sweet desserts are of no interest.

• NICOLA PAONE

207 East 34th Street
LUNCH, MONDAY TO FRIDAY; DINNER, MONDAY TO SATURDAY. CLOSED SUNDAY.
Reservations: 889-3239.
Credit cards: AE, DC.
Very expensive.

Here lunches the *National Review*, William F. Buckley's hobby. Extreme liberals avoid the place on the assumption that its eponymous proprietor must surely be a card-carrying Fascist, but though neither political posters nor any other factional signs are in evidence, there are indications that Mr. Paone is an ardent conservator of ancient values. His menu is one such. You cannot, for example, get a bite of food in this place that you could not have got in scores of New York Italian restaurants back in the days when northern and southern Italian cooking were respectively defined as Neapolitan and Sicilian. Yes, this is something of a reliquary. Its somber solidity will put you in mind of certain old stone museums in which are housed arcane collections no one ever looks at. Those who visit this museum, however, are here to consider not an ancient culture, but their own. Nicola Paone is the house of the almost dead. Those in attendance are well fed, sit at their dinners upright and past stoicism, register nothing. It is a posture that, you will recall, surrounded you on your last visit to a house of worship.

Upon a time every fourth Mediterranean restaurant on Manhattan Island was fitted out as your basic wine cellar. Like most of them, this survivor does not take the theme terribly seriously. This cellar, for example, has mock windows, barred, that look out on painted landscapes and town streets. Tile rooftops protrude into the room on all sides, there is a gurgling fountain, a fruiterer's display, strings of garlic on the walls, a bowl of oranges on a shelf, a basket of onions on a tray stand. You walk on a floor that is of great square stones. The back of your armchair is of webbed leather. Often the background music is a plinking guitar, and a guitar hangs on one wall. As your waiter explains, Mr. Paone is a musician, is the soloist in his own singing commercial. In fact, Paone may come by and tell you the one about the customer who dials information and asks for this restaurant's number, whereupon, so the story goes, the operator sings it—889-3239— just the way Nick himself sings it on the air. You figure the tale has been told a thousand times.

Nostalgia takes over, and you order the cold antipasto. Sure enough, here is that slice of salami of sainted memory, that sheet of ham over more-or-less ripe melon, the dab of clammy caponata, the ice cold stuffed mushroom, the bitter slice of roasted red pepper, and the lumpish lump of mozzarella. Next time your good sense takes over, and you go for the baked clams, eight fresh littlenecks in their shells, their oiled breading delicately browned. Do not, however, conclude that clams in any form are this establishment's forte, for the white clam sauce you may have on your spaghetti seems like something prepared at the beginning of the week for daily reheating as needed—the clams are flat and leathery, utterly without seafood sparkle. The lasagna, though undistinguished, is inoffensive—a weighty compendium of firm pasta and melted cheese pinked with a primitive tomato sauce.

Even in its earliest days, the Paone menu suffered from a slight case of the cutes, listed ordinary dishes by irrelevant names—among them baci-baci, boom-boom, night-gown, the last of which consists of two gargantuan roulades of veal, eggplant, and cheese that oozes from the ends like an extrusion—the dabs of tomato sauce on the cylinders do nothing to leaven their tasteless weight. The snapper is browned—through and through. The chicken cacciatore is an honest dish, big parts of a big, rather tasty bird in a decent mushroom sauce. Your steak is a little tough, and, though ordered rare, quite medium —still, this is beef of good blood flavor.

On the wagon an assortment of layer cakes: a pignoli cake that is notable for its nutty flavor and for the layer of rich whipped cream at the center; chocolate ricotta cheesecake that is intense and rich—and heavy; a strawberry-banana shortcake composed of good fruit, good whipped cream, dull pastry.

★ IL NIDO

251 East 53rd Street
LUNCH AND DINNER. CLOSED SUNDAY.
Reservations: 753-8450.
Credit cards: AE, DC, MC, V.
Expensive.

One of the most popular restaurants in New York, but all it ever takes to reserve a table is a quarter for the phone. Of course when you arrive, you may well find a waiting crowd ahead of you that would itself fill a restaurant. Thus has Il Nido solved the no-show problem. For everyone who decides not to keep his word, there are two who regret keeping theirs. When a restaurant, because of near-unanimous praise, is taken up by those who wish only to be secure in what they like, the management may be tempted to write off the discerning, to discontinue operation as an eating place, to carry on solely as a money machine. A fool's money, after all, is as good as anyone else's, and that kind will show up in hordes, get cranked through, make their contribution, and go home content if the evening carried a seal of prior approval. If a few have the sense to be offended, even to leave, well, there are always others adding themselves to the end of the line. Il Nido still serves good food, an occasional dish as good as it ever was, but as its commerce is no longer with a clientele of its own, rather with an anonymous populace that eats where it is told, the place perpetuates but does not renew itself, which is stagnation. When the lady at the book mechanically assures you that the wait will be "no more than a few minutes," while those being seated tell you that forty-five minutes have passed since the hour of their reservation, you know you are in the hands of the dehu-manized. Your hope, if not your faith, is somewhat renewed by the dining room staff's courtesies, even though they are expended mainly on those on whom they are wasted.

The physical Nido is as engaging as ever. The anteroom to which you enter, three tables and a tiny bar, a dark, dark-gray and rather spiffy prelude to the stylized farmhouse that is the restaurant proper, a big, rambling, softly lit place in which deep-brown half timbers and ivory-colored rough plaster are dramatically juxtaposed with walls of paned mirroring that are jewel-like and crystalline. You are seated, before white-linened tables, on the dark-brown banquette that rims the dining rooms, or on handsome black-enam-eled side chairs. Wherever you sit, you are hard by others—nary an inch of this precious New York real estate goes to nonprofit ends.

What is given as "fresh mushroom salad" is not as fresh as it once was—still, the great mound of thin slivers (they are only a little limp), dotted with nuggets of celery and bits of strong garlic, has been dressed with an intense and fragrant green olive oil that quite overcomes any flatness of the main ingredient. Mushrooms again, chunks and lengths of sautéed woodsy porcini, moist of the strongly seasoned oil in which they were done, arranged on crusted triangles of polenta—but the dish really comes alive only when the good house Parmesan is grated on. Similarly the many-textured spaghetti bolognese, firm pasta and a nubbly meat sauce, just touched with cream and tomato, that, though sound, lacks depth until that cheese is added. What are given as ravioli malfatti are not pasta at all, but balls of spinach bound with ricotta cheese and moistened with a bright, elemental tomato sauce—once again the dish lacks real sparkle (it comes across as little more than strong spinach) until the magic cheese is added.

Some perfectly nice broiled shrimp are served with a coarse, sour sauce of anchovies and capers that, when sampled straight, does this really terrific imitation of your finest Worcestershire sauce, though when only a tiny amount is applied to the crunchy shrimp, a bit of life is added. The moist red snapper is joined, in its briny tomatoed broth, by a handful of littleneck clams—the mollusks, unlike the moist fish, are less than tender, a bit less than utterly fresh. You opt for a chicken dish, and again, you are served food that is more than decent, less than interesting. The pollo scarpariello is many nuggets of boned, browned, strongly salted chicken mingled with slivers of artichoke, the two in a sticky sauce in which you encounter a sliver of strong garlic now and again—all the dish needs is real chicken flavor. Saltimbocca is the surprise winner, the scallops of juicy, nicely browned veal overlaid with thin slices of smoky, salty prosciutto, the meats, in a pale, herbed, and winy sauce, garnished with a clump of pungent spinach. You do well to pass up the à la carte vegetables, among them sautéed artichokes that uncannily mimic the canned product and fried zucchini that, being a little soggy and not a little limp, amount to an audacity in a town that is almost obsessed with crispness and lightness in this item.

The pungent cheese that redeems so many of the dishes may be had straight—nuggets of it are served with strong black olives. The arugula salad you choose to have with it is brought to you with cruets of too-sour wine vinegar and pallid olive oil—you ask for "the good oil" and a tall bottle of the real thing is delivered. The zabaglione is hot, winy, frothy, reaches you mounded up over ripe strawberries in a large wineglass. The cheesecake is the Italian article, but denatured, for it is almost powdery, its wetness gone—happily good strawberries and raspberries are added to the plate.

★★NIPPON

155 East 52nd Street
LUNCH, MONDAY TO FRIDAY; DINNER, MONDAY TO SATURDAY. CLOSED SUNDAY.
Reservations: 758-0226.
Credit cards: AE, DC, MC, V.
Medium priced.

Long the Cadillac of New York's Japanese restaurants, expensive and complacent, Nippon, recently compelled to remove from the premises it occupied for twenty years, has relocated a couple of doors to the east. The complacency, however, has stayed put. Nippon has never, for example, bothered to print up a menu that is wholly comprehensible to anyone who has no Japanese, and as there are no captains on the floor, only waiters and waitresses, and as the menu is extensive, complete exegeses are out of the question. And while the most recent of midtown's more ambitious Japanese restaurants have brought to New York spaciousness, clarity of design, and that special Japanese integration of spareness and luxury, Nippon seems merely to have compressed its former operation into a smaller store. It is not that every appointment in the new place is, individually, unappealing to the eye. Nor is it that a restaurant is obligated to provide the newest in design in every new installation. It is, rather, that the familiar is especially oppressive when, no matter which way you turn, it is no more than eighteen inches from your nose. (By special request—and, you may be sure, just by accident—you may have yourself assigned to a certain curved table at which the occupants, one and all, are necessarily facing a pillar at about that range.) Surely, every element in this place is a tribute to Japanese craftsmanship. But, just as surely, the silk upholstery would look less like molded plastic, the hardwood tabletops less like Formica, the grass-green carpeting less like artificial turf, and the wood-and-rice-paper lanterns less like the same old wood-and-rice-paper lanterns if only there were a little less of all of them per cubic foot. The main dining room, such as it is, is surrounded by smaller rooms—if there are a number of you, and you reserve one of these spaces, you will be able to eat in relative comfort, as do many of the knowing Japanese who frequent Nippon.

They frequent it because, its discomforts notwithstanding, the food is the genuine article, upon which subject you may well be warned at once: Some of it is so genuine that it is listed in a separate box under the warning words SPECIAL FOR "CONNOISSEUR." For "connoisseur," read "Japanese." Such items as salted sea cucumber, preserved herring roe, and preserved squid have, variously, such gaminess and/or animality and/or minerality and/or just plain sliminess, that there may be no point in your getting half drunk to get to know them, since you will never want them sober anyway. But you are suffering from culture shock, not bad food, for the intense little dishes have the impact of authenticity, albeit entirely separated from the more familiar one of easy deliciousness.

For nonconnoisseurs, there is the impeccably fresh raw fish in the sushi and sashimi; a preserved cod-roe dish, pink and granular, in which the strong and salty seafood flavor is striking against the lemon you squeeze on; a little dish of sautéed eggplant, rich and slightly charred, served with vivid ginger and soy sauce; a tofu dish called ganmodoki, a warm knob of the bean curd, spongy but firm, threaded with vegetables; a duck dish called aigamo-hasamiyaki, consisting of salted slivers of the rich meat, intensely flavored of their own fat, mingled with shafts of scallion and moistened with a strong black oil; and a so-called beef salad in which the thin, barely cooked slices of meat are served, sprinkled with sesame seeds, over crisp greens in a polished soy sauce dressing that has an almost glassy oil finish.

Order salmon in the manner called shioyaki, and you receive a fresh slab of the pink fish, its charred skin still attached, the meat of intense flavor. The tuna teriyaki is of equally fresh fish, in a dark, clinging sauce that potentiates its flavor. What is given as "lobster gusoku-ni" is of lobster chunks in their shell, moistened with a slightly sweet sauce that somehow mingles with and emphasizes the sweetness of the lobster itself. Chicken shichimi-yaki is a deeply brown-crusted—almost blackened—chicken served in the syruplike sauce that is the basis of its dramatic crust. When something must be cooked at the table, it is well if there is an empty place, for the tables are small, and the cooking apparatus every bit as large as it needs to be. The beef sukiyaki made this way is a good version of the usual thing. A new dish on the menu, called aigamo-yuan-nabe, is prepared with duck, which is poached not only with the usual vegetables but with slices of orange as well—they add a nice piquancy to the mellifluous meat.

The best drinks with this cooking are sake or beer or both. All the familiar Japanese beer brands are available in their regular and in their bottled "draft beer" versions—of which Sapporo is the best.

• NISHI NOHO

380 Lafayette Street (at Great Jones Street)
DINNER.
Reservations: 677-8401.
Credit cards: AE, DC.
Medium priced.

The overnight success of the huge Tower Records store, at the corner of Fourth and Broadway, has engendered emulators in other lines. Establishments for the on-premises consumption of food, for example, have materialized nearby in numbers, most of them lacking only the escalator to rival the monumentality of the Tower itself. The rash will, you may be sure, spread in all directions. This efflorescence to the east is Japanese, a descendant twenty times the size of the successful Nishi on Amsterdam Avenue. Like the original, Nishi NoHo is jet black throughout. Build a black store this size, with elaborate adornments and spots casting beams of light through the cavernous, dimly lit space, and you have simulated a movie palace—this one is fitted out with red carpeting, illuminated silken kimonos on the walls, and coppery pillars rising grandly through the space. No popcorn counter—instead New York's most romantic sushi bar, off in its own little dark corner.

The city's Japanese are doing so well as entrepreneurs that few remain loyal to the working class. Accordingly Japanese restaurants now hire locals to staff their dining room floors, with the result that you no longer have to settle for Western food to get yourself scorned by a dancer between assignments. Here is a fellow right beside your table, pad and pencil poised—he has asked for your order, and the beginning of your recitation is his cue to pirouette for an impromptu exchange of anecdotes with a passing colleague, complete with muffled shrieks.

Most of the colors in the sushi spectrum are here, from the pale translucence of fluke or yellowtail, to snowy crabmeat streaked with dark pink—alone, or with a bit of pale-green avocado in the California roll—to rosy red tuna, through the glistening brown of grilled eel. The raw fish is fresh—now and then this or that is a day older than you want it—and the vinegared rice is sweet and sticky, dotted with sesame seeds in the California roll, but of all items in this department, eel is the winner, the thick shafts of firm, warm meat at once sweet, oily, and strongly oceanic on their platforms of white rice. There are little hot dishes and little cold ones. Among the hot ones: shrimp dumplings, knobs of fluffy shrimp forcemeat in tender noodle wrappers; and conch barbecue, a conch shell set among three stones, the sliced meat of a conch in its aperture, the whole production aflame in brandy—the sea-gamy seafood is nicely flavored by the treatment, but also toughened. Among the cold ones: resilient lengths and slivers of octopus in mild vinegar; and a distinctly loud marinated salmon that you cleverly render palatable by dipping it in soy sauce you have fortified with wasabi. There are also dishes recognizable as main courses, and though the apricot chicken casserole, a fruity and stewlike solidity, is merely decent, the poached whole porgy (its crisp surface suggests it is exposed to the fire before it is served) is of fresh fish in a strong, thickened, almost harsh soy sauce—the porgy is surmounted by strands of ginger.

Domestic desserts: a rich thick chocolate pie with a bit of orange flavor—its whipped cream is thin; a mandarin chiffon pie that is vibrant of citrus—it is surfaced with a slick yogurt icing; and Mount Fuji, a giant wine glass crammed with four balls of vanilla—the obvious sweet is topped with crème de cacao and warm chocolate sauce.

★★ODEON

145 West Broadway (at Thomas Street)
LUNCH, SUNDAY TO FRIDAY; DINNER, DAILY.
Reservations: 233-0507.
Credit cards: AE, DC, MC, V.
Medium priced.

At any given time you can count on the point of one elbow the restaurants in New York that manage to make it as both trendy and first class. So lower your sleeve and button the cuff, for with the 1987 departure from this place of Patrick Clark, its once chef, the Odeon menu has been attenuated, the dishes are less often than in the past of bright conception, and, finally, their execution sometimes misses their intent. Odeon is now one of the many eating places around town in which the victuals are but an eminently satisfactory background to whatever foreground business you are otherwise about, whereas upon a time you may well have come here solely to eat. While the Clark minitragedy got itself acted out, an even lesser one was taking place. As a hot destination, Odeon has cooled—though it is far from ice cold, and occasionally both the bar and dining room are full up. But most nights a phone call an hour ahead will get you a table, and if you show up without a reservation, it is rare to wait through more than a single drink at the bar before you are seated. But do not assume a causal connection between the first decline and the second. Trends feed on themselves, not on good food, and when new trends come along, the trendy would not be themselves did they not pursue them. You do miss the costumes. Everyone in the place appears to be wearing whatever he had on when, shortly before he got here, he decided this was where he wanted to go. One is unable to distinguish this crowd from the set at the Kiev, on Second Avenue at 7th Street, except that from time to time Odeon still gets the rich and famous, albeit they are here in twos and fours for impromptu dinners of no occasion, whereas in the old days this is where they celebrated themselves.

The management tacitly acknowledges the decline. The tables are now clothed in soft white paper, not linen, albeit there is still a flagon of ice water and a shot glass of toothpicks on every table, and the floor staff is fewer in number than in the old days, even on busy nights, so getting the attention of someone attentive is not the snap it once was. The background music these days extends from E. Fitzgerald, J. Garland, and L. Pavarotti, through grand and light operatic choruses of Verdi and Gilbert & Sullivan, to such occasional special treats as Un Bel Di to a soft rock beat. A cynic could read desperation in those tapes, an attempt to bind a contemporary clientele to the era evoked by the old cafeteria setting that is Odeon—the easy-to-mop terrazzo floor, the easy-to-wipe-down chairs of plastic cushions mounted on steel tubing, the mirrors all about, the Deco bar with its green-glowing clock encircled by pink neon, the little mural more-or-less in the style of the murals the WPA put in public buildings back when painters (unlike those whose declining presence here indicates that they have found ritzier spots with more flattering prices) benefited from government priming of the artistic well. The high-ceilinged place is still illuminated by hanging white globes, the venetian blinds in the windows are still the old-fashioned ones of wood slats and wide ribbons, you still hang your coat on a pipe rack, or on the hooks affixed to the columns that rise through the room. And the *Times* truck still drops a pile of papers just inside the front door every night, so if you leave after the delivery, and you are going home alone, you may console yourself that the paper is safer.

The culinary decline is more in the art than the mechanics—the ingredients, for example, are not at fault. And with respect to these warm clams, nothing else is either, the half dozen fresh littlenecks, in their shells, warmed through but not toughened under the hollandaise, touched with fresh thyme and lightly browned, that conceals them— if the dish is flawed, it is in its presentation, for the clams are arranged around a tangle of seaweed, which, when the dish arrives and is swung into place before you, creates for a moment an atmosphere reminiscent of certain low tides. Fresh thyme again, an almost overwhelmingly heady fragrance and flavor of it, in the sauce in which is placed this great mound of salad—watercress, shredded cabbage, shiitake mushrooms—around which are situated three immense sea scallops, fresh, rich, and prettily browned. The terrine of duck liver is the kind of thing you do not see around much anymore, in these days of America's own foie gras, which, as if to show off the stuff, is usually served in its pure state. Still, there is much to be said for the old-fashioned adulteration, the olea-ginous meat converted into a cool, rich, judiciously seasoned paste, heightened with brandy, garnished with a dab of stewed, sweetened onions, and very good with the supplied buttered toast. But then there are these eggplant ravioli—firm and tender pasta, an eggplant filling of clear enough eggplant flavor, and a tomato sauce of almost astrin-gent sourness, three parts in hopeless search of an excuse for being together.

Lotte is not New York's most popular fish, being ugly to look at and of fugitive flavor, but if it has popularity at all, its consistent presence on this establishment's menu is part of the reason. What twenty years ago was a fish that local fishermen did their best to exclude from their nets is today one that many places have learned to deal with, while many more think they have. At Odeon it is almost always well handled, either by adding flavor to it, or by treating it so carefully that it loses none of what it has. In this prepara-tion, the boned medallions are sautéed, mingled with artichokes and peppers and crou-tons, and set on a layer of strong spinach—it is almost startling that in this context, the delicate flavor of the fresh fish is vivid. To say that Odeon obtains good ingredients, unfortunately, is not to say it *always* does. This chicken, for example, though judiciously roasted within its herbed skin, is not identifiably a chicken by way of any flavor of its own. It is, moreover, garnished with a triple-decker consisting of three stiff rectangular pastry shelves separated by two thick layers of mashed potato—the house calls it a napoleon, but a mashed potato sandwich is a mashed potato sandwich. Order the cas-soulette of lamb, and you are delivered a dinner plate covered with a one-inch depth of tangled green noodles of distinctly, if indeterminately, leafy flavor. The lamb is part of a stew that comes in a brown pot, in it also chunks of lamb sausage, onions and baby carrots, and a dark broth that is powerfully garlicked—you pile the stew on the noodles and proceed, ultimately to perspiration. Your venison arrives in nuggets that are skew-ered with prunes and mushrooms, the charred meat tender, fibrous, blood-juicy, and of distinctive, vaguely sweet venison flavor—the meat is well garnished with chestnuts and herbed rice.

You are informed early that, in the event you want to order one in advance, soufflés are among the desserts. They are of a certain size—small enough for one, large enough two—and sometimes they are offered in flavors you do not associate with soufflés, pineapple, for example, which, when the fruit is present in a moderate dose, makes for a lively hot sweet, this one handsomely risen, moist, and light. The bête noir is a slightly cool chocolate layered affair, the deepest layer a thick mousse, the whole in a pool of chocolate sauce—a good thing of its type, much chocolate intensity with no distractions. The mocha hazelnut torte is moist and nutty in its pool of cassis sauce. The calvados cheesecake is not what it sounds like, merely a heavy cheesecake, of no distinction, that cannot be rescued by the calvados-flavored ragoût, of apples, currants, and walnuts, in which it is set.

★★OMEN

113 Thompson Street (near Prince Street)
DINNER. CLOSED MONDAY.
Reservations: 925-8923.
Credit cards: AE, DC.
Inexpensive.

Old meets new is, inevitably, the SoHo theme underlying all other SoHo themes. For into a neighborhood that is a very reliquary of nineteenth-century New York every fashion streams. Since Japanese restaurants make up an even faster-growing industry on Manhattan Island than three-card monte, it is not surprising that several of these sprightly enterprises have popped up downtown. This one is all of a piece with its chosen neighborhood, for within the confines of a deep and narrow old store, rice-paper-and-wood lanterns and paneling have been shrewdly combined with old brick, ancient door and window frames, a venerable hardwood floor. The Japanese touch has lightened the potentially grim space. The illumination is bright but not glaring. The young Japanese waiters and waitresses are cheery. They wear Western clothes—long dresses, sweaters with patched elbows, purple pants, high-heeled shoes. The Japanese background music seems to come from far away, as if the restaurant were spacious. And lots of Japanese come here—not those throngs of businessmen in Ivy League suits that crowd the uptown Japanese restaurants, but Japanese families, Japanese couples, even integrated Japanese showing this place off to American companions. Whoever you are, it is assumed you are comfortable with Japanese ways. You are brought a small hot towel soon after you are seated (and you are not told what to do with it). And, except by special request, the only implements you are given are chopsticks—unfortunately those little splintery ones that come, attached at one end, in paper sheaves.

Omen is not only the name of the restaurant but of the first-named dish on its menu. Everybody orders it. You get a big bowl of hot, dark broth, a basket of hot noodles, a plate of fresh vegetables, with ginger, and a dish of roasted sesame seeds. You add the solid ingredients to the broth, eat the solids with your chopsticks, drain the bowl by lifting it to your lips. The broth is stout, the vegetables fresh, the sesame a fragrant note in the rousing dish.

Perhaps as a result of a meaning revised in translation, almost everything on the menu is identified as an appetizer. There are, in fact, dozens of little dishes that, if judged only by their size, do not qualify as main courses. Among them: oden (not omen), thick slices of the earthy radish called daikon and a pouch, fashioned of bean curd, stuffed with a meat-and-noodle filling, served in a hot, ginger-flavored broth; kaki no shirasu-ae, a light, herbed bean curd paste studded with orange shafts of sweet, ripe persimmon; oshitashi, one of two dishes of this name, this one a cool, salty, and smoky dish, crunchy of its principal ingredient, raw cabbage, which is mingled with fungus and bean curd; goma-ae, cool and moist spinach, quite crunchy, mixed with strands of mushroom, flavored with sesame. No sushi here, but the sashimi is of impeccable seafood—strong mackerel, smooth and deep-red tuna, velvety slivers of pale squid. More of that squid is one of the ingredients of ika-no sumiso-ae, in which it is mingled with green pepper and soybean paste—the cool dish is oceanic, fruity, a little acidic. The dish called yakijake is a small portion of skinned salmon, carefully broiled, hot and salty, fresh and flaky, of vivid flavor. Omen's shrimp tempura is not the ultimate, but the batter is light, the shrimp are of clear flavor, the chunks of vegetable that are mingled with the seafood (a disk of yam, a sheaf of beans) are fresh and crisp. In the special department called chicken appetizers you will find enoki-no tosazu-ae, a little bowl of watercress and mushrooms and slivers of chicken, served cool, in a dressing that is sour and sparkling. Closer to what you think of when you think of chicken is the item called sansho, hot chicken, boned and browned and glistening, tender, moist of chicken fat, lightly coated with oil that is dark with soy sauce.

All this food is light, and you will want to bulk up your dinner with rice, here served with barley. You may have your rice and barley plain; or with chiso—the dark, sharp preserved leaves of an obscure Japanese plant; or as the "special rice of the month," which has included the likes of mushrooms, green vegetables, and eel mixed into the light grain.

Fruit, green-tea or red-bean ice cream, or those little dumplings called ankoro mochi (which do this really terrific imitation of bubble gum) are the desserts. The so-called Sapporo draft beer (which comes in one-pint bottles) is splendid with this food. Sake is available, as well as strong Western booze, but cocktails are not mixed.

★ ONINI

217 Eighth Avenue (at 21st Street)
LUNCH, SUNDAY TO FRIDAY; DINNER, DAILY.
Reservations: 243-6446.
Credit cards: AE, DC, MC, V.
Medium priced.

You may say that the new Onini lacks the charm of the original, but it lacks also the discomforts. You may add that the spiffy new place is just another example of quasi Deco on the cheap, but then it is no longer hole-in-the-wall on the even cheaper. Chelsea gentrifies apace, and Onini keeps up. The place is bigger, airier, shinier—and, oh yes, dearer, for there is money in this neighborhood now. Above black-painted lower walls today's Onini has been faced with pale cloth that is patterned with vague, floating squares and circles, like nursery wallpaper seen through a mental fog—it does not offend, neither does it amuse. The background music, on the other hand, is often Benny Goodman. The place holds a scant two dozen white-linened tables, in rows, around them little black side chairs with straw seats. The façade is glass, to the ceiling, and at an Eighth Avenue windowside table, you enjoy an unobstructed view of the grimy closet-size shops across the street (sure to shuffle off when their leases come up), among them a few mint, fresh-painted enterprises that signal things to come. Until the things come, however, presumably including additions to the mini Restaurant Row that is Eighth Avenue between 14th and 23rd Streets, Onini is still the best source of Italian food within walking distance of the General Theological Seminary.

There is nothing Italian, however, about this watercress salad, the giant mound of greens dotted with firm white beans, the whole in a citrus-flavored vinaigrette that drenches more than dresses it—still, a rousing first course. Oysters Onini are five of the lightly breaded, oiled, baked bivalves, very tender in their half-shells, each joined by chunks of tomato and warm mozzarella—the fresh oysters retain their oceanic sweetness in the sturdy setting. On occasion the place offers veal sausages, three halves of browned sausage (bifurcated the long way) set in a thick and creamy sauce that is fragrant of tarragon—the sausages lack a little something in the way of succulence, but the good sauce enriches them. Much in the way of pasta: fusilli in a rather harsh, heavily salted marinara sauce into which sun-dried tomatoes have been cooked—the dish is aggressive rather than assertive; fettuccine al Gorgonzola, an elemental dish of little more than the firm noodles and the strong melted cheese—simple, rich, unimpeachable food; and tortelloni (really tortellini) with pesto—the flavor of the pale green stuffing is indistinct but immaterial in the presence of this heady, creamy, and basil-fragrant green sauce, which is dotted to good effect with walnut halves.

Onini's distinction is the dishes it does that no one else does. Consider the oysters and shrimp primavera, a salty, lightly cooked stew of the two shellfish with red and green peppers, zucchini, carrots, and arugula, the seafood of sweet flavor, the pale garlicky broth oiled and vigorous. The sautéed trout is a firm, fresh fish, browned a little, cooked through but juicy, set in a sauce of lemon and anchovies that is thick with fresh parsley. The bird is not a distinguished one in this dish of chicken with eggplant, but the firm white meat is buried under a great mound of the sautéed vegetable, flavored with sage and threaded with the strong bacon, and that redeems it. The cryptic listing "Arista" refers to a double pork chop, the two-story knob of meat, lodged in the crook of its ribs, and partially cut through between them, is supple and creamy-white within browned surfaces that have been treated, as has that incision, with herbs and balsamic vinegar. Good lamb chops too, the eyes of browned meat spread with an earthy, garlicked hash of wild mushrooms. On occasion the house offers a carefully done steak, the big, fibrous, tender, and blood-juicy slab of meat surfaced with peppercorns and adorned with a thick layer of herbs.

Though you are fed copiously at Onini, the house cheesecake seems the right dessert, the genuine Italian article, weighty, wet of its ricotta cheese, browned and sugary, dotted with black raisins. The stewed fresh fig is garnished with whipped cream and berries. And the stuffed prunes are packed with a filling of prune puree that has been fortified with brandy—they, too, come with whipped cream, and with crisp slices of Granny Smith apple.

The waiters and waitresses know the menu and, moreover, as you learn by reference to that document, wear shirts by Susan Ann Thornton.

★ ORSINI'S

26 East 63rd Street
LUNCH, MONDAY TO FRIDAY; DINNER, MONDAY TO SATURDAY. CLOSED SUNDAY.
Reservations: 644-3700.
Credit cards: AE, MC, V.
Very expensive.

The original (West 56th Street) Orsini's was, in its early years, chichi, the stylish went there, the jet set. Anyway, the people who went to Orsini's in order to gape at that crowd were persuaded that those they saw were they, and some were. The trendy, however, are by definition responsive to shifts in fashion, while those who pursue them are often unaware of the changes. Thus, after a time, the seen were supplanted by those who came to see, and Armando Orsini, proprietor there then, and here now, shifted gears a little to accommodate his new trade. Among the vogueish Armando mingled as one of the crowd, but from the camp followers he remained a little aloof, which was all right with them—after all, they sought out Orsini's in the first place to be among their betters. Anyway, his aloofness was only coy flirtation—patronize him well, and he would let you get close. Eventually he permitted himself to be taken over by that crowd, the tasteless rich.

He even took on some of their characteristics, so that when the time came, as he saw it, to semiretire, it was to a restaurant in Florida that he repaired. Florida is where you learn that though you are perhaps ready to semiretire, you are not ready to die. If you have life, a year or two in the Sunshine State, and you gladly turn in the ones you have left for one last act in New York. Tall, handsome, silverhaired eagle Armando is back, the Herbert von Karajan deportment intact, stiff upper torso and all that, the game strut as of the stubborn wounded, the head a little back, though now and again he bends forward to allow, with good-natured mock ceremony, a hennaed lady on her way out to kiss each cheek. As long as Armando's clientele lives, Orsini's lives. When he decided to reenter the business in New York, the dwindling but still sufficient tribe of his adorers rushed to his new place. He knows them by name, they come to hear him say it.

But for Armando to learn a name, that takes time, and until he knows yours, you are an outsider. As he is happy to have it around that there is never a time when you do not have to wait for a table at Orsini's, and as he nevertheless must take prompt care of his regulars, you may well wait for your table no matter how hard upon the hour of your appointment you show up. That suitable tables stand empty is not the point. Consider, for example, the situation in which Armando's unfortunate maître finds himself for having attempted to seat you at once: Armando, suddenly short of breath, his eyes bulging for the moment before their lids drop to half mast, as, nostrils at flare, he enunciates in staccato Italian a Martian could understand that the intended table is too good for these types, that they may wait until something undesirable opens up. The poor maître turns to you, apologizes for his error, shows you to the bar, you serve your time.

These are the premises late, briefly, of QV, before that of Quo Vadis through countless changes of management. The installation opted for by the current interests is closer to the ostentatious opulence of Quo Vadis than to the severe austerity of QV, while it skirts the derisibility that characterized both. Make a hard right after your dealings with that maître, and you are in a subsidiary dining room adjacent to the cushy little bar, a pale Italian sky on the ceiling overhead, short banquettes along each side of the room, over one of them an ornately framed mirror, over the other, in oils, a mutt asleep on a bed as garnish to a large self-involved odalisque—she does not distract, but, then, those that do have been bought up. The main dining room, cubical, somewhat cavernous, has been tamed with mirrors and decorative old paintings on the pink walls, by tall tied-back curtains (their floral pattern is like that of the curtains upstairs at the old Orsini's) over the window, while the ceiling high overhead retains the mural, from all previous administrations, of a dark mythic scene in a heaven somewhere. The floor is of marble blocks in a brickwork pattern, the sconces on the walls are of old-Roman inspiration, the service plates are of hammered brass, the banquettes of a richly colored nubbly cloth, the armchairs massive. It is a setting that is meant to flatter the way an ornate hotel lobby flatters. If you are here in this obviously important place, it says, you deserve to be. Later, the size of your check repeats the statement.

"Funghi boscaioli" are "mushrooms wild," and this salad thereof, big fungic slabs in a bowl formed of a great leaf of red lettuce, has freshness, firmness, a dressing of good oil, everything except the earthy flavor of wild mushrooms at their best. Vitello tonnato is thin-sliced veal in tuna sauce, and in this version you willingly overlook the thinness of the caper-dotted sauce in consideration of its vivid lemoned-tuna flavor, but you hesitate to forgive veal that is brown-edged and dry, as if sliced for lunch and served for dinner. Pappardelle are broad, thick ribbons of pasta, and here they are served in a sauce of porcini mushrooms so sliced that the noodles and mushrooms mimic each other, not to mention that the thick, dark sauce by its weight mimics both—the impeccable ingredients notwithstanding, the unrelieved heaviness is off-putting (especially as you must cope with or divide a full order—no half orders of pasta served). Not to worry, you happily dispatch solo your full plate of gnocchi di ricotta e spinaci, for these little dumplings of chopped spinach and soft cheese are at once rich and sticky and light, of a fugitive succulence, and they are fortified by the bit of ground Parmesean on each of them that is browned just before serving.

The red snapper is baked in parchment paper with fresh vegetables, in the course of which the vegetables become soft and wilted, while the fillet loses a bit more of its own flavor than it gains from the treatment—out of the oven three or four minutes sooner, and the dish would be perfect. The salmon is well grilled, in the course of which nothing transpires to undo its slightly less than fresh state, and neither its mustard sauce nor its caper-dotted red pepper sauce conceal that condition. The baby chicken is also grilled well, but you judge from the metallic flavor near the bone that somewhere between the chicken factory and your plate the little bird suffered an unscheduled interruption of its refrigeration—too bad, for the crisped skin and fresh rosemary are lively. But Orsini's turns out to be an estimable scaloppine house, the thin-sliced veal pale and juicy within its lightly browned surfaces, very nice when served "all' Orsini," with crunchy slivers of artichoke and sweet glistening-green peas; just as good with these woodsy porcini mushrooms in an herbed and winy sauce. The loin of lamb is medium rare, the way you ordered it, and its lamb flavor is in evidence, but the meat is bloodless, as if the loin were grilled in advance and sliced to your order.

In this crowd meats are followed by sweets, cheese is not offered. You point out to your captain that there must be Parmesan in the house, that it is an ingredient of certain dishes, is added to others at the table. Sure enough, chunks of aged Parmesan, hard and strong, can be produced, very good with a salad of fresh greens (also not listed) that is served in a lively vinaigrette. The hazelnut and apple tart is moist and fruity and of vivid nut flavor in its pool of creamy sauce. The "four chocolate dreams" are a chocolate truffle, a ball of intense chocolate ice cream, strands of black and white chocolate, and strands of white chocolate affixed to strands of orange rind—one of the minor fantasies of a chocolate freak. The poached pear is the winner, the huge peeled fruit firm, sweet-spiced, and of heady pear flavor, its good, slightly gritty texture intact, painted on one side with chocolate in its pool of berry sauce.

You are expected not only to dress properly, but to arrange yourselves according to Armando's preferences. When, at a table for two, for reasons of their own, a gent seats himself with his back to the wall, the lady opposite him, Armando tells them in passing that they are sitting "the wrong way."

★ ORSO

322 West 46th Street
LUNCH AND DINNER.
Reservations: 489-7212.
Credit cards: MC, V.
Medium priced.

Ezra Pound and Elizabeth Taylor, I. F. Stravinsky and D. H. Lawrence, Heming-way and Callas, Richard Wagner and Laurence Olivier—what have they in common? Nothing, of course, except fame. And yet their photographs and those of dozens of others (mostly black-and-whites in black frames) are densely assembled on the walls of this one place, in the way celebrity pics, in olden days, were hung in restaurants to memorialize eminents who had fed on the premises. Of course Orso is not misrepresent-ing. Surely all the world knows that Wagner hated Italian food, and that Stravinsky's most rooted phobia was of being waited on by unemployed actors and actresses. The photos are, rather, propitiatory, are directed at whoever cares about whatever. Movies are your bag? Here is John Huston. You like baseball? Ted Williams was the hitter of the century. You loathe Norman Mailer? Have a look at Gore Vidal. All you types, Orso announces, this is your place. Mr. Joe Allen (who owns the restaurant Joe Allen) is proprietor here, and he has calculated that if theater posters could make Joe Allen a hangout for theatrical types, the photo gimmick could target another population seg-ment: those who can read, write, hear, or watch television.

He has calculated shrewdly. The theater is one of the places television watchers go when they are not tubing it, and that set packs this dining room during the early evening, stuffs and sedates itself, leaves in time to collapse into their seats as the curtain goes up. Then, after eight, the literate appear—albeit in lesser numbers, many of them in or of the theater rather than at it—and Orso becomes quite civilized, the laughter is not so gaudy, neither is the clothing. Make no mistake, subtly but surely, the photos flatter these cultureds even if they never glance at them, and the sprinkling of ballplayers and pols among the aesthetes tickles their most common conceit—that for all the richness of their inner lives, they are one with ordinary man. Similarly the physical Orso, which pretends to unpretentiousness, its few-steps-down, ochre-painted, and well-lighted inte-rior much like those of Italian places that were one or two to a block in New York's Italian neighborhoods a couple of generations ago. The tables are surrounded by assorted rough-painted chairs that look like found objects rehabilitated. And you are waited on by young people in white shirts, four-in-hands, long white aprons—they have posture, presence, the correct weight for their height, and, in a few instances, what has come to be called attitude. As headaches are caused by a lack of aspirin, attitude results from a lack of love—or applause.

From a bilingual menu that changes daily: gamberi in padella, the nicely sautéed shrimp moist and crunchy, though their iodine does not work well with the red onions and sundried tomatoes that are their sauce; sautéed clams in their shells buried under chopped tomatoes and a mash of leeks, the vegetables fragrant of thyme, the clams resilient of their overcooking; carciofi fritto, which look like deep-fried artichokes and taste like deep-fried anything, though they are well crisped, take on life when you squeeze on lemon; grilled mushrooms with grilled leeks, picnic food that, on the way to the beach, has risen a bit from its icebox temperature; vitello tonnato, roast veal, quite rare and tender, in a rich and lemony tuna sauce that is dotted with tart capers; tripe, the unexpected winner, the many gummy lengths of innard, a little chewy but not really tough, in a creamy tomato sauce that is thick with chopped vegetables, served with a charred crust of bread that is moist and heady of its garlicked oil.

Order pizza bread, and you get a great pile of the crackling chips, glistening with garlicked oil and salty, lively. But order the pizza alla siciliana, and the circle of pizza bread has all the liveliness of a Passover matzo, while the many ingredients arranged on its surface—olives, peppers, mushrooms, and onions among them—are like a mingling of loose change from many currencies. Occasionally risotto is listed, the fluffy rice buttery, parsleyed, studded with chunks of chicken liver—your waitress abandons her attitude, grates on the Parmesan with abandon, which gives the dish depth and strength. The spinach gnocchi are in a creamy tomato sauce that cannot redeem their gumminess On the Italian side of the menu the grouper is listed as grouper—in either language this is fresh fish judiciously sautéed, and the herbed mushrooms and radicchio with which it is done are, respectively, earthy and pleasingly bitter. The pan-fried liver reaches you as a giant pile of little slivers—you wish they were crisper, bloodier at their centers, but garlic and much Italian parsley manage to make the dish.

The Parmesan that did so much for the rice is just ok straight, and the fruit you may have with it varies—from the like of these firm seedless grapes to these not-quite-ripe strawberries. The pistachio ice cream is nut-studded, sweet, cold. Unfortunately the poached figs are equally cold, therefore flat, as is their cream cheese filling. The apple tart is warm, thin, its fruit hardly more than a film, a good airy thing under its thick whipped cream.

★★OYSTER BAR & RESTAURANT

Grand Central Station, lower level
LUNCH AND DINNER. CLOSED SATURDAY AND SUNDAY.
Reservations: 490-6650.
Credit cards: AE, DC, MC, V.
Medium priced.

If you think you know from fresh, you should have some fish at the Oyster Bar. After a few months of casual seafood, chosen from French menus, or Italian ones, or whatever, come to the Oyster Bar to brush up on freshness basics. This is not the only New York fish restaurant at which the fish is fresh every time. There are a few others (at a couple of which there is perhaps more finesse in the kitchen than here). But no one else offers thirty or so varieties of fish and shellfish in just-caught condition every day. (The Oyster Bar even prepares the stuff lots of different ways.) In seafood, freshness may not be all, but you cannot make really good seafood dishes without it.

In the mid-1970s this place was taken over by new interests, after an extended mori-bundity that had just climaxed in a muffled whimper. But, though there had been a demise, there had been no decay, for this place had been built—more than fifty years before—as an integral part of Grand Central Station, which is to say it would take a wrecking ball to make it crumble even a little. Spiffed up, the place at once revealed its ancient grandeur, quite unspoiled. And you can see it now. The main room, entered from the lower level, is at least a short block long. Under a lofty vaulted ceiling of glinting sand-colored tiles, and walls of maple-stained wainscoting with old marble at the base, there is an acre of tables at one end, a furlong of white countertop, in a repeating S, at the other. You walk on red tiles, you sit in armchairs, or on the banquettes that are along the edge of the room here and there. Or you eat in the saloon, a separate depart-ment at the east end, accessible via a flight of steps down from the entranceway near the low end of the ramp at 42nd Street and Vanderbilt. It is not only the stairway access to the saloon that makes it seem subterranean. The room is windowless and clubby looking, like a speakeasy or a cavernous den. The walls of wood stripping are hung with nautical prints, ships' models behind glass, mountings of big game fish, varnished and glistening. A bar runs along two sides of the room—fifty may water easily along its length. Several dozen gingham-topped tables take up most of the floor. At the late end of mealtimes, when the big main room is sparsely populated, this room may be two-thirds full and cheery. When busy, either room provides enough noise to distract you.

Clams and oysters are sold by the piece. You can come here, order one of each listed oyster, plus a littleneck and cherrystone, and go home sated. On a good day there are as many as ten varieties of oyster available, and if you order an assortment, your waiter (in the main room) or your waitress (in the saloon) will tell you which is the Chincoteague, which is the Malpeque, etc. You will find that the little Belon oysters are as sweet as melon, the Chincoteagues briny and strong, the Cotuits a complexity of fruit and oil and the ocean. By late in the evening the more exotic varieties usually run out, so if you want to sample those Belons or Box oysters, you are more likely to find what you want at lunchtime, or before 7:30 at dinner.

This place has taken to smoking fish (no, not a new fad), and it does a delicate job of it. You get smoked sturgeon, thin slices spread across a big plate, light, ever so slightly soapy (which smoked sturgeon can be ever so excessively), the smokiness at once re-strained and vivid—the horseradish sauce that garnishes the pale meat is sharp, even though it is mostly whipped cream. The smoked salmon is pale, moist without being oily, so tender it is almost fugitive—capers and chopped onions are served with the pink fish, but they should be used with restraint or they will obscure the salmon. The Point Judith herring these days is not much more than ordinary pickled herring. The clams Cassino are plump cherrystones, not buried in breading, just touched with it, and with a bit of bacon—the big clam shells are standing in a film of herbed butter, and the warm clams have a strong and tangy flavor. If you are lucky enough to come when she-crab soup is on the menu, do not pass it up. This is the famous Carolina soup, here made with Maryland crabs, presumably the female of the species, and the resulting bowl is a thick, buttery, subtly spiced, and steamy richness that is dense with sweet white crab-meat.

The impeccable freshness of the ingredients is not, however, invariably matched by their preparation. Lotte is a fish that swims all over the Atlantic. It has never been popular in New York because it is (1) ugly to look upon when whole and (2) rather obscure of flavor when cut up and cooked. Here it is served in hefty chunks that the menu refers to as "tournedos," their surfaces handsomely browned, with a sauce béar-naise that is presumably intended to compensate for the slightness of the flavor of the fish. The sauce, however, is as green as grass, as sweet and thick as molasses. The fish is pretty good if you substitute lemon for the sauce. That béarnaise is particularly hard to understand in light of the pretty good hollandaise that comes with the carefully broiled, fresh, and flaky bass. There is broiled halibut steak, and it falls into tender flakes that are velvety and snowy. In season there is shad and/or shad roe. The fish is floured and browned, the white meat sealed in the buttery crust. But the roe is probably parboiled before its final preparation, and it is a little dry, more like grit—less like caviar—than this dish at its best.

The shellfish stews are homey, big chunks of sea scallop, for example, in a hot and buttery cream broth that is red and spicy with fragrant paprika—the soup is a little briny from the juice of the scallops. The Pacific Coast's renowned Dungeness crab is sometimes available. They must fly it in on a Concorde, for the big crustacean seems to be as fresh as the local items. You get one crab to a serving, it is bright red, cold, it entirely occupies a long platter, and it is garnished with strong, mustard-flavored mayonnaise. There is abundant meat in one of these beasts if you know where it is stored and have the patience to dig it out. A Dungeness crab is about twice the work of a lobster, but this is sweet seafood and worth the bother.

Steaks and chickens are available for inlanders; mixed seafood dishes, complex stews, seafood omelets; shore dinners after 5 P.M.; and live lobsters—you can pick yours out.

Most of the desserts are old-fashioned American items: a cool, custardy banana cream pie, intensely banana flavored, touched with slivered almonds; rice pudding, a frothy, cinnamoned, raisin-studded sweet, obvious but good; a whole-wheat apple pie, on occasion, the grainy crust around nuggets of tart apple, only lightly sugared; blueberry pie, a deep-purple filling of the jellied little fruits filling the lard crust to plumpness—too bad it is served so cold.

A new menu is printed daily, prices written in next to those regular dishes that are available that day; a dozen or so special dishes of the day written in as well.

By now everyone knows that the Oyster Bar serves nothing but American wine, almost one hundred different bottles from four states.

★★PALIO

151 West 51st Street
LUNCH, MONDAY TO FRIDAY; DINNER, MONDAY TO SATURDAY. CLOSED SUNDAY.
Reservations: 245-4850.
Credit cards: AE, DC, MC, V.
Expensive.

Proud, plump Tony May steps from the shuttle elevator that has just descended from his second-story restaurant to its street-level bar, on his face spectacles and a serene smirk. It is shortly after a favorable item in the press, and Tony has been force-feeding himself and happily choking on all the reservations he can get, never mind such details as the physical limitations of his room. The throng angrily leaving, after waiting to no end long past the time of their reservations, commingles with an equal number arriving to begin the same ordeal. May is unperturbed, in fact loves it, winks at a group of his pals to let them know they will get special handling, rides back up. But even he cannot unseat those who, having been fed late, choose to stay late, so the pleasure of his somewhat nettled friends, when they must wait five minutes to be seated out of turn, lacks the thrill of that privilege conferred at once. But May is the kind of man who, having picked your pocket the last time he saw you, wants you to know there are no hard feelings. When finally you are at your dinner, he stops by to ask if everything is all right, obviously confident that you will drop your fork and rise at his coming. When you do not, he figures that is your problem, not his, and saunters off, unconcerned and amused.

The room to which you enter is a big cube, a horseshoe bar of polished gray stone filling most of it, black cocktail tables with little black chairs along two sides. The lower walls are wood paneled, the upper ones faced on all four sides by a wraparound mural, in hot colors, celebrating the breadth of man's cultural achievements, with particular emphasis on horse racing—Palio is a biannual festival in the Italian town of Siena, a wild horse race around the town square one of its main events. The Palio bar has been taken up by the after-5 office set for reviewing the day's frustrations—and, after a couple of drinks, for exchanging confidences. "Last week he says change to low heels in the office, the high ones catch on his loopy rug. Now he says go back to high ones, they look better. He's a real rat, but isn't he gawjiss? You should see his wife. I don't know how he stanza." This to background music by Handel or Mozart.

Cleared for departure by the man who tends the book, you elevator up to the restaurant proper, find yourself at the end of a long, high-ceilinged room of grand proportions, its floor massive blocks of gray-brown marble (carpeting in the aisles), the walls wood, the white ceiling divided by intersecting beams into large squares, at the center of each a recessed light within a protruding collar of polished brass. Two low wine racks divide the room into three parts—and somewhat undo its sweep. The tables, covered with pale beige linen in which a pattern of slightly darker threads is woven, and set with brass service plates, brilliantly painted tiles at their centers, are surrounded by capacious armchairs of black-painted wood with black-upholstered seats. Just above the tan leather banquette that runs the length of the room down one side, small mirrored panels have been installed, above them a series of brilliantly colored flags, bold insignia thereon—palio means flag, and the winner of that horse race gets one. Your captain is in black-and-white formals, the waiters and busboys are in colorfully adorned white jackets, and the sommelier, a metal cup on the chain around his neck, chews gum (or something). He serves you a bottle of white wine. You tell him it is quite cold enough, ask him to leave it on the table. "Certainly," he says, and goes off with it.

Too bad he has not gone off instead with your marinated eel, disks cut from a cold roulade of the soured, somewhat jellied fish—it is assertive but of little character, strong rather than strong flavored. Happily, he has also left behind what is given as "stuffed saddle of rabbit," which you would probably characterize as a terrine. Either way, you receive two thick slices cut from a loaf, hefty chunks of tender meat, of vivid rabbit flavor, well fatted but not fatty, packed tightly together, herbed, dotted with sharp olives, filmed with velvety olive oil, and cleverly garnished with a clump of cold spinach. Surely you can count on your thumbs the number of midtown restaurants that list kohlrabi, a troublesome vegetable of elusive flavor and, sometimes, stringy texture. Palio's kohlrabi is not exactly flavorsome, but it is tender, and the hollowed-out stem is served filled with a hot, rich, and well-seasoned sweetbread puree, the entire dish in a pale sauce that is thick with Parmesan cheese. The place makes exceptional rice, and you may have a mound of the nubbly, winy, abundantly parsleyed stuff dotted with morsels of frogs' legs—a strong admixture of garlic potentiates the flavor of the satisfying dish. Frogs' legs again, this time mingled with slightly chewy potato gnocchi, the little dumplings green of the herbs with which they are flavored, the two in a dark, stout, and briny sauce. The trenette, thin flat strands of pasta, are a dark, grayer green, for they have been prepared with squid and its ink—the pale seafood itself seems to glow in this dank setting, and the

258

well-oiled and tomatoed sauce is salty, vibrantly sea-gamy, invigorating. The rice and pasta dishes are sold only as full orders.

A peculiarity of the menu: within categories—e.g., cold appetizers, pasta, seafood, meats and fowl—all dishes are one price. They tend therefore to be of unequal profitability, perhaps in compensation for which your main course of shrimp involves but five of the crustaceans, wee examples at that, but these are sweet, crunchy shrimp, their lightly browned surfaces dotted with fresh herbs, and they are garnished with a rich puree of zucchini that is strewn with tiny, crisp strands of deep-fried leeks—bits of garlic liven the good dish. Three lengths of dark-pink salmon fillet, rolled around a salty, heady stuffing of ground olives dotted with pink peppercorns, are served on a handsomely contrasting layer of strong spinach—the fish itself is not of notable flavor, but still, a dramatic dish. Come here once, and you will do well to opt for quails, the boned bodies, browned and glistening, bursting with a rich, earthy stuffing of duck livers and mushrooms. The medallion of veal, though hardly browned, is a bit dry anyway—the flavor of the dish is in its sautéed eggplant and zucchini and in its lightly tomatoed sauce. The roast lamb is a couple of substantial slices of rare, tender meat in a sauce of balsamic vinegar that could just as well be of anything at all, for it is thick with organ meat, assertively livery.

You may do better here concluding your dinner with salad and/or cheese than with something sweet. Among the salads: cool white beans and bits of onion in garlicked oil; skinned sections of orange and slivers of endive dotted with cracked peppercorns; tiny slices of raw baby artichoke, lightly oiled, mingled with matching slices of sharp Parmesan. That good cheese and several others may be had in larger quantities if ordered separately—they are at room temperature and on view in a transparent roll-top display cart. The tirami su is a vapid example of the cloying sweet. The black polenta pudding is a dark, grainy muffin—not quite bread, not quite cake—in a tangy red-berry sauce on one side of your plate, a sauce of rich white chocolate on the other. The cheesecake is one of the big winners—it is textured, weighty, dotted with candied fruit, moistened with a sauce that is cool and liquored. The millefoglie is another, a large sandwich formed of two circles of light, flaky pastry, much cool, tangy zabaglione—it is made with white wine—and fresh berries.

At the end of the evening, May is still on his feet, this time tripping after an abundant, low-cut blonde headed for the facilities. He is being as witty as possible at the back of her head. She is tossing answers back over her shoulder and not slowing down.

• PALM and PALM TOO

837 Second Avenue (near 45th Street); 840 Second Avenue (near 45th Street)
LUNCH, MONDAY TO FRIDAY; DINNER, MONDAY TO SATURDAY. CLOSED SUNDAY.
Reservations accepted at lunch; for four or more at dinner at Palm Too: 687-2953 and 697-5198.
Credit cards: AE, DC, MC, V.
Very expensive.

How are the lowly fallen! Inelegance was the Palm's reputation, but first-class lowdown is more than just a gross menu and sawdust on the floor, about all that are left at the Palm and its across-the-avenue satellite. As it is more than a room with occupied pews that makes a congregation, it takes more than the trappings to make the Palm.

Needed also are zealots, those who live the whole life, not just the weekly visit. This place was made by the hardheaded, guys who smoked unfiltereds, drank beer, ate like pigs, and all at the same time. Nor was the Palm ever, as its reputation once had it, merely a media hangout. Anyone could eat here, no matter how conventional his day's work. But most who did expressed thereby the real selves hidden within their two-piece uniforms. They turned from their phony jobs to what they saw as honest, simple pleasures: boisterousness, vulgarity, intoxication, gluttony, surfeit. The true Palmist, secretly or not, detested every effete thing else. Only here was he himself.

Today the Palm is a mechanical replay of the old place. The crowds (somewhat diminished, but still impressive) come, have drinks, address the mammoth lobsters, go. They are like modern-day pilgrims who by day walk the paths of the divine, by night sleep in a motel. These followers know nothing of the excess that was the foundation of the early believers' ecstasies. These days, after dinner, the parishioners depart with their mates, upright as they came. Appropriately, the Palm is now a chain. In eight big cities and East Hampton, the worshipers go through sanitized versions of the old rites. It is not that the food by its type or the servings by their size are less carnal than they were, rather that without the attentions to them of pop-eyed, red-faced participants, they become exhibits in a museum. Today's Palmist comes from across the water, is fresh from the shower, drinks Amstel Light, *shares* a lobster (takes home the claws), skips dessert. He comes, in short, to lie to himself about himself. He does not even mind that, on arrival, he is greeted by courteous, albeit aloof, automatons in business suits, that it is occasionally not necessary to wait for a table, that the waiters in their putty jackets do so well here with their limited skills that some of their contentment is expressed as courtesy (this is less true in Palm Too, where many members of the younger floor staff are still in the early surly stage, which usually lasts about a decade). Though at the original Palm, the nearby *Daily News* is still a source of self-conscious cynics who, by their presence here, mean to make plain their unwillingness to swallow whole anything that will not fit in a shot glass, most of the customers in the original store are here to tell you that this is a great country, and there are still plenty of ways to make a living in it despite not knowing anything. Palm Too gets a younger set, more or less the next generation. In fact its little bar has a life of its own, in which everyone smokes, talks sports, and leaves big tips to the bartender, who is one of their own. These are guys who come with their girlfriends and, after they marry, come alone. As one man alone explains, while on his fifth or sixth something-on-the-rocks, "I'm only twenty-nine, but I got to be shop steward because of the girl I'm married to's father." The Palm and Palm Too are sawdust on the floors, painted cartoons on the walls and ceilings, white-linened tables, hanging white globes for illumination, and four-bladed fans for moving the smoke. The original Palm has an upstairs much like the downstairs, was once a speakeasy. Palm Too is its child of the late seventies. When tables open up in one Palm while there is still a long wait in the other, customers may carry their drinks across the street and get seated. Anyone who tells you he can distinguish the food in one Palm from that in the other has delusions of acute discrimination.

As all the world knows, the Palm has no printed menu, the waiters recite only a fraction of what is available, a smaller fraction more if pressed. The complete menu is posted upstairs at the back of the Palm, on the wall between the bar and front window in Palm Too. Most of the food in both these places is now nowhere: raw littleneck clams that are sometimes flat, though on occasion the eight cherrystones in the clams oregano suffer only from a bit of toughness in their blunt, herbed, dark-browned breading; an abundance of crabmeat that, if it is not frozen, is nevertheless without the sweetness and sparkle of the fresh article—it needs its bright cocktail sauce, which you may be disinclined to fortify from the supplied cup of horseradish, even though a previous customer was apparently content to break through the crust to get at the good part; a fillet of red snapper the size of an open book that has been cooked through and blackened to seafood anonymity; lamb chops that are so overcooked, though delivered promptly, that you suspect they are prebroiled, heated to order; a dry veal chop that has lost utterly the bursting juiciness of the thing done right; beef à la Dutch, a pile of slightly sour potted meat with a pile of flat noodles, the two in a forceful gravy that is thick with onions and green peppers; cottage-fried potatoes that are warm, tasteless potato chips; fried onions that, though not greasy, lack onion character. And yet, the items for which the Palm has always been known are admirable. The immense sirloin steak is fibrous and tender, its charred surface stretched by the bursting blood-juiciness within—the meat even has the flavor, rare nowadays, that is the mineral sharpness of aged beef. The giant lobsters are tails the size of a heavyweight's forearm and claws that will do as King Kong's bloodshot eyes. They have been broiled from scratch (not steamed first), and as their own juices have not been diluted by alien moisture, and as they are taken from the fire before they dry out, they have an extraordinary intensity of marine flavor. When the hash brown potatoes are right, they are crusty, potently seasoned, of a clear potato flavor that is at once plain and pungent; when they are wrong, they are greasy, flat.

For dessert there is cream-cheese cheesecake, and for overwhelming richness devoid of finesse, this is a good example of the type.

★ LE PALMIER

37 East 20th Street
LUNCH, MONDAY TO FRIDAY; DINNER, MONDAY TO SATURDAY. CLOSED SUNDAY.
Reservations: 477-6622.
Credit cards: AE, DC, MC, V.
Medium priced.

Except that the cylindrical fish tank behind the bar (in it brilliantly colored fish and convoluted structures of coral) recalls a scene from your last bout of delirium with tremors, the up-front drinking area of this vast, high-ceilinged place, what with its fronded walls, the soft blue-gray composition surface of the bar, and the pastels and pale wood all around, looks like a health food setting, not a drinking scene. This whole place, in fact, is tone deaf, unattuned to the world around it, so that here at the center of this booming part of town, the dinner hour finds Le Palmier populated by a sampling of what remains of Gramercy Park gentility, attracted here by the gardeny pink-and-green fantasy that is the dining room, what with its palm trees, pink linen, pink carpeting, pink side chairs with pink-upholstered seats. Even the brick walls have been daintified by stylized palm trees rendered in whitewash and copper-colored tiles. Withal, the place looks unfinished, like a stage set seen from the wings. And when the air is filled with the noodlesome "live" "music" of a gent at the keyboard of a device that resembles the inevitable leftover panel from an assemble-it-yourself furniture kit, you know the place is groping.

Anyway, you can always get a table here at the dinner hour, and if you go for the fresh coriander soup, you are sure of at least one plate of exceptional food, the yellow-green substance at once creamy, rich, light, alive with the vibrant scent and taste of cilantro—the preservation of which in hot food is an achievement, for the flavor of this herb is fugitive, can be lost in all but the most restrained cooking. So you figure maybe the man in the kitchen is a soup man, next time you make it the mussel bisque, and sure enough, the bisque itself is at once briny and earthy, but the oysters that could be a nifty note in this setting have been defeated by their overcooking. And then there are these sea scallops provençale, which are flat under their garlic and parsley—you apply a dab of the tomato purée that is at the center of your plate to each bite of seafood to help it along. What is listed as "warm salmon" arrives cool, which is too bad, for these were probably perfect little fillets five minutes before they reached you, alive in their citrus-flavored sauce. Your confit of quail is spooned out to you from a little oval ramekin, the parts of the bird and chunks of strong black olive, in their dark and spicy sauce, placed beside a salad of good greens in a lively dressing. The wild mushroom canneloni consist of thin pasta sheets formed into a tube around a mushroom hash that seems actually meaty— the constructs are moistened with a bit of chive butter.

The snapper is browned and snowy and tasteless. The skin-on fillet of pompano is better, clearly pompano, and prettily adorned with chopped tomato in its parsley butter. And the fricassee of lobster and artichokes, morsels of each arranged around firm spaghetti, is quite impeccable in its pale-pink shellfish sauce. The veal chop is nicely browned, though the slices of apple in its sweet-spiced calvados sauce are distractingly sugary. Prunes in a port wine sauce, it turns out, are a harmless setting for sautéed sweetbreads. And the "grilled mignons of beef" seem rather coarse meat for what you assumed was filet mignon, while the sauce, of white raisins and Armagnac, has a raw-alcohol quality that overwhelms the dish.

A very nutty block of coconut mousse is dotted with chunks of sweet, chewy dates, is served with sheets of pineapple and curls of brown-and-white marbleized chocolate, all in a pool of passion fruit purée—a showy and amusing dessert. Something given as "noir & blanc" is a chocolate fantasy of mousses, more of those chocolate curls, and chocolate sauce, in all of which you fail to discern either the listed cognac or almond biscuits. Aurore is a dessert cooked onto your plate—pears and figs and almonds and a sauce, the top browned in the broiling, the pears of clear flavor, the figs lost in the setting, the almonds a crisp note. What goes as opéra consists of little towers cut from a brown-and-tan layer cake and set in a cool and creamy coffee-flavored sauce.

★ PAOLA'S

347 East 85th Street
DINNER.
Reservations: 794-1890.
Credit cards: AE.
Beer and wine.
Medium priced.

Restaurants as latter-day Woodstocks may be getting all the attention now, but the custom of the hole-in-the-wall as eating place persists. Consider, for example, this sliver of real estate. It is hardly more than a dim path from a front door to a kitchen, but in it you could easily delude yourself that you are in a corridor between a cellar and a dungeon. By the feeble light of the rococo fixtures on the walls, you are able to discern that, under a murksome stamped-tin ceiling coated with deep-blue enamel, and within dark-red walls, Paola's is hung with mirrors, flowers in wall pots, greenery in the front window. You can see that on the white-linened tables, there are more flowers—these in little hand-painted, vases—and flickering candles. But in such darkness, you are aware mainly of darkness—unless you get a table at the rear, near the portal to the kitchen, and choose to look in. The lace curtains are tied back, and you may see for yourself that Paola's is a family enterprise: surely the teen-aged stripling in kitchen whites is kin to the cheerful, well-fed young woman in charge of the dining room; and where but in an Italian family restaurant would the workers at the stoves and sinks be enjoying Verdi on the tape deck.

From the brief menu of mostly vigorous food, you may begin with the bruschetta, dark, crusty bread spread thick with a chopped, herbed, and well-oiled mixture of tomatoes, cheese, and raw garlic—fresh, invigorating food. Just as fresh, but more soothing than rousing, is the mozzarella fresca, a soft pancake of the pale, pleasantly gummy cheese, moistened with a light vinaigrette, strewn with herbs, garnished with sprigs of basil, arugula, and slices of juicy tomato.

Perhaps you should ask that the mussels be omitted from your linguine pescatore, for they are poorly cleaned and add a rank cast to the entire dish—which is otherwise of firm pasta, a stout red sauce, sweet little clams, and crunchy shrimp. This place uses thick spaghetti, and the hefty strands are of the right weight for this solid Amatriciana, a spicy tomato sauce that is thick with sautéed onions and strands of Italian bacon—add cheese, and you thicken the sauce further, and at the same time potentiate its elemental flavors. Good tomato sauce yet again, this time on the cappelletti, each of which is a circle of pasta upon another, the packages thus formed stuffed with a fluffy and lightly seasoned filling of ground meat. The house will serve one pasta dish as two halves, but half orders are not prepared.

The gamberoni are big sautéed shrimp, of a sweet oceanic flavor, moist of the oil they were done in, pungent with garlic. You may have your chicken simple—morsels of it that are browned, buttered, and lemony; or less simple—combined with lengths of salty, gamy sausage in a stout sauce. The big veal chop is sautéed with herbs—you wish it were moister. The lamb chops are better, pink and blood juicy, touched with rosemary, garnished—like most of the main courses here—with hefty, oiled slices of potato that are mingled with slivers of garlic. The usual sautéed spinach and escarole are on the menu, and they are fine. But then there is something given as grilled radicchio, which reaches you as a mound of blackened leafy slivers that have a good bitter edge—the hot lettuce is served with lemon.

Paola's version of tirami su is a weighty layered affair, the rich cheese combined with a liquored and coffee-flavored cake and dotted with chunks of chocolate. If that strikes you as much after a substantial dinner, the cool zabaglione will not seem like much less—the winy froth is thick and smooth, overlaid with slices of ripe strawberry.

★★PARIOLI, ROMANISSIMO

24 East 81st Street
DINNER. CLOSED SUNDAY AND MONDAY.
Reservations: 288-2391.
Credit cards: AE, DC.
Very expensive.

New York's most expensive Italian restaurant, Parioli began as a simple place, on First Avenue. But long before its move from the original site the establishment took on the high solemnity, high prices, and high-style food for which it is known today. Its plebeian origins, however, remain, in the person of Mr. Rubrio Rossi, its ever present founder and host, a gentleman whose close-cropped hair, tailored clothing, and formal bearing, whatever their studied purpose, are the manners and trappings of your basic butler. (If you have never yourself employed a butler, you may be intimidated, as many are, by Parioli's atmosphere, which consists in large measure of Rossi's church warden air. Members of the staff certainly are, for they go through their chores, some of them, as if their proctor were permanently installed on their shoulder.) Still, Ruby's act almost convinces, and it is not until some heavy spender grabs him by the elbow—with the oily companionability of one who ingratiatingly asks a favor while knowing it cannot be refused—that he shifts down to the same low-obedience gear in which his underlings operate all the time. Rossi inclines his head, listens, runs to do the fellow's bidding, perhaps to adjust the air conditioning, hastens back to determine if the new climate is satisfactory, clasps his palms together as he makes his getaway, smiling all the way. You figure that, despite his prosperity, when he sits down to feed himself at the end of the night, he does not eat what he wants, but what is left.

Your entrance is to New York's most sober bar, the tipplers do not smile, the ice cubes do not clink. But things pick up in the aisle just beyond it, where you find (when it is not being wheeled through the dining room) a wagon of cheeses—rows of cylinders, blocks, pyramids, disks—that, taken together, look like an architect's model of a small town. A little further, and you are in the principal dining room, a square space, softly lit, in which about fifteen large linened tables, spotlighted flowers on each, are distributed across a dark-carpeted floor, enough space between them for even that big cheese trolley to be wheeled up to any one. Here you are in the grandest room, a couple of stories high, of the parlor floor of an old Manhattan townhouse, its fireplace huge (and now in disuse), its ceiling carved. Two of the tables are at couches situated under windows that look out on a kind of atrium, covered over by a sloping glass roof, on the far side of which a smaller dining room with a handful of tables enjoys a quasi-outdoor setting. The rooms have been Italianized with a coat of neo-Renaissance mottled ochre, and the walls are hung with a few bizarre paintings that, by their indifference to esthetic effect, establish that Parioli makes no false claims—this is a place for pleasure, you spend a lot of money here, you do not pretend that anything lofty is going on. Parioli has in fact always appeared to be a clubby place, one to which dirty old men with filthy money brought their nieces. At the original site, it was usually busy, but not with a large following, rather with what looked like a few devotees who came often. That has changed somewhat since the move, for as the restaurant gets more and more recognition in the press, and more and more traffic from those who follow fashion, it is less of a lure to those who covet privacy. Couples composed of a lady listening and a gentleman making promises have been replaced by pairs between whom the promises have been, often regrettably, kept.

Presumably in honor of the modified tone of the clientele—the present crowd is more inclined than the former one simply to take the place at the face value of its lofty cost—Parioli's kitchen bothers less than it used to with details of product. What are given, for example, as "delicate baby artichokes" may reach you coarsened and leathery, and their pungent green-olive stuffing, though of good flavor, in no way puts the dish in line with its billing. Then there is the carpaccio d'agnello, which, though the title leads you to expect raw lamb, the subtitle describes as "cooked to a turn." Anyway, the lamb is cold and very rare, the edges of the thin slices are browned, and they are served with a dollop of sauce that has a good red-pepper intensity—the dish adds up to mildly diverting picnic food. So if it is cold meat you want, and you come here when vitello tonnato is available, have that, for the silver dollars of pale, tender veal are under a smooth tuna sauce that is at once rich and sparkling of its oil and lemon. If you are to have pasta here only once, you will do well to make it the trenette ai funghi porcini, the firm but tender strands in a creamy and polished sauce, thick with chunks of wild mushroom, that is of an almost overpoweringly woodsy fragrance. What Parioli calls fedelini, you call spaghetti—the pasta is served in an otherwise good red sauce, well oiled and sweetened with onions, that is fortified with jalapeño peppers, which make the sauce hot, but not in a way that fits it—their heat and flavor come off as appendages to the dish, not parts of it. But the tortelloni are good, the big packages of green pasta, filled with well-seasoned ricotta cheese, are light despite their solidity, and they are in an oily and redded sauce that is fragrant of herbs.

When the scampi are good, they are very, very good, the big grilled shrimp sweet and crunchy in their peppery butter—but at times one or more are tough, and at times as many are touched with iodine. Rossi goes to the trouble of obtaining copies of the Italian swimmer called branzino, labels them "Adriatic sea bass," overcooks them not much, but enough to water their flavor—still this is good fish, the seafood juicy of the white wine in which it was baked, and it is roused and enriched by its creamy tarragon sauce. The younger the chicken, the milder its flavor, which is why broilers are seasoned, browned, basted with tasty fat. This place offers 21-day-old birds (broilers-in-training) at $30 per, as if their meat were to be prized more or less in the way the fur of unborn animals is prized. The things are roasted with truffles, reach you browned and moist, but the treatment cannot offset their pallidness—as with the gentlemen's nieces, youth is their sole appeal. More birds, veal birds, in which the thin-sliced meat, rolled around an olive-accented stuffing, is browned, braised, and served in a winy cream sauce that is studded, strikingly, with sweet peas. Like the dining room itself, the veal chop is two stories high, two protruding ribs to prove the point, the great knob of supple meat cooked through but still pink and bursting with moisture—the mélange of mushrooms, broccoli florets, and strands of root vegetable with which it is topped neither adds nor detracts, and the sauce in which it is set, though only vaguely the "tarragon sauce" it is called, is earthy, creamy, enriching. Steaks in many sauces, a winner the filet mignon in a tangy caper sauce that contrasts dramatically with the velvety red meat.

Parioli knows how to sell cheese. The cart is wheeled to your table, sent for or not, and a well-schooled captain tells you of his wares for about five minutes—unless you interrupt, and direct him to explicate only the items that stir your curiosity. Italian, French, Spanish, English, and American cheeses are here, all in good condition. Whatever you select, include some Parmesan—just a couple of flakes from the giant block will rouse you for dessert. When you have chosen your cheese, you are brought a silver tray, on it a labeled bottle of port and a decanter from which the wine is actually poured. You ask the price, and the gentleman proffering the stuff winces (at Parioli, no one asks prices), mumbles that a glass is $16.50.

The legendary chocolate cake is deep and sharp, is enriched by a thin layer of almost black chocolate cream, is frosted with confectioners' sugar, is garnished with rich whipped cream. The zabaglione is hot, winy, frothy, on raspberries that, unfortunately, are a little hard.

★★★ LE PÉRIGORD

405 East 52nd Street
LUNCH, MONDAY TO FRIDAY; DINNER, MONDAY TO SATURDAY. CLOSED SUNDAY.
Reservations: 755-6244.
Credit cards: AE, DC, MC, V.
Very expensive.

Here are brought together much of what is new in French cooking and all that is traditional in the prosperous at their pleasure. There have always been local eating places that, because they did not attract the fashionable, appealed to the comfortable, restaurants to which the folks repaired simply to be among their own happy kind. That this place is now one of their repairs suggests that the new cookery is getting old (which, of course, is not to judge it, or to suggest it is on the way out).

There has been a Périgord at this site for more than two decades now, during which time the restaurant has changed both hands and appearances. Its current looks—at last—are actually prepossessing, though the setting is more flattering than diverting, one in which a soft and rosy boudoir glow confers on those within it a look of broad-spectrum well-being, everything from health to wealth. The room has always been weighted down by its low, low ceiling, but portions of the ceiling have been carved away, and a network of handsome crossed beams has been installed—they lighten and make airy the formerly oppressive overhead. The walls all around are covered with textured cloth on which is printed a muted pattern of flowers and leaves. The plush carpeting matches the velvety, deep-rose banquettes and capacious booths that rim the room on three sides. Flowers are everywhere, and the china and crystal on the white-topped tables glitter under the spotlights positioned among the ceiling crosspieces. The ladies glitter too, anyway their shimmering dresses, jewelry, lacquered fingernails (nary a woman in the place with fewer than ten). The gentlemen, on the other hand, give off a firmer light—that of the burnished dome, the pink and shiny clean-shaven cheek, the heavy silk tie—and are content to be known by how expensively are turned out their spouses. Still, people come here neither to be seen nor to gape. They are a civilized and satisfied set, thank you, and they number among them many from UN missions nearby. Foreign languages definitely spoken here. Both the locals and importeds choose this place, in part, because the dining room staff nurtures their contentment with the intelligence and courtesy they take as their due.

You enter Le Périgord to an anteroom, in it a display of cold hors d'oeuvres, one of them a full-grown snapper, poached and skinned, the big fish just about filling the great platter on which it is set. If the swimmer catches your eye, you may well choose to start your dinner with a portion of its firm and glistening meat—from its sweet and characteristically nutty snapper flavor, you judge that the fish was fresh when prepared, and its herbed mayonnaise livens and enriches it. For cold seafood more complex, you refer to the menu, among its listings lobster in aspic, the muffin-shaped compacture of tender morsels bound at the top by a cool jelly that is thick with herbs and cracked pepper, the construct set in a green pool that is a parsley sauce tart with lemon. Seafood in a green sauce again, this time what is given as "saumon mariné demi-doux à l'huile épicée," gravlax to you, albeit a French version, the slick, oil-marinated slices of red fish, strewn with sprigs of fragrant dill, only slightly sweet, this green sauce of watercress and lime, its tanginess in nice contrast to the supple salmon. If the words "duck confit" call to your mind hearty, spicy food, set aside your preconceptions when you order the duck confit appetizer, for in this presentation you receive slivers of the preserved fowl that, trimmed of fat, are interleaved with thin, matching slivers of cool, ripe pear, the fruit a foil to the duck in much the way that a pear can be the moderator of strong cheese. If there is a spare $10 among your effects, pay the premium for the duck foie gras, for the combination of lightness and richness that is the essence of foie gras is here emphasized by an artful sautéing of the sliced organ meat—it is moist, pink, soft within its browned and glistening surfaces, and it is served in a dark sauce, cloves of garlic in it, that, despite its assertiveness, only underscores the liver. No spare cash required for the sweetbread crêpe, morsels of the organ meat and chunks of wild mushroom that are sautéed, moistened with a dark sauce, wrapped in a thin pancake, and served in a buttery white sauce that has been livened with vinegar—that white sauce is like a clever bonus, for the crêpe and its contents are complete without it.

Mediterranean fish, sometimes one kind, sometimes another, are offered. When the variety is rouget, prepared in the way the house styles "provençal," you do well to look no further. Rouget is a firm, red-skinned, white-meated fish of a sweet taste that, though delicate, is vivid. The fillets you get here, their skin crisped and spicy, have all their flavor, and they reach you on a mound of strong spinach, the two set in a pale, nubbly sauce, buttery and a little tart, that is dotted with herbs and bits of tomato. Your lobster may be had grilled, but think twice before passing up the lobster "à la crème d'estragon," for this way, the meat of the crustacean is enriched and perfumed by a creamy sauce that is suffused with fresh tarragon—a wondrous dish. When your duck arrives, so does the scent of dill, for the hot food is strewn with many sprigs of the herb, and their aroma is the setting for a dish that otherwise has no dill in it. The bird, suffused with lemon, is served in slices and parts that are arranged on a thin sheet of crisped potato, everything moistened with a polished, slightly tart red-wine sauce, and garnished with slivers of browned, bittersweet endive. Little may be said for these fillets of veal, for with veal there is always the danger—as here—that it will come across as little more than nameless protein. The veal "arlequin," however, is just about redeemed by its sauces (one slice is in a pale and acidic lime sauce, the other in a red and vibrant lobster sauce) and by its garnishes (strong spinach, carrots of exceptional natural sweetness). Instead of liver and onions, there is a variation, the great crescents of sautéed pink meat under a veritable carpet of minced scallions (with chopped parsley), their sharpness a nice foil to the rich organ meat. Under the heading "Le Plat Classique," there is one item, "boeu faux carottes, vielle façon," old style, that is, the morsels of meat—a pyramid of them at the center of your plate in an herbed and fat-rich sauce—still fibrous, their surfaces retaining much of the rough texture of their browning, though they have been stewed until tender, the beef surrounded by a ring of shiny, bright-orange inches of sweet carrot, their near hardness a good textural note in this setting.

If you remember to order it when you order your dinner, you may have an airy, raspberry-flavored soufflé for dessert, deep-pink and shot through with bits of berry under its browned and risen top—your waiter makes an incision and spoons in a winy raspberry sauce. The lemon pie is tangy under its meringue top. The pear tart is moist and fruity on its flaky pastry. You may have a slice of rather light but otherwise conventional crème caramel. The lemon-raspberry mousse is a dull layered affair—happily, your waiter garnishes it with fresh berries.

★★PERIYALI

35 West 20th Street
LUNCH, MONDAY TO FRIDAY; DINNER, MONDAY TO SATURDAY. CLOSED SUNDAY.
Reservations: 463-7890.
Credit cards: AE, MC, V.
Medium priced.

If, unfortunately, you recall the brief fashion for cacophonous Greek nightclub-restaurants that addled New York for a few years in the seventies, you may well take one look at this place and flee, for it sports every visual taverna cliché that you reflexively associate with twenty thousand watts of amplification, loudspeakers at three-foot intervals along the walls (the facilities not excluded), a regiment of bouzouki players, and a hoarse, maniacal contralto, her mouth around a microphone, screaming incomprehensibly her head off in twelve languages that border the Mediterranean. Be calm—Periyali, but for its standard look, is not that. For those of you who came in later, however, know that in the taverna (the Greek equivalent of, roughly, the trattoria) the light is low, the walls are of coarse white stucco, except where—and this is essential—they are of massive stones, the wooden benchlike banquettes are equipped with thin cushions (both seats and backs), and kitchen implements and photos of the old country hang on the walls. Among the permissable variations are the white cloths that, draped from beam to beam, lower this ceiling; and with respect to the floors, they may be either of wood, as they are in this main dining room, or of old red tiles, as in this establishment's small back rooms. With respect to what is served, retsina, a terrible tasting Greek white wine is always on the wine list, but is never ordered by Americans. (There is some question as to whether it is ordered by Greeks once they have been exposed to other wines.) And the food is usually predictable and tolerable, which is where Periyali nervily skirts tradition—Greek cookery is not a culinary wonder of the world, but, as in any cooking, when the ingredients are right and the dishes fresh made, as they are here, it is better than other food less carefully prepared.

Another thing you will almost always see in a New York taverna—displays of appetizers, desserts, what have you. But here you will do well to overlook the assortment of vegetables that, by their appearance, may put you in mind of certain Italian displays of this type. Though this is perfectly good food, there are better ways to begin your dinner here. But, for the record (and for vegetarians), an assorted plate of these items may include a spinach risotto, the dark and oiled rice threaded with the green; marinated mushrooms that have more mushroom flavor and less astringent sourness than run-of-restaurant mushrooms à la Grecque; florets of cauliflower with timidly hot green peppers; a mingling of beets and onions; whole okras that are mushy in their tomato sauce; strands of decent red peppers, oiled and roasted; and, at the center of your plate, a baked tomato packed with a sweet-spiced stuffing of rice and pine nuts. All that is fine, but finer still are: taramosalata, the familiar red-roe paste in a version that is smooth, lively of its lemon, and of a briny sparkle possible only in the just-made article; melitzanosalata, a rather too-blenderized version of the familiar eggplant mash, but its freshness and subtle liveliness save it; gigandes skordalia, big white beans on a thick, oiled, and well-seasoned paste of garlic and potatoes; octopus, the long, rough-textured tentacles firm but not rubbery, blackened by grilling, moistened by an herbed and oily sauce; tiropeta and spanakopeta, light pies of flaky pastry, the former filled with feta cheese of real strength, the latter, which is tubular, with good spinach.

If you wish, you may have your snapper grilled, but have it roasted, and it arrives, still wrapped in its crisped skin, buried in a dense, garlic-flavored sauce of tomatoes and onions, the fish itself firm and juicy. Of course there is moussaka, and the ground lamb in this one is of powerful, muttony flavor, to which the charred eggplant is a vigorous zest—the top, happily, is not a gooey white sauce, is browned and crackly, is sprinkled with more of that ground lamb, a bit of cheese as well. The tender lamb chops seem to have been oiled and seasoned before their grilling, but this only potentiates their flavor —and, oddly for a Greek restaurant in New York, you may have your lamb rare if you want it that way. Withal, the winner is the rabbit stew, the great nuggets of meat, on the bone, white and juicy and powerfully flavored by the spicy redded sauce, thick with whole onions, in which they have been done.

The rice pudding is nubbly, custardy, sweet—too bad it has been in its cup a while, and that a thin skin has formed across the top. Good baklava, of almonds (rather than the walnuts that, in New York, are usually the nut of choice), the honey-sweet nut paste, mingled with crisp slivers, interleaved with flaky pastry and set on a good cake base. What are called "diples" are coils of fried-in-oil dough that you eat with honey—an amusing sweet. Your waiter suggests Greek coffee. You ask what that is. He describes it. "Sounds like Turkish coffee," you say. "Yes," says your waiter, "but we're not allowed to say that." The coffee, half liquid, half sediment, and very strong, is good with some of Periyali's homey cookies.

★ PESCA

23 East 22nd Street
LUNCH, MONDAY TO FRIDAY; DINNER, DAILY.
Reservations: 533-2293.
Credit cards: AE.
Expensive.

Finfish, shellfish, a dash of pasta, and a couple dozen buzzwords of contemporary cookery, such are the surefire ingredients that are the culinary recipe for this place. The formula yields fashion without style, serviceability without (seafood) character, anonymity. Pesca is the Gimbel's of fish restaurants, albeit at Bloomie's prices. Nothing terribly wrong with the place, you understand, but it is informed not at all by any passion for the produce of the deep. What this house does to seafood is what Hollywood does to a novel—licks it, as it is put, denatures it to broaden its base of acceptability. For all its fanciness, and there is a lot of it, the food tastes as if it were prepared according to the precepts of *Joy of Cooking*. Dinner here, and you will rarely come away imagining that the smell of the briny lingers in your nostrils. But while the place has subtracted much that is fundamental to seafood restaurants, it has also, happily, left out a lot that is too often included. The ceiling is not festooned with hairy fish nets, there is no hardtack in the breadbasket, you do not stub out your cigarette in a seashell.

Not that Pesca is coy about what it is about. The place is, in fact, hung with scores of oils, watercolors, engravings, prints, all of them watery—fish or shellfish, ships or seascapes—and all handsomely framed and boldly hung, the only three-dimensional deviation a big white-enameled sailfish that, your host assures you, is a sailfish coated with white enamel, not the plastic model it could easily be. All this in a long, high-ceilinged room that is wide at the front, where it accommodates, in addition to tables and chairs, the bar and piano, the latter inaudible when the place is filled and noisy, and at other times tinkled with sufficient softness neither to distract nor divert. Between the cream-colored stamped-tin ceiling and the polished wood floor, the room is painted a shiny pale pink that glistens in the soft light of overhead spots. The white-linened tables are surrounded by bentwood side chairs with green-upholstered seats that, by their skimpiness —they are about as big around as dinner plates—seem to make an exaggerated assumption about the slimming properties of a seafood diet. It is important to know of Pesca that it is an operation as much as it is a restaurant, a place in which you may find yourself processed rather than catered to, for though certain members of the staff are sweet, a number of the veterans go through their resentful paces as if sentenced to this place by you. Maybe they do not like fish.

The smoked tuna is notable for how the intensity of its smoke flavor obscures the seafood quality of the fish, and for how the thin slices of brownish meat are wet rather than moist—the jigger of good sesame dressing served with it does not rescue the event. But then there is the gravlax, the supple cured salmon in a version that is salty rather than sweet, heady of dill, very nice with its thick, sharp mustard sauce. A couple of little handsomely browned pancakes studded with kernels of corn garnish the bluefish sausage, which reaches you in a green sauce that is spicy of the hot green peppers that account for its color, but the plump sausage itself, though juicy and well seasoned within its casing, is certainly no expression of bluefish, could be any fish. And the seafood chowder, though its redded broth is hearty, is studded with dice of fish that, though not invariably fresh, are always overcooked, and with mushy cubes of vegetable.

Each day there is a pasta of the day, and you only have to read the list of ingredients —for example, farfalle (bowties) in a tomato-and-basil sauce, with sundried tomatoes, eggplant, and shrimp—to know that the sauces are compendia of attractive-sounding parts that have been added to one another but not really transformed into anything new. And each day there is a risotto of the day, and the grain, cooked in stock, has good flavor, nicely accommodates the ingredients—they vary from time to time—added to it.

When soft-shell crabs are in season, Pesca obtains the best of them, tiny ones that have just shed their shells, but sautés them in a rather gingerly way, so that they are hardly crisped, and serves them in a sauce of red bell peppers that makes sense only because the crabs need the help. But the roasted lobster is fine, its crunchy stuffing of wild rice and chopped root vegetables a good textural foil to the firm, sweet meat. And the broiled salmon steak is exemplary, glinting moist and pink within its browned surfaces—the fish gains nothing from the good mustard sauce served with it. Then there is this grilled pompano, which though not off, is low enough on pompano taste to make you suspect the fish was frozen, or on ice for days on end—its loose sauce of capers in crème fraîche livens it. Whatever you do, skip the cioppino, a San Francisco stew here made with noisome mussels, lobster that is toughened by its overcooking, scallops, dice of nameless fish, and innumerable vegetables—the spicy broth is invigorating, perhaps you should ask for it straight.

The fruit-custard tarts come, often, on rubbery pastry, and the custard itself is sometimes a bit leaden. The nutted chocolate tart is intense, its black icing more so. First-rate whipped cream is served with the desserts.

★ PETALUMA

1356 First Avenue (at 73rd Street)
LUNCH AND DINNER.
Reservations: 772-8800.
Credit cards: AE, MC, V.
Medium priced.

This offshoot of Elio's began as a California restaurant with an Italian accent. That did not work out, and success came only when Petaluma caught up with what, after all, was surely its destiny. Today it is, in all but name, Elio's, Jr., is ninety percent Italian and proud of it, and the menu items that remain from the eclectic past—crab cakes, goat cheese salad, Siamese chicken—are stepchildren left behind by previous spouses. Of course Elio's, Jr., is not Elio's. You do not find pizza at Elio's, and sometimes you cannot find a waiter here. Gents who regularly dinner with the guys at Elio's are at Petaluma the night they get the kids, grandly urging them to order anything they want. Elio's is the dining room, Petaluma the rec room. But of the many eating arenas around town that, by their spaciousness, informality, and snacky menus, sell themselves as youthful repairs, Petaluma is the one that addresses itself specifically to scions of the civilized. Sometimes the parents themselves come, unaccompanied by child, and they feel free to hang their jackets over the backs of their chairs. Petaluma occupies the no-man's-land heretofore known as Generation Gap.

The site of this coming together is a big, pink, L-shaped store arranged on a couple of levels, a good-size bar just inside the corner entrance, a pizza oven behind a counter at the elbow's inner turn. Big windows front on First Avenue and on East 73rd, great columns of faux marble rise through the space, and the black-and-white diamond pattern of the asphalt-tile floor and the vastly unrelated hangings on the walls partially undo the calm of the soft light—as does the insistent but not loud background music (now soft rock, now music of the thirties and forties), as does the alternately frenetic and becalmed action of the staff in the aisles.

On display near the pizza station are the makings of the antipasto misto Petaluma, and you submit yourself to your waitress's good will, permit her to assemble a plate according to her lights. Comes presently a lively assortment, slices of pungent salami and chunks of sautéed zucchini, a crunchy salad of white beans, cool rice dotted with bits of olive and sweet peas, roasted red peppers suffused with oil, more. Cold first courses of greater seriousness, however, must be ordered individually: smoked tuna, sliced thin and spread all across a good-size plate, adorned with fresh artichoke hearts and moistened with olive oil of vivid flavor; slivered fresh mushrooms and pungent arugula covered over with slices of hard, sharp Parmesan, nothing else on the plate but that good oil again; vitello tonnato, the pale veal under a lemony sauce that is dotted with capers, but as tuna sauces go, this is lemon sauce, the fish but a remoteness. As to that pollo Siamese, it probably hangs on in this foreign situation because of the peanut sauce served with it, which is at once fruity, of strong nut flavor, and fiery hot, for the chicken, though handsomely browned and glistening on its wood skewers, reveals little flavor of its own —the unlikely arugula garnish is probably just lost.

Lost also is the waiter who passes your table in search of his station. You stop him, ask, as a matter of information, whether half orders of pasta may be ordered. As "yes" or "no" would take too long, he suggests you discuss the subject with your own waiter. It is enough to get you thinking that Petaluma is where waiters go when they are fired from Elio's. Anyhow, no is the answer, and you begin dinner with a serving of spaghetti pescatore that could end it as well, firm pasta, clams and mussels in their shells, scallops and shrimp out of theirs, all fresh-tasting and all sweet (but for a bit of iodine in the crunchy shrimp), the herbed red sauce briny and stout. Two or three rice dishes are usually listed, sometimes risotto con porcini, the mound of moist grain earthy of the chunks of wild mushroom with which it is dotted—spooned-on cheese thickens and deepens the hefty dish. Bits of sharp and salty green olive are the life of the pizza quattro stagioni, the crackling circle of bread surfaced with glistening cheese and adorned with mushrooms and artichokes, thin slices of good browned ham over the top.

For your collection of buzzwords in unlikely places, consider the listing "polpa de granseole Maryland," crab cakes to you and not bad; fluffy, browned, crusted patties of the sweet seafood served with a red-pepper mayonnaise that is rich and spicy. The veal itself is the making of the piccata alla vernaccia, the pale and juicy meat roused to subtle but real life by the wine and shallots of its sauce and the herbs that cling to its surface. Four lamb chops reach you with their ribs extending beyond the rim of their plate, the eyes clustered at the center and overlaid with sautéed onions, mushrooms, and pungent little black olives, powerful flavors that do not obscure the strong meat.

The issue of whether "Thaitian vanilla bean cheesecake" is Thai or Tahitian remains unresolved even when you have eaten it, the standard stuff between a graham cracker crust and a slick white icing. The raspberries are a bit more than ripe in their winy zabaglione sauce. The chocolate cake is intense, but suffers for being cold at the center.

★★LA PETITE FERME

973 Lexington Avenue (near 70th Street)
LUNCH, MONDAY TO FRIDAY; DINNER, MONDAY TO SATURDAY. CLOSED SUNDAY.
Reservations: 249-3272.
Credit cards: AE, DC, MC, V.
Expensive.

Having redefined the "neighborhood restaurant" in terms that disregard cost, La Petite Ferme gets by on the custom of those who are indifferent to that factor. There are not so many of them that they may be relied on regularly to fill this restaurant, but the rent on the real estate occupied by the empty tables is taken care of by the premium built into the prices paid at the others. Anyway, this Farm provides value for the extra dollars. The food is better than at places with names like Mama Mia's or Maman Marmite, the service is more civilized, and the charms (by definition, neighborhood restaurants have charms) are more charming. 'Twas not ever thus. Upon a time La Petite was a minuscule (20-chair) place in the Village, and it was the rage, a destination, chichi, for in that tiny store was served the most elemental French food—that in the days when what was called "all those fancy sauces" (a/k/a haute cuisine) *was* French cooking in New York. This second incarnation is considerably larger than the original, it has shifted a couple of culinary steps away from the first store's Spartan cookery, and those moves toward normality account for the restaurant's altered status—no one remembers the last time anybody talked about this place.

This is a deep, soft-lit narrow room, dark carpeted, half timbered, furnished with bare tables, their thick wood tops sealed, the chairs around them those little upright things of wood dowels and straw, cushions on the seats, that are charming but dinky, not for the broad of thigh. The tables are set with matte-finish clay-white china (blue flowers painted on), with wildflowers in crockery pots, with white candles in big hurricane lamps, with plaid dishcloths for napkins. It is all *slightly* cluttered, every other table, it seems, tucked into a corner or turn of this somewhat compartmented room, which contributes to the restaurant's relaxed air. The place may be defined by what, on the upper East Side, it is not—it is not a Third Avenue Italian restaurant/saloon, or a celebrity showcase, or the snowy fantasy of the day's hottest restaurant architect. So it gets a nice crowd, albeit genteel.

As if in mockery of the canapes, at once elaborate and minuscule, to which many of New York's more ambitious restaurants these days treat you, here you are presented with a plate of potato chips, warm, crisp, salty, of real potato flavor, apparently just made. While you are working on this unlikely beginning, and considering whether it is cricket to ask for more, your waiter comes by with the wood-framed blackboards. One of them bears a list of white wines on the front, reds on the back. The other is the menu, and he holds it under his chin—the way a grammar school child presses a prize-winning drawing to his chest—while reciting (from memory!) the brief list, which changes from day to day. The mussels, however, seem always to be offered, and this is one of the increasingly rare places in which this inglorious mollusk is never rank, reaches you with all its clean flavor showing, the great mound of black shells in a thickened vinaigrette that makes a delicacy of the orange-tinted meats. Still, you do well to pass those up when you are offered also the shrimp with salmon quenelles, the shrimp, barely cooked, of the clearest, most elemental ocean sweetness, the warm pink dumplings light and of vivid salmon flavor, the two garnished with strands of red and green pepper in their rich herbed butter. But do not mistake those salmon quenelles for these so-called salmon medallions, a composition formed into a sausage within a crêpe, and served in slices in a yogurt sauce adorned with caviar—the sauce is fine, but the seafood is just an indeterminate solidity. The artichoke is carefully poached, the heart retains its good gritty texture, and it is nicely roused by the lemon sauce with which the hollowed vegetable is filled. Sometimes there is cauliflower soup, and this is mother's milk food, white and hot and homey, rich but not thick, livened by paprika, textured, chunks of the vegetable at the bottom of the bowl.

It is the custom of this place not to list lobster on the blackboard, but always to offer it, the waiter referring to it as a specialty. It is served in what the house calls a white butter sauce, which is light, delicately herbed, slightly winy, just the enrichment for this smallish, judiciously poached crustacean. Salmon yet again, this time slender pink fillets prettily set on a dark, olive-green sauce that is a buttery, well-seasoned purée of strong spinach. Those seafood dishes notwithstanding, the monkfish may be this kitchen's most notable accomplishment, for the meat of this swimmer is known for the flavor it lacks, while here the white fish—given as rôti of lotte—is crusted in the making, then served in a red-wine sauce bordelaise, which creates a lively complexity of textures and flavors. If the blanc de volaille au poivron et estragon is low on chicken flavor, that deficiency is offset by the heady tarragon-and-red-pepper sauce in which the crisped and juicy bird is served. You anticipate a steak when you order the filet de boeuf au madère, but the tender beef seems almost potted in its winy sauce—good food, but not what you expected.

First-class Brie is unobtainable on this side of the Atlantic, but the Brie served here, just a little runny, in a snowy crust, and of earthy flavor, is as close as you can come. The papaya sorbet tastes like papaya, the kiwi sorbet like a concentrated intensity that is an improvement on the fruit. The mixed berries reach you in the bowl of a big wine glass, over them a thick and smooth and liquory sauce sabayon. The strawberry tart is a triangle of pastry on which stand, in close rows, huge, utterly ripe strawberries—thick, stiff whipped cream is served with the tart.

★★★ PETROSSIAN

182 West 58th Street
LUNCH AND DINNER.
Reservations: 245-2214.
Credit cards: AE, DC, MC, V.
Very expensive.

For the more or less recherché foodstuffs with which it is specifically identified, this is the place. Part of the reason, of course, is that Petrossian is not merely a restaurant, but also the standardbearer of the Petrossian name and of the foods the Petrossian family produces, imports, distributes widely: black caviar and other fish roes, sturgeon and other smoked fish, foie gras. (You find other items on their menu, but almost no one comes here and fails at least to sample the specialties of the house.) Accordingly, what is put before you of those wares is impeccable, will tend to be recorded in your memory as exemplars by which you will judge those foodstuffs in other places—in, say, the Russian Tea Room, this establishment's natural competitor around the corner, which, for all its charms, cannot be counted on every time to serve up caviar like what you get here. Maybe no one sells the little black eggs to restaurants as carefully as Petrossian does to walkers-in off the street, and probably very few restaurants know all there is to know about handling the stuff, but those are not your problems, so when you get a yen for these goods, and there is a stack of large bills you are unable to launder, dinner at Petrossian will do much to finesse that problem.

With respect, however, to the physical restaurant, Petrossian's lure is identical to that appeal of caviar that has nothing to do with its quality, only with its luxe. Partly for that reason, comes here a foppy crowd of those who work as hard spending their money as making it. The restaurant is expensive, they figure it must be part of the good life, a conviction reinforced by the appointments: walls that are tinted mirrored glass or burled wood, a floor of polished granite, deep-pink drapes of silken gauze, panels of mink on the gray leather banquette, bronze statuary, flowers and gold-rimmed plates on the tables, and a sailing ship—the family emblem—embroidered into each of the carefully ironed napkins. You enter to a bar, nothing so vulgar as bottles on display behind it, to which passersby who have been unable to swing an impromptu table may repair for picnics of beluga, toast, and Mumm's. To your left is, how you say, the deli, the wares behind a counter, the counter behind red ropes. It offers, in addition to takeout, the paraphernalia—silver dishes, gold-colored caviar spatulas, and the like—by way of which Petrossian makes rite of the consumption of its victuals, and by way of which you may do the same in the privacy of your own rec room. Chez vous, however, you will probably have to do without the services of the Petrossian staff, gentlemen in mustard-colored jackets who seem to be chosen for the sauvity and weight of their continental accents.

Black caviar is the roe of sturgeons, and most of the world's supply comes from fish that swim in the Caspian Sea, Black Sea, rivers nearby. The kinds you encounter most often—beluga, osetra, sevruga, to put them in descending order of their cost—are named for the species of sturgeon from which they are taken. (A tiny quantity of pale "golden" caviar is also produced, from the species sterlet, but you will not find it on restaurant menus.) So-called pressed caviar is a compacture of roe, usually osetra or sevruga, that has been damaged—though its texture does not match that of the more expensive stuff, and though it is usually more heavily salted, there is something to be said for the saltier taste when the caviar is rolled in blinis. Though beluga is the most prestigious, you need not be shamefaced about ordering osetra or sevruga—the three are not, after all, grades. Beluga caviar is of the largest, palest-gray eggs, is the most subtly flavored. Osetra resembles it closely. Sevruga eggs are tiny, almost black, have the strongest flavor. What distinguishes all the caviar served here is its perfect texture, the clarity and freshness of its flavor, the utter absence of the fishiness you sometimes detect in restaurant caviar—which indicates imperfect storage somewhere between those Eastern waters and your table.

The best way to acquaint yourself with the varieties of black caviar is by way of what the house calls Les Années Folles (mad times), a $104 repast that begins with thirty grams each (a bit more than an oz.) of beluga, osetra, sevruga (which you spread on triangles of toasted white bread, a substance of so little character that it takes nothing from the caviars themselves), the flavors of which are marine essences, pure and primordial. You are then served pressed caviar with blinis, rather pallid wheat pancakes, to which you apply crème fraîche and then caviar, and which you then roll into cylinders that, if you have done your job neatly, you eat with your fingers. The binge involves one more self indulgence before dessert: smoked salmon, moist but not oily, of vivid fish flavor and subtle but unmistakable smokiness, the great circle of thin, pink meat, clinging to its cold plate, served only with that toast, no other garnishes, and it needs none. Other items of cured seafood on the menu: salmon roe, great red-orange globules, glistening and clinging to one another, of which you are served a dollop the size of a plump apricot set at the bottom of a round, thick-walled, straight-sided glass dish—these eggs are brinier than sturgeon roe, and their flavor is powerful even when smothered in crème fraîche and wrapped in blinis; cod roe, four ovoid dollops of the sticky, pale-pink stuff, strong but not really gamy—you may even detect a bit of sweetness under the salt surface of the flavor; smoked sturgeon, five substantial strips of the supple fish, at once smoky and soapy, the latter quality not a negative, just the closest approximation to the odd flavor of this singular swimmer; smoked trout, of which you are served the four skinned and boned pink quarters of a salmon trout reassembled in the shape of the whole fish— this is the most delicate smoked trout in town, and unlike what you get in many places, this meat retains its moisture, is almost fluffy; and smoked eel, briny and oily, the most vigorous of these items. Order what the menu refers to as a whole goose liver, and you are brought an amalgam cut from a loaf—you can only complain a little, for the cool liver is almost overwhelmingly oleaginous: meat as butter.

Petrossian also lists a substantial menu of more-or-less straight French food: a standard mousse of duck liver; a pâté of sweetbreads, encased in a flaky pastry with a crown of dark jelly, that is a little flat; lobster and scallops en croûte, the two, with spinach, between leaves of rather doughy pastry, and in a saffron sauce that does not rescue the merely fancy dish; roasted quails, their skins barely browned, but the meat of strong quail flavor, served with slices of tart apple in a brown sauce with white grapes—fancy food again.

Rich, stiff whipped cream and fresh berries are added to just about any dessert you order: the good crème brûlée, served unheated from the dessert cart, the custard light under its crackling top; the strawberry cheesecake, which is very fluffy for its richness; the pear tart, half of a firm, glistening poached pear set in a nutty almond cake; the mocha cream tart, intensely coffee-flavored pastry cream within layers of light, moist cake.

★★PIETRO'S

232 East 43rd Street
LUNCH, MONDAY TO FRIDAY; DINNER, MONDAY TO SATURDAY. CLOSED SUNDAY.
Reservations: 682-9760.
Credit cards: AE, DC.
Very expensive.

The anteroom just off the street is fresh and spiffy, and so you look twice at the brass sign. Both times it reads the same:

THIS PLACE

HAS

BEEN HERE

SINCE

MAY 1, 1932

The situation is cleared up a little when you pass into the main room, where there is another sign much like the first one, but different:

THIS PLACE

HAS

BEEN HERE

SINCE

JAN. 3, 1984

If the restaurant looks familiar, as if you have been coming to it for fifty years, be aware that it is not the physical surroundings you recognize, but the style. For when Pietro's moved its fifty-year-old steakhouse—from the second and third stories of an ancient structure on the corner of 45th and Third to this big street-level spread a few blocks to the southeast—it did not undertake to replicate the props of the original set. It could have been done, but there are not, for example, any choice windowside tables next to false windows. That fondly remembered steamy closet of an open kitchen, complete with perspiring crew, is gone. Even the density and noise have been left behind. Only the spirit, much of the staff, and the food made the trip intact. The customers followed on their own.

Though the new quarters are unlike the old, the differences are not a function of the passage of five decades between their inceptions. Whether by design or mistake, what Pietro's has created is a brand-new Depression steakhouse, one that could have been put together just this way in the days when alcoholism was a federal offense, not a disease. The place is all rough plaster and dark wood, with rows of white-linened tables surrounded by simple chairs. These are on two levels, the only dimly contemporary note, and if you like to think that way, you may choose to believe that the two-level layout is a remote reference to the two stories of the old place. The engravings on the walls are a gesture to the received notion that the blank spots on restaurant walls ought to be occupied by framed objects. There is a bar up front (probably installed the moment Repeal was ratified) and curtains on the front window. Your host is cordial even if he does not know you. And the waiters, in their dark-blue linen jackets, are courtly and professional —they know the menu, they hear you talking, and they rarely make mistakes. You may well conclude that this place will be at this site until the next thirties. And if things continue here the way they have been going since the days when Charles Curtis was Vice President, the next century will see Pietro's populated by well-fed burghers with their wives and descendants, white-shirted executives with their customers, and guys from the nearby *News* with girls from the nearby *News*.

None of them is preoccupied with thoughts of "nouvelle" or "nouveau," or even of "northern" or "Italian" or "cuisine," or, most assuredly, of "balsamic vinegar," when they commence their dinners with, say, great sheets of strong, dark red, fat-rimmed, and gamy ham draped over slices of melon that, they hardly notice, are less than utterly ripe. They do just as well with what is listed, under salads, as "Chopped," a huge, lively mélange of onions and tomatoes, lettuce and watercress, and strands of salty anchovy, all in a tart and forceful dressing. The Caesar, however, is no match for the Chopped—it seems to be prepared in large batches during the course of the evening, not mixed to order, and your allotment may be somewhat wilted, having been in its dressing for a time. Eight littlenecks are most of the so-called Clams sauté, a bit of breading and a pool of parsleyed and shallot-sweetened butter the balance—the clams are fresh, but this still comes off only as fun food.

Like most Steak Row steakhouses, this one has an Italian side, so there is pasta. Many of the noodle dishes are the ones you would have found in New York Italian restaurants in the days when cars had running boards. If, for example, before you die, you want one last dish of spaghetti and meatballs, think of Pietro's as the place that is holding an order with your name on it. Until then, you are better off with the spaghetti in white clam sauce, a standard version of the familiar dish, the firm pasta mingled with lots of fresh clams in a buttery brine that is loaded with garlic and parsley. But there are also rarities in this department, including an exceptional ziti dish in which the ribbed tubular noodles are mingled with minced broccoli and much garlic, and lubricated with lots of butter—you strengthen the dish by adding ground cheese.

You get a slab of swordfish here the size of an art book—it is fresh, browned, glistens of butter on the outside and of its own moisture on the inside. A two-and-a-half pound lobster will cleanse you of $35, and you can get one here that is truly broiled—not steamed and then broiled. But there are Steak Row places where that big bet is more likely to be a winner than Pietro's—the place has been known to give lobsters a bit too much fire. Lots of chicken dishes, but you will do well to note the item that calls attention to itself (1) by being more expensive than the others and (2) by carrying the company name. Such is Chicken à la Pietro, great meaty chunks of the crisped bird (they have real chicken flavor) buried in a tangle of sautéed onions (blackened a little and sweet) and strands of crunchy green pepper. The veal chop is hearty, big and browned and juicy, but you are sometimes served a loin chop here, not a rib chop, which is certainly not what you had in mind. The lamb chops, however, do not disappoint—you get a pair of three-rib chops, the nuggets of red meat moist and of high lamb flavor within their charred surfaces and rims of crisped fat. You get just about perfect broiled steaks here, that is, the meat is fibrous, tender, blood-juicy, accurately prepared—and handsomely charred in the process. But even Pietro's cannot bring back the prewar steer, and as in all steakhouses, the beef is sometimes a little low on its essential ingredient: beefiness.

The French fried onions are dark, crinkly, and sweet. But, as you know, meat's real other half is the potato: the shoestrings are crisp, fresh fried, have real potato flavor; the lyonnaise are big deep-fried disks under moist slivers of sautéed onion, but the au gratins are the big winner, the dice of crisp tuber judiciously seasoned in their rich and creamy sauce, the cheese topping artfully browned, pully, and a little sharp.

The standard cheesecake is sweet, weighty, slightly vanilla flavored, browned on top, cool. The powerful zabaglione is hot, winy, fluffy. Rum cake, fruit, and ice-cream items are the balance of the dessert list.

★★PINOCCHIO

170 East 81st Street
LUNCH AND DINNER.
Reservations: 650-1513.
Credit cards: AE, DC.
Beer and wine.
Expensive.

Formerly an unmarked one-room hole-in-the-wall that often went unfound even after an intense search, Pinocchio is now a two-room hole-in-the-wall that often goes unfound even after an intense search. Certain charms, however, were lost when Pinocchio was doubled. It is, for example, no longer necessary, at certain tables, to rise and stand aside when the front door is opened. But, as ever, even when you have found the outside, you will have difficulty making out the inside. Pinocchio is dimly lit, and it is somber within its dimness—burlap curtains, brick or dark-brown walls, a deep-maroon stamped-tin ceiling. Some illumination is produced by feeble electric lights that are enclosed within hanging flora of colored glass—clusters of grapes and the like. On close inspection you will discover that there is white linen on the tightly assembled tables, terra-cotta bas reliefs on the walls, as well as photographs and—this is important—venerable Metropolitan Opera Company bills. The proprietor, you see, is a devotee of Italian vocal art, and, early and late, and sometimes during the shank of the dinner hour itself, the earnest beseechments of legendary Italian tenors quicken the air. Sometimes Mimi departs with the last diner.

This is a busy place, the kind in which spaciousness is sacrificed for the delights of dense conviviality. There is always room for one more at these tables. And if, in the enlarged establishment, the hired help that has been added to the original family staff is occasionally amateurish (it is a rare night when you ask for nothing twice), the jolly crowd does not think that matters much.

Carpaccio—just-cut thin slices of raw beef—is adorned with a tart green sauce of capers and herbs. Bresaola—gamy, air-dried beef—reaches you under a film of good olive oil. Genoa salami—the hard, purple sausage, fatted and garlicked—is served hot, under a generous storm of strong grated cheese. Though you find two sautéed mushroom caps a meager apportionment, these are fresh and crunchy, and their seasoned mushroom stuffing is of intense flavor under its toppings of hot, pully cheese. Around town the word "crostini" usually refers to some variant of chopped liver on toast. Here the word is used with the modifier "nostri," so do not be surprised when what you get is a hot open-face sandwich—a layer of anchovies, another of strips of red pimento, and a top one of melted cheese on the crusty slice of bread.

White and dark-green noodles, slivers of veal and strong ham, fresh peas and carrots, all in a buttered wine broth, make a paglia e fieno unlike others you regularly find. The hefty tubes of pasta called penne and a sauce of cream and cheese, with capers and bits of bacon, go as penne palermitana, which is just as rare. The house primavera is made with fresh vegetables and perfectly al dente spiral noodles (fusilli), but the dish lacks the surprising quality of this establishment's best pasta.

No fish is listed on the menu, but some is usually offered: sometimes salmon puttanesca, the pink fish in a light tomato sauce sharpened with olives; on occasion poached salmon, in a broth dotted with fresh vegetables. Both dishes are good, but would benefit from fresher-tasting fish. And sometimes there is trout poached in red wine—the fish is served in a smooth, buttered, and somewhat tart sauce prepared from the cooking liquid.

The lemon chicken—white meat from a mature bird—has much chicken flavor and, happily, nothing candylike in the lemon sauce. Another lemon sauce, this one frothy, on the veal piccata—the carefully sautéed meat is adorned with disks of lemon and much fresh parsley. The restaurant's saltimbocca has always been elegant—thin slices of veal and ham in a delicate white-wine sauce. Among the most pungent dishes in the place is the liver torinese—an herbed and creamy sauce, thick with bits of bacon, binds the slivers of dark organ meat.

What Pinocchio calls caffè nonno you would call a glass of zabaglione with espresso poured over it—dessert and coffee for the price of dessert alone. When the zabaglione is cold, it is thickened with whipped cream and served over ripe berries—you cannot fault it. Moscovita di ciocolata is not exactly a chocolate mousse—more like strong chocolate ice cream under thick whipped cream. On that order, but more elaborate, is the budino al caffè—mocha mousse studded with bits of chocolate and served, in a sundae glass, under whipped cream. When you come to the bottom of the glass, you find a macaroon soaked in coffee and chocolate. The melon in raspberry-brandy sauce is rousing.

The menu is changed often, so you will not always find what you seek.

★★IL PONTE VECCHIO

206 Thompson Street (near Bleecker Street)
LUNCH AND DINNER.
Reservations: 228-7701.
Credit cards: AE.
Medium priced.

Asphalt-tile floors, light- and dark-tan walls (a random assortment of art and posters thereon), rows of tables occupied by locals in casual clothes—drinking, mostly, carafe wine and enjoying the low prices and good food. Those who are not eating are at the tight little bar in the front room, drinking, probably waiting for a table to open up. You will find little here but basics, and nothing to complain about.

You will find fresh raw clams that are tiny, sweet, cold. You may also have them as clams posillipo, a massive mound of the steamed littlenecks in a hot red broth, herbed and oily. (You can have fresh mussels made the same way.) You will find shrimp oregan-ati, big sweet ones, albeit only three, in a strongly salted oil that is flavored with oregano and much lemon.

Everybody orders the unlisted linguine alla Johnny, the al dente noodles in a peppery red sauce that is thick with shrimp, fish, great chunks of plum tomato. The carbonara is creamy, sharpened with Italian bacon, made fragrant with fresh parsley. Amatriciana is this establishment's simplest red sauce—it is served on thin spaghetti, it is aggressively seasoned, and it is superb when it is made thick with ground cheese. The manicotti is elemental, little more than ricotta cheese stuffed into pasta pillows and baked in tomato sauce—it arrives sizzling.

No bass on the menu, but it is usually present in the kitchen. You may have yours broiled, touched with thyme, moistened with a light, lively tomato sauce. The zuppa di pesce is a bristling platter of mussels, squid, shrimp, fish, all in a briny red broth. The place obtains chicken that tastes like chicken, converts it into chicken Ponte Vecchio—slices of boned white meat under red peppers in a pale wine sauce. The same good bird goes into the chicken cacciatore, in which the smooth and winy red sauce is thick with mushrooms, onion, garlic. When rabbit is available, the pale and tender meat is served in a sauce much like that one. The veal paillard is of veal pounded out to the size of a big platter and grilled until it is blackened a little but still moist—you bring it to lively life by squeezing on lemon. The veal francese is lightly crusted with its eggy batter, lemoned, parsleyed—a delicate dish. Indelicacy is the name of the veal chop. It is not listed, but is usually on hand—the house makes it many ways, but in all cases you get a chop the size of a club, juicy inside, charred outside, of an unmistakable sufficiency.

The provolone will open your eyes and clear your sinuses. The pleasantly wet Italian cheesecake is dotted with black raisins. The hot zabaglione is frothy, loaded with marsala.

★★POSITANO

250 Park Avenue South (at 20th Street)
LUNCH, MONDAY TO FRIDAY; DINNER, MONDAY TO SATURDAY. CLOSED SUNDAY.
Reservations: 777-6211.
Credit cards: AE, MC, V.
Expensive.

Word in the press has it that one of the powers behind this place made his mark as a director of television commercials. This is confirmed by your waitress, who also tells you that when the fellow shows up for work here, he goes at once to the book, to peruse the list of reservations—and marks with a big asterisk any name he recognizes as eminent. What puzzles her, she goes on, is that then he does no more, that the celebs are granted no special favor. You suggest that the man is just reassuring himself, keeping score of his importance, that one who has taken the TV-spot road to the top is, willy-nilly, doomed always to wonder if he could have got there on the legit. She looks at you as if you are deranged.

Of course, making a winning restaurant—these days anyway—does no more to firm the ego than does making a sixty-second movie to sell another man's poison. The populace warms to a restaurant for the same reason it guzzles Pepsi—because it is told to. The poor restaurateur does not know whether he is loved for his restaurant or his publicity. And when he is himself a graduate of the hyping game, the dilemma is garnished with a twist of irony. Too bad, for Positano could have succeeded on its merits alone—the place is spiffy, the food is good, and (do not discount this) the prices are a bit lower than in many of the other spots around town that were conceived with chichi in mind.

Though the place is a great big cube of a room, two tall stories high and well lighted, it avoids the day's fashionable starkness. This is accomplished in part by the colors chosen for the shiny surfaces of its walls and massive columns—very pale coral, and very pale, *pale* green; and in part by the material chosen for the windows (walls of glass, really) on Park and on 20th Street—they are hung with a filmy gauze, which is pleated and softly lit. You enter to the corner of a street-level L, tables and booths in the legs to your left and right. Within that angle, two higher levels have been installed: A few steps up is the bar, the centerpiece of the place, the handsome counter, of dark green marble squares, framed in pale wood, the stools occupied by those who are patiently waiting—for a table, or for the appropriate stranger; a few steps farther up, and you are on the top deck, a row of tables along the back-wall banquette and a handful of additional ones along the brink, from which you may look down at the bar and at the often hectic scene all around it. That pale wood is repeated in the upholstered chairs and the unlinened tables—in the latter it frames a slick pea-green composition surface that some observers have taken for marble, but which is in fact something euphemistically known as "poured marble." Poured marble, you understand, is to marble as pig Latin is to Latin.

A sprightly thing much like a salade Niçoise is given as "Insalata di Positano." In it the *canned* tuna manages to be quite inoffensive among the balls of firm potato, slivers of black or green olive, strands of scallion, and an abundance of tart capers, all strewn with fresh, fragrant basil, and moistened with this restaurant's silken olive oil. Less familiar is this artichoke dish, cuscinetti di carciofi, in which the fresh sections of heart, the tender part of the leaves attached, are dipped in batter and fried—the sweet root taste is vivid within the browned surfaces, and the hot morsels are cleverly garnished with lightly dressed tomatoes under fresh basil, and with cool mozzarella.

Half orders of pasta are not prepared (and there is a $1 charge for splitting a full order), so bring with you someone whose pasta tastes are like your own, and have this penne con melanzane, in which the hefty tubes of noodle, firm but not tough, are in a dense, potently seasoned tomato sauce that is sharp with charred eggplant and heady with still more of this establishment's beloved basil—ground cheese fortifies the vibrant food. You order the linguine alla giudea, and if the night is a busy one, you may find that you can no more twirl the slender strands than you can wind chopsticks—and the sauce, of bacon, escarole, and black olives, reveals no evidence of the first and little flavor of the second. But if you come here only once, you will not choose pasta from this part of the menu at all, you will have instead the risotto con porcini, the hot mush of firm rice powerfully flavored of the profound stock in which it was cooked—the dark, enriched grain is redolent of the nuggets of wild mushroom with which it is studded.

The grilled lobster is itself flawless, firm, moist but not wet, sweet of its oceanic flavor, but its breading, which is crisped on the surface, is dull and mushy in the cavities into which it has been stuffed. The swordfish steak is half an inch thick, almost as big as the plate on which it is served, mahogany striped of the grill on which it was broiled, and fresh—on it, as on a heraldic field, you find two snow peas and a rich, dark-red sundried tomato. The carefully broiled snapper is just as fresh, and its flavor is potentiated by the vinegar and mint with which it is prepared. Skip the veal chop, for though it is nicely sautéed, its sauce—thick with little pickles, pickled onions, and nuggets of cucumber—defeats the subtle meat. Have instead the rabbit—chunks and slices of the moist, browned game under a mound of soft, slivered celery and onions. A couple of nicely roasted little quails, browned and juicy and of strong flavor, reach you gleaming in their smooth, fennel-flavored sauce.

At Positano you do well to conclude your dinner with salad—the place gets good tomatoes and serves them, variously, with strong anchovies, sharp onions, a decent fontina cheese, always the fresh basil, and a dressing of first-class oil. The sweet desserts are just sweets, among them the "tart bebé," a liquored white cake with custard at the center and a candied cherry on top; and the tirami su, an obvious, heavily rummed, layered thing of thick cheese, nuts, and much sugar. The ricotta cheesecake is sturdy but not heavy, sweet, vaguely fruited.

★ PRIMAVERA

1578 First Avenue (at 82nd Street)
DINNER.
Reservations: 861-8608.
Credit cards: AE, DC, MC, V.
Very expensive.

All money is fungible, even old and new, brands of it that have more in common than just their interchangeability. Though new money is spent in search of status, the old on its preservation, in those respects neither is disbursed with any discrimination. Staid solidity is what lures old money here, while the new pursues the old. Which is not to say that Primavera is without merit as an eating place, rather that its success is a function mainly of its success: having got away for as long as it has with selling food (at wondrous prices) that is only occasionally better than very reliable (though never less), it now merits the highest of all restaurant ratings: unquestionability. The place is packed nightly with folks who, simply by being here, are satisfied that their evening is well spent. Watch them, note how little attention they pay to what they eat, and yet how content they are, how certain of themselves. Dinner at Primavera is irreproachable, like getting to your feet for the playing of the national anthem. The restaurant is a safe house, a place where you may turn off your competitive alert. Fridays and Saturdays, it is thick with those from across the rivers, Sundays with a bankerly and lawyerly Upper East Side set, though every night at least some members of both opposing factions are on hand, the outlanders in molded hair, jewelry, padded shoulders, and seashore tans, the locals, often present in family gatherings, notable less for what they wear than for the consistency of dress among the generations, the sons and grandsons, daughters-in-law and girlfriends, like the presiding parents themselves at these upright rituals, one and all models in Brooks Brothers ads.

It is a carpeted, hushed, clubby space in which they are all so comfortable, the wood-beamed walls faced with coppery silk on one side of the room, with handsome brick on the other. The windows are hung with lace curtains, and there are huge bursts of flowers on their sills. On the white-linened tables there are pots of flowers in little baskets, gold-rimmed service plates with the restaurant's insigne, in gold, at their centers. The tables are surrounded by graceful side chairs with seats upholstered in apricot suede. You almost take Primavera for a tasteful installation that has aged gracefully to its present condition. But the restaurant gives itself away, very much in the manner of the man who rents a tuxedo and then wears it with his yellow shoes. For after the architect's work was finished, the proprietors apparently took over, hauled a big load of art up here probably from the Washington Square Outdoor Art Exhibit (in, one likes to imagine, a station wagon), and proceeded to hang the hilarious stuff all over the walls. The customers do not complain. Neither do the members of the staff, who, from busboys to the host himself, are in formal black-and-whites—with black shoes.

What with fresh ingredients—in dishes prepared just when you order them—you almost never get a bad plate of food here. But if, for example, you have had seafood salads in some of the city's jauntier Italian restaurants, you will find Primavera's as forgettable as it is unimpeachable, the abundant serving of fresh squid, shrimp, scallops in a dressing that is barely lemoned, let alone garlicked—you expect this dish to be rousing, instead it is almost weighty, more like what you want later in your dinner. But then there is this hot first course of sautéed shrimp, a perfect simple thing, the big crustaceans sweet and crunchy, roused by the herbs, lemon, and white wine in which they were done. If it is mushroom time, your waiter brings to your table a basket of big Italian wild mushrooms, encourages you to have some of them grilled as a first course. Sound advice, for they are meaty, earthy, and they are done in oil of heady flavor, though the promised garlic is at best an obscurity.

The pasta list is led, of course, by capelli d'angelo primavera, and, sure enough, this is the quintessential Primavera dish, thin spaghetti that is judiciously cooked and firm, utterly fresh vegetables, and little in the way of vigor—still, good food, especially when plenty of cheese is spooned on. You figure that there will be more life in what the chef is inspired to prepare especially for the day, so you go for a whimsical spaghetti dish made with arugula and sauce marinara, only to find that little has been done to give either component cause to do business with the other. Though blenderized to a creamy puree, the house pesto is powerfully fragrant of its fresh basil—you accept lots of grated Parmesan, as much for its texture as for its pungent flavor.

It is perhaps unfair to describe the grilled baby salmon as hospital food, but the pale-pink fish, barely touched with oregano, moistened with oil, and delicately browned, for all its freshness, seems designed principally to exacerbate no condition. If you must have seafood as a main course, that yummy shrimp appetizer is available in a full portion. And when soft-shell crabs are in season, this place gets good ones—the shells barely perceptible—and browns them handsomely. Additional perfect and perfectly harmless sustenance may be taken by way of the pollo alla forestale, juicy chicken just out of the sauté pan, plus the vegetables, mushrooms, and ham with which it was done—those promising ingredients notwithstanding, the dish is merely a model of inoffensiveness. Similarly the uccelletti alla finanziere, veal rolls stuffed with spinach and prosciutto in mushroom sauce—you do wish there were cheese in the package and/or that the roulades had been browned before they were finished and/or that they were served in something more vigorous than this smooth, pallidly seasoned, creamy tomato sauce (it would be perfect in some other setting), which is thick with mushrooms that seem never to have been sautéed. But then there is this veal chop valdostana, the huge eye of meat bifurcated latitudinally, a layer of ham inserted, but, despite what the menu says, no cheese—not a shortcoming, for the thick browned chop, bursting with pink moisture, is invigorated by quite another mushroom sauce, this one rich and winy. If you come here in springtime, when baby goat is offered, that may well be the item to have. If you hesitate at the idea of eating goat, be assured that a baby goat is nothing like an old goat. Its meat is, in fact, sweet and tender, and as if to establish that the house is not hidebound to culinary gentility, you are provided with a mammoth serving, a veritable hillock of the charred nuggets of dark meat.

If, to this point, dinner has had a sedative effect, some aged Parmesan with one of the brightly dressed house salads will rouse you. The apple tart is not bad, though you wish it were not sealed in syrup. The St. Honoré is a complex layered affair involving custard, whipped cream, chocolate cream, candied fruit, good pastry—it is notable for its freshness. The chocolate cake is light, but not especially intense. Many of the regulars conclude their dinners with the fruit plate—sliced apples and pears, bunches of grapes in a couple of colors, chunks of various melons, orange slices, all mounded over cracked ice. The fruit plate does not include berries, which are available separately—sometimes wild strawberries from far-off places served with good whipped cream.

★★PRIMOLA

1226 Second Avenue (near 65th Street)
LUNCH, MONDAY TO FRIDAY; DINNER, DAILY.
Reservations: 758-1775.
Credit cards: AE.
Medium priced.

New York's love affair with Italian food might have dwindled decades ago were it not regularly restimulated by new settings in which to carry on. In recent years, moreover, the life expectancy of the romance has been extended by a fresh style of Italian cookery, one that makes fewer demands on an aging lover than did the weighty stuff that used to obtain. About as far as you can come from, say, a 1950's Little Italy spaghetti-and-meatball store is Primola, which in its light look is as remote as California, in its food as distant from the past as a bottle of clear, bubbly prosecco from the inky chianti—it was made of tree bark and bugs, and you drank it ice cold—that used to be sold in green bottles wrapped in straw.

All is sunny, pale wood and cream, snowy linen and abundant light, rows of tables and chairs, a print or watercolor on any panel of wall not occupied by a light fixture that is a glowing semihemisphere, greenery in the corners. Two elements somewhat undo the openness and simple comfort of the place: The area around the bar, to which you enter, is under a lowered, hard-surfaced section of the ceiling, and as the crowd waiting for tables is often dense (Primola overbooks, and a wait of thirty minutes past the hour of your reservation is not unheard of), you are subjected, while you wait, to a piercing din; and the rear of the restaurant has for some reason been raised a couple of steps, creating a low-ceilinged somewhat segregated room that is apart from the airy commodiousness of the rest of the place. Withal, Primola is comfortable, convivial of the crowd that fills it.

Along one short side of the bar stands a counter, its top a slab of pink marble, on it a display of the dishes that, taken together, make up what is listed as Gli Apri Bocca di Franco, which is not so literally translated as "A selection from the chef's buffet of seasonal vegetables." With a bottle of balsamic vinegar, another of vividly green olive oil, arrives your crowded plate, on it slices of browned eggplant, deeply oiled, overlaid with mozzarella cheese, circles of tomato, fresh and fragrant basil; great mushroom caps filled with a spicy stuffing of crunchy vegetables; another vegetable stuffing, this one packed around sweet mussels in their half-shells; firm white beans mingled with minced scallion greens and overlaid with circles of red onion; a pungent caponata, mostly eggplant, accented with cracked black olives and sour capers; morsels of cheese that have been marinated and enriched in seasoned oil—all the items stand apart from one another, for their components are fresh, retain their individuality. A couple of lively first courses the like of which you do not find elsewhere: thin leaves of raw salmon, marinated with fennel, their surfaces whitened a little by the treatment, their interiors red and juicy, the pool of marinade on your plate bright and tangy; and filetto di vitello Harris, little sheets of pale, tender veal arranged over leaves of bitter radicchio, strewn with arugula, and moistened with a mustard dressing that is at once rich and sharp.

Have pasta here once, and you will do well to make it spaghetti ai frutti di mare, the very thin noodles in a red sauce—of exceptional briny vigor—that is dotted with fresh clams and mussels in their shells, crunchy shrimp, slivers of squid. Order pasta a second time, and you will do almost as well with the spinach dumplings, the soft morsels, melted cheese between them, arranged on a tomato sauce that is tart and a little creamy —ground Parmesan rouses this dish. Spinach again, this time in the one rice dish listed, risotto verde, the great mound of buttered grain bright green of the pureed spinach with which it has been blended—once again, add enough ground cheese and the dish becomes heady.

Little in the way of finfish on the printed bill of fare, but sometimes the house has on hand baby snapper, the fillets of white fish firm, fresh, moistened and powerfully flavored by an herbed and winy sauce from the pan in which it was sautéed. What goes as pollo al balsamico e rosmarino is a dozen chunks of chicken, browned and glistening, mingled with slivers of garlic, infused with the herbs and sweet vinegar of its sauce. The veal paillard is less than gloriously browned, rather too thoroughly cooked through. There is much more of interest in these unusual medallions of blood-juicy beef—Parmesan cheese has been melted over them to dramatic effect, and they are garnished with braised and bitter endives.

There is fruit, but little in the way of cheese. The handsomely browned cheesecake is touched with chocolate, is almost puddinglike in its good, weighty wetness. The lemon meringue pie is a little sweet and vividly sour on its dark and crumbly pastry.

★ PROVENCE

38 MacDougal Street (near Prince Street)
LUNCH AND DINNER. CLOSED MONDAY.
Reservations: 475-7500.
Credit cards: AE.
Medium priced.

You approach the book, and your French-accented host, who guards it, turns to give you his attention, when—the phone rings. The caller, who wishes to reserve a table, is put on hold ten seconds into the transaction so that another caller may be asked to wait please before he makes, as it turns out, a cancellation, during which exchange the phone, you guessed it, rings, this unseen supplicant desirous of switching his eight-thirty to nine-thirty ("Can you make it ten?"), a discussion interrupted by a caller who...

You assume that when all this began the principals wondered which of their partners made the deal with Satan, since what started out, by the look of it, as a stab at a living—on an investment in, solely, the key to the door—has become the kind of success from which one ordinarily wakes up. For this is the former Gordon's, where a number of enterprises of that name failed, and in this revival, in which little more than the walls have been retained, even less has been added, surely nothing that resonates to the new name. A couple of airy chandeliers, the big bar, much carved-wood paneling, and tall paned windows on MacDougal Street are front-room holdovers from the original clubby installation. But the upper plaster walls are filmed—smeared, actually—with ivory-colored paint that appears to be running, as are the walls of the densely tabled back room (unadorned except for a grossly pitted gray chair rail), while the so-called garden beyond it, a trellised urban yard with a fountain at the center, is much as it was as the main attraction of the predecessors. Throughout, the tables are covered with white butcher paper, the chairs are dinky, the crowd is noisy, the waiters, in jeans, white aprons, white shirts with four-in-hands, thump through like the driven, feed hundreds each night before looking up from their tasks to breathe.

All the fuss is ostensibly about these blunt renditions of the food of southernmost

France, among them: a hot fish soup, brothlike and of strong, almost gamy fish flavor—in it a garlic-smeared crust—that rather loudly reminds you of soups that made you sweat in Marseilles; a so-called brandade d'Avignon, a hot version, made with potatoes, of the garlic-flavored salt-cod paste that lacks the coarse elementality of the usual cool article; a gâteau d'aubergines that is a layered and drab-colored eggplant thing incorporating two strata more colorful than the others, a red one of sautéed peppers, a green one of spinach, the entire construct thoroughly oiled and of vividly seasoned vegetable flavor; a tepid pissaladière that is a rectangle of chewy bread spread with a pulpy onion paste and adorned with six black olives, tiny and strong, and a single glistening anchovy; and these tartines de roquefort, a couple of thick triangles of toasted French bread liberally coated with a paste of the Roquefort—the cheese is softened with butter and a little brandy, made nubbly with chopped walnuts.

The printed—well, scrawled and photocopied—menu lists five dishes that are served only one day each week, one of them Friday's bouillabaisse, a hot, vigorous, and well-oiled version, thick with chunks of fish, many mussels, a few shrimp, and served with bread crusts that are spread with a heady garlic sauce. Sunday there is couscous, a rare presentation thereof in that the stewing broth, traditionally served separately, reaches you in the kind of steel pouring pot that holds the milk for coffee on diner counters—otherwise this is but a copious statement of the familiar idea, chickpeas and root vegetables, chunks of meat and of fowl, everything cooked too far, but well before the point of total defeat, and mounded over a hillock of the couscous grains, all of which you moisten with the broth from that creamer and invigorate with a hot paste served on the side. The word aioli refers to a kind of mayonnaise in which garlic is incorporated, but it denotes also a variable dish served with it, the variation here made up of steamed cod, florets of broccoli and cauliflower plus slices of blanched tomato, among other vegetables, and quarters of hard-cooked egg, the parts arranged in a circle around a ramekin of the rich and heady mayo—the elements are fine, amount really to an amusing means of enjoying the contents of that ramekin. The rabbit is coarse-breaded and greasy in its thick mustard sauce. The rare-roasted lamb is many slices of good meat within a ring of pungent spinach—the potent dish is garnished with limp ratatouille. The tender and accurately prepared steak is not of the tastiest beef, and the French fries served with it have been fried, fried, and refried, have not only the shape but the texture of matchsticks.

For dessert, you will do well with the crème brûlée, which though sometimes more than browned on top, actually charred, is fluffy. Your fruit sherbet may be moistened, for an extra charge, with liquor of the same fruit. The tart tatin, though of good caramelized-apple flavor, is mushy. And the terrine d'orange, a slice cut from a loaf that is a chunky compacture of denatured orange, is in a white-chocolate sauce that surely cannot restore what has been pointlessly lost.

This is SoHo, but not the SoHo of trendy painters and their commission retailers, rather of corporate and professional drudges by day, self-consciously self-styled swingers by night—that one may eat here rather cheaply is much of what lures them.

★ PRUNELLE

18 East 54th Street
LUNCH, MONDAY TO FRIDAY; DINNER, DAILY.
Reservations: 759-6410.
Credit cards: AE, DC, MC, V.
Very expensive.

A designer's restaurant, one in which nothing was held back, and yet New York has never quite taken it up. The problem is not the food at the price—many lesser places are more popular—rather that for all the luxe of this interior, and for all the warmth of its coloring, it is but a display of itself. Prunelle does not embrace you, rather it shows itself off to you, demands your attention, competes with you. Even when the restaurant is suffering from one of its frequent spells of the quiets, you get the feeling, toward the end of dinner, that it is time to go someplace where you can talk. The installation even fails at what it undertakes. The walls have been faced with burled wood that is the color of certain Cremonese violins and as highly polished as a new car, and you are meant to be overwhelmed, but the ceilings are simply too low for the wood to achieve its intended imposing sweep, and the placement here and there of great bursts of brilliantly colored flowers before glinting rectangular mirrors, though very pretty, fail as jewels on the gown, diminish the effect that unlimited honey might otherwise achieve. For the rest, there are dun-colored carpeting and a grape-colored banquette, comfortable armchairs with sloping arms around the big, well-spaced, white-linened tables, courteous gentlemen in formals cruising the aisles.

The only thing for it is a patron in every seat, a crowd to warm the place in a way the appointments do not. But they will not keep coming back for the likes of this marinated seafood, three little mounds, of sliced lobster, scallops, minced shrimp, each in a different vegetable context, none of them a clear expression of itself, the cold sautéed mushrooms at the center of the plate and the cold artichoke heart they are mounded over equally devoid of flavor, the thick herbed dressing no help. Similarly the gravlax, which, though prettily served as a great dark-pink floret, is without liveliness or fishiness, sweetness or tartness, is merely tender, supple meat of a certain dim familiarity. You do somewhat better with what is given as salade "Charlie," the principal fault of which is that the disparate ingredients are all at different temperatures—warm grilled scallops, strands of tepid chicken, ice cold greens, wild mushrooms at room temperature—pine nuts, bits of red pepper, and minced chives make the dressing lively, and while it is certainly not essential that every ingredient of a dish be as cool or as warm as every other, in this instance each mouthful is a disconcerting surprise after every previous one. All of which matters not at all, for when you come here you simply order the snails, served with "leurs oeufs," which is to say "their eggs," the snails plump, tender, a little resilient too, arranged as if pouring out of a puff pastry cornucopia (which you wish were flakier), everything set in a dark, herbed, and winy sauce that is thick with minced vegetables and with hundreds of the tiny eggs, their presence a nice nubbliness.

Nowadays, when you have become accustomed to the charms of salmon cooked rare, it is something of a comedown to encounter a steak of this fish that lacks the promising red blush at its center. That aside, the darne de saumon is utterly fresh and certainly not overcooked in its herbed and buttery sauce. A bit of overcooking is, however, the problem with the lobster, for the chunks of sweet meat, buried in noodles of three different colors and varying widths, is less than juicy, though the pink and honeylike shellfish sauce that moistens the seafood and the pasta and the surrounding vegetables does much

287

to redeem. In this self-consciously fancy place, the main course the house titles after itself, poularde Prunelle, is a homey one, a crusty and vigorously seasoned potato pancake, upon it a browned breast of chicken that is redolent of the flavor of chicken fat, crunchy walnut halves on that, the whole in a dark and winy sauce—sturdy food. Usually there is game, sometimes venison, the slices of rare meat—marinated, earthy of its marinade—arranged around the sides of a mound of buttery wild rice, cranberries and a fruity currant sauce its good foils.

For some reason apples and kiwis are shown with the cheese, but when you request pears, it turns out that good ones are hidden away somewhere in the kitchen, can be brought to you peeled and sliced. Stilton, Roquefort, a rich and creamy reblochon, and heady goat cheeses are offered. After the cheese you will have little interest in the cheesecake, which turns out to be the usual thing, albeit purpled by the stewed blueberries in which it is served. The soufflé Prunelle is a blob of soufflé, bits of raspberry embedded in its skinlike browned surface, whole raspberries all around, the sweet sauce hot and lemony. Withal, the apple tart is the dessert to have, as much a pie as a tart, the bottom pastry dark, the top one pale and tender, between them myriad flakes of crisp, tart fruit interleaved with nut slivers.

★★QUATORZE

240 West 14th Street
LUNCH, MONDAY TO FRIDAY; DINNER, DAILY.
Reservations: 206-7006.
Credit cards: AE.
Medium priced.

Like a gay young blade of grass that, simply not knowing any better, shoots out of a crack in a heavily trafficked sidewalk, so has this place jauntily sprung up in the grim chasm (West 14th Street) that separates outer Greenwich Village from lowest Chelsea. You could have shown that the very idea was out of the question. You could have pointed out that the site is neither here nor there—and that where it is is nowhere. But, in fact, the new restaurant was immediately spotted by citizens on both sides of this border. They noticed at once the handsome deep-red façade and big gold letters by which it announces itself to its dowdy arrondissement. That front, however, will shed its luster in time, become familiar, and, thereby, be subsumed by its surroundings. But it is unlikely that the spanking interior will lose any of its freshness soon, for this is the niftiest joint to hit 14th (West *or* East) in decades.

Quatorze is a spiffy bistro and a well-bred brasserie. It is plain and fancy. Up front, you are standing on a floor of white tiles when you are at the trim, marble-topped bar. Then you walk on handsome oak through the pale-lemon-yellow dining room just beyond it. Along the wall on your left, under inset rectangular mirrors, runs a plush banquette of burgundy velvet, a row of white-linened tables-for-two before it. There are bigger tables across the aisle, then four more, one in each corner of a small square area at the back. There is handsome dark-wood trim here and there, and a few great big posters that, without cluttering the place, cleverly temper its spareness. The light is soft but not dim. And the ladies and gentlemen who wait on you are efficient and know well the brief menu from which they work.

Oysters are sold by the oyster, they are fresh, cracked open only when you order them. There are usually a couple of varieties on hand, among them big rich Wellfleets, and the smaller but more interesting Malpèques, which are somehow both sweet—even fruity— and briny. Order the smoked chicken breast, and you get three substantial slices of good, mildly cured white meat—but the hit of the plate is the sauce, which is a thick whipped cream sharpened with strong horseradish. The jambon persillé is a nice enough version of the usual thing, a mosaic of chunks of ham in a firm jelly that is green with parsley—it is garnished with sharp black olives and strong mustard. What the house calls terrine is a singular thing in which layers of cold sliced beef are interleaved with layers of spinach or carrot—the meaty dish has a stunningly variegated texture, and its tastes are at once mingled and distinct. The red-lettered first course is the chicory salad, a giant mound of crisp, pleasantly bitter greens dotted with nuggets of good, strong bacon, and dressed with a hot and tangy vinaigrette. If there is cold beet soup when you come, know that this is not just another chilled and pureed vegetable. The deep-pink liquid is thick and nubbly and creamy, its beet flavor pure and fresh.

A big comedown is the fettuccine with tomato and basil. The dish begs to be simple and dramatic, a condition that cannot be achieved if one element is a lifeless mash of the green herb—the pasta is served with a ramekin of ground cheese, which changes things without improving them. But then there is this grilled salmon, the fish itself moist and sweet, crusted in the making, of clear flavor, its sauce choron stunning, thick and rich, fragrant of tarragon, chunky with the bits of tomato that make it pink. The grilled chicken, served in parts, is eminently well prepared, the skin crisp, the meat cooked through but still moist—too bad the bird itself is a pallid one. But there is a better bird, the roast duck, of which you get a couple of substantial sections—they are nicely browned, their meat is not fatty but is imbued with the flavor of fat, and they are set in a smooth sauce dotted with fiery peppercorns, a striking contrast to the rich meat. Sometimes there is roast pork, and you are served two supple inch-thick slices of the pale-pink meat, each of them turned upon itself, like an eccentric heart—a garlicked and fragrantly herbed stuffing is in the crease, the meat is set in a sweet, sticky sauce, and it is garnished with chunks of crusted potatoes, sour red cabbage, and disks of crisp, barely sautéed zucchini. Choucroute has a place of honor on the menu, its own red box. But, though it is entirely edible, it is no more, for the cabbage would be lifeless without its juniper berries, and the sausages and pork are solid but not diverting.

Quatorze makes a point of offering a very respectable sauternes by the glass. If you had some with your oysters (do not judge the combination until you try it), and liked it, have some more with your (do not judge the combination until you try it) Roquefort, of which you get a wondrously firm, creamy, and sharp example here. The sweet desserts include a striking pear tart—the slivers of ripe fruit are separated from the crumbly pastry by a layer of creamy marzipan; a warm apple tart—a circle of thin, overlapping slices of browned, crisped fruit, lightly sugared, on a shortbread pastry; and a crème caramel.

★★RAGA

57 West 48th Street
LUNCH, MONDAY TO FRIDAY; DINNER, DAILY.
Reservations: 757-3450.
Credit cards: AE, DC, MC, V.
Medium priced.

A "raga" is an Indian musical form, and on the walls of this restaurant of that name are displayed many Indian musical instruments—among them sitars, vinas, and rubābs —all of them beautiful to look at. At certain hours of the evening, Indian music is performed here. And if, admittedly, the idea of background music in restaurants is generally a bad one, Indian music is another matter. It has the power unobtrusively to charge the atmosphere of the room in which it is being played in such a way that, while the music may go almost unnoticed, all other experiences are slightly heightened. For a moment you may actually feel that you are in India, even if you have never been there. Be advised that the effect is intensified by a judicious intake of alcohol.

Raga is a big place, at once cushy and stately, with slender wood columns rising through the great space to the beams they intersect on the distant ceiling. You walk on plush carpeting of hot colors in sinuous stripes. The walls are covered with coarse raw silk, and in addition to those instruments, they are bedecked with colorful cloth hangings that have woven into their patterns bits of glinting metal, like tiny mirrors. One whole side of the dining room is given over to an elaborate building façade of dark, intricately carved wood, complete with columns and their capitals, windows and doorways. When seated, you are in big red-upholstered chairs before large tables on which candles burn in dark glass globes. The center of the room is divided—by partitions and planters—into islands, each of which holds a single large table, most of them suitable for six or more. In this very civilized restaurant, where the service is almost always sweet, you will sometimes be offered one of these commodious accommodations, without your asking, even when there are fewer of you than the table was designed for. What, you wonder, is wrong with the Indian ego, that it does not recognize its need to put you in your proper place right from the start.

The cold appetizers include dal papri, a mildly spicy, vigorously stimulating dish of lentil chips and chopped potatoes in a tart yogurt sauce; chaman ki chat, morsels of fruit and sweet potato in a tamarind sauce that is fruity and spicy; and murg ki chat—that same fruit sauce on small slices of chicken and chunks of potato. The hot oysters Bombay reach you in a big scallop shell—they are fresh and tender, and they are set in a thick sauce that is mostly ginger-flavored onion. What is listed as "crabs Goa" is a hot, spicy paste of crabmeat, tomatoes, onion, and oil—remarkably, the sweet flavor of the crabmeat is not wholly lost in this setting. Murg ke pakore is a chicken dish of little chicken flavor, but the slices of meat are reddened, blackened, beautifully crisped, and they are good with the fruit chutney or the spicy, creamy sauce with which they are served.

Salmon is rare in Indian restaurants, but Raga serves it, as machali masala. It consists of moist, fresh salmon steaks immersed in a thick, smooth, mildly garlicked sauce of onion and tomato. Jhinga tandoori is shrimp that have been grilled in the hot Indian oven called a tandoor. The shrimp are handsomely reddened and mildly spiced, and they are fresh and crunchy, but you do wish this preparation did not—perhaps inevitably— dry them out. That oven is kinder to lamb. Rann-e-Khyber, a dish prepared only for two (and served in an amount that will hold three or four), arrives as a substantial mound of gargantuan knobs of charred meat under rings of strong onion, slices of green pepper, and disks of tomato. The lamb is firm but not tough, of strong flavor, its darkened surfaces vividly spicy, and under it is a pool of the dark brown marinade that has dripped from the meat. The lamb vindaloo is much lamb, combined with crunchy little pickled onions and browned potatoes, in a sauce that has in it seeds of spice that burst with fragrance when you bite into them—this dish can be fiery if you tell your waiter you want it that way. Gosht palak—chunks of lamb in a succulent and spicy spinach mash —can satisfy the most primitive kind of food lust. In the hillock of rice called nizami biryani, you will find, as you mine your way through it, nuggets of lamb and potato— there is saffron in the dish, a touch of fruitiness, the fragrance of fresh coriander.

The good vegetable items include baingan bhurta, an herbed and strongly seasoned eggplant paste; mutter paneer, hot- and sweet-spiced peas with chunks of Indian cottage cheese; palak paneer, more of that solid cheese, this time buried in spicy, well-oiled spinach. Order rice, and the fluffy grain comes dotted with fruits and nuts. Naturally, there are condiments, and they range from raw onions in a fierce oil that can remove the fillings from your teeth to sweet mango chutney to cool yogurt.

As in most Indian restaurants, most of the desserts will merely puzzle the Occidental palate. The rasmalai are delicate little cheese balls adorned with pistachios—you can eat them and just about not notice them. The Indian ice cream called navrang kulfi is divertingly flavored with saffron and cardamom, but it is creamier than you want your ice cream—anyway, it is billed as a breath freshener. The kheer is a honeyed rice pudding studded with nuts and fruits—it is at least cool and refreshing.

★★RAKEL

231 Varick Street (at Clarkson Street)
LUNCH, MONDAY TO FRIDAY; DINNER, MONDAY TO SATURDAY. CLOSED SUNDAY.
Reservations: 929-1630.
Credit cards: AE, DC, MC, V.
Expensive.

Confidence, not to say audacity, is here at work, for while New York now shows signs that it harbors about as many eating places as, so to speak, it can feed, and while by way of the 1986 tax law more of the eaten-out dollar is charged to the eater's account than at any time since the administration of Joseph R. McCarthy, Rakel is that most chancy of restaurant essays: a big place, a pricey one, and situated at a remove from most of the city's money. The enterprise is, in fact, almost wistful, the last word a little late, another Empire State Building—which, you will recall, was conceived in the giddy twenties and completed just in time for the really good part of the great Depression. Rakel, on the other hand, is a monument to quite another (restaurant) era—specifically the years between the ascensions to the presidency of Gerald Ford and Nancy Reagan— and it encapsulates the spiffiest architectural and culinary restaurant styles of that time.

This is Greenwich Village, but Rakel's design antecedents are in SoHo, where the gutting and refurbishing of vast, unlikely commercial spaces for restaurant uses began. In the old days the results were mostly gaunt and functional, but in this highly evolved example of the type, though it necessarily retains, even exploits, some of the more gargantuan elements of the giant store as found, and though its lines and surfaces are in the genre's hard-edged, slick tradition, the effect is muted, hushed, gently aglitter. The soft-gray room is wide and deep, two massive columns along its lengthwise axis rise to the ceiling two tall stories overhead. You walk on dark carpeting, venetian blinds hang in the tall windows on two sides, the glassware and china gleam on the linened tables. On the wall behind the long bar, there rises a stylized skyline, stark and dark, in slight relief. The aural background is occupied by Bach, Beethoven, and Billie Holiday. The place is cool—you may find it cold—but its false notes, two huge surrealistic paintings to either side of the skyline, probably intended to warm the room up, just compromise it without mitigating the mild severity.

You are waited on by young gents who keep up with the ever-changing menu and discuss it with you intelligibly, albeit he who commends the "fried oysters con feet of leeks" is no more reliable than his French, for though the confit is a well-seasoned and buttery little vegetable hash, of vivid leek flavor, the oysters themselves are loud within their coarse batter. You are better off with the crab cake—the deep-browned patty is a bit rubbery, but its spiced crab flavor is fresh, and the so-called coulis of crab in which it is served, though it seems not at all like a seafood puree, is sweet and polished. Foie gras two ways: The "mosaique" is a pâté, threaded with truffles that impart nuttiness and a bit of crunchy texture to the rich forcemeat; the poached foie gras is the whole glistening liver, hot, plump, and light, garnished with a little cloud of shredded radish, and set in a nubbly sauce of sherry vinegar. A more voluminous cloud—almost a bird's nest—of deep-fried strands of leek reaches you surrounded by salted, crisp-fried slivers of sweetbread, the vaguely Oriental dish moistened by a tangy sesame vinaigrette. Each day there is a pasta of the day, sometimes very thin spaghetti in a thick red sauce, dense with slivers of ham, that is livened with needle-thin strands of orange rind—cheese invigorates the good dish.

You figure that in the sautéed salmon deference is being paid to both fashion and qualm, for though listed "medium rare," it is served cooked through—excellent fish, living pink, clear flavor, and all that, but a comedown when you have been promised something better. You conclude, however, that simpler failings explain the salmon, for the "rare" roast tuna reaches you as billed, like a perfectly made "blue" steak, the slices of fish a glistening beef-red at their centers, a pale, cooked pink just under the charred, peppered edges—it is served, with a mound of strong spinach, in a buttered sauce that is thick with more of that coarse-ground pepper. Plump scallops and crunchy shrimp are the shellfish of the "shellfish ragout," despite which title they are supplemented by chunks of finfish, all the meats mounded up, in a soup plate, over spaghetti that is set in a deep pool of oceanic broth—the dish comes with crusts of bread that are spread with a vibrant garlic paste. The lobster you looked for but did not find in the shellfish ragout may be ordered straight, poached. The tender crustacean morsels reach you, in a wonderfully intense pink sauce of the lobster roe, between a layer of pungent arugula and a crusted little pancake of potato. Sometimes there is rabbit, and if the pale meat has lost some of its distinctive flavor, you are consoled by its tart sauce, by the little sandwich garnish of rabbit-liver puree between crisp potato disks, and by the pleasantly gummy, fragrantly herbed gnocchi that also accompany this game.

Come here once, and the dessert to have is the chocolate tart, a disk of almost black bittersweet chocolate, so light, moist, and smooth that you cannot really call it cake, in a pear puree that is textured with bits of fruit, the item's third element an egg of rich vanilla ice cream. The three-citrus tart is a tangy, almost fluffy custard in a browned pastry cup—it is set in a crimson raspberry sauce that is strewn with orange sections. The crème brûlée is light, its caramel top crisp and tender. Among three ice creams the prune-Armagnac, thick with patches of dark fruit, is the winner; the hazelnut, with its grittiness of chopped nuts, is not bad; and the banana is exaggeratedly intense, like candy.

★★★ RAOUL'S

180 Prince Street (near Sullivan Street)
DINNER.
Reservations: 966-3518.
Credit cards: AE, MC, V.
Expensive.

A pioneer SoHo settler, this place was chichi in the neighborhood's early days, but has been less than all the rage for a couple of years now. It is out of style because it has not kept up—and that is the only reason, for you eat as well here now as you ever did. Back when SoHo was being settled, improvisation was much of the mode, and a seemingly thrown-together enterprise purveying French country cooking in a weather-beaten saloon was the perfect setting for public display of the pioneers' open-minded spirit. But the haste with which SoHo shed its bohemianism dazzled even the most cynical observers, for as soon as uptown money showed on the scene, swank was in. Oh, sure, you could still convert an old store into a dinner house, but you had to make sure the place looked like a room or two borrowed from the Museum of Modern Art.

Raoul's is the place with the neon beer signs in the front windows and cream-colored stamped-tin walls, with white butcher paper on the tables and, in the back room, car-seat booths with two-tone plastic upholstery and chromium trees for your hat and coat. The front room has the bar—waxed on the mirrored wall behind it are the names of the available beers and the prices of those dishes (steak pommes frites, pâte maison) that you may order if the bar is where you want to eat. Against the wall opposite is the long black banquette, a line of tables before it, that, to some tastes, is the restaurant's choice seating; for with your back to this wall, the bar scene is right before you, also the entrances and exits of Raoul's somewhat depleted but still colorful clientele, and also—with a few turns of your head this way and that—the whole array, motley and helter-skelter, of the establishment's paraphernalia. Some of this stuff came with the premises, and much of it was added by the present interests: a couple of ancient electric fans, complete with drooping wires, that, in honor of the air conditioning, are never turned on; a portrait of General Charles André Joseph Marie de Gaulle; a couple of photographic landscapes with, in the extreme foreground, a single human female breast each; a huge Toulouse-Lautrec poster; exposed pipes; an ancient stove on which are displayed the house desserts; not to mention oils and etchings and framed mirrors and, on the rear wall, the chalked menu, the only really legible one in the place—for you are still expected to select your dinner here from the tiny slate you are handed, which bears scratchings (many of them, at a guess, in French) that appear to have been polished almost to extinction by centuries of erosion. Nobody cares, about that or much else, for this is a jolly place with a vociferously contented crowd, its shortage of trendies making it the closest thing in SoHo to a neighborhood restaurant for adults.

You get spanking oysters, opened when ordered, fresh and cold and sweet, served with a spiky sauce mignonnette—they are best, however, with lemon and ground-on pepper. The house usually has on hand either poached leeks or asparagus—they are cool and crunchy, and they are in a sparkling vinaigrette that is thick with chopped egg whites and minced red peppers. The country pâté is firm and pink and pungent, very good with its sharp mustard and with this restaurant's chewy, slightly sour, and distinctly earthy bread. Occasionally sautéed wild mushrooms are offered—the delicate chanterelles woodsy, and the black, rough-textured morels sweet, almost fruity, in the dark and winy sauce. But still, if you come here when the blackboard lists ris de veau en salade, look no further, for these cool, slivered sweetbreads are at once buttery and light—actually delicate—in their herbed and creamy dressing.

Much good seafood: the smallest soft-shell crabs, their carapaces like flaky pastry, browned and crisped in hot butter, and strewn with crunchy sautéed almonds; a whole baby salmon, boned, butterflied, and grilled, the charred skin clinging to the expanse of fresh pink meat, a little dish of intensely tarragon-flavored sauce béarnaise on the side; turbot, the genuine article, from, how you say, the other side, but fresh, strong of that particular swimmer's singular flavor, the pair of fillets of almost ephemeral texture within their crisped, parsleyed surfaces, and served to you—stunningly—on a platform of warm, buttery leeks. Apparently Raoul's has something going with sweetbreads. After doing that thing with cool ones as a first course, it produces these hot ones, thin, crisp slivers of the rich but light meat in a winy sauce that is dense with crunchy black morels. The good liver is sliced thin, arrives deeply browned outside and blood-pink inside, is served in a tart vinegar sauce that contrasts strikingly with the organ meat's strong flavor. And once in a while there are these paupiettes de veau, roulades formed of thin sheets of veal wrapped around an airy forcemeat of yet more veal, the fluffy stuff herbed and judiciously seasoned and steamy within the browned veal wrappers, the big knobs moistened with a sauce that is thick with wild chanterelles.

Oddly, Raoul's offers no cheese. You can get a good salad of fresh greens and respectable tomatoes in a tangy vinaigrette. Some of the desserts seem commercial and are boring—among them a ponderous chocolate Grand Marnier cake. But then there are what the house refers to as fruit tarts, which seem more like clafouties: They are probably made on the premises, they have been variously offered with cherries or the small pale plums called mirabelles, the crunchy fruits set in something that is more akin to browned custard than to pastry—they are homey and satisfying.

This place has had a bad press, but that is mostly judgment too timid to contradict appearances. Only a handful of restaurants in town turn out old-fashioned French cooking as good as this.

★★★ LE RÉGENCE

37 East 64th Street
LUNCH AND DINNER.
Reservations: 606-4647.
Credit cards: AE, DC, MC, V.
Very expensive.

What distinguishes this place from others in its posh French class is the almost magical quality of its intimidation, magical because nothing about the way Le Régence is run ought to scare anyone off. Yet even on Saturday night, when Manhattan Island is regularly invaded and swarmed over by foreign bodies in Detroit cars, the crowd here is made up, almost homogeneously, of folks who bear lightly their tons of old money, a set that, by practice, has become this establishment's natural trade. Is it not a comfort to know that there is a restaurant in New York to which you may repair, drop two or three hundred dollars on dinner, and not find yourself among those who would rather mortgage the mortgage than not outspend you?

Surely it is the situation and look that effect that effect, for though Le Régence is only just outside the midtown maelstrom, it is deep in the heart of Park Avenue country, in the determinedly old-world (albeit slick, Hôtel Plaza Athénée, namesake of a legendary Parisian lodgment whose gracious dining facilities are in one respect echoed, though certainly not replicated, in these dining rooms. You approach them through a cool, stony lobby and then through a cushy, softly lit cocktail area in which, at certain hours, you may be mildly diverted by a gentleman who has at his disposal a larynx and 88 keys. The sounds he produces do not, however, follow you to your dinner, which transpires in a cream-and-turquoise Louis the Ornate interior that, glittering with crystal, is reflected and re-reflected in mirrors all around that extend the place to all horizons. Le Régence is a central room surrounded by a number of smaller rooms, the one in the middle under a barrel ceiling that, painted to resemble a cloud-dotted summer sky, is a reference to the outdoor court of the Paris antecedent. You are seated in armchairs of simulated leather framed in carved wood, or on sofas of antiqued velvet. The plywood paneling and lumberyard moldings applied to the walls have been cleverly painted, simulate, to the dim-sighted, hand work. You walk on plush carpeting. And, but for the flowers all around and the white linen and white trim and the sparkle of glass, all is aqua or aquamarine, jade or blue-green, with here a touch of teal, there a hint of mint. By now you know you are to wear your crimson dress. The help wear their black-and-whites, are unfailingly cordial, answer your questions willingly, knowledgeably. Among them there is a sommelier complete with small saucer on a chain around his neck—he is a rare sommelier, acknowledges that he has not tasted personally the wine you have chosen from among the scores on his list.

In the eternal relay race by way of which New York's haute cuisine kitchens change hands, Le Régence has countered the piracy of its original chef by the acquisition, for advisory and intermittent participatory services, of the Rostangs, père et (deux) fils, they of two two-star restaurants in the old country, one on the Riviera, the other in Paris. What with yet another of their countrymen always in place in New York, the food seems to vary not at all with the family's comings and goings. Consider, for example, this salmon tart, a circle of dark and flaky pastry, on it a layer of rich crème fraîche threaded with strands of sweet onion, the two hidden under thin, overlapping slices of delicate but vividly flavored salmon that are adorned with little sprigs of dill, everything warm but not hot—and weightless, actually fugitive, food that seems to satisfy while burdening you not at all, like a dream dish, one that may be consumed perpetually. Fear not, the ethereal quality of that tart is not the mark of all the food, you may actually eat and experience the beginnings of satiety, as when you do away with this lobster salad, the little crustacean in four parts, the tail two of them, the claws one each, leaves of heady basil clinging to the moist, supple, sweetly oceanic meat, which is in nice contrast to the sharp greens, in a tart dressing, on which the seafood is set—an arrangement of delicate baby carrots intertwined with the lobster's little claws adorns the plate. This place offers real langoustines, that is, Dublin Bay prawns, which, technically, are not prawns at all and not found in Dublin Bay—but that is another story. Anyway, they are steamed in their shells (a preparation that preserves all their flavor), and the meats are extracted and served, in a pool of sauce that is at once polished, tangy, acidic, and of a briny pungency, within a circle of pencil-thin asparagus spears—a stunning dish. What goes as galette d'artichauts is an artichoke mousse studded with morsels of sautéed foie gras, and that liver, remarkably, potentiates the flavor of the vegetable, as does the creamy vinegar sauce in which the construct is set—you do wish that the garnish of small sections of artichoke bottom were not rather hard, their trimmed leaves not a bit too fibrous for consumption.

Much seafood on the right hand side of the menu, including pompano, a great side of the fish under a thick layer of coarse-chopped black olives—it is moistened with a bit of smooth, sweet sauce and garnished with browned, buttery fennel, the perfume of which pervades the dish. Your pigeon is described as "laqué au vinaigre et au miel," which is to say, lacquered with vinegar and honey, and sure enough, the browned bird, in four parts, reaches you glistening—you were asked how you want it, and if you answered that you want it the way the chef likes to make it, it reaches you medium rare, the meat moist, redolent of its fat within the coppery skin, and garnished, strikingly, with a little muffin of garlic custard. You are perhaps a bit dismayed at the paucity of your serving of veal, a couple of nuggets the size of large golf balls, but there is no quarreling with the crisp browning of their surfaces, within which all the meat's juiciness is sealed, nor with the rich and winy sauce in which they are served, nor with the sprigs of rosemary that are lively relief to the sturdy food, nor with the little strips of browned-in-clarified-butter potato slices that add vivid potato flavor and crackling texture to the dish. The sliced lamb is good, the tender, roasted meat blood-pink and of frank lamb flavor, but it is notable especially for the deep-brown vinegared mash of shallots on which it is dramatically served.

What goes as Irish cassis is a big wine glass half filled with currants, the fruit in its jelly, over the top a quarter inch of thick, rich cream—forgettable. The gratin de framboise consists of a soft meringue, raspberries, and a light honey- and orange-flavored sauce—not memorable. The goût de chocolat is an assortment of many chocolate things, cake and mousse and ice cream among them, all of intense chocolate flavor, and all set in a cool lemon sauce—fine, but not what you come back for. You do well with the passion fruit soufflé, a great mound of the light, creamy, fruity confection, hidden under it a so-called "coconut shell" that is in fact a coconut pastry—a nice foil to the fluffy sweet.

★★LE RELAIS

712 Madison Avenue (near 63rd Street)
LUNCH AND DINNER.
Reservations: 751-5108.
Credit cards: AE, MC, V.
Medium priced.

The folding doors that form the front wall of this restaurant are pushed aside when the weather is fair, exposing the place to the pedestrians and vehicles on Madison Avenue, and vice versa. Sometimes a handful of tables are even set up on the sidewalk, under a little awning; champagne is kept cold in buckets, and this restaurant's menu items—bistro food with a light touch—are dispatched as casually as possible by the revelers who disport themselves thereat. They betray much contented awareness that the ease with which they lead this good life is on display. Of course, you cannot have a party on the sidewalk and act as if you were in your own dining room. Not even if you swallow your entire bottle of blasé pills.

Le Relais is a Parisian restaurant, bustling and contented. Its ivory-colored walls are hung with dozens of prints and engravings, and with big mirrors that have their tops tilted forward, so that from any seat in the house you get a voyeur's view of lots of other seats in the house. The International Set crowds the little bar at the front. They wear Riviera tans, Savile Row flannel blazers, brevities from Fifth Avenue. One smashing lady, all of whose hair has migrated to the left side of her head, chats with one gentleman, holds in abeyance another by placing her hand on the back of his, and swivels her eyes and watches with shock the entrance of a third, who, goddammit, is accompanied by a lady all of whose hair has migrated to the left side of her head.

Folks who do not know any better get all dressed up to come here. But this is an easygoing place, at which gentlemen in tennis sweaters and ladies in prominently labeled denim are quite at home. Some of the food on the constantly changing menu could be picnic food, such as the pâté of chicken livers, a very spreadable brandied and buttered paste that is crunchy with hazelnuts. The cool lentil salad is dotted with bacon and onion and fragrantly herbed in its tangy dressing. A slivered endive, adorned with bits of strong, creamy Roquefort cheese and moistened with good oil, makes a rousing first course. As does the cold bass, the pale and moist white meat in an herbed dressing that is sharp with mustard.

The bass again, this time hot but served in an uncooked lemon-and-oil dressing that is herbed and lightly garlicked—a slightly daring and very stunning dish. Le Relais is one of the few places in town where the carpaccio appears to be sliced to order: The tissue-thin leaves of raw beef are blood-juicy, and they are served with a great dollop of rich, tomato-flavored mayonnaise. The sautéed chicken is a good bird, its wine sauce polished, its title—poulet à l'estragon—incomprehensible, the tarragon being not in evidence. Hefty slices of lamb, charred at the edges, as rare as you want them at the center, are served as noix d'agneau Nesselrode—good, tender meat, of mild but clear lamb flavor, in a creamy calvados sauce that is at once sweet and slightly acidic.

The fruit tarts, sometimes apple, sometimes pear, are elemental, made on light, flaky, barely browned pastry. The chocolate mousse is rich, dark, intense but not excessive—it is served with whipped cream that is the genuine article, rich and light. You may have strawberries with that whipped cream, but some of the fruit was selected through rose-colored glasses. The bombe pralinée is an icy-cold compound of cake and ice cream and hazelnuts, served under more of that whipped cream—a heady sweet.

★ REMI

323 East 79th Street
LUNCH, SUNDAY TO FRIDAY; DINNER, DAILY.
Reservations: 744-4272.
Credit cards: AE, DC, MC, V.
Expensive.

It even looks noisy, loud white stripes on the dark-blue banquettes, cacophonous red, yellow, and gray light fixtures (albeit of genuine, imported, do not accept imitations Venetian glass—this place has Venetian leanings) on the semi-gloss walls, a babel of little framed prints all around that seem to chatter incomprehensibly about their indistinct Venetian subjects, brandished crossed pairs of gondola oars mounted on the low ceiling overhead (in recesses that, though padded, are apparently as acoustically transparent as the fabric on your loudspeakers). The busy movement through the aisles of the waiters in their bold-striped shirts is a considerable addition to the general visual din, as is the guests' boisterous speech to the aural, their loudness, of course, essential, for they are in competition with the clangor that is built into this hard-surfaced place. The closeness of the tables in the not large room, especially those along the banquettes, adds to your sense that the world is here much with you, as does the affectionate nudge of your waiter's hip against your shoulder when he leans to pour wine for the table adjacent to your own. You may find it hell, you may find it jolly, it depends on your mood, which depends on whether you have a drop before coming—which, it is suggested, you occasionally do, for with care you eat well here, though only the born lucky should trust their luck.

Luck is smiling—well, grinning—on you when you choose the endivia con sardine e ravanelli, a bowl filled with crisp, cut-up endives, thin disks of red-trimmed radish on top, among them silvery strands that are sour, salty, herringlike fish fillets—the salad's mustard dressing is vigorous. But the corners of her mouth then fickly turn down, and she permits you to stumble into the radicchio e grana con polenta—nothing wrong with the decent greens, and the slivers of Parmesan suffer only by their paucity, but the star-shaped chunks of polenta are mushy, without flavor, their surfaces hardened rather than crisped in the toasting. Smoked goose at its best has a vigorous spiced-meat flavor, but here it is pallid stuff, the salad served with it of much more interest in its strong horseradish dressing. But then there is this carpaccio, the meat fresh cut, its raw-beef flavor clear, on it a little mound of heady arugula under slivers of sharp Parmesan cheese—you pour on liberally the green olive oil.

Dark bigoli are a Venetian pasta made with whole-wheat flour and shaped like spaghetti. The noodle has a grainy flavor that is clear even in its herbed and well-seasoned onion sauce, which is accented with bits of anchovy. White noodles too, among them mezze maniche con salsiccia e finocchio, short tubes of pasta in a slightly creamy and enriched tomato sauce, nubbly with chopped sausage and minced fennel, that is potentiated by the addition of ground cheese. Each night there is a risotto of the night, sometimes risotto primavera, the pile of rice dotted with bits of celery, zucchini, carrot, and strikingly sweet red pepper, all the vegetables of vivid flavor among the million moist grains.

You wonder about the elemental-seeming entry "steamed salmon," order it, discover that it is salmon, elementally steamed. The fillet is fresh, firm, has lost only a bit of its oil and flavor in the processing, is served on a little platform—buttered disks of zucchini and yellow squash—is garnished, the hit of the show, with a great column of scalloped potatoes, browned, firm, and creamy. More potatoes, these mashed, thick, heavily seasoned, with another fish, grilled snapper, in what is called a wine and onion marinade —the pearly strands and the bit of warm broth a sweet foil to the good snapper. Order a chicken breast, and you get both sides nicely browned, moist but cooked through, of real chicken flavor, the garnish of wild mushrooms woodsy and redolent of garlic. With respect to the rack of lamb, however, the garlic the menu leads you to expect is remote, though the chops themselves, rarer than what you asked for, are firm and tender, their edges nicely crisped.

Once again the Venetian star, a big, quarter-inch-thick six-pointer of zabaglione broiled on its plate, the winy, eggy fluff nicely heightened by the browning, and very striking is the egg of vanilla ice cream set at its center—you do wish the sweet were not garnished with white strawberries. The crème brûlée is sugary, which, taken together with its admixture of lemon, makes it candylike and cloying. The wine-poached pear is firm and fruity, the little cannoli served with it crusty and crisp, the custard filling cold, smooth, and sweet. The chocolate cake is rich, intense, of a crunchy nutted texture.

★★RENÉ PUJOL

321 West 51st Street
LUNCH, MONDAY TO FRIDAY; DINNER, MONDAY TO SATURDAY. CLOSED SUNDAY.
Reservations: 246-3023.
Credit cards: AE, DC, MC, V.
Medium priced.

Of the dozen or so French restaurants in the theater district, this is the one that, more than any other, has departed from the old Broadway-bistro formula. René Pujol is even influenced a little—a *very* little—by carryings-on usually associated with restaurants of the Madison Avenue French persuasion: Raw salmon you can get, even fishes that are jetted in from across the Atlantic. What is perhaps more to the point are the notes of clarity and lightness in dishes that elsewhere in this neighborhood are, traditionally and to this day, overwrought and weighty. But while the place is drawing back somewhat from blunt assertiveness in its cuisine bourgeoise, it has so far refused to deviate from the uncompromising kitsch of its cornball appointments: a beamed ceiling, crockery and varnished copper on the timbered walls, a brick fireplace (complete with a fake deer's head over it), an old grandfather clock (with swinging brass pendulum and quarter-hourly chimes), French-countryside murals. The place is not so much a restaurant as a flash forward to a twenty-fifth-century museum, in which is recreated a characteristic public eating place on the isle of Manhattan, serving French food to the subaristocratic classes in the era before the dawn of civilization.

With callous disregard of its effect on your appetite, the savages present you, as soon as you are seated, with a pot of rillettes, a paste of pounded and seasoned pork and fat, which you are meant to apply copiously to slabs of bread—with butter, if enrichment is required. The natives extract the roe from certain fish and serve it as red caviar, the mound of russet-orange globules accompanied by white disks cut from sharp red radishes, strong chopped onion, a great dollop of sour cream, lemon, warm buttered toast —a rousing appetizer. And they trap lobsters at the bottom of the sea, boil them, remove the crustaceans' meat from the shells, cut it up, serve it warm—in a dressing that is little more than seasoned oil—mingled with strands of crisp vegetable on leaves of tender lettuce and endive. Salmon is marinated raw, with dill, and the great sheet of tender, pink meat is served with a sour, tangy, and caper-studded mustard sauce, and with lime, the juice of which makes the dish sparkle.

Seafood is this kitchen's strength. You get a whole Dover sole, fresh, firm, skinned and filleted and sautéed, its buttered and browned surface glinting. Most days there are a couple of fish of the day—sometimes a splendid red snapper stuffed with a fluffy mousse of sole, blanketed with a stout lobster sauce, and garnished with a little mound of bay scallops; and sometimes fresh salmon, broad slices of it, in a winy cream sauce that is laced with tart sorrel, this fish, too, garnished with scallops. If you want the scallops without the fish, the little morsels are sometimes served combined with julienned vegetables in that same sorrel sauce. The shellfish winner, however, is the lobster "au wiskey," in which the chunks of lobster meat are served in a polished red sauce—at once sweet and biting and briny—that has been fortified with liquor. You get sweetbreads that are as light as soufflés, floured and lightly browned, their dark-red sauce sharp with green olives. Thin slivers of veal are served in a rich and creamy sauce that is thick with mushrooms and heady with brandy. You wish that the blocks of beef in the boeuf bourguignon had been cooked longer, for they are a little resilient, not at all integrated into a steamy, stewlike mass, which is what you expect this dish to be. The rack of lamb is of good meat, accurately roasted, cut into tender little chops that are blackened and salty around the edges. The rack is made only for two. So is the Chateaubriand, that great knob of tenderloin, roasted until it is a deep mahogany on the surface, still bright red within, and served with a sauce béarnaise that is abundantly salted, powerfully fragrant of its tarragon.

In season, perfect berries are served here—raspberries, strawberries, blackberries even—with excellent whipped cream. Both the pear cake (a layer of cool pear filling at the center of the light spongecake) and the orange cake (spongecake again, this one wrapped in paper-thin slices of orange) are served in pools of crimson raspberry sauce.

★★LA RÉSERVE

4 West 49th Street
LUNCH, MONDAY TO FRIDAY; DINNER, MONDAY TO SATURDAY. CLOSED SUNDAY.
Reservations: 247-2993.
Credit cards: AE, DC, MC, V.
Expensive.

Originally designed not to offend, La Réserve, after a few years on the scene, has now undertaken not to bore. The interior, of course, is unchanged (perfect innocuousness cannot be improved), but the food no longer comes across as the work of a born apprentice promoted as a reward for loyalty. And the help in the dining rooms these days is notably sweet.

It has been suggested that this is where W & J Sloane went when it died. The cushy carpeting, wood paneling, and scored mirroring are the perfect setting for banquettes upholstered in a glistening fabric of peach pink and skin pink and for period side chairs —with plump seats and oval backs—done in shimmering velvet the color of lime sherbet. The place is illuminated by chandeliers that are big clusters of light fixtures of milkish convoluted glass—the illumination they give off is a kind of glowing pallor. "La Réserve" is "the game preserve," and throughout the front and back rooms of this place, the walls are faced with large murals of wildlife—quail, grouse, egrets, and such—enjoying themselves and looking beautiful in woods and bosky dells, beside lakes, bays, and streams. Though the paintings are handsome and decorative—you divert yourself by identifying the species they depict—and despite the help they get from the stands of greenery here and there around the rooms, they cannot redeem the mindless posh of this installation. Only the cheering effect of a full house humanizes this place, so if you chance to come on a slow night, it is well if you have brought with you company that is easier on your eyes than are the surroundings.

Focus on your friend, and get yourself an order of, say, lobster cream soup. It is ladled into your soup plate, at your place, over a couple of waiting quenelles that are surmounted by strands of root vegetable. The quenelles are fluffy and of sweet fish flavor, the vegetables are crisp but tender, and the soup itself, though creamy, is light, and it has a deep lobster flavor that is at once succulent and a little sharp—you will probably be pleased when, having dispatched the oceanic stuff, the big pot is brought back and you are offered more. Salmon and scallops that have been marinated with dill are served garnished with thin slices of cool lime: the fish is light, subtle, almost fugitive, lacks the sugariness of the usual gravlax, but the scallops are a bit soggy—still the well-balanced seasoning, the heady flavor of the dill, and the presence of whole coriander seeds make this a striking dish. Dill yet again, this time whole sprigs of it arranged over slices of duck liver. The dish is described as "sauté à l'hydromel," and a waiter explains to a nearby table that "l'hydromel is an herb." Of course it is not, it is mead, and you do note a slight honeylike sweetness to the browned, pinguid, and yet light meat—the dill is striking against such rich stuff, but the centers of each very rare slice are unfortunately a bit cool. You order snails, and you are brought an oval-shaped silver dish with a silver lid. The top is lifted off, and a complex aroma of herbs, wild mushrooms, and sweet spices invades your space—the sauce is creamy, the mushrooms earthy, and the plump snails have the flavor of the good stock in which they were done.

The house does much with fish out of French waters. Consider the rouget, filleted, grilled—and crisped—with its skin on, the slices of firm and buttery fish served in a pool of beurre blanc—the surprising notes of sweet-spice flavor you get in every other bite are the whole cloves with which the fish is studded. Then consider the turbot, a remarkable ocean fish that needs no help, but which does well no matter how it is treated. Here three fillets are set in a delicate and enriching brown sauce, one of them adorned with lemon grass, the other two with black caviar—almost any dish can be improved by elimination of caviar, and here the roe used is nothing special, but this is fresh turbot, ocean sweet, delicately done, and it has all its flavor. The roasted chicken is shown to you whole, taken away, returned to you as the boned breast in two parts, legs attached. The glazed skin is browned and shiny, the pale meat is of real chicken flavor, and the bird is served in a powerfully herbed and well-fatted sauce that is thick with crunchy whole shallots—though they are cooked, and sweetened thereby, they retain much of their bite. La Réserve turns out a quite superb sirloin, the firm, tender, fibrous, and blood-juicy steak done to perfect rareness—this is sautéed beef, neither seared nor charcoaled, and its unsullied flavor is very good with the tarragon and bone marrow that dominate its sauce.

If you put yourself in the hands of your waiter, he will repair to the kitchen and choose for you the cheeses that are in good condition—they are fine with the house salad of sharp greens, chopped tomato, endive, and a tart dressing prepared with velvety oil. You may have for dessert a fluffy mass of Grand Marnier soufflé (it is subtle, only mildly liquored) in a crêpe envelope that is strewn with confectioners' sugar—it is served with orange sections and a crimson raspberry sauce. The chocolate cake is remarkably light for its richness, the tarte Tatin deeply caramelized on its flaky crust, the black currant mousse rather sugary, though of good fruit flavor.

★★RESTAURANT RAPHAËL

33 West 54th Street
LUNCH, MONDAY TO FRIDAY; DINNER, MONDAY TO SATURDAY. CLOSED SUNDAY.
Reservations: 582-8993.
Credit cards: AE, DC, MC, V.
Very expensive.

It is sometimes observed that the market is never wrong—any more than a wild animal is wrong. It wants what it wants. You do not argue with it, you satisfy it—and maybe grow rich. You may of course abjure wealth, go your own way, and retain something that you flatter yourself to call integrity. Still, it is not as simple as that. For though the market is never wrong, it reserves the right to be one thing one day, another another.

You may be willing slavishly to follow it, but it does not show the way clearly. Each of its new secrets may be told in a new language, and it is understood readily only by those who are willing to give up languages of their own—adaptable types, that is, those who are defined by what they are tuned to, as a radio takes its inspiration only from the station to which it is dialed. Pity poor Raphaël Edery, proprietor here. He wants to satisfy the market, but only with difficulty does he tune to anything but himself. One look at the gentleman—tall, slender, trim-tonsured, erect in his well-tailored suit, of a charm that is carefully measured—and you grasp at once that the source of his austere taste is no radio station. Upon a time, ironically, Edery's preferences pleased the market, and the sterile restaurant in which he served his then trendy (and very good) food, at lofty prices, prospered. These days, you can reserve a table for dinner on thirty seconds' notice, even though he has tried, albeit in his own way, to give the market what it wants: the once prix fixe menu is now à la carte, the imposed, and resented, surcharge for gratuities has been dropped in favor of the American system, and the monastic appointments have been made, well, less monastic. But the spirit is not in it. Restaurant Raphaël does not resonate to the market's wavelength. For real success, M. Edery will have to wait for the return of that time when what the world wants is, once more and probably briefly, what he is inclined to give it.

But this is a big city, in it there do live others with tuning like Edery's, and for them today's Restaurant Raphaël has charms. It remains a narrow room, a brick wall opposite an ivory-painted one, short crossbeams overhead. Where Raphael reproductions once hung, on the brick-walled side, there are now lighted sconces mounted on shield-shaped mirrors, and the dark upholstery on the banquette under them has been replaced by a light, flowered tapestry cloth that shows up also on the straight-backed chairs surrounding the tables across the way. Underfoot the carpeting is rust colored, delicately patterned, and there are flowers here and there. The back of the restaurant is a small room with a tile floor, a table in each corner, walls that are muraled to suggest you are in an ancient fortress, looking out through stone-framed apertures onto bucolic, paradisian vistas. Further back, through glass doors, there is a prettied back yard in which, when the weather is fine, you may drink and/or eat. Though the captain on the floor is, as ever, formally dressed, the waiters nowadays are in white shirts, four-in-hands, aprons to the knee. The changes are meant to make the place cozy—they help, but do not entirely undo its spare, skeletal quality.

You set such observations aside, however, when presented with this egg of chicken liver mousse, which is accompanied by another of onion marmalade, the former rich, smooth, nutty, the latter cool and sweet, the well-dressed salad served with them unusual for the black raisins with which it is dotted. Salad again, a mound of excellent greens in a tingling dressing, upon it hot slices of duck confit, the preserved meat moist, a bit spicy, of clear duck flavor—with them are what are given as "celery chips," which look like potato chips, taste like nothing at all, add a nice textural note. Snails without shells, five of them, plump and tender, are arranged on the circumference of a pool of buttery sauce that is green with herbs, at the center a sandwich formed of two light puff pastries, within it two snails more, and a pink, tart tomato sauce. An enriching tarragon sauce almost rescues the red snapper ravioli, a heavy filling in packages formed of somewhat rubbery pasta.

A small lobster—judiciously poached, so that it is firm, tender, and of sweet flavor —is handsomely served, the front and rear ends of its red carapace at opposite sides of its circular plate, the white meat at the center surrounded by fettucine that is intertwined with fresh vegetables, everything bathed in a light and creamy lobster sauce. A couple of fillets of fresh salmon, nicely browned, cooked a bit past the perfect point, but not dry, are served in a pale and mild artichoke sauce that is pinked by dabs of tomato sauce. Much good flavor is imparted to the broiled chicken by the herbs you find stuffed under the charred skin. And quite a bit is imparted to these browned and tender medallions of beef by the wild mushrooms with which they are sautéed, and by their dark and winy sauce.

When the house prepares what it calls "cheesecake made with crème fraîche," what you get is a white disk the size of a hockey puck—it is not only, as you expected, creamy and cheesy, but also smooth and light, and the thing reaches you in an intense red-berry sauce that is strewn with mint leaves. The cool and strong-flavored chocolate mousse is thick and sticky, conditions emphasized by the chopped hazelnuts with which it is densely coated. What is given as a "feuillantine" is many, many thin leaves of hot pear on a flaky pastry, under it a strong caramel sauce, above it a cloud of glinting spun-sugar threads. On a thin circular pastry that is hardly more than a pancake, a great swirl of apple slices mounds to a peak at the center—the hot tart is blackened a bit at its points, and lemon underscores its fruitiness.

★ LA RIPAILLE

605 Hudson Street (near 12th Street)
DINNER. CLOSED SUNDAY.
Reservations: 255-4406.
Credit cards: AE, DC, MC, V.
Medium priced.

Though with respect to numbers the species *bistro rustica* is dying out, most extant specimens are healthy, suggesting that the decline is a function not of any inhospitality in the ecosystem, but of a tendency among the survivors, in reproduction, not to revert to type. When the pimplous and blithely forgetful lad who waits on you here goes off some day to open a place of his own, his restaurant will not be a candlelit farmhouse serving la cuisine bourgeoise. Which is too bad, for these establishments have their uses. Enter one, note the stupendously familiar appointments, and you are instantly focused solely on the occasion. In this kind of place the setting always reassures, your back is safely to the wall. So hypnotic is the effect, in fact, that when La Ripaille's grandfather clock strikes the hour, you hardly notice it, which is perhaps why it has the habit of striking it again a few minutes later.

White plaster, wood beams, glazed brick in the dim light, wildflowers and dried grasses in baskets on the walls, antique tapestries, too many white-linened tables for the knotty space. In search of isolation, you request the table at the extreme back, the one beside the unused fireplace, for though it is distressingly proximate to intermittent loud crashes from the kitchen, it is larger than the other tables for two, and the space around it is sufficient so that when the radiator nearby is spitting steam, the table may be moved to the outer edge of its hot orbit. Withal, La Ripaille is not appreciated for its perverse charms, is frequented mainly by first daters and bargain seekers who, by sharing this course, choosing that one arithmetically, skipping the other, eat cheaply here. It is depressing to find yourself among those who grow tender over candlelight and kidneys.

From a menu that changes daily, you begin, in the spirit of the place, with the pâté de campagne, and you are served a better-than-everyday slab of the traditional compacture, the amalgam of meats at room temperature, vigorously seasoned, just a little gamy, good with hot mustard and with this establishment's fluffy white bread. Les escargots, too, are integral to this kind of place, but these snails deviate misguidedly, come in a lightly creamed tomato sauce that is only vaguely touched with basil, and the snails themselves are of little flavor. You find that what La Ripaille calls a "feuilleté de champignons sauvages" is made with, mostly, mushrooms that are not very savage at all, only a few of the wild mixed in with many of the tame, but the pastries are flaky, the mushrooms sport much earthy flavor, and their herbed cognac sauce is rich. Pasta has taken a permanent place on menus of this kind, and here you are sometimes offered large round ravioli stuffed with a mild Roquefort cheese filling, the sharpness of the cheese gentled by an herbed and creamy white sauce.

Skip the trout—it is not off, you understand, it is just not on, has no trout flavor, and the slivered almonds that could add a bit of drama lack crispness. Better are these quails, for though the nicely browned birds are identifiable as quails mainly by their size, their mushroom stuffing is pungent, and their madeira sauce is winy, deep, a little sweet. Better still is this liver, the thick slices crisped, pink, blood-juicy at the center, strikingly set off by the chunks of good bacon with which they are strewn. You are attracted to the noisette d'agneau by the description "au thym frais," you figure the lamb has been prepared with thyme. Maybe, but these slabs of pink meat have little taste but their own, as does their somewhat greasy sauce, the herb figuring only as a garnish of a few sprigs.

You are saddened by the lack of cheese. Your waiter commiserates. You point out that there must be cheese on the premises, that there is Roquefort in the ravioli. You are brought Roquefort, but with the regretful explanation that, as it is not on the menu, you cannot be charged for it. Though crumbled, this is perfectly good cheese, and with the money you save on the gratis dessert, you buy more wine rather than inflate the tip. The frozen lemon soufflé is informed by the notion that there is a point of interest halfway between ice cream and sherbet. There is not. The apple tart is of good, slightly sour fruit and decent pastry, but its sauce is icky. The winner is the bombe pralinée, the dense, cold ice cream threaded with candied hazelnuts.

★ RITZ CAFÉ

2 Park Avenue (entrance on 32nd Street)
LUNCH, MONDAY TO FRIDAY; DINNER, MONDAY TO SATURDAY. CLOSED SUNDAY.
Reservations: 684-2122.
Credit cards: AE, DC, MC, V.
Medium priced.

Fish and shellfish in mostly Southern and Sunbelt preparations, a score of still wines from California (none from anywhere else), 50 beers from 20 nations, and the drop-by social-club character of those old New York neighborhood seafood restaurants (they had names like Fin 'n' Claw and The Chowder Bowl) to which, in the years before the culinary and cultural revolutions, forlorn locals repaired for overcooked fish and for a little human contact, after the nine-to-five, with other than the spouse or the man on the late-night news. Such is the Ritz, but a contemporary expression of the genre, so the human contact is more than a matter of exchanged civilities with some waitress in a smock and change apron, or a nod but no smile to the newt at the next table. At the Ritz there are, in fact, bars specifically set aside so that the social aspect of your visit may be integrated with the refective. The one is a bar bar, the other an oyster bar, and the brief blackboard menus that hang behind them enumerate the light dishes over which you may, lubricated by, say, a Belgian beer or Napa chardonnay, have at the contemporary newt you find at your elbow. For some reason it is the oyster bar of the two at which most of the post-office pursuits are pursued. You lean to your left to follow one that is well underway. Says the she-newt: "Why should I? I don't even know your *name*." The he-newt: "Bob Kramer." The she-newt: "Mine's Karen Delaney."

At this site, some years back, the New York branch of La Coupole did, happily, a quick demise. The Ritz has modified the big place to its own purposes only a little, and there remain the huge boxy Deco light fixtures hanging from the high ceiling and the abundance of pale-wood paneling down below, to which have been added that oyster bar just inside the 32nd Street windows (mollusks and bottles of beer on display on ice), wood partitions with etched glass tops that cut up the space a little, and, along the east and north sides, high-walled booths within which the occupants are almost but not quite enclosed—on busy nights people wait at the bars for these booths to open up. You eat at tables covered with white butcher paper.

The Café, in advertisements on the air, avers that fish not sold the day it is received is discarded, that, therefore, what you get here is invariably fresh. Perhaps an unstated distinction is being made between finfish and shellfish, or perhaps the house is unaware that suppliers may sell less-than-fresh seafood, or perhaps the Ritz's handling of what it buys is sometimes careless enough to undo the goods in a day's time—anyway, you order the warmed oysters with citrus beurre blanc, and they have the dreary flatness of dinner oysters that were already quite dead while you were still at lunch. Still, that is not the rule here (though the incident may incline you to initiate bar friendships over beer instead of bluepoints). There are, for example, these first courses of salmon: unimpeach-able Nova Scotia served as a couple of open-face sandwiches on grainy black bread, a circle of red onion on each, garnished with a salad of tomatoes and fresh greens in a dressing made lively by the capers with which it is dotted; and, more interesting, fresh salmon cured with mint and bourbon, the thin slices of clear-tasting pink meat seem-ingly candied by the liquor, but in a way that makes their freshness brisk. The fried calamari is a great mound of the battered slices of squid, fairly tender, fairly crisp, and therefore in need of something spicier than—you guessed it—the fairly hot red sauce. Plenty of heat in the conch fritters, however, still these patties are nameless, of little conch character, get by on the basis of their spice, nubbly texture, browned surfaces. The Maryland crabcakes, unlike most crabcakes in Maryland, consist principally of crabmeat. You will not object, for these crisped and spicy little seafood hamburgers are of vivid crab flavor, and they are nicely garnished with a tart relish of onions and peppers. That same seafood, however, is something of an obscurity in what is given as homemade egg noodles tossed with Maryland crabmeat—the flavor is present, but the substance hardly at all, and the crunchy florets of broccoli dominate even the dark sauce, which is flavored with basil and weighted with mascarpone.

As the item is a main course, you probably anticipated, with respect to these grilled shrimp, a number greater than four. The menu calls them large, you call them meso-morphic—still, nice crustaceans, blackened and crunchy, lively in their pimento vinai-grette. The swordfish steak is handsomely grill-marked, only a little overcooked, takes well to the herbed and garlicked butter with which it is moistened. The fried catfish, fluffy within its crackling, peppered crust, is served in a jalapeno relish that is hot but not quite searing. And the herbed and garlicked codfish is a little dry of its roasting, a condition not relieved by the exhausted sautéed tomatoes and zucchini served with it. The lively sauce that is most of the Portuguese codfish bake—it is thick with celery, onions, black olives, green peppers, slices of stout sausage—could get along without the codfish very well.

If the title "Jack Daniels Chocolate Ice Cream" leads you to expect something spirituous, be aware that this is just chocolate ice cream. The apple pie is tart in its good lard pastry, is studded with black and white raisins, is garnished with rich vanilla ice cream. The crème fraîche cheesecake is a dull amalgam between a lively graham cracker crust and a slick black icing.

★★ROSA MEXICANO

1063 First Avenue (at 58th Street)
LUNCH AND DINNER.
Reservations: 753-7407.
Credit cards: AE, DC, MC, V.
Medium priced.

The generation trained to stoic patience by around-the-block movie lines provides much of the crowd that, reservations or no, waits calmly—contentedly, even—for tables here. These are the grown-ups who, back when they were majoring in success, sought out Mexican food because what went by that name was the cheapest hot meal within a dollar's worth of gas off campus. Having learned to abide that stuff, they are, willy-nilly, nuts about Rosa Mexicano's *haute* version of the real thing. If this menu is not precisely a compendium of Mexican-home-cooking familiarities (and why should it be), the ingredients and the spirit are the closest thing to south of the Rio Grande anywhere north of Buttermilk Channel.

You enter to a front room dominated by two serving stations, each of which exemplifies an important side of this operation. First, the bar, a crowd of human beings with, at its center, a counter—it shields the man behind it from the horde before it. His job is to take orders fast, make change fast, hit you up when your glass is empty. Chosen for the part is an all-American type, rangy and lithe. Farther along is the open grill, set before a tiled wall. Here steaks, chops, chickens, and whole fish, variously marinated or otherwise flavored, are charred in a fire, then sauced and garnished (to be picked up on the fly by the young waiters and waitresses who patrol this place). Chosen as grill tenders are a couple of gentlemen from Rosa's homeland, swarthy and black haired in their kitchen whites. The front room houses tables as well: a few under the front windows (avoid the one closest to the bar, for the crowd impinges); several more along the bar a few feet away (the crowd presses on these, too, and you may perspire in this part of the room from the heat of the grill); a short row of semiprivate booths with their own little arched roofs; and, at the rear, a single large table under a sunburst mirror. The back dining room is a big square space rimmed by a banquette that is overhung, all around the perimeter, by an arched canopy of rough stucco. At the center of the room a low, broad pot of tropical greenery flourishes under spotlights.

Rosa Mexicano is softly lighted and hot pink throughout, which, in combination with the orderly arrangement of its appointments, gives the place a kind of subtropical formality. That, however, is somewhat undone by the clientele, which consists in large measure of that set of restaurant-going New Yorkers who patronize eating places not to eat in them, but to have been to them—to be able to talk about having been to them. They are a community, they like to think they know one another intuitively, like members of the same species, and adjacent couples along the back-room banquette initiate conversations with their neighbors (invariably about food or restaurants) as readily as they ask their waiter for the check. One such enthusiast thinks nothing of objecting strenuously when he overhears you ordering the white sangria, insists on pouring you a glass from his own pitcher, to dissuade you, is triumphant when, after you concede that the stuff is watery and flat, you switch to beer. Another opinion maker virtually abandons her dinner to share with the unfortunates beside her a torrent of food thoughts, among them, "I don't think there's really that much difference between Nouvelle and Japanese-French," for which her paralyzing clincher is, "do you?"

The avocado is much of Mexican cooking, and to start your dinner with it in one of its seemingly purest forms, you order the hot avocado soup, a thick and creamy puree of the rich fruit that is spiced, soured a little with lime juice, and fortified with chicken stock. For avocado more complex, there is guacamole, and nowhere in town is a greater production made of it than here. A serving stand is wheeled to within a couple feet of your table, on it the ingredients, and also a molcajete, the legged, rough-textured bowl, carved of volcanic rock, that is basic to the Mexican kitchen. Here it is used as the mortar (a plain wooden spoon is the pestle) in which the avocado (one of those good black ones, with the pebbly skins and nutlike flavor) is mashed and flavored. You are asked if you want your guacamole hot, and if you really do, you must insist, otherwise it will be only tepidly spiced. Strong or mild, this is wondrous stuff, and though it is crunchy with chopped onions and fragrant of coriander, its secret is in those excellent avocados and in the last-minute preparation—the dish is served in the molcajet, filled to the rim, and one order is enough for two. The stuffed jalapeños are the shells of three of the famously hot green peppers, packed with sardines in their oil, and garnished with tomatoes and pickled onions—a primitive, violent, and rousing dish. The salpicon is of crabmeat that is sautéed with onions, herbs, and peppers, and then chilled—it gets a little flat going through those changes. For something like it, but brighter, there is the ceviche of red snapper, in which the morsels of fresh fish, "cooked" in an herbed and spicy lemon-juice marinade, are presented to you in a small bowl lined with thin slices of tomato—the snapper retains much of its sweet flavor among the herbs, onions, and peppers in which it is prepared. Among the few tortilla dishes on this menu there are these flautas, slender tubes formed of the cornmeal pancakes, filled with chicken, and served with what the menu calls crème fraîche, but which seems like an extremely rich mayonnaise—the good dish is garnished with cold chopped tomatoes that are mingled with fresh, fragrant cilantro.

From that grill: a whole snapper, the skin a blackened, powdery parchment, the meat within it fresh, moist, and of clear flavor, garnished with cool, soured onions and warm rice studded with black beans; pork chops that have been marinated with hot spices, so that when they are grilled, their flavor is almost like that of strong beef; skewered sausages—thick, black, sticky blood sausages and spicy meat sausages alternate on the slender blade with onions and tomatoes, and with peppers of killing heat—the job of these chiles is to flavor the other items, which they do effectively, and you are safest sampling their taste only in what was next to them; and a shell steak, good beef, tender and rarer than you wanted it, strewn with sautéed peppers—hot, but approachable— and onions. From the kitchen: a skinned breast of duck, of strong duck-fat flavor, but not fatty, set in a sauce of chiles and green tomatoes that is strong, sweet, vibrant; and what goes as tamal en cazuela, a homey dish, not unlike a bowl of cereal with strands of chicken and tangy mole sauce in it, melted cheese over it—stout, elemental food.

Little in the way of desserts: The papaya ice cream tastes a bit like papaya, and is soft. The cool sautéed pineapple, with coconut and walnuts, seems like something spooned over ice cream for an extra quarter.

★★RUSSIAN TEA ROOM

150 West 57th Street
LUNCH AND DINNER.
Reservations: 265-0947.
Credit cards: AE, DC, MC, V.
Expensive.

Once the preconcert and pretheater crowd has left, by a little before eight, you can walk in here any night of the week nowadays and get a table. Even a full house at Carnegie Hall, next door, rarely quite fills the Tea Room, as it once did, with après-musique night people for late supper, albeit the remains of this set, unlike the earlier crowd, are New Yorkers mostly, oldish mostly, a population group that, as it thins, leaves this ancient establishment more and more to vacationers and night-outers from points beyond the rivers. Certain of the consequences of RTR's decline are either sad or happy, or perhaps they are both. Consider, for example, the matter of the choice booths in the front room. Upon a time they were, if not quite sold to the highest bidder, easier to come by if you were known to the gent at the book as one who remunerates for small favors. Nowadays the poor man works on spec. You ask for a booth, you get one if one is available. And whether or not you are going to give him a fin for his largesse he does not know for sure until you have—or leave having not.

There are eight of those semielliptic booths, five on your left as you enter, just past the coatcheck, and three on your right, just before the bar. They are choice in that, while the tables for two in the dining room proper are cheek to cheek, within these cushy enclosures you are insulated from those around you; they provide a good view, sometimes diverting, of the goings and comings of all who enter and leave; their very scarcity makes them valuable; and, as they are still reputedly set aside for the mighty, your presence in one (especially if you dress extravagantly) engenders murmured speculation among the plebes who pass by, en route to the everyday dining room, as to who you may be. Moreover, for all the Tea Room's fabled opulence and glitter, this more dimly lit of its two rooms is the site of the restaurant's most charming physical asset, the sweeping mural—maybe years ago it was black on white, today it is black on brown—of the view, from behind sheltered tables and chairs and waiters and customers, of a Paris sidewalk café at the turn of the century, a broad boulevard in the middle distance, horse-drawn carriages on it, trees and grand hotels beyond. Nothing in the Tea Room is like anything in that mural—except a certain civilized spirit having to do with human beings going about the respectable business of their pleasures, and the beauty of it. The Tea Room is a hundred painterly paintings on dark hunter-green walls, the golden tinsel and shiny red balls that are the year-around Christmas decorations, the gay clash of lipstick-red banquettes and vivid-pink linen, scores of gleaming brass samovars, and, not least, the waiters—some have been here for decades—in their belted cossack shirts of brilliant scarlet. You will not believe for a moment that you are in the Union of Soviet Socialist Republics, but you may well forget you are in New York, for the Russian Tea Room is an enclosed world—some people seem to think it is Hollywood, so that, while New York's musical community is less in evidence than it once was, west-leaning bicoastal types still aim themselves here when they are in town, faces you have seen on the big and/or little screens, anonymous bronzed guys with plural starlets in tow, liver-spotted producer types garnished with acolytes.

All of which is nearly enough. But, big but, you came to eat, maybe beluga caviar at $45.75 the ounce, or osetra at $41.50, and they are imperfect. The steak ordered rare that arrives medium rare is not a disaster, just a disappointment. But caviar that is of something other than clear, untainted ocean flavor, though technically caviar, is, unlike the steak, remote from the thing you were after—luxury and perfection. It is not that the imperfection would be tolerable at a lower price. The price is irrelevant, is evidence that caviar is a luxury, but is not what makes it one, and, as it happens, in this luxury perfection is of the essence. Even the red salmon caviar is sometimes off and dry. Have your caviar with blini, and the ceremony is all it ever was, the heady grain flavor of the stack of fluffy pancakes in their little pot, the enrichment of drawn butter and thick sour cream, the waiter forming all the ingredients into cylindrical packages, the champagne and/or vodka (from a selection of two dozen) that can convert the ritual of caviar-and-blini consumption into a minor orgy. But if the caviar is not equal to what you have come to expect by way of memory of luckier, flawless days, your expected orgy is approximately holding hands.

A modernization of the RTR menu has been announced, and though the menu items are mostly what they have always been, certain dishes, though still well made, seem denatured these days. The Tea Room's eggplant orientale was once vigorously garlicked and deeply oiled. Today it is a harmless substance that, when spread on the pumpernickel supplied with it, is detectable only as a moisture, though some of its old character is in evidence when you eat it straight. As to the chopped liver, if not your mother, then your grandmother did better, for this stuff, though fresh-made, is a pastel version of the vigorously seasoned and deeply fatted real thing. Happily the herrings are all they ever were: the matjes herring dark and supple, sweet and tart and salty; the pickled herring astringent and rousing in its silvery skin. Withal, if you come here but once, you will do well to begin your dinner with the hot borscht. If this dish has been tinkered with, it was not to its detriment. The red soup still has the depth of a profound stock, a complexity that is the yield of a judicious balance of herbs and vegetables—you add cool sour cream according to your taste, and from time to time you pause in your consumption of the soup for a bite of pirojok, the light, flaky meat-filled pastry served with it.

Certain dishes cannot be prepared in large quantities and then served over the course of a long night—in time they fade. Maybe that is not the explanation for this beef Stroganoff, but much of the meat buried in this sour cream sauce is of a depressing gray and a stubborn resilience. The Tea Room's brisket is the safer beef, the long, thin, narrow slices of juicy meat, tender despite their distinct fibrousness, in a strongly seasoned and vegetable-sweet broth—the brisket is fine with or without its sharp horseradish sauce. If your memory of the luli kebab is of homey, peasanty lamb meatballs, peppered and weighty, sadly learn that the item has been refined. The new dish of the old name is a good one, light and juicy, but the change seems like the premature expression of the end of an era. So if it is lamb you want, opt for the shashlik Caucasian, nuggets of the straight meat, skewered with slices of onion, pepper, tomato, the fresh vegetables blackened at the edges, the lamb red within its charred surfaces. Probably at the insistence of the insurance company, your waiter pierces your chicken Kiev before putting it at your place, for hot melted butter is supposed to spout from the incision. Sometimes it does, but sometimes it merely dribbles out, which is too bad, for the event is most of this dish, its looks (the thing resembles a plump roll with a golden-brown crust) much of it, while as food the roulade of white chicken, made juicy by the mildly dilled butter that has melted within it, is of almost no flavor at all—of course it remains one of RTR's most popular dishes. Each night there is a fish of the night, sometimes fresh, filleted, skin-on snapper, the skin touched with citrus flavor, the whole in a pale white-wine sauce.

The Camembert on the menu is also in the refrigerator, where you will sensibly permit it to remain. The strawberries Romanoff are mildly liquored berries, mostly ripe, served with sugared whipped cream. You are directed instead to the baklava, chopped walnuts and pistachios, of an almost liquorlike honeyed sweetness, between layers of flaky pastry; to the halvah, a good example of the sugared paste of ground nuts and grain; to the kasha à la gourieff, a white cereal sweetened with a purée of apricots and adorned with slivered almonds—here too the consultant who has been tinkering with this menu shows his hand, for the cereal is decorated with slivers of kiwi as well. He has also been at the cranberry kissel, a thickened and slightly sweetened purée of cranberries that, in the old days, you enriched with heavy cream—now it is served with what your waiter frankly calls half-and-half, which merely waters it.

★★SABOR

20 Cornelia Street (near Bleecker Street)
DINNER.
Reservations: 243-9579.
Credit cards: AE, MC, V.
Medium priced.

Though you have, very likely, never been to Cuba (and though in fact the only Cuban in this long, narrow store is one of the waiters), you will, probably, be persuaded at once, by the appearance of the place, and later by the food, of this establishment's Cuban "authenticity." Everybody is. Judging only by the food you get in New York's other Cuban restaurants, what differentiates Sabor's is only its superiority. The food is the genuine article, at least as genuine as it is anywhere else in town.

But in choosing its appearance, Sabor was guided not by the gaudy looks that are traditional in Manhattan's Cuban restaurants, but by the plain look of cafés and simple restaurants in Spain and in the old parts of the old cities of the Caribbean islands. The room is painted ivory and dark tan, the wooden floor is dark reddish brown. The ceiling is of stamped tin, ceiling fans hang from it. There are straw baskets on the walls, green plants here and there in the dining room, as well as in the front window. There is a tiny service bar at the back, and when a Caribbean rum drink is being prepared in the blender, conversation at the rear of the restaurant halts, for Sabor—especially at the back—is something of a sound box. You put a little noise in, you get a lot of noise out. Between frozen daiquiris, Latin music jangles from the speakers. When the place is busy, there is a bit of boisterousness from the sometimes loudly self-satisfied clientele, for it is easy to spend freely on lots of food and wine when prices are this low. Sabor is a jolly place, and though it is loud it never seems inappropriately so.

Your waiter (the chap with one earring), when you mention to him that your table is remarkably small, cheerfully agrees with you, as if you are exchanging pleasantries. When you ask if there is a wine list, he informs you that there is. Actually to see it requires a more pointed approach. He is perfectly nice, you understand, just a little out of it sometimes.

Sabor is never out of escabeche, a firm, cold, sour side of a small fish, surrounded by crisp vegetables—onions, celery, diced carrots, green peppers, salty green olives, capers —all in the tart pickling marinade. The marinated squid is cold, but spicy hot, the circles of tender meat mingled with hot red peppers. And you can get shrimp (camarones picantes) prepared the same way—the house obtains very good shrimp, and if you eat them carelessly, your lips will burn for a while after. The hot appetizers include empanadas, triangular dumplings of browned pastry filled with ground sausage that is both fiery and a little leaden—earthy food; and frituras de malanga, fritters composed of garlic-flavored chunks of a Caribbean root vegetable—the flavor is not immediately distinctive, but lemon converts the nuggets into more-than-pleasant hot morsels. Sabor's gazpacho is more watery than oily.

For fancy fish, you order the poached red snapper, which reaches you whole in a casserole dish, head and tail on, under a thick blanket of sauce that is green with parsley, winy, tart of its capers and lime juice, oily and garlicked. The snapper is fresh, perfectly cooked, moist and flaky. For humble fish, you opt for the bacalao à la Vizcaina, a weighty stew of salted codfish, heavy with potatoes, sharpened by capers and olives, served in a strong tomato sauce. For all its weight, the dish is not leaden. Sabor serves chicken in a so-called curried prune sauce, with whole prunes and mushrooms: These spices are not packaged curry powder, and they make the dish remind you a little of good Indian cooking; the chicken is stained dark from being cooked with the sweet fruit. There are more of those prunes in the pot roast of beef, but this *is* a heavy dish, the slabs of meat are a little dry despite a moist stuffing of sausage, fruits, capers, and olives; even the dark and winy sauce does not quite redeem the tasty but ponderous meat. Ropa vieja is an odd component of Cuban cookery, which non-Cubans usually eat once. This is because the name means, and the dish often resembles, "old rope." The way this dish is usually prepared in New York's Cuban restaurants, the shredded meat is as resilient as hemp, resulting in a marathon for the jaw. Sabor's version, however, is by comparison a piece of cake, the mound of dark strands in an oily tomato sauce flavored with cloves and cinnamon—a striking dish. Pretty good black beans and rice are served with just about everything, but certain vegetables available à la carte are also of interest, among them yucca, another Caribbean root, this one white, hefty, with a texture like that of yams, served in a garlic-flavored oil—strong and primitive food.

The little individual key lime pies are made on a very ordinary crust, and the pale-yellow chiffon reveals little citrus flavor—the superb whipped cream helps. The flan is something the precise likes of which you have tasted every one of the thousand times you have ordered flan. And the roulade of sponge cake and custard, wetted down with liqueur and orange juice, is an obvious sweet. The big winner is coco quemado, a hot, sweet, nutty coconut dessert, made with sherry, flavored with cinnamon, and served with more of that terrific whipped cream. If that does not suit, there is fresh pineapple on hand.

★ SAL ANTHONY'S

55 Irving Place (near 17th Street)
LUNCH, SUNDAY TO FRIDAY; DINNER, DAILY.
Reservations: 982-9030.
Credit cards: AE, DC, MC, V.
Medium priced.

The crowd here drinks Sambuca after dinner, having graduated from drinking it before dinner. Up life's ladder and all that. Their motto is: If you've made it, flaunt it. That is to say, go to the right places. That this is one of the right places is easy to see. For it is brilliantly illuminated, in part by the gilded sconces that are mounted on mirrored walls and on walls of glazed brick. The place is a veritable gallery, abundantly hung with framed art. You are paraded to your table by your smartly turned-out host, across luxuriant carpeting, serenaded along the way by background music of the big-band era, including much Sinatra. (In this crowd, a dissenting opinion about Frankie is the moral equivalent of declaring for the mayoralty of Irving Place on the Homosexual Party ticket.)

You look around and you spot a proportional relationship between age and girth. It is as if the naturally accreted rewards of years of feeding at Sal Anthony's well-filled plates are being displayed as proudly as the dark blue suits, silver four-in-hands, shiny dresses, and bulky jewelry that figure in many of the costumes here. Almost all the foods that fuel these enlargements could have been found on most New York Italian menus thirty years ago—Ol' Blue Eyes grew up on this stuff.

Your Caesar salad is prepared for you and a friend (one order serves two) beside your table in a great wooden bowl—crisp romaine lettuce, crunchy croutons, strong anchovies, and plenty of cheese, but the salad's garlic is remote, and a single egg yolk is not enough to thicken this much dressing; still, this is lively and tasty food. Fresh squid and shrimp and octopus, plus chopped celery and black olives, all in a mildly garlic-flavored vinaigrette, make up the slightly pallid seafood salad—you squeeze on the lemon and bring it to healthy life. A lightly oiled and well-seasoned breading—mingled with (unfortunately) dried oregano—is the crisp brown crust on the hot and steaming clams oreganata.

A half order of lasagna will hold you—the great block of layer upon layer of firm but tender noodles is interlarded with hot cheese and ground sausage: The whole is cloaked in a red sauce of no breed, much viscosity, tartness, spice. Fresh clams, split cloves of garlic, salt and pepper and parsley, clam juice, and hot oil constitute the white clam sauce that is served on linguine—consume a full order of this at moderate speed and you will find that a film of sweat has materialized on your brow. The fettuccine filetto di pomidori is of perfectly good noodles, but the sauce is more pureed than the title leads you to expect—you look in vain for chunks of tomato.

Every day, a fish of the day, including, at times, grouper in brodetto, a huge slab of the snowy meat in a briny white-wine sauce—simple, striking food. Sometimes the scampi are loaded with iodine, the ruination of an otherwise well-made dish in which the crisp shrimp are in an herbed butter that is touched with the flavor of basil. A big production here is the so-called seafood combination, in which an abundance of those shrimp, as well as clams and mussels and squid, are served up in a hot, tomato-flavored seafood broth—stout food. Chunks of crisped chicken, slivers of browned garlic, and a sprinkling of herbs add up to what the menu refers to as "chicken olive oil & garlic"— obvious and good. You can get one veal chop or two (there is a slight discount on the second)—they are pale, pink but not bloody, crosshatched with black grill marks, very good with a bit of the lemon that is supplied. The place does well with a regular sirloin steak, but sometimes it offers a butterflied version (two thinnish steaks) pan fried with garlic—lots of salt and onions, too, in the very flavorful preparation.

The cheesecake is wet, weighty, nutted, its alleged admixture of anisette undetectable, its garnish of whipped cream a redundancy, the thing itself a perfect example of Italian cheesecake—if you get it the day it is made. Crisp cannoli tubes are filled with a cool, sugary, liquored custard—an intentional excess. The strawberry tart, on light sponge cake, is very nice. The zabaglione is not always winy or frothy.

★★SALA THAI

1718 Second Avenue (near 89th Street)
DINNER.
Reservations: 410-5557.
Credit cards: AE, DC.
Inexpensive.

This Thai place looks like a barely transformed domestic place. Except for a handful of framed Oriental scenics, it could be an Upper East Side saloon, though the absence of a predominantly positioned liquor bar troubles that interpretation. The restaurant is carpeted, trimmed with brass, has gilt-framed mirrors set in its walls—all those of a distinctly Third Avenue anonymity. But one small clue makes it clear that the establishment is an outlander on its turf: The slight-of-build, black-haired young gentlemen who wait on you are unfailingly courteous—even when they deny you chopsticks (explaining that in Thailand they are not used, and that they are available in most Thai restaurants only because customers expect them).

Bigger clues are in the things the young men bring you, which are, how you say, alien but accessible (though occasionally searingly spicy—the house rates the dishes from three asterisks [***] down to none, with the highest ratings for the hottest dishes). The boys will deliver, for example, this cold spring roll, a log the size of a baby's forearm, its wrapper a sheet of noodle, its contents chunks of sausage, slivers of meat, bean sprouts and crabmeat and chopped cucumber, over all that a tangy and fruity tamarind sauce. That one is mild. Considerably hotter is the squid salad, a two-asterisk dish that may strike you as worthy of three, for the slivers and strands of tender seafood, with crisp onions and scallions, are in a truly searing lime-juice dressing.

What the menu refers to as "the most famous Thai dish" is made here in an exceptional version. Called pla lad prig, it is a whole fried fish, fresh and moist within its crackling crust, covered over with a thick paste that is pungently garlicked and fiery. A frequent special is something described as "broiled salmon Thai fines herbes." This is good fish too, under its herbed and garlic-flavored shrimp sauce, and it is served on crunchy fresh spinach. The sautéed shrimp with onions and chile peppers are mingled with mushrooms and greens and bits of garlic as well—this is only a mildly spicy dish, but extremely lively by virtue of its contrasting elements. The word "curry" shows up all over this menu. It does not mean what you think, but refers, rather, to dishes in which coconut milk is a principal ingredient. These coconut sauces tend to be not weighty— they are hardly more than liquids—but their coconut flavor is vivid, and when the sauces are hot, the spiciness potentiates the coconut flavor. There are "curries" of scallops, chicken, pork, beef, those meats mingled, variously, with basil leaves, sweet peas, slivers of red pepper, bamboo shoots, scallions—the dishes are all good, the individual ingredients always distinct among the others. Mee krob, the crispy Thai noodle dish, is not very crispy; but the pad Thai, which is something closer to a Western noodle, is fine, the strands threaded with flakes of cooked egg, scallions, shrimp.

No desserts are listed.

★★SALTA IN BOCCA

179 Madison Avenue (near 34th Street)
LUNCH, MONDAY TO FRIDAY; DINNER, MONDAY TO SATURDAY. CLOSED SUNDAY.
Reservations: 684-1757.
Credit cards: AE, DC, MC, V.
Expensive.

This is the lost restaurant, the remembered one. Perhaps it is only imagined, and never existed. It is, in any case, the model, the one from which the others departed—to become less and less restaurants, more and more public theaters, scenes of self-display. Salta in Bocca remains the opposite of that. It is respite, where everything comes to a halt. You go there the way you go to your mistress's apartment. You do not leave a number where you may be reached. It is even pink.

Your host is a tall, thin, quietly dressed, Italian-accented gentleman. His manner of easy courtliness would be the envy of any aristocrat. Women love him. And so, apparently, does his staff—their unfailing politeness and discretion devolve from his. Even the physical restaurant has the good manners not to be distractingly prepossessing: a barroom, a dining room, and, beyond that, down a few steps, a smaller dining room with mirrored walls, which make it seem spacious. The rooms are rimmed with red banquettes, the walls are deep salmon pink, the carpeting is dark, the linen is white, the light is soft. What few adornments there are achieve their purpose—the place does not seem bare. In fact it glows a little, is welcoming.

When hiding out here, you should try the food: the zuppa di vongole, hot little clams in their shells, briny and sweet, in a pool of parsleyed and buttery wine sauce; scampi saltati, three big sautéed shrimp, crunchy and of vivid flavor, in a mellifluous sauce that is herbed, buttery, smooth; spiedino romana, the long, multilevel, deep-fried skewered sandwich of bread, cheese, ham, dark and pully in its stout sauce of oil, chopped capers, anchovies. Or have some pasta: firm trenette, thin flat noodles, in a pesto sauce that is wildly fragrant of fresh basil, garlicky, buttery rich; fettuccine casalinga, broad noodles mingled with sweet peas, sautéed onions, and slivers of strong ham in a thick cream sauce; spaghetti al sugo, the familiar thin noodle in a well-seasoned and meaty dark sauce.

The red snapper is fresh, its sauce livornese heavy with cracked black olives, capers. Chunks of good sautéed chicken bathed in garlicky oil go as pollo scarpara. The livers of that bird go as fegatini di pollo veneta, and they are crusty, pink inside, come in an herbed and winy sauce that is threaded with onions. The veal paillard is of pale, tender meat, it is charred in its quick grilling, and it sparkles when lemoned. But the costoletta bolognese—a huge, butterflied veal chop stuffed with ham and cheese—is miraculous for how light it is despite the weightiness of its ingredients. You can get pungent sausages—coarse and crusty and spicy—in a dense marinara sauce that is thick with red peppers. All the vegetables are good, the salads spanking.

The ricotta cheesecake is cool and weighty, made lively by candied fruit. The St-Honoré is of unimpeachable pastry filled with good whipped cream and chocolate cream. The house zabaglione tends to be low on marsala, a little bland.

At lunchtime this peaceful repair can be a madhouse.

○ SAM'S

152 West 52nd Street
LUNCH AND DINNER. CLOSED SUNDAY.
Reservations: 582-8700
Credit cards: AE, DC, MC, V.
Medium priced.

Intended as an evocation of all that is all-American, Sam's has captured something of the thirties and forties, complete with a life-size buffalo-nickel high up over the center of the racetrack-shape bar, and a foursquare layout and terra-cotta color scheme that recall the Horn & Hardart Automats in which, in those days, the buffalo nickel really did reign. There is even an open kitchen at one end of this big space, just as in the Automats there were steam table counters at which H&H patrons could pick up hot food dispensed by white-garbed functionaries who had been graduated to the status after years as busboys pushing carts of dirty dishes through the aisles. There is even a big painting, just as in certain old Automats there were murals that resembled the WPA art in public buildings. Some days even Sam's background music is of the era—Benny Goodman, Billie Holiday—but other times the sounds are the two competing soundtracks going at once that is the recipe for certain contemporary aural opiates. It is appropriate that in this American third part of the Equitable Center's restaurant triptych—it began with the French Le Bernadin and the Italian Palio—Sam's should choose a Depression theme, for surely Black Tuesday did more to determine the history of the 20th Century than the mere machinations of European rulers. It seems, however, that the theme was not so much chosen as found after the fact, for there are signs that the intentions were Wild West (not just that bison, but also these cacti, which, in great terra cotta pots, stand on massive pedestals about the room, reach toward the lofty vaulted ceiling, are echoed in smaller cacti in tiny pots on the tables, which latter will eventually disappear as more and more of them are blithely dropped into the glove-leather pouches of contemporary carpetbagger woman).

The dribbling away of purpose culminates, if that is the correct word, in the menu, which, such buzzwords as *southern* braised chicken, *New York* shell steak, and *crab cakes* of unnamed provenance notwithstanding, is about as American as the UN. That the crab cakes are charged to no locale you understand at once, for they seem to be fabricated of a paste reduction of the original foodstuff, and their ice-cold tomato sauce does little but dramatize their tastelessness. Now don't go way, for the grilled shiitake mushrooms are earthy and meaty and the roasted red peppers of intense flavor on their crisp greens, in which are mingled crunchy nuts and, too bad, ropy green beans. Okay, now go way, for the chicken livers seem precooked, recooked, and overcooked, cannot be redeemed by their burnt "frizzled" onions, while this paste of fresh and smoked salmon, though of clear flavor, is of a claylike density—it would be less of a comedown were it not called a "mousse." You are directed to a simple pasta dish—cavatapi (pasta shaped like coiled telephone cord, in two-inch lengths) in a chunky, herbed, and well-seasoned tomato sauce—and away from the onion, blue cheese, and rosemary pizza, which is onion soup on white; and from the assorted vegetables on whole wheat pizza, which is sauce primavera on All-Bran.

The sautéed black bass is fish all right, while the herbed polenta served with it, under it, actually, is something like the first solid food you take after a couple of weeks in intensive care. Because it is braised, the chicken is wet, but it has no more flavor than the pebbly rice served with it. The lamb chops, though they have picked up no flavor in

315

the grilling, would be not bad if not for their sauce, which resembles canned beef stock thickened. And Sam's burger is at once blood red and bloodless, as if the patties are wrung out, then grilled.

The nut strudel, a sweet-spiced nut paste encircled in a sugared pastry and set in an icky vanilla sauce, is at least an excess. The two-colored frozen praline terrine tastes like a Dixie Cup. It is the misfortune of the yam cinnamon custard to taste the way it reads.

• SAM'S CAFÉ

1406 Third Avenue (at 80th Street)
DINNER.
Reservations: 988-5300.
Credit cards: AE, DC, MC, V.
Medium priced.

Mariel Hemingway, the lady behind this place, likes cows, has painted Sam's milk-white, brands her menu with a checkered taxicow, hangs dairy posters on the wall behind her bar, attracts healthy young milk-fed calves to her store, where—it is all a wicked trick—she corrupts them, feeds them chic eats and booze (nary a milkshake on the menu), pointing the young, pink-cheeked Hamptonists-in-training down the road to red-nosed Montauk decadence. In fact, Sam's is very much your Route 27 luncheonette, waterside ice-cream parlor, airy, open, and casual, the candlelight dimness and white table linen notwithstanding. The Café is a front room and bar, a corridor past the kitchen, a back room with a peaked, crossbeamed ceiling, three square skylights in one of its sloping sides. The dining rooms are hung with big, bold, modern art, but the paintings do little to solemnize the proceedings. Your waiter, for example, clutches awkwardly under his arm the uncorked bottle of wine belonging to the table next to yours, while with pencil in teeth and groping for his order pad, he indicates by nods and a grin his eagerness to hear your wishes. It is well to be ready for him, his visits being intermittent—the quarter-hour interval between the request for and delivery of your own bottle of wine, for example, he attributes airily to "the computer." Such lackadaisicality disturbs this crowd not at all.

The menu has a mild case of the cutes, viz, "Fish Today," "Pasta Today," "Polenta Today," the last a winner when you find leaves of fresh mint between the blocks of cornmeal and the pully melted cheese with which they are surmounted, an herbed and creamy tomato sauce enriching the entire dish, the mint an inspired lively note. Probably someone grabbed the wrong bottle when seasoning the grilled endive and wild mushrooms, for the otherwise good food—both items well oiled and handsomely browned, the endive crunchy and with a good bitter edge, the mushrooms firm and earthy—is seasoned with a sweet spice that is either misplaced here or just a bad idea. The steak tartare is a burger-size patty of raw beef that, though fresh-ground, is inelegantly over-spiced, pasty for lack of oil, in need of the egg yolk with which it is not topped. Sam's salad is a big plate of food, much strong fennel, watercress and sweet snap peas, slivered beets and shredded carrots, a ramekin of spicy dressing on the side.

"Pasta Today" may be penne with four greens, the firm tubes in good, fragrantly garlicked oil, but the greens—spinach and basil among them—and oil do not make a sauce, and the dish is simply a meeting of parts that refuse to combine. That young man with the wine under his arm warns you that the grilled tuna is rare unless you specify otherwise. You specify samewise and get a slab of fish that, though nearly raw at the center, as promised, lacks the lively resilience of raw or barely cooked fish at its freshest —it is in fact mealy, fish made according to a fashion not quite understood. Opt instead for the roast chicken, the prettily browned sections of moist bird flashing about as much chicken flavor as chickens ever have these days—it is garnished with scalloped potatoes, browned and potently seasoned in their thick cream, and with corn on the cob that lost its sweetness to long cooking long before you got it. The green peppercorn steak is a slightly chewy sirloin in an inelegantly assertive sauce of brandy, cream, and pepper, each ingredient, miraculously, in too great a proportion to both of the others.

The chocolate cake would be perfect with a glass of cold milk if it were not itself at refrigerator temperature. The crème brûtée is a bit thick, its caramelized top like unto a sheet of glass. The strawberry shortcake is prepared with something very close to a real biscuit, the cream is rich, and the berries are fresh and more or less ripe.

★ SANDRO'S

420 East 59th Street
LUNCH, MONDAY TO FRIDAY; DINNER, MONDAY TO SATURDAY. CLOSED SUNDAY.
Reservations: 355-5150.
Credit cards: AE, DC, MC, V.
Medium priced.

This place is named for its chef, Sandro, and there is even a line drawing of the big fellow on the front cover of the menu. If that alone does not satisfy you, not to worry, for during dinner he favors the dining room with several live appearances. In fact, while you are in the very act of ingesting, he may suddenly materialize right beside your table, a great white presence. You judge by his confident smile that he fully expects you to drop your fork, swallow hard, and tell him how much you love the food you had been hoping to eat undisturbed. But tell him instead that he ought to put on a clean jacket before emerging from the kitchen and that, moreover, his cavatelli are lumpish, and the result is the same: delight. He is one of those who, after his mother diagnosed him as wonderful, never sought a second opinion. Soon Sandy is in the dining room again, this time to the delirious applause of a big table of birthday celebrants, for he is proudly bearing a tray that has on it a suckling pig. He has carried a corpus from a kitchen, but you could swear from looking at him that he just pulled a battleship out of a hat. Several kind things may be said about this restaurant, most notably that the food is nothing like what the chef's rapt self-confidence leads you reasonably to fear.

Slightly posh Mediterranean subtropical rusticity is the intended effect, and the hand-painted crockery on which the food is served, the red-tile floor, the stucco columns, and the pale-linen walls—adorned only with globular white lights that are prettily trimmed with red and green—all hint at it. The potted palms, however, suggest a Caribbean hotel coffee shop—and it is especially difficult to overlook their presence if you are seated where the fronds tickle your ear. Still, this is an open, airy, comfortable place. It has, at the center of its dining room, one table that is unlike all the others—it is long, unlinened, and communal, and you can sometimes get a seat at it when the rest of the place is booked up. You probably prefer privacy, but bear in mind that Sandro's does its own laundry, and on busy nights when the dryer cannot keep up with the demand, a regular table may be spread with wet linen. "Not wet," says your host—you have upset him—"damp."

The seafood salad is not wet either, for it is only lightly moistened with its dressing of excellent oil. It comes off simply as nuggets of fresh shrimp and slivers of squid, their flavor intensified but in no way masked—the salad is served with leaves of endive. What goes as "zampone e polenta con crema di fagioli" reaches you as disks of a grainy, porky, and sweet-spiced sausage, moist and rich, garnished with chunks of browned polenta and a mash of white beans—a good, weighty first course.

Certain events lead you to conclude that the training program for new employees may be bypassed if a waiter can prove he is illiterate. You ask one fellow to elucidate, please, the spaghettini with lemon. He explains that it is made "with lemon." You devise a better way to find out, and order it. Pasta, of course, is weighty stuff, somewhat more so when it is firm, as this spaghetti is, and yet the parsleyed and creamy lemon sauce in which it is served is fruity and bright, and though the dish is solid, it is stimulating. Not so these cavatelli, cylindrical nuggets of rather leaden pasta, albeit in a tomato sauce that is nicely enriched and fortified with pecorino cheese. The fettuccine with fish and mushrooms reaches you as broad noodles and little morsels of fungi, the "fish" evident only as a sweet oceanic flavor, as if the fettuccine has been cooked in a seafood broth—the earthy mushrooms are striking against the briny noodles. A big winner is the ravioli ai ricci di mare, in which the squares of pasta are filled with sea urchin roe (you take this on faith, for they come off as squares of pasta filled with nothing at all) and served in a tomato sauce that is studded with tiny scallops—the red sauce is well oiled, strikingly succulent, and the scallops give it sturdy texture and good seafood flavor.

Lowish prices are the policy of the place, low profit is not. Accordingly, some servings are ample, others scant, depending on the ingredients. That $6 spaghetti in lemon sauce, for example, filled its big plate, while those ravioli with scallops did not quite hide the bottom of a dish just like it. But even forewarned, you are dismayed to discover that a main course of "jumbo" prawns amounts to three not overfed shrimp. They have been lemoned, touched with tarragon, baked—and they are sweet shrimp, if a little dry, but they are not dinner. At the price of those three crustaceans, you may have instead two whole baby octopi. Be forewarned, baby octopi this young look like balls of twine, but their tender meat—which seems to have been grilled, for it has a slightly charred taste—is fine, though its otherwise worthy tomato sauce, fortified with anchovies and olives, makes no music with this seafood. A good tripe dish is sometimes offered, called tripe alla Mozart. Now, though Wolfie is known to have liked mainly wine, women, and veal, the very irrelevance of honoring him with innards might well have appealed to his well-documented taste for the absurd. Anyway, you get a great mound of the tender and gummy strands of pearly tripe, and they are mingled with just as many thin strands of carrot in a sweet, sticky, and mildly peppered sauce—good food. The strong flavor of the juicy baby lamb chops is set off dramatically by their sauce of balsamic vinegar. Sometimes there is goat, and though it is listed "cacciatora," the excellent meat—tender, salty, remarkably sweet—is served with but a trace of sauce. A steak listed as "la mia pizzaiola," which is translated as "Sandro's way," is probably not your way, for the distinctly overcooked little sirloin is set in a pool of tomato puree and topped with melted mozzarella cheese—no improvement on the cheeseburger. A $2.50 menu item is listed as "The Salad Cart, our own flavored oils and vinegars," and though the cart is on display, when you try to get anything but the standard house salad, your waiter must repair to the kitchen for S's permission. Permission denied.

You are assured that the listed lemon ice cream is ice cream, not sherbet. It is sherbet. The poached pear is mushy, lacks fruitiness—the unexpected nugget of Gorgonzola cheese attached to its base is the best part of the dish. What the menu refers to as an apple tart is a light and lightly nutted cake, chunks of moist apple within it at the bottom. And what it refers to as crema di polenta is a syrupy blenderization of cornmeal that is prettified with raspberry sauce and strewn with grated coconut—an obvious sweet.

• SANTA FE

72 West 69th Street
LUNCH AND DINNER.
Reservations: 724-0822.
Credit cards: AE, MC, V.
Medium priced.

Mexican, gone slightly chic, which is to say, carpeting, pink linen on the tables, changing exhibits of contemporary art on the walls, and $5.50 for guacamole. The place consists of a small barroom, a front dining room, and a back room, all dark pink, with white woodwork. The three gas-fire "fireplaces," the potted palms, and the potted cacti are probably meant to suggest, respectively, the hot, lush, and parched aspects of the North American tropics. But the bright light and cacophonous reverberance of this often crowded, hard-edged place will suggest anything but the slowed rhythms of warm climates.

The basket of corn chips and the little jug of scorching relish are very much what you remember from less pretentious Mexican joints (albeit here they are in rather spiffy containers), but at Santa Fe you nibble at the former, dipped very judiciously in the latter, while downing your own very personal frozen margarita. Not only does the menu list the drink in two sizes ($4 and $7), but it is standard practice for a table of, say, six to generate a margarita order consisting of two regulars, very little lime; one regular, lots of Cointreau; and three large, hold the salt. You do not hear requests for easy on the tequila.

That guacamole, its cost notwithstanding, is blenderized or whipped or something, and its clear avocado flavor, well spiced and lemoned, cannot overcome its toothpaste texture. The seviche appetizer is of shrimp and scallops—the seafood is fresh, but somewhat undone by the very obvious fruitiness of the citrus marinade in which it was steeped. Mexican fun foods: There are nachos, in which cheese and meat, sour cream and beans, hot peppers and bits of tomato are served with a crisp tortilla; and there are quesadillas, a meatless, soft-tortilla member of the same family, with cheese inside, guacamole and hot peppers outside. Both of those are fine, but Santa Fe has found no method for raising them above the regular run of such things, in which the ingredient called flavoring never seems quite to substitute for the one called food.

Your waiter, when you order swordfish and lamb chops, surmises that you must be regulars, for, says he, those are the best things in the house. Both are marinated, the fish until it is soggy (it is still that way even after it is prepared), the lamb until it has lost much of its meat texture, as if it were tenderized. Both are grilled over charcoal, pick up a nice carbon flavor in the process, but at the bottom line, both are net losers, less than what they started out as. Enchiladas Suizas and chimichangas are listed, and their fillings of cheese and chicken and beef, and their garnishes of refried beans and sour cream, are fine, but finally the food lacks sparkle, individuality, life. Marinating, seasoning, crisping, and burying in goo are no substitute for foodstuffs being permitted, at least a little, to be what they are. Combination plates of tacos, enchiladas, tostadas, and rellenos are offered, and you are encouraged to compose your own assortment.

The so-called lemon soufflé is really a mousse—but it has a terrific lemon flavor, the taste and texture in it of minced rind as well, and it comes with an intense raspberry sauce and good whipped cream. The slightly tart and crusty apple crisp is raisin studded and dotted with bits of pecan—it is served with more of that good whipped cream.

★★SANTERELLO

239 West 105th Street
LUNCH, SUNDAY; DINNER, DAILY.
Reservations: 749-7044.
Credit cards: AE, MC, V.
Medium priced.

For decades—and until quite recently—pizza, steam-table spaghetti, and the universal red sauce were about all that went for Italian food on Manhattan's vast Upper West Side. If you strolled the neighborhood in those days, wherever you went, there were the natives accosting one another on the street to enter into passionate exchanges on the subject of why cannot we have real Italian food over here like what they have downtown and crosstown? Now, at last, the West Side has at least some of it. This place has been purveying the Upper West's best Italian food for several years now.

Santerello is very much your snug side-street repair, brick walled and low ceilinged, carpeted, candlelit, dim. You will probably not notice the art that is casually hung on the walls, but the bursts of flowers here and there are illuminated by ceiling track lights, and they are the bright spots in the room. Almost as bright are the waiters. They are conversant with the menu and discuss it with you in the manner of one human being to another. On the upper West Side, that is the equivalent of finding a resident string quartet in an SRO hotel.

These gents will inform you, for example, that the marinated-seafood appetizer is of squid and scallops, shrimp and mussels, and even tender little clams, all firm and fresh in their lemony dressing. The mozzarella fritta is a simple thing, blocks of cheese, battered and deep fried—the cheese is warm and pully within its crisp surfaces, plain and utterly satisfying, quite lively when you squeeze on lemon. If the words "sfogliata ripieno" do not call to mind a vivid image, imagine a couple of slices cut from a long, plump, warm strudel—the pastry wrapper is at once flaky and rich with fat, and it is filled with a hot, light, and well-seasoned stuffing of meat and cheese.

You may have your red sauce dotted with shrimp in the dish of thin spaghetti that goes as capellini d'angelo con gamberi. Or you may have it spicy, as part of the fusilli (corkscrew-shaped pasta) all' amatriciana—this one is a bit smoky of its Italian bacon. Or you may have it fragrantly herbed as in the linguine alla Santerello—this sauce is hardly more than hot slices of tomato, and it is thick with salty ham and heady with fresh basil.

Each day there is a fish of the day—you have reason to suspect that when there are two of them, yesterday's has become today's. Sometimes it is broiled swordfish—fresh, fibrous but still moist, and enriched with butter that is made sharp and tangy with lime and minced chives. But Santerello has served a dish that could be called tuna with a past. Scampi here are more than what that word usually means—the shrimp are big and crunchy, and they are browned in a garlicky, oregano-flavored butter that is thickened with bread crumbs, Parmesan cheese, and slivers of ham.

Good chicken dishes: one of them the breast in a pungent Gorgonzola sauce that is populated with bits of ham and fresh green peas; the other the legs, which are slit, stuffed with herbed ricotta, and served in a weighty sauce of tomato and zucchini. At least one good veal dish: artfully sautéed scallops of the pearly meat in a strongly seasoned cream-and-marsala sauce that is dense with fresh mushrooms. And good combinations: for one example, the spezzatino di vitello Santerello, wherein chunks of chicken, veal, and shrimp are stewed and served in a powerfully tarragon-flavored sauce that is textured with rice; for another, the spiedini alla uccelletto, an assemblage, on a skewer, of marinated veal and sausages with slices of bacon, the row broiled and blackened a little and served on rice.

You are advised to conclude your dinner with the good house cheese—more than respectable Parmesan and provolone are usually on hand—and some fresh greens in a bright vinaigrette, for the sweet desserts may well turn you off upon presentation: Examples of each of the four are crowded onto a plate and set at the center of your table. Your slight interest in this excessive display declines even further when your waiter, presumably acting on instructions, points with an index finger at each sweet—at a range of about three inches—and describes. For the record, a dark cake allegedly made of macaroons is rather breadlike, and a mountainous item of pastry, whipped cream, and Grand Marnier is merely a mound of goodies. The cannoli—a crisp pastry tube filled with rich, thick custard and bits of candied fruit—is a perfectly good example of the thing.

★★SCARLATTI

34 East 52nd Street
LUNCH, MONDAY TO FRIDAY; DINNER, MONDAY TO SATURDAY. CLOSED SUNDAY.
Reservations: 753-2444.
Credit cards: AE, DC, MC, V.
Very expensive.

The prime mover behind this place has been quoted as saying that he named the restaurant for the composer, because, as he put it, "I like his music." (He does not specify whether it is the music of Alessandro Scarlatti he likes or that of his son Domenico.) He has said further that this restaurant is meant to be the Italian counterpart of La Côte Basque. (And you wonder if he has ever encountered the familiar opinion that La Côte Basque is the most beautiful restaurant in New York.) There are, of course, those who do not mind telling you that they just happen to have very good taste. And you are not at all surprised to discover, one look at this installation, that you disagree. Scarlatti (the restaurant, not either of the composers) is luxe for the sake of luxe, posh without a theme, opulence with no point of view. If you strip away the adornment, there is nothing left. The place does not look as much like a fancy restaurant as like the stage set for one (just as those who frequent it—en masse, anyway—look less like prosperous people than like caricatures thereof).

The huge chandeliers are clusters of gauzy, glowing lampshades among ropes of weighty crystal, and the matching sconces are mounted on silken walls. You walk on plush carpeting, are seated on bouclé banquettes or on plumply upholstered period side chairs with oval backs. Almost all the surfaces are beige, the glow of the place is pink, and there are, here and there, panels of dark-tinted mirror, walls of gilded glass. Modern paintings are all about, but they seem to have been chosen for their tendency to disappear into the background. On every white-linened table there is a single flower—and also a single candle in a tulip-shaped tumbler formed of smoky glass. You can tell the waiters from the busboys by the good braid on their shoulders.

But what you are served here is solid food, none of it fantastical. The seafood salad, for example, varies little from dishes of that name you have had in restaurants that do not look at all like prefabricated boudoirs: fresh-cut slivers of squid and slices of shrimp, with a little celery for crunchiness and strands of red pepper for color, all in a dressing of velvety oil. Grilled shrimp, scampi, are listed as a first course, but among the main courses you will find scampi ribelli—shrimp baked with mozzarella. If the house will not make a small portion, seriously consider sharing a full order with a passerby, for this is a striking scampi dish, the sea sweetness of the crunchy crustaceans (a touch of iodine notwithstanding) striking under their film of lightly browned cheese. In the pasta department the house sometimes offers assortments, and if the idea of three farinaceous items on a single plate strikes you as excessive, know that when the three are wisely selected, they set one another off dramatically—and seem not at all repetitious. Consider these golosi, moist dumplings, at once rich and light, of spinach and cheese; alongside soft, thimble-shaped gnocchi (of noodle dough, not of potatoes) that yield eagerly to the pressure of your tongue—and that are greened with a buttery pesto sauce heady with fresh basil; alongside tortellacci (big ravioli) that are stuffed with a fluffy ricotta filling and served in a simple tomato sauce that is tart and sparkling. A couple of rice dishes are also offered, one of them risotto ortolana, in which the mound of earthy grain, moist of the deep broth in which it was cooked, is studded with mushrooms and chunks of sweet vegetable—the addition of ground cheese and/or black pepper potentiates the sturdy food.

There are simple seafood dishes, among them fresh and firm striped bass in a sauce livornaise—tomato, black olives, capers—that is smooth and strong and salty. There is also a complex one that is listed as a specialty of the house—zuppa di pesce, in which the tail of a small lobster and the whole of a big shrimp, three tender clams in their shells and three sweet mussels in theirs, slices of squid, whole bay scallops, and a slab of fish (on the way down from the zenith of its freshness) are served on a great platter, all the elements dressed with a dark, tomatoed, hot-spiced, and briny sauce. You get a rare chicken dish here, pollo cipriani, in which the mild-flavored bird is in an herbed red sauce that is dotted with peas and mushrooms (nothing unusual there) and also, surprisingly, with a couple of good shrimp—the touch of seafood brininess offsets the chicken strikingly. The scaloppini santa elena is in a wine sauce that is graced with good mushrooms and chunks of crisp artichoke, but the veal itself has been carelessly sautéed, is somewhat overcooked inside, not at all browned outside, and amounts to a mere carrier for the sauce. The good veal chop valdostana—a great nugget of pale meat with a layer of ham and cheese at its center, a huge rib protruding from its side—is notable for the sweet black raisins in its creamy mushroom sauce. When wild broccoli is in season, it is offered here—the crunchy and bitter leaves and stems in a pool of hot oil, and accompanied by, at your captain's suggestion, a couple of strong, gamy sausages.

Whatever salad greens you want may be had in a good dressing with some strong Parmesan cheese. Order zabaglione, and you may see the eggs separated by your captain, and whisked over a flame, right in the dining room—the hot froth reaches you thick, winy, and fluffy. At considerable additional expense the zabaglione will be served to you over ripe raspberries, even in that fruit's local off-season. The zuppa inglese is a fresh, moist, multilevel affair dotted with fruits and nuggets of chocolate, layered with white cream and chocolate cream, stained red here and there, and soaked in rum—if you like that kind of thing, this is a spectacular example of it. If you prefer a simpler thing, there is the délice, in which layers of meringue are interleaved with chocolate cream yet again and whipped cream, the whole strewn with slivered almonds. For something simpler still, the house has on hand some good, ripe melon.

★ SEA GRILL

30 Rockefeller Plaza (at 49th Street)
LUNCH AND DINNER.
Reservations: 246-9201.
Credit cards: AE, DC, MC, V.
Expensive.

For decades now, Rockefeller Center has been respectable. No one any longer points to it as the perfect, offensive symbol of superior economic man's triumph over lesser economic man. When it was declared a landmark, dialectical arguments were not raised in opposition. You are today free, in polite company, to praise its architecture without offering countervailing provisos about the rapacious accumulation of wealth that made it all possible.

Perhaps mindful at last of the altered climate, the interests behind the Center have now deleted the somewhat honky-tonk public accommodations that for years, presumably as a sop to the masses, surrounded—and in summer occupied—the sunken middle of the plaza. (The plebes never did show much appreciation for them anyway.) In their place have been substituted establishments in which even a Rockefeller might eat. The flagship of the new food-service facilities that now rim the skating rink on three sides (and spill forth umbrella-shaded tables onto it during the warm-weather months) is this one. Of course, the ungrateful riffraff—the idle, the young, tourists, others among the underutilized—continue to frequent the plaza. So a means had to be found by which the right folks could gain access to the restaurants, from points outside the Center, without coming into contact with the throngs of gawkers and loungers that sometimes crowd the approaches from Fifth Avenue and the side streets. Accordingly, glass bubbles have been erected on 49th and 50th. You may drive, or be driven, right up to a bubble. Each is manned by a uniformed attendant. And between each of them and the eating places below them an elevator shuttles. The attendant summons the elevator for you and even presses the button. The experience is as nifty as knowing a password.

It is from the bubble on 49th that you drop to the Sea Grill. Once below, you learn that the name tells only half the story, for it is not just the fashion for seafood that this place is following, but the rage for regional American cooking as well. Accordingly, the restaurant has been done up in a style of domestic suburban that, fortunately, is cushy enough in the rendering to offset its natural anonymity. The place is wood paneled and carpeted, with living-room armchairs and sofas for two arranged around white-linened tables that are big and, mostly, far apart. Glassy wine racks are all about, flowers and glinting brass here and there. Into a couple of shallow tile pools water splashes. At the eastern end of the place is the spiffy exposed kitchen, wrapped in glass. Near it is a little bar and a handful of cocktail tables (at which, when you are served a drink, you are also served a cocktail napkin of neatly pressed linen). If you get a table at the long northern wall—it is mostly glass—you may look out at the skaters in winter or, in summer, at diners in Paris café chairs eating among the planters, palms, and umbrellas. You, too, may eat out there, under the huge golden statue of Prometheus, the waterfall behind him, and the skyscrapers, at once massive and soaring, that rise all around.

You do wish that more of the food were as good as the best. Take, for example, what is given as "three poached shrimp, Texas champagne" (your basic shrimp cocktail). It consists of giant shrimp reclining side by side—they are pink, firm, devoid of iodine, and devoid of any other flavor as well; and of that "champagne," a wonderful mustard-flavored cocktail sauce—but still, cocktail sauce. The sausages of shrimp and scallops are presumably in part of those same crustaceans, for they are utterly tasteless and cannot be saved by the vivid shellfish and saffron sauces that come with them. But the oysters Rockefeller (maybe in response to some sort of duress) are flawless: four half-shells on a mound of warm coarse salt, each filled with a creamy, spicy, heavily Pernod-flavored spinach puree; and, submerged in each shell, a tender and sweet little oyster. Order the Sea Grill chowder, and you are brought morsels of finfish and shellfish in a deep plate, and some thick red liquid in a cup—the latter is poured over the former, but the seafood remains pallid despite the spiciness of that smooth soup. The angel hair pasta with tiny clams is notable for the dozen fresh and tender littlenecks in among the firm noodles, and for the briny, well-parsleyed broth. Among the non-seafood appetizers is a good one called golden oak mushroom salad, in which the truly woodsy strands of wild mushroom are served with slices of warm, rich duck liver in a mildly spicy dressing.

Of the half-dozen fish that are prepared on the grill, you get a big tuna steak, hand-somely charcoal striped, the fresh fish only slightly dried, lively in its tomato vinaigrette; a filleted whole pompano, also fresh, but its delicate flavor quite defeated by heavy charring, the warm, buttered citrus sections with which it is served robbed of their liveliness in this handling; and a wall-eyed pike (you do your best not to stare), yet another delicate fish, this one out of fresh water, and this time gently grilled, the meat firm and a little oily, the green sauce—of fennel, watercress, garlic, and onion—a pungent and fragrant foil to the white meat. Skip the grilled lobster, for in the strenuous effort not to overcook it, it is sometimes taken untimely from the fire, and served neither rare nor yet quite white. A version of the San Francisco fish stew called cioppino is served here—the heavy tomato sauce, thick with onions and peppers, is studded with fish and shellfish, none of them outstanding, the mussels distinctly rank. Perhaps the restaurant has chosen the wrong emphasis for itself, for one of its red-meat dishes is among its best—the beef tenderloin, two nicely sautéed disks of tender red meat, each surrounded by a slice of rich duck liver, the whole dish moistened with a red-wine sauce the spiciness of which suggests—subtly, interestingly—Worcestershire sauce. The à la carte vegetables can be fine—tender and firm asparagus, or hefty, nicely browned disks of zucchini; but the pan-fried potatoes—a pancake of browned strands under a bit of sour cream and melted cheese—is terrific one time, cordlike and tasteless another.

The cheese-and-fruit plate is of terrific American fruit, but also of American cheeses doing bad imitations of European ones. The big end-of-dinner winner is the key lime pie, a tangy, fruity filler on a dark graham cracker crust, a great thickness of whipped cream on top. What the Grill calls strawberry shortcake, you call strawberries, whipped cream, and sponge cake in layers, but it is not bad for that. The apricot mousse layer cake is of fluffy mousse and good preserves, but the cake itself is chalky. The almond pound cake is rather heavy, with almonds around the rim. If you would like a glass of milk, this place has the classic chocolate cake to go with it.

★★SERYNA

11 East 53rd Street
LUNCH, MONDAY TO FRIDAY; DINNER, MONDAY TO SATURDAY. CLOSED SUNDAY.
Reservations: 980-9393.
Credit cards: AE, DC, MC, V.
Expensive.

You approach the place through a courtyard that fronts on 53rd Street. It has been planted with a stand of trees, and at night their branches glow, softly but vividly, with the amber and golden lights strung along them. The walk through those trees, though it is just a brief moment of tranquillity, is equal to at least half a Valium—and you can even mix it with alcohol. There is calm again inside. The dining room is a lofty space, all wood and the colors of wood. It manages, in the Japanese manner, to be at once spare and luxurious. The substantial wooden tables are as sturdy as concrete. The upholstered armchairs receive you in an affectionate embrace. The baskets and pottery and prints that are spotted around the room soften a little what might otherwise be its severity, without compromising its quite grand simplicity.

The most irritating thing about the Japanese is that whenever they undertake to do something the West already does, they find a way to do it better. Take, for what is only the most recent maddening instance, this item listed as "smoked salmon." Seems fair enough, lots of countries smoke salmon, and every denomination has one virtue or another. But this Japanese entrant seems, magically, to combine the forthrightness and subtlety that in all other varieties are mutually exclusive. These glistening orange sheets are of a fish flavor that, though it is vivid, is somehow clouded by the slight oiliness, smokiness, and textural delicacy of the diaphanous stuff. As in almost all Japanese restaurants that do not have sushi bars, the sushi and sashimi here are not up to the best in town—these are good little morsels, but they lack that utterly unfaded freshness of these things at their best. On the other hand, such a commonplace as shrimp tempura (sometimes prepared here of large, very delicately flavored shrimp from Japan) is encased in a fried batter that seems little more than crispness and air—you dip the delicately crusted crustaceans in their sharp black sauce to spice them. Crabmeat shumai are firm, plump crabmeat dumplings, some of them wrapped in spinach, some in an omeletlike sheet, all of them of clear crabmeat flavor—they are served with shredded vegetables, sharp mustard, a pungent soy sauce.

The listing "shio broiled fish" makes reference to a method of fish preparation in which salt is applied to the skin of the fish before broiling. The salt causes the fat under the skin to break down and saturate the meat during cooking. The technique imparts so much flavor to the fish that even a relatively pallid variety like tilefish is served—charred and juicy—sporting a pure, powerful flavor. What is called stuffed sole consists of four cutlets of good fish spread with a seasoned paste and served in a red sauce that is sweet, acidic, strongly garlicked. The striking fish is garnished with broccoli florets, the color and crispness of which are in well chosen contrast to the crimson sauce and pale fillets. Seryna lists steamed fresh fish, a dish in which the variety varies from day to day. When snapper is prepared this way, you are served the fish boned, but with its pink-metallic skin gleaming, the whole set in a pool of almost caustic dark sauce and strewn with leaves of coriander. Little of that strong sauce clings to the fluffy, sweet fish—just the right amount, it seems, to strengthen it without obscuring its good flavor. What the house mysteriously calls crabmeat steak is actually a complex dish in which crabmeat appears three ways: as broiled crabmeat legs, lightly charred, tender and a little spicy; as domino-shaped blocks of a kind of spicy egg-and-crabmeat-and-vegetable gelatin, much like a highly stylized gefülte fish; and a heavily oiled sauce that is strongly flavored of crabmeat shell. The three are about as different from one another as foods can be and still be, clearly, alike.

If you want steak—sirloin or filet mignon—it comes with a Japanese rock set in the wooden frame in which it is carried to your table. The rock cannot be brought to you the way, say, a plate is brought to you, because it has been heated to 400° F. Your steak comes already sliced, but raw, and though your waiter or waitress will gladly pepper it and then rock-grill it for you, piece by piece, you can do that yourself after getting instructions as to how many minutes on the rock will yield what degree of doneness. Once you have started cooking, the rock is good for about 15 minutes of use before it cools down. If you eat slowly, you may send for another rock. Anyway, the method turns out lovely chunks of this restaurant's good beef, which you may dip in your choice of a couple of sauces—one of which seems to have Worcestershire sauce in it, and the other of which is a tangy relative of ketchup. Yet another modified Westernism in connection with this dish—it is served with an odd little dish of herbed potato sticks and something that does a good likeness of whipped cream. (In French fries, apparently, the Japanese have not yet taken the lead.) After you have mastered doing your own steak, you are ready for shabu-shabu, in which you dip slices of rosy beef in the pot of boiling stock and wine that has been hooked up right on your table. When you have done with the meat—having dipped the briefly simmered morsels in a nutty sesame sauce before eating them—you are ready to cook up some mushrooms, scallion greens, seaweed, blocks of bean curd, and clear noodles in the same stock. These you flavor with a strong sauce of citrus and vinegar. The ingredients are good, and the food is good—the dish coming off as a dozen textures and flavors, each of them simple, but dramatic in relation to the others—but you may find that it requires more work than you want to expend when you have to pay as well.

To a Japanese, slippery arrowroot noodles dipped in fruit syrup may seem like dessert. To you they will probably seem like food only for thought. The Japanese melon sometimes offered here has a slightly dry austereness—it bears the same relationship to your idea of melon as does herbal tea to a pastrami sandwich. When there is papaya, have that—it is ripe and juicy and solid and sweet, and very good after the food here.

★★SIAM CUISINE

410 Amsterdam Avenue (near 80th Street)
DINNER.
Reservations: 874-0105.
Credit cards: AE, DC, MC, V.
Inexpensive.

This restaurant's spiffy little bar—with the polished mirror behind it reflecting the rows of glinting bottles—seems like a modern appliance in a primitive kitchen. From the looks of the floor, it appears that someone attempted to paint it—and failed. On your second look at the ceiling, you realize that the acoustic tiles are really squares of plywood. When the installers were surfacing these walls, they chose one material—and then, when that ran out, another, so there is pastel-blue paint, vaguely patterned wallpaper, white brick, and, at the back, a wall that is almost entirely mirrored. Withal, the place is not ramshackle, is in fact cheery, and it often fills with a casual neighborhood crowd that is of the West Side's old, preswinging style—the earnest, steel rimmed, and bearded in the company of the earnest, steel rimmed, and unpainted.

Though the first section of the menu is headed "Appetizers," for a really rousing first course you will select from among the items listed as salads. Three of these, the squid salad, shrimp salad, and beef salad, consist of, respectively, strands of fresh and tender squid, whole crunchy shrimp, and slices of good browned beef, each mingled with crisp vegetables, among them cucumbers, peppers, onions, scallions, and snow peas, all in a fiery lime-juice dressing. The makeup and proportions of these added ingredients vary from squid to shrimp to beef, and also from time to time, but the salads are especially stimulating when fresh and fragrant coriander leaves are present in abundance. You may think of satés as Indonesian or Malaysian dishes, but they are part of Thai cooking as well. A small order of chicken saté consists of three substantial lengths of white meat that have been flavored with a spicy and fruity marinade. The shafts of meat are impaled on wood skewers, broiled until they are flecked with black but still moist and shiny, and served with a thick peanut sauce that is sweet and spicy. Naturally the Thai noodle dish called mee krob is on the menu here—this is a great tangle of deep-fried rice noodles (in this version dotted with bits of pork and a few shrimp), moistened with a mildly spiced tamarind sauce that is of a honeylike sweetness.

You get a nicely deep-fried whole fish here, the surface crusty; the pale meat moist and flaky and fresh tasting—it arrives under a spicy-hot sauce that is thick with red peppers and peas, and with chunks of pineapple that are a striking note in this setting. What is given as "chicken curry (green)" reaches you as a steel pot of hot, oiled broth (mostly coconut milk) that is laden with strands of coconut, red peppers, sweet green peas, and an abundance of good chicken. If you come to this place just once, do not miss the marinated rabbit, which consists of large chunks of the sautéed meat, lightly crisped and tender, mingled with more of this establishment's ever-present sweet peas, and moistened with a spicy sauce that is redolent of garlic.

Western desserts seem bizarre after Thai food, but to satisfy what must be a real demand, the restaurant obtains a good chocolate cake.

★★SICHUAN PAVILION

310 East 44th Street
LUNCH AND DINNER.
Reservations: 972-7377.
Credit cards: AE, DC, MC, V.
Medium priced.

The dreary situation that is today's New York Chinese-restaurant scene has been brightened some by the return of Sichuan Pavilion—happily, to new quarters. Recall the high-ceilinged, brightly lighted color boxes that were the rooms of the old place, and you know what the new one is not. But remember the old Pavilion's food—what it was when the restaurant was new and at its best—and here it is again. The new look has come to us from China by way of California, that is, the flower paintings, framed calligraphy, and panda art are subsumed in a comfortable—almost cushy—haze of soft light and unstained wood. The well-spaced tables are linened, the chairs are padded, and the floor is carpeted. The big central dining room is rimmed by smaller rooms usable for parties. Etched-glass windows overlook the row of enclosed tables on 44th Street.

This is the place with the limp dumplings. They look like you could drape them over a clothesline. Not so easy, however, for the noodle casings are slippery of the black, oily, hot, and hot-spiced sauce they are served in—the fillings, firm nodules of pork force-meat, are vibrant of their complex seasoning. The beef strips in a small steamer come, you guessed it, in a small steamer—it is filled with the just-done slivers of meat, fibrous and very tender, spicy-hot and aromatic. The smoked fish fillets are made smoky, black, and a little spicy by their treatment—the fish, clearly, was fresh when it was prepared, and its pristine oceanic flavor gleams through. Still, that fish is akin to dishes you have had in dozens of Chinese places, while other cold appetizers here hold surprises: tangy chicken, for one, thick slices of white meat cut from a tasty bird, moistened with a black sauce that is at once salty, winy, fragrantly perfumed—the dish is marked with a star, but it is far from violently hot; and tangy rabbit, long strands of the firm meat mingled with grassy greens that impart a citrus acidity to the rousing dish—the moisture is a smooth oil that carries the fiery spice, and the dish is sprinkled with crisp sesame seeds.

In a box at the center of the menu are listed ten dishes under the heading "first time served in America." Many of these were so described at the old place, so the claim is now strained. Still, this is where to look, for here you will find the likes of "dry sautéed squid," which would better read "sautéed dried squid," for it is made—by design—not of the fresh article, but of the preserved, the gamy accent and slight resilience of which, in this mass of bean sprouts, shredded pork, and much else, gives the dish such assertive character that your waiter lowers his pad when you ask for it, looks you over, inquires if you know what you are doing—you reassure him by confessing a helpless addiction to the stuff. Still working the box, you order "tinklin [sic] bells with ten ingredients," and the components are wheeled to your table on a serving stand, where they sizzle viciously when transferred to a hot frying pan. The dish is not, as its name leads you reasonably to fear, just another Chinese compendium, substantial but confusing. In fact, its elements —little mushrooms, crisp disks of water chestnut, scallion whites and scallion greens, slivers of pork, emerald snow peas, crunchy shrimp, and more, all filmed with a light, glistening oil—retain their individuality in the complex setting. The "tinklin bells" of the title are small dumplings, somewhat doughy ones that pick up a bit of crispness in that last-minute sautéing, and their starchy weight is in nice contrast to the sprightlier items in the dish. What is given as "crispy whole fish" is just that, the giant sea bass in a pool of sauce that is thick and dark, smooth and oily, fiery hot and dense with scallion greens. A silken, slightly sticky sauce binds the diverse elements of the Sichuan-style lamb: slivers of meat that taste slightly burnt, chunks of fragrant garlic, delicate ears of baby corn, lengths of scallion—the food is heady of fresh ginger and powerfully hot of the red peppers (dangerous to eat) you find hidden among the other elements. Most of the dishes go well with the crunchy pan-fried noodles—a crisped tangle dotted with vegetables and meats. The spiced string beans are, pleasantly, a little tough—they reach you under strongly seasoned ground pork.

★ SIDO

81 Lexington Avenue (at 26th Street) (new address)
LUNCH AND DINNER.
Reservations: 686-2031.
Credit cards: AE, MC, V.
Inexpensive.

Despite the loss of your job, and the consequent difficulty keeping up your alimony, child-support, mortgage, maintenance, garage, health-insurance, club-membership, and back-tax payments, you are determined to maintain your man-about-town persona. But to do so, clearly, you must become a man about another part of town. Enter a heretofore hidden side of your personality, the shrewd ethnic sampler, one who knows where the real food in this town lies hidden (not that fancy uptown stuff), who knows where genuine New Yorkers eat, who knows that honest cooking can always be spotted by the unpretentiousness of its price tag. The hard part is holding a straight face while explaining this to the girlfriend.

You automatically reject restaurants burdened with self-consciously prepossessing appointments, and you embrace almost without hesitation Sido, your one demur a reaction to the scattered handful of pictures on the walls (the assorted subjects share a Middle Eastern theme, including this intimate, quite smashing, all tan closeup of a great sand dune), because their seemingly random placement suggests that they are positioned vainly, that is, to conceal structural blemishes. The foursquare room sports upper walls of mock brown stone, lower ones of mock brown wood, a floor of dark-gray flagstones. You are shielded from the unnecessarily sumptuous white cloths on the tables by the sheets of plate glass that protect you from them. And though you would prefer bare bulbs, you permit yourself to be amused by the garish hanging lamps and wall sconces that the interests behind this place have installed, in deference to the tawdry taste of the locals. All the place lacks, really, are broken chairs and shaky tables. Instead, there is recorded pained wailing, to which even the waiters, to whom this music is presumably familiar, do not tap their feet.

Many of the charge-account delinquents and credit-card junkies who frequent Sido have found here a single menu item that will feed satisfactorily two hungries. It is called Sido Mezzo and consists of eight items from the appetizer menu that, together with the basket of warm pita that accompanies it, may well hold you until your next dinner invitation. The components are, moreover, good to eat, a condition having nothing to do with the modest $12.95 price of this Levantine smorgasbord: hummus, a particularly nutty and oil-rich version of the chickpea-and-sesame paste; baba ghannouj, baked eggplant ground to a coarse spread, flavored with lemon juice and oil, this example quite smoky; tabboulee, the chopped salad of parsley, onions, tomato, and bulgur wheat that, in this instance, is mostly fresh parsley in a bright lemon dressing; cold grape leaves, the little cylindrical packages of moist, sweet-spiced rice dotted with pine nuts and wrapped in tender leaves that have a nice parchment quality; yogurt of a creaminess and tartness unlike any yogurt on your grocer's shelf; dreary cheese; an unfortunate kibbee made with fowl rather than lamb, the hot dumplings of grain and ground chicken (or whatever) packed not only with nuts and vegetables but also with giblets, which do not provide what the lack of lamb takes away; and falafel, hot, crunchy, spicy, well-garlicked, and artfully deep-fried balls of grain and ground chickpeas.

The unencumbered among you may consider a main course. The chicken couscous is a great plate of the grainlike semolina fluff, and another deeper plate of the stew (chicken, firm potatoes, and rather soft carrots and chickpeas the principal ingredients) in an inch of its murky but deeply flavored stewing broth—the flavor of the good chicken has been potentiated by the herbs, spices, and vegetables with which it was done. The shish kebab is many morsels of strong lamb, long marinated, quite tender, blackened a little, and strewn with raw onions.

Kanafi is the good dessert—rose-water custard under pine nuts and threads of coconut. The bakhlava is a perfectly good filling of honeyed nuts between layers of rather heavy pastry.

★★SIGN OF THE DOVE

1110 Third Avenue (at 65th Street)
LUNCH, TUESDAY TO SUNDAY; DINNER, DAILY.
Reservations: 861-8080.
Credit cards: AE, DC, MC, V.
Very expensive.

As the aged and infirm return to religion—just in case it develops, hard upon the last moment, that there is something to it—so have the interests behind this old hustle given themselves over, here in the fading years of New York's grand restaurant spree, to quality. But surely visitors from the land west of the Hudson, who for decades provided this former trap with most of its commerce, continue to produce as many more of themselves as ever; and certainly the dollar's diminuendo makes Manhattan a tourist attraction of greater cost effectiveness than other world-class metropolises not susceptible to unscheduled changes of government; ergo, one must conclude that the Dove's new policy is no response to short-term need, that, rather, someone has seen the light. All kneel.

The new order does not, however, extend to the visual and aural spheres. You check your coat, and you are led past a gentleman at a baby upright whose harmless tinklings follow you to your table, which is in one of two grandiloquent dining rooms, each a few stories high, lofty archways between them. One is covered over by a great domed stained-glass skylight, the other by a ceiling painted in a mauve-and-gray pattern of roiling ocean, its effect, upon prolonged consideration, gastrointestinally unsettling. You lower your eyes to walls of brick bathed in rosy light, to statuary, to huge mirrors that face each other, east-west and north-south, and that reflect and re-reflect the rooms in endless repetition, so that it is as if the Dove extends from First Avenue to Fifth, from P. J. Clarke's to J. G. Melon. There are tied-back gauze curtains on the tall windows, flagstone floors, bouquets of flowers on the white-linened tables, big bursts of them here and there around the rooms—everything awash in soft light. This kind of thing still draws the outlanders, some from not so far off, and here they are, lounging in their chairs, soaking up the luxury, she in a fleecy cashmere sweater trimmed with mink, he in a doeskin suit, neither aware that the fancy food they get here now differs from the fancified stuff they loved in the past.

Fancy indeed is this casserole of oysters, the dish with which, if you come here once, you wisely begin, the fresh, plump mollusks, out of their shells, warm, of vivid oyster flavor, served in a light, creamy, and briny broth that is threaded with dill and dotted with diced vegetables—tomatoes, zucchini, and much crunchy fennel among them. Your order of eggplant terrine is a couple of thick slabs cut from a layered loaf that is many slices of the named vegetable, among them a layer of red peppers, the two vigorously seasoned and suffused with garlicked oil. A stuffed pasta pancake goes as "duck confit and shiitake ravioli," the forcemeat within the folded noodle sheet of spicy duck flavor, thin strands of celery and chive upon it, meaty slices of sautéed mushroom around it, all in a good, strong, mushroom-flavored sauce. Hot, crisp, and salty parts of quail and cool mushrooms are arranged around a salad of baby lettuce and artichoke hearts in a dressing made with good oil, but the warm ingredients argue with the cool ones, and the artichoke hearts are much like those you find in cans.

In this establishment's fanciful version of the French fish soup called bourride, slivers of rich scallop, a split prawn, its meat sweet and firm in its half shells, and morsels of supple lobster are arranged, with tiny spears of baby asparagus, over a mound of enriched cabbage, everything set in a pink and polished crayfish sauce. Your crosshatched slab of Norwegian salmon is on occasion a bit overcooked, a little dry—still, this is fresh fish, nicely set off by the warm greens on which it is arranged, and by the mushrooms and artichoke hearts around it. Pale and tender meat, handsomely browned, cooked through but juicy, such are the medallions of veal—they are surmounted by the good sautéed wild mushrooms that show up in just about every second dish in this place, and they are garnished with strong spinach that is adorned with a little muffin of wondrously rich garlic custard. The boneless rack of lamb is serious fun food, the slices of pink meat, spicy within their charred edges, forming half a circle, the other half an arc of brown-edged slices of fried potato, the two served with two sauces—a dollop of intense red-pepper puree, and a so-called herbed aioli that is rich, but rather mild for this company.

The lemon mousse cake is a cool and acidic custard on a light shortbread pastry. The raspberry mousse cake, pink and fruity, is intensified by a crimson raspberry sauce. The pear tart is of thin, delicate slices, the apple tart is of great caramelized nuggets, both are on flaky pastry, and both come with fist-sized dollops of rich, tangy crème fraîche.

★ SISTINA

1555 Second Avenue (near 80th Street)
LUNCH, MONDAY TO FRIDAY; DINNER, DAILY.
Reservations: 861-7660.
Credit cards: AE.
Expensive.

The name of the place is a reference to the chapel, and there hangs on one wall a replica of a detail from its famous ceiling—specifically from the section in which is depicted God's creation of Adam. Moreover, when you crush out your cigarette, you do so on an ashtray the surface of which is a picture of the chapel's interior. It was a fortunate coin flip indeed that determined which illustration would go on the wall, which on the ashtray. This enterprise is in the third or fourth generation of Upper East Side restaurants serving Italian food in clubby surroundings, and it does owe much to its predecessors. But, though it was supposedly Michelangelo himself who said, "When I steal, I kill," Sistina does not bother. It is, in fact, at once the most slavish and most bloodless rendition yet of the Elio's-Parma-Lusardi's theme. Except for a couple of palm trees, a mirrored back wall, and that unfortunate reproduction, it could pass for a prefab. When this style originated, there was, behind it, an idea. Now it shows up wherever there is the lack of one. You know what to expect: the little bar up front; smooth ivory-colored walls; lots of wood trim—in this case unstained oak, sealed and shiny; a polished-wood floor; and rows of white-linened tables. The room is well lighted, pallid, and, somehow, nude, but when there are lots of customers, that helps dress it up.

If you have been to these places, you may recognize some of the help—there exists a battalion of brusquely efficient, mostly Italian waiters who bounce around within this restaurant league like billiard balls at the break. You, however, may go unrecognized, in which case your host, desperate to exercise power, denies you the table of your choice with an excuse chosen purely for its transparence. You express your preference for a certain square corner table that can hold no more than four. He expresses his regrets, explaining that it is reserved for six. Eventually it goes to three, with the dining room half empty all evening. But when a veteran neighborhood waiter is on hand, spots you, and informs the authorities that you are a substantial client hereabouts, your host is suddenly all accommodation. The man's infirmities are real ones, but somehow, he generates little sympathy. After all, he is affiliated with a restaurant that is better than he is—anyway, the food is.

As soon as you are seated, get yourself an order of fried zucchini. The lightly battered strands are hot and crisp, and you will need something to nibble on during the time you waste deciphering the menu, for it is replete with the likes of "filetti di sogliola gran successo," and "pollo alla Sisto IV," which is to say, names of dishes that would mean nothing to you even if Italian were your first language and Italian cooking your second. You must ask questions, but you probably know without asking what means "vitello tonnato." At Sistina it stands for an abundance of good, cold veal under a thick, well-oiled, judiciously seasoned, and vividly tuna-flavored sauce—you wish it had not been quite so thoroughly blenderized, but fortunately, the contrasting capers are sprinkled on afterward. The carpaccio is a bit of rather icy raw beef that is strewn with shavings of good Parmesan cheese, garnished with slices of lemon, and served with a jigger of cool, sour, salty sauce that is green with parsley. When your host comes by to deliver the spiel about the specials of the day, he carries with him a basket of wild mushrooms from Italy. They look pretty frightening in their gnarled and twisted uncooked state, but do not let that keep you from the crostini di polenta ai porcini, in which the fragrant and pungent sautéed mushrooms—mingled with firm white beans and moistened with the good to-mato-dotted oil in which they were prepared—are served over toasted cornmeal crusts.

Among the mostly good pasta dishes: big tubes of rigatoni in a four-cheese sauce—of mozzarella, fontina, Gorgonzola, and Parmesan—that has a winy, almost brandylike intensity of cheese flavor; tonnarelli (read linguine) primavera, in which the fresh vegetables and delicate pasta are bound in a creamy sauce that is pinked with tomato; and linguine ai frutti di mare, wherein the slender noodles, mingled with an abundance of mussels and clams in their shells, squid, little scallops, and crisp shrimp, are served in a briny white broth that is dense with parsley and threaded with slivers of garlic.

You may have that seafood pasta in red sauce instead, which is a little like having the caciucco alla Mediterranea (it would go as zuppa di pesce in most places), in which the shellfish are augmented by slabs of finfish, chunks of octopus, and crusts of toasted bread—the solid ingredients are all fine, but the parsleyed and garlicked red broth is thin. The good shrimp you found in the zuppa may be had in quantity in what is given as scampi "sorpresa"; the "surprise" is that the browned and crunchy little shrimp—they are in an herbed, pinked, and buttery sauce—are sprinkled with still more of this kitchen's beloved capers. Each day there is a fish of the day, sometimes swordfish, which is variously described to you as broiled or grilled—anyway, it seems to be no more than heated through, is neither browned nor crisped, and though its sauce is ostensibly of butter and lemon, you must add more of the latter to give the dish life. But the chicken molisana needs no such help—the chunks of browned bird are really just background for these disks of spicy sausage and sections of sweet red pepper, all of which are in a stout, tomato-reddened sauce—a hefty dish. The names of some of the menu items are references to the house theme. Thus, scaloppine Buonarroti (presumably one of Michelangelo Buonarroti's favorite dishes), a construct of nicely sautéed scallops of veal, thin slices of tomato, leaves of very good ham, and, over all of those, many disks of browned zucchini, the entire production moistened by a sauce that is notable for its intense olive-oil flavor. What Sistina calls fegatini meraviglia, you call liver veneziana prepared with chicken livers. Still, nothing wrong with that, and the crusted little meats, pink inside, mingled with slivers of sweet onion, are fine in their winy sauce.

That waiter who knows everybody—he shakes your hand as if you once saved his life—has a casual way of taking orders, regularly gets them wrong, smiles cooperatively when you order Parmesan cheese, and then delivers a lovely plate of peeled fruit with fontina and Gorgonzola. His resentment at having to make the change is hard to miss, which does not alter the cheese—it is flinty and strong. One waiter explains to you that the dessert called "delice" is of chocolate, lemon, and meringue. Later his partner refreshes your memory: chocolate, vanilla, and almonds. You opt instead for the chocolate mousse cake, which is the usual thing. The crème brûlée is soupy. The melon balls and strega are a terrific combination, would come off perfectly if the melon were riper. Sometimes the house serves good raspberries in balsamic vinegar—when offered those, have those.

You order the fish of the day, swordfish, and only when you get your check do you discover that, at $18, it is more expensive than anything on the printed menu. But another time, when, during the course of the evening, the house has decided to treat you with care, you find that the prices on your check have been entered, then rubbed out, then written over. In its final version, this remarkable document has a half order of pasta at less than half the price of a full order, and cheese at a 25 percent discount from what it went for earlier in the week. If you care what you spend, get quotes up front.

★ SMITH & WOLLENSKY

797 Third Avenue (at 49th Street)
LUNCH, MONDAY TO FRIDAY; DINNER, DAILY.
Reservations: 753-1530.
Credit cards: AE, DC, MC, V.
Very expensive.

If you have recently telephoned for help to one of America's great corporations—to have, say, your typewriter repaired, or to get your sewing machine wired for electricity—you have perhaps noticed that the so-called service personnel with whom you deal have developed a way of speaking formerly peculiar to recorded announcements. Sometimes it is difficult to determine whether what you say is being responded to by a human or a digital intelligence. Even witticisms, which you essay in a desperate try to draw out what remains of the mortal in your respondent, are met with mechanical comebacks. Fortunately, this form of human decomposition is not yet widespread in the restaurant game. But you are a bit thrown when, upon addressing yourself to one of Smith & Wollensky's young, overgrown bartenders with the words, "Do you have Moosehead?" the galoot responds with, "Yes, and we pour it proudly." Maybe he thinks that by modeling his language after product commercials, and his manner of speech after that of airwaves hucksters, he will attract the attention of one of the thousands of executives who, at the expense of the very corporations whose products are so drearily peddled, pack this place daily. You do like to think the poor fool is just looking for a job—but the obvious pleasure he takes in his mastery of this manner and idiom disputes that fond reading.

You are at the bar because, though you arrived on time for your reservation, and though tables are available, the foppish young gentleman at the book this day is one who enjoys exercising what small power he has managed in life to accrue. He sends all comers to the bar for a ten- or fifteen-minute cooling-down period, and then grants tables, now to these two, now to those three, as if he were dispensing alms to mendicants—the distribution always in something other than the poor beggars' order of arrival. And if for some reason he dislikes you altogether, he may forget you indefinitely—until you make a scene. It appears you have to be his type, or his idea of S&W's type, which, as it happens, is a quite specific one. This is a male species (its ladies are only in waiting), it is cleanshaven, cigared, blazered. It watches football in winter, golfs in summer. It does beer and booze. In fact you figure at first that the enforced prelude at the bar is for the purpose of selling extra drinks to customers who will often have nothing stronger than pop once their boulders of beef are before them. (And it is true that, though the establishment sports a dozen-page, computer-printout multinational wine list, a tour through the restaurant's many rooms and regions turns up maybe one working bottle of wine per dozen occupied tables.) But when others are handling the seating, it is sometimes conducted equitably—at least it is when there is no more room at the bar.

This is the place that, in the late seventies, appeared on the scene having unashamedly composed for itself a style formed of characteristics lifted from the most successful steakhouses in New York. It borrowed so well that today it appears to be doing more business—anyway, under one roof—than any of its models. (In its earliest days it even operated without printed menus—in the manner of the Palm and Christ Cella—but that particular idiocy was soon abandoned.) Of the qualities it endeavored to replicate, the basic one was age. S&W was built to look as if it had been here forever. Composed of areas at various levels, each of them furnished somewhat differently from the others (just tables and chairs here, booths there, a big banquette yonder), the sprawling place—all wood-floored and buff-colored—looks like a normal-size restaurant that, by accretion of now one additional space, now another, became a mammoth one over time. The sense of history is reinforced by the dozens of pieces of art and artifact—mostly Americana—that, it is easy to believe, were accumulated over the years, each piece mounted or hung wherever there was room. The dining rooms and bar are dripping with duck decoys, models of historic vehicles, primitive paintings, an ancient horse-and-buggy weathervane, sporting prints, more. Some things have been added during the restaurant's actual years: little brass-colored plates (tacked up behind the bar, at the entranceway to the central dining room, elsewhere), each of them engraved with the name of one of the establishment's regular customers, dead or alive—Hal Horowitz, Jim Lewis, L. Baxter Chamberlain, &c—for S&W is a fraternal place; and a second story much like the first—though noisier, for it does not benefit from the acoustic ceiling that, on the lower level, modulates the sounds of the vociferous crowd. Upstairs or down, the place is patrolled by waiters who wear putty-colored jackets, shirts and ties, white aprons—as in ye olden days.

Just as the restaurant looks to have been here since Prohibition, nothing about its printed menu suggests that the document postdates World War II—that is, if you imagine the decimal points one place to the left. But when the shrimp cocktail arrives, you are promptly back in the present, for this restaurant's illusionism overrides all but economics, and so the half dozen crustaceans that were once the usual allotment are expressed, in the S&W rendition, as four. These are not bad shrimp, big, crunchy, and devoid of iodine, but of shrimp flavor they have not much. The lobster cocktail, however, is a minor masterpiece, the entire little beast snug in its split red shell, cool but not cold, firm but not tough, moist but not wet, of sweet oceanic flavor—obviously, it was prepared and cooled not too long before you ordered it. And the lump crabmeat is more than its equal, a great mound of iridescent nuggets of firm but delicate meat, each of them of a marine sweetness that suggests crabs fished from the water the very day. The shellfish cocktails are served with two sauces—a vibrant cocktail sauce that sparkles with sweet spice, and a creamy ginger sauce that is greened with chopped spinach. Shellfish aside, you may begin your dinner with prosciutto and melon—three broad paper-thin sheets of strong and salty ham over three crescents of fairly ripe melon; or with the thick and pleasantly sticky pea soup—it is hot and spicy hot, and it is poured into your broad soup plate from the tin cup in which it was carried from the kitchen.

In this busy place the fish of the day is truly of the day, and you may have here the like of this great side of red snapper, the utterly fresh fish, redded and browned, falling into tender flakes of pale meat that retain all their distinctive snapper flavor. Opt for other than fish, however, and things begin to go—downhill. You order a broiled lobster, and, as is the way of this place, you are presented with a lobster that is first steamed and then broiled, which is quite another article. Steaming and then broiling is supposedly a means of lobster preparation that combines the advantages of two methods—it sounds reasonable but does not work out that way, and the so-called broiled lobsters here are usually somewhat stringy or tough, unlike the strictly broiled ones you get at, say, the Palm or Christ Cella. With respect to the chopped steak, S&W makes the mistake all steakhouses make—it prepares its immense chopped steak as if it were an unchopped steak, so if you want yours, say, rare, you will get a chopped steak that, though it is rare at the center, is brown and dry throughout its outer half inch. If you have sometimes wondered why coffee-shop hamburgers are often better than steakhouse chopped steaks, it is because coffee shops do their hamburgers on a griddle (or, occasionally, in a pan), and a hot, flat metal surface is the only source of heat that will hold the moisture in a chopped steak—or hamburger—while cooking it through. The sirloins are big, blackened a little, accurately broiled, and tender—but a bit dry, and of less than the beefiest flavor, even for these days. And the veal chop, even when it is pink, lacks juice, comes across as a great slab of lovely chicken—and if it is broiled chicken you want, there is the genuine article here, sold as lemon pepper chicken, the skin of the big bird tart and spicy and handsomely crisped, though once in a while you get a bird that seems to have been inadvertently derefrigerated somewhere along the line, so that it has some of the off flavor sometimes found in supermarket chickens. You get sensational hash browns here, the big serving actually a kind of pancake of firm little cubes and slices of potato, the top crusted and dark-browned, the interior moist and glistening of its oil, the whole strongly but judiciously seasoned. The cottage fries are like good hot potato chips, and the onion rings are sweet, if rather heavily battered and a little greasy.

Naturally there is cheesecake, and it is the usual rich, creamy, sugary thing, albeit a good version thereof. Fruit tarts are offered, sometimes a pretty good one of pear on a nutty pastry. The hot deep-dish apple pie is a square of toast over crisp slices of apple and dark raisins, all in a thin vanilla sauce. You can always have ice cream.

(Attached to S&W's southern flank, on 49th Street, is an annex called Wollensky's Grill, a small and clubby two-level barroom/dining room plus about a dozen and a half tables under an awning outside. Not many worse sites for outdoor eating can be found in

New York, for the 49th Street crosstown bus passes regularly, a mobile cloud of gas fumes in its wake. The Grill has its own menu [though you may order from the S&W menu if you wish], lower prices, inferior food, and sullen help.)

★★SOFI

102 Fifth Avenue (near 15th Street)
LUNCH, MONDAY TO FRIDAY; DINNER, MONDAY TO SATURDAY. CLOSED SUNDAY.
Reservations: 463-8888.
Credit cards: AE, DC, MC, V.
Very expensive.

Dreams need work. Realize a fantasy, find its faults. Here someone has been given his dreamy head, and voilà, a setting in which is fulfilled every designer's ultimate fantasy, a room in which is incorporated every idea his other clients rejected. Surely the fellow persuaded himself that it all, can you believe it, "works." And it does for one mildly amused visit. But you will not discover new layers of satiric meaning (the kind you look for if you look at all) on subsequent encounters—the joke sustains only one hearing.

Sofi is, moreover, huge, a couple of stories high, and under its distant ceiling, which is the green of surgical gowns, the walls have been mottled to the effect of a rosy-colored dawn seen through mists not yet burnt off. But the morning light is ample enough for you to discern that the raised area at the front of the restaurant, directly under the big windows that look out on burgeoning lower Fifth, is broadloomed, furnished with L-shaped sofas done in pale, flowered chintz, and with wicker chairs, some of them the color of that ceiling, around the little tables at which drinks are served. The dining room proper is dominated by four giant columns in a line along its axis—their stippled surfaces are shadowy at the bottom, as if they have been splattered by passing vehicles during slushy weather—whim amok—and they are topped by elaborate finials that appear to hang rather than support. The mezzanine on one long side is a comfortable part of the place—large tables, some of them beside a few more of those sofas—despite its excellent view of the other long side, which is dominated by two huge food-and-flora still lifes (or are they subtropical Christmas trees), that threaten at each end. Between them, on the lower level, the long bar is backed by a mirror triptych within overarching wood frames. Down here there are rugs—in the styles of many lands—on the red-tile floors, and along the sides a number of those sofas yet again are the seating for some good-size tables. (The tables for two, however, are about right for a cigarette and a cup of coffee.) At the back, the open kitchen of the previous tenant has been modestly concealed behind a massive folding screen of mirrored glass framed in dark-stained wood. The waiters and waitresses are in men's dress shirts, the bowties on their wing collars vivid black chokers around their youthful necks. One of them hangs around while you look at the wine list, which offers a dozen-and-a-half wines by the glass. Say you: "How nice, you have a cruvinet." Says he: "Yes, but tonight we're out of it."

You may decide that whoever put together the physical place was mindful of the menu, for it, too, is diverse—beyond any possibility of national culinary identification. Happily, though you take in your surroundings all at once, you eat only one dish at a time, beginning, if you are wise, with skate, ten anchovy-size strips of the white fish, their clear marine flavor intensified by a light marination, arranged on their plate like the spokes of a wheel, at the center a mass of so-called tomato salad that is more like a deep, dark vegetable stew, between the spokes dark-green dabs of a pesto sauce that is nutty, pungent of its cheese, heady of fresh basil. Four spokes of another wheel, these broader and deep pink, are smoked salmon that has been warmed, no less, which heightens its salt, fish, and smoke flavors, the strips of seafood in a creamy sauce that is nubbly with minced fennel and celery. On three slabs of cured tomato at the edge of a mound of green salad are placed three egg-shaped masses of eggplant caviar, their eggplant flavor, however, remote—you spread the stuff on the crusts of bread that come with it, and wonder what you would guess it to be on the blind. You would wonder not at all about the identity of this terrine of cassoulet, a block cut from a loaf of the meats and beans that are the usual cassoulet components, sautéed until its surface is crisped and dark brown—no, you would know at once that this is hash, albeit good hash, but unmistakably the coarse and fatty thing, in no way disguised, never mind elevated, by the sticky sauce in which it is served.

Rigatoni are ribbed tubes of pasta; here they are stuffed with a mildly seasoned mash of Swiss chard and ricotta, and they are served under a "fresh tomato sauce" that is hardly more than warmed, chopped, herbed tomatoes, albeit very nice for that. What Sofi calls rotelle, you call fusilli, the corkscrew pasta mingled with little florets of broccoli, lengths of green bean and red pepper, and with nuggets of salmon that would be perfect were they perfectly fresh—this is an odd dish in that there are just the solids, barely a trace of liquid, so when your waiter offers cheese, cheese on a seafood dish being a further oddity, you go for it anyway, and sure enough it does nothing but append itself, one more element among others that have not been made into a whole.

Happily, the lobster Castlebay (you take it on faith the dish is of Hebridean extraction) will help you to forget all that, the white meat, out of its shell, under a cloud of long, thin, crisp-fried potatoes, the whole set in a pool of pink, creamy lobster sauce that is of sharp shellfish flavor, in it lengths of chive, strands of red pepper, bits of garlic and of ginger—you encounter those oddments as occasional bursts of surprising, almost shocking, invariably pleasing flavor. The dim taste of monkfish is here roused by the bits of strong prosciutto with which the fish is studded—you are served a row of morsels of the firm seafood arranged down the center of your plate, on one side a simple burnt-orange sauce that is of red peppers, on the other a complex greenish one that is dominated by fennel, slightly bitter baby turnips and sweet baby carrots two of the good vegetables that adorn the colorful dish. Duck, as you may know, no longer arrives looking like duck. Here you are served a semicircle of somewhat rare slices of the juicy and quite ducky meat in a rather sweet vermouth sauce, the meat garnished with a pungently seasoned eggplant mash, several leaves of cooked endive, in each of them a slice of roasted red pepper, and a dollop of tapénade that is of powerful black-olive strength. That is good duck, but this is even more interesting quail (though the dish is dominated by a whole, rich foie gras at the center of the plate), the sautéed parts, of unmistakably strong quail flavor, in a winy, meaty sauce that is thick with a many-textured hash of black bread and vegetables—that abundance of foie gras, however, gives the dish an almost overwhelmingly pinguid cast. Notable veal, the three substantial scallops of pale, tender, juicy meat handsomely browned, strewn with fresh basil, and served in a greened sauce that is muddied, thickened, and sharpened by ground pecorino cheese and crushed fava beans —that basil is a stunning note in this setting. A platform of well-oiled eggplant under a strong tomato sauce, thin slivers of sautéed zucchini strewn over it, is the centerpiece for your roast lamb, little slices of good meat surround it, the two in a bit of moisture that is mostly the roasting juices.

Here has been ennobled banana cream pie, now called a tart, the thick, sweet, and pale-yellow custard, of concentrated banana flavor, on a browned pastry under a cloud of fluffy whipped cream. More whipped cream, this time touched with Grand Marnier, is the bulk of the strawberry napoleon, the balance three leaves of crisp, flaky pastry and fresh strawberries, the tiered affair in a crimson pool of berry puree. Whipped cream yet again, this time with poached fresh pineapple, cool and sweet, the two between thin, crisp coconut pastries, on the sandwich confectioners' sugar, under it a creamy sauce. With the chocolate cake the whipped cream is just a garnish, as is the little ball of chocolate ice cream under its leaf of pure chocolate, as is the ball of vanilla coated with crushed macadamia nuts—the cake itself, nutted and strong, is slicked with black icing.

★ SUKHOTHAI

149 Second Avenue (near 9th Street)
DINNER.
Reservations: 460-5557.
Credit cards: AE, MC, V.
Inexpensive.

In the heterogeneity that is the so-called East Village (made up, as it is, of flower children gone to seed, residual Ukrainians, philistines named Punk, artists starving and otherwise, and gentrificators clinging against the future to tenement investments—not to mention chemical entrepreneurs and other unpaid-in-full members in good standing of the underground economy), this innocent place seems to have no place. It caters to its neighborhood in no special way, is a Thai restaurant like others in most respects, just does, how you say, its thing. It is situated, one flight up, in the midst of a row of boisterous restaurants-cum-sidewalk cafés: to the north of it, Bandito at No. 153 and Art Café at No. 151, and to the south, Pier Nine at No. 149. To enter this place on, say, a hot summer night from swarming streets—picking a path between the guzzler-gawkers at Art Café and those at Pier Nine—is to leave the neighborhood behind. Not that Sukhothai gets its traffic from other parts of town, rather that new rules take over when you enter it. That is to say, even though you are in the East Village, when someone asks you to extinguish your cigarette here, you do not respond by blowing smoke in his face.

It is not that the house has a nonsmoking section (it has not) or regulations of any kind, rather that the seemingly innocent demeanor of the Thais who run it, and the spacious, almost religious calm and cool of its dark and lofty interior, tend to soothe the passions of self that inform the sizzling arrondissement around it. The place is much brick and dusky plaster, unlinened tables of dark wood (a placemat of soft cloth at each place), and a plain wood floor, greenery all about, Thai art and mirrors here and there. Those materials and appointments notwithstanding, the dining room is in no way threadbare, has about it, in fact, a kind of well-worn baroque luxuriance. But there is also, appended to the front of the place and in quite another mode, a little "terrace" enclosed almost entirely in glass and suspended one story over Second Avenue, a handful of tables in a setting that, with its abundance of plants, on the windowsills and hanging from the skylighted ceiling, is rather jungly—but for the hot-pink neon sign in the front window that announces Sukhothai to the world.

Like most Thai eating places, this one assumes, sensibly, that non-Thais will have difficulty pronouncing the names of Thai dishes. Accordingly, the dishes are numbered, and you may order them by their numeric designations. Tod mun pla, for example, is

Appetizer No. 1, firm chunks of fresh kingfish, darkened by their marinade, spicy, and fragrant of coriander leaves; haar keon, No. 2, for another, four shrimp wrapped in the bean-curd skin in which they were fried, served with a dish of sweet and slightly spicy oil. The satés are No. 3 on the list, and you may choose to have yours of beef, pork, or chicken—choose the last, and you are served many morsels of pale grilled meat on their skewers, the chicken saturated with the herbs and spices in which they have been steeped and set in a redded peanut sauce. Have any of those in preference to Appetizer No. 4, the so-called Thai egg roll, the somewhat greasy though crackling casings packed with a nameless vegetable mass. The soups make up a separate category, and you take it that No. 1, po-taak, is the most ambitious of them, for it is the most expensive, and is offered only in a serving suitable for two. It arrives over a portable stove, the soup in a vessel shaped like a doughnut bifurcated horizontally, a flame poking through its hole. The broth is grassy, tart of lime juice, spicy hot, and after a few spoons of it you may well remove your jacket and hang it over the back of your chair—the soup is abundant with chunks of seafood and mushrooms.

You note that of more than fifty listed items, Seafood No. 16 is the only one the house pushes with especial pride. "Highly recommended," reads the menu. Sure enough, the steamed whole fish (it reaches you, up to its waist in the broth in which it was done, in a fish-shaped metal dish over a small fire) is fresh, supple, moist, and permeated to heady effect with the flavors—herbs and vegetables, ginger and pork—that infuse its liquid. Of the several deep-fried fish, No. 14, pla preow whan, has a skin that is at once leather and crusty, is fine in its sweet and sour sauce of peppers and onions. Pad phed is one of those Thai dishes dominated by fired-up coconut milk—you may have yours made with chicken, beef, or pork, and however you have it, the liquid, thick with red and green peppers and strips of water chestnut in addition to the meat, is of a sweetness and complexity that is clear despite its fiery spiciness. The nuur yang nam tok is another hot dish, this one of beef, the crusted little slivers of tender meat mingled with onions and strikingly moistened by a tangy lime-juice sauce. Of the familiar rice noodle dishes, pad thai and mee krob, Sukhothai's are sweeter and less lively than most versions around town.

For dessert there is a coconut pudding of which it may be said that it has the texture of pudding and the flavor of coconut. Beer is the drink with this food, and the Thai beer served here—Singha—is good, assertively hoppy, a little fruity.

★★SUSHIZEN

57 West 46th Street
LUNCH, MONDAY TO FRIDAY; DINNER, MONDAY TO SATURDAY. CLOSED SUNDAY.
Reservations: 302-0707.
Credit cards: AE, DC.
Medium priced.

A recent tabulation comes up with one Japanese restaurant in Manhattan for every two manhole covers, the ratio constantly growing. To the Japanese, the differences among these eating places are surely as clear as the distinction to native New Yorkers between Luchow's and Lutèce. Locals, however, rarely can tell one morsel of, say, tuna sushi from another—so long as the fish is fresh. Occasionally, however, one Japanese restaurant becomes more popular than others. There are theories about this, the most convincing being that such places have something (very) subtly Western in their style. You cannot point to a dish and say this or that restaurant's version has an Occidental accent, only that in such places, whether or not they are also popular with the Japanese, New Yorkers are secure with the food. There is no compromise of Japanese style, you understand, only a certain overtone that happens to sound a distant Western bell. (You will get arguments about this from those who insist that their favorite Japanese restaurants are *echt* Japanese. Do not argue back—you are merely being misunderstood.)

Such a place is Sushizen. At the center of the city's midtown business district, it is often crowded for lunch. But, happily, in the evening you can usually come by any time, get yourself seated at once, share your waiter with few or no competing diners. The room is gray-carpeted, painted pale green, sports lower walls of raw silk. The establishment's few physical oddities include: backlighted circles of glass, about the size of wine-bottle bottoms, cut into the gray carpeting along the path from the front of the dining room to the one-step-up sushi bar at the back; one long wall the upper portion of which consists of bas reliefs over bas reliefs, a 10-inch-deep simulation of mountain range after mountain range (not a surprising technique for citizens of a small, crowded nation); and, the winner, the handsomely patterned suspenders on the unfailingly courteous pink-shirted waiters.

Sushizen serves sushi, all the common raw-fish varieties, among them tuna and fatty tuna and salmon, fluke and bass and yellowtail, each of them fresh, made with vinegared rice that is just this side of too sticky, that side of not sticky enough, garnished with brisk ginger, and with the violent wasabi with which to fortify the soy sauce you dip the constructs in. It also produces a few rarer sushi items: cool, silken octopus; smoky, sea-gamy eel, seemingly sugar sweetened, deeply oiled but not oily; and, the last word, sea urchin, the piercingly loud orange flesh set on a low platform of rice within a deep bracelet of seaweed, in the spare room at the top, if you so request, a raw quail egg, its yellow eye staring up at you forlornly from its imprisoned position—strong food, and the egg does not make it mild.

The non-sushi dishes include, naturally, first courses and main courses, and you may as well make your dinner of several of the former as one of the latter, for there is nothing inherently one or the other about most of them except their amount: eel again, that same smoky dark meat, this time sprinkled with sesame seeds and formed into a cucumber-wrapped roulade from which slices are served to you on a wood board, the warm, complex, many-textured disks garnished with wasabi and ginger; spinach, cold and fresh and acidic, under a cloud of shaved bonito (a cured-fish fundament of Japanese cooking), and set in the dark and stout broth in which the vegetable was done—bracing, particularly when dipped in the special soy sauce served with it; fried chicken, the moist meat of clear chicken flavor within its crisp and slightly tangy batter; yellowtail collar, a great triangular section of the fish, which you more or less break open—within the browned skin you find masses of particularly sweet white meat; dumplings, their salty pork fillings herbed, spicy, and light within the delicate noodle wrappers; negima, a variant of the familiar dish, served in squat little packages, the shafts of asparagus crunchy within the tender wrappers of thin-sliced beef, the vegetable augmented by one chunk of cheese per unit—the presence of cheese is of course surprising, as is the fact that it does not harm the dish; broiled eggplant, firm and well oiled, this also topped with great tangles of shaved bonito, which here does impart a vague ocean flavor; chopped conch, a little tough, strewn with tiny sticks of seaweed, the conch of vivid marine flavor, as are the two red fish roes with which it is mingled.

★ TABLE D'HÔTE

44 East 92nd Street
LUNCH, SUNDAY; DINNER, MONDAY TO SATURDAY.
Reservations: 348-8125.
No credit cards.
Beer and wine.
Medium priced.

Conversion of ancient storefronts to contemporary eating places has rarely been achieved with so little rehabilitation of so rickety a site. And though this tiny place has been around several years now (and presumably turns a profit), those in charge have apparently concluded that its charm is in its worn condition, for they have preserved its every dent and bump through all seasons. Actually, except for the stamped-tin ceiling, which has rents in it like the tears in a pair of stylish old jeans, nothing about the place is actually broken down. It just looks as if no plasterer has been near these walls, no scraper at this floor, since the school days of those who here own and operate. It appears that they moved in, painted the floor red, everything else white (including the two four-bladed fans that hang from the ceiling), installed a tiny kitchen (just curtains conceal it from the dining room), and, you figure, placed the crockery and the cookware and the early Americana on the walls where they would conceal the holes and cracks. Intent on preserving the ambience established by these initial measures, they then fitted the place out with an assortment of eight tables (left unlinened) that would be antiques if age were the only standard, surrounded them with what would be chairs if four legs and a seat the size of *Time* magazine defined the species. Still, this old brand of innocence does beguile a little, and it gets an assist from the one element that was probably unplanned: What with the easy circulation between the kitchen and you, Table d'Hôte offers not only homey surroundings, but also the smells of home cooking.

Do not, however, be deceived by those aromas. The food here aims for contemporaneity. The brief menu—a handful of appetizers, of main courses, of desserts—changes each month. Herewith most of the items on one of them: cold leeks, a little overcooked, but in a good dressing that, though fortified with bits of jalapeño pepper and soured with capers, does not overpower the vegetable; crostini, four substantial crusts of toasted dark bread covered with a fresh liver paste that is fragrant of sage; a salad of arugula (a bit wilted), endives, and sun-dried tomatoes, all in a good dressing, with it a couple of crusts of French bread adorned with little slabs of creamy goat cheese; another salad, one that suffers for the soft overripeness of the sliced avocado you find among the perfectly good watercress, fennel, cherry tomatoes.

Some impeccable seafood: a fillet of fresh, moist Norwegian salmon, all its sweet flavor intact, served in a silken dill sauce; and tiny, crisped soft-shell crabs in a butter that is nubbly with minced scallions. The chicken breasts are nicely browned, actually sport a bit of chicken flavor in their sauce of red peppers and mustard—in which the latter quite obscures the former. The filet mignon is wrapped in bacon, sautéed with green peppercorns—this is tender meat accurately prepared, and the spicy, somewhat creamy sauce is fine, but the smokiness of this bacon is an inelegant touch in the otherwise well made dish.

The chocolate pot de crème is wonderfully smooth and intense under its rich whipped cream and sprig of mint. That whipped cream yet again, this time on the lemon tart, the tangy custard on a crumbly, buttery pastry. The almond mocha-cream dacquoise is a rather heavy layered affair that, happily, is leavened and brightened by a thin layer of

341

raspberries. A good shortbread pastry, fresh strawberries and blueberries, and a smooth custard make up the good fruit tart.

No hard liquor. Wine is $15 and up on the short list, but you may bring your own and have it served to you for a corkage fee.

★★TAMU

340 West Broadway (at Grand Street)
LUNCH AND DINNER.
Reservations: 925-2751.
Credit cards: AE, DC, MC, V.
Inexpensive.

A typhoon is what a hurricane is called on the other side of the world, and in season, Indonesia gets lots of them. Earthquakes, on the other hand, are enjoyed all year around. So if you have been putting off your first trip to the Malay Archipelago because rolling turf makes you seasick and you are afraid of losing your hat, you will have little trouble persuading yourself that this corner of West Broadway and Grand is, at least for the time being, Borneo. Few people in town will argue with you. And anyway, the food is good.

If you have seen thirties adventure movies about equatorial Asia, you have seen the appointments with which this place is furnished: potted palms, commodious chairs of cane and bamboo, hanging lamps of pale straw that cast a soft glow on the white-linened tables. Your napkin is a heavy, fleecy, brilliantly colored cloth. Your menu is mounted on a large square of pasteboard that is bound in elaborately printed cotton. You are waited on by dark-haired, mocha-skinned young gentlemen in white trousers, crimson shirts, brimless native hats of patterned cloth. Their courtesy is apparently boundless. This store is old, high-ceilinged space, two-story windows along two sides. Accordingly there was room enough to build in a mezzanine. Downstairs there are walls of white plaster, a bar, big tables that look out on West Broadway. But the stairway at the center of the room leads up to what has become this restaurant's preferred seating. Up here the brick walls are hung with native art; you are protected from the short drop off the edge by a retaining wall of blond wood; and on the mezzanine you are out of the crisscross traffic—from and to the stairs, the bar, the kitchen, the facilities—that makes the lower level less than serene on a busy night.

The printed menu is a reproduction of a handwritten document of almost irresistible orthographic charm. Gado-gado (all anglicizations of native words are taken on faith from the masterpiece itself), for example, is described as "a delightfull collections of vegetables mix to perfection and leced with savory dressing made with peanut butter." Is also yummy. Includes potatoes, cucumbers, carrots, zucchini, cabbage, plus noodles and hard-cooked eggs, all in a dark and tangy peanut sauce. For a salad more akin to what salad means to you, there is asinan, which is characterized, with enviable accuracy, as "mixed fresh garden Vegetables and bean cakes, vinegar dressing prepared with Indonesian spices and Brown Sugar." The saté madura is a hot first course of chicken that is allowed to marinate in its thick, spicy, and garlic-flavored sauce before it is broiled—the white meat is powerfully flavored, lightly charred, and the dark sauce is rich and thick without being at all fatty or cloying. Saté bali is much like the saté madura, but with nuggets of firm, tender beef in place of the chicken.

Order sambal goreng udang, and you will be brought "jumbo fried shrimp season with tropical erbs and yello coconut sauce, lemo grass, Indonesian bay leaf, ground nut meg." This dish is actually better than its write-up, the dark and crunchy crustaceans in a sauce that is at once sharp and fruity, flavored of onions and scallions and coconut milk, sweet-spiced and a little hot. What goes as ikan bumbu bali consists of two great chunks of codfish, moist and crusty, in a slightly sweet, ginger-flavored vegetable sauce—this is enough like Chinese fried fish to suffer by the automatic comparison to the best versions of that. Ayem goreng is a dark chicken dish, the meat of the bird fried until it is pleasantly leathery on the outside, served with mushrooms in a dark sauce of dazzlingly complex spiciness. Ayem panggang is boneless chicken, charred and juicy, in a sauce that is fruity of lemon grass, tangy of its ginger. You will be delighted to learn that there is a section of the menu called "Lambs." In that department you will find gulai kambing, gamy chunks of meat in a hot sauce that is fragrant with clove, slightly sharpened with scallion greens. Rice and a spicy eggplant stew are served with most of the main courses. If you wish to taste lots of the menu, you order the rijsttafel, in which a dozen different dishes are included.

Firm, ripe mango, honeylike in its sweetness, is the right dessert after this food. The fried bananas are good too—they are hot, ripe, soft, and sweet within their dark, cinnamon-flavored crusts, and they are served with excellent whipped cream. Dismayingly, if you order tea, you get a cup of hot water and a selection of tea bags.

★★TANGO

43 West 54th Street
LUNCH, MONDAY TO FRIDAY; DINNER, MONDAY TO SATURDAY. CLOSED SUNDAY.
Reservations: 765-4683.
Credit cards: AE, DC, MC, V.
Medium priced.

Anybody can turn up yet another decent Japanese restaurant. They are everywhere, like occupied cabs. The trick is to find one that does not remind you of a hundred others. You are in especial luck if the place you find is, moreover, a little better than most, a phenomenon like one of those cabs disgorging a passenger right where you are standing, so that you may have it for yourself. You may have Tango for yourself, for though it has its lunchtime followers from nearby office buildings, by night it is often a sleepy place. You find it glowing only very softly on its quiet side street. You consider its posted menu, which offers little to suggest that it differs from a thousand other places. You enter to the inevitable sushi bar, from behind which men grin brightly at you, looking friendly while wielding knives. Their station faces a narrow brick-walled aisle that leads to your basic Japanese dining room at the back, in which there are beams on the ceiling, wooden slats over rice paper to simulate Japanese windows on the walls. The place is mostly pale gray, with pale-gray table linen covered by plate glass. Somehow, plate glass, no matter how transparent, never looks like table linen. The waiters and waitresses are angelic, unless you hang around after closing time—when they want you to go home, so that they can eat. Then they become firm. The waitresses pad around in ravishing kimonos. The waiters are in black and white, like the fellows who work in Italian restaurants on Third Avenue. The uniform, however, is all the resemblance. You ask one of these gentlemen why a Japanese restaurant is named for a Latin-American slow dance. He explains that it is not, that long ago, when Japan was politically districted differently from the way it is now, one of its prefectures was called Tango. He explains also that the word in Japanese has no other meaning. When pressed further, he carefully avoids stating directly that anyone connected with this place could be guilty of pride of origin. "Maybe," he says, "the owner is from there." Then he smiles a little wickedly.

Then he brings you fresh abalone steamed in Japanese wine, and it occurs to you that you may never have tasted abalone before, for these thin slices of fibrous but tender seafood have an almost nutlike flavor—they are arranged like the sides of a polygonal tent over a mound of fresh spinach, all in a pool of dark and salty broth. You order boiled octopus and set yourself for lengths of tentacle with suckers attached. You receive instead tepid, delicate slivers of the pale meat, mixed with like slivers of cucumber, the two dotted with bits of seaweed, the three set in a lightly oiled soy sauce broth—the interplay of these flavors is at once gentle and dazzling. An ice cream scoop of grated horseradish is covered over with globules of glistening salmon roe, over all of which your waiter or waitress pours some soy sauce from a little pitcher on your table—a bright, rousing dish. The eggplant appetizer—better known as nasuno-misodengaku—reaches you as a great slab of the warm, succulent vegetable in the shape of a flat fish, the skin still attached to the bottom side, the whole spread with a warm, fruity soybean paste. There are simple dishes too, like the deep-fried bean curd, little blocks of the soft, comforting stuff, the fried surfaces slightly darkened and leathery. You dip the bean curd in soy sauce to which you have added fresh ginger, horseradish, chopped scallions.

When Japanese restaurants first came to New York in numbers, tempura was something of an astonishment to the locals. This was deep frying, sure enough, but the crisped batter was so light and free of grease that it could hardly be thought of in the same unhealthy, fattening breath as the American counterpart. During the decades since then Japanese frying standards in the big city have slipped, and a lot of what now goes as tempura lacks air and, if you handle it, leaves your fingers oiled. At Tango, however, you may be reminded of your first experiences with this remarkable form of cooking, for not only are the shrimp sweet and the vegetables fresh and crisp, but the batter is gossamer-like, has no more weight than cotton candy. At about the time you first tried tempura, you also were introduced to sushi, raw fish mostly, combined—along with other ingredients—with vinegared rice. Here the fish is fresh, the rice is tangy, the soybean wrappers are firm and tender, and the variety of seafood is extensive—red roes, tuna, mackerel, shrimp, bass, more. You need not have your seafood raw. Seafood suki comes in a great pot with a wooden cover. In its broth you will find lobster and crabmeat in their shells, octopus and clams, mushrooms and scallions, much else. Sounds good? Not so good as most of the dishes here, for the seafood is overcooked—much of it is tough—though the broth in which it is prepared is pungent and complex. The so-called barbecued eel is sweet and blackened, the meat so rich it seems fatty. What the house bills as Japanese tartar steak does not rival the best of the West, but the fresh-ground beef is fine with the horseradish and chopped scallions with which it is spread—you must add soy sauce for the essential seasoning.

★ TAPIS ROUGE

157 Duane Street (near Hudson Street)
LUNCH, MONDAY TO FRIDAY; DINNER, MONDAY TO SATURDAY. CLOSED SUNDAY.
Reservations: 732-5555.
Credit cards: AE, MC, V.
Medium priced.

Back in the beginning, it made sense, a French bistro for TriBeCa—and, TriBeCa being what it is, there was no reason not to spurn all bistro clichés and make it a glitzy one. Back then, only the food was out of place, being terribly ordinary, occasionally worse. Sure enough, Tapis Rouge was hot for a time, members of the downtown set forewent an occasional Odeon evening in favor of dinner here. After a while the place seemed to have quite firmly installed and stabilized itself in its community, and you probably would have predicted that any improvement in the kitchen would reinforce the entrenchment. But it is as if Tapis Rouge is fated always to be missing a piece, for with the improvement in its cookery the place has suffered a parallel diminution of support from what ought to be its natural clientele, TriBeCa locals. And, as if hastily to plug the gap through which that custom leaked away, replacements have been lured from foreign parts. You see folks here, especially on weekend nights, that you figure were brought en masse by bus, the kinds of couples in which, ever since the honeymoon, the husband has been calling the wife Mother. Says one such Mother to her opposite number, "Tappiss Rose, what's it mean?" Says the opposite number, "I think they served tapas when they first opened."

Tapis Rouge is, first, a little barroom, in it the single table at which you may smoke; then a little aisle; then the dining room, through all three of which, on a painted-black floor, runs the long Red Carpet of the title. Its brand of glitz is Deco, the shiny black pilasters on its pale wood walls mounted with Deco light fixtures, and where the walls are not of pale wood, they are panels of either clear or black tiles of mirrored glass—an icy effect. Art hangs between the pilasters—faux cubism, faux expressionism, faux fauvism, et al—high-backed black side chairs surround the white-linened tables. On the ceiling a square is formed by four rows of papillar protuberances that glow in the manner of lights. The waitresses are in long white aprons, gray button-down shirts, and black, knitted four-in-hands. They appear to have been chosen for their youth and for their looks— and they get lots of looks.

You will be distracted even from those distractions by a singular oyster dish among the first courses. The so-called "stew" of oysters, potatoes, and small onions is a mingling of the warmed-through mollusks, which retain all their uncooked oceanic sweetness and brine, firm slices of potato of vivid potato taste, and whole small onions that have given up all but a little of their bite, the three in a creamy and buttery sauce that is nubbly with clumps of parsley. Eat here once, and, barring an allergy, that is the item to have. Eat here twice, however, and you may be permitted the crabmeat terrine, a square cut from a block that is formed of fresh crabmeat, garlic mayonnaise, bits of red pepper and green herbs—the fresh, rousing stuff is garnished with a good salad and a relish of minced tomatoes and scallions. On occasion you are offered duck rillettes, the spiced meat pounded with its own fat, but this is mild stuff, lacking the strong seasoning needed to balance the richness, though the garnish is fine—a green salad with walnut halves in a sprightly dressing. The terrine of venison is made with port, lots of it, and the wine's fruitiness underscores the good flavor of the meat.

The red snapper is marinated, seems to have lost its own flavor and gained nothing in the treatment—the fish reaches you in a sour broth that is thick with peppers, and it is garnished with a slab of onion topped with browned melted cheese, altogether an inexplicable essay. These quails, packed with a mushroom dressing, would be fine were they not tied up in lengths of ordinary bacon, which, unfortunately, and apparently intentionally, transfer their flavor to birds that do not need it, are overpowered by it. There is, however, happily, this tender veal chop, juicy and pink within its browned surfaces, and served in a strong mustard sauce. And, if you are here on Wednesday, there is this couscous, a broad plate of the little couscous granules, two of the fiery hot lamb sausages called merguez, a pot of stew—many vegetables, chunks of beef, sections of moist chicken—that you spoon over the couscous, and a little ramekin of almost violently hot sauce with which you modify the dish according to your taste and tolerance. Other days, other specials, among them cassoulet on Thursday, pot au feu Friday, choucroute Saturday, all at $16.

The standard lemon tart is citric and sweet, more a chiffon than a custard on its flaky crust. The almost black chocolate mousse cake is fresh and of good intensity in its polished milk-chocolate sauce. The espresso parfait is a column of ice cream of potent espresso flavor—it is topped with and surrounded by rich whipped cream.

★★THAI ROYALE

1668 First Avenue (at 87th Street)
DINNER.
Reservations: 876-5640.
Credit cards: AE, DC, MC, V.
No liquor.
Inexpensive.

One way or another, there is always something innocent about a Thai restaurant. This place, for example, is innocent of current trends in restaurant interior design. The dining room is assembled of such parts as glazed brick and pale wood, carpeting and Danish bentwood chairs (with caned backs and stuffed plastic seats), and, on the walls, framed mirrors and presumably Thai art, all of which bespeak innocence in definitive form: the absence of sophistication. And, oh yes, the help—especially the lady who runs the place—all of whom regard you and treat you with a smiling wide-eyed goodwill that would deter a hangman.

If you have read Thai menus before, you have read most of this one. And if you have had chicken saté before, the oil-moistened lengths of browned white meat, on their wood skewers, will not in themselves reveal to you anything new, though the hot peanut sauce with which they are served is striking for its silken freshness. More chicken, this one called garry-puff, in which the ground meat of the bird, flavored with fragrant Eastern spices, is packed into triangular turnovers of light, flaky pastry. Certain first-course salads seem intended specifically to rouse either your appetite or you. Pla-pa-muk is one, squid bodies packed with a fiery squid stuffing and mingled with onions and herbs in a hot dressing that is touched with lime. The beef salad, yam-nur, is a craggy mound of hefty strands of browned beef, resilient and fibrous, but not tough, intertwined with onions, and moistened with a searing dressing that is heady of coriander.

Among finfish, the menu mentions only sea bass, but sometimes snapper is available in the same preparations. The steamed snapper, for example, is the utterly fresh whole fish, firm and moist in its pink and silvery skin, in a dark ginger-flavored broth dotted with good mushrooms. Goong-ob-mo-din is described, in part, as "broiled shrimp," so you are a little surprised to be presented with a covered pot in which the shrimp are buried in masses of herbed noodles—you season the steaming food with a hot citrus-flavored sauce. For plain abundance you turn to gai-yang, half a big chicken, marinated with ginger and garlic and browned, good the way it is, though a fruity sauce is served with it. The duck item called ped-gra-tiem is heavily garlicked and salty, and the meat, though skinned, is rich of fat—this is an honest and weighty dish that will not appeal to all.

The proprietor of this place is related to the proprietor of an Italian restaurant in another part of town. That may explain the availability of tartufo for dessert. But sweets do not really make much sense after this food.

★★TRASTEVERE and TRASTEVERE 84

309 East 83rd Street; 155 East 84th Street
DINNER.
Reservations: 734-6343; 744-0210.
Credit cards: AE.
Beer and wine.
Expensive.

One imagines that, once upon a time, in the section of Rome for which these restaurants are named, the practice grew up of serving working-class dinners to working-class folk on a single plate: meat or seafood on one side of the plate, salad on the other. One further imagines that the trickle of cool salad dressing that, inevitably, invaded the hot-food territory is the basis of the cookery that, in these two restaurants, is represented for the first time in New York. This historic accident, now encouraged to occur scores of times per night on dinner plates in these eating places, has so delighted New York that the first timid effort to bring this food here—the tiny Trastevere on 83rd Street—was hardly a year old before it was busily spawning an enlarged version of itself only a few blocks to the northwest. Of course, there is more to Trastevere's cooking than hot food touched by cold. And almost all that these places do, they do well. The menus of the two branches are identical, and the cooking at the two is indistinguishable.

The first place these pioneers opened is only a little wider than a refrigerator but at least twice as deep. Into it they fitted almost a dozen tables, a table for four being about the size of a long-playing record. Anything larger is set aside for large family gatherings (and at the end of the evening, management, friends, and relatives assemble at one of these, knee-to-knee, and eat things that, you note, are not offered guests). To offset the crowded conditions, the lights are turned off. To find out more about where you are, take the flickering, dripping taper from your table and hold it aloft. You will espy that high on one wall is hung a photograph, in full color, of Italy's World Cup championship soccer team. Mention this to any waiter, and he will stop on the spot to share with you his amazement at his countrymen's accomplishment. Engravings of Roman buildings may also be perceived, as well as, inexplicably, autographed glossies of American movie stars. When the place is filled, the waiters negotiate the so-called aisle like latecomers crawling to theater seats. The second store is twice as big and just as crowded. Otherwise, its relationship to the first place is roughly that of Tavern on the Green to a tavern. The darkness is real, but the bricks are artificial. The engravings are here, but not the soccer team. It was the original, tiny place that got most of the praise in the press, so it gets the publicity followers from the Lanes, Drives, Roads, and Crescents—they never utter a peep of complaint when their dinner plates impinge, necessarily, on the air rights over their laps. The bigger store gets the locals. They like the extra room on the tables for their elbows, and the food is just as good.

It includes spiedino alla romana, a multilayered, deep-fried hot sandwich of charred bread, melted cheese, strong ham, in a thick and powerfully garlicked sauce of anchovies and oil. The hot vegetable appetizer for two is composed of sautéed vegetables—zucchini, peppers, mushrooms, broccoli—in a garlic-flavored oil, sometimes accompanied by crisp slices of tomato in tart vinaigrette. Be warned that on occasion the mussel appetizer is of rank mussels, which is too bad, for when the mussels are fresh, the dish is fine—dozens of mollusks mounded up in an inch of thick, buttery tomato sauce that is loaded with garlic. This is the place for pasta primavera. The very thin spaghetti—capellini—is firm, and the peas, zucchini, broccoli, and tomato with which it is mingled are in a hot, garlicky oil that has taken on the flavors of the fresh vegetables.

Among the main courses that are served with salad, and thereby are sauced with its dressing, are sole, scampi, and a big, pounded-thin breaded veal chop—each is artfully sautéed. The salad is of lettuce and tomato, and the tart vinegar dressing livens the disparate items as if it were made just for the purpose. The good chicken dishes include pollo gaetano, in which the browned chunks of bird are served in a wine sauce that is dotted with mushrooms and garlic.

The desserts include a rather Italianate napoleon—the custard is dense, the layers of deeply browned pastry heavy. A sometimes available cream puff is of good chou pastry, real whipped cream, and a hot chocolate sauce of intensity and polish. The tartufo is a great nugget of chocolate-studded chocolate ice cream concealed within a cloud of that good whipped cream.

★★LA TULIPE

104 West 13th Street
DINNER. CLOSED MONDAY.
Reservations: 691-8860.
Credit cards: AE, CB, DC, MC, V.
Expensive.

This one is run by a former schoolmaster and his wife, he the church usher out front who, wearing a thin smile in which are blended sanctity and tolerance, leads you to your table, she the wholesome-looking lady in charge of the kitchen who, her involvement perhaps more supervisory than participatory, sometimes arrives at the front door when her last customers are on brandy. Mr. & Mrs. exchange the smiles of greeting, on such occasions, of mates who have found bliss through mutual respect. The restaurant, moreover, though French in its food and much else, has about it a peculiarly American self-satisfaction of spirit, as if its success confirmed not only the business sense of those who run it but their goodness as well. You see regulars who, after responding to their host's sweetish greeting not from his plane, but from one a few steps down, settle into their chairs with the contentment of those coming off a frisson of anointment. Of La Tulipe's state of grace, however, discretion is the better part. Why test a proven condition? Now that the restaurant has found its way, it is set. Its brief menu, for example, which is almost frozen (from time to time one or two items are changed), is supplemented by little in the way of special daily dishes—often as not, none is offered. Happily, however, the perfections that can compensate for so narrow an aim are here often in evidence. All of which is as it should be, for La Tulipe is the restaurant of those who take no chances, and are content to have none taken on their behalf.

It is also, though run by Americans, determinedly French, particularly a first encounter. The room to which you enter has been fitted out with an impeccable French accent. The zinc bar, the brass-rimmed marble-topped tables surrounded by café chairs, the BYRRH poster and the ABSINTHE-BAILLY clock, the floor of dark-stained wood, the wildflowers, and the dozens of prints and old menus on the walls (Pyramide, Le Pavillon) would be in place in Paris itself. There are even a couple of white-linened tables in this room, off in a corner at a banquette of brown corduroy, where you can sometimes get seated when the place is otherwise booked up. Eating in the bar is a quieter and, surely, a visually more diverting experience than dinner in the dining room proper, a formally laid out room, crowded with tables and chairs, that is convivial solely by virtue of the humanity that fills it, and fills it with noise, for its deep-red walls, inlaid rectangular mirrors, and dark carpeting add up to a weighty environment only slightly leavened by the prints and flowers here and there.

You are waited on by an earnest staff that is in large part French, and you order from a menu that is almost entirely French. Not French at all is the pinched spirit that determines the size of certain helpings. Consider, for example, the mousse de truite fumée, a wondrous substance, buttery, creamy, judiciously salted, and of vivid smoked-fish flavor, of which you are served a coiled ribbon that, unwound, would generously butter the surface of a ladyfinger—it is garnished, in kind, by strands of roasted red pepper that, though of high flavor, are of elusive substance, comprising as they do a volume that would get lost in a shot glass. Perhaps an effort is made to play quantity off against quality, for you get, if not an amplitude, at least a sufficiency of the séviche de saumon, a pink obelisk of salmon slivers in a crimson pool of tomato puree—the fish would be fine had it been delicately "cooked" rather than lengthily soaked in its marinade, yielding fish that, though rousing, lacks breed. What goes as mosaique de porc is a chunky, meaty, well-fatted, and spicy terrine in which nuggets of pork and tongue, with pistachio nuts, are bound in a firm jelly—the thin slice is in a tart and oily dressing that is thick with herbs. Order the gâteau aux aubergines, and you are served yet another slice cut from a loaf, this one hot and two-sided, one side a mass of pungent goat cheese, the other a layering of eggplant and tomato, the flavor of the eggplant—which is saturated with oil but not oily—dominant, the strong stuff garnished with roasted red peppers, once again, and sharp black olives. Now that first-class foie gras is produced on this side of the Atlantic, it is on menus all over town. At La Tulipe, the minuscularity of your serving, a single thin slice that perfectly fits the crust of buttered bread under it, is somewhat offset by the judicious sautéing of the liver—its surface is handsomely browned, and the rich meat within is hot, pink, and moist—and by its dark sauce, which is fragrant of herbs, thick with white raisins.

Though the papillote of red snapper has been served here for years, it has never been mastered. The fish reaches you in the balloon of paper in which it was steamed—unto, on occasion, a tasteless mush redeemed neither by the buttery broth in which it is set nor by the good vegetables by which it is surrounded. But then there is the poached halibut, the fresh, supple, snowy steak in a mash of sautéed tomatoes—intense, herbed, chunky—and moistened with a warm vinaigrette that is heady of fresh dill. Another dense tomato sauce, this one powerfully flavored of fresh tarragon and dotted with bits of vegetable, is the red part of the navarin de homard—the white part is the meat of a baby lobster, its ocean flavor sweet and clear even in the context of its powerful sauce. The confit of duck is peppery meat of vivid duck flavor in crackling skin—it comes with nubbly lentils and with sautéed wild mushrooms that are at once buttery and earthy. For some reason, though you are served plenty of duck, a comparative paucity of squab is deemed a sufficiency, little slices of the dark meat in a sticky sauce, the squab flavor livery and strong, the meat arranged around a mound of shredded cabbage that is over-laid with crisp vegetable strands. A grilled filet mignon that is perfectly decent (though overcooked by about one full stop) remains only that despite the ham, minced scallions, and browned, crusty potatoes served with it.

Mostly good desserts: La Tulipe Marie-Louise, rich vanilla ice cream and slivered almonds in a tulip-shaped pastry cup—black, intense chocolate is spooned on at your table; a warm apple tart that is moist and sweet, the rich whipped cream served with it fortified by a bit of liquor; an icy, sweet, smooth lemon sherbet that is roused by the Stolichnaya poured on as it is served; a nutted chocolate cake, under a slick black top, that is strongly flavored of its coffee pastry cream; a floating island—filmed with cara-mel—that is distinguished by the ground hazelnuts embedded in its base; an apricot soufflé (it must be ordered at the start of your dinner) that is of concentrated dried-apricot flavor—its cap is spooned off when it is served, rich whipped cream is inserted, the cap is returned.

★ "21"

21 West 52nd Street
LUNCH AND DINNER. CLOSED SUNDAY.
Reservations: 582-7200.
Credit cards: AE, DC, MC, V.
Very expensive.

Published word has it that the new interests here spent $4 million refurbishing the old club, but from what is visible you conclude that it took imaginative accounting to produce that bottom line. Perhaps the big ticket was meant to lure the curious to the sight of what that kind of money can buy, and sure enough "21" is doing better business than before the rehab. But little about the spiffed appointments suggests that "21" is anything but what it has always been: a restaurant/saloon for eternal collegiates down-stairs, a dining room to which they may take their visiting parents one flight up. You first notice that the place is exaggerating itself when you telephone, ask to make a reservation, get switched to a recorded message to the effect that "all our lines are busy" and that a "reservationist" will be with you shortly. It turns out you always get a table, no problem.

The famous front door is opened for you by a doorman dressed like an executive trainee. You enter to the freshened anteroom and, on your right, a Ralph Lauren living room, a score of wing chairs in tan leather, broadloom carpeting with the symbol "21" woven in (it carpets all the public rooms other than the bar), Remingtons behind glass, and, of course, the big TV, a sporting event on its screen if at all possible—the room longs for a gray atmosphere of cigar smoke, and the nearby cigar stand, a plaster horse in place of a cigar store Indian beside it, is always staffed. But before you get that far, you are greeted by guys in tight suits who, if they do not like you (and if they do not know you, and if you do not present yourself with the kind of mindlessly hearty greeting—

"Great to be here," for example, "just great"—that identifies you are one of their own, they do not like you), they go through the words and gestures of hospitality with the flatness of delivery and stiffness of carriage of the man who escorts you in to meet the members of your court-martial. But once you have shaken off these automatons, you are in the hands of normal human help, men (mostly) who have figured out that, though the proprietors of this place (the new ones as well as the old ones who are still about) may be content to concern themselves mainly with their friends, the staff are tipped by everyone —even those to whom the strutting Jacks and Charlies of this organization are just so many floorwalkers, men who have made themselves vicariously important by sucking up to those who have done it directly. But the new owners here know from the books of account that during its last years in the old hands the restaurant's we-got-it-made style was bluff, that even the granitic businessmen who were the core of its trade during the seventies and eighties had begun to spend more of their time and money in eating places that served food for adults in grown-up surroundings. The substantial culinary and modest physical changes the new interests have undertaken are calculated to attract new customers without scaring off the old.

For the old there is still the so-called bar, the big downstairs playpen—three building lots long—that, divided into three bays, is ideally laid out for application of the class distinctions that so delight the upperclassmen who come here (frosh and sophs take solace in propinquity). The bar itself (no stools) adjoins one long side, while the red banquette that rims the rest of the room extends into it at two places (where the formerly separate buildings adjoined) to effect the trifurcation. The bays are numbered (not by sign, but by common usage) according to the original house numbers, 21 being the most privileged, 19 next, 17 Siberia. All this would make no difference, for the accommodations are equivalent throughout, except that if you are deemed no better than 17 material, and tables are available only in 19 or 21, you will wait, however long it takes, no matter the hour of your reservation, for something to open up in 17, while walk-ins who are cronies of the house will be seated at once in other parts of the room. This privilege is the fundament on which the fuss is based—the CEO of Universal Link & Joint does not have to wait around while one of his salesmen is being seated; and, moreover, when the chief exec is led promptly to a table, he knows that those at tables nearby, whoever they are, are the right sort. (You will be pleased to learn that, on the other hand, admission to the attended rest rooms is first-come-first-served, and that, presumably to circumvent incidents, there are no public drinking fountains.) The room is dimly lit and low-ceilinged. There are silver bowls of pretzels on that stand-up bar, brass spitoons under its brass rail. There are plaques on the walls, tankards and decanters and the like on built-in shelves, Peter Arno cartoons all about (they satirize the smart set that once frequented this place), and, hanging from the low overhead, and the pride of "21," hundreds of objets des métiers, model airplanes of every conceivable number of engines and every known airline, autographed footballs, football helmets and baseball helmets, baseball bats and baseballs and a New York Yankees shirt, scores of toy trucks with their immortal corporate emblems (Texaco, Whirlpool, Chevron, Super Foods, Sweet 'N Low, Family Circle, Dannon), and such proud artifacts as a Wheeling Steel pail, a dump truck, a telephone, the Yellow pages, microphones of local radio stations and license plates of neighboring states, a roll of Reynolds Wrap, a Goodyear blimp, a bowling pin, a miniature case of booze, an ivory tusk, a rifle, a pistol, several hard hats—the emblems and tokens, that is, of everything that underlies this restaurant, what a wise man once referred to as "enough junk for a lifetime of throwing out." Most of the seating is on that meandering banquette, the tables before it, under red-checked linen that is overlaid with white napkins, as tightly assembled as seats in a theater. Men like all this because it has the jostling conviviality of a men's eating club, women because it has the jostling conviviality of a men's eating club.

Downstairs is where you find what remains of the old menu (the preparations improved), together with many new dishes, some of them meant to express in contemporary terms the style of the original place: a Maryland crab cake, which the captains push, having noted that old customers easily take to the handsomely dark-crusted and cilantro-flavored patty of sweet seafood in its pool of tomato-dotted horseradish cream; an assortment of smoked fish, eel, sweet salmon, and good sturgeon among them, served with a salad of fresh greens in a nut oil dressing, and with little crusts spread with herbed cream; a terrine of short ribs, the big dice of coarse meat, bound to nuggets of root vegetables by a dark and strong-seasoned jelly, served with a thick and creamy horseradish sauce; and (also served upstairs) beluga caviar with buckwheat blinis, the globules black and gleaming and sticky (your captain endears himself to you by spooning from the can an oz. that is at the very least an imperial oz.)—you spread the stuff on silver dollar-size pancakes that are crisp and grainy under their thick sour cream. The famous "21" burger is still listed, and it still comes with a sheaf of thin green beans and house-made potato chips, neither noteworthy, but the burger itself is denatured, lacks beefiness, is like a dish invented by a Frenchman who had never before encountered ground beef as a basic ingredient, for its core of herb butter waters the blood-juiciness that underlies even the wildest burger variant—that the thing reaches you overdone on its slice of grilled bread is almost beside the point. So if it is one of the listed "House Specialites" you are after (the category includes several sandwiches and both omelets and scrambled eggs with a selection of additives), you will do better with the lobster sandwich, a great mound of lobster salad, slices of crimson tomato on top, bound in a good herbed dressing—it is set on a strip of bacon on a slab of brioche, and it is garnished with a lively, crunchy cole slaw. The baked salmon in its blackened crust of basil is a dish that gains little in return for its sacrifice of salmon character, for the basil has lost most of its perfume in this treatment—still, this is fresh fish, firm and moist. The sage roasted rack of lamb reaches you as four big chops, supple, glistening pink, and of vivid lamb flavor, but the sage is only a suspicion thereof.

The big upstairs facility has been for some reason transformed from a grand but slightly decrepit hunting lodge into a hotel dining room. The wood-paneled lower walls have been refinished, and the grim plaster of the upper walls has been covered over with padded, off-white bouclé. The chandeliers glow brightly, the emblemed carpeting is cushy, the banquette has been covered with fresh red vinyl, the tables are set with beige linen and pretty flowers in glass bowls, and the chairs have been fitted with little chemises to clothe their backs. Ceremonial cups, big platters and trays, and samovars, all of gleaming silver, stand on shelves and counters and ledges all about. Massive wood columns rise through the room, intersect wood beams that cross the ceiling.

Upstairs the menu is an utter departure from that of the old "21," unless you think of these pan-fried shrimp as just an up-to-date shrimp cocktail—these are crunchy little crustaceans, butterflied and in their shells, coated with herbs that are browned and crisped in the making, altogether impeccable except for the touch of iodine with which one or two are tainted. The gratin of cod (it shows up also on the bar menu) is simple, gratifying food, the mash of strongly salted and vividly flavored fish, at once solid and fluffy, in a little stainless steel casserole that looks like something you ate out of in your army days—but the slice of grilled bread that protrudes like a sail from its surface is hardly the right foil to this dry food, and the billed Parmesan crust is a visible tan, but an invisible flavor. The delicate lobster ravioli, in their pale, chive-threaded sauce, are notable for the slivers of browned, earthy chanterelles with which they are topped. And then there is the picatta of foie gras—three substantial slices of the rich, hot meat reclining against the sides of a pile of rice noodles that are mounded over slices of hot apple in a polished brown sauce—a good dish but for those noodles, which are chewy rather than crisp, fail as textural contrast. Among the main courses, the fillets of striped bass, skin attached, are fresh and firm and sweet, nicely set off by their fennel-and-mushroom garnish; the duck stew is striking for the clear flavor of the browned and stewed morsels of meat and for the fresh root vegetables added to the thick sauce shortly before it is served; the noisettes of lamb, in a vaguely Italianate sauce that is lightly tomatoed and heavily peppered, are pink and velvety under their herbed garlic crust; and the sirloin steak, fibrous, blood-rich, tender, is dramatized by the cracked peppercorns with which it is coated, the whole pink ones with which it is sprinkled, the buttery bourbon sauce in which it is served.

One dessert menu upstairs and down: a sugary and very cinnamoned rice pudding dotted with raisins in its fluted oval ramekin—it is lumpy enough to seem home-made; a warm and nutted apple tart, on a rather doughy pastry, that benefits from the ball of good ice cream with which it is topped: a so-called "fruit soup" that amounts to a fruit salad of many berries served with an intense almond ice cream; a dreary lime parfait—the cold and hard green disk tastes like toothpaste; and, a sushi-shaped item that is a sleeve of chocolate sheeting filled to the waist with gooey mousses—one chocolate, the other raspberry—to the top with mushy raspberries.

★ UNION SQUARE CAFÉ

21 East 16th Street
LUNCH AND DINNER. CLOSED SUNDAY.
Reservations: 243-4020.
Credit cards: AE, MC, V.
Medium priced.

Your waiter wants you to know he is on your side, that the advice he gives is deeply considered, derives from his intimate familiarity with the ins and outs of each and all of the house dishes. Of one item, says he, "It's something I myself feel very comfortable recommending," of another, that it "gets my personal seal of approval," of a third, that it is "particularly tasty," this last in the manner of someone sharing a deeply felt experience. After the man has waited on you a number of times, you figure out that his recommendations—confidences, really, if you take them as they are given—apply solely to special dishes of the day, never to those items that are constants of the printed menu. Under instructions to push what the house wants to get rid of (items it will not be selling tomorrow), he is the fervent company man. Ignore his advice, however, and he has been rehearsed for that eventuality as well. "A *very* good choice," goes he, or "I compliment you on your selection"—and you puff right up. Nor is he finished with you yet, for his problem is not merely that he has been programmed and, thereby, dehumanized—some waiters and waitresses here do bend the rules, and their performances, in the interest of their sanity—but that his perfect fit in this determinedly friendly place devolves also from his mindless socialization of—everything. When, eventually, he serves your dinner, it is with "Now I'll just put this swordfish right down here in front of the lady . . . and I'll put these grilled onions right here between the two of you so that both of you can reach them . . . and now I'll put this veal chop right here in front of the gentleman . . .

and I'll just pour some more of this Chardonnay into your glasses..." (Consider, say, a barber of this persuasion. "Now I'll just grasp this lock of your hair in my left hand... and with my scissors I'll just snip three-eighths of an inch from the ends..."). To the highly trained who work this floor, no one has ever suggested that there are among the customers grownups.

Contemporary New York is, however, inured to the peculiarities of contemporary service, and the Café is today a sprawling, convivial, popular place, albeit one in which an attitude of amused disbelief comes in handy. You enter to a long bar, beyond it a dozen tables or so, a handful more on the mezzanine a flight up. The main dining room is up front, opposite the bar, a square room a few steps down, abundantly but gently lit, the tiny spotlights on the low ceiling like soft-glowing stars. The restaurant is pale ivory throughout, the lower walls are deep green, the floor is plain wood, palms and bursts of flowers are here and there, and the rooms are hung with handsomely framed art. Not all, however, is tasteful. A couple of whimsical murals (not, happily, in the dining room proper) appear to have been done in finger paints by artists on trips. Though one of them is of frolicking nude ladies, the Café des Artistes has nothing to worry about—an instant Howard Chandler Christy it is not, nor will it incite to uninhibited behavior.

Neither will this tangle of hearts of palm and roasted red peppers, the two, bound in an anchovy-thickened vinaigrette, over leaves of arugula—a salad that might be just a little titillating were the sand perfectly rinsed from the green. But then there is this miniature antipasto, a patty of melted scamorza (a soft cheese much like mozzarella), a slice of strong prosciutto, and a substantial mound of chopped tomato in a dressing that is heady with fresh garlic—a rousing plate of food. Those tomatoes appear again on the open-faced bruschetta, a big, crusty slice of sour and grainy bread that has been sautéed in olive oil and garlic, the tomato, with fresh basil, piled thereon. What is given as "bombolutti ai modo mio" consists of short, thick tubes of pasta mingled with coarse-ground sweet Italian sausage, the two moistened with a creamy sauce that is fortified with ground cheese—an abundance of fresh parsley livens the pungent dish. More pasta, penne alla puttanesca, this version of the red anchovy sauce rather obvious for the sour and salty dominance of its capers and green olives—the unbalanced dish is, however, well made, the pasta firm, the strong sauce of complex texture. There is, rarity, a regularly listed risotto in an appetizer-size portion—the rice is nubbly, moist with oil and tomato, dotted with chunks and slivers of shrimp and squid.

The lobster salad is probably fine if you get here early, but a lobster poached and cooled some hours before you eat it has lost, you will discover, its liveliness and sweetness. You do better with seafood made to order, broiled swordfish, for example, the cooked-through steak, firm and juicy, in a buttery peppercorn sauce touched with lemon. But if you have seafood here just once, opt for the sea scallops, nine of the plump morsels arranged in a circle at the perimeter of their plate, each of them deep-browned and crisped, the pale meat rich and juicy within the crusty surfaces, at the center of the plate a huge, crunchy shrimp on a platform of braised endive, everything set in a rich, slightly sweet, lightly saffroned sauce—the sauce wonderfully livens those scallops when it is soaked into their crackling surfaces. Good sweetbreads, the big, crisped morsels in a winy sauce that is dotted with bits of mushroom and red pepper. You are asked how you want your veal chop, which is always a bad sign, for veal is not beef, is not yet itself when rare, no longer itself when well done. You specify medium, it arrives close to raw—but is nicely rescued by a second exposure to the fire, whereupon it is served to you under its second melting dollop of fragrant sage butter. The marinated lamb steak, handsomely crosshatched by its grilling, is tender, the strong-flavored meat enriched by the oil of its marinade. The Café makes much of its à la carte vegetables, among them oiled and grilled red onions that retain their bite and crunchiness; and mashed turnips, the hillock of pleasantly bitter froth overlaid with slivers of crisped shallot.

You cannot beat this raspberry tart, firm and utterly ripe berries, light pastry, a lemony cream between them. The almond cake is fresh and nutty, moistened with a lightly liquored sauce of Italian cream cheese, and garnished with a few of those good raspberries. The apple tart is hot, the thin slices of Granny Smith apple separated from the pastry by what the house calls apple butter, which resembles dark, sweet-spiced apple sauce. Concentrate, and you will detect the apricot flavor of the apricot ice.

★★VAŠATA

339 East 75th Street
LUNCH, SUNDAY; DINNER, TUESDAY TO SUNDAY. CLOSED MONDAY.
Reservations: 650-1686.
Credit cards: AE, DC, MC, V.
Inexpensive.

In this time capsule you see women arrive in cloth coats that have fox pelts—complete with heads—attached to the collars. Sometimes they wear their hair in long braids tied across their heads. Particularly on weekend evenings and at Sunday dinner gentlemen of years wear their best three-piece dark business suits here. Vašata is a Czechoslovak restaurant—but, more important, it is a survivor. Of the Central European eating places in this part of town that have held fast for a couple of decades or more, this is the one that has lost the least with the passage of time. Now that many of the old places are either gone or no longer themselves, Vašata has become the natural home not only of the neighborhood's Czechoslovak population but of nationals from neighboring states as well. You hear German spoken here often, assorted Slavic languages, sometimes Hungarian. You do not know what is being talked about, but the dis-harmony of the languages and the conservative bent of the clientele give you confidence that an insurrection is not brewing.

Vašata simulates a comfortable upper-class European country inn. It is well lighted, beamed and timbered, adorned with colorful pottery, carpeted, rimmed with a brightly colored leatherette banquette (into which you sink rather further than you expect before you reach a support level). The burghers assemble contentedly around tables that are covered with snowy linen. Here is kept alive the credo that the comfortable are the worthy.

Be advised that Czechoslovak food often is (a) heavy to a degree that life has not prepared you for and/or (b) composed of parts of the animal that life has not prepared you for. Pickled calf's brains on toast, for example, the slippery gray matter cold and sour and rich—you will be relieved that it comes with a thick, tart tartar sauce. The headcheese is of chunks of meat and organ meat bound like a mosaic in a firm, dark jelly—the spicy stuff is good with white vinegar, lemon, or both. The ham salad is easier on the mind—lots of ham, in thin slivers, in a tangy mayonnaise dressing. On occasion the restaurant's herring is a little soft, sour rather than tart. And the breaded mushrooms, quartered and fried—slightly greasy and in a way that is at once convincing and a little off-putting—are lightened by that good tartar sauce and fresh lemon.

Birds are Vašata's strength. Sometimes there is goose, good fat flavor in the dark meat—a brown sauce of herb- and vegetable-flavored stock is supplied, but it is pooh-poohed by your waiter, who suggests that it is a concession to alien styles. Duck is always on hand, and sometimes you see orders of the roasted bird streaming out of the kitchen a half dozen at a time. The ducks are meticulously roasted—crisp skin, the hot meat fat and juicy—but if you automatically expect a fruit sauce with roast duck, know that here the bird is served only with a gravy of its own roasting juices. The boiled beef comes in thin slices—if you have yours with dill sauce, you will note that it is mild, and that the sharp taste of the meat is vivid through it. Whenever you feel up to something truly leaden, have the veal à la Vašata, a heavily breaded cutlet surmounted by bacon and chicken livers, over all of which you pour a stout gray gravy. When sautéed chicken livers are on their own, they are mingled with onions and bound in yet another thick gravy—not an elegant dish, but impossible to fault on its own standards. The pork chops Serbien are not much lighter, but they are moistened with a slightly acidic tomato sauce and with sautéed tomatoes and green peppers, which brighten the dish.

Much is made here of the matching of vegetables to meats. The waiters affect an expertise, but close study has shown that what they aim for is color contrast—pale sauerkraut (very good) with dark chicken livers; beets with boiled beef. Of course, there are dumplings—their density is such that you are always surprised when they manage to soak up this kitchen's gravies.

A pureed-chestnut wafer coated with chocolate is served with whipped cream—it is the kind of sweet you love if you grew up with it. Likewise the chocolate-covered macaroon. Here the palacsintas are rather doughy, but the house serves lots of them—folks from the old country apparently find them just right. Vašata's coffee is strong and fresh—a blessing after some of this food.

Customer: "May I have a check?" Waiter (grinning delightedly): "I am a Czech!" You get the impression he has made the joke before.

★ VICO

1603 Second Avenue (near 83rd Street)
DINNER.
Reservations: 772-7441.
No credit cards.
Beer and wine.
Medium priced.

Here is a narrow, simply furnished store that modestly presents a modestly priced menu to New York's oh-so-moneyed Upper East Side. What means? Means an understanding that the moneyed get that way, at least in part, by loving bargains more than anybody. Moreover, what with recent amendments to the American way of life enacted by the Congress, deductions—real or imaginary—are worth less to you than they used to be, and your corporate employer, what with the diminished federal subsidy, is stickier than in the past about the way you spend the shareholders' money. It has got to the point where honesty, if not the best policy, is at least a contender, especially when you factor in the risks, for cheating just does not pay as well as it used to—it may be cheaper, is certainly safer, to eat on the cheap on the level. In fact Vito can be seen as part of a counter-expense-account revolution, for the place even abjures credit cards, and what it saves thereby presumably accounts in part for the sanity of its charges. And if the folks who fill it are here on the nights when they are not calling their spouses out-of-town buyers, then who needs those little green slips anyway? Other questions pertaining to retail stores that deal only in cash will be treated of in a separate chapter.

One building lot wide, and tapered at the back to accommodate this old building's stairway to the floors above, Vico is a bright oyster-white room with a plain wood floor, a ceiling that is stamped tin here, plaster there, a row of linened tables down each side next to the long walls. Black-and-white photographs of the old country (Italy), rather casually hung, are the sole adornments. The place has been tidily put together, is spiffy, even cozy despite its hard edges. You loosen your tie as you enter, very likely hang your jacket over your chair—only to put it back on when the vigorous air conditioner rouses itself. Your waiter is in jeans and a white polo shirt, his cordiality none the less for his informality. When the room is full, you spend time adjusting to the well-reflected noise.

If you want diversion while you consider the menu, an order of fried zucchini about the size of half a soccer ball can usually be produced quickly, the slender threads, their light batter crisped and browned, very nice when you have squeezed on the half lemon that the house supplies all dressed up in a cheesecloth pant. Your fresh-cut and beefy carpaccio parmigiano is a red sheet across your plate, and when you investigate the bump in the middle, you find a mound of fresh arugula hidden underneath—there is not much of the billed cheese grated on, but, on request, you are provided with good oil to moisten the meat. The grilled vegetables—a sliced baby eggplant, endives, much radicchio—are browned, saturated with oil, of clear flavor. But when the house has on hand New Zealand mussels or scallops (and their coral-colored roe) on half-shells, have one of those: the down-under mussels, in their green-edged shells, exceptionally sweet and tender in the garlicked and tomatoed broth; the little scallops delicate under their herbed, crisped, well-seasoned breading. Pasta: linguine with white clam sauce, the firm noodles, slick with oil, surmounted by several littlenecks in their shells, several more out of them, all fresh and tender—a bit of garlic strengthens the dish; penne puttanesca, the hefty tubes in a tomato sauce that is powerfully invigorated by anchovies, black olives, capers, hot pepper; fusilli Vico, the spirals in a nubbly meat sauce that lacks depth, lacks also the richness and earthiness the listed ingredients—cream, wild mushrooms—lead you to expect.

Your whole snapper is grilled, displayed to you, and, if you wish, skinned and boned —the firm and moist white meat is eminently good enough to eat plain, but it is much invigorated by the slightly minted sauce that you may have spooned on. The pollo campano is several parts of an undistinguished bird, but they are nicely browned, and they are mingled with chunks of eggplant, red pepper, tomato, are moistened with an enriched tomato sauce, reach you under a film of melted, pully cheese. Eschew the costolletta di vitello pepata—the buttery green-peppercorn sauce is fine, but the thick veal chop is underdone and bloody—in favor of the veal chop Milanese, the meat pounded out until it is the size of its plate, upon it a lettuce and tomato salad the dressing of which soaks into the crisp-fried breading of the pale, tender meat.

Chocolate salami is chocolate in the shape of, and with the appearance of, you guessed it. Slices of the stuff, in which bits of white cake stand in for a salami's nuggets of fat, reach you protruding like snails from a mound of good whipped cream, all in a strawberry sauce—a fun sweet. The tirami sù is cool, rich, liquored, is of strong coffee flavor, is buried under chocolate shavings. When there are berries, they are served in abundance, they are ripe, and they come with the good house whipped cream.

Off-the-menu dishes tend to be pricier than listed ones.

★ WATER CLUB

500 East 30th Street (on northbound service road of FDR Drive)
LUNCH AND DINNER.
Reservations: 683-3333.
Credit cards: AE, DC, MC, V.
Expensive.

As a method of adding eating places to the local scene without using up valuable real estate, in-the-river construction is not as good as suspending restaurants from dirigibles just above well-trafficked intersections. (Arrive at the appointed hour, whistle, and the maître drops a rope ladder.) But until that airborne millennium, when earthbound eateries have been made into much-needed housing of various kinds (Tavern on the Green, for example, will finally be officially designated an outpost of the zoo), the Water Club is the shortest trip you can take and still tell your friends you are going out of town for dinner.

Do you think it was the water and the passing boats that suggested the yacht-club trappings? Anyway, it is a big boathouse façade that overlooks the Drive, and it is to walls of nautical prints that you enter when you make a left into the bar. Here there is even a fireplace, complete with flames, at which you may warm the soles of your Top-Siders after a blustery day on the spray-washed decks. The dining room, about half a block long, parallels the river, and is windowed, floor to ceiling, on the east and north. Look uptown, and you see the Manhattan skyline over the green-and-white signs of the FDR Drive. To the east tugboats and barges challenge the East River's treacherous currents. Peer beyond the water, and you espy the big red Pepsi-Cola sign, the *Daily News* sign, black smokestacks against a murky sky—the industrial heartland of Queens. Though the view is not classic, it is at least a little thrilling, so window tables are the choice ones, though the stepwise arrangement of the levels of the room provides a pretty good view from anywhere. But for the French café chairs that surround the tables, the furnishings are straightforward. Signal flags hang from the white skylighted ceiling, and brightly colored models of boat hulls and mock portholes with brass fittings adorn the long white wall. However, the nearby navigable water and the seagoing paraphernalia notwithstanding, the intended spanking nautical freshness comes off as innocuous country club cleanliness. One of the problems is the player of this baby grand piano—the music he produces is the kind that makes you want to jump up and dance with your minister. And then there is the crowd, consisting, in large measure, of the contented professionals who staff the nearby world-famous medical institutions. They are suited, tonsured, stripe tied, properly spoused. To these standard-bearers of the American way of life, the conviction is sure and certain that the tree of liberty must be refreshed from time to time by the blood of patients.

James (says your captain, "My name is James if you want me," which seems to suggest that even when you cannot see him, he can hear you) makes a great show of asking who gets the oysters, who gets the smoked salmon, etc., and so it is that eventually someone serves the right items to the wrong diners, a chronic complaint here. But the oysters are fresh, and interesting varieties from distant waters are sometimes available. Order your oysters fried, and you get eight bluepoints, hot and crusty, but devoid of the warm, somewhat briny sweetness of deep-fried oysters at their best—lemon helps. Two smoked salmons are on the menu, one of them Irish—the pale-pink meat just a little salty, tangy, delicate but of unmistakable fish flavor, garnished with chopped onion, capers, lemon, and, unfortunately, the kind of pasteboard dark bread that comes, already sliced, in supermarket packages. The Club is studiedly American, so the ham you get with your melon is Smithfield—this is swell meat, smoky and salty, tender, even delicate despite its vivid flavor, and it is served with good fruit. But the country pâté is unmistakably French, the strong and well-fatted meat studded with crunchy nuts. The sometimes offered, and definitely Italian, vitello tonnato consists of three tongue-shaped slices of cool veal, each spread with a creamy tuna sauce, a mound of capers on each tongue tip. The corn-and-crabmeat chowder is thick, sweet of the yellow kernels, but despite the palpable presence of abundant crabmeat, the soup has little seafood quality.

The broiled whole snapper arrives in its skin, is fresh and firm and juicy; but the so-called sauce provençale that, fortunately, you arranged to have served on the side will strike you as little more than tepid stewed tomatoes. With respect to lobsters, by "broiling" the house means steaming and then charring, a cosmetic but devastating preparation, so you get yours steamed. This is a fine lobster (about two pounds for $26), moist and of clear, sweet flavor, but it has been done too long, is a little tough. Moreover, other difficulties attend upon eating lobsters here. Careful measurement reveals that the lobster platter, the plate for shells, the plate for your companion's main course, a couple of vegetables, a bottle of wine, water glasses and wineglasses, bread and butter, bread-and-butter plates, salt and pepper, and an ashtray require a minimum of 784 square inches of table space, even when laid out with the aid of a computer. Tables for two here provide only 576 square inches, so you must dismiss the bread, the small plates, the ashtray, etc. What you have here, you see, is a grand restaurant informed in its layout by two-bit economics. The myth of the Maryland crab cake survives, though here as everywhere, including Maryland, the dish is a triumph only of institutional cooking, a discipline in which food is "stretched" until it becomes—well, Maryland crab cakes. Crabmeat has the relationship to crab cakes that corn has to cornflakes. But then there is this superbly roasted duck (you may have it crisped or not), firm, delicately fibrous, of striking duck flavor, strewn with whole chestnuts. And then there is this so-called Connecticut rabbit stew, hefty chunks of pale meat, on the bone, in a thick, spicy, garlicky, and fragrantly herbed sauce in which you will also find lengths of crisp carrot, mushrooms, chunks of good bacon. And then, again, there is this roast beef, a gigantic chop of less than blood-strong flavor, but velvety and tender, the darkened seasoned rim a nice accent to the pink meat. Much is made of what the house calls its "market fresh" vegetables, but the big platter of them, served for two, includes the likes of hard, rather than crisp, carrots; dried-out and coarse broccoli; tough string beans. The hash brown potatoes are a little crusty, pleasantly salty, but you wish they had the frankly strong and greasy quality of hash browns at their best, instead of this misplaced delicacy. The mashed potatoes colcannon are buttery, very nice with the cracked peppercorns and chopped scallions and onions with which the puree is sprinkled. The menu promises Kentucky limestone lettuce with Stilton cheese, but you get the greens with a rather sour cheese dressing instead—and some of the leaves are black and wilted.

The service is briskly semicompetent. Says your captain on almost every visit, "Your waiter will be right with you to tell you about desserts," and by the time anyone shows up you have lost interest. When someone does materialize, he suggests something you would call a Paris-Brest, but which he rhymes with Harris-East. Anyway this is a fluffy mocha mousse wrapped in a crisp almond crust. The linzer torte is exceptional, the strawberry shortcake fun, the apple pie a little mushy, the strawberries mostly ripe. You may have superb whipped cream with any of the desserts.

★ WINDOWS ON THE WORLD

1 World Trade Center
LUNCH, DAILY; DINNER, MONDAY TO SATURDAY.
Reservations: 938-1111.
Credit cards: AE, DC, MC, V.
Expensive.

It all began about a decade go, when denim was high fashion, and brand-new Windows on the World, in its aerie on the 107th floor of the World Trade Center, decided to disallow (as it still does) "jeans of any kind." At the same time, no rule was instituted against clothes that were just plain ugly. Naturally, under the circumstances, members of the local smart set were compelled to deduce that they were not wanted here and ever since, have stayed away from the place as if it were the Empire State Building. Come to Windows on the World today, and you are surrounded by the folks you left behind when, after college, you headed for New York instead of back home. They even bring what are called the kids. But if Windows is nothing like a New York restaurant to New Yorkers, it is all exoticism to visitors from west of the Hudson. The wonderland view is even more spectacular from the restaurant than from the plane they arrived on, and the menu lists dishes not found in *Joy of Cooking*.

For the tourists who come to this place, the experience is a continuation of their air travel. They must call ahead to reserve a place, stand in line at ground level to check their coats, form an orderly crowd for the next elevator up. When they disembark at 107, they are met by a uniformed traffic coordinator, who directs those looking for Windows down a long passage—the Hall of Mirrors—to yet another line, where they wait for table assignments and the escort who will parade them to their place. That hall is a corridor of, you guessed it, mirrors, but also of vapid photomurals of New York. In addition, it has on display, on brass pedestals, four boulders of raw crystal, each identified by a plaque—Eurasian pegmatite, African rose quartz, etc.—the glinting rocks about the size of small barrels. The crystals look like something terribly educational from the Museum of Natural History, and they set the tone of this sexless place. For when you are finally seated, you are in a huge dining room that has all the character of the well-lighted interior of a jumbo jet, with beige linen on the large, well-spaced tables and pale leather and nubbly cloth all about, every appointment chosen for its vivid neutrality.

Of course, you come here not for the surroundings, but for the view. Accordingly, the place is as steeply tiered as a sports arena, and from virtually any point in it you may look out—through three-story-high floor-to-ceiling windows—either east to Brooklyn, Queens, and beyond and/or north over the length of Manhattan Island to the Bronx and points above. At night, if your table is beside a window, it is as if the Milky Way itself were spread out below, studded with blocks of masonry and glinting crystal and cut through by black rivers that are bridged by chains of stars.

For years, the performance of this establishment's kitchen was taken as evidence that as soon as it gets far enough off the ground, all food turns to airline food. Nowadays, that remark is something of a cheap shot. For though you can still get dinners here that will cause you to experience (associatively, of course) turbulence, it is also possible, if you choose carefully, to be distracted from the vista around you by the food before you. Among such turbulences and distractions (some of which you will find, and some not, on the restaurant's frequently changing menu), there is an appetizer of marinated salmon, the cool slices of dark-pink meat moist with oil and suffused with the flavor of fresh dill; big, plump sea scallops garnished with leaves of crisp endive and a mound of thin haricots verts threaded with strands of red pepper, all the elements moistened with, and made vaguely Oriental by light dressing of sesame oil; and the mussel bisque, an oceanic broth that is light, albeit creamed, briny, and of clear mussel flavor. The agnolotti are not bad, the little pasta packages filled with pesto and served in a white sauce that is dotted with chopped mushrooms and tomatoes—on occasion, the sauce is loose and milky when you want it to be rich and creamy. Among the first courses to skip are these leathery little snails in a harshly seasoned butter, and this pâté of duck liver, which is cold and rather nakedly meaty.

Fish cannot be much fresher, or of sweeter taste, than these sautéed fillets of red snapper, but the pecans with which they are not the note of striking contrast they would be if the snapper were moist. Crayfish meat, chunks of good lobster, and crisp nuggets of dilled cucumber reach you in a smooth and supple crayfish sauce—a good dish, of light, clear flavors. A salmis is a troublesome but rewarding preparation in which a bird (usually) is first roasted and then braised. Windows does a pheasant that way, and it arrives very moist and very strongly flavored (functions of braising in good stock), and also handsomely browned (a function of the roasting). The pheasant's dark, winy sauce is made of the braising liquid. You can get quite impeccable lamb chops here, big, plump doubles, paper stocking on their ribs, a bit of seasoned butter on their charred surfaces. But much of the food seems tailored to what is assumed to be the taste of out-of-towners. You ask for your venison rare, but it reaches you bloodless, the otherwise decent medallions of tender meat in a slightly fruity sauce that is studded with slices of prune and threaded with stringy filaments of pomegranate.

For dessert, get yourself an orange soufflé—it is hot and fluffy, at once tart and sweet, with a good flavor of rind in it—or fresh berries, which come with good whipped cream. The other sweets include a pear tart that lacks fruitiness, a lemon tart that is gooey, a floating island that may well be marshmallow, and a cold raspberry soufflé that is certainly mother of bubble gum.

On the regular list—over a hundred wines from more than a dozen countries—you will find decent bottles for as little as $8, none as high as $50. Ask for the encyclopedic complete list, and you are handed a file folder holding twenty-six typewritten pages stapled together (by reference to this document, you may arrange to spend as much as $400 for a bottle).

★ ZAPATA'S

330 East 53rd Street
LUNCH, MONDAY TO FRIDAY; DINNER, DAILY.
Reservations: 223-9408.
Credit cards: AE, DC, MC, V.
Inexpensive.

A Mexican hole-in-the-wall with wobbly tables and shaky chairs, paper place mats on the red linen, low light from dim lanterns. On the walls are depictions of dangerous Mexicans with drooping mustaches, cigarettes hanging from their lips, big hats, and bandoliers of bullets crisscrossed on their chests; also Mexican artifacts of indeterminate purpose; also a vanity mirror (the glass is ovoid, and about the size of the human face) set in a rectangular wooden frame at each corner of which is mounted a cloven hoof with attachments up to, approximately, the fetlock—this is one of the many elements that give this place its distinctly neighborhood feel. Another is the staff, hustling waitresses who are accustomed to discussions about anything but food, and whose pride is their ability to deliver as fast as the kitchen can prepare, never mind how slow you eat—your courses may get backed up right under your eyes, a severe problem when the tables for two are about big enough for a couple of cocktails and an ashtray.

Still, the place is popular. People come here after the office when they are spending their own money, for the prices are low. And the menu, though it consists mostly of dishes selected from that culinary subcategory known as Manhattan Mex, includes among its familiarities the makings of first-rate dinners, if you know where to look.

Look among the appetizers for the ceviche of red snapper, which is served in a stemmed glass, the many chunks of fresh fish submerged in a spicy-hot tomato-and-lime marinade, which is heady with coriander and thick with chopped onions. Come once, and that is the first course to have. But the guacamole is fine, seems just made, is chopped rather than blenderized, dotted with bits of tomato, quite salty—it comes with corn chips protruding like sails from the thick, green mash. The nachos, seasoned cheese melted onto crisped tortillas, are hearty, and you find a thin layer of green peppers—hot and oily—between the two.

The restaurant serves tacos, enchiladas, tostadas, burritos, tamales, stuffed peppers, flautas, all with the usual fillings and coatings and toppings—and of course with garnishes of rice and refried beans. If you have had these items in other places, you know what you will get here, though this place turns them out with a bit more flavor and a bit less leadenness than the run of Mexican restaurants. But what distinguishes Zapata's from its competition are some of the meat and chicken dishes. The mole verde, for example, is made with a bird that has real chicken flavor, and the green-pepper sauce under which it is buried is thick and spicy, substantial without being heavy. That same good chicken is most of the mole poblano—the familiar dish offers no surprises, though the almost black chocolate sauce has good depth, and a nice, thick, almost chalky texture. The place offers veal in a hot red chili sauce, but this is coarse veal and it makes a coarse stew. Have instead the cabrito—goat—which is offered the same way, for this meat, at once sweet, resilient, and distinctly wild tasting, is just right in the powerful sauce.

The desserts—custards, guava with cream cheese, mango with cream cheese—are the usual thing.

★ LE ZINC

139 Duane Street (near West Broadway)
LUNCH, MONDAY TO FRIDAY; DINNER, DAILY.
Reservations: 732-1226.
Credit cards: AE, MC, V.
Medium priced.

Here congregate, and intermingle unconflictingly, Wall Street and its attendant banks and law firms; contemporary artists and their attendant dealers, collectors, hangers-on; and, of course, in this neighborhood, those defined more but what is unfortunately referred to as their lifestyle than by their manner of supporting it—the loft dwellers. Many who frequent this place fit two of those categories. An art-collecting stockbroker living in a loft makes it in all three. In fact, it may be the loftlike aspect of Le

Zinc that brings together its heterogeneous crowd, for it is a barn of a place in which some of the appointments suggest a decision on the part of the new tenants to make do (for the time being, of course) with oddities found on the premises. How else account for the dark-wood Chippendale frames around the exit to the street and the entrance to the kitchen? Surely the upright piano that now stands just inside the front door is something the previous occupant figured it would cost more to move than lose. And obviously the new tenants decided to go with the functional old wood floor until other essentials could be taken care of. Withal the raw space has been well served by its improvisational treatment. There was a special on maroon paint, and the walls are therefore a potent shade of barn red. And instead of spackling, prints and paintings and big framed mirrors have been hung wherever there were cracks or scars in the old plaster. From the vaulted ceiling hang four-bladed fans, also cheerful chandeliers that are great clusters of glowing white bulbs. The tables, in long rows, are covered with white linen, are surrounded by simple side chairs, and the place is patrolled by diligent and forthright waitresses and (mostly) waiters in white shirts and long white aprons. Le Zinc is rare in that it is convivial even when less than filled. And in good weather, you can sometimes get a table out front, under the awning on the Duane Street sidewalk.

By way of its menu, its prices, and of how its habitués use it, Le Zinc is a French bistro. Bear this in mind firmly, and you will make the most of the place. You will for example gravitate eagerly to the pâté de campagne, which the menu describes as "homemade," and which embodies all the qualities of that dish in its pristine primitive form. You rarely get pâtés of this type anymore, aged a few days, it seems, its flavors melded, pink at the center and dotted and rimmed with creamy white fat, touched with sweet spice and more than touched with garlic, a little gamy of its meat—with strong mustard, white bread, and cold red wine, it is these days a fond memory. But when you spot an entry like "saumon de Norvège mariné au citron vert," it is wise to smile with knowing dubiety, for sure enough the lime of the title is nowhere in evidence, the stuff tastes like straight smoked salmon (though quite ok for that), and, to elaborate the confusion, when later you get your check the item is written in as gravlax. The salad of preserved duck is perhaps not bistro food as in olden days, but it is in the spirit, a satisfying plate of food—watercress, spiky greens, mushrooms, radicchio, all those, in their good tart dressing, overlaid with an abundance of dark strands of strong-flavored duck. Each night there is a pasta of the night, on occasion what the house calls fettucine carbonara. You may choose not to call it carbonara, for it is eggless, but you cannot deny what the enriched sauce of ricotta cheese does for these firm noodles, and you cannot but regret that the bacon crumbled on top, for all its perfect crispness, is the kind of thing you get in coffee shops with scrambled eggs, a blindly misplaced element in this setting, where Italian bacon would do so well.

Though your medium-rare steak pommes frites arrives vastly overcooked, you encounter no problem in arranging to have the job done over. Entrecôte No. 2, happily, is medium rare, handsomely crosshatched by the grill, tender and blood-juicy, garnished with French fries that are thin, light, and of good potato flavor, if not exactly crisp. Of the steak tartare it may be said, much in its favor, that it is of beef just ground, but it is sour, insufficiently enriched with egg yolk and/or oil, too grossly black peppered, lacks the special balance of richness and strength that makes a steak tartare. La grillade de poulet grillé et saumon fumé au basilic is identified as one of the house "spécialitées," which is presumably to say no one else makes it. As to the basil, it is apparently omitted in the off season, for this is some very nice chicken and some more of that variously identified smoked salmon you encountered among the first courses, alternating sheets of the two over spinach in a light sauce—perfectly decent food. Still, there is better food in the bistro department, the cassoulet, albeit the usual abundance of white beans, some-how not leaden, and buried within it you encounter a bird's leg, two kinds of sausage variously assertive, chunks of pork that are mostly fat, but, being the size of children's blocks, easy to put aside (they add good flavor to the hefty food), everything in a lively, redded sauce.

The tart tatin lacks the quality of caramel. The crème brûlée is cold, thick, sugary. The chocolate mousse is rich and sticky, dark and intense—too bad it was spooned into its cup an hour or two before you ordered it, has developed in the meantime a thin skin. The good sherbets are concentrated, fruity rather than sweet.

SEYMOUR BRITCHKY'S RESTAURANT LETTER

Every month Seymour Britchky publishes a supplement to this book. A private guide to New York's newest restaurants, *Seymour Britchky's Restaurant Letter* is available to readers by subscription only. The *Letter* is the one source of reliable opinion on the scores of new restaurants that open in New York each year—too late for inclusion in this volume.

In each monthly newsletter Mr. Britchky also takes a look at changes that are taking place in some of the city's older restaurants—established eating places, of high standards and low profile, that tend to be forgotten in the excitement about hot new spots.

For an insider's view of the ever-changing New York restaurant scene, subscribe to the *Restaurant Letter* today.

One-year subscriptions (12 monthly issues) are $25
Two-year subscriptions (24 monthly issues) are $45

Please make your check payable to:

Seymour Britchky's Restaurant Letter
Post Office Box 155Q
New York, NY 10276

You assume no risk when you subscribe to the *Restaurant Letter*. If you are not pleased with the first issue, for any reason, you may have a refund—in full—by return mail.